About the a

GW00537744

André Odendaal is the vice-chancellor's writer-in-residence and honorary professor in history and heritage studies at the University of the Western Cape (UWC). He received his first degrees from Stellenbosch University and his PhD from Cambridge University. Thereafter, he spent thirteen years at UWC, where he started and directed the Mayibuye Centre for History and Culture in South Africa. In 1996, he was appointed founding director of the Robben Island Museum, democratic South Africa's first national heritage institution.

During the 1980s, André was involved as an anti-apartheid activist in the United Democratic Front (UDF), the South African Council on Sport and the National Sports Congress. In 1987 he attended the much-publicised Dakar conference in Senegal between the ANC and a large group of 'dissident' Afrikaners, which is discussed in this book.

After running organisations for twenty years, he started working full-time as an independent researcher, writer and publisher in 2015. Since *Vukani Bantu!* (Rise Up You People!) in 1984, he has authored or co-authored a dozen books. The most recent are *The Blue Book* (2012), *The Founders* (2012), *Cricket and Conquest* (2016), *Divided Country* (2018), *Pitch Battles* (2020), *Robben Island Rainbow Dreams* (2021) and *Swallows and Hawke* (2022). He has also published and co-published twenty books under the imprint of his African Lives series.

For dear comrade Edgar —

Dear Comrade President

Oliver Tambo and the Foundations
of South Africa's Constitution

Warm fond wishes,

André Odendaal
with editorial contributions by Albie Sachs

Bayete Tambo Albie
1/6/24

PENGUIN BOOKS

Dear Comrade President:
Oliver Tambo and the Foundations of South Africa's Constitution

Published by Penguin Books
an imprint of Penguin Random House South Africa (Pty) Ltd
Reg. No. 1953/000441/07
The Estuaries No. 4, Oxbow Crescent, Century Avenue, Century City, 7441
PO Box 1144, Cape Town, 8000, South Africa
www.penguinrandomhouse.co.za

Penguin
Random House
South Africa

First published 2022

1 3 5 7 9 10 8 6 4 2

Publication © Penguin Random House 2022
Text © André Odendaal/ASCAROL 2022

Cover photograph © Mark Reinstein / Getty Images

PUBLISHER: Marlene Fryer
MANAGING EDITOR: Robert Plummer
EDITOR: Lauren Smith
PROOFREADER: Dane Wallace
COVER DESIGNER: Ryan Africa
TYPESETTER: Monique van den Berg
INDEXER: Sanet le Roux

Set in 10.5 pt on 14.5 pt Minion

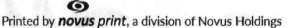

Printed by **novus print**, a division of Novus Holdings

MIX
Paper from
responsible sources
FSC® C022948

ISBN 978 1 77609 668 8 (print)
ISBN 978 1 77609 669 5 (ePub)

'First of all, we have to build concepts and attitudes, we have to evolve and project an outlook, we have to destroy archaic ideas and notions and replace them with revolutionary ideas. We do all this through the medium of language as well as by our actions. But in our actions we are carrying out decisions and pursuing goals which have first been conceived in our minds and expressed in words, in language.'

– Oliver Tambo, handwritten letter to an unnamed comrade, November 1970

Contents

Foreword

DURING MY TWENTY years of studying history formally, I always felt a
great divergence between what I learnt within the university setting and
what I learnt outside of it.

That divergence owed not so much to my professors' shortcomings – they were
all brilliant in their own ways and contributed towards the histories of southern Africa in ways that were radical, especially during the apartheid era. What
was missing in this formal history education was that thing I have come to call
'umbilical sense'. That is, an African sensibility of knowledge that emerges from
a deep connection to place, people, traditions and stories.

While it has long been obvious that the precolonial histories of the indigenous
peoples of South Africa have not been well told in the mainstream academic
world, it is generally taken for granted that the history of the liberation struggle
is well and extensively documented. This is because there is a long tradition of
both liberal and radical left history-writing in South Africa. More recently, in the
post-apartheid years, much has been written about the African National Congress,
its past and its present in government.

Having grown up in the ANC and spent parts of my childhood in exile, however, I was always struck by how academic writing on the ANC was bereft of an
inner lens or perspective. Even though the factual details were there, the analyses
of the ANC's history seemed to lack an appreciation of the very rich way in which
the humanity and struggles of people emerged in the context of a generous, com-
munitarian intellectualism and liberation ethic.

André Odendaal's style of writing about African pasts is distinctly different.
I was first drawn to this when I picked up *The Founders*, his path-breaking book
on the origins of the ANC. It was the first time I had properly encountered André's
work, and I was particularly struck by the palpable Africanism conveyed in his
narrative style. His penmanship captured, with idiomatic sensitivity, the intellectual modalities and ethos of the black political traditions that many of us grew up
with and which we heard and came to internalise through familiar song, speeches,
umrabulo. At the height of South African student protests for the decolonisation of university curriculums, Professor Xolela Mangcu lamented the fact that
'One hundred and fifty years of black intellectual thought remain outside the

social theory curriculum in South Africa'. He chose eight 'defining texts' about 'how black people in Africa and the diaspora have interpreted the meaning of social existence and out of such processes ultimately gave meaning to the social ideals contained in the South African constitution'. Alongside books by Biko, Mqhayi, Mamdani, Bernal, Du Bois, Olaniyan and Sweet, Mangcu's list included Odendaal's *The Founders* as one of the canonical texts for a curriculum on African intellectualism.

In *Dear Comrade President*, Odendaal does this again in the service of sorting out reality from myth in the history of the making of the South African Constitution. He sets out to explain the 1980s genesis of the Constitution, for some reason still a scarcely known or written-about story. In the process he challenges certain present-day misconceptions about it, chief among them the idea that the Constitution was somehow a foreign-inspired concept that had little rooting in the African tradition, or in the past of the ANC's form of Africanism. He also firmly rebuts the logical extension of this critique, which is that the ANC adopted constitutionalism because it had been defeated and was forced to negotiate.

Dear Comrade President invites debate by implicitly addressing what I have come to call 'constitutional scepticism', a pervasive feeling among the young that the ANC 'sold out' a more radical project to deliver a constitution that has betrayed the people of South Africa. By revealing the archive and investigating it meticulously, we are challenged to consider how we can debate the origins of the South African Constitution properly if we do not, for a start, know the actual history of its emergence. In debates on decolonisation, I have taken the strong position that the archive of African action itself, no matter how contradictory and incomplete, is where the process of epistemic reconstruction and debate begins.

Odendaal thus makes a significant contribution to the current academic and public discourses at a time of significant political contestation as South Africa's democracy gets tested by hard political and economic realities, and perhaps most of all a sense that we are failing to live up to our own promise that we could be far, far better than our past. *Dear Comrade President* makes the case that the path to 1994 was indeed a history of African-rooted initiative, agency, intellectualism and political genius, based on solidarity with inclusive universal perspectives, against a backdrop of global power inequalities and the systemic violence churned out by centuries of colonialism and apartheid.

The rise of this constitutional scepticism has been troubling to many who lived through those years of struggle and negotiation, and it must be more so for those grounded in and knowledgeable about the long history of constitutionalism as a principle within the ANC dating back many charters, including the historic Africans' Claims document of 1943, nearly eighty years ago.

From the outset, the author addresses these present-day concerns by setting the modern traditions of African nationalism as the ground upon which constitutionalism grew. He argues that scepticism regarding the Constitution and questions over its authentic connection to the goal of black liberation tend to 'underestimate the African agency involved' in the making of modern South Africa. He contends also that there is a kind of flattening of the past in the context of public discourse that has taken the quick-to-conclude routes of social media. People 'too often conflate or transpose dates and events from three decades ago, offering as truth generic assumptions that can be disproven when holding a microscope to the facts'. He explains, 'I've therefore attempted to carbon-date the unfolding developments, illustrating and explaining developments step by step, year by year – almost month by month – from 1986 to 1990 to show how the template for a new constitution and new society was forged.'

Dear Comrade President provides us with a kind of prenatal scan of the Constitution's umbilical roots, as well as a road map for understanding the unfolding development of constitutional principles, guidelines and strategies of the ANC and its aligned internal partners such as the UDF, COSATU and the SACC between 1985 and 1989, which shaped the decade to follow. For the ANC and its partners, constitutional planning was always interlinked with the four pillars of struggle, namely mass action, underground struggle, armed action and international solidarity. The reader is taken back to the Kabwe conference of 1985 and to the ANC's modest headquarters 'situated discreetly between Cha Cha Cha and Cairo Roads' in Lusaka, where Oliver Tambo convened his Constitution Committee and gave them their mandate in January 1986.

At Kabwe, the ANC dealt with its own moral code as a revolutionary movement. Oliver Tambo guided the ANC into adopting a Code of Conduct by which it would hold itself to a high standard of humanism and ethics in undertaking its revolutionary armed struggle – an extraordinary step for any movement to take in the middle of a war against an enemy armed to the teeth. The same can be said of its earlier signing as a non-state party of the Geneva Conventions. This kind of deliberation about the moral content of the struggle is what set the anti-apartheid struggle apart from so many others. Odendaal meticulously documents how the internal sense of democracy and moments of self-reflection led by Tambo generated the almost counterintuitive concepts and strategic ideas for a future constitution of South Africa, so that the ANC would not be outmanoeuvred by the time negotiations merged.

What I found interesting is how Odendaal brings across Tambo's visionary instinct for how to prepare the movement and how to identify the right combination of thinkers and doers to execute the tasks he felt were necessary. Here you see key exceptional figures around him: Hani the military hero, Mompati the forceful and trusted aide, Mbeki the diplomat, Jordan the thinker and key link to the Constitution Committee, Slovo the strategist, and Maharaj the brilliantly versatile Vula underground commander – all different characters operating in complementary compartments in a complicated environment. Acknowledging that the National Executive Committee did not have the capacity, space or time to do the job themselves, he also worked with colleagues to bring some impressive ANC intellectuals into his Constitution Committee.

As Odendaal puts it, 'Knowing that nearly all wars end at a negotiating table, and judging the balance of forces to be tipping in favour of the liberation movement, Tambo instructed his new think tank to formulate the principles and draft the outlines of a constitution for a future non-racial, democratic South Africa.' Pallo Jordan emerges as one of the intellectual forces advising Tambo on the possible alternatives for a South African future. Odendaal shows that, in the context of the many ideas circulating at the time on how stable post-conflict societies might be built – including many right-wing and unprogressive ideas on the international stage – Jordan drew from the revolutionary aims of the Freedom Charter and comparative revolutionary experiences to rebut any arguments for group rights, as these would uphold the status quo. Instead, he argued almost heretically for a Bill of Rights and multiparty democracy. Odendaal does not ask us to take anything for granted. After all, much of history looks inevitable in hindsight. Rather, he insists on immersing the reader in the detail of how the ideas unfolded, and how arguments were made and reformed during the early years of the Constitution Committee's work in Zambia.

The author is uncharitable about the intellectual role of the 'other side' and speaks back to the attempts by National Party intellectuals of the time to rewrite themselves as enlightened reformers. Even if De Klerk shared the Nobel with Madiba, Odendaal wants it noted that the change agenda came from the liberation movement. He argues that 'the regime and its agents were *not* enlightened visionaries driving change or willing co-authors of a new democratic order in South Africa; they were latecomers to the idea. Bereft of political alternatives, the apartheid establishment ... was dragged to the negotiating table after 1990 – where it again failed to control the process as it had intended to do.'

It is a characteristic of Odendaal's history-writing that he ties together the threads of modern ANC intellectualism by mapping out the long genealogies of family and struggle. He seems to do this for two important reasons. Firstly, he wants to show that the ANC was an intergenerational project, carried through families and communities at all levels of black African society in South Africa. As such, the kin relations among the various ANC families such as the Jordans are explained, conveying the indigenous links to royalty and clan that many within the ANC came from. Secondly, Odendaal wants to make it clear that the nationalist struggles in South Africa were international and consciously cosmopolitan, products of a particular kind of African universalism, while having unquestionably indigenous roots.

This valuable study opens new ground for understanding the genesis of democratic South Africa's Constitution and should serve as inspiration for more such work. Reading it provides me with certain pointers in this respect. Firstly, Odendaal is particularly comfortable in Eastern Cape history; he connects the dots with ease and one can feel that the weight of the book lies in this genealogical terrain. This should invite more writing in other geographies that lays bare the other indigenous genealogies around which the ANC formed.

Secondly, in *Dear Comrade President* the documents have, of necessity, dominated the narrative so that the still untold story of the evolving constitutional guidelines and planning can be laid out. Odendaal tends to be fastidious about what the documents say, since he is meticulously documenting evidence of the origins of ideas. Interviews with some of those who were there are also included but feel somewhat secondary to the paper archive. The broader archive – interviews, art, creative writing – could be explored in future studies.

Thirdly, it goes without saying that today the massive historical erasure of women needs to be redressed so that their roles are brought properly into history. In his postcolonial histories of the colonial game of cricket, Odendaal has led the field in writing about the history of women in modern sport in South Africa, going back to its nineteenth-century origins. In this latest book he shows how decisive steps were taken in the 1980s to address the deep-seated patriarchal nature of the ANC, such as at Kabwe, the important In-House Seminar in 1988, and the important Women's Seminar in 1989. We see a cast of familiar women's names such as Gertrude Shope, Ruth Mompati, Lindiwe Mabuza, Barbara Masekela, Brigitte Mabandla and Frene Ginwala, as well as an emergent cohort of newer leaders and thinkers, and a sense of the intense debates on women's rights during the deliberative democracy of the ANC as the concept of a constitution was debated. New works that go further on women in history are essential.

There are some fascinating details and moments that jump out at the reader, such as one of the principles that emerged in the Foundations of Government document of February 1987, which called for the 'outlawing of the advocacy or practice of racism, fascism, Nazism, tribalism, chauvinism or regionalism'. This struck me as being so specific to what were then living, recent memories of fascism in Europe as well as the problem of the Bantustans and Inkatha's then violent regionalist ethnic-separatist politics. I was reminded of how much living in a specific time compels one to address issues as they appear and are known in the moment. Remarkably, however, the general trajectory of constitution-making that followed was able to encompass all these thoughts through more universal language by 1996, a mere decade later. The intricacies of the debate on the redress for victims of forced removals in the context of overall dispossession may be illuminating in the context of current land debates. Another early point of agreement was that the Constitution could not 'entrench the rights of property', a clause that remains to this day but is still contested for what is perceived as its inability to proactively compel the democratic state to radically expropriate land in the name of historical justice.

I felt it was symbolic that I engaged with this book from my current academic home at the Nelson Mandela University in the Eastern Cape. In its former incarnation, the university had 'Metropolitan' in its name, and its identity was more as a city university for the young who needed to be professionalised. Once the decision was taken to adopt the Mandela name proper, I felt a great existential and ontological weight come upon me as an African in relation to how we convey the story of our roots and our liberation to new generations with all its granularity and complex twists, its oft-forgotten turns. I therefore accepted the task of writing this foreword with a sense of real responsibility. I can commend *Dear Comrade President* as a thoughtful, original and timely work of great relevance, which underlines that Africans in South Africa, working in solidarity with democrats of all hues across the globe, imagined and engineered their own freedom against great odds. This is the kind of history our students and young historians must engage with and build on.

PROFESSOR NALEDI NOMALANGA MKHIZE
Acting Director of the School of Governmental and
Social Sciences, Nelson Mandela University, Gqeberha

Acknowledgements

*D*EAR COMRADE PRESIDENT is the latest in a line of dissertations, books and articles I've written over the past forty years on the history of the freedom struggle and the deep African roots of constitutionalism in South Africa. In that time, many individuals and institutions have supported my research and writing, and I thank them all once again here.

This book emerged from close collaboration with Albie Sachs, a struggle icon and judge in the first Constitutional Court of democratic South Africa. We bumped into each other by chance at an intimate memorial service for our mutual friend Sadie Forman at Amy Thornton's home late in 2014.[1] While we mingled with Denis Goldberg, Tanya Barben, Terry and Barbara Bell, and other comrades of Sadie's, Albie invited me to join a project on the making of the South African Constitution that he was busy launching. ASCAROL – the Albie Sachs Trust on Constitutionalism and the Rule of Law – would be the vehicle that commissioned me to write the story of the ANC's Constitution Committee, from its founding in Lusaka-based exile to 1990, ending where most accounts of the constitution-making process in South Africa start.

It has been a special journey working with someone with Albie's immense intellect, insights, humane sensibilities, courage and vast insider knowledge of the decade-long South African constitution-making process. Through the six years it took to nurture and produce this work, it was difficult to decide on the authorship because we worked so closely together. At times it was going to be my work. At times we were going to be co-authors. However, we decided that the most accurate description for *Dear Comrade President* is that it is authored by André Odendaal, with acknowledgement to the editorial contributions made by Albie Sachs. It is necessary to make this distinction for various reasons. Firstly, I have developed a distinctive approach in my writing on the African roots of constitutionalism in South Africa over the past four decades. It would have been a different book if we had been co-authors. Secondly, I set out, as a priority, to guard against this becoming a sweetheart project for a famous actor in history. The book had to be different, regardless of how outstanding the many 'Albie books' are.[2] To do this, and to ensure its integrity as a collective rather than individual story, I had to put some distance between me and Albie. This was a challenge, given his strength of personality and the sheer weight of his contribution to the making of the Constitution. It required me to act cautiously, to sometimes resist Albie's charm and enthusiasm, to look for contestation and contradictions and not just seamless progress. And, yes, to bump heads with him occasionally in order to retain my voice as author.

Albie is a giant in this story. Not one mention of his many historical contributions or editorial suggestions was put in without me first giving this close consideration. Often, contributions and material of his – though not undeserving – were left out in case these unsettled my attempt to prioritise the collective story or ensure the bigger picture was explained. The omitted fragments must await the necessary biography to come.

I am satisfied that the unusual challenge, this unusual intimacy with a subject, and dance with subjectivity, has now led to the kind of book I envisaged. But our close cooperation also needs to be recognised. Our many long conversations have become part of my special inheritance as a historian, activist and individual. I can say the same about my valued engagements over the past few years with Mac Maharaj and Pallo Jordan. Their book *Breakthrough: The Struggles and Secret Talks that Brought Apartheid South Africa to the Negotiating Table* (Penguin Books, 2021) in many ways provides the connecting context for this story and has similar aims of helping to decolonise accounts of the transition to democracy in South Africa. The time spent with these three remarkable South Africans has given me insights and understandings that money could not buy.

Albie and his editor Alexandra Dodd gave the first draft of this manuscript a comprehensive edit, suggesting cuts in length, adding valuable detail – for instance in the biographical details of people he knew intimately in the chapter on NADEL – and helping to polish the manuscript in skilful ways. I have acknowledged this by citing material and memories particular to him as 'A.L. Sachs and A. Dodd edit, Cape Town, 10 September 2020' (and, as mentioned, recognising him on the title page), while still writing about him in the third person. Albie's edits draw mainly on his previous writings and his interviews with Stanley Sello in 2007 in which he contextualised and explained the ANC Constitution Committee material he donated to the UWC/RIM Mayibuye Archives, which Pat Fahrenfort later transcribed. I chose to use these 211 pages of transcriptions, which still need final editing and critical attention, only on rare occasions in order to prioritise the primary sources – the original meeting documents and Constitution Committee correspondence.

I thank Albie for understanding the need for us to work apart at some distance and for me to create a narrative that seeks to amplify my particular 'voice'. It has been an immense privilege to work with him. Thanks, too, to co-editor Alexandra

Dodd; Albie's trusted support person Susan Rabinowitz; Jill Singer, and ASCAROL's trustees – Vanessa September, Nazreen Bawa, Vincent Saldanha, Kate O'Regan, Thuto Thipe and Moshoeshoe Monare – who have been supportive and patient.

In April 2018, I decided to phone Zola Skweyiya to ask for his assistance. It was becoming clear to me that he would be a key figure in this book. I had met him once in Lusaka and then on the UWC campus after his return from exile, followed by intermittent passing encounters. The phone rang, the answer button was activated, there were background voices, but no one spoke. The next day I heard the sad news: Zola had passed away. It was a great loss for the country, and for this small project. Three of his fellow Constitution Committee members – Jack Simons, Kader Asmal and Teddy Pekane – had also passed by this stage. However, I was lucky to have made contact with and received support from two other members of the Committee, Ntozintle 'Jobs' Jobodwana and Brigitte Mabandla, while Thuthukile Skweyiya and Manana Pekane kindly provided family photos, and Louise, Rafiq and Adam Asmal gave me permission to go through Kader's papers at his Alma Street home. These I roughly sorted and boxed for the family, and they have now been reunited with the rest of his documents, which are kept in two separate parts in adjoining rooms in the UWC library, curated by the UWC/RIM Mayibuye Archives and the UWC Archives respectively. The core research material for this book came from the Asmal Collection and the Albie Sachs Collection, which is also housed at the Mayibuye Archives, as well as the Jack Simons Papers at the University of Cape Town and the official ANC archives located at the University of Fort Hare. Given the nature of its journey home, parts of this ANC collection are also to be found at Mayibuye and at the University of the Witwatersrand. The staff and archivists at the different repositories were more than helpful. *Ndiyabulela*, Luvuyo Wotshela, Ike Mamoe, Vuyo Feni-Feda, Lunga Poni, Zalisile Cakacaku, Nomthandazo Jaza and Vuyani Booi at the liberation archives at the University of Fort Hare; Andre Landman, Isaac Ntabankulu and Clive Kirkwood at UCT Special Collections; and Mariki Victor, Stanley Sello, Andre Mohamed, Tracey Lamberg, Zikhona Mhlontlo, Andile Ngcaba, Graham Goddard, Hamilton Budaza, Esther van Driel, Babalwa Solwandle and all of the team at the UWC/RIM Mayibuye Archives. It was a joy to do research in a repository that I helped start, and no request was too much for my namesake Andre, the historical papers co-ordinator, who grew up in exile and studied at Solomon Mahlangu Freedom College.

The work of Heinz Klug and Joseph Jackson on the Constitution and Constitutional Guidelines has been especially relevant to me. Thanks to Heinz for the periodic discussions and for sharing material with me. His and other material from Albie and others received without an indication of the archival source is acknowledged as 'ANC Archives (on file)' in the endnotes and has been filed. Phoebé and Hein Gerwel generously gave me access to Jakes Gerwel's papers at his home in Belhar. Similarly, Christelle Terreblanche and her siblings kindly gave me access to their father Sampie Terreblanche's papers. Thank you to Tony Trew for talking to me briefly about the Consgold meetings and to Mac Maharaj for providing me with copies of Tony's and Michael Young's original notes of those meetings. These helped beef up the related chapters considerably. Mac, Pallo Jordan, Russell Martin, Hugh Macmillan, Max du Preez, former Constitutional Court judge Johann van der Westhuizen, Riaan de Villiers and Christopher Saunders, along with Albie, took the trouble to comment on my drafts. I spent many enjoyable hours with Gordon Metz, Adam Asmal and Grant Atkinson in eThekwini, Tshwane, Johannesburg and Cape Town, interviewing Maharaj, Sachs, Roelf Meyer and Thabo Mbeki. We thank them for giving us the time.

My appreciation to Professor Nomalanga Mkhize for agreeing to write the foreword and to Marguerite Poland for her friendship, empathy and encouragement. They share with me a world of ideas that finds beauty in dancing through a rich past of African sensibilities, imaginations, agency, achievements and intellectualism. Many others helped. My gratitude for their support and encouragement to Katie Mooney, David Wallace, Zolile Mvunelo, Razia Saleh, Verne Harris, the late Drusilla Yekela, Luyanda Mpahlwa, Denis Goldberg, Luli Callinicos, Sylvia Neame, Gabriele Mohale, Xolela Mangcu, Mwelela Cele, Mandla Langa, Barbara Hogan, Hassen Ebrahim, Baleka Mbete, Mike Savage, Vusi Pikoli, Neo Lekgotla laga Ramoupi, Noel Solani, Khwezi ka Mpumlwana, Abigail Thulare, Jeremy Wightman, Charlotte Imani, Mthunzi Nxawe, Bridget Impey, Pamela Maseko, Tim Wilson, Shan Balton, John Young, Charlene Willatt-Bate, Archie Henderson, Bob Edgar, Ciraj Rassool, Ian Liebenberg, Jeff Opland, Athambile Masola, Michael Weeder, Tyrone August, Vusi Khumalo, Rashid and Yana Lombard, Julian Williams, Mary Odendaal and Ra-ees Saiet for their support and encouragement. My switch to writing full-time in recent years has been enriched by new opportunities and a new support network of colleagues and friends. I have expressed my appreciation to many of them in *Pitch Battles* (2020, p. 430), but thanks again, and my apologies to anyone I have missed.

These acknowledgements started with the explanation of a special personal relationship and debt I owe. They end with a few more. Next to Albie, I must also single out for particular appreciation Tony Tabatznik and his Bertha Foundation for the generous support that has enabled me to research, write and publish full-time for a number of years. Tony has a passion for defending human rights and freedom of expression and supporting radical causes against 'big brother' control. He has been generous beyond measure in his support of my writing and publishing projects, including the launch of the African Lives series with its twenty titles so far. Our collaboration has led to a level of productivity that exceeded the expectations I had when I set out to do 'a second PhD', with the support of my wife Zohra Ebrahim, following a somewhat unconventional, two-decade-long career in charge of various institutions. My sincere thanks to him and to Bertha.

Then, arising from my recent work, UWC offered me a three-year fellowship as writer-in-residence, based at the Centre for Humanities Research (CHR). I am very grateful to the rector, Professor Tyrone Pretorius, whose initiative this was, as well as the dean of arts, Professor Monwabisi Ralarala, CHR director Dr Heidi Grunebaum, Larry Pokpas, Beulah Hendricks and Ramesh Bharuthram for their welcomes. It is professionally very satisfying to have this late-career opportunity to reconnect with an institution that has profoundly impacted my life and thinking.

Above all, my thanks to Zohra Ebrahim for the immeasurable support she has given me over our thirty years together. Writing is a wonderful but solitary, consuming process. Those close to you often feel even more the loneliness that is part of the journey. My hard work has come at a cost to Zohra. I am very grateful to her for her love and companionship and the big sacrifices she has made for me. She and our children – Rehana, Adam and Nadia – enrich my life and keep me young.

Robert Plummer and the team at Penguin Random House South Africa put the cherry on the cake. Robert, editor Lauren Smith, proofreader Dane Wallace, designer Ryan Africa and publisher Marlene Fryer were always professional, friendly and considerate on their way to finalising this book.

I trust that *Dear Comrade President* will nurture an appreciation among South Africans for the priceless legacy left by the generations who struggled against injustice and generated the inclusive and soaring values embodied in the Constitution of democratic South Africa – many still to be realised.

Finally, 'them' and 'they' are perhaps the words with some of the most harmful connotations in the English language. They underpinned the concept of apartheid. The Constitution is an 'us' document, with a common humanity and inclusivity at its core. May we, in an unequal, post-truth world – here at home and all over the globe – stand in solidarity, not sit back, when indignities and violence continue to be visited on those who face prejudice and socio-economic exclusion and are marginalised, 'othered' and unfairly discriminated against.

ANDRÉ ODENDAAL
Sunningdale Road, Cape Town,
12 January 2022

Abbreviations

AAC: All-African Convention
ANC: African National Congress
ANCYL: African National Congress Youth League
ASCAROL: Albie Sachs Trust on Constitutionalism and the Rule of Law
AZAPO: Azanian People's Organisation BC Black Consciousness
BC: Black Consciousness
BCM: Black Consciousness Movement
CALS: Centre for Applied Legal Studies (Wits)
CDF: Conference for a Democratic Future
CEDAW: United Nations Convention on the Elimination of All Forms of
    Discrimination Against Women
CHR: Centre for Human Rights (University of Pretoria)
CIA: Central Intelligence Agency
COSATU: Congress of South African Trade Unions
DLCA: Department of Legal and Constitutional Affairs
ECC: External Coordinating Committee
EPG: Eminent Persons Group
FLS: Frontline States
FRELIMO: Frente de Libertação de Moçambique (Mozambique Liberation Front)
GDR: German Democratic Republic
ICRC: International Committee of the Red Cross
IDAF: International Defence and Aid Fund
IDASA: Institute for a Democratic Alternative in South Africa
LHR: Lawyers for Human Rights
LRC: Legal Resources Centre
MDM: Mass Democratic Movement
MK: uMkhonto we Sizwe
MPLA: Movimento Popular de Libertação de Angola (People's Movement for the
    Liberation of Angola)
NAFCOC: National African Federated Chamber of Commerce
NAT: Department of National Intelligence and Security
NEC: National Executive Committee
NECC: National Education Crisis Committee
NIS: National Intelligence Service
NUM: National Union of Mineworkers

NUSAS: National Union of South African Students
NWC: National Working Committee
OAU: Organisation of African Unity
PAC: Pan-Africanist Congress of Azania
PMC: Politico-Military Council
RIM: Robben Island Museum
SACBC: South African Catholic Bishops Conference
SACC: South African Council of Churches
SACP: South African Communist Party
SACTU: South African Congress of Trade Unions
SADET: South African Democratic Education Trust
SADF: South African Defence Force
SANROC: South African Non-Racial Committee
SASO: South African Students' Organisation
SG: secretary-general
SOMAFCO: Solomon Mahlangu Freedom College
SWAPO: South West Africa People's Organisation
TRC: Truth and Reconciliation Commission
UCT: University of Cape Town
UDF: United Democratic Front
UFH: University of Fort Hare
UN: United Nations
UNISA: University of South Africa
UNITA: União Nacional para a Independência Total de Angola (National Union for the Total Independence of Angola)
UNTAG: United Nations Transition Assistance Group
UWC: University of the Western Cape

Introduction

THIS WAS A call to arms. Buoyed by the unprecedented depth of militant resistance to apartheid inside South Africa, Oliver Tambo announced in his annual 8 January address that 1986 would be the 'Year of Umkhonto we Sizwe – the People's Army'. It was the seventy-fourth birthday of the exiled African National Congress (ANC), and Tambo's message was for South Africans to make apartheid unworkable and South Africa ungovernable through four pillars of struggle: armed action, mass mobilisation, underground work and international pressure.

Meanwhile, unknown to the world, the soft-spoken science and mathematics teacher and aspirant Anglican priest turned revolutionary had also set more discreet plans in motion. On that very day, he launched a secret seven-member think tank in Lusaka. He named it the Constitution Committee and assigned it an 'ad hoc unique exercise' that had 'no precedent in the history of the movement'.[1]

Knowing that nearly all wars end at a negotiating table and judging the balance of forces to be tipping in favour of the liberation movement, Tambo instructed his new think tank to formulate the principles and draft the outlines of a constitution for a future non-racial, democratic South Africa. When the time came to talk to the apartheid government, the movement would thus be prepared and holding the initiative in the fledgling days of national liberation, freedom and democracy. Furthermore, the very process of taking the lead in negotiations could help unite South Africa and hasten the political collapse of apartheid.

For the exiles, life in Lusaka was far from comfortable. Many of them – women and men – were living in tough conditions, sleeping on the ground in the local townships. For years, cadres in the ANC exile community queued for food and clothing from the organisation and received a stipend that was just enough to buy vegetables at the market or get cigarettes and a beer. One of the Committee's seven, Penuell Maduna, slept on the floor in a Lusaka 'compound' for months before securing a mattress. 'Chawama was a slum,' he recalled. 'The fact that I might have regarded myself as a lawyer was neither here nor there … There were no chairs in my house in Chawama. We stood around a petroleum drum to drink whatever … you people had brought us … So imagine these lawyers, high-flyers in the ANC … Professors, etc., standing around an oil drum.'[2]

It was also a time when danger lurked everywhere. Men wearing balaclavas crossed borders with silenced guns to eliminate opponents of the apartheid state. Opening an envelope or the doors of a car could get you killed (see Chapters 1, 20 and 29). The threat of South African commando raids was constant, prompting Zambian president Kenneth Kaunda to give Tambo sanctuary in a guest house on the grounds of his official residence.

The Constitution Committee members were well aware of the stakes. Some years earlier, Professor Jack Simons had been conducting study classes for combatants of Umkhonto we Sizwe (MK), the armed wing of the ANC, at the Novo Catengue training camp in Angola. He was evacuated a week before SADF planes 'flattened' Novo, as he observed in his diary.[3] Penuell Maduna fled Swaziland after being advised that a South African hit squad was on its way to take him out. He crossed the border to Maputo to stay with Albie Sachs, who himself would lose an arm and the sight of an eye when a bomb was planted under his car during the course of the Committee's story.

Ranging in age from thirty-four (Maduna) to seventy-eight (Simons), the seven initial Committee members were all men. From diverse backgrounds and with richly different life experiences, they had trained, studied and worked on five continents. All were intellectuals and activists totally dedicated to the liberation struggle. Zola Skweyiya and Shadrack Lehlohonolo 'Teddy' Pekane had both been among the earliest recruits to receive military training from MK before earning PhDs in law from Eastern European universities. Simons and Sachs had received PhDs in England. Kader Asmal was dean of the law school at Trinity College in the heart of Ireland's beautiful capital city of Dublin. Maduna and Zingisile Ntozintle 'Jobs' Jobodwana had qualified as attorneys in South Africa before going into exile in Swaziland and Lesotho, respectively. Brigitte Mabandla, who joined them later on, had a law degree from the University of Zambia.

The Committee's first meeting on that historic day in January took place in a small office consisting of a few structures in a builder's yard, accessed either by a sanitary lane or through a neighbouring shop. This was the headquarters of the ANC in exile, situated discreetly between Cha Cha Cha and Cairo Roads near the city centre of Lusaka. It lacked basic office equipment – even photocopiers were rare items – yet the ideas and strategies that emerged from this seemingly insignificant space would come to shape the course of a country's history.

Step by step, Tambo's think tank started deliberating. The Committee's work was to be kept confidential between itself and the National Executive Committee (NEC), and they regularly reported directly to Tambo, typically starting their correspondence with the words 'Dear Comrade President'.

Drawing on the intimate archives of the participants, *Dear Comrade President* explains the unfolding of this process, which fundamentally influenced the history of contemporary South Africa. Why, where and how did it happen? What were the first written words? When were they put on paper? By whom? What were the values they espoused? How did their work fit into and influence the broader struggle? What were the major controversies, and how were they resolved? This book answers these questions in ways that have not been done before, and provides new insights into the purposeful first steps taken in the making of South Africa's Constitution.

The outcome of the Committee's work was profound. While the broad struggle led to the oppressed people in South Africa reclaiming their self-determination and national sovereignty, the Committee helped lay the conceptual foundations of the country's constitutional democracy. Tambo, often referred to as 'the Chief', saw to it that attention would be focused on the central drama of the South African constitution-making process: on one side were advocates of inherently racist concepts of group rights and power-sharing by representatives of ethnic groups, and competing against them were those who wanted a united non-racial democracy with a constitution and Bill of Rights that would protect the rights of every individual and promote socio-economic transformation.

Within days, the Committee decided that as a core matter of principle, a new constitution should only be drafted on South African soil by a democratically elected body created along the lines of a constituent assembly like the one that had drafted the constitution of India. In the meantime, the ANC would establish certain key principles to be placed before South Africa's own assembly in due course.

Several core documents played a role. The first, already sitting on the desks of Tambo and the NEC, was a 1985 paper by Pallo Jordan titled 'The New Face of Counter-Revolution' (see Chapter 3). Despite this being a time of insurrectionary resistance and 'people's power', Jordan's context-sketching paper went against the run of play, arguing that the ANC should come out openly in favour of a multi-party democracy with a Bill of Rights guaranteeing the individual freedoms of every South African. This would allow the ANC to take the initiative and pre-empt various counter-revolutionary strategies being developed by conservative and liberal think tanks of the right-wing establishment in South Africa and abroad. These counter-revolutionary strategies were all based on some form of group rights, and aimed to thwart the liberation movement's drive for unfettered self-determination and national sovereignty in South Africa.

The Constitution Committee produced a second key document within a short time; by mid-January 1986 they had what they called 'The Skeleton' (Chapters 4–9). Two years of intense toing and froing of documents were to ensue, often with heated arguments.

Tambo forwarded the Skeleton to a subcommittee of the ANC's National Working Committee (NWC), which challenged the document as premature and not revolutionary enough (Chapter 10). After its deliberations, the NWC forwarded certain recommendations to the Constitution Committee. The secret think tank incorporated and developed these further and the Skeleton mutated into a document called 'The Foundations of Government' (Chapters 11, 13 and 14). The NEC discussed this document in October 1986, with seventeen members of the ANC leadership weighing in with their own very diverse views before accepting the document in principle (Chapter 15). The basic template for the future was in place.

The Constitution Committee was in a rush now to release the Foundations for discussion among the broad membership, along with an explanatory 'Statement of Intent' (Chapters 15 and 17), but for more than a year it was held back from doing so by the NEC (Chapter 23). The leadership rejected the Statement as clumsy, and this document was canned. Further discussions ensued, and eventually Tambo stepped in to edit the Foundations himself – his first and only direct involvement in the writing process (Chapters 25). In early 1988, the Committee and the NEC finalised a text now titled 'Constitutional Guidelines for a Democratic South Africa'. Thus, with intense discussion all the way through, the Skeleton had morphed into the Foundations of Government, which in turn had been transformed into the Constitutional Guidelines (Chapter 26).

The leadership then placed the Guidelines before its membership – for their 'unconstrained appraisal' – in a five-day In-House Seminar held in Lusaka in March 1988. Attended by over 110 delegates from more than twenty countries in which ANC members were based, the In-House Seminar produced additional textual modifications (Chapters 26 and 27). The revised Constitutional Guidelines were distributed internationally and inside South Africa for comments (Chapters 32 and 33). After thirty-three months of internal ANC discussions and more than a dozen drafts, the Guidelines became part of the incipient process of talks about the possibility of official 'talks about talks'. ANC representatives tabled the Guidelines for discussions with proxies of the regime and its National Intelligence Service (NIS) at the Consgold meetings held in England in August and December 1988 (Chapters 31 and 32).

All those involved in drafting the Constitutional Guidelines were men, until Brigitte Mabandla joined the Department of Legal and Constitutional Affairs (DLCA) in 1987. And there were only two women out of the more than thirty NEC members overseeing the work of the Constitution Committee. They were the doughty head of the Women's Section, Gertrude Shope, and the equally forceful Ruth Mompati, who played a key role as administrative head of the secretary-general's office. At the time, these two, together with the late Lilian Ngoyi and Florence Mophosho, were the only women to have served on the seventy-five-year-old ANC's highest body. So, the ANC – characteristic of the time – was profoundly patriarchal in nature. Though policy positions proclaimed women as equal partners in the struggle, the reality was that they faced 'traditional' attitudes on a daily basis and had generally been relegated to secondary roles in the organisation. But women's voices from within, strengthened by deepening international struggles for gender equality, brought about changes. A decisive albeit gradual turnabout on the women's issue became visible from the mid-1980s onwards. At both the Kabwe conference in 1985 (Chapter 1) and at the 1988 In-House Seminar (Chapter 27), it was resolved that liberating women from discrimination by gender, race and class – in society and inside the ANC – was essential to giving real content to the idea of national liberation. Most importantly, in December 1989, the ANC held a second internal seminar in Lusaka to 'entrench issues specific to women' in the Constitutional Guidelines. This seminar was given the status of a policy conference, and critically dissected and challenged historic gender discrimination, setting in motion a process that had a profound influence on the future of South Africa, starting with twelve changes to the previously approved Guidelines for a future constitution (Chapter 36).[4]

Finally, separately from the Constitution Committee but with Jack Simons involved and various clauses from the Constitutional Guidelines included, a special drafting team working closely with Tambo came out with the Harare Declaration in August 1989 (Chapters 34 and 35). Its purpose was to get the international community behind the ANC's plans for the future. It flowed from positive and negative lessons learnt after the Battle of Cuito Cuanavale, when the United Nations' involvement precipitated and propelled the processes leading up to independence in Namibia. Tambo had set up a team to draft a declaration ensuring that the liberation movement would be at the helm in determining the processes and principles governing negotiations for an end to apartheid and establishing a constitutional democracy. The Organisation of African Unity (OAU) and the ANC took the Harare Declaration to the UN, where it was adopted by acclamation by the General Assembly in December 1989. With hindsight, it is clear that the Harare Declaration was a stunning diplomatic success for the ANC. It provided an internationally agreed-upon framework for the transition from apartheid to democracy, tying the apartheid government into a process it could not wriggle out of. The framework called on the South African government to release political prisoners, let exiles return, withdraw troops from the townships and permit free political activity. It also envisaged the creation of a united, non-racial, democratic South Africa and set the template on how that should be achieved.

The Constitutional Guidelines provided the conceptual base that allowed the ANC to open up this new terrain of struggle in the late 1980s, going hand in glove with the practical preconditions for action contained in the Harare Declaration. Negotiations within a clear framework now became a fifth pillar of the struggle that would lead to official talks in 1991, followed by a transfer of power and national self-determination and democracy in 1994. These are the documentary foundation stones of our democracy. Placing them in sequence, we can see a straight line of thought and formulation running from 1985 right through to the signing of a new constitution for South Africa in 1996. As envisaged by the Constitution Committee at its first meeting in Lusaka in 1986, it had been adopted on South African soil by democratically elected representatives of the people of South Africa. The only change was that the body that adopted it was called the Constitutional Assembly not the Constituent Assembly.

For various reasons the foundational developments in the making of the Constitution described in this book remain poorly recorded and understood. Four decades on, few analysts, commentators and university academics or students know about the foundational documents, debates and personalities in any great depth, which is not the case in many other countries.

In a literature survey, historian Christopher Saunders has expressed surprise that so little is known about the making of South Africa's democratic Constitution, 'especially on the way it evolved over time, how it was contested and yet agreed to, and where the ideas embodied in it came from.'[5] This is what *Dear Comrade President* sets out to start explaining.

Saunders further notes that historians have left the field to legal scholars who, as a rule, have failed to explain or analyse the historic roots of the Constitution, concentrating their writings on the post-1990 period instead. Again, this book attempts to address this lacuna by concentrating almost entirely on the 1985–1990 period. During this time, the author argues, the ANC moulded the constitutional template for the future, and made its implementation possible by simultaneously coordinating a multipronged struggle that backed the regime into a corner.

Weighty, broad-canvas accounts of the politics of the 1980s, whether via biography or big-picture historical overviews, provide few details about this formative process of constitutional planning within the ANC. This is, to an extent, understandable. Consider, for example, the challenges faced by Luli Callinicos in her 683-page biography of Oliver Tambo, and Mark Gevisser in his even thicker 892-page tome on the life of Thabo Mbeki. Their works had, out of necessity, to analyse and discuss a multitude of complex personal, organisational, national and geopolitical issues traversing a longer period than this book covers, in addition to the overarching task of creating life histories. And so too do overview histories like SADET's massive multivolumed *The Road to Democracy in South Africa*, David Welsh's *The Rise and Fall of Apartheid* and Thula Simpson's fat *History of South Africa: From 1902 to the Present.*[6] These substantive books either overlook the work of the Committee or deal with it in a mere handful of pages. While the Guidelines might get a mention, the micro-steps that led to their adoption by the ANC and where they fitted in a multipronged struggle are virtually ignored. In these narratives, dramatic big-picture issues such as armed struggle, exile, negotiations, apartheid, the nature of the state, famous political actors, global geopolitics, etc., demanded their space and subsumed the story that this book seeks to tell.

Dear Comrade President takes a single issue, follows a single strand of the ANC's struggle and remains focused on it in ways that reveal something fresh about the Constitution's origins and, hopefully, about the ANC and South Africa's history more broadly. It shines a light on aspects of 1980s politics that are not yet fully understood, showing how the Constitution Committee's work in developing the Constitutional Guidelines from 1986 onwards was closely interconnected with, and deeply influenced by, other aspects of the broader liberation struggle.

Dear Comrade President is therefore deliberately selective, constraining itself as a story and in terms of the material used to illuminate this one strand of a remarkable history. It is about both fragment and form, attempting to explain this broad historic process in ways that are clear and readable and also capture the microclimate in which the Constitution Committee worked, bringing alive the intimacies of place, relationships, daily life, the dangers of exile and the different personalities involved. In particular, *Dear Comrade President* stresses the importance of African agency in the shaping of the Constitutional Guidelines and the making of the Constitution. It reveals that of the first 130-odd people to participate in the shaping of the ANC's Constitutional Guidelines and constitutional planning process between January 1986 and March 1988, 80 per cent were African cadres, with Oliver Tambo and Pallo Jordan being the senior protagonists. Similar demographic proportions were evident at the important women's seminar that beefed up the Guidelines in December 1989, this time with two-thirds of the over 100 participants also being women.

The details presented in this work underline the homegrown origins and essence of the Constitution. By doing so, the book rejects the notion that the Constitution and its fundamental principles were somehow handed down from on high by external, 'un-African' forces in a sell-out of sorts. One common assumption has been that it was the collapse of the Berlin Wall in November 1989 that caused the ANC to adopt a constitutional approach. However, the facts do not substantiate these claims. The ANC's NEC had already endorsed the Foundations of Government document (which unambiguously proposed a constitution guaranteeing a multiparty democracy and Bill of Rights to protect every person) *thirty-seven months earlier*, in October 1986. Indeed, this was a few weeks *before* Oliver Tambo first met with the reformist-minded president of the Soviet Union, Mikhail Gorbachev, who some inaccurately believe coerced the 'ANC communists' into opting for constitutional options, as a kind of South African version of glasnost and perestroika.

Committee member Brigitte Mabandla states plainly: 'Get used to it. This was our plan and our values informed it.' Her message is that, like it or not, those modern-day sceptics who loudly make such claims should learn their history.[7]

This book also attempts to counter the often incorrect or simplistic popular assumptions about the ANC's constitutional planning and the politics of the 1980s. These, too, are rooted in the above-mentioned ignorance about the topic. Academics, politicians and the public alike too often conflate or transpose dates and events from three decades ago, offering as truth generic assumptions that can be disproven when holding a microscope to the facts. I've therefore attempted to carbon-date the unfolding developments, illustrating and explaining developments step by step, year by year – almost month by month – from 1986 to 1990 to show how the template for a new constitution and new society was forged.

For example, the story that the NIS was already negotiating with the ANC by the time a dramatic meeting in Dakar happened in July 1987 is simply not true.[8] Concrete talks about the possibility of official 'talks about talks' (not negotiations) only took off properly in 1988, and became substantive two years after Dakar in mid to late 1989, when the imprisoned Nelson Mandela met with P.W. Botha, followed by a meeting between the ANC and NIS in Switzerland.

Dear Comrade President also refutes the Hollywood narrative that elements of the apartheid regime were somehow enlightened visionaries who, nudged by British and American envoys, became equal co-authors of South Africa's democracy and constitution. When F.W. de Klerk, successor to the bellicose P.W. Botha, stood up in the last white parliament on 2 February 1990 to announce his reforms, the apartheid government had already been boxed in politically, leaving it with limited room to manoeuvre. Some six weeks before that date, the Harare Declaration – drawn up by the ANC in tandem with the internal Mass Democratic Movement (MDM) and the leaders of the Frontline States and the OAU, and then adopted in turn by the Non-Aligned Movement of 'Third World' countries, the Commonwealth grouping of more than fifty countries and, by acclamation, the UN General Assembly – had already set in concrete the internationally supported minimum conditions necessary for negotiations and the 'normalisation' of South African politics.

The point above helps illustrate a key argument made in *Dear Comrade President*, namely that that the regime and its agents were *not* enlightened visionaries driving change or willing co-authors of a new democratic order in South Africa; they were latecomers to the idea. Bereft of political alternatives to their apartheid world view, weakened by insular thinking and faced with the inability of repression to bring 'order', they were dragged to the negotiating table after 1990 – where they again failed to control the process as they had intended to do. Hollywood narratives in films like *Endgame* (2009), and books by writers from the apartheid establishment such as Niël Barnard and Willie Esterhuyse, claiming foresight and enlightenment on the part of the system, need to be better contextualised and fundamentally re-evaluated and debunked (see Chapters 31 and 32). Nelson Mandela and Aziz Pahad, who were prominent in the earliest substantive talks from 1988 onwards, were surprised to discover how clearly uninformed Barnard, Esterhuyse and other members of the white establishment were about the dynamics of the freedom struggle and broader South African history. Mandela's experience was that his 'new colleagues' were largely ignorant about South African politics outside their narrow white-minority world and that they 'knew little about the ANC [although] they were all sophisticated Afrikaners, and far more open-minded than nearly all their brethren'.[9]

Thus, from the mid-1980s, while a climate of insurrection swept the country, the ANC and its internal allies wove constitutionalism in as one of the distinct threads of an enormously complex, multifaceted and sometimes contradictory struggle during a decisive – indeed epochal – moment in South Africa's history. *Dear Comrade President* now details this 1980s genesis of the intense process of struggle, negotiation and constitutional planning that ended formal apartheid and led to the birth of a new nation.

It is necessary to follow the Constitution Committee's activities and thinking from 1986 onwards to see how this happened, and how constitutionalism and negotiations became a key pillar of the ANC's thinking, strategy and tactics in the second half of the 1980s. In following this one distinctive strand, the book also brings to light little-known aspects of broader ANC culture and South African politics and history. It also brings out the way the ANC interacted with many other political and social forces at home and further afield who contributed their own thought, energy and activity to the bringing down of apartheid.

Some striking facts emerge from an exploration of the archives containing the key foundational documents mentioned earlier. The first is that Tambo established the intellectual foundation of the Constitution, drawing heavily on a paper he had commissioned Pallo Jordan to prepare (Chapter 3). In his own particular manner, he was in charge at all times. He navigated the process through the various structures of the ANC and chose his moment late in the day to make his own direct and significant intervention (Chapter 25).

The second is that in plotting this new strategic path in the 1980s, Oliver Tambo, the Constitution Committee and the ANC symbolically and concretely connected with, and drew inspiration from, a deep history of African constitutionalism in South Africa. They were drawing on a long tradition of theorising and mobilisation by black intellectuals and activists going back well over a century from the 1860s onwards, which led to the first proto-nationalist organisations, newspapers, demands for the franchise, and creation of national networks in the 1880s, 1890s and early 1900s.

This process of mobilisation has been dealt with in depth by the author in his earlier writings.[10] Taking off from there, *Dear Comrade President* argues that understanding the twentieth-century liberation struggle and ANC strategies in the 1980s and 1990s requires an understanding of this deeper historical context too, also in relation to the ANC's internationalism and operation in exile. Even though the ANC was founded in 1912, four of its first five presidents had already travelled abroad to study *before* 1900.[11] The earliest generations of intellectuals and activists protesting discrimination and political exclusion in colonial South Africa – like those operating in the difficult but rich terrain of exile – drew on international ideas and developments from the start, as part of their African aspirations to become global citizens and shapers of a new society in South Africa. This knowledge should encourage us to take a long view of the struggle for democracy and its fundamental concepts and ideas.

Key 1980s actors and planners – like Oliver Tambo and Pallo Jordan – had direct linkages to earlier generations of constitutionalists. The president, secretary-general and other leaders often referred to their own organisation's pre-exile past to explain the strategy it was adopting. The ANC's demand for a constituent assembly in the late 1980s and early 1990s was consistent, too, with earlier demands by African spokespeople for a national convention to create an inclusive political order.

The calling of the South African Native Convention in Bloemfontein (Mangaung) in 1909 was in response to the 'colour-bar' clauses of the constitution of the new Union of South Africa and led directly to the founding of the ANC as the 'Native Parliament' three years later.[12] In 1923, the ANC adopted a Bill of Rights for South Africa. Its tone was deferential and its terms limited, but it articulated the idea of everyone having certain fundamental rights irrespective of race, colour or creed. Then, in response to the 1936 Native Trust and Land Act and the final removal of Africans from the voters' roll in the Cape

Province in 1935–36, the ANC helped call together the All-African Convention (AAC), which was meant to be 'the most representative national convention ever of chiefs, leaders and representatives of all shades of political thought'.[13]

A few years later, during World War II, the ANC adopted the Africans' Claims document, a clause-by-clause response to Churchill and Roosevelt's Atlantic Charter, which laid out the basis for a post–World War II era of human rights and freedoms. The Atlantic Charter gave rise to the formation of the United Nations in 1945 and the adoption of the Universal Declaration of Human Rights by the UN in 1948. The Africans' Claims document included a comprehensive Bill of Rights and set the benchmark for the future. It unequivocally demanded the same full citizenship rights for colonised people as those claimed by the former colonisers in the developed nations, including rights to equal justice, freedom of residence, freedom of movement and freedom of the press; free education and equal social security benefits; recognition of the sanctity of the home; the right to own land and 'engage in all forms of lawful occupations', etc.[14]

The 1955 Congress of the People, which adopted the Freedom Charter, and the 1961 All-in African Conference's call for a national convention in the post-Sharpeville era, at the time South Africa became a republic, were more well-known steps that perpetuated the convention idea.

The goal of the All-in African Conference was unambiguous: 'We demand that a National Convention of elected representatives of all adult men and women irrespective of race, colour, creed or other limitation be called by the Union Government not later than May 31, 1961; that the Convention shall have sovereign powers to determine, in any way the majority of representatives decide, a new non-racial democratic Constitution for South Africa.'[15] The discussions in this book about the role of the Freedom Charter in the mid-1980s (Chapters 1 and 8); the presence of Thembu king Sabata Dalindyebo at Kabwe (Chapter 2); the intellectual pedigree of Pallo Jordan, who drafted 'The New Face of Counter-Revolution' (Chapter 3); and the way the ANC in exile engaged with global debates and networks (Chapter 5) all illustrate the link with this long tradition of constitutional politics. At the opening of the In-House Seminar in Lusaka in March 1988, secretary-general Alfred Nzo stated that the Constitutional Guidelines were extensions of these earlier clarion calls. Many of the words and ideas articulated in these early pronouncements, particularly in Africans' Claims and the Freedom Charter, would run straight through into the new constitution in the 1990s.

On an ideological level, too, this author has shown that debates about the elusive and shifting connections and balances between 'Africanism' (and Black Consciousness) and 'non-racialism', which remain key issues in South African life today, started not with Steve Biko or Barney Pityana in the 1960s, nor Sobukwe in the 1950s or Lembede and Mda in the 1940s, but with the constitutionalists of the nineteenth century.[16]

But these continuities were not seamless. Shifting economic, political and social contexts resulted in regular ruptures and contradictions in broader politics, as well as contestations within the ANC itself, as revolutionary Marxism, direct-action defiance and different ideological tendencies (including Gandhian passive resistance) emerged, asserted themselves and vied for space. Zwelethu Jolobe has reminded us that 'revolutionary movements and organisations consist of many coalitions, factions and individuals who sometimes have conflicting interests', and it is important to recognise this in the broad-church movement led by the ANC as well.[17] Nevertheless, constitutionalism was indisputably in the DNA of the seventy-three-year-old ANC when it decided in 1985 to reconnect – in a different context and in an altogether more assertive manner – with a tradition that had long been central to its politics until Sharpeville, the subsequent bannings and the unforgiving repression of apartheid put it on a new trajectory of self-defence via armed struggle and the revolutionary seizure of power. Hopefully, this process of reconnection and the complexities and contradictions that accompanied its unfolding – this time in tandem with mass mobilisation, underground activity, armed attacks and international solidarity action – are reflected in the pages that follow.

Oliver Tambo led the ANC for the entire thirty years of its exile era, holding the liberation movement together against huge odds. In August 1989, he arrived back in Lusaka from a knees-to-chin journey in a small aeroplane arranged for him by President Kenneth Kaunda. He had flown to Dar es Salaam in Tanzania where his team received important advice from Julius Nyerere, then to Harare in Zimbabwe, to Gaborone in Botswana and, finally, to Luanda in Angola, to secure his plan for the South African negotiation process and the exiles' return home. That night, after a further session of dotting the i's and crossing the t's on the Harare Declaration that would give the African continent a critical role in bringing down apartheid and ushering in a new constitutional order, Tambo collapsed, incapacitated by a stroke (see Chapter 34).

The Constitution Committee's Zola Skweyiya was in the room and called for help as he tried to make 'the Chief comfortable on a couch. Tambo's work had been done. His journey was over. But a new chapter in the history of South Africa was about to be written.[18]

This book ends as Tambo and the other Constitution Committee members return to South Africa in 1990. The Committee morphed into an expanded constitutional think tank with a contingent of home-based legal heavyweights including

Pius Langa, Arthur Chaskalson, George Bizos, Dullah Omar, Bulelani Ngcuka, Essa Moosa and Fink Haysom. Tambo landed to a huge welcome at Johannesburg's Jan Smuts Airport, which was later renamed after him.

The remarkable process that started in the backrooms between Cha Cha Cha and Cairo Roads in Lusaka on 8 January 1986 ended ten years, eleven months and two days later when the new Constitution of democratic South Africa was signed into being by Nelson Mandela on 10 December 1996 in Sharpeville. That document was the product of deep-rooted African imaginations and struggles grounded in the lived experience of generations of dispossessed and disenfranchised South Africans.

The task of recognising the African agency at work in creating a new country, as well as decolonising the story of this transitional slice of South Africa's history, is very much overdue. The dispossessed and disenfranchised people of South Africa gathered support from democrats throughout the world and became the architects of their own freedom in a struggle stretching across generations. The oppressed wrested justice from history and defined the contours of their own destiny. They imagined, engineered and won freedom. It was not given to them. That is the bottom-line conclusion of this book.

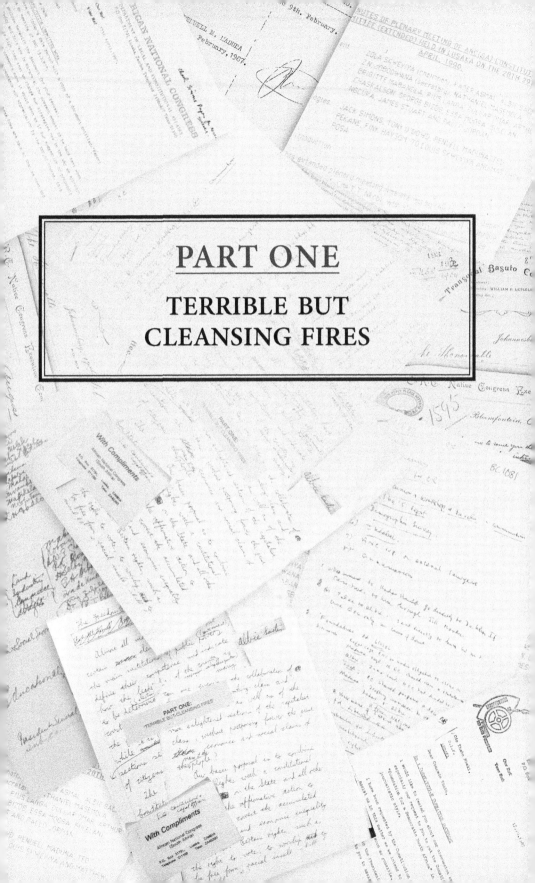

PART ONE

TERRIBLE BUT CLEANSING FIRES

1

The 'Council of War' at Kabwe

'The darkness that has shrouded our country for so long is now lit by flames that are consuming the accumulated refuse of centuries...'

– Oliver Tambo, 16 June 1985[1]

IN THE WINTER of June 1985, a little-known mining town in Zambia became a signpost to South Africa's future. Hundreds of fired-up ANC exiles converged on Kabwe, 140 kilometres north of Lusaka. The mood was hot, with strong feelings brewing about the state of the organisation, and about the discontent and tragic deaths in the military training camps in Angola. The organisation's leadership was being stretched in its attempts to keep control of operations across forty countries on various continents as it approached a quarter of a century in exile.

It was the first major consultative meeting since the ANC adopted the revolutionary policy document 'Strategy and Tactics' at Morogoro in neighbouring Tanzania sixteen years before. Chris Hani and some of his comrades had risked possible execution for a memorandum raising dissatisfaction with the conduct of the ANC leadership and their inability to start military operations against South Africa's apartheid rulers.[2] Like Morogoro, the Kabwe conference was called because of intense pressures facing the movement, both internally and on a broader level.

'Back home', as the delegates would have said, one town and region after another had erupted since August 1984. Portions of the country threatened to become 'ungovernable', a new word in the national lexicon. The 1983 Tricameral Constitution introduced by P.W. Botha's government was denied the legitimacy its apartheid drafters had hoped it would achieve. As the urban revolt spread, black local councils collapsed. Symbols of government were attacked and torched. Perceived collaborators were dealt with harshly, some subjected to grisly necklacing. The army invaded townships. Extrajudicial killings by the security forces intensified. One massacre followed another, and mass funerals held on football and rugby fields became the order of the day.[3] These tumultuous liturgies of pain further politicised the besieged communities. In Angola, there was the internal matter of abuses that had been happening in ANC military camps.[4]

It was in this context that ANC missions and branches throughout the world had been discussing theme papers that were to be presented at the consultative conference. Issues on which decisions were to be taken included how to ensure that all the elements of the struggle could be brought together in a coherent strategy to bring down apartheid; what the ANC's attitude towards whites in South Africa should be; how the organisation could strengthen its administration and ensure legality in its ranks; and whether non-Africans should be allowed into its top leadership. The conference would also elect a new leadership by secret ballot.

The Kabwe delegates did not know where they were to meet. Heightened security meant the venue – the President's Citizenship College, just outside the town – was kept secret until the very last moment. Albie Sachs remembers the excitement aboard their bus:

> No one knew where they were going. There was lots of laughter. Chris Hani teased Jackie Selebi, saying that rations would be short and Jackie would be forced to get fit. Jackie fired back with a quick retort. We were on edge but enthusiastic. For months, in our separate branches all over the place – some in America, some in Angola, some in Mozambique – we had been debating position papers on a whole range of issues ranging from how the struggle should be taken forward to whether non-Africans should be allowed onto the national executive of the ANC. After some hours, the bus stopped and we were told that we were in a place called Kabwe. We saw Zambian soldiers all the way round the building we were going to meet in. Only then did we get details about a massacre by apartheid hit squads in Gaborone two days before.[5]

On the night of 13–14 June 1985, South African security forces had crossed the border into Botswana and attacked several ANC safe houses identified by informers in the capital, Gaborone. With fifty to sixty tanks, helicopters and jet fighters in position in nearby Zeerust in case Botswana retaliated, notorious Vlakplaas operatives and their henchmen killed several ANC members as well as innocent civilians, among them nationals from Somalia, Lesotho and the host country. Twelve died, and others were injured.[6] Mrs Hilda Phahle from Johannesburg explained how her son George 'Baldhead' Phahle, her daughter-in-law Lindi Phahle and her cousin Joseph Malaza were killed:

> The SADF [South African Defence Force] arrived swearing and behaving like people well-drugged and drunk, ordering George to open the door ... Instead of opening, George and Lindi ran into his bedroom, locked the door, and pushed his portable piano against it. Lindi threw herself face down in a corner. George fell over her as a sign of protection. There was nothing impossible with these murderers. They blew the door open, pushed it and the piano fell against

[his other son] Levi's bed under which he was hiding. God spared him to tell the story [though Levi was 'adversely affected'].[7]

Using disinformation circulated by the notorious spy and killer Craig Williamson, the *Sunday Times* in Johannesburg (edited by another government informer, it was reported later[8]) sensationalised the raid with a front-page story titled 'The guns of Gaborone', a play on *The Guns of Navarone*, a Hollywood movie starring Anthony Quinn, Gregory Peck and David Niven.[9] Weapons later acknowledged to have been planted by the assassins were depicted in the newspapers as captured evidence of the ANC's terrorism.

Also murdered was the talented artist Thami Mnyele, who was due to take up a scholarship in the Netherlands. Mnyele was a member of the Medu Art Ensemble[10] based in Gaborone and had worked closely with fellow artists such as the writer and underground commander Mongane Wally Serote; poet Willie Keorapetse Kgositsile (then teaching at the University of Botswana); Baleka Mbete, head of Medu; and its treasurer Mike Hamlyn, who was also killed that night.

The Phahles' bombed bedroom door and smashed piano, along with the murdered artists, summed up a broader truth: the frontline in South Africa was shifting into every sphere of life and invading even the most personal spaces. In May that year, Vernon 'Rogers' Nkadimeng had been killed in Botswana by a letter bomb.[11] His father, John, was heavily involved in the Kabwe preparations as secretary-general of the South African Congress of Trade Unions (SACTU) and was a long-standing ANC NEC member. This bitter news reinforced the vision of the conference delegates, all of whom saw themselves as part of a revolutionary movement against which the enemy could strike at any place, at any moment.

Zambian president Kenneth Kaunda, known simply as 'KK' to the ANC, was putting fellow Africans at the disposal of the South African freedom fighters, even as he and his fellow frontline leaders came under sustained pressure from the Botha government to withdraw facilities from the ANC. Charles Nqakula, then a newly exiled journalist and Umkhonto we Sizwe underground operative, was accustomed to small secret meetings of underground cells and recorded the sense of awe felt by the 250 or so representatives at the opening of the conference. MK members led the singing and dancing. The atmosphere was 'phenomenal'. As Oliver Tambo led his NEC onto the stage, 'there was momentary silence followed by thunderous ovation ... There they were before our eyes, the leaders of the revolution.'[12]

After a performance of Enoch Sontonga's moving anthem 'Nkosi Sikelel' iAfrika', which 'stayed with participants for a long time' after Kabwe, Tambo predicted that the conference would go down as a decisive moment in history:

The days we spend here will live forever in the records of struggle as marking a turning point in the history of all the people of South Africa. Our conference will be remembered by our people as a council of war that planned the seizure of power by [the] masses, the penultimate convention that gave the order for us to take our country through the terrible but cleansing fires of revolutionary war to a condition of peace [and] democracy.[13]

In the ANC president's eyes, Kabwe would prepare the organisation for the final revolutionary push for power and a people's parliament of the future, which would reflect a genuine South African national congress comprising all 'national groups'.

The 250 delegates had arrived from every country in the world where the ANC had members, including forty countries that had official ANC missions. Besides the twenty-two-person NEC, delegates included 'all our diplomatic functionaries – the chief representatives, commanders and other members of our army, political organisers, trade unionists, administration, production, health and cultural workers, propagandists, students and other members who are employed outside the ranks of our organisation'.[14]

Hugh Macmillan, who taught for many years at the University of Zambia, has written about the intense, open discussions that happened in the run-up to Kabwe. For example, the thirty-five delegates from Zambia were chosen after months of preparation, during which strongly conflicting viewpoints were expressed. This included a regional conference in Lusaka in April that lasted for five days and involved the establishment of five commissions. In his book *The Lusaka Years*, Macmillan concludes that the ANC allowed internal criticism in a way that was unique among liberation movements. In his view, critics who claimed there was no internal democracy in the exiled movement were unaware of the real efforts made by both the ANC and its ally the South African Communist Party (SACP) to promote political education and get members involved in political life.[15]

On the other hand, Stanley Manong, an MK commander in Angola, was angry with what he regarded as failures of the ANC leadership, and he arrived at Kabwe determined to speak his mind. He, too, was moved by the proceedings, noting that the conference began on a sober note for John Nkadimeng, Rogers' father, who was seated at the podium next to Tambo. It had been only a month since his son had been assassinated by letter bomb, but despite his deep concerns, Manong approved of Tambo's rousing opening speech to the conference, recalling that 'It was carefully thought through, highly articulate and interspersed with the use of impeccable English as its trademark...'[16]

Manong was also struck by the president's revelation, in the presentation of the NEC's political report, that the ANC leadership had sought to have secret talks with Steve Biko and that, 'Shortly before his death, Biko had agreed to meet the leadership of the ANC ... [including] Tambo himself ... in a secret venue in Swaziland'. Acknowledging the growth of the Black Consciousness Movement as a 'distinct' force since the last consultative conference in Morogoro, the ANC recognised it as 'part of the genuine forces of the revolution', without hiding the ideological differences existing between them.[17]

A letter from political prisoners on Robben Island and in other jails, signed by Nelson Mandela, was read to the conference, evoking 'indescribable emotions' among the participants.[18] Those in 'apartheid's dungeons' reiterated their loyalty as ANC members and added, 'As you know, we always try to harmonise our own views and responses with those of the Movement at large ... ever conscious of the crucial importance of unity, and of resisting every attempt to divide and confuse.' The message added that all discussion and planning had to be 'invariably subjected to the overriding principle of maximum unity. To lose sight of this basic principle is to sell our birth right, to betray those who paid the highest price.'[19]

The conference endorsed this call for unity. In a call to the people of South Africa, it declared that 'true liberators should not fight among ourselves. Let us not allow the enemy's dirty tricks department to succeed in getting us to fight one another.'[20]

The conference also resolved that, in pursuing unity, it was important that all the people be organised and mobilised, in the towns and the countryside, including those in the Bantustans. Progressive traditional leaders had always been an important constituency for the ANC, and at the conference this historical connection was emphasised by the presence of Sabata Dalindyebo, the exiled king of the Thembu, who would not long afterwards pass away in Lusaka.

The conference delegates paid tribute to the unifying role the United Democratic Front (UDF) had played in the country since its formation in August 1983. Tambo said the ANC 'was pleased, to say the least, when the UDF was formed because that created a platform exactly for united action'. The ANC's desired united front was one that covered all political organisations, all ideological trends, each fighting on its own specific front, but with an understanding that there was a common purpose to bring down apartheid and unite South Africans. If some of these groupings differed (on the Freedom Charter, for example) 'we accept that' but, for the sake of overthrowing the regime, 'let us act together'.[21]

Tambo's basic analysis was that the apartheid system was in a deep and permanent general crisis from which it could not extricate itself.[22] The violence of the state reflected this: because the regime could not rule as before, the Botha government had brought its military forces into the centre of apartheid state structures. These developments reinforced thinking among the Kabwe delegates that armed struggle would continue to be central to overthrowing the violent apartheid system, and the main aim remained the seizure of power by the people. The conference made a special call to those working in the system 'who administer the cruel laws against the people' to 'earn your place in the free South Africa that is coming, by organising to turn your guns against your masters: let your typewriters speak the truth. Let there be no place where the enemy can rest.' Here it specifically called on 'those in the army, police and prison services of the regime and its Bantustan puppets' to respond.[23] In these circumstances, the ANC and MK needed to pursue 'a heightened and co-ordinated political and military offensive'.

But armed struggle was not assumed to be the sole means of bringing down the racist regime. The focus was to step up the all-round political-military offensive, a strategy reinforced by the growing mobilisation within the country in the 1980s. The Kabwe conference confirmed that there were four interrelated pillars of the ANC's struggle: underground organisation, mass mobilisation, armed action and international solidarity. The ANC re-emphasised that 'the black workers are of special importance in the mass activity of all our people and are ... the backbone and leading force in our struggle for national liberation'. The Commission on Strategy and Tactics confirmed that there was 'unanimity' that the 'primary perspective' continued to be People's War which would, after protracted struggle, lead to insurrection.[24]

The internal morality of the revolutionary forces themselves occupied much attention at the conference. One of the key documents adopted was a code of conduct, the need for which had been highlighted in a report by the Stuart Commission, which Tambo had appointed to investigate the harsh abuses suffered in the ANC's Angolan camps and the subsequent mutiny by some MK members. Albie Sachs was prominent in its drafting. The code of conduct, like the ANC's participation in international forums and its support for international conventions, expressed the organisation's intent to live up to the highest standards of organisational behaviour under the exceedingly difficult circumstances of exile and armed struggle. Members had perforce to operate as underground revolutionaries from a tenuous base under conditions of strict secrecy in often life-threatening situations, but, as Heinz Klug has pointed out, the ANC in exile 'continued through the years to make appeals to law' as well as to 'work within the international legal environment provided by the United Nations and the post–World War II system of decolonisation and human rights'.[25] For example, ANC lawyers were involved in the formation of the UN Special Committee against Apartheid in 1963; the Special Committee's work in spearheading the imposition of sanctions against apartheid South Africa in 1967; the 1973 declaration of apartheid as a crime against humanity under the International Convention on the Suppression and Punishment of the Crime of Apartheid; the UN arms embargo imposed under Resolution 418 of the UN Security Council in November 1977; and in the debates and negotiations to include liberation struggles in the Geneva Convention Protocols I and II governing the rules of war, becoming the first liberation movement to commit to treating captured enemy combatants as prisoners of war.[26] Against this background, and following the Angolan camp abuses, Tambo and the leadership now sought to introduce the internal code of conduct and various internal structures and processes to give effect to it.

Recalling the impact that the code made on the participants, Nqakula describes how the 'communist and brilliant lawyer, Albie Sachs, his face embellished by his wonderful smile ... went up to the conference lectern to deliver one of the most thought-provoking policy positions in the history of the ANC Alliance which Tambo had asked him to develop'.[27] According to Nqakula, the code of conduct was the clearest illustration of how extraordinary the ANC was, given its underground status and the fact that it was involved in a revolutionary struggle. It 'introduced a moral ethos into everything that was done in the name of the movement by its members, including the leadership, and laid down rules as a personal badge of morality and honour in the struggle for South Africa's liberation'. And, he noted, 'The centrepiece of the Code was humanness and morality – even in the handling of exposed security agents infiltrated into ANC ranks by apartheid security forces.'[28] Its first paragraph quoted clause five of the Freedom Charter starting with the principle that 'All shall be equal before the law'.

The code, as presented by Sachs, was enthusiastically endorsed by the conference. It included the following lines:

In fighting for justice in our land, we must ensure at all times that justice exists inside our organisation – our members, the people of South Africa, and the people of the world must know and feel that for us justice is not merely an ideal but the fundamental principle that governs all our actions. Accordingly, we must at all times act justly in our own ranks, train our people in the procedure of justice and establish the embryo of the new justice system we envisage for a liberated South Africa ...

The ANC is fighting for peoples' power, and in the last analysis, it is the same power of the people that all the organs of the ANC, including the judicial organs, express. The people want justice and the people want to be protected both against external exploiters and against abusers within their own ranks. Accordingly, the people want proper institutions to guarantee the just exercise of their power.[29]

To cover military discipline, Kabwe also agreed on an Umkhonto we Sizwe 'Military Code', which unambiguously stated: 'The political leadership has primacy over the military. Our military line derives from our political line. Every commander, commissar, instructor and combatant must therefore be clearly acquainted with the policy with regard to all combat tasks and missions.'[30]

Kabwe also dealt with the problem in both MK and the ANC of widespread patriarchal attitudes and gender discrimination (and sometimes abuse) that women faced in exile. The report of the Commission on Ideological and Political Work included a section on 'The women's question'. It concluded that the tendency to refer women's issues to the Women's Section needed to change. The organisation as a whole needed to take responsibility, both in terms of political approaches as well as relationships within the working life of the organisation. The report conceded that there were cases where men in the ANC, 'because of traditional attitudes, use their superior positions to take advantage of women'.[31] In the Angolan camps, as Ruth Mompati testified, there were sometimes gender imbalances of six women to two hundred men in a camp and the result was strong pressure on the women to start unwanted sexual liaisons.[32] The commission concluded that it was vital to 'stop practices that were unethical and contrary to the high principles of the organisation'. Remedies were suggested. Programmes asserting the equality of men and women had to be embarked on. Urgent measures should be introduced to ensure women participated at all levels of the struggle, including the forward areas and underground. Positive discrimination was needed in the deployment and employment of cadres. Unit and branch meetings needed to discuss and promote these perspectives. The Women's Section – led by Gertrude Shope and staffed by fifteen of the roughly 400 cadres deployed in Lusaka at the time[33] – needed to be strengthened and there was an urgent need for the ANC to learn from the experiences of countries such as Vietnam, Cuba and Nicaragua. A national seminar on the women's question was proposed, to set out a theoretical basis and plan for the emancipation of women. The starting point had to be the recognition that women suffered triple oppression in South Africa – on the basis of race, class and gender. The commission concluded that Tambo's speech at the first national women's conference in Luanda in 1981, where he said 'we should stop pretending that women in our movement have the same opportunities as men', should be a guide.[34]

Many delegates wondered if the emphasis given to seizure of power would exclude the possibility of negotiations between the ANC and the apartheid regime. The theme of negotiations was openly canvassed, with Tambo declaring:

The NEC is of the view that we cannot be seen to be rejecting a negotiated settlement in principle. In any case, no revolutionary movement can be against negotiations in principle. Indeed, in our case, it is correct that we encourage all forces, particularly among our white compatriots and in the Western world, to put pressure on the Botha regime to abandon the notion that it can keep itself in power forever by the use of brute force.[35]

The president raised the possibility of talks with white South Africans, as well as of developing closer linkages with Western countries, many of whom were traditionally antagonistic to the ANC but now showed interest in establishing and maintaining relations with it as a result of the growing strength of the movement. Tambo specifically mentioned that the growing crisis of the apartheid system was causing sections of the ruling classes to look for ways of defusing the conflict in South Africa.

Among these are elements from the big capitalists of our country, representatives of the mass media, intellectuals, politicians and even some individuals from the ruling fascist party. Increasingly these seek contact with the ANC and publicly put forward various proposals which they regard as steps that would, if implemented, signify that the racist regime is, as they say, moving away from apartheid. This poses the possibility that our movement will therefore be in contact with levels of the ruling circles of our country that it has never dealt with before. It is absolutely vital that our organisation and the democratic movement as a whole should be of one mind about this development to ensure that any contact that may be established does not have any negative effects on the development of our struggle.[36]

Tambo ended his contribution on the topic of possible negotiations and contacts with Western countries by saying, 'If we seriously consider ourselves as the alternative government of our country, then we need to act and operate both as an insurrectionary force and a credible representative of a liberated South Africa.'[37]

Yet although the president and others pertinently raised the possibility of future negotiations, the final conference communiqué was quiet on the prospect of a political solution to the conflict. Its only comment on the topic was that the ANC could not even consider the issue of a negotiated settlement while its leaders remained in prison, and would continue to campaign for their immediate and unconditional release.[38] At this stage, negotiation posed more of a threat than an opportunity to the ANC, which was fully aware that the regime and its allies were seeking to thereby divide the movement, demobilise the mass struggles and improve its own tattered reform initiative abroad, selling false hope with no intention of either transferring power or ending apartheid.

Constitution Committee member Penuell Maduna maintains today that at this memorable conference Tambo was saying 'for us when the conditions are conducive, propitious [for negotiations], the ANC will be more than ready; that was spelled out explicitly'.[39] But his 'more than ready' view was not backed up by the speeches, records and atmosphere at Kabwe.

Meanwhile, it was clear what the guiding vision of the ANC would continue to be. Concluding its deliberations on the eve of the thirtieth anniversary of the Freedom Charter, the Kabwe conference adopted a special resolution underlining that the Charter expressed the legitimate and fundamental interests of the majority of the people and remained the only basis for the genuine liberation of all the people of South Africa. It was 'the lodestar pointing the way to freedom'. The conference hailed the internal democratic movement – the coalition represented by the UDF and other ANC-aligned groups – for its struggle to advance the objectives contained in the Freedom Charter, and also thanked the UN and other international bodies for observing the Charter's thirtieth anniversary.[40]

In keeping with the Charter's opening line that South Africa belonged to all who live in it, black and white, the participants decided that it was important to 'win as many whites as possible to our side ... [and] continue to pose the alternative of a united, democratic and non-racial South Africa'.

A key function of the conference was to ensure that the NEC and the top leaders of the organisation were democratically elected, but before elections could be held, the conference had to decide whether or not non-Africans could be members of the NEC. White, Indian and coloured people had been founder members of MK, and many people from other 'national groups' were being recruited into the ANC's underground structures. ANC branches outside of South Africa functioned on an openly non-racial basis. The understanding in the ANC, however, had been that its senior leadership positions would be reserved for Africans only. The idea of dropping this limitation provoked lively debate. Kader Asmal and Brian Bunting spoke against the proposal, the latter saying that no one could accuse him of being anti-white or anti-communist, but that he didn't believe the mass of the people were politically ready to accept whites in the leadership. Yet one MK member after the other declared that, if white comrades were prepared to lay down their lives for the people's struggle, it would be ridiculous to say they could not be full members of the organisation at all levels. Professor Jack Simons, sitting at the back of the hall, shouted, 'Open door!'

In the end, the vote was overwhelmingly in favour of opening the NEC to all members on a non-racial basis. The conference confirmed that ANC membership was 'open to South Africans of all races who accept the policies of our movement'.[41] Seventy-two years after its founding, James Stuart (Hermanus Loots), Reg

September, Mac Maharaj, Aziz Pahad and Joe Slovo – perhaps the apartheid regime's prime public enemy and bogeyman – were voted in on a secret ballot as the first coloured, Indian and white members of the NEC.[42]

An expanded NEC of thirty people was elected for a five-year period, bringing in a new generation of leaders. Eleven new members joined the nineteen re-elected. Two former office holders, whose conduct had been widely regarded as having contributed to discontent and rage in the camps in Angola, were not re-elected. The five youngest members – including Chris Hani (who received the most votes), Pallo Jordan and Thabo Mbeki – were forty-three years old at the time.

Tambo and others continued, at times, to use the earlier ANC language of 'national groups', which was derived from 1950s 'four nations' thinking that regarded Africans, whites, coloured people and Indian South Africans as forming communities to be organised like the four spokes of the Congress wheel. At the same time, Kabwe uninhibitedly adopted the language and core values of 'non-racialism', which the new UDF and the trade union movement were popularising through their energetic struggles – beamed live all over the world – across community and ethnic lines within South Africa. At the press conference following Kabwe, Tambo and other ANC spokespeople explained the ANC's conscious use of the word 'non-racialism' rather than the 'multi-racialism' of the 1950s: 'Multi-racial does not address the question of racism. Non-racial does. There will be no racism of any kind and therefore no discrimination that proceeds from the fact that people happen to be members of different races.'[43]

2

'Will Comrade King Sabata Please Come to the Microphone'

ONE OF THE big moments at Kabwe came when the recently exiled king of the Thembu, Sabata Dalindyebo, was invited to the platform. Having arranged for Charles Nqakula, the Cradock-born ANC journalist and MK member, to be his interpreter, the 'Comrade King' addressed the audience animatedly in isiXhosa. For those present, this was a unique occasion emphasising both the ANC's linkages with important constituencies within the country and its ties stretching into the past. They highlighted the deep African roots of constitutionalism in South Africa, as well as the central role that the small town of Cradock played in its political evolution.[1]

The Thembu kings had been involved in early constitutional politics from the time of the first king Dalindyebo in the 1880s and 1890s. In those decades, the first independent black newspapers, breakaway 'Ethiopian' churches and proto-nationalist organisations in South Africa emerged in the eastern Cape. These groups included the Native Educational Association, Imbumba Yama Nyama (the union of black people), numerous local 'native vigilance associations' or Iliso Lomzi (the 'eye of the nation') and, most significantly for the long term, the South African Native Congress (SANC), formed in King William's Town on 7 July 1891. The SANC or Ingqungqutela was not only a founder member of the South African Native National Congress (SANNC, later to become the ANC) formed in 1912 but can also be regarded as its forerunner.[2] As its name indicates, the SANC wished to unite Africans throughout South Africa, and from 1902 onwards it played an important role in helping to set up similar congresses in the Transvaal and Orange Free State after the South African War.

Unusually for the colonial world at the time, black citizens of the Cape Colony were allowed the vote on a common voters' roll (until 1936) if they had certain educational and property qualifications. By the end of the 1880s there were already some 20 000 registered black voters in the colony. They started their own independent newspapers – *Imvo Zabantsundu* and *Izwi Labantu* – and used these to mobilise the voters, determining the outcome in several constituencies in the eastern and western Cape. Driven by African notions of Ubuntu, Christian teachings of equality and British liberal values of individual freedom, these schooled people emerged from the many British missionary institutions in the region and laid the platform for the new organisations and new forms of politics that would lead to the later formation of the ANC. They used as their motto the phrase 'dubula ngo siba' or 'shoot with the pen', saying that the African people had to take on the colonisers at their own game of constitutional politics through lobbying, voting, petitions and the press if they wished to survive in the colonial world.[3] They were, in a sense, the nineteenth-century equivalents of the digital natives in today's technological revolution.

Dalindyebo was the first mission-educated Thembu king and became profoundly involved in rallying and supporting the earliest black voters, as well as their newspapers and organisations. From the first elections in the new Thembuland constituency in 1888, the large body of African voters there would first meet at Dalindyebo's Great Place before deciding which white candidate to support. He was said to be the head without which the Thembu body could not act.[4]

The Thembu National Church, started by Nehemiah Tile, was also one of the first 'Ethiopian' or breakaway churches that made themselves independent of the missionaries. The rebel minister also happened to be prominent in the new politics, and, in a gesture of defiance, he declared Dalindyebo the head of the church, in the same way that the British sovereign was head of the Anglican Church.[5]

In 1905, Dalindyebo travelled to England with Dr Walter Rubusana, one of the SANC founders, who had translated the Bible into isiXhosa. He actively supported the establishment of the SANNC and is said to have sent 200 cattle as a gesture of goodwill to their founding conference in Bloemfontein in 1912.[6]

Years later, in the 1920s and 1930s, the young Nelson Mandela lived at the Great Place of the acting regent Jongintaba Dalindyebo and was brought up to follow in his father's footsteps as a traditional advisor to future Thembu leaders. He grew up with the regent's children, and his agemate and cousin was the future king Sabata Dalindyebo. Wedded to education, the Thembu royals sent Mandela to the prestigious Clarkebury and Healdtown schools, and he went on to become the first member of the royal family to get a university degree. As writers have noted, particularly Xolela Mangcu, Mandela's leadership traits and both his heroic and pragmatic strands of political thinking were shaped by his growing up in the Thembu royal household. It was here that he observed the regent and his court at work in Mqekezweni, and was exposed also to the workings and debates of the Bhunga or General Council in which both his father and the Thembu regents and their advisors participated.[7] In their book *Nelson R. Mandela: Decolonial Ethics of Liberation and Servant Leadership*, Busani Ngcaweni and Sabelo J. Ndlovu-Gatsheni contend that his efforts in the 1980s and 1990s to focus on negotiations and national unity were not due to wishy-washy ideas of rainbowism, but 'the extension of a decolonial notion of Ubuntu, which went beyond copycat reactions to western modernism (war and Nuremberg-like retribution) to develop a new African paradigm of humanism where "many worlds fit harmoniously"'.[8] Mangcu indirectly backs this up by adding that Mandela's peace-making abilities come from his belonging to the Thembu i-Xhiba house, whose traditional role had been to mediate conflict in the kingdom's royal family.[9]

Sabata Dalindyebo succeeded Jongintaba as king in 1954. In 1962, as politics in South Africa were being redefined in a time of upheaval, he headed an opposition to the apartheid grand plan. The National Party (NP) was about to launch the hated Bantustan system, with Transkei as the first 'self-governing' homeland. It is not generally remembered that Sabata followed the ANC's pre-banning tradition of constitutionalism by proposing an alternative constitution. A Congress newspaper noted confidently that he did this with 'the unanimous support of the 400 000 tribesmen of Thembuland who gave allegiance to [the] Paramount Chief'. Working with the ANC and supported by Winnie Mandela, Sabata proposed replacing the government's model with a constitution that provided for 'full democratic rights for all the people of the Transkei, African, Coloured, Indian and white'. Moreover, 'all members of the TTA [Transkei Territorial Authority] to be elected whether chiefs or not, and Transkeians of any colour to be MPs, Cabinet Ministers, Prime Minister or President'. Sabata also called for full independence from South Africa after a transition period of five years, during which the state's contribution to the project would have to be increased many times the current budgets.[10]

This was not the kind of independence that Pretoria had had in mind. Summoned to a meeting with the chief magistrate of the Transkei, Sabata brought only one of his counsellors with him, a potent snub to the big white chief or *makulubaas*, as apartheid administrators liked to style themselves. The official was 'angered' that the king did not stand up when he spoke to him, and when he noticed two lapel badges that Sabata was wearing to show his political loyalties. One bore the words 'Amandla ngawethu' and the other had the face of the imprisoned Nelson Mandela on it.[11]

Sabata, the chief who opposed the Bantustans, and Mandela, the African nationalist leader who was in prison, had the same great-grandfather: Ngubengcuka. Ngubengcuka had cooperated strategically with the British to protect Thembu interests against perceived hostile neighbours. In an irony of history, another of his great-grandsons, Kaiser Matanzima (Mandela and Sabata's second cousin), became the regime's most prominent collaborator in implementing the Bantustan system. As president of the self-proclaimed Republic of Transkei, this minor Thembu chief ended up on the side of the apartheid enemy.[12] He persecuted Sabata and other opponents of his Bantustan and was reviled by the liberation movement. By 1979, Matanzima had forced Sabata Dalindyebo into exile, where he was to die in 1986.[13]

The apartheid government's logic behind the Transkei's creation was that if other 'homelands' followed Matanzima's lead by agreeing to a pseudo-independence, then the indigenous African people, already dispossessed of their land, would no longer qualify to be South Africans, and white domination over 87 per cent of the country's surface area could be maintained under the cloak of democracy. As Hendrik Verwoerd, chief architect of apartheid, put it, there would be black domination in black areas, and white domination in white areas.[14] The imprisoned Mandela was given several offers of release by Matanzima and P.W. Botha on the condition that he live in the Transkei, but he rejected these terms because accepting them would have given legitimacy to the Bantustan system.[15]

At Kabwe, Comrade King Sabata Dalindyebo openly aligned the Thembu people with the ANC as his grandfather had done. In a resonant voice he delivered his message in the form of a story about a villager in the backwoods where men still wore nothing but red blankets to cover themselves. One of the men was married and had a son called Tyomphayo. One day, the man was attacked by an assailant bearing a *kierie*. During the beating, the blanket slid from his shoulder, but when it reached his waist, he quickly grabbed it, using both his hands to cover his crotch. His wife shouted to her husband to fight back, saying, *'He wena, yise ka Tyomphayo akuboni uyaphela? Yeka umnyanzelo lo ulwe!'* ('Hey you, father of Tyomphayo, do you not see you are being finished off? Leave your penis and fight!') Nqakula struggled to translate the vivid narrative word for word. He recalls that 'The delegates on the podium who understood isiXhosa, such as O.R., Mbeki, Makana, Piliso, Hani, Sizakele Sigxashe and Jordan, were laughing their lungs out. But how could I say something like that in the presence of the struggle luminaries in the hall? "Crotch" is one thing. But Sabata said "umnyanzelo" – "penis". I was so shocked that I softened the interpretation.'[16]

There was general merriment in the hall, but the delegates understood the seriousness of the point being made: that the ANC should drop its stance of not attacking civilian targets. Yet although there had been murmurings in the corridors that the whites would never stop killing black children until they had to bury their own, no one came to the platform to offer support for what the Comrade King had alluded to. No one stood up to contradict him either. The delegates laughed along with the story, gave the Comrade King a prolonged round of applause and went on with the business of the day. This was the conference's gentle and respectful way of reaffirming a long-standing ANC position of not attacking 'soft targets'.[17]

———

A month later, the deep intellectual and political continuities within the struggle played themselves out through events that unfolded in Nqakula's birthplace. The Cradock Four, brutally murdered by the apartheid security police, were buried there. The footprints of the past led right up to the open graves where comrades sang the struggle lament 'Senzeni Na?' ('What have we done?') as the coffins were lowered into the ground.[18]

One of those being buried was Fort Calata, grandson of Canon James Calata, who as ANC secretary-general had been instrumental in reviving the organisation in the late 1930s and early 1940s. Fort was so named because when he was born in 1956, his grandfather was being held in the Old Fort Prison in Johannesburg (now home to the Constitutional Court) during the long 1950s Treason Trial. At the mass funeral of the four young activists, the SACP flag was unfurled openly for the first time in many years alongside that of the ANC. In a country where having the name Nelson Mandela scratched on a coffee mug could get you four years in jail, the people were in the process of unbanning the ANC themselves. And, this author noticed, high up on the wall of one of the houses to which mourners were invited after the washing of hands was a picture of Canon Calata. It was a small black-and-white photograph framed in green and gold, the banned colours of the ANC, discreetly but incontrovertibly linking the past and the present, the current revolutionary struggles and past constitutional approaches.

A gentle Anglican priest and educator, Canon Calata was fiercely loyal to his African roots. He had run a famous choir and was a historian of the ANC. His comrades fondly recalled his lectures and his singing in jail during the Treason Trial.[19] His hometown of Cradock had been the venue for the ANC's annual conference in 1953, where it was decided to convene the Congress of the People. In the same way that Sabata Dalindyebo's presence at Kabwe symbolised historic ANC linkages with traditional leaderships, Canon Calata was not only a religious minister and part of the school tradition referred to above that gave rise to the first black protest groups, but also chair of the Rharhabe Royal Council.[20]

Nqakula recalls festivities in Cradock where 'we saw Calata always at the elbow of the King and decided it must be an ANC event.'[21] When the British king George VI visited South Africa in 1947, Calata accompanied Chief Archibald Velile Sandile to King William's Town to welcome the monarch. In doing so he was emulating another *mfundisi*, the legendary Tiyo Soga, who was the first South African to have a biography written about him.[22] In a mirror-image event in 1860, nearly a century before, Tiyo Soga accompanied Velile's predecessor, King Sandile, to the same town to act in a similar diplomatic capacity, reading a message of welcome to Prince Alfred, son of Queen Victoria, before accompanying the British prince and his Xhosa royal guest by boat to Cape Town.[23]

At Canon Calata's funeral in 1983, Charles Nqakula, Steve Tshwete and other underground activists used the occasion to re-establish an ANC presence in the town. The murdered Four were likely to have been among the young activists who draped the old man's coffin in the banned flag and toyi-toyied from church to graveside with it on their shoulders, to the displeasure of the local ministers.[24] Two years later it would be their turn to be buried in a ceremony that reverberated around the country, etching the town of Cradock into the map of the world as a site of struggle.

3

A New Dimension of Strategy and Analysis

AFTER KABWE AND the Cradock murders, events unfolded quickly in South Africa. On the evening of the Four's funeral, apartheid president P.W. Botha imposed the first of several states of emergency, giving his security forces unprecedented power to contain the growing unrest in the country. Soon thereafter, it was announced that he would make a major speech in Durban on 15 August 1985 to lay out plans for dealing with the escalating crisis facing his government. The world was led to believe that a big policy shift was imminent. Expectations were raised that Nelson Mandela might be released.

The speech was a damp squib. An ill-tempered, finger-wagging Botha failed to cross the Rubicon, as promised. The value of the rand dropped. International pressure on the regime increased. Daily scenes of security-force violence against ordinary South Africans flashed on television screens around the world, and Britain, the United States and other sympathetic Western countries began to distance themselves from their apartheid ally. International banks feared for their investments and started calling up loans, dropping the country into an economic crisis.

A month later, on 14 September 1985, a private jet landed at a game reserve in Zambia with the most powerful businessman in South Africa on board. He was Gavin Relly, head of the mighty Anglo American Corporation, the biggest company listed on the Johannesburg Stock Exchange by far. He had approached President Kaunda to facilitate a meeting with Oliver Tambo. The business establishment was reaching out to the 'terrorists'.[1] And, unbeknown to the public, even as the insurrection deepened, the ANC leadership was preparing itself, post-Kabwe, to take its first far-seeing steps towards future negotiations and related constitutional solutions.

Straight after Kabwe, Oliver Tambo had invited Pallo Jordan to prepare a paper analysing the various constitutional options being punted within South Africa and how best the ANC should respond. They were at the height of the fervour to make apartheid unworkable and South Africa ungovernable, and Jordan, newly elected to the NEC and head of the ANC Department of Research, was a revolutionary thinker with an unusual intellectual pedigree and fiercely independent mind. His paper was titled 'The New Face of Counter-Revolution', and it introduced a new dimension to the debate. He proposed that the ANC publicly commit itself to a Bill of Rights and multiparty democracy in a united South Africa. This was a brave argument coming from a revolutionary Marxist located in the very boiler room of the struggle just a few months after the 'call to arms' at Kabwe. Jordan argued that such a declaration would enable the ANC to take the initiative and pre-empt various counter-revolutionary strategies being developed by conservative think tanks in South Africa and abroad. His second challenging proposition was that, instead of attacking the nascent black bourgeoisie, the revolutionary movement should actively woo this class, so that it did not succumb to the temptations being dangled before it by President Botha and an anxious capitalist ruling class.

Jordan's independent-mindedness was seen to flow from his remarkable intellectual and life journey. His mother, Phyllis Ntantala, was from the Sukwini, a formerly Khoi clan that had been absorbed into the Xhosa kingdom during the seventeenth century. She put great store by missionary education. Her father, George Govan Ntantala, had been educated at the Anglican College in Zonnebloem, Cape Town, together with the sons and daughters of other Xhosa and Sotho notables. From their school they could look across the bay at Robben Island where Maqoma and other of their relatives were imprisoned for opposing British colonialism. Phyllis was a feminist thinker and activist decades before it became mainstream. She was described in an obituary as 'One of South Africa's great – and largely unheralded – fighters against apartheid and for women's rights'.[2] Her memoir, *A Life's Mosaic*, vividly describes the intellectual and political milieu in which she (and later Pallo) grew up.[3]

Pallo's Fort Hare–educated father, Dr Archibald Campbell 'A.C.' Jordan, made a series of pioneering accomplishments. He wrote what has been described as the first great novel in isiXhosa. This was *Ingqumbo Yeminyanya* (*The Wrath of the Ancestors*), published in 1940. In 1946, A.C. became the first African to be appointed as a lecturer at the University of Cape Town (UCT) and received his doctorate in 1957. In 1972 he published *Towards an African Literature*, a collection of essays originally published in the *Africa South* journal edited by Ronald Segal. This study was the first to research and celebrate the writings of the nineteenth-century figures who formed the first protest organisations in South Africa from the 1880s onwards.[4]

A.C. Jordan was an African intellectual who embodied and transcended the dichotomies of this time. While fulfilling his role as a mission-educated 'New African' who was secretary of the Fort Hare university cricket club, he was influenced by left-wing Marxist ideas, like many other leading thinkers and intellectuals worldwide in that decade of global depression and anti-fascist struggles. His novel describes the tensions between the lives and ideas of missionary-educated Africans and traditionalists in the 1930s and 1940s, and this exploration of changing African identities was part of his multifaceted world of ideas.

Among Jordan's peers was Govan Mbeki, who followed a similar left path. Like Govan, A.C. was part of a generation of formative radical African intellectuals who started exploring the intersection between national and class struggles. They proceeded on divergent paths. Mbeki became a follower of the Communist Party of South Africa (CPSA). The woman who married him, Epainette Moerane, was one of the first women to be active in the Communist Party. Jordan initially joined the ANC but switched his allegiance to the All-African Convention at the end of World War II. The AAC was affiliated to the Non-European Unity Movement, which was heavily influenced by Trotskyite thinkers in Cape Town. In 1945, A.C. became head of the aligned African Teachers' Association. After university, he taught for some time in Kroonstad in the Orange Free State, where he studied for his master's degree and learned Sesotho.

A.C. had a reputation as a brilliant teacher.[5] His influence in national life was demonstrated by the fact that A.P. Mda (who founded the influential ANC Youth League with Anton Lembede, Tambo and others) named his son Zanemvula, after one of the characters in A.C.'s famous isiXhosa novel. Zanemvula later became known as 'Zakes' and is today one of South Africa's most celebrated novelists. In *Sometimes There Is a Void* he wrote about reading his first book at the age of eight – it was Jordan's *Ingqumbo Yeminyanya*.[6]

So, when Pallo Jordan wrote and spoke, he did so as part of a milieu whose extent and intergenerational depth we must understand. Brigalia Bam, who comes from the same eastern Cape school and university milieu as the likes of Tambo, Mandela, the Mbekis and the Jordans, remembers well how there were once discussions about which of the two prodigies from well-known intellectual families was the brightest – Thabo Mbeki or Pallo Jordan? Jordan's mother, of course, 'had a fierce pride in Pallo and did not hold back on her views on this matter,' recalls Bam.[7]

As Pallo grew up, the revolutionary socialism of his parents was imprinted on him. Friends from wide backgrounds were invited for dinner and discussions. Yet the precociously bright son of UCT's first African academic could not, on the grounds of his colour, register as a student at the same university because of the misnamed Extension of University Education Act of 1959. For two years, Pallo went informally to imbibe what the campus had to offer, sitting in on English and history courses, his father's isiXhosa classes, and Professor Jack Simons' Comparative African Government and Law classes, which were a magnet for political activists. Jordan was on the hill at UCT on 30 March 1960, the day that Philip Kgosana led a march of thousands of residents from Cape Town's townships to the Caledon Square police station. He recalled the feverish excitement: 'We were sipping Cokes in the Students Union and quickly rushed down to the highway to hitch rides to town.' After listening to Kgosana, they soon found themselves in front of police headquarters. There were heated discussions 'abuzz with polemics' among the small group of black students gathering at what they dubbed Freedom Square at UCT: 'The only students whose opinions were in any way relevant were those who had committed themselves to the Pan-Africanists and their voices now carried the weight of thousands.'[8]

Barred from the dormitories, the swimming pool, athletics and even from socials, the few black students who had been granted special permission to study at UCT were reminded every day that they were different. For example, Johaar Mosaval, who went on to become the principal dancer of the Royal Ballet Company in Britain and is now in his nineties, recalls having to dance alone behind a separating line drawn on stage, facing scowls from troupe members, when Dulcie Howes recognised his talent and invited him to practise with her class.[9] Professor William Pick, who went on to Wits and Harvard in a later era, has written about how he and his fellow 'non-European' medical students had to leave the room at UCT when post-mortems were done on white bodies.[10]

A.C. Jordan went into exile in the early 1960s after leaving South Africa illegally to travel to the USA on a study sabbatical. His wife and family joined him after being slapped with one-way exit permits by the government. Pallo Jordan's disrupted intellectual journey continued in exile in tumultuous fashion. Having enrolled at the University of Wisconsin, he was refused an extension of his student visa because of his student activism, including his protests against the Vietnam War, and he had to suspend his studies and leave the US in 1967. He relocated to London, where the noted South African scholar and poet Mazisi Kunene initially put him up. In this city of exiles, he immersed himself in political and intellectual work on and off campus. This was a time of revolt and revolution in South-East Asia, Latin America and decolonising Africa, as well as in Western and Eastern Europe, where events such as student uprisings in Paris and the Soviet invasion of Czechoslovakia were creating ferment.[11]

He intended continuing his studies, but his application to Sussex University, where his later comrades Thabo Mbeki and the Pahad brothers, Essop and Aziz, were studying, was turned down. His path would be to become a revolutionary activist intellectual rather than follow his father into academia.

Between 1972 and 1974, like many in London's ANC exile community, Pallo earned his bread and butter working with fellow South Africans at Abbey Life, a life assurance company whose founders included Joel Joffe, one of the defence lawyers for Mandela and the other Rivonia trialists. Joffe had been forced out of the country like so many that decade.

After Mozambique and Angola obtained independence, Jordan returned to Africa, and from 1977 to 1990 he worked out of Luanda and Lusaka, becoming head of the ANC's Department of Research for a total of nine years. Comrades in Lusaka remember his brilliance, and his voracious appetite for reading, writing and debating. In her autobiography, Helena Dolny describes vividly Jordan's scholarly stature in Lusaka:

> As he began to talk people fell silent, listening attentively. He cut a tall striking figure, his trademark scent of patchouli drifted faintly over the conference room. There was always gravitas in his delivery. He was revered amongst his comrades. His intellectual prowess was something they were proud of; the progressive intellectual debate had been too long dominated by whites ... He was also respected because he had survived some of the worst of the ANC's abuse of its own comrades. Someone had tried to label him a spy, and he'd spent time detained in a pit. He seemed to rise above harbouring any bitterness. He expected no special privileges as a member of the ANC's higher echelon. When I first met him in Lusaka he was living in spartan conditions in the building that housed the ANC's library in the suburb of Makeni. All of this meant that his comrades listened to him with special pride.[12]

But, as Dolny indicates, being a leading thinker in the movement meant that Jordan's path was not a smooth one. He was subjected to sharp and powerful criticism from within the exile hierarchy. His straight-talking and dissenting theoretical positions often diverged from the schematic revolutionary dogma of some senior persons and the paranoid tendencies of others. In 1983, he was arrested and interrogated by Mbokodo ('the grinding stone'), the name given to the ANC's internal security wing. Pallo was held in what he described as a 'hokkie, a sort of chicken run outside Lusaka'. Concerned comrades, including Wolfie Kodesh, one of the founders of MK and a member of the ANC logistics department, and no doubt more senior comrades, finally prevailed on the leadership to get him freed from a rough spell under interrogation. '*Here* [Lord], man', Wolfie said, 'we were frantic. It was a dangerous situation. We had to go and knock on doors.'[13]

Earlier, Jordan also had the misfortune of being present when one of his closest comrades and co-workers was assassinated. As head of research in the ANC, he worked with the formidable writer and intellectual Ruth First and others from home such as Rob Davies, Alpheus Manghezi and Sipho Dlamini who, after the independence of Mozambique in 1975, had created a base at Eduardo Mondlane University in Maputo. Their platform was the Centro de Estudos Africanos (CEA), where they interacted with an array of radical scholars, including the director Aquino de Bragança. First was the director of research. But tragedy struck on 17 August 1982. Jordan, De Bragança and another were speaking to First in her office on campus when a parcel bomb exploded in her hands, killing her instantly. The assassination had been ordered by Craig Williamson and carried out by the security police's bomb-making squad in Pretoria. Jordan suffered a perforated eardrum, which left him deaf in one ear, and he was lucky to survive.[14] Rob Davies was delegated by the ANC to accompany President Samora Machel to the scene that evening. He wrote, 'The image of blood and flesh splattered all over the cracked wall and the ceilings is something I will never forget.'[15]

Ruth First's work and tragic death, as well as the mention above of Phyllis Ntantala, Nomaka Epainette Mbeki and Brigalia Bam, serve as a reminder of the constant presence of women at the heart of the freedom struggle. Though few women were in positions of power in the liberation struggle and they are largely missing from its master narratives, they were always part of the living, breathing fabric of the drama playing itself out in exile.

Jordan's narrow escape during the assassination of Ruth First and his deten-tion by his own movement also underlined the great personal risks and danger that struggle strategists and intellectual thinkers faced in shaping their ideas. He realised 'how fragile life is'. The 'near-death experience' in Maputo and the 'near oblivion' in Lusaka, he said, 'shook me a great deal'.[16]

Jordan's briefing paper for Tambo and the NEC on 'The New Face of Counter-Revolution' started by noting that the air was thick with 'rumours and specula-tions about the possibilities of some dramatic [reform] breakthrough in South Africa'. The problem was that most of these were rehashed versions of old themes. That was not to say that no change was happening. 'Indeed,' he wrote, 'the very outpouring of speculative writings and premature predictions is a sign of the extreme fluidity of the situation.'

He then identified some of the important sources of thinking on reform. In left circles there were two main trends: 'one which dismisses these changes as cosmetic while the other traces them to profound structural and ideological pres-sures within the South African capitalist system'. But the paper focused its attention on the thinking of the English-speaking liberal establishment and liberal-minded Afrikaner *verligtes*. For them, 'the system of apartheid, as it operates at present, is untenable and should be scrapped'. The classic economic liberals saw apartheid as threatening their class interests and wanted it changed 'to create the space for capitalism to assert its essential rationality'. Others advanced political and moral reasons for change. The enlightened Afrikaners, influenced by European models of consociationalism, supported liberal positions but were in favour of a pluralism that not only stressed individual rights but also how 'individuals coalesce into groups in pursuit of their common interests'.[17] Moreover, these ruling-class thinkers had black allies among those participating in apartheid structures in South Africa.

Jordan dealt in detail with the interlinked efforts involving the initiatives of the Anglo American mining group, the Progressive Federal Party, the *verligte* wing of the NP and the Buthelezi Commission. He noted that while all these purported supporters of 'reform' differed in some way, they shared three key positions. Firstly, when they criticised apartheid, the analysis was 'extracted from its material foundations' and the critics 'treat it as if it exists as a "pure" phenomenon – the ideology and practice of the National Party'.[18] Secondly, their plans had moved away from the idea of a unitary state to advance the ideas of federalism and consociationalism based on the protection of group or ethnic interests. Thirdly, all these actors saw the purpose of reform as being 'to pre-empt revolutionary change – its essence is counter-revolution'.

It was Jordan's 'considered opinion that "reform", talk of reform and all the reformist political model-building we are witnessing, are eleventh hour counter-insurgency ploys, designed to snatch white domination (as distinct from apartheid) from the jaws of defeat'.[19]

He also gave particular attention to the writings of Harvard scholar Samuel P. Huntington, who had designed US counter-insurgency strategies in Vietnam and whose views had gained credence among liberals and *verligtes* in South Africa. Huntington's 1981 book and 1985 visit to South Africa had a significant influence on the 'reform' thinking of government and establishment academic think-tank members.[20] He proposed a top-down model of change based on limited political reform and calculated repression that had to be implemented 'from positions of relative strength, when the incumbent government can still dictate the terms'. According to Huntington, 'The government that is too weak to monopolise counter-revolutionary repression is also too weak to inaugurate counter-revolutionary reform'.[21]

The essence of Jordan's analysis and his 'proposals for an effective counter' were twofold. Firstly, the principle of 'one person, one vote', as demanded in the Freedom Charter, was no longer enough – elements of the ruling class were prepared to concede this. The ANC needed to 'differentiate ourselves from them' and, therefore, 'universal suffrage must be linked to the demand for a unitary state'.[22] He wanted the door to be shut on any notion of group or ethnic politics that would advantage ruling-class interests and weaken the power of a future central government through minority or other vetoes. Moreover, it needed to be made clear, and 'be unequivocally stated and understood within our movement', that such a future scenario would 'mean a state and a government dominated by the African people'. Anything else would be 'transparent double-talk' and in fact 'racial discrimination at the expense of Africans'.

Secondly, he framed the middle ground as the area of contestation. The ruling class was offering the black middle class soft options and at the same time painting the ANC as hostile to their interests. Jordan wrote:

> We must at all costs work towards detaching this elite from the ruling class, not merely rendering it neutral but committing it to our objectives. We would suggest that the best means of doing this at the juncture would be the adoption of a Bill of Rights. The name we give it will not be that important but the constitutional rights and liberties it will embody will make a tremendous impact on the political scene at home and abroad. We do not suggest that such a Bill of Rights replace the Freedom Charter, quite the contrary. It should in fact be an extensive and comprehensive exposition of the rights and liberties South Africans would enjoy under an ANC government. Such a document could take many forms. We could model it on similar documents from other countries – the Declaration of the Rights of Man and of the Citizen, comes to mind. Or we may come up with a totally new conception. Whatever form it takes it will explicitly declare apartheid, racism, fascism and Nazism illegal and punishable offences.[23]

Jordan went further, warning the ANC that it needed to look critically at its own thinking and complacent revolutionary rhetoric:

> We shall also have to explicitly pronounce ourselves on the question of political pluralism (i.e. a multiplicity of political parties and political space for the loyal opposition). There is a sad misconception which has taken root amongst us, that radical social transformation is only possible under one-party rule. This notion must be dispelled and laid to rest once and for all. It is neither intrinsic to revolutionary change that one party dominate the political process nor is it in fact the case in most socialist countries. In the countries where this is the case, particular historical circumstances created that situation and not the imperatives of revolution. Subject to the provisions of the maintenance of democratic values and the suppression of the crime of apartheid, there is no reason, in principle, why we should oppose a multi-party system. We would submit that as long as the ANC and its allies are capable of demonstrating through political argument, debate and open contestation that we have both the correct policies and practical ability to address the burning social and

41

political problems facing the people, we have nothing to fear from such a system.[24]

Telling the NEC not to romanticise one-party states was, at that time, a dangerous departure from the orthodoxy of many in the ANC and SACP, but it helped redirect the liberation movement and change the course of history. Finally, Jordan argued that in a strategic and tactical sense,

> The immediate political advantages of adopting such a Bill of Rights will be that it puts the ball in the courts of our opponents amongst the ruling class – on its right, centre and left. The Inkatha leadership and other pro-ruling class forces who oppose us will also be compelled to define their position in relation to it. If we adopt and publicise the document at the appropriate moment, it will become the focal point of political discourse inside the country. No one, even our worst enemies will be able to ignore it, and as such it will be an intervention that puts all other options in the shade. The question of timing will be all important (provided the idea is acceptable) so as to project the ANC even more firmly as the only viable alternative to continued racist domination.[25]

According to Jordan, there were two features and failings of Huntington, and by extension his South African academic admirers. Firstly, they brought the 'think tank' into fashion and elevated social scientists into social engineers, 'who could manipulate human beings and entire societies in very much the same manner as their counterparts in the natural sciences manipulated chemicals and other inanimate matter'.[26] Secondly, while maintaining the pose of a 'disinterested outsider, who views the entire panorama with keen, objective eyes', these scholars failed to sufficiently examine the merits and demerits of the forces for social change because of their 'prior commitment to the social order'.[27]

'The New Face of Counter-Revolution' was a remarkably prescient diagnosis of the South African situation and arguably one of the most influential pieces of writing in the shaping of modern South Africa.[28] Here, during a key point in an insurrectionary moment, amid the popular rhetoric of 'people's war', was a grounded Marxist intellectual and struggle leader cautioning against revolutionary romanticism, bad practice and some of the liberation movement's basic assumptions, saying the organisation needed to address some of the holy cows of its ideological orthodoxy. His clear articulation of the future of the ANC as a multiclass organisation in a multiparty democracy was remarkable, coming when it did.

This revolutionary was advancing progressive constitutionalism to complement other interrelated forms of struggle in the final push to winning power. His ideas, including a Bill of Rights and multiparty democracy, went far beyond the territory where a professed liberal-minded establishment of white politicians and academics inside South Africa were prepared to venture, ideologically or politically. Although some paradoxically claimed to be carrying the flag for 'democratic liberalism' in South Africa, they generally supported group rights and most of them baulked at the idea of an unqualified universal franchise.[29] The scenarios Jordan presented anticipated almost exactly how the process was to unfold in the next ten years.

Tambo sent the neatly typed memo to the NEC with a covering note in his own hand. The ANC president stressed the importance of understanding the various constitutional models Jordan had raised: 'We are poorly briefed and are lagging behind on the ideas being thrown about among the enemy's "think tanks" in their quest for a way out of the apartheid crisis that leaves the system intact ... The whole issue needs a thorough and comprehensive study by a collective, which is being set up as part of the reorganisation of our work, following the National Consultative Conference.' Tambo's note ended with the salutation 'In the Year of the Cadre' (1985) and his spidery initials underneath.[30]

Pallo Jordan now moved into the centre of ANC planning for the future. After Kabwe, he became administrative secretary of the NEC, working at the 'deliberately obscure' Cha Cha Cha Road headquarters close to the central post office, together with the other members of the NEC secretariat: Ruth Mompati (secretary in the SG's office), James Stuart (secretary of the External Coordinating Committee, or ECC) and Joe Nhlanhla (secretary of the Politico-Military Council, or PMC). The quartet thus coordinated the four main operating arms of the organisation. Working alongside them at HQ in the president's office were three of Tambo's support staff: Thabo Mbeki, Tony Mongalo and Cecilia Masondo. Mbeki was an NEC member, head of the Department of Information and had been a trusted political secretary to Tambo since his early thirties. His position was upgraded to head of the president's office. Fellow NEC member Tony Mongalo was deputy political secretary to Tambo, and Masondo, who lived in a cottage at the back of the house of Jack and Ray Simons, was his 'ultra-loyal' administrative secretary.[31]

These appointments were part of implementing the Kabwe resolutions that 'there should be a permanent NWC secretariat'. A typed Kabwe report also states that 'Conference was informed about the existence of an inner core of the NEC called the Group of Five or Presidential Committee'. This consisted of veteran leaders of the alliance – secretary-general Alfred Nzo, treasurer-general Thomas

Nkobi, SACP chairperson Dan Tloome, SACTU general secretary John Nkadimeng and SACP general secretary Joe Slovo – who played an important stabilising role behind the scenes.[32]

At the first meeting of the NEC after Kabwe, Oliver Tambo started shepherding through the changes that were discussed at the watershed conference, such as the formation of an NEC subcommittee to look at the prospects for negotiations. The President's Committee was mandated to oversee the organisational rearrangements agreed to at Kabwe.

The core of the NEC negotiations subcommittee was provided by the people in key operational positions. Johnny Makatini, head of Foreign Affairs, proposed that Jordan chair the new subcommittee and not necessarily someone with legal experience.[33] The other members appointed by the NEC were Thabo Mbeki, James Stuart and Simon Makana, a long-standing official in the Department of National Intelligence and Security (NAT) and NEC member since Morogoro in 1969.

Following up on 'The New Face of Counter-Revolution', Jordan once again made a crucial intervention by drawing up a second discussion document called 'Submission on Negotiations' to complement and translate into practical action the ideas he had put forward earlier. This eleven-page document formed the basis of the shorter report called 'A Submission on the Question of Negotiations', which the subcommittee submitted to the NWC on 27 November 1985.[34]

Jordan noted in his paper that the ANC had 'quite correctly' held to the armed seizure of power as its goal, but that 'the question of talks, negotiations and a settlement that was not preceded by a relatively protracted war was outside our ken'. He added 'that this is no longer realistic in the present day', which did not mean putting 'all our eggs in the basket of talks' but that 'a perspective of a negotiated transition has begun to open up'.[35] Talks could be a way of 'winning at the conference table or consolidating what we have won on the battlefield ... pursuing our political objectives employing other means, or to supplement our conventional means'.[36]

Besides these strategic possibilities, Jordan warned of a further danger: 'we must today begin to contemplate a situation in which we could be forced into negotiations under less than optimal conditions'. The intentions of imperialism coupled with the ANC's dependence on the vulnerable Frontline States and 'the diplomatic and moral support of Africa' meant this kind of coercion was a real possibility for the ANC. It had happened in Zimbabwe, when the Patriotic Front party was corralled into the Lancaster House talks and agreement in London, and the tactic of drawn-out 'talks' was used to 'wind down' or dilute the struggle of the South West Africa People's Organisation (SWAPO). The ANC needed to avoid such pitfalls, including the possibility that the Eminent Persons Group (EPG) – set up by the Commonwealth countries at their summit in Nassau the month before – would lead to an 'analogous result' where the ANC was offered terms that seemed to break drastically with the regime's previous position but 'nonetheless fall short of what we want'.[37]

Drawing on lessons from revolutionary France and Russia, as well as Vietnam and neighbouring liberation struggles, the optimal goal would therefore remain the seizure of power, but *without prioritising armed combat*. Jordan said it should preferably be via an ANC-led mass democratic movement that grew in strength and 'can visibly emerge as the chief determinant of the pace of events, able to intervene through mass action at any given juncture'. From this basis, it would neutralise the enemy's capacity to suppress the liberation forces, bolster MK's armed interventions and move rapidly towards a situation of 'dual power' where the mass democratic movement not only 'commands authority [even if in an informal sense] ... but can wield it in opposition to the enemy's power and finally overthrow him'.[38]

The ANC also had to work out less favourable fallback possibilities than this, he warned.

In its shorter submission, Jordan's NEC negotiations subcommittee pointed to some key aspects in any such negotiation process for the ANC. Firstly, it would need to be fully prepared and clear on the preconditions for negotiations to guarantee the integrity of the process before, during and after talks, so that 'the movement – in its entirety' – could operate freely without hindrance (a condition made repeatedly). Once these preconditions were won, the plans for talks would be worked out, including the shape of the table and who sits where, leading to a national convention or, ideally, a constituent assembly 'after the transfer of power from the regime'. The ANC and its allies would also have to ensure that there were only two main negotiating parties: itself and the regime. This was so that the forces of reformism did not use the plethora of other actors to nullify the ANC and shift the discussion to the centre and right, thereby retaining the essence of the old system. These groupings would instead have to align themselves with either the system or the mass democratic forces. However, the ANC needed to earn its spurs as a vanguard force – not assume the right – by actively winning over the middle ground through the Bill of Rights and multiparty system, as Jordan had earlier advocated. It was important 'not to drive the now disintegrating ruling class forces back into unity'.[39]

Finally, the NEC subcommittee of Jordan, Stuart and Makana declared that 'when we reach the conference table we should have our own set of concrete constitutional proposals (not merely the Freedom Charter), otherwise we will be forced to react to the other side's proposals'. It made four concrete suggestions to the NEC in this respect:[40]

- It was of 'paramount importance that our leadership keeps itself briefed and fully conversant of the thinking and plans in the enemy camp'.
- The NEC must 'immediately set up a constitutional think tank under the supervision of [an NEC] sub-committee', whose task would be to 'draft proposals to place before the NEC' within three months or so.
- The proposed NEC subcommittee would in addition be 'responsible for studying and familiarising the leadership with the experiences of our allies in this region and beyond who have either passed through or are engaged in negotiations in order to learn negotiating tactics and pick up tips on specific situations'.
- Finally, Jordan's research unit, which had already started work on the alternative constitutional models emerging from the ruling classes, and which had started a number of projects in tandem with the Economists Unit headed by Sindiso Mfenyana to cost and operationalise the vision of the Freedom Charter, would now have to 'speed up our programmes and tighten the time frame'.[41]

In arguing for a new constitutional think tank and a quick response to Commonwealth and apartheid initiatives, Jordan argued that 'we can no longer afford the luxury of allowing our academics and intellectuals to vegetate in an ivory tower or to isolate them because we fear "maverick" ideas. Let us face the reality that the NEC has neither the time nor capacity to undertake all the tasks on its own. There is no reason why properly supervised working groups cannot be established to handle some of these problems.'[42]

Jordan's far-seeing papers and the report of his subcommittee prompted the NEC to open up a whole new sphere of operations. The key ideas therein would in future guide the ANC's broad responses to the issue of negotiations and a future constitutional dispensation in South Africa. The views he presented no doubt owed a great deal to collective thinking in the ANC leadership, but they were articulated in his distinctive manner. From then on he would, as administrative secretary of the NEC, be at the centre of the movement's constitutional planning. It might be that Tambo had handpicked him for this role straight after Kabwe because as early as 26 July he had informed Tambo (after conferring with him at a meeting in Addis Ababa, Ethiopia) that he'd been liaising with comrades in London about involving them in the process.[43]

What about the crown prince, Thabo Mbeki? At this stage he was nowhere to be seen. He did not attend any of the NEC subcommittee meetings. Its report stated, simply, that 'owing to other commitments [he] was unable to participate'.[44] This would become a refrain at NEC level as well in the years to come.

Thus it came to pass that, by the end of a momentous year, Oliver Tambo and the NEC were ready to launch an ANC counter to the ruling-class think tanks Jordan had warned against in 'The New Face of Counter-Revolution'. Firstly, the Department of Legal and Constitutional Affairs was launched, headed by Zola Skweyiya. Secondly, Tambo created the Constitution Committee, a separate new think tank chaired by ANC veteran Jack Simons. It is this think tank that forms the main subject of our book.[45]

'At this point the ANC stands poised to make the rendez vous with destiny', Jordan concluded. 'Everything depends on our tactical acumen. We cannot fail'.[46]

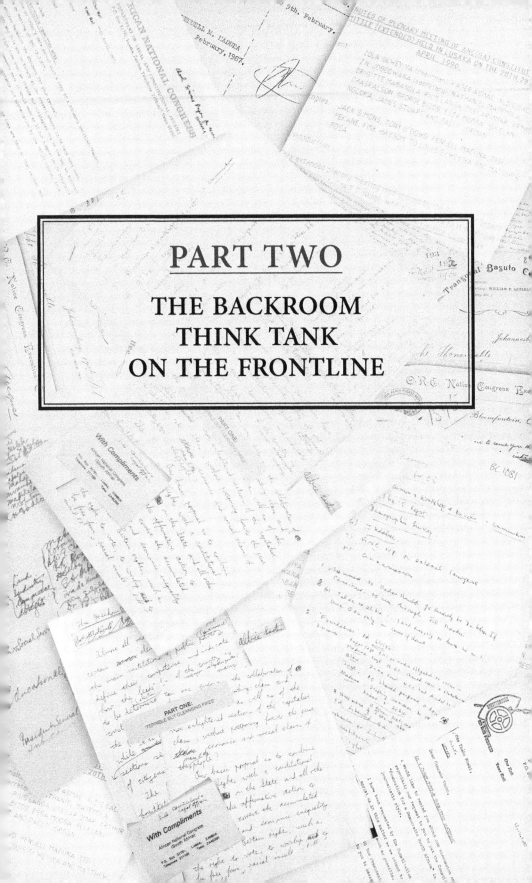

PART TWO

THE BACKROOM
THINK TANK
ON THE FRONTLINE

4

A Historic Gathering in a Builder's Yard off a Sanitary Lane in Lusaka

T HE EIGHTH OF JANUARY was the most important day of the year in the ANC calendar. It was the birthday of the organisation and the president had been issuing an annual 8 January statement since 1979. Over Radio Freedom he outlined the progress achieved in the year gone by and set down the objectives and organising theme for the struggles of the new year.

The year 1986 marked the ANC's seventy-fourth birthday. Seated next to Alfred Nzo and Thabo Mbeki and looking dapper in a suit and pinstriped shirt, President Oliver Tambo announced in his 8 January message that this would be the Year of Umkhonto we Sizwe, the People's Army. At the same time, he underlined that armed struggle should not be isolated as the sole instrument of liberation. Rather, victory would demand the 'maximum unity of all our fighting contingents and the democratic movement' and a coordinated focus on all four pillars of struggle – the others being underground work, mass mobilisation and intensifying international solidarity against apartheid. He welcomed the launch of the giant new labour federation COSATU (Congress of South African Trade Unions), which had added 'enormously to the strength of the democratic movement as a whole' and highlighted the role of the army and the rousing of the masses to make the country ungovernable and apartheid unworkable as the insurrection proceeded in value-based, politically directed ways.[1]

In those days, before social media and instant messaging, the 8 January statements had to be smuggled into South Africa. One year, for instance, four thousand audio cassettes were made for distribution inside the country, thanks to Swedish sponsors. Though dissemination of the statement was illegal in South Africa, activists in the mass movement comprising the UDF, trade unions and community groups would be waiting to receive copies or verbal feedback so that they could build the essence of the address into their strategising and activism.

Luyanda Mpahlwa listened to 1986's 8 January statement as a university student and was subsequently sent to Robben Island for his efforts to make apartheid unworkable. He shook his head in animated surprise many years later when he heard that that Wednesday was also the day Oliver Tambo launched an ANC Constitution Committee to start planning for a new South African constitution and the political negotiations that would go with it.[2]

The Committee's first meeting took place at the ANC's backyard HQ between Cha Cha Cha and Cairo Roads in the city centre of Lusaka. It was reached via guarded steel gates at the end of a sanitary lane or through a neighbouring shop. A rare photograph of the president's office in 1988 shows photographs of Tambo's imprisoned law-firm partner, Nelson Mandela, the host country's president, Kenneth Kaunda, and Zulu king Cetshwayo adorning one of the walls. Two shields alongside the latter image served as an explanatory metaphor for MK's defensive armed struggle, as well as celebrated the inspirational Zulu army victory over the invading British forces at the Battle of Isandlwana in 1879.

The NEC chose seven cadres for the new think tank: Professor Jack Simons, Dr Zola Skweyiya (also referred to by his *nom de guerre*, 'Zola Bona', in the notes by Simons), Ntozintle 'Jobs' Jobodwana, Professor Kader Asmal, Penuell Maduna, Dr S.L. 'Teddy' Pekane and Dr Albie Sachs. They were men with a broad range of life and legal experience. Tambo and the ANC leadership decided that the Committee should be chaired by Simons, who was one of the oldest and most respected Lusaka cadres and an adviser to the president on some key issues over the years. With his distinctive gravelly voice, he would clear his throat before speaking and was used to commanding attention. And people listened.

To convey the importance of the Committee's task, Nzo and 'the Chief' or 'OR', as he was called, went in person to give the members their mandate and help frame their discussions. In contrast, however, the members arrived in dribs and drabs, showing little outward sign of the energy and commitment with which they would tackle their new task. Only four of the seven – Skweyiya, Asmal, Maduna and Jobodwana – were present with Tambo and Nzo on the first day.[3] For some reason, the chairperson himself had not been advised of the meeting. Someone was sent to fetch him from his home at 250 Zambezi Road in the suburb of Roma, close to the university. But Jack was nowhere to be found and missed the first afternoon.

Albie Sachs would only be flying in from Maputo later that evening. He held a permanent government position as head of research in the Mozambican Ministry of Justice, and the Committee later prevailed on Alfred Nzo to request President Samora Machel to give Sachs leave to attend Committee meetings. Teddy Pekane arrived on day three for reasons not given.

The Committee had before it three documents: the Freedom Charter, the Constitution of Zambia and part two of the third Ruth First Memorial Lecture, which Sachs had presented in Maputo a few months earlier. Its title was 'Towards the Reconstruction of South Africa: The Constitutional Dimension'.[4]

It would have made sense to include Jordan's seminal paper on how the ANC could seize the initiative in relation to a vision for a new constitutional dispensation in South Africa, but it is not mentioned in the minutes and Sachs does not recall seeing it there, nor is it in his extensive collection of papers, or those of Simons and Asmal. The only obvious explanation is that it was held back as a classified and confidential document still to be fully analysed by the NEC. Nevertheless, Jordan was head of the NWC's constitutional subcommittee at the time and had been tasked to work with this new activist think tank. The Constitution Committee invited him to join their meeting on the final day.[5]

Secretary-General Nzo started the proceedings by announcing the members of the Constitution Committee. Though he was to have relatively little interaction with the Committee's debates and discussions, his office facilitated the organisation of its activities and meetings. He explained that the group had been set up by the NEC and that 'it was not the legal unit of the ANC' – in other words, it was separate from the recently established DLCA,[6] even though several Constitution Committee members – Zola Skweyiya, Teddy Pekane, Jobs Jobodwana and Penuell Maduna – would participate in both.

Tambo then explained the 'purpose for the formation of the group, the terms of reference generally, [and] the scope and nature of its work'. According to the minutes, he made nine key points:

- The movement should try to anticipate current developments in South Africa and their political effects.
- 'Racist S.A.', the USA and Britain were looking for a constitution that would be acceptable to them. This would, of course, be 'a constitution that entrenches the former positions of the oppressors', structured in 'such a way as to avoid a future S.A. envisaged in the Freedom Charter'. So the effort and recommendations of various research groups and committees of think tanks set up by the regime should not catch the ANC unprepared.
- 'We should not be found responding to initiatives brought to us by other people.'
- 'The group will have to investigate various constitutional proposals and look even beyond the Freedom Charter.'
- 'The group will be expected to draw [up] a constitutional framework' but this 'shall not be a blueprint prescription of the future constitution of S.A.'
- 'The group's task is to assist the NEC in tackling some of the major constitutional problems it might be required to solve from time to time.'
- 'The work of the group will be confidential between itself and the NEC.'
- 'The group will consult and cooperate closely with the NEC on various important issues.'
- 'Democratic lawyers at home will have to be consulted from time to time as their input will be necessary and important.'[7]

After Tambo's introduction, 'the comrades of the group participated in discussing the nature and scope of the task'. It was pointed out that this 'was an ad hoc,
unique exercise anticipated to work very rapidly' and had 'no precedent in the
history of the movement'. 'It was the feeling of people that the end of apartheid
is not very far away and the USA and the regime were for opportunistic reasons
showing an interest in future constitutional arrangements.'[8] There was clearly
a sense of urgency about the task at hand and a feeling, mentioned later in the
minutes, that 'the group's work should not betray our struggling masses because
S.A. is their patrimony'.[9]

In the language of the time, the constitution was 'a new terrain of struggle'
where much depended on 'the balance of forces'. Would it be possible to not only
make the language and logic of constitutionalism compatible with revolution but
to advance and give texture to the process of liberation? The challenge was to
find meaningful ways of harmonising the concepts, vocabulary and discourse
of constitutionalism with the ANC's concepts, vocabulary and discourse of revolutionary struggle.

The preliminaries continued into day two, Thursday 9 January, for which
Tambo and Nzo were once again present. Sachs had arrived and Simons had
been tracked down. The latter got off to a bold start, taking seriously the mandate
to work 'very rapidly'. Even as the Committee members were settling in with a
discussion about their administrative needs, including secretarial support, funds,
office equipment and accommodation, he promised Tambo and Nzo that the
Committee would produce a preliminary report to the NEC 'within a week'.[10]

One of the first rough handwritten notes Simons made as chair was 'Keep ahead
(avoid Lancaster House)', referring to the Zimbabwean independence settlement
finalised with external parties in London in 1979.[11]

An exiled liberation movement operating in a dangerous hood does not accommodate itself in a midtown office block with a big sign on the front door. So,
besides Tambo's HQ in the backspaces of the city centre near the main post office,
where this first Constitution Committee meeting took place, the ANC set up
various other offices around Lusaka, as well as safe houses where documents
could be stored in case of attacks.

The working home of the Constitution Committee was at the movement's
property in Sheki-Sheki Road in the suburb of Emmasdale on the outskirts of the
city, where it set up a garage for its 'mechanical engineers'. The property had
on it a two-storey building that accommodated the offices of Secretary-General
Nzo, Treasurer-General Nkobi and the accountant Dan Tloome. It was known
as Alpha. This was also the workplace of four Lusaka-based members of the

Constitution Committee – Zola Skweyiya, Teddy Pekane, Jobs Jobodwana and Penuell Maduna – in their capacity as the first four members of the newly established DLCA.

It made sense for the four full-time members of the department to act also as the secretariat and administrative base for the Committee. An office on the second floor of Alpha was set aside for them.[12] Here the Committee would plan for a future constitution for South Africa, while in the garage below the mechanical engineers 'serviced' the movement's cars – and fitted vehicles with false compartments which were loaded with weapons for secret missions into the country.

Perhaps the most daring of the clandestine operations involving the garage were the African tours run by British anti-apartheid volunteers working secretly with Manny Brown and other ANC members in London. The volunteers set up a Hinterland Tours company to serve as a cover. Using a ten-ton, four-wheel-drive Bedford army-model truck, specially converted in Britain by Koeberg bomber Rodney Wilkinson, they undertook forty 7 000-mile round-trip journeys between Nairobi and Cape Town up to 1994, each time stopping in Lusaka to pick up one ton of arms and delivering them in South Africa undetected. Veteran gunrunner Stuart Round explained that the truck would stop for a 'service' at the ANC's garage in Lusaka, where thirty-two handmade wooden boxes would be packed into four-inch-wide secret compartments running the length of the vehicle under the seats on each side. Each box contained an assortment of plastic-wrapped AK-47 rifles, Makarov pistols, ammunition, hand grenades, tins of TNT and limpet mines.[13]

Next door to the garage, Pekane, Jobodwana, the young Maduna and their senior, Skweyiya, head of the new department and deputy chair of the Constitution Committee, would straight after the first meeting with Tambo get down to their task.

5

'KK', 'OR' and Comrade Jack

THERE IS A photograph of the African music icon Miriam Makeba singing into a microphone during a visit to Lusaka. She looks magnificently commanding in her pose, comfortable about her place in the world. Accompanying her is a smiling pianist with a handkerchief in his top pocket. It is President Kenneth Kaunda himself. The pair are captured in a moment that reveals something deeper than politics with a capital 'P'. KK was known for using his handkerchief to wipe his tears when speaking in public, and here he is caught in a moment that is untouchably rich and deep. It sums up perfectly both the breadth of the exile experience and the intimacy and depth of the bonds that Oliver Tambo and the ANC had developed outside South Africa in the two decades after it set up its HQ in Lusaka. A unity that goes beyond the speeches and flag-waving of politics is made palpable. The partnership between KK and the ANC – and 'OR' personally – embodied a powerful African solidarity that was playing a key role in the bringing down of apartheid.

Tambo was both a natural democrat and a seasoned constitutionalist, who had absorbed from Chief Albert Luthuli and the likes of Professor Z.K. Matthews the political traditions that had preceded him.[1] Constitutionalism was in his DNA. He had helped found the ANC Youth League in the early 1940s when the Africans' Claims document, which included a Bill of Rights, was adopted. He strongly supported the Freedom Charter, adopted a decade later. He drew up the 1959 ANC constitution with Luthuli and worked closely with him as ANC secretary-general and later vice-president. Working with Nelson Mandela in the only African law firm in Johannesburg, Tambo learnt directly how the law could be used both as an instrument of oppression and as a weapon to fight it:

> To reach our desks each morning, Nelson and I ran the gauntlet of patient queues of people overflowing from the chairs in the waiting room into the corridors … the delegations of grizzled, weather-worn peasants from the countryside who came to tell us how many generations their families had worked a little piece of land from which they were now being ejected. Our buff office files carried thousands of (similar) stories (from the towns) and if, when we started our law partnership, we had not been rebels against South African apartheid, our experiences in our offices would have remedied the deficiency.

We had risen to professional status in the community, but every case in court, every visit to the prisons to interview clients, reminded us of the humiliation and suffering burning into our people.[2]

One of Tambo's responsibilities at the Kabwe conference was to oversee the update of the ANC's statutes. He was meticulous about documents. The ANC archives at Fort Hare contain voluminous records in his own handwriting. A great listener, he would ordinarily be the last to speak at a meeting, but he always came well prepared. He was punctilious, a throwback to his days teaching science and mathematics at St Peter's Secondary School in Rosettenville, south of Johannesburg.

After the Sharpeville massacre in 1960, Mandela went underground to provide leadership to the resistance in South Africa, while Tambo was sent abroad to rally international support for the struggle and set up new bases. As the heavily travelled acting president of the ANC in exile, he got to know different political and legal systems first-hand. In one day, as Albie Sachs has explained, he would take a plane from the one-party state of Zambia under the leadership of Kenneth Kaunda, to the People's Republic of Mozambique headed by Samora Machel, and then be driven to meet King Sobhuza II in the Kingdom of Swaziland, before returning 'home'. He insisted on attending the funeral of the forty-two victims of the Maseru massacre with King Moshoeshoe II of Lesotho, despite the danger of having to fly over South African airspace. Somehow, he managed to establish good personal relationships with all these politically diverse leaders.[3]

Tambo also became internationally admired for his great diplomatic skills. Olof Palme, the social democratic premier of Sweden, became a close friend. Tambo would go on to speak with eloquent authority to Mikhail Gorbachev at the time of perestroika in the Soviet Union, as well as Sir Geoffrey Howe, the Conservative foreign secretary in Margaret Thatcher's government, and George Shultz, the secretary of state in the Reagan administration.

A thoughtful, soft-spoken person, he helped to reconfigure what a revolutionary leader could be. Albie Sachs recalls that when he spoke, 'You felt that truth was being conveyed openly and honestly in its most direct form. The emotion lay in the thought, not in the power of delivery.'[4]

The practice of looking outward to gain support for developing constitutionalism with an African idiom for South Africa had roots that went as far back as the 1830s, when Dyani Tshatshu (son of an amaNtinde chief, who had undergone both the traditional circumcision ceremony to manhood and conversion to Christianity) travelled to England to appear before a select committee of the House of Commons in London. Over the course of the journey, he criss-crossed the country, speaking to audiences of thousands. He was part of a delegation headed by the missionary Dr John Philip. In his two-day testimony, Tshatshu proposed that the English set up colleges with a classical curriculum for Africans in the Cape Colony. '[T]hen the Caffres would have a House of Commons, and a House of Lords, and then they would only fight like the English with a news-paper ... Then will come a time when the assegai will be put down and nations will only fight with a book and paper.'[5]

Tshatshu's journey abroad was followed by those of Tiyo Soga, the first black ordained Christian minister in South Africa, in the 1850s and 1860s. Nathaniel Mhala (Umhalla) and a Zonnebloem cohort of students went to study in Canter-bury in the 1860s. In the 1880s, the first enfranchised black voters, newspapers and proto-nationalist organisations in the Cape Colony networked with international humanitarian groups like the Aborigines' Protection Society. The activists and intellectuals who formed the South African Native Convention in 1909, and then the modern-day ANC, which emerged in 1912, were mobilising against the colour-bar constitution of the first new Union of South Africa (which came into existence in 1910) and they sent protest deputations to Britain. By this time, several hundred South African students had studied in the USA as well. What emerged was a uni-versal African perspective envisaging an inclusive South Africa.[6]

The new sensibilities were demonstrated by, for example, the talented young Charlotte Manye (later Maxeke), who toured Britain with the pioneering African Native Choir in the 1890s. She studied at Wilberforce University in the USA, where the pan-African scholar W.E.B. Du Bois was one of her professors. She initiated an alliance between the African Methodist Episcopal Church (which had been started by free blacks during the slavery era in the USA) and leaders of the incipient African or 'Ethiopian' church movement in South Africa. She also became the first black South African woman to complete a university degree.[7] Simi-larly, in 1904, Pixley ka Isaka Seme, then a law student at Columbia University in New York, won a widely reported-on debating competition with his speech on the regeneration of Africa, declaring that he aimed to become 'Attorney-General for his people' and that Africa had generated 'precious creations' of various kinds and was destined for a new future that would be 'spiritual and humanistic':

> Already I see her chains dissolved, her desert plains red with harvest, her
> Abyssinia and Zululand the seats of science and religion, reflecting the glory
> of the rising sun from the spires of their churches and universities. Her Congo
> and her Gambia whitened with commerce, her crowded cities sending forth
> the hum of business and all her sons employed in advancing the victories of
> peace – greater and more abiding than the spoils of war.[8]

The 'new Africans', in the words of Ntongela Masilela,[9] were preparing themselves to be global citizens who shaped a future South Africa. The inherent impulse
was not to exclude and restrict in a parochial, self-isolating manner, but to reach
out to the world and engage with it. They did so via deputations to Britain, the
Africans' Claims document responding to the Atlantic Charter, and pan-African
conferences. This tradition of external engagement continued steadily during the
twentieth century.[10] Exile broadened the circle as tens of thousands of South
Africans left the country from the 1960s onwards and roamed the world, encount-
ering a multitude of new experiences and ideas, most notably the influence of the
anti-colonial and anti-imperialist movements of that time.

Working with the international anti-apartheid movement took ANC members to every part of the globe. They established a strong presence at the UN in
New York, and at the OAU headquarters in Addis Ababa. By the mid-1980s, they'd
opened quasi-diplomatic public offices in around forty countries, bringing them
into contact with political leaders from all continents.

Drawing on these rich contacts, lived experiences and journeys, the Constitution Committee was able to assess the strengths and deficiencies of many different
constitutional models throughout the world. Their vision was not informed by
a need to follow outside forces or to conform to any specific, externally imposed
ideology. Rather, it drew on everything they had learnt, especially in Africa, to give
constitutional substance and texture to the principles of the Freedom Charter.
They were able to draw on their lived experience and continental solidarity as
Africans when shaping their vision of a post-apartheid South Africa. The result was
the idea of a progressive, transformative, post-dictatorship constitutional model
for South Africa. At its core would be the establishment of a new sovereignty based
on the will of all the people, in which there would be a multiparty democracy
guaranteeing fundamental rights for all.

In keeping with the ANC ethic of connecting with the world rather than with-
drawing from it, the members of Tambo's Constitution Committee had trained,
studied and worked on several continents.

Jack Simons grew up in the rural western Cape. In 1937, he earned a PhD under
the famed Professor Bronislaw Malinowski at the London School of Economics,
where his fiery political advocacy led to an order of expulsion, later suspended.
This was at the time of the Great Depression in Britain, hunger marches, and
resistance to fascism and Nazism. Simons returned to South Africa as a communist, as did his later comrades Bram Fischer and Dr Yusuf Dadoo.[11]

Hired by UCT to teach a course called Native Law and Administration, he
transformed it into the study of Comparative African Government and Law. His

classes were packed, with non-registered students sitting at the back to enjoy the brilliant classroom dialogues he provoked. One of these students was Albie Sachs, who remembers the intellectually vivacious way in which Simons contrasted the British colonial system of indirect rule using traditional leaders with the French and Portuguese colonial systems based on assimilating a small class of indigenous collaborators to become more French than the French and more Portuguese than the Portuguese. Simons demonstrated that when apartheid was introduced to systematise racism in South Africa, it was modelled on indirect rule as imposed by the British in the colony of Natal. He also opened the students' eyes to the fact that African communities in South Africa had strong notions of social solidarity, indigenous law and conflict resolution.

Simons was detained without trial for several months in 1960 after the Sharpeville massacre. His pedagogical fame increased when he returned to his UCT classroom with the words, 'As I was saying before I was so rudely interrupted ...' The students drummed long and loud on their desks in response.

Simons' wife, Ray Alexander, was general secretary of the Food and Canning Workers' Union. Their home in Cape Town was often filled with workers, mainly women from coloured and African communities. His classic book *African Women: Their Legal Status in South Africa* describes the notion of the triple oppression of African women.

Jack and Ray went into exile in 1965 after they were both banned from carrying on with their work in South Africa. They travelled to Britain via Lusaka, and Jack took up a fellowship at the University of Manchester. In 1967, they returned to settle in Lusaka. Simons was appointed as a professor of sociology at the University of Zambia. In 1969, the couple published their classic *Class and Colour in South Africa*.

As in South Africa, their home became a centre for people involved in the freedom struggle. Penuell Maduna recently recalled: 'It was the first time I saw a house with so many books. There was a book around him all the time, so we go there and we have our meetings, etc. The camaraderie among all of us, the mutual respect, the opportunity to debate a whole lot of things ... Those discussions I sorely miss even today.' And guests were always treated to pawpaws and avocados from their garden, served by 'Comrade Jack' and 'Comrade Ray', as they came to be known.[12] Ray regularly sent avocados to London too, hand-delivered by a roving exile to friends like her former Cape Town comrade Sadie Forman.

After teaching at the University of Zambia, Jack's pedagogic skills were put to the fullest test in a completely different setting: the ANC military camps in the Angolan bush. His students there were the scores of young men and a few young women who had escaped from South Africa after the Soweto uprising of 1976 and who had subsequently joined MK. Conditions in the camps were unpleasant. In his diary, Simons wrote: 'Mosquitos (how they bite in bed!), flying ants, moths, hornets – plus crawlers – the lizards, cockroaches, beetles that invade the room in a flash if a door or window is ajar.'[13]

Over the following years, hundreds of students were enthralled by his provocative debating style. Instead of pouring out authoritative pronouncements, he would have the students pose and debate hard questions about the nature of society, social structures, forms of leadership and political theory. On 14 March 1979 the South African military sent Canberra bombers to attack the Novo Catengue camp. They blasted to smithereens the structure where he and his students gathered for their classes. Ronnie Kasrils reported afterwards that there was just rubble where the bombs had fallen. This was the highest award any professor could receive. Fortunately, Simons and his comrades received the 'honour' in absentia. Prior intelligence had alerted the camp command to the impending assault, and a malaria-stricken Comrade Jack and the others were evacuated on 13 March. The tunnels of the Benguela Railway, running close to the camp, were used as air-raid shelters.[14]

According to Hugh Macmillan, who was close to Simons for over a decade, his most important role 'was as one of Oliver Tambo's most trusted advisers'. Tambo often invited him to NEC meetings, asked him to edit the disciplinary code for MK and included him in key discussions, such as a Revolutionary Council/NEC meeting in 1978 to discuss new strategy after Tambo's visit to Vietnam, and a crisis gathering in 1984 to prepare for a meeting of the Frontline States in response to the Nkomati Accord.[15]

Politically seasoned, intellectually combative and administratively efficient, Jack Simons proved to be an effective chair of the Constitution Committee. In his first session of chairing on day two, he drew on Marxist understandings of the 'national question' to float the idea of the 'multi-national' nature of South Africa's 'plural society' in which 'tribal and national groups' could perhaps be 'accommodated side by side in a way that expresses the ambitions of our people'.[16] Perhaps this was part of a kite-flying exercise, but the Committee 'came out very, very strongly for a non-racial vision' in which 'the foundation for acknowledging diversity was on a common platform' based on political recognition of individual rather than group rights.[17] From Simons' shorthand notes, it was clear from the start that the Constitution would therefore not provide for a federal state. Tambo stated that the 'ANC has said no to Federalism', although he did add the rider, 'but the committee may wish to explore it'. He was also emphatic: 'We want total departure from colonial structure'. Skweyiya noted that 'Federation would perpetuate race and tribal divisions'. And Kader Asmal, who inputted nine points in his preliminary thoughts on the topic, including the 'Danger of being bemused by white anxieties', added: 'Federation in Nigeria is divisive and leads to fragmentation'.[18] By the end of day two, the group had concluded that federalism would 'entrench white minority rule and preserve [its] former class property position and economic power base'.[19] The future democratic South Africa would have to be a unitary state.

6

The Quartet in Sheki-Sheki Road:
The Core of the Constitution Committee

LIKE SIMONS, ZOLA SKWEYIYA had also earned a doctorate in Europe, but his life journey could not have been more different. Tall, deeply thoughtful, outwardly stern, with a reserved manner, he had learnt at a young age how fierce apartheid law could be. He was born in Luyolo township near the picturesque harbour of Simon's Town in 1942. In 1965, Luyolo was declared a white group area and destroyed in a single day. It had been home to a community of 1 500 people. Resident Mzimkhulu Mamputa recalled: 'One day the location was there. The next day it was gone, with families forcibly removed to a township they didn't know, and which many of them hadn't even heard of. The trucks came in and families were told to pack up their possessions and load them onto the vehicles. What we couldn't squeeze in had to be left behind.'[1] Brigitte Mabandla remembers that the first time she saw Skweyiya in tears was when he spoke about these forced removals.[2]

He joined the ANC Youth League before completing his studies at Lovedale and the University of Fort Hare, where he took part in underground ANC activities and was 'amongst the first to join MK', in 1961. Sindiso Mfenyana explains in his autobiography how Govan Mbeki and other senior figures in the movement had carefully selected the finest students from the university to go into exile based on their leadership qualities and their districts of origin.[3] Skweyiya and Chris Hani were among these Fort Hare alumni. They were part of the seven-person MK regional committee in Cape Town and left with twenty-six others in a group led by Mark Shope on a long journey into exile, walking in 1963 across the border into Botswana and then going by lorry and train via Northern Rhodesia (Zambia) to Tanzania, where they linked up with Oliver Tambo and the ANC leadership in Dar es Salaam.[4]

Within three months, Skweyiya had been sent to the Soviet Union for military training. Among his comrades were some of those who would embark on the ANC's first armed incursions during the Wankie Campaign in what was then Rhodesia in 1967. However, he was destined to follow the route of diplomacy and administration. During the 1970s, he spent six years studying in the German Democratic Republic (GDR) and graduated with a doctorate in law at the University of Leipzig in 1978.[5] Like all exiles from Africa, he had had to adapt to a cold climate, learn a new language and go through a whole gamut of new experiences in Erich Honecker's Germany. Ike Mamoe recalled that the South African students had to learn to speak German from the start and that, although this was tough, there was also much fun to be had enjoying the opportunity to study and socialise in a country that 'did not have primitive attitudes' reflected by the racial restrictions of home.[6] Even so, Skweyiya would point to many aspects of life in the GDR that he felt were alienating the government from ordinary people. He was never afraid to express his own views when called upon. Although he did not feel that his legal training there gave him sufficient preparation for the nitty-gritty of transforming the legal system in South Africa, he returned to Africa with impressive qualifications and made steady progress through the leadership eche-lons of the movement.

His next stop was Addis Ababa. In addition to representing the ANC at the OAU from 1982, he was also the organisation's representative at the UN Human Rights Commission, attending its meetings every year from 1984 onwards. The OAU posting gave him the opportunity to learn first-hand what life was like under the Dergue government after the assassination of Haile Selassie and the destruction of the monarchy. He also got an overview of governmental systems throughout independent Africa and saw leaders from all over the continent in action. His daily work was literally Afrocentric: physically, it was undertaken near the heart of Africa, and conceptually it involved coming to grips with views throughout the continent on the liberation struggle in southern Africa.

While learning diplomatic skills and participating in the functioning of an international institution of special significance for South Africa, Skweyiya also kept up to date on the latest strategic thinking at the highest levels of the ANC leadership and communicated to the OAU the kind of support the liberation struggle was seeking.

All these experiences helped hone a character marked by an ability to listen and observe in a quiet manner. He had an acute mind and enjoyed reading. Dr Zweli Mkhize remembered him as a 'revolutionary democrat' with 'a cool temperament, never overtaken by emotion'.[7]

When the DLCA was set up, he was withdrawn from Addis Ababa to become its head. Maduna, Jobodwana and Pekane joined him in the office at Alpha. They came to constitute 'the secretariat' of the Committee, with Jobodwana as scribe and secretary.

While Skweyiya was more a listener than a talker, saying only what was necessary, when necessary, Penuell Mpapa Maduna loved nothing more than to participate in a robust and serious political argument. Ebullient and intense, he was a great storyteller and always quick to get people around him talking, engaging them in debate. The youngest member of the Committee, he was a product of the Black Consciousness era of mobilisation and reflected the often-mixed influences and political strains influencing that movement.

His grandmother, like his mother, was a domestic worker and went to her grave carrying her ANC card signed by Walter Sisulu. She introduced Maduna to political work by using him to courier clandestine ANC material when he was just eleven years old. One day, he came home from the Eshowe Government Bantu School in then Natal, proudly displaying a shiny new coin given to each pupil. His uncle angrily commanded him to go outside and throw it away, which he reluctantly did. Only later did his uncle explain that the coin obnoxiously commemorated ten years of South Africa being a republic.

After getting a first-class matriculation pass, Maduna enrolled at the University of Zululand. In 1973, he tried to resuscitate the South African Students' Organisation (SASO) branch that had been closed after the raids that followed the assassination of Abram Onkgopotse Tiro by parcel bomb the year before.

On 18 June 1976, two days after the start of the Soweto schoolchildren's uprising, Maduna was detained for thirteen months and tortured. '[It was] not just the use of fists, the kicking ... They actually were hitting you in your most sensitive parts of the human anatomy using wet towels to hit you between your thighs ... The pain that goes to the head was immeasurable.'[8] Twice he was put on trial. In the first case, his attorney was Griffiths Mxenge and his advocates were Ismail Mahomed and Thembile Lewis Skweyiya (Zola's cousin). In a passionate address to Justice John Milne, Mahomed said that his clients had loudly and unashamedly cried out for justice, but that there was no proof that they'd done anything in the cause of a banned organisation. Justice Milne agreed and acquitted them. In the second case, Maduna's advocate was Pius Langa, who also succeeded in getting an acquittal.[9]

After being released, Maduna completed his studies and went to work in the office of Priscilla Jana, who was very active in defending people charged with political offences. Once while at the office, he looked out of the window and saw security police running into the building. Noticing some documents lying on the photocopier where Renfrew Christie and another comrade had earlier been working, he picked them up, put them in his briefcase and walked past the police as they entered. Only afterwards did he discover that the pages were copies of a plan of the Koeberg nuclear power station. He passed them on for delivery to the ANC in London, possibly contributing to a successful operation to place explosives in the heart of this top-security site.[10]

To avoid further police harassment, Maduna crossed the border into Swaziland, where he got a job at Victor Day Dlamini law firm, allowing him to earn a living while continuing with his ANC activities. In 1983, the ANC received information that he was being targeted for assassination and instructed him to proceed immediately to the Namaacha border. When he arrived, carrying a small bag containing little more than his toothbrush, he was met by Jacob Zuma, who drove him down to Albie Sachs's apartment in Maputo. Maduna recalls that, although working with whites was not new to him, 'what was strange was putting up under the same roof as a white man ... I didn't even know that whites had dreams as well ... I hadn't been in any white person's bedroom before ... it was very, very interesting, live together, cook together'. Albie taught him how to prepare ratatouille, he prepared township cuisine, and they shared 'our love of classical music', slipping in cassettes to listen to Bach and Mozart.[11]

After being joined by his wife and baby child, Maduna stayed on for months, waiting for his next posting. During this time, while Sachs quietly completed reports in Portuguese for his work in the Mozambican Ministry of Justice, Maduna would hold forth in fierce political debates with various ANC comrades who gathered there. One of the participants was Chris Hani, whose wife Limpho and two daughters had also come to stay in the apartment after their neighbours in Maseru were killed by South African commandos mistaking them for the Hani family.

Maduna's next move was to the ANC office in Mazimbu in Tanzania, where the ANC school stood. Later he was posted to Zimbabwe to assist in the office of the chief representative, Judson Kuzwayo. While there, he registered for an LLB at the University of Zimbabwe. He graduated in May 1986, while busy with his work in Lusaka with the new DLCA and the Constitution Committee.

Though the youngest on the Committee, he participated in some of the earliest tentative contacts with South African insiders. In 1984, when Professor H.W. van der Merwe from the Centre for Conflict Resolution in Cape Town twice visited Lusaka after an invitation from Gertrude Shope, it was Maduna who accompanied him to Tanzania. On the second visit he was part of a three-person delegation, together with senior leaders Thabo Mbeki and Johnny Makatini, which met with Van der Merwe and the Afrikaner newspaper editor Piet Muller.[12] Like some of the other Committee members, his future would, from then on, be shaped by the constitutional and legal struggles and developments that lay ahead in South Africa.[13] Together with Asmal, Sachs and Skweyiya, he was one of four members of the Constitution Committee who remained at the heart of the constitutional planning process for the next decade, providing valuable continuity from the moment of that first meeting with the Chief.

———

Ntozintle Jobodwana was the Committee's official scribe. His correspondence, often handwritten, now occupies the archives, evidencing his centrality in the process. He grew up in Khwetyana village in Newlands Location near East London, where his father was a school principal and instilled in him a lifelong appreciation for education. Newlands had a long history of political organising going back to the early 1900s when *Iliso Lomzi* or 'Eye of the Nation', a strong branch of the early SANC, predecessor of the ANC, was formed there.[14] Jobodwana was educated in Khwetyana until Grade 6 and then moved to nearby St Luke's Higher Primary, followed in 1963 by the well-known Lovedale College, where Thabo Mbeki, Chris Hani and many other of his exiled comrades had also studied. Immediately, there was a student strike because the medium of instruction in social studies was changed to Afrikaans (followed by arithmetic in 1965 and mathematics in 1966). Jobodwana points out that 'conceptualising in English was already a daunting task' and now this. For technical and science subjects to be in Afrikaans was 'upsetting and overwhelming, [and] stunned our parents but there was little we could do'. Long before the Soweto uprisings in 1976, he says, there were protests against Bantu Education and the use of Afrikaans. He remembers that after the bannings and prior to the Rivonia arrests, the senior students and teachers who constituted 'almost the whole leadership of the Lovedale-Fort Hare [Youth League] underground cell' had either fled the country, been detained or been sent to prison. Those left behind were too junior to lead underground cells and people were 'gripped with fear'. He was one of the leaders when the next protests at Lovedale broke out in 1966. For this he was expelled. From 1969 onwards he studied at the University of Fort Hare, before being admitted as an attorney in East London in 1976, where he set up his own office in the giant dormitory township of Mdantsane the same year. Those were tumultuous times in South Africa, and in 1977 Jobodwana slipped over the border into Lesotho. In Maseru he started practising as an attorney once again.[15]

The next big disruption in his life came five years later, in December 1982, when the SADF crossed the border and killed forty-two people, including thirty ANC members, in a night-time massacre in Lesotho's capital.[16] He was deported straight after the Maseru raid. Arriving at Maputo airport early in 1983, he realised his short-term UN travel document had expired and he couldn't even leave the airport. 'That is when I went direct to Lusaka', Jobodwana says. He did not want to be caught in limbo and sent back to South Africa.[17]

It was thus, via an unplanned, circuitous journey, that this trained lawyer from eMonti (East London) arrived in Lusaka in 1983. Besides a stint of military training in the GDR, where he was given instruction in 'military engineering' and 'military blasting techniques', as well as military intelligence and counterintelligence,

Jobodwana remained in Lusaka. That is how he came to be incorporated into Skweyiya's DLCA and the Constitution Committee in 1986, and he lived in the city for eight years.

Like Maduna, he remembers that life was tough but Lusaka was 'a very important place to be as it was our headquarters'. Zambia faced destabilisation by the apartheid government and others because of its support for the liberation movements to the south. Sanctions led to economic depression and 'there was a scarcity of food and other basic commodities'. At the same time, wave after wave of new ANC arrivals were coming after their expulsion from unreliable Swaziland, Mozambique after the Nkomati Accord in 1984, and Lesotho after the 1986 coup against Leabua Jonathan. There were also Namibians and some ZIPRA/ZAPU cadres from Zimbabwe who did not want to live under the ZANU government, and as comrades 'we drank and socialised in local bars ... much to the chagrin of the leadership'. The only affordable beer was the 'brown bottle' – the unlabelled local Mosi beer.[18]

Jobodwana remembers that the cadres were not living in camps as in Tanzania and Angola but were incorporated into local communities. 'Our children were attending local schools and became our local language interpreters', with many inevitably becoming fluent in Chinyanja. They lived mainly in high- and medium-density areas – the older, poorer parts of Lusaka, such as Lilanda, Kabwata, Libala, Chilenje, Nyumba Yanga, Chawama and Mutendere. It was a big day when a local train service was introduced, running from Lilanda through the central business district to Chilenje. Jobodwana was eventually able to buy a new house in Nyumba Yanga. The leadership lived in the low-density areas like Woodlands and Kabulonga. Security was tight because of a fear of South African cross-border raids and, therefore, 'we wouldn't generally know the place of residence of our leaders'.[19] Pallo Jordan, for example, came to stay in Avondale, where for three years he shared a house with Zola Skweyiya at the very time that they were working on the constitutional planning process. Steve Tshwete lived a block away and Chris Hani (sharing a house with some MK soldiers) stayed on a farm just outside the suburb. When work allowed, these four and other close comrades met almost weekly to socialise. This would have enabled Skweyiya, as deputy chairperson of the Constitution Committee, to stay in touch with Jordan, the NEC liaison the Committee reported to, even though they worked in different parts of the city – Jordan at HQ alongside Tambo, and Skweyiya at Alpha, with Secretary-General Nzo.[20]

Albie Sachs recalls that the scribe 'was perhaps the only member of the Constitution Committee who actually looked, dressed and spoke like a lawyer'.[21] Jobodwana was soft-spoken, well organised and less inclined than the other members to stray from the legal issues at hand and into ANC political discourse. If the other members of the Committee presented themselves as activists who had taken up law as part of the struggle, he came across as a lawyer who had taken ANC thinking into his legal activity. 'I had that professional background,' Jobodwana explains.

S.L. Teddy Pekane was one of the quiet heroes of the liberation struggle. Skweyiya described him as having 'a humble demeanour that belied his extraordinary achievements'.[22] Born in Newclare, Johannesburg, he and his family were victims of apartheid removals that forced them to relocate to Meadowlands, Soweto. He completed his matric at Musi High School in Pimville, Soweto.

In 1964, at the age of twenty, he was among the first groups of young people who left the country to join MK. After military training in the Soviet Union, he returned to the ANC's Kongwa military camp in Tanzania and went on to serve in various positions at the Nkomo military camp in Zambia. Pekane spent several years in Bulgaria, where he obtained a PhD in international and public law in 1981. He then returned to Zambia to work in the ANC Treasury as director of projects and later joined the DLCA.[23]

Both he and Jobodwana were members of the National People's Tribunal chaired by NEC veteran James Stuart. This was the internal ANC court set up after Kabwe to establish more formal legal processes in the ANC. Jobodwana and Pekane effectively became 'judges' appointed by the NEC to adjudicate on serious transgressions of ANC codes and general disciplinary cases. Such disciplinary cases had previously been dealt with on an ad hoc, case-by-case basis, but now the ANC was attempting to introduce a system of due process with agreed procedures and an independent judiciary enjoying an arm's-length distance from the department in which such misdemeanours occurred. The tribunal's task was to determine guilt or innocence and recommend sentences to the president, who 'would usually' refer these to the ANC's version of an appeal court: the 'Review Board' consisting of Ruth Mompati, John Motshabi and veteran SACP leader Dan Tloome. Then, the 'sentence would be confirmed by the President and carried out'.[24]

According to Maduna, the existence of the tribunal did not wipe out all abuses, but it certainly reduced them drastically. In particular, it made the ANC security officials – Mbokodo, referred to as 'our rocks' – accountable. He had once been appointed as one of the defence lawyers:

the instruction ... was we must conduct a proper tribunal and ... behave as though we are lawyers in a court of law. So I was instructed to defend people who had infiltrated the ANC – not just to brush our teeth, but to kill us. Tambo says: 'Forget about all of that. Treat them as you would treat clients who [had] instructed you to act for them in a court of law.' ... We interrogated our own rocks ... cross examined them ... Suddenly they had to account for what they were doing.[25]

In one case he cross-examined a defendant who had fathered a child with some-one he hadn't known was a leading underground combatant in MK. The regime had arranged for this man to get out of the country in the hope that he would infiltrate the ANC as a 'sleeper' who would be in place and available to receive instructions at a later stage. The tribunal accepted Maduna's argument that the defendant had received no instructions and did not even know what his task was; 'he was just happy to be out of the clutches of the apartheid regime'. On this basis, they acquitted him. Some people in the NEC who were listed as targets criticised Maduna, saying he worked hard to get people who had come to kill them off the hook or pleaded in mitigation for them.[26]

Pekane was also kept busy in two other areas, both involving travel. When dangerous missions had to be undertaken to neighbouring countries, he and Skweyiya – senior members of the Committee and trained first-generation MK soldiers – would be called on first (see Chapter 20). Jobodwana, also a trained MK operative, remembers that they were

in and out of Botswana, Swaziland and Lesotho arranging for the immediate release of MK operatives; those who happened to have been captured, and in detention, arranging bails, making sure they are not abducted or handed over to the enemy.[27]

There were also matters like impounded ANC cars that had to be seen to in these cases.

Then there was the international travel. Every year, Pekane and the other Constitution Committee members would represent the ANC at a round of inter-national conferences, developing valuable contacts and lobbying support for victims of the successive states of emergency in South Africa. For example, early in 1987, he, Maduna and Jobodwana visited the GDR (a unitary state) and federal Czechoslovakia to look at constitutional models and the transitional arrange-ments that occurred there after World War II.[28] In the same year, Skweyiya asked permission for Pekane to be seconded to work full-time in Harare to help organise the highly significant International Conference on Children, Repression and the Law in Apartheid South Africa. As Jobodwana put it, 'I recall in a year, I would be in Geneva for the February/March United Nations Human Rights Commission sessions and then later [in] the same year attend the UN August/September Human Rights Commission sessions in New York City.'[29] This travelling and the work for the DLCA and the Constitution Committee was perfect diplomatic training. In 1989 it led to Teddy Pekane being appointed chief representative in Brussels, where he continued to promote and write about the Committee's work.[30]

7

The Two Insiders from Outside Lusaka

T HE CONSTITUTION COMMITTEE had two legal thinkers based outside Lusaka: Kader Asmal and Albie Sachs. Asmal lived in Ireland and Sachs was working for the FRELIMO government in Mozambique. Both had been recommended to Tambo by Pallo Jordan.[1] Both were prodigiously talented, academically highly qualified and had long histories of involvement in the struggle. The fifty-year-old Sachs had participated in the 1952 Defiance Campaign and the seminal Congress of the People in 1955. Asmal had become involved in the establishment of the British and Irish anti-apartheid movements as a student in the early years of exile.

Starting at the first meeting, these two intellectual heavyweights would butt heads from time to time. Sachs recalls: 'Kader, sparky, bright, lots of international experience, quick turn of phrase and a fantastic personality. I would say it happened more than once that Kader and I were in competition over ideas. But we had a very strong relationship; very respectful of each other even if at times we were jostling you know to have the last word on a particular question ... one of the strengths was the diversity of personalities on the Constitution Committee.'[2]

Born in Stanger (KwaDukuza) in Natal in 1934, Asmal was lively, quick-tongued, incisive and gregarious. When the Sharpeville massacre occurred in 1960, he had been studying at the London School of Economics, where he completed his LLB and LLM degrees. From 1963 to 1991 he worked as a law lecturer and dean of humanities at Trinity College, Dublin. At a Boycott South Africa campaign party, he met Louise Parkinson, a young Englishwoman involved in the Campaign for Nuclear Disarmament and civil liberty activities. She remembers him as 'this skinny creature in a large black sweater'. They married within a year, with the approval of Oliver Tambo and Dr Yusuf Dadoo. Asmal could not return to South Africa because his wife would have been classified as white and would not have been able to live with him, so they remained in Britain and Ireland, and became central figures in the ANC's international solidarity work. Asmal was a founding member and treasurer of the British Anti-Apartheid Movement and, later, founder and chairperson of the Irish Anti-Apartheid Movement (IAAM), in which he and Louise served for twenty-seven years. He was a long-time vice-chair of the

International Defence and Aid Fund (IDAF) for Southern Africa, which surreptitiously channelled large sums of money to secure legal defence for anti-apartheid activists in South Africa. He'd also served as legal advisor for the South African Non-Racial Olympic Committee (SANROC), which spearheaded the international sports boycott. He held several prominent positions in Irish organisations, such as the Irish Federation of University Teachers and the Irish Council for Civil Liberties.

Asmal's expertise lay in international law. A warm-hearted and engaging speaker, he stood back for no one and was fond of quoting his friend Seamus Heaney and other poets and writers from his adopted land. He jokingly referred to himself as 'the only Indian South African Irishman in the world'. Two future Irish presidents who studied at Trinity College – Mary Robinson and Mary McAleese – paid tribute to the role his vivacious teaching played in awakening their political consciousness. For three decades, he was a familiar figure at UN and international anti-apartheid fora.[3]

Prompted by his country's unique circumstances, Asmal chose to specialise in international law at a time – the decade of decolonisation – when it was undergoing significant changes, including acceptance of the principle that all people have the right to national sovereignty and self-determination.[4] He was involved in the formation of the UN Special Committee Against Apartheid in 1963, and worked closely with its indefatigable head, Enuga Reddy, for many years. The committee spearheaded the imposition of sanctions against apartheid South Africa in 1967 and the declaration of apartheid as a crime against humanity in 1973 under the International Convention on the Suppression and Punishment of the Crime of Apartheid, which came into force in July 1976, a month after the Soweto uprisings. The same year, Asmal was one of the rapporteurs at the World Conference for Action Against Apartheid in Lagos, which led to an arms embargo being slapped on the regime under Resolution 418 of the UN Security Council in November 1977. For the next three years, while also serving on the International Commission of Inquiry into the Crimes of the Apartheid Regime, the Dublin-based law professor was involved in the debates and negotiations to include liberation struggles in the Geneva Convention Protocols I and II governing the rules of war. The ANC became the first liberation movement to declare that it would treat captured enemy combatants as prisoners of war (a gesture not reciprocated by the regime). In November 1980, Asmal accompanied Oliver Tambo, Alfred Nzo and Thomas Nkobi to Geneva for the signing of a declaration to this effect with the International Committee of the Red Cross (ICRC). He declared that while the South African rulers disregarded 'all norms of humanity', 'we have always defined the enemy in terms of a system of domination and not a people or race'.[5] The upshot of these moves was that international law legitimised freedom struggles against despotic rule.[6]

Asmal described the signing of the ICRC declaration as 'a great moment in the history of our struggle':

> the ANC's status was affirmed, and this opened the doors to participation in all kinds of forum and also to much greater levels of support from the international community in general and the UN in particular. No longer were liberation movements assumed to be a bunch of thugs and murderers, but instead they came to be treated as organisations with legitimate grievances against despotic states ... Here was a document that established the moral basis of our struggle.[7]

Kader Asmal's presence on the international anti-apartheid circuit inevitably made him a target of the disinformation and dirty tricks of the Bureau of State Security (BOSS). A file of materials, some from Irish government archives – including the Taoiseach's office – which he received decades later, show how the apartheid intelligence agencies sought to exert pressure on him via their Irish counterparts and the questioning of his activities at Trinity College.[8]

Albie Sachs was the main architect of the new Code of Conduct adopted at Kabwe. Given his writing skills and the broad character of his legal experience, Sachs was also made the regular 'rapporteur' of the Constitution Committee. Born into a political family, he was given his first name in honour of Albert Nzula, a young communist leader who died shortly before he was born, allegedly in a Stalinist purge while he was visiting the Soviet Union. His mother, Ray Edwards, had worked as a typist for the Communist Party and ANC leader Moses Kotane. Aptly, he first saw the light of day at the Florence Nightingale Hospital in Johannesburg, a short walk across the street from the Old Fort Prison, where the Constitutional Court of democratic South Africa stands today.

On his sixth birthday, during World War II, Sachs's trade unionist father, Solly, wrote that his birthday wish for his son was that he become 'a soldier in the fight for liberation'. Solly Sachs had founded the Garment Workers' Union, which organised Afrikaner, coloured and African women into one of the strongest forces of the labour movement at the time. Though expelled from the Communist Party in the 1930s for what was then called 'right-wing deviationism', he remained a militant union leader until the 1950s, when the apartheid government placed him under banning orders that forbade him to attend any gatherings. Though not trained as a lawyer, he became famous as a litigator, constantly in and out of court. His last case involved his attendance at a gathering of workers on the City

Hall steps in Johannesburg in defiance of his banning order. After being sentenced to six months' imprisonment, he went to the Appeal Court in Bloemfontein himself to argue that the banning orders were invalid because of their vagueness. His junior in court, wearing his first suit, was seventeen-year-old Albie, then a second-year law student.

Albie was inspired to become an activist after listening to a lecture on the poets Federico García Lorca and Pablo Neruda by the Afrikaans writer Uys Krige. These poets were part of the anti-fascist struggles in the 1930s and connected the intimacy and longings that Sachs loved in poetry with the grand public events of the world.[9] In 1952, Sachs led four white youths to sit on seats marked 'Non-Whites Only' in the Cape Town General Post Office as volunteers in the Defiance of Unjust Laws Campaign.

He soon became a member of the illegal underground SACP (from 1953 to 1963) and part of the Modern Youth Society (they couldn't call themselves 'socialists', so they called themselves 'Modern'), where his comrades included Denis Goldberg, Ben and Mary Turok, George Peake, Joseph Morolong and Amy Thornton, all of whom subsequently went to jail.[10] He attended the Congress of the People in 1955, where the Freedom Charter was adopted. A few months later, he received a five-year banning order that restricted his activities considerably but did not prevent him from receiving a UCT law degree and setting up practice as an advocate at the Cape Town Bar in 1957 at the age of twenty-one.

Much of Sachs's legal work consisted of defending people such as Annie Silinga (a well-known activist who refused to carry a pass), black trade unionists accused of striking illegally, and the writer Alex La Guma, who was charged with breaking his banning orders. Sachs frequently defended Gilbert Hani, a civic leader in Cape Town's Langa township, on charges brought against him based on his opposition to Kaiser Matanzima, the Transkei homeland leader collaborating with Pretoria. Some years later, he defended Gilbert's son Chris Hani, and Archie Sibeko, with whom Chris had worked in the underground, against charges of being in possession of ANC pamphlets. They were sentenced to prison, but Sachs helped them escape from the country while still out on bail.[11]

In 1963 Albie himself was thrown into prison and spent 168 days in solitary confinement under what was then called the 90-Day Law. On his release, he ran from the centre of town to Clifton Beach and threw himself, fully clothed, into the waves. Two years later, he was placed in solitary confinement again and subjected to torture by sleep deprivation. Sachs's *Jail Diary*, in which he recounts his experiences of detention, was later adapted into a play for the Royal Shakespeare Company and broadcast by the BBC. Living in Britain from 1966 to 1977, he completed a PhD in law at Sussex University and taught for six years at Southampton

University. In 1977, he moved to newly independent Mozambique, where he became fluent in Portuguese and worked as a law professor at Eduardo Mondlane University for six years before being recruited to work as head of research in the Mozambican Ministry of Justice in 1983.

His participating in the Mozambican revolution had a major impact on his legal thinking. Sachs embraced the unifying, anti-racist and transformative processes of People's Power and wrote a book about popular justice in Mozambique.[12] But as the years passed and the country became engulfed in civil war, he was persuaded of the importance of political pluralism. He saw that if no space was left for opposition, it did not disappear but went underground and got powerful external backing. Similarly, although deeply impressed by the integrity, effectiveness and popularity of community courts at the local level, he discovered that the absence of legal codes and processes affected the poor and vulnerable the most. The financially secure relied on their political or other connections. It was the poor who needed the law. These ideas were sharp in his mind when Tambo asked him to draft the Code of Conduct.[13]

The Constitution Committee members who gathered in Lusaka in that second week of January 1986 were totally dedicated to using their legal skills to overthrow apartheid and create a democratic South Africa. In addition, they had exceptionally rich experiences in seeing how the law operated in different countries. Their single mission was to stop the use of law as an instrument of oppression and convert it into an instrument of emancipation.

Against the background of Kabwe and the mandate presented by Tambo, the secret committee's deliberations for a new constitutional dispensation proceeded from the very beginning out of a desire for fundamental change in South Africa. This was underpinned by a strong concern that Western countries, which had supported Pretoria in the Cold War context, would continue to identify with and support the interests of the white minority.[14] It was clear to all that the basic starting point in drafting a new constitution would be the Freedom Charter. This document had by now achieved enduring status as an inspiring vision for a free South Africa. For the ANC, it was the rock on which its struggle was based. When a member joined the organisation, they swore allegiance to the principles of the Charter. The challenge for the Constitution Committee was to translate the Charter's vision into a constitutional document that could be implemented in a liberated South Africa.[15]

8

Translating the Vision of the Freedom Charter into a Constitutional Document

'In all our discussion the Freedom Charter has to be the group's point of departure
... [it is] legally binding [and] we have to translate [it] as a basis of a constitution
... the group cannot revise the Freedom Charter as it came from the people of
South Africa themselves.'

– Minutes of the Constitution Committee's first meeting,
Lusaka, 8 January 1986[1]

THE MINUTES OF that first Constitution Committee meeting on 8 January 1986 declare that their main aim was to translate the principles and programmes of the Freedom Charter into an operative constitutional document, thereby setting the constitutional foundations of a South Africa without apartheid. This discussion started in earnest on day three, Friday 10 January. By then, Jobs Jobodwana had minuted more than fifty issues and suggestions in bullet-point form. These were narrowed down into five discussion items: 'Freedom Charter, Political Structures, Organs of Power, Bill of Rights, Forms of Representation'.

Albie Sachs was given the task of introducing the topic. To get the ball rolling, he distributed a two-page paper on 'The Freedom Charter and the Constitution', and 'a lengthy discussion on how the contents of the Freedom Charter could be incorporated into a constitution ensued'. After the discussions, 'Cde Albie was asked to revise his paper', inserting specific recommendations from members.[2]

This revised paper, which was later presented to the NEC, opened by explaining that, while the Freedom Charter had a constitutional character and was like the general principles and sections on citizens' rights rolled into one, it could not serve as a constitution. For a start, it did not define the structures of government:

Almost all modern constitutions have certain elements in common. They set out the main institutions of public power (government), define the competence and indicate how the leadership of the country is to be determined (election, hereditary succession, religious position). In addition, many constitutions contain sections dealing with the general principles of the society, while it is even more common to find sections setting out the specific rights of citizens, sometimes in a section called a Bill of Rights.[3]

The Committee had to enlarge the significance of the Charter by transforming it from a programme for the future into the centrepiece of a constitution.

Jack Simons' notes on day three show that Asmal and Sachs spoke several times on the issue, with the former saying that 'We need only propose to [the] NEC a preamble that will incorporate concepts of the FC'. The latter, however, 'insists that [the] FC should be incorporated'. Asmal countered that although it was a fundamental document, 'incorporation does not mean necessarily a reproduction of the FC as a single document'.[4]

Jobodwana's formal minutes faithfully incorporated these positions. The Committee decided the Charter could be incorporated into a constitution in several ways. The first would be to 'distil' the Charter's principles and inscribe them 'into the relevant parts of the Constitution'. The second would be to 'incorporate the full [actual] text' of the Charter's ten clauses 'as they stand' as an introductory section of the constitution under the heading 'General principles'. The third would be to 'disperse' excerpts from the Charter throughout the constitution, 'locating them where they belong, but not necessarily using the whole text'.[5] In the end, the Committee explained things in the following way:

> The advantage of incorporating the text as a whole (shorn of its preamble and conclusion) is that it is a document that is well-known and balanced, that came from the people and is already part of the history of the people. It follows the approach adopted by many revolutionary constitutions of incorporating goals of the society as a programme binding on the state, but does so in a language that is acceptable to non-revolutionaries.[6]

However, this option was not really feasible. It did not follow the format of normal constitutions and, more importantly, 'to include the entire text is to encourage lawyers of all sizes and shapes to examine the details and create problems for the new government'.

Penuell Maduna proposed that the Committee go through the Charter clause by clause, considering its relevance for a new democratic constitution for South Africa. The minutes of the revised document show that the following comments (recorded here beneath each clause) were made:

THE FREEDOM CHARTER

We, the People of South Africa, declare for all our country and the world to know:
that South Africa belongs to all who live in it, black and white, and that no

government can justly claim authority unless it is based on the will of all
the people;
that our people have been robbed of their birthright to land, liberty and
peace by a form of government founded on injustice and inequality;
that our country will never be prosperous or free until all our people live in
brotherhood, enjoying equal rights and opportunities;
that only a democratic state, based on the will of all the people, can secure to
all their birthright without distinction of colour, race, sex or belief;
And therefore, we, the people of South Africa, black and white together
equals, countrymen and brothers adopt this Freedom Charter;
And we pledge ourselves to strive together, sparing neither strength nor
courage, until the democratic changes here set out have been won.

1. The People Shall Govern!

Every man and woman shall have the right to vote for and to stand as a
candidate for all bodies which make laws;
It was felt that the right to vote should stipulate an age limit.

All people shall be entitled to take part in the administration of the country;
*The reference to 'all people' entitled to take part in the administration should
exclude all those who participated in the criminal activities of apartheid, and
those who were 'mentally disabled persons' or had 'legal impediments'.*

The rights of the people shall be the same, regardless of race, colour or sex;
All bodies of minority rule, advisory boards, councils and authorities shall be
replaced by democratic organs of self-government.
*It was asked whether 'all bodies' should mean 'law-making bodies or elected
bodies'.*

2. All National Groups Shall Have Equal Rights!

There shall be equal status in the bodies of state, in the courts and in the
schools for all national groups and races;
*There was concern that requiring equal status for all national groups and races
in the bodies of state could pander to ethnicity if 'equal status' was interpreted
to mean proportional representation for ethnic groups. This was exactly what
the ANC wished to avoid. The rest of this clause was accepted:*

All people shall have equal right to use their own languages, and to develop
their own folk culture and customs;
All national groups shall be protected by law against insults to their race and
national pride;

The preaching and practice of national, race or colour discrimination and contempt shall be a punishable crime;

All apartheid laws and practices shall be set aside.

3. The People Shall Share in the Country's Wealth!

The national wealth of our country, the heritage of South Africans, shall be restored to the people;

The mineral wealth beneath the soil, the banks and monopoly industry shall be transferred to the ownership of the people as a whole;

All other industry and trade shall be controlled to assist the wellbeing of the people;

All people shall have equal rights to trade where they choose, to manufacture and to enter all trades, crafts and professions.

The Committee decided not to discuss this clause at that stage and to await the report of the ANC Economic Commission, which had the special task of looking at questions of economic freedom.

4. The Land Shall Be Shared Among Those Who Work It!

Restrictions of land ownership on a racial basis shall be ended, and all the land re-divided amongst those who work it to banish famine and land hunger;

The state shall help the peasants with implements, seed, tractors and dams to save the soil and assist the tillers;

Freedom of movement shall be guaranteed to all who work on the land;

All shall have the right to occupy land wherever they choose;

People shall not be robbed of their cattle, and forced labour and farm prisons shall be abolished.

Again, the Committee felt that discussion should await the report of the ANC Economic Commission. Its understanding, according to Jack Simons' hand-written notes, was that the Committee would concentrate on the 'legal and political system', while others more qualified should work on the aspect of a future 'economic model for SA'.[7]

5. All Shall Be Equal Before the Law!

No-one shall be imprisoned, deported or restricted without a fair trial;

No-one shall be condemned by the order of any Government official;

The courts shall be representative of all the people;

The Committee felt that the NEC should specify how courts should be constituted and recommended that future courts include community representatives even at the top level.

Imprisonment shall be only for serious crimes against the people, and shall aim at re-education, not vengeance;

The police force and army shall be open to all on an equal basis and shall be the helpers and protectors of the people;

All laws which discriminate on grounds of race, colour or belief shall be repealed.

6. All Shall Enjoy Equal Human Rights!

The law shall guarantee to all their right to speak, to organise, to meet together, to publish, to preach, to worship and to educate their children;

In addition to several comments made, it was the opinion of the group that the ANC Education Council should look into this clause and give a critical analysis of its implications. The question of private schools was raised as these might be used to promote racialism and class differentiation. There was a strong concern within the ANC that private education not be used to maintain white privilege in future. Rights to speak, publish, preach, worship, etc. shall not be inconsistent with the provisions of the Charter or constitution.

The privacy of the house from police raids shall be protected by law;

All shall be free to travel without restriction from countryside to town, from province to province, and from South Africa abroad;

Pass Laws, permits and all other laws restricting these freedoms shall be abolished.

Some members felt that the privacy of the house could be regulated and modified by legislation and that the same could apply to travel restrictions and pass laws.

7. There Shall Be Work and Security!

All who work shall be free to form trade unions, to elect their officers and to make wage agreements with their employers;

The state shall recognise the right and duty of all to work, and to draw full unemployment benefits;

Men and women of all races shall receive equal pay for equal work;

There shall be a forty-hour working week, a national minimum wage, paid annual leave, and sick leave for all workers, and maternity leave on full pay for all working mothers;

Miners, domestic workers, farm workers and civil servants shall have the same rights as all others who work;

Child labour, compound labour, the tot system and contract labour shall be abolished.

It was felt that this clause constituted the programmatic aspect of the Constitution and did not have to be interfered with.

8. The Doors of Learning and Culture Shall be Opened!

The government shall discover, develop and encourage national talent for the enhancement of our cultural life;

All the cultural treasures of mankind shall be open to all, by free exchange of books, ideas and contact with other lands;

The aim of education shall be to teach the youth to love their people and their culture, to honour human brotherhood, liberty and peace;

Education shall be free, compulsory, universal and equal for all children;

Higher education and technical training shall be opened to all by means of state allowances and scholarships awarded on the basis of merit;

Adult illiteracy shall be ended by a mass state education plan;

Teachers shall have all the rights of other citizens;

The colour bar in cultural life, in sport and in education shall be abolished.

The minutes simply record 'for the ANC Education Council'.

9. There Shall Be Houses, Security and Comfort!

All people shall have the right to live where they choose, be decently housed, and to bring up their families in comfort and security;

Unused housing space to be made available to the people;

Rent and prices shall be lowered, food plentiful and no one shall go hungry;

A preventive health scheme shall be run by the state;

Free medical care and hospitalisation shall be provided for all, with special care for mothers and young children;

Slums shall be demolished, and new suburbs built where all have transport, roads, lighting, playing fields, creches and social centres;

The aged, the orphans, the disabled and the sick shall be cared for by the state;

Rest, leisure and recreation shall be the right of all:

Fenced locations and ghettoes shall be abolished, and laws which break up families shall be repealed.

The Committee agreed 'in principle' to leave this clause intact. However, there were various questions and comments on the issue of housing and shelter: Do we protect people's rights to houses? What to do with all-white suburbs? It was stipulated that the constitution should not be designed so as to prevent government from embarking on programmes of reconstruction. Similarly, the state should be obliged to pass laws ensuring that the consequences of apartheid did not manifest themselves after independence.

10. There Shall Be Peace and Friendship!
South Africa shall be a fully independent state which respects the rights and
sovereignty of all nations; South Africa shall strive to maintain world peace
and the settlement of all international disputes by negotiation – not war;
Peace and friendship amongst all our people shall be secured by upholding
the equal rights, opportunities and status of all;
The people of the protectorates Basutoland, Bechuanaland and Swaziland
shall be free to decide for themselves their own future;
The right of all peoples of Africa to independence and self-government shall
be recognised, and shall be the basis of close co-operation.
*The Committee agreed to retain all the sentiments expressed in this clause
except for the provision dealing with the former protectorates, Basutoland,
Bechuanaland and Swaziland, which had achieved independence.*[8]

Let all people who love their people and their country now say, as we say
here: THESE FREEDOMS WE WILL FIGHT FOR, SIDE BY SIDE,
THROUGHOUT OUR LIVES, UNTIL WE HAVE WON OUR LIBERTY.

The Freedom Charter was referred to no less than twenty-four times in the
sixteen-page minutes of the Constitution Committee's first meeting. In the
decade to come, the ANC and the Committee would stick unwaveringly to the
Charter as its basic departure point – helping, in this way, to determine the future
constitutional form of democratic South Africa along the lines envisaged by the
movement since the 1950s.

After its session on the Freedom Charter on Friday 10 January, the Constitution
Committee turned its attention to the next agenda points, which dealt with structures of government. The discussions ran over into day four, Saturday 11 January.
Sachs was given the key task of being rapporteur and was once again 'requested to
produce a memo' for final discussions and for the Committee's promised report
to the NEC.

9

The Skeleton

ANDREWS MOTEL ON the outskirts of Lusaka where Albie Sachs stayed for the week of the Constitution Committee's first meeting was, he recalls, the kind of place where there was a fixed menu, the swimming pool was empty and there was hot water to shower, but not every day. It was here that the Committee's rapporteur sought to produce materials that would capture their discussions and become the initial documents that would eventually influence the fortunes of a country.

More concerning than the discomfort, however, was that at times 'it was a place where we felt very scared', Sachs remembers.[1] Botha's SADF had struck at ANC targets in Lusaka only six months earlier, shortly before the Kabwe conference. Oliver Tambo's notes for his meeting with Gavin Relly's business delegation shortly afterwards were written on paper with the letterhead of President Kaunda's state house residence on it, because the threat to Tambo was so great that KK had given him shelter on the grounds of his personal residence.[2]

Sachs recalls how exposed he felt at the Andrews Motel when enjoying a brief reunion there with Denis Goldberg, who had been his comrade in the Modern Youth Society in Cape Town in the 1950s and had later joined MK. He and Sachs were hugely happy to see each other and talked excitedly as they walked non-stop around and around the empty swimming pool. But the climate was such that they kept their eyes on the sky in case helicopters flew in to drop commandos to take them out.[3] Goldberg had been captured in Rivonia and served twenty-two years in prison. The ANC had called him to Lusaka to explain to the NEC why, when stuck in the small, isolated, whites-only section of Pretoria Central prison away from his comrades, he had accepted an early release offered by P.W. Botha. The NEC accepted Goldberg's explanation and he remained a veteran in good standing in the organisation.

As rapporteur, Sachs used his break time from the meeting to synthesise the Committee's discussions. In particular, he used the meeting's adjournment from after the Saturday session to Tuesday to prepare documents for the fifth and final day. It was then that the Committee members discussed and worked out the first outline of a constitution for a future liberated and democratic South Africa – what they called 'The Skeleton'.

As the Constitution Committee fully understood, there were several reasons why the Freedom Charter could not be a constitution, only the basis for one:

the Freedom Charter says nothing about what kind of legislature or executive the country should have, whether the government should be Presidential or Prime Ministerial in character, the territorial division of the country (for purposes of central, regional and local government), how many Chambers the legislature should have, or whether elections should be by proportional representation or in single member constituencies. Nor does it deal with questions such as official languages, the flag, where the capital should be, or even with the name of the country (at the time the Freedom Charter was adopted, South Africa was still a monarchy; the Charter did not require that it become a republic).[4]

Therefore, the members decided to make a start on a skeleton constitution that could be fleshed out and elaborated in future. They noted that 'Any constitutional document drawn up at this stage must of necessity be incomplete and provisional ... because we still await clear guidelines on questions such as economic policy and education, and because we lack important politico-demographic information.'[5] The questions regarding the economy and education were to be referred back for specialist input from the economic policy and education units. The Committee felt that the leadership should also make provision for in-depth research into key areas that it and the leadership would need to consider in drawing up more concrete plans.

The Skeleton started with a rough preamble comprising the first and fourth sentences of the Freedom Charter, followed by nine points culled from 'The statement of the problem' in the memo on 'The Preliminary Nature of the Constitutional Document', which Sachs had drawn up after the discussions of the previous few days.[6] Though not yet written out as a distinct document, these first eleven clauses suggested as suitable for a preamble to the first democratic constitution for South Africa read as follows:

DRAFT ONE: The Skeleton, drafted by the Constitution Committee, 8–14 January 1986:

Preamble
- South Africa belongs to all who live in it, black and white, and no government can justly claim authority unless it is based on the will of all the people;
- Only a democratic state, based on the will of all the people, can secure to all their birth right without distinction of colour, race, sex or belief; [and it]
- Grants to the oppressed majority their just national rights;

- Outlaws racial discrimination in all its forms;
- Ensures the complete dismantlement of apartheid structures and their replacement by democratic ones;
- Prevents the resurgence of racist policies and programmes, whether in their old form or new ones;
- Overcomes the effects of centuries of racial domination and inequality by ensuring a substantial redistribution of wealth and the complete opening up of access to facilities for all;
- Encourages the active involvement of all sectors of population in government and economic and cultural life;
- Promotes the habits of non-racial thinking, the practice of non-racial behaviour and the acquisition of a genuine, subjectively-held patriotic consciousness;
- Creates conditions for the speediest achievement of these goals with the least possible disruption to the tranquillity of the country and to the production of the goods and services necessary for a decent life for the community as a whole; [and]
- Guarantees the security necessary for the achievement of the goals set out in the constitution.[7]

These can be regarded as the first words in the drafting of the Constitution of modern South Africa. The phrase 'SA is constituted as an independent, non-racial democratic State' could be added to the preamble, the minutes noted.[8]

Following on the preamble, the minutes for 14 January 1986 list eleven more parts to make up the Skeleton, as follows:
- Name of the country
- Symbols
- Official languages
- Coat of arms
- Capital
- Organs of government
- Regional and local governments
- Commissions
- Fundamental rights and duties of citizens
- 'Declaration of international aspects'
- Transitional legal arrangements[9]

Under each of these eleven headings, the Constitution Committee made various comments and observations:[10]

Name of the country

The name 'Azania' was used by some of the political opponents of the Congress movement, such as AZAPO, and the Committee considered the idea of a completely new name for the country. In the end it concluded that 'Africa' needed to be part of the name in order to identify with the continent. 'Democratic Republic of South Africa, Lundi and Maluti [were] considered but no recommendation made.' Simons noted that the emphasis on 'Democratic' may be big enough to offset historical antecedents of continuing with the name South Africa.[11]

Symbols

The first democratic parliament would decide on these but the Committee, though not in favour of a one-party state, accepted the black, green and gold of the ANC as appropriate colours for the national flag. For the anthem, the Committee felt it had to be 'Nkosi Sikelel' iAfrika'. There was a 'strong sentimental attachment to our anthem' and tampering with it would be 'worse than tampering with the Freedom Charter'.

Official languages

The Freedom Charter guideline was that 'all languages shall have equal status'.

Coat of arms

This was for the NEC to consider.

Capital

'Leave the topic for the time being.'

Organs of government

The Committee wrote a detailed six-page summary of its discussion on this issue, identifying the two major issues: the type of government (presidential or prime ministerial) and the voting system (constituency-based or based on proportional representation).

In the first case, the Committee tentatively proposed a three-tier leadership system. They looked at France, the United States, Latin America and Britain, as well as at former British colonies, now independent, and discussed the merits and demerits of governmental systems in operation there. Their preliminary preferences were for an executive president, as 'we feel that the country will need strong, clear and directly legitimated leadership, especially in the early years of the new Constitution'. There was a provisional view that consideration should be given to an American-style vice-president, who would be a running mate for the president, ensure that the succession was smooth in the case of death, and who could exercise important functions inside the ANC itself. There should, in addition, be a prime minister, a third leading figure in the government, who could chair the normal business meetings of the Cabinet and steer legislation through Parliament.[12]

Regarding the voting system, the Committee's initial preference was for directly elected MPs in a single-member constituency model, rather than proportional representation. This had already been the practice in South Africa for seventy-five years for white voters and it would encourage the formation of national parties. Why change something that was already well known? The answer did not lie simply in a '"pure" theory of government' but rather in an understanding of the concrete conditions in the country and of how the goals of the Freedom Charter could best be achieved. For example, given rigid segregation patterns, could constituency boundaries be drawn in a way that encouraged cross-race voting patterns? And what needed to be done to ensure that all sections of the population were well represented in Parliament?

Aware of the painful history of migrant labour, the Committee felt that special care should be taken on how migrant labourers would vote. If they did so in their areas of work, this would help to undermine ethnic identification, but their views on the question should be canvassed. To better understand conditions on the ground, the Committee recommended that the ANC undertake more detailed studies on the national demographics and the political system before it made a final decision on both the leadership structures and electoral models. 'In general terms, we feel that the Constitution should be manifestly fair and democratic and not loaded in favour of the ANC. But at the same time, it would be foolish to gratuitously introduce provisions which weakened the electoral prospects of the ANC.'

Regional and local governments

The Constitution Committee emphasised that local and regional government needed special consideration for three reasons. First, they deal with concrete issues directly affecting the lives of the people, such as housing, services and education, which would be important priorities in a changing South Africa. Second, they involve large sectors of the population directly and actively in questions of government. Third, they would be the scene of direct transformation in people's lives.

The situation at that level was fluid at the time, given that P.W. Botha was trying to reshape the system of government through the Tricameral Parliament and new black local authorities. On the other hand, incipient organs of People's Power were attempting to collapse and replace state structures at the local level. Regions 'should not substitute for the centre', and 'all the people in all the areas' should be encouraged to think of themselves as South Africans. Still, local government was a key area of life and needed to be part of the proposed demographic and political survey. The ANC required 'more precise information than we possess at present', including the financial implications of any proposed policies.

The ANC could draw on people's support in Soweto, for example, but investigations were necessary to ensure that reactionary white–black alliances did not defeat them in Greater Johannesburg. Similarly, breaking up huge areas like the Cape Province into smaller administrative regions would make sense, but caution was needed to 'avoid permitting the term "regions" to become an apparently neutral description for a South Africa divided into ethnic homelands'. These remained, in effect, isolated and 'permanently underdeveloped feudal and reactionary units'. Democratic organs of self-government had to be built everywhere and boundary demarcations should be drawn at both local and regional levels 'to ensure that rich and poor areas were included side by side'. These levels had 'important implications for finances' as well as for breaking down patterns of inequality.[13]

The Committee underlined that decisions on the future needed to be based on hard facts and realities on the ground.[14]

Commissions

The Committee recommended a constitutional clause that made provision for the repeal and review of apartheid laws. All laws 'not repugnant to the Constitution' could remain in force until amended or repealed. Those that were restrictive of freedoms could be listed on a schedule and repealed automatically.

They also recommended the establishment of three commissions to act as watchdogs over the process of change: an affirmative action commission, a constitutional commission and a public service commission.

Pending new legislation, the affirmative action commission would deal with those laws that were 'obnoxious because of their racist character but which had important practical consequences', such as the payment of teachers' salaries. A future government would also have to give special attention to traditional or customary law, but this did not need to be a constitutional question 'unless it is felt [contrary to the Committee's belief] that exceptions to the section on "Fundamental rights and duties of citizens" should be made so as to permit inconsistent traditional law practices to continue'. Here the Committee felt that some 'long overdue reforms', such as the 'subordinate position of African widows', should be 'immediately effected' and that, as in Mozambique, legislation should also provide for community courts to function at grassroots level.

As the current apartheid-minded judiciary was 'the last organ that could be given the position of watchdog of the Constitution', the Committee recommended that a new constitutional commission be established under the control of Parliament to supervise the application of the Constitution. It would advise Parliament and liaise with the affirmative action commission. The Committee felt that 'it would be unthinkable to entrust the vast programme of social and economic reform contemplated by the concept of affirmative action, to the scrutiny of these judges. Parliament is the place where social and economic issues are decided.'[15]

Thirdly, the Committee recommended a public service commission, which would 'supervise access to and promotion' of public services within the bureaucracy of government, and make sure it developed a democratic and non-racial character as quickly as possible while causing the least possible disturbance to functions such as transport and communications.

Great attention would ideally be paid to the people appointed to all three commissions, given the transformation goals they needed to advance. The Committee believed that the president should work with a parliamentary committee to make these appointments, so that both the executive and legislative branches of state would be involved.

Fundamental rights and duties of citizens

The Committee's basic proposal to protect every citizen entailed the adoption of a Bill of Rights that guaranteed certain inviolable rights for all. It was argued that there should also be a constitutional requirement on the state and all other bodies to advance affirmative action – drawn from United States precedents – which the Committee called a 'key and innovative concept in the South African situation'.

With affirmative action as a fundamental departure point, the new democracy would be able 'to take active steps to alter the structures of inequality inherited from the past', and make sure those steps were 'legally enforced with the full power of the state'. The Committee advised that the Freedom Charter and the UN and OAU charters on human rights be used to define citizens' rights in accordance with the desire to redress historical inequality. While the Universal Declaration of Human Rights adopted by the UN in 1948 upheld the classical liberal rights of individual freedom, including voting rights and freedom of speech, worship and movement, later UN conventions extended these to include social and economic protections, such as the right to food, health, housing and education. The African Charter on Human and Peoples' Rights, adopted in Nairobi in 1981, went still further. It encompassed people's rights to peace, development and environmental protection. The Committee felt that these could provide a foundation for post-apartheid transformation in South Africa too.[16]

'Declaration of international aspects'

This paragraph established that there be a constitutionally inspired counterbalance to the basic freedoms set out in the previous paragraph. It affirmed that South Africa would follow international conventions in which 'the practice of national, race or colour discrimination and contempt shall be a punishable crime'. There would be 'overriding constitutional provisions preventing the dissemination of racist ideas'. The Committee also felt that 'the promotion of tribalism and tribal division should be covered in the same way'. In a country where 'our constitutional draft presupposes in general a multiplicity of parties and the existence of what is referred to as political pluralism', the electoral act would not permit parties and campaigns 'restricted on a racial or tribal basis' or any campaigning 'promoting the perpetuation or re-introduction of apartheid'.[17]

Transitional legal arrangements

Envisaging that the final constitution would be in place before elections or a transfer of power, the Committee made it clear that 'the constitution we draw up … would have to be complemented by another document which attends to the arrangements necessary to ensure the transition from the apartheid to the democratic constitutional order'. This would deal, for example, with the creation of a non-racial voters' roll, whether the constitution would come into effect through a national convention or a referendum, and with the transitional legal provisions relating to the proposed three commissions.

Finally, the Committee felt the ANC should indicate that its constitutional proposals were provisional. Should the struggle lead to the seizure of power, 'it would be possible to propose a new version of the transition plan reflecting more advanced forms of people's power'. In these circumstances, if it so wanted, the ANC could 'proclaim a new constitution' in the same way as had happened in Mozambique and Angola.[18]

The Constitution Committee understood it was virtually impossible to determine or pre-empt the final form of the constitution. It could not be ready-made. Its final shape would be determined by the balance of forces existing at the time of the transition to democracy. But the Committee had made a start. The day that they agreed on those first words was Tuesday 14 January 1986. It took another ten years, ten months and twenty-seven days before the constitution for a new democratic South Africa was finally signed into law in Sharpeville on 10 December 1996.

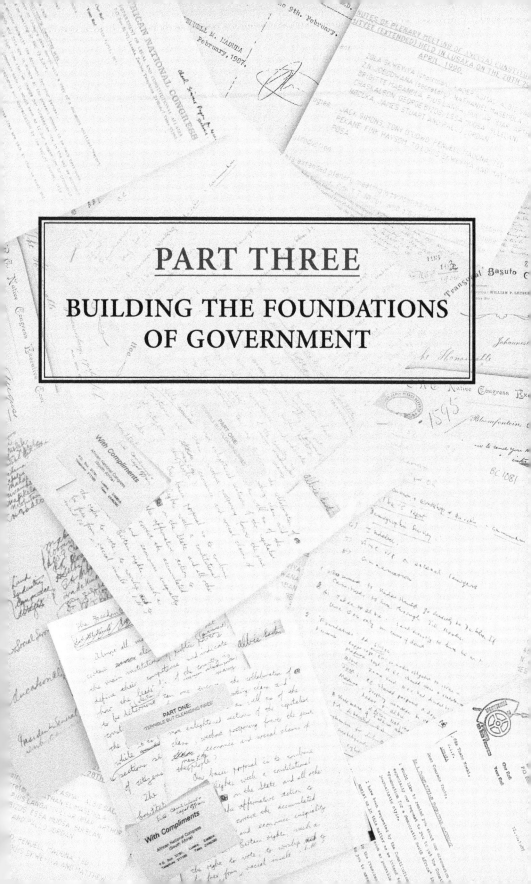

PART THREE

BUILDING THE FOUNDATIONS OF GOVERNMENT

10

Joe Slovo's Misgivings

O N THE SECOND day of the Constitution Committee's meeting, the chair-person had promised to deliver its first report to Oliver Tambo within six days.[1] The promise was duly fulfilled and the first 'ANC Constitution Committee Report to the NEC' was handed to Tambo on 15 January 1986 and forwarded to Secretary-General Nzo the next day.[2] It included several attachments: Jobodwana's sixteen pages of minutes, and three reports authored by Albie Sachs in his role as rapporteur: 'The Freedom Charter and the Constitution', 'Our Objectives in Draft-ing a Constitution', and 'The Preliminary Nature of the Constitutional Document'.[3]

Before closing, the Constitution Committee also gave itself homework to do. Kader Asmal, the 'Comrade from Ireland', who had the resources of Trinity College in Dublin at his disposal, would 'collect various precedents and other material for the group's resources', so they could examine closely both Western bourgeois and 'revolutionary democratic' constitutions. Skweyiya and Maduna would look at the constitutions of neighbouring states, and the ANC Research Department would be asked to prepare dossiers of material, including on 'opposi-tion (racist) thinking' inside South Africa.[4] They decided to rope in London-based Tony O'Dowd, a communist, lawyer and close colleague of Joe Slovo, going back to the time they had studied together with Ruth First, Nelson Mandela, Harold Wolpe and other struggle figures at Wits University in the post–World War II years.

In his covering letter to the Committee's report to the NEC, Jack Simons under-lined to their 'Dear Comrade President' the need for action and feedback from the leadership, the specifics of which were included in the report.[5]

In the section 'Our objectives', the Committee noted that the main aim was to set out the constitutional foundations of a South Africa without apartheid, based on the values of the Freedom Charter. This would fit in with the aspirations of the overwhelming majority, be actively anti-racist (in the same way that the American constitution outlawed slavery) and encourage a sense of common citizenship among all the people. The future constitution would have to be an operational document that defined the structures of government, the principles in terms of which it functions, and the relations between it and individual citizens. It would also have to be an educational document that enshrined core values and was a positive point of reference for society. The Committee stressed that 'such a document should be presented in accessible language and have a clarity and coherence of vision which makes it easily understandable to all our people'. It needed, at the same time, to be a signal to the international community. 'Anything we craft must have a quality of argument and presentation that carries conviction' and builds support from international organisations such as the UN, OAU and the Non-Aligned Movement to governments and NGOs all over the world.[6]

There were five key questions that the Committee felt the NEC had to consider and give guidance on:

- how to deal with the 'so-called problem of power-sharing or the rights of minorities';
- how to reconcile freedom of speech, organisation and electoral activity with the need to combat the dissemination of racial and tribal hatred;
- how to devise an electoral system and appropriate structure of government that would encourage the achievement of the principles contained in the constitution;
- how to establish forms of regional government that would be consistent with the aims of the constitution;
- how to maintain an ongoing legal and administrative system while rapidly dismantling the legislative and institutional structures of apartheid.[7]

These five questions involved explicitly political decisions that needed to be made by the core leadership of the ANC. To begin with, an area of the constitution dealing with calls to safeguard so-called minority rights would have to be drafted with special care. The Committee warned that this issue should be managed in a way that both built unity in a fractured society and prevented any future subversion of democracy – e.g. that 'even if the people get the vote, they shall never really govern'.

At the same time, the Committee explained to the NEC that 'while the aspect of allaying fears of minorities – whether legitimate or illegitimate – should never take precedence over guaranteeing the rights of the majority, the importance of not unduly alarming middle sectors, and of encouraging division in the ranks of the enemy should not be lost sight of'.[8]

The ANC's NWC subcommittee consisting of the Lusaka-based NEC members met regularly and directed and supervised the work of the ANC in between scheduled meetings of the broader executive. These happened infrequently because NEC members were dispersed throughout the world. The NWC was run by a strong general secretariat of key officials: the secretary-general and his deputy, three full-time secretaries who were also full-time NEC members, and the admin secretaries of the External Coordinating Committee and Politico-Military Council, the two important operational arms for external affairs and matters inside the country, respectively. Both the ECC and PMC reported to the NWC.[9]

On 14 January, Tambo had set up the NWC subcommittee that would liaise with the Constitution Committee and 'charged [it] with the responsibility of reading and studying the report ... in order to guide the NWC during its discussions'.[10] It consisted of three key NEC members: Pallo Jordan, Joe Slovo and Simon Makana.

Joe Slovo was a former advocate of the Johannesburg Bar and was current MK chief of staff and Communist Party theoretician. He'd been one of the founders of MK and was later chosen as general secretary of the SACP. Simon Makana was yet another of the numerous struggle activists educated at Fort Hare University. He came from Middledrift in the eastern Cape and had been an NEC member since the Morogoro conference in 1969. Nicknamed 'Nkokheli' (leader), he was assistant secretary of the Revolutionary Council, an NEC subcommittee whose task was to coordinate ANC actions inside South Africa from 1969 to 1976. He was then promoted to director of NAT for the next four years. In 1980, Makana was replaced by Mzwai Piliso and given the lower rank of NAT head of processing and information, while serving once more on the Revolutionary Council (1980–83).[11] He was later given the important diplomatic responsibility of setting up the first ANC embassy in Moscow as 'Chief Rep' to the Soviet Union.[12]

Though we have no minutes to verify the exact details, the Constitution Committee report, as we will see below, generated immediate excitement in the ranks of the ANC's leadership in Lusaka, but they sent out mixed messages. The NWC subcommittee met on 18 and again on 25 February 1986 to discuss the report, and the NWC itself probably met just after that. Neither got back to the Committee with the clear mandate it was seeking, and it was months before they sent a formal reply.

On 21 January 1986, three days after the new NWC subcommittee first met, Jack Simons received a phone call to his Lusaka number, 254 519, at his home, Entabeni, on Zambezi Road. It was Joe Slovo, and he was unhappy with the basic departure points outlined by the Constitution Committee. He said Oliver Tambo was due back in Lusaka the next day and he 'will want a response'. Simons was sufficiently concerned by the call that he drafted two foolscap pages of notes on the conversation. According to these, 'JS embarked on a long and rambling discourse'. Simons 'heard him without interrupting'. He noted that 'while picking his way cautiously and refraining from anything like a criticism of the Report' – perhaps 'careful to avoid giving offence' to Simons by criticising something he had endorsed – Slovo 'expressed misgivings'. Simons observed that 'his talk raised many points taken at random without an apparent logical sequence'. The activist professor noted eight of these, 'not necessarily in the order here listed':

1. Was it wise or fruitful to produce a draft of a proposed ANC constitution at this stage?
2. Transfer of power might be remote and take place in circumstances quite unpredictable.
3. Unlikely that ANC would face the regime for a discussion of constitution. If we were asked to negotiate, we might reject the offer. We are too weak at present to enforce our conceptions.
4. Possible that an interim period, referred to in Report, might last for a long while.
5. Discussion of such issues as Executive President or Prime Minister appears unreal; they present no departure from existing structure.
6. Doubtful whether we will need Bill of Rights, or Commissions such as those listed in Report. For whose benefit are they included?
7. Probable that at this stage we should go no further than a general statement of intent. Repeating our determination to institute universal franchise and remove all racial discrimination.
8. There was no urgency. We were not being confronted with constitutional systems to which a response was needed.[13]

Jack Simons responded politely. He told Slovo that to state that 'such a project was ill-advised, being premature and perhaps harmful, could be a political judgement and usurp the role of the NEC'. Far from running on its own, the Committee had closely followed the NEC brief delivered by the ANC president himself – to make the Freedom Charter the 'core or base of our proposals' and to consider a 'suitable constitution' that will 'give effect to the aspirations of the oppressed'. The Committee's report specifically asked the NEC to make political decisions to guide it, 'which amount to the kind of brief that the NEC failed to deliver' in the first place. Without such guidance, the options the Committee had explored were 'almost unlimited'. Therefore, if Slovo felt the venture was untimely or otherwise unwise, he should persuade the NEC to put the project in cold storage.[14] Meanwhile, said Simons, 'the Committee would remain in existence, prepared to act as and when called upon'.

Simons had asked Tambo that the Constitution Committee be given a reply by 22 January 1986, the day after the Slovo call.[15] This did not happen. But the matter had clearly got the lines buzzing in Lusaka. The Committee's reports generated considerable discussion and, indeed, differences of opinion between the three NWC subcommittee members on both their content and how the Constitution Committee should proceed with its mandate. A stalemate arose. Reporting after their second meeting on 25 January, Jordan, as the scribe, noted politely that 'a consensus emerged around a number of crucial questions', but 'a number of differences also arose ... some of which remain unresolved and hinge upon the interpretation of the mandate the Legal and Constitutional Commission [*sic*] received from the NEC'.[16]

On 27 January, a concerned Simons wrote to 'Dear Comrade President'. He said the Committee planned to 'resume our discussions early next month but only after receiving a brief from the NEC in response to the issues raised in our memorandum'. He said to Tambo: 'I want very much to obtain a directive about the further activities of the Committee ... Can we meet?'[17] Simons' wish was granted. Tambo spoke to him the same day and then contacted 'Si' (Simon Makana), who told him the NWC subcommittee response was 'ready and being typed'.[18]

When Simons had not heard anything by 30 January, he wrote to Ruth Mompati in her capacity as administrative officer at the secretary-general's Alpha offices, saying, 'I thought that a copy would be sent to the Committee by now, but this has not happened.' Mompati replied the same day. She apologised for the delay and said Jordan's subcommittee had been given a deadline and were to report in a day or two. Meanwhile, the Constitution Committee's report had been given to all NEC members so that when they met they would already have studied it.[19]

Mompati was a trusted aide of Tambo's and an influential figure in Lusaka. In the fifties, she'd worked as office manager with him and Nelson Mandela in their convention-defying law practice in Chancellor House in downtown Johannesburg. She was among the first ANC comrades to leave the country in 1960. She helped establish the first external mission and HQ in Tanzania along with Duma Nokwe, J.B. Marks and the duo trained at Pius XII University College: Thomas Nkobi and Mendi Msimang.[20] In addition to her role as administrative secretary in the secretary-general's office, she also served on the PMC, which became the executive arm of the NEC in relation to all matters pertaining to the conduct of the political and military struggle inside South Africa.[21] She became a regular contact person for the Constitution Committee.

On 7 February 1986, Mompati conveyed the leadership's formal response to the Committee's first report in a letter delivered to Simons at Entabeni. Although the letter was from her as the administrative secretary in the office of the secretary-general, it was signed on her behalf by Jordan, the administrative secretary of the NEC and its hands-on liaison person with the Constitution Committee, who worked closely with Mompati.

Looking at the documents today, one is struck by the way in which the supremacy of the NEC is constantly affirmed, as well as by the emphasis given to formal decision-making in keeping with specific mandates.

The Constitution Committee, too, consistently acted in a collective manner. It took care to share tasks and made formal decisions only at full meetings. Zola Skweyiya also made a clear distinction between the work of the DLCA and that of the Committee, even as the four Lusaka-based Committee members in the DLCA took responsibility for the Committee's administrative tasks. The Constitution Committee's correspondence shows that the ANC had set practices for formal communication with the leadership in the president's and secretary-general's offices, as well as a multitude of other structures responsible for the internal and external work of the ANC, the most important of these being the PMC and ECC.

Mompati and Jordan informed Simons that the NWC had made four observations about the report:

1. The type of constitutional framework that the lawyers' commission envisages appears to be a conventional liberal-democratic framework rather than a framework arising from a revolutionary struggle. Perhaps it might be wiser to explore beyond this limited horizon.
2. Is the constitution that is envisaged a transitional constitution, which we anticipate will operate within a definite time frame?
3. Do we conceive of the constitution that will emerge as principally a mobilising instrument or as a tactical tool in the event that negotiations are forced upon us?
4. How do we frame a constitution which can translate the slogan 'Peoples Power' into reality by making a framework of government that ensures that the government will always be subject to the people?[22]

Mompati concluded by saying that 'at the end of the day there was general consensus that our lawyers had done a magnificent piece of pioneering work' and 'our critique is tempered by the recognition that this is the first occasion on which the ANC has even attempted to give constitutional expression to its programmatic demands'.[23]

From the Mompati letter, it was clear that the NWC had also met after the two inconclusive meetings of its subcommittee. Almost verbatim comments from the meetings of both these groups are to be found in the missive she sent to the Constitution Committee. It laid out three steps to be followed in the subsequent constitutional planning process. Firstly, Jordan's NWC subcommittee would draft clear political guidelines, taking account of the NWC's critique, 'to serve as a basis for a joint meeting between the NWC and the lawyers' commission'. Secondly, the so-called lawyers' commission 'shall prepare a brief for the NWC on the various options posed in its document'. The NEC wanted more clarity on matters such as the relative benefits of proportional representation over direct representation, the presidential system over the prime ministerial system, and so on. Then the Committee also had to prepare a briefing paper on how to deepen People's Power perspectives constitutionally by looking at such matters as the constitutionalisation of the role of mass organisations and constitutionally endowing the state with power to limit and redefine the rights of private property.[24]

Simons replied briefly on 11 February: 'Steps are being taken to place these and related matters before the Committee as soon as its members can be brought together. I shall keep you informed of the progress.'[25] He also corrected Mompati on the status of the Committee: 'Please note that the President has named us the Constitution Committee; and that the title "the lawyers commission" is inaccurate.'[26]

He had already circulated the communication to his colleagues and called a meeting for Wednesday 12 February. They'd planned to have a meeting of the full Committee in early February, though in the end only the Lusaka members were able to attend. The reply from the NWC had taken longer than expected, making it impossible to arrange for Asmal and Sachs to attend in time.[27]

When the local members met on 12 February, Simons handed out what he called a short aide-memoire he had drawn up in response to the NWC report. Here he replied directly to three of the NWC's questions and strongly affirmed the Committee's position: 'Though provisional, our proposals embody propositions, principles and concepts that express our revolutionary demands and the aspirations of the oppressed majority. These principles are permanent and will appear in every constitution proposed by the Revolution.'[28]

With his characteristic exhortation that the president 'told us the need of constitutional proposals is urgent', he advised that the Committee push ahead despite the absence of Asmal and Sachs. However, the locally based members would 'refrain from taking decisions until the full Committee is in session'. In the meantime, the aide-memoire could be used 'to stimulate discussion'.

11

A Call for Clear Political Guidance

A FTER THE RUSH of activity in the first month of the Constitution Committee's existence, an unexplained silence fell over the process from March to
August 1986. For six months the president and the NWC remained mum despite
the urgent approaches of Jack Simons and his Committee, who did not stand
back from showing their growing frustration.

The Committee's first question was how it should respond to what it regarded
as the somewhat inappropriate and belittling stance the NWC had adopted
towards its January report. It was felt that the Committee as a whole should convene to develop a formal response to Ruth Mompati's letter. Jack Simons informed
Mompati that the Committee would have a plenary session early in March and
that the team was glad that Pallo Jordan's subcommittee would be drafting guidelines in preparation for a joint meeting between the NWC and the Committee.
Requesting a prompt response, he said that it 'would help us greatly' to get these
before the March plenary of the Committee.[1]

The archives show that the NWC did in fact hold a follow-up meeting on
18 February to discuss the matter. I have been unable to access the minutes, but
the NWC mandated Jordan's subcommittee to finalise and draft the guidelines
requested by Simons. The three members – Jordan, Slovo and Makana – convened
again on 20 February and Jordan wrote up the results on 23 February, without
forwarding them to Simons and the Committee.[2] (See Chapter 14 for details.)

For reasons not clear from these documents, the leadership then went quiet
regarding the next steps in the constitutional planning process. Neither the NWC
subcommittee's guidelines nor the six-page outline of the NWC discussion on
18 February or Jordan, Slovo and Makana's own deliberations on 20 February
were forwarded to the Constitution Committee as promised. The Committee was
ready to take off, but a long period of frustration lay ahead for them.

Strained by the lack of response from the NWC and the consequent cancella-
tion of planned meetings, Simons wrote to Tambo for the second time in a month
to politely request a personal consultation on Tuesday 4 March.[3] He also sent the
Comrade President an advance copy of his reply to the NWC, which would only
be formalised and circulated after his Committee had approved it at their next
meeting a month or so later.

There is no evidence that Tambo met with Simons as requested on 4 March. No meeting possible in February! No meeting possible in March! The Constitution Committee now set April as the date for its full plenary. But by the end of March, they still had not heard from Jordan. Nothing was coming through about the guidelines and the promised meeting with the NWC.

Early in April, frustrated by the silence from Jordan and Mompati, Simons and Jobodwana circulated the Committee's original January report to NEC members directly. Copies were also forwarded to heads of the other two arms of the alliance in exile: Dan Tloome, chairperson of the SACP, and Stephen Dlamini, president of SACTU. This was a brazen circumvention of the NWC subcommittee. Jobodwana warned that if the NWC didn't send their guidelines soon, there was 'the likelihood that another opportunity for such a discussion as you propose, may not recur until June or July 1986'.[4]

Sachs recalls the distress felt by the Constitution Committee members: 'We had received a clear mandate to go full-steam ahead from Tambo himself. For Kader and myself, travelling to Lusaka required complicated advance planning. We were all raring to go. We understood the political dimensions of our work and we had no problem at all working under the direction of the NEC. It was not for us to determine the policy of the organisation. All we wanted were clear political guidelines and they simply never reached us.'[5]

Finally, after a wait of nearly three months, the Constitution Committee met for its second full plenary meeting on 7 April 1986. At the top of the agenda were 'Reading of NWC's CC report on preliminary nature of constitutional document' and 'Cde Jack's reply and discussion thereon'. The minutes note that after Simons' opening remarks, the meeting expressed concern that the Constitution Committee had not been furnished with political guidelines as promised by the NEC in its letter of 7 February 1986. It was moved that 'we demand a meeting with the NWC' the next day at 8 a.m. Only then would the Committee know 'what the nature of our second report shall be'.[6]

Zola Skweyiya was asked to phone Mompati to convey the Committee's demand for a joint meeting. He came back with confirmation that they could meet the next day at ten in the morning. For the next five hours, the Committee worked on a list of topics that needed to be discussed with the NWC delegation. There were ten altogether, and a presenter was chosen for each one.

Sachs had to catch a flight back to Maputo the next day, so it was decided he should make the first presentation. The topic would be the key one currently facing the leadership: 'What kind of a constitutional document does the NEC want'? His draft was discussed at length and small but important changes were made. The Committee decided to add a concluding sentence that read, 'In any constitution there shall be a special provision made for workers' rights and [the] place and role of trade unions.'[7]

Mompati arrived at the appointed time the next day but was accompanied only by fellow NEC/NWC member James Stuart. She announced that it was not possible for the Committee to meet the NWC subcommittee, as two of the latter's three members were out of the country, including Jordan, who was in New York.

In addition, Mompati apologised to her comrades because the political guidelines were not yet available. She made no reference to the seventeen-point framework of guidelines that Jordan had already drafted in February. Was the leadership still not in agreement on this issue or did they believe that the political circumstances were not yet right for releasing these guidelines? Perhaps it was felt that only a meeting of the full NEC could give the go-ahead for a matter of such importance. Mompati explained that she would reserve for the consideration of the NEC questions on matters to which she could not provide a satisfactory reply. As it turned out, these matters included virtually everything under discussion. For the two days of the meeting, she and Stuart simply took notes, asked questions and reserved replies.[8]

As agreed, Sachs started with his presentation on day one of the joint meeting before flying out. Rapporteur Teddy Pekane noted the three main points in his input on the kind of constitutional document the ANC needed. To start with, it was 'not for the ANC to draft the constitution' but it should provide the basic guidelines for a future constitutional framework. Next, the leadership needed to have a clear understanding of three different constitutional models, namely a liberal democratic constitution, an anti-fascist constitution and a People's Power constitution. He said further that at this stage the ANC should produce a 'set of papers analysing and exposing ANC policy'. These would help in 'converting strategy and tactics into constitutional language'.[9] On day two, 9 April, the remaining Constitution Committee members made their presentations. The topics were a multiparty system (Skweyiya), non-central government bodies (Maduna), a demographic survey and land ownership (Asmal), what an entrenched Bill of Rights would entail (Jobodwana), the place and role of trade unions (Simons), the land question (Maduna), nationalisation of monopolies and trusts etc. (Skweyiya), the concept of a mixed economy 'in our context' (Simons) and, finally, the state apparatus (Asmal).[10]

Teddy Pekane neatly summed up each presentation in the meeting, giving a good sense of how ANC members and the Committee saw these different issues in early 1986. On the land question, for example, Penuell Maduna noted that the Freedom Charter provided guidance and the NEC 'must tell us what type of approach it is thinking about – nationalisation is one option' and this had to go with 'safeguards such as equity and production'. He said, 'We want the NEC to make a declaration that the land rights denied our people over the centuries will be restored'. He concluded that 'on the land question there can be very little compromise if ever'. Similarly, Skweyiya noted that the NEC would have to 'give guidelines how nationalisation will take place without diminishing production and efficiency'. The ANC's Economic Unit needed to give this matter serious attention and, he warned, state monopolies had to be guarded against.[11]

The Committee members were asked to prepare short notes on the themes of their individual presentations for formal presentation to the NEC. After speaking about these constitutional issues with Stuart and Mompati, the Committee withdrew to discuss matters on its own. Among the outstanding discussion points were the approaches from various international legal scholars and bodies. Professor Bob Seidman, an expert on law and development from Boston University, who was advising SWAPO, had written offering his support, which the Committee accepted. However, relying on a heavily sceptical Simons and Asmal, the Committee rejected working with the Foundation for International Conciliation, which had earlier met with a delegation including Thabo Mbeki and Zola Skweyiya, and the Institute for Social Inventions, chaired by Nicholas Albery and directed by David Chapman, which submitted a pro-proportional representation discussion paper on 'An electoral system for South Africa'. It was felt that these two Europe-based bodies were driving dubious neo-apartheid agendas.[12]

These plenary meetings became the prototype for the Committee's work over the next two years. Four plenary sessions were held between 1986 and January 1987. Each lasted several days and was well minuted. In between the plenaries, the Lusaka members met in general monthly operational meetings and communicated regularly with each other. The Constitution Committee's administration continued to be carried out by its four locally based DLCA members, Skweyiya, Maduna, Pekane and the busy scribe Jobs Jobodwana, with an active chair working through Jobodwana.[13]

After the inconclusive April meeting with Mompati and Stuart, Jobodwana was mandated to discuss formally with the secretary-general the Committee's need for guidance and feedback from the leadership. The outcome was that he and some of the others in Lusaka met with Alfred Nzo on 9 May 1986.

Perhaps because it was not getting the responses it sought, the Constitution Committee took great care to ensure that the entire leadership and chain of command were kept up to date with developments. Jobodwana therefore copied in Tambo, Mompati, Stuart and treasurer-general Thomas Nkobi on the next memo.[14] In it, Jobodwana asked the leadership for support to strengthen the new DLCA. The

volume of the department's work had increased so much that it had become necessary to increase the secretarial services and personnel of the department and the
Constitution Committee. The secretariat met and decided that Comrade Stanley
Mngadi, who had studied in Bulgaria and was currently in Mazimbu, should join
the secretariat as research officer. His focus would be on current local and constitutional developments in South Africa.

Following on the Constitution Committee inputs at the meeting with Ruth
Mompati and James Stuart in April 1986, its members had by the end of July
completed nine papers on the different aspects of the constitutional planning
process discussed there. Only two of the identified research areas – the demographic survey and the state apparatus – were 'not yet received'.[15]

Meanwhile, the Committee was also gearing up to increase its involvement in
the growing number of meetings and consultations happening with external parties, including the potentially exciting prospect of making 'physical contact with
persons from SA who have special knowledge of matters falling within the range
of our mandate'.

12

Confidential and Urgent: Opening up Channels with Lawyers from Home

MEETING CLANDESTINELY AT the Ghanaian embassy in Harare, Zola Skweyiya, the tall, stern head of the DLCA, greeted his shorter, warm and softly spoken cousin (or brother, in Xhosa tradition) Advocate Thembile Lewis 'Luwi' Skweyiya with intense feeling. They had not seen each other in twenty-three years.

The meeting had been carefully prepared. On 19 April 1986, Oliver Tambo wrote to Zola reminding him of instructions at the founding of the Constitution Committee to consult with democratic lawyers at home.[1] While noting that such contacts would enrich and enhance the scope of the department's work, Tambo emphasised that they should be carefully coordinated since linking up with people in South Africa was already the main work of the PMC.

Skweyiya lost no time. Within a month he'd set up a meeting with Lewis, then based in Port Elizabeth, and Kwenza Mlaba, an attorney from Durban who appeared to be Skweyiya's main contact for dealing with cases inside the country. Lewis Skweyiya had been educated at the Healdtown and Lovedale mission schools, before graduating with social science and law degrees from the then University of Natal. He first specialised in civil and commercial work, but in recent years had undertaken the defence of political activists from the ANC and other struggle organisations. One of a tiny handful of pioneering black advocates, he managed to establish a relatively successful practice despite suffering constant indignities in the apartheid courts.[2]

Zola and his DLCA staff drew up a draft agenda for the meeting, then discussed it with Joe Nhlanhla, the secretary of the PMC responsible for internal operations. He also copied it to the offices of the president, secretary-general and treasurer-general, as well as to James Stuart and Ruth Mompati. The result was nine jointly agreed-upon discussion points covering questions and strategic issues from the ANC's perspective.[3]

Jobs Jobodwana then met with Secretary-General Nzo and followed up with a letter conveying the Committee's position. In this he noted:

We are glad to have your assurance that our committee should take an initiative in conducting research into constitutional development affecting our movement and act in this capacity as the eyes and ears of the NEC. We shall re-orientate our work accordingly by making contact with specialists and interested parties inside the country and elsewhere for opinions and information regarding constitutional developments both among supporters of our struggle and its enemies. For this purpose it is necessary to make physical contact with persons from SA who have special knowledge of matters falling within the range of our mandate. We understand the NEC will approve of such contacts and authorise expenditure involved. Our committee will naturally keep you informed of the discussions and decisions taken, if any.[4]

The extreme sensitivity of the task and the secrecy under which the DLCA and the Constitution Committee worked were emphasised when the members arrived in Harare for their meeting on 19 May 1986. Former NAT head of security and ANC chief representative in Zimbabwe, Jan Mampane (aka Reddy Mazimba), explained that Zimbabwean government officials wished to attend, and he felt it would be undiplomatic to refuse their request. The Lusaka quartet – Skweyiya, Jobodwana, Maduna and Pekane – promptly removed three points from the lengthy agenda because they 'constituted sensitive matters of a political nature of operational import'. These could be later discussed in private with the two visitors from home.

The four drew up a detailed twelve-page report of the meeting headed 'Confidential and Urgent', and the NEC was specifically asked to respect this so 'as not to prejudice our future meetings with the lawyers from home'.[5] To protect Skweyiya and the link with his close relative, Lewis Skweyiya, the ANC in Harare sent correspondence to him under the name of 'Cde Zola Bona', an exile *nom de guerre*.[6]

The meeting, held at the Ghanaian embassy, started with an ANC briefing before the duo from home provided an extensive analysis of the judicial system and existing lawyers' bodies in South Africa. Lewis explained that he had appeared as an advocate before the benches of all the provincial divisions of the Supreme Court of South Africa, and had personal contact with the judges on a professional level.

The ANC wanted to know which of the professional lawyers' bodies in South Africa 'might be referred to as progressive, liberal or reactionary', what their relationships were to the struggle and to the ANC in particular, and how 'the conservative legal profession' could be drawn into 'the mainstream of our political struggle'. Among the bodies discussed were the Black Consciousness–aligned Black Lawyers Association (BLA); the Natal-based Democratic Lawyers Association; a grouping from the eastern Cape, Border and Transkei (which planned to start a similar provincial body after claiming the BLA was 'racist'); the liberal Lawyers for Human Rights; and the left-oriented Legal Resources Centre (LRC), 'who are mainly ex-NUSAS office bearers'. One of the priority actions agreed on was the formation of a new national body, and the ANC and its allies in the movement were called upon to help with this.

The meeting's second session was more confidential in nature. It was devoted to devising the most effective way of providing funds for the legal defence of activists who had been charged with political offences in South Africa. Lewis Skweyiya and Mlaba forcefully argued that the ANC should devise ways of channelling funds to various attorneys in every region. ANC cadres did not always get adequate and timely legal support, and one particularly tragic example of this was Andrew Zondo, an MK soldier who was charged with detonating a bomb in a supermarket. Zondo was tortured and mentally incapacitated and did not get legal representation until a late stage and so was sentenced to death and executed.

In addition, there needed to be 'a fair distribution of work' among black lawyers. They reported that

political cases have become a lucrative business inside the country. This is so because of the high legal fees demanded and the length of time political cases take. As a result there has now come into existence some firms of lawyers who are noted for handling political cases in certain regions serving the whole South Africa. The anomaly arises when, say, a Priscilla Jana flies all the way from Johannesburg to Durban, Ciskei, Transkei and other places in S.A. at almost one and the same time ... Certain firms of lawyers hold in trust huge sums of money from various sponsors, but are reluctant to release part of the money to other firms of attorneys defending political cases and [who] are in need of legal fees.[7]

The duo said that there were lawyers whose services were not being used who could be instructed in confidence, and that it was necessary to promote other black firms.

In the third session, the DLCA team held a separate meeting with the Zimbabwe Association of Democratic Jurists (ZADJ), briefing their counterparts on the conservative think tanks being set up inside and outside the country to do research into various constitutional models that might be suitable for a future South Africa. The ZADJ responded that they were aware of 'such enemy manoeuvres' and were willing to help. This aid would include sending a trusted core of its members into South Africa to undertake missions for the ANC. It would also collect and share material, organise seminars for lawyers from home, and seek support from the University of Zimbabwe to train members of liberation movements recognised by the OAU.[8]

After receiving the report of the lawyers' Harare meeting, the ANC leadership in Lusaka issued a press statement publicly announcing the existence of the DLCA and its desire to reach out to democratic lawyers back home. The statement went on to put into the public domain, for the first time, the possibility of negotiations. It explained in an extremely tentative and indirect way that, among the many matters of mutual concern discussed, were

- The much-publicised general talk about some remote possibility that sanity may prevail in our country and that a round-table discussion, involving all the people of South Africa, may be held.
- The frequently discussed proposed constitutional changes, which some people said should involve the introduction of a Bill of Rights.[9]

The report-back from Harare was well received. The president and NEC shortly afterwards directed that a broadly based preparatory committee be established to initiate a meeting between South African democratic lawyers and the ANC. Skweyiya then called on Ruth Mompati, Joe Nhlanhla, James Stuart, Tony Mongalo and 'Cde Norushe' (SACTU) to personally drive the initiative within their defined areas of operation.[10]

On his return to Lusaka, Zola Skweyiya asked the NEC to give urgent attention to the matter of financing legal defences. Then he and Penuell Maduna went to London, where they were met by Kader Asmal, who flew in from Dublin. The three of them worked on a plan to better coordinate activity internally, find more equitable ways of funding progressive lawyers, and provide more efficient support for ANC cadres and their dependants who had been arrested, imprisoned or were awaiting trial. They then met with the IDAF in August to give input on how best the ANC could pursue its huge secret funding programme for victims of apartheid repression.[11]

Defence and Aid, as it was initially known, was set up in the 1950s when Canon John Collins of St Paul's Cathedral in London agreed to raise funds and provide support for the 156 trialists in the long-running South African Treason Trial. His efforts were complemented by an internal support group. The organisation also provided support for Nelson Mandela and his comrades during the famous Rivonia Trial in the early 1960s, helping to ensure they were not sentenced to death. Thereafter banned in South Africa, the IDAF became part of the underground struggles against apartheid, devising an ingenious 'barriered system of legal firms' using Swiss bank accounts to secretly channel hundreds of millions of rand into South Africa to support trialists and their families via 'respectable' organisations and individuals who were persuaded to act as supposed donors. This humanitarian support came mainly from the Scandinavian countries. By 1990, the IDAF was paying twice as much in support of political trialists in the country as the state's entire legal aid budget for criminal trials – R35 million versus R17 million. The *Observer* newspaper commented that it became 'possibly the South African legal profession's most reliable employer, with more than 150 attorneys and 80 advocates on its books', though few realised where their payments were coming from.[12]

After returning from London, Skweyiya reported to Tambo that the IDAF was due to meet soon with Reverend Beyers Naudé, the secretary-general of the South African Council of Churches (SACC). Skweyiya had suggested that the DLCA be present 'as its political input would be required in this regard'. The SACC was one of the biggest distributors of funds inside the country for legal defence in political cases. The Harare discussions had pointed to the need for all parties to be on the same wavelength on these matters.[13] For example, distress had been caused by the fact that Andrew Zondo had not qualified for support under SACC policy.

13

The Dilemma

'How do we frame a constitution which can translate the slogan "People's Power" into reality by making a framework of government that ensures that the government will always be subject to the people?'
                    – Ruth Mompati to Jack Simons, 7 February 1986[1]

WHEN SKWEYIYA AND his comrades returned from the talks in Harare in May, there was still no substantive feedback from the president or NEC on the Constitution Committee's first report in January. June, July and August came and went, but still there was no response.

The Committee members were puzzled that Oliver Tambo, who had given them the clearest possible mandate to go ahead and to whom they reported directly, remained silent. At the Committee's first meeting he had given them a full briefing and emphasised the need for speed. He had also, apparently, encouraged Mompati to give quick initial feedback in response to the Committee's first report. But although routinely invited to all their meetings in the months that followed, he had not met with them again or sent any written communication that we know of.

The Committee knew, however, that Tambo had a punishing schedule. He travelled regularly and engaged widely with internal and external parties on the way forward. This included the first discussions on the issue of negotiations. Furthermore, his health was deteriorating. At the end of 1985, he was put off work and sent to the Soviet Union for treatment. He'd had a mild stroke in 1982 and his doctors warned him that the constant flying, changes of climate and overwork 'may well push a fragile balance out of equilibrium.'[2] But his treadmill routine continued. In February 1986 he travelled to Sweden to address the Swedish Parliament and met UDF leaders from South Africa. The next month he had important discussions in Mozambique, where he attended the funeral of Moses Mabhida, general secretary of the SACP. Afterwards, he boarded a long flight to Cuba. There, he and Thabo Mbeki met Fidel Castro and had a debate with him about the Freedom Charter as the basis for the future.[3] In May, Tambo went to Malaysia, India and France, and on the sixteenth of that month he took charge of a meeting in Lusaka between the ANC NEC and the high-level Eminent Persons Group representing the Commonwealth heads of government.

Since February 1986, the EPG had been shuttling between P.W. Botha, the imprisoned Nelson Mandela, the ANC in Lusaka, the UDF and COSATU, with a view to creating a climate conducive to negotiations. Moreover, Tambo's visit to Paris had been undertaken in preparation for a meeting between the Soviet Union and Cuba with SWAPO and the ANC over the possibility of a political settlement in Namibia. The ANC itself was now having to engage openly and formally on the possibility of negotiations.

The Constitution Committee saw a role for itself in these 'talks of talks about constitution'. On 11 May 1986, shortly before Tambo and the NEC met the EPG delegation, Jobodwana wrote:

Our committee is generally aware of meetings and consultations as for instance the Eminent Persons Group in South Africa and outside. We do our best to follow these events by examining reports in the press and journals, but should like to have access to more authoritative sources which we assume are available by the NEC. We shall be grateful if material of this kind can be made available to us to study and report. We assure you that the principle of confidentiality will be strictly observed.[4]

On 19 May, two days after the NEC met with the EPG, Simons sent Jobodwana a set of nine documents the NEC had used in its preparations for that meeting. Interestingly, two of these had been written by Simons himself for the NEC: a summary of a P.W. Botha speech and a document on 'A Possible Negotiating Concept' sent to the ANC by the EPG.[5] The ANC boxed cleverly against the EPG. It decided 'to be firm but not hostile' and to 'place the EPG on the defensive ... by viewing it in the light that K.K. suggests', i.e. as an additional vehicle for advancing sanctions. The ANC reasoned that it was premature to talk of negotiations because Botha was only using the idea to buy time. The ANC would 'avoid any formulation' that invited a third party to be involved as facilitator or chair, as it would then risk being sidelined in the process. Finally, in line with thinking since Jordan's recent paper, the ANC 'had no objections to an entrenched Bill of Individual rights' but opposed group rights of any kind.[6]

However, 19 May 1986 was also the day the EPG saw its mission being scuttled by Botha. Their delegation was in Cape Town when his forces hit what they called 'ANC targets' in Botswana, Zimbabwe and Zambia – all countries that the EPG had visited. Pallo Jordan recalls the aeroplanes coming over Makeni at tree height. Botha also proclaimed a new nationwide state of emergency, and thousands of anti-apartheid activists were detained.[7] The ANC's political standing grew in the wake of the EPG. Jordan, in his late 1985 presentations, had flagged the possibility of the ANC being under undue pressure to talk prematurely, but this risk now slid away. Western countries imposed sanctions as the ANC desired, and conservative Western leaders started talking to the organisation for the first time. This under- lined that the ANC could not be excluded from any future negotiations – a point that the regime would concede only two years later in 1988.

At the height of these dramatic political events, Tambo was sent to East Germany for medical treatment for his heart. In April he had reminded Skweyiya about the importance of staying in touch with lawyers from home, but on the debates between the NWC group and the Constitution Committee the president was keep- ing a distance. According to Albie Sachs and others, it was part of his leadership style to give his colleagues in the ANC leadership the space to debate and absorb on their own the matters that were being raised by the Committee. He was also aware of his difficult dual role as president of the ANC on the one hand, and commander-in-chief of MK on the other. His biographer Luli Callinicos noted that this 'at times put an intolerable strain on him'.[8] Tambo was not going to push hard one way or the other.

The EPG outcome ended up giving the NEC a breathing space, but it had yet to resolve a key uncertainty: how to translate its firmly held notion of 'People's Power' into constitutional terms that harmonised with the Freedom Charter.

In 1969 the ANC had adopted its 'Strategy and Tactics' document at Morogoro, after nearly a decade of exile and illegality at home. This had marked a decisive move towards seeing liberation coming from revolutionary struggle with a strong armed component. It closely identified with anti-imperialist Third World liber- ation movements from Vietnam in Asia to Nicaragua in Latin America, and ongoing liberation struggles in Africa, such as those in Mozambique, Angola and Guinea-Bissau. The discourse of revolution, including the seizure of power and class analysis, became the bedrock of much thinking in the exile movement.

The overthrow of the fascist dictatorship in Portugal by middle-ranking army officers of the 1974 Carnation Revolution was inspiring. But more import- ant was that liberation movements had achieved independence in Angola and Mozambique after years of armed struggled. The MPLA in Angola and FRELIMO in Mozambique both proclaimed new constitutions based on concepts of People's Power. After the Soweto uprising in 1976, MK recruits from South Africa were being trained and housed in camps in the People's Republic of Angola, while people from all over the world, including South Africa, were coming as 'cooper- antes' to offer their skills in support of the Mozambican revolution.

As Joe Slovo pointed out, 'during these periods the basic political content of the ANC was moulded in the socialist countries ... from 1970 onwards we started sending people in large numbers to the GDR, to Bulgaria, to the Soviet Union and so on, and they were brain washed in Marxism'. He would later say, 'Thinking back on it now it horrifies me to remember the kind of things they were taught. As a socialist, as I am now speaking, very mechanical rubbish Stalinist concepts.'[9]

The concept of People's Power was reinforced by the insurrectionary climate inside South Africa itself, where the people were being called on to make apartheid unworkable and the country ungovernable. From late 1984 onwards, People's Power increasingly became part of the discourse and drive of popular internal politics. By the end of August 1984, local government structures were being attacked and rendered inoperative in various parts of the country. Street committees and alternative local structures were set up. People's education and other programmes became popular.

Daryl Glaser has written about the 'indeterminacies' of the two models the ANC was trying to reconcile but which could not be definitively resolved. This was in part because the Marxist-inspired, National Democratic Revolution (NDR), People's Power model and the constitutional democracy model were two theories that 'speak past each other, having never expected to meet on ground where their respective ideologues would need to find a common language'. The places where they did meet throughout the twentieth century were in struggles against fascism in the 1930s and 1940s, and in struggles for national liberation in the 1960s to 1980s. In these situations, Marxists, on the one hand, felt obliged to put aside pure class analysis to build broad fronts with non-socialist forces against tyranny. On the other, non-Marxist democrats recognised that in those life-and-death struggles, a constitutional solution would need to go beyond formal rules to incorporate fundamental socio-economic and political changes in society as a constitutional goal. 'Despite their discordant relationships, the two logics are not irreconcilable', Glaser concludes.[10]

It was against this background that the Constitution Committee had to consider the very brief NWC feedback from Ruth Mompati on 7 February 1986, with its implicit critique that the Committee was somehow unable to grasp the essence of a constitution suitable for a People's Power approach. Position papers on various topics relevant to the debate were prepared for the leadership. Among these were three written by Simons, Sachs and Maduna respectively, each dealing specifically with People's Power. These would accompany the aide-memoire Jack Simons had written to respond to the NWC subcommittee's queries.

After observing that 'certain misgivings' on the part of the NWC 'necessitate remedial action', and foreseeing problems should the liberation movement become ideologically divided, Simons also proposed that the Committee discuss recommending to the NEC the formation of a new national front embracing parties that had the same revolutionary perspectives, ideals or aims, and that the SACP, SACTU and the ANC (while retaining some autonomy) should form a single organisation, goal and platform. He feared that in future 'under the usual conditions of ballot box rivalries' the three organisations 'might become rivals in a ruthless war of words, to the delight of our enemies and dismay of the people ... Under such conditions of disunity, it is conceivable, even likely, that governments will cease to carry out the will of the people'. To prevent such a disaster, the first practical precondition for People's Power was to preserve the 'existing unity of purpose and action before and after the revolution' and move towards 'some kind of fusion' organisationally.[11] The Constitution Committee quietly withdrew Simons' thought-provoking position paper, with its seeming applicability to South Africa even today, and it was not taken further with the leadership in tandem with the Committee's other papers.

To help the NEC understand the conceptual differences between various constitutional models, the Committee asked Albie Sachs to explain to Ruth Mompati and James Stuart the distinctions between liberal-democratic, anti-fascist and People's Power constitutions when it met with them in April 1986. He subsequently wrote up his ideas in a short paper, setting out the options that the leadership faced:

> The basic difference between liberal democratic and People's Power constitutions is that the former purport to be neutral on the question of who exercises power in the state, whereas the latter take a declared constitutional position – based on class analysis – on the question. Put another way, liberal democratic constitutions presuppose that power vests in the institutions of government themselves and that the essential function of the constitution is to establish the 'rules of the game' as to who holds the reins; People's Power constitutions, on the other hand, confirm that power in any state belongs to classes or class alliances, which use the institutions of government as means of exercising such power.
>
> Several consequences flow from the distinction:
>
> First, liberal democratic constitutions are silent on the nature of power in the state, while People's Power constitutions expressly legitimate a defined form of class hegemony or domination.
>
> Secondly, liberal democratic constitutions do not accord any overt recognition of political parties, while People's Power constitutions expressly recognise a leading or vanguard role in relation to society as a whole and to the state apparatus in particular of an identified party or alliance of parties ... [T]he issue is not simply whether the state is one-party or multiparty, nor whether the constitution institutionalises a party or not. One-party states may be fas-

cist, liberal capitalist or socialist. Multiparty states as well. Many conservative African states institutionalise a single party.

Thirdly, liberal democratic constitutions tend to regard the state as a necessary evil that has to be controlled through separation of powers and a Bill of Rights, while People's Power constitutions regard the state as a major instrument whereby the people achieve their right to progress and development. Thus, People's Power constitutions emphasise the harmony of objectives of the three basic institutions of the constitution, namely, the legislature, the executive and the judiciary, while outlining their separate functions. Similarly, People's Power constitutions, while affirming individual rights of citizens, refer also to citizens' duties or responsibilities, and indicate that these rights and duties are exercised in a context which does not permit a restoration of the overthrown power.

Fourthly, liberal democratic constitutions leave open the question of social and economic programmes, or only deal with them indirectly, for example, by consecrating the rights of private property in a Bill of Rights, while People's Power constitutions expressly impose on the state a duty to fulfil a defined socio-economic-cultural programme. One consequence of this is that new constitutions emerge in a liberal democratic state as a result of the failure of institutions (France at the time of De Gaulle), while in a People's Power state they result from their success – the realisation of one constitutional programme requiring the formulation of another.

Fifthly, liberal democratic constitutions imply that the army and other instruments of power are neutral, responding to the command only of the elected government, while People's Power constitutions recognise the existence of politicised armed forces to defend the gains of the people's struggle.

Finally, constitutions are normally complemented by separate electoral laws, which differ considerably depending on whether the state is liberal democratic or People's Power in character. While the principle of universal suffrage and secret ballot is common to both types, there are major distinctions in relation to the way candidates are selected. In addition, People's Power constitutions sometimes deprive persons directly implicated in crimes or policies of the overthrown regime of the right to elect or to be elected.

These are the main differences. There are a number of other constitutional variants that cannot be correlated with the existence of liberal democracy or People's Power. Thus, either system might be unitary or federal (the USA and the USSR both call themselves unions, but in fact from a constitutional point of view both are federations). Equally, either type may be presidential or prime ministerial. (Maurice Bishop was the Prime Minister of Grenada, the first former British colony to follow the road of People's Power.)

What would the implications of a People's Power constitution be for South Africa? It would declare that South Africa is a state of national democracy in which the formerly oppressed masses, uniting around themselves all patriotic forces, exercise power. It would institutionalise the revolutionary alliance headed by the ANC as the vanguard force in society and government.

It would impose on the state a duty to carry out a programme of social, economic and cultural transformation.

It would institutionalise changes in the judiciary, armed forces, security apparatus and civil service, putting them at the service of People's Power.

It would outlaw activities designed to defeat the programme of transformation or to restore or perpetuate apartheid.

The electoral law would give the alliance headed by the ANC, working together with democratic mass organisations, a leading role in the selection of candidates.

In short, People's Power establishes itself first, then proceeds to institutionalise itself. The process of institutionalisation, including the adoption of a constitution, cannot be predicted in advance. What can be done in advance is to publish a general political programme which defines the basic goals of the post-liberation society.[12]

In the end, Sachs came back to the same answer as Simons and the Committee: 'A People's Power constitution published in the absence of People's Power is virtually a contradiction in terms.' In other words, the balance of forces at the time the liberation movement took power would determine what shape a constitution could or would take.

Pallo Jordan's subcommittee and the NWC as a whole were clearly struggling to come to a conclusion on the most appropriate constitutional model for a future South Africa. They had been asked to clarify the Committee's mandate and respond to the draft document, but had remained silent for months, except for the brief, non-committal responses via Ruth Mompati and James Stuart. Joe Slovo, a key military figure in pursuing armed struggle and insurrection aimed at the seizure of power, had expressed to Simons his severe doubts about the very notion of pursuing constitutional options for the future. He dug in his heels again at the NWC meeting in February, as can be judged from the formal report of the discussions by Pallo Jordan.

Summarising the NWC's reservations regarding the Committee's initial offering helps explain why – the leadership were grappling with some of the core political strategies and goals of the ANC alliance with the SACP and SACTU, and a fierce debate was happening in the top echelons of the movement.

In analysing the Committee's first report, Jordan, Slovo and Makana were complimentary in various respects, but felt that the Committee's approach was 'too wedded to liberal democratic notions with some slight modifications'. Its framework was 'very similar to conventional bourgeois-democracy and not a framework arising from or created by a revolutionary struggle'. They argued that

> While we recognise that it is difficult to predict the shape of future institutions there are however already some indications in the embryonic forms of popular power that are being thrown up in the course of the struggle; that new and more far-reaching forms will emerge and that our constitutional thinking must necessarily accommodate these.[13]

For some reason, the trio had read the Committee as merely seeking to adapt the '1910 constitution' of South Africa, rather than departing radically from it, saying that 'Over the past three years, especially since Nkomati, the ANC has been at pains to explain to the world that we are not fighting for the [mere] democratisation of the 1910 constitutional framework ... Quite the contrary!'

The Constitution Committee was, in fact, *ad idem* with Jordan's subcommittee on these points. It wanted a complete break with the essence of the past constitutions, and Simons had stressed that although 'Our Committee refrained from sticking labels on the draft scheme', it was not meant to be a liberal democratic constitution. 'If pressed, we should probably opt for such description as a "Constitution for South Africa's National Democratic Revolution".' He said this title fitted the sentiments of Tambo's opening address at Kabwe – 'We are Revolutionaries, Internationalists, Africans!'[14]

The NWC subcommittee also wanted to go beyond formal 'non-racialism', as in the US Constitution (which nevertheless left institutionalised racism in place), to a 'practical non-racialism' that should outlaw racism in 'theory and practice'. Regarding reconciling civil liberties and popular power, it felt that 'in every respect priority must be given to the defence of popular power and the securing of the aspirations of the majority'. This meant supporting the principle of affirmative action or positive discrimination 'even if this undermines the principal of equity'. The freedom of speech, assembly, the press and of 'peaceful petitioning' would also be circumscribed in a similar conditional way. The NWC subcommittee found 'rather unfortunate' the paragraph by the Constitution Committee that 'the legitimate fears of minorities should be addressed'. This, they declared, would be 'a form of pandering to the racial bigotry of whites'. It was their 'considered opinion' that the role whites played in the struggle would decide their future position. Therefore, 'encouraging division in the enemy ranks cannot be absolutized to a point that it jeopardises the aspirations of the majority'. (Once again, this was a point the Constitution Committee itself had made – Asmal's previously quoted statement of the 'Danger of Being Bemused by White Anxieties', for example.)[15] The NWC subcommittee also felt that in referring to the current constitution and general concepts like Roman-Dutch Law and company law, the Constitution Committee was mistakenly assuming aspects of South African law to be 'racially neutral'. They insisted that 'we cannot conceive of a democratic state retaining the services of the present judiciary'. The NWC subcommittee declared that they 'would advocate the dismissal of all of them; if there are indeed "noble exceptions" these can be rehired into a body of democratic jurists established by the new state'.

Jordan, Slovo and Makana were divided among themselves on matters such as property rights and the electoral system for the future. On property, they agreed 'we cannot entrench the rights of property', but one voice was in favour of maintaining a 'diplomatic silence' over the rights of churches and private schools, while another felt that secular and religious matters should be treated in the same way, and schools should not be allowed to become 'a device for securing crucial areas of white privilege' as had happened in Zimbabwe. On the electoral system, one view was that the system to come was an 'irrelevancy', while another asserted it was 'crucial for the ascendancy of the liberation forces and as such needs to be closely studied with particular attention to the present demographic distribution largely determined by racist laws'.

The discussions were so intense that, as convenor, Jordan had to report on their differing positions to the NWC and NEC. His report-back had three main subheadings: 'The areas of consensus', 'The areas of difference' and the subcommittee's proposals to the NEC.[16]

When the full NWC discussed these matters, its language was less outspoken than in the above conversations, but it was clear that 'The ANC must champion the rights of the majority whether we come to power by force of arms or through a negotiated settlement'. A constitutional document that 'does this' was needed and it had to be flexible enough to deal with the changing balance of forces during the fluidity of a transition period.[17] The NWC suggested also that the Committee 'study the experience of the People's Democracies in Europe'; indeed, Simons and Sachs would subsequently visit the USSR, and Pekane, Jobodwana and Maduna the GDR and Czechoslovakia.

There was therefore an ambivalence within the NWC on which way to go. But it was also already clear from Jordan's 1985 paper and Tambo's address at the Committee's first meeting in January 1986 that the one-party option was unlikely. It would be a 'grave' strategic error, Tony O'Dowd warned in June 1986, because

'Such a proclamation would invite all the other political organisations to unite in an anti-ANC coalition. We, however, must strive for just the opposite – an anti-government coalition in which a variety of allies will join us.'[18]

The Constitution Committee had traversed most of the issues raised by the NWC members and shared the overall bias towards majoritarian interests and redress. The question was how to translate the political goals of the struggle into constitutional terms. Sachs was invited to speak directly to the NEC on the differences between a liberal democratic constitution, a People's Power one and a third model, which he and the Committee called 'an anti-fascist or post-dictatorship constitution', and remembers how excited he was at the prospect. The chance to address the top leadership was an important moment. There were about twenty NEC members sitting in clusters around desks and wherever they could find a spare seat. As if to set the scene, the first speaker was Chris Hani expressing concern that comrades were all running on the soft road towards talking to the enemy. Instead, they should be putting their energy into the hard task of getting people and supplies back into the country. The next to speak was Thabo Mbeki. He ignored what Hani had said and informed his comrades about contacts he was developing on what he called 'the diplomatic front'.[19]

Sachs was asked to discuss the points made in his paper about the different constitutional prototypes that should be considered. After discussing classical liberal democratic constitutions such as those of the United States, and People's Power constitutions like the one in Mozambique, he gave information about constitutions drafted in Eastern and Western Europe after the defeat of Nazism and fascism in 1945, and in Portugal after the revolution in 1974. What these anti-fascist constitutions had in common was that they not only provided multiparty democracy and votes for all, but they also embodied clear commitments to programmes of social and economic advancement for all the people. In this respect, it was highly relevant that communists and socialists, who had played leading roles in the resistance to Hitler and Mussolini, had been very active in the constitutional negotiations. Similarly, in the case of Portugal, communists and socialists who had led the opposition to the dictatorship had also played a key role in the development of a new democratic constitution. Sachs reflects:

In speaking to the NEC, I was at pains not to express either a personal preference or a preference on behalf of the Constitution Committee for any of the three constitutional prototypes. I knew, however, that the majority of the NEC would intuitively feel that a classical liberal democratic constitution would be unduly protective of the existing patterns of hugely skewed property ownership and sociocultural domination. At the same time, we had seen in Angola and

Mozambique that constitutionally entrenching one party in power had been followed by bitter, externally supported civil war. Millions of refugees, child soldiers, the nation torn apart, ceaseless war, bitterness without end – this was not what we were fighting for.[20]

Fuller debate needed to be held at the top levels of the ANC before the Committee could proceed in any clear direction. The new language of emancipatory constitutionalism was still too much for the ANC to absorb without deeper engagement. In addition, the organisation as a whole was suspicious that Pretoria and its allies could use talks about talks as a strategy for relieving the increasing pressure being put on it. Tambo had therefore tried to make it clear that the ANC would only get involved if certain basic conditions were met and the talks did not become a 'device to quell internal demands and weaken external pressure'.[21] However, when P.W. Botha ordered cross-border raids and imposed a national state of emergency on 19 May 1986, when the EPG was in Cape Town, it strengthened the belief among many NEC members that intensifying the push for a seizure of power was the most logical strategic path for the ANC.

Above: ANC president Oliver Tambo, with his head of office Thabo Mbeki and secretary-general Alfred Nzo, at the press conference in Lusaka on the organisation's 74th birthday, 8 January 1986, calling on South Africans to make apartheid ungovernable. On the same day, Tambo launched the secret ANC Constitution Committee and assigned it an 'ad hoc unique exercise' that had 'no precedent in the history of the movement'

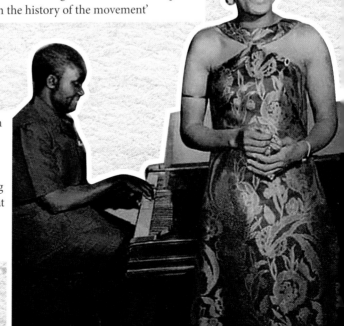

Right: African music icon Miriam Makeba accompanied on piano by Zambian president Kenneth Kaunda in a photograph that captures the deep solidarity, going beyond politics with a big 'P', that Tambo and the ANC received in exile from their African host countries

Left: Pallo Jordan, ANC head of research, administrative secretary of the NEC and chair of the NWC's Constitutional Commission or working committee. His groundbreaking analysis in 1985 helped lay the foundations for the ANC's decision to add constitutionalism to its strategic armoury during the decisive struggles of the late 1980s

Below: The thinkers and ideas of the 1980s struggles were connected to deep-rooted intellectual and political networks stretching back generations: Jordan's mother, Phyllis Ntantala, pictured on the cover of her autobiography (*left*), and his novelist and literary scholar father, Prof. A.C. Jordan, at UCLA in 1962 (*right*)

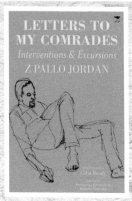

LETTERS TO MY COMRADES
Interventions & Excursions
Z PALLO JORDAN

Amandla! Matla!

Pallo.

Z. Pallo Jordan.
Director of Research

A Life's Mosaic

The Autobiography of
PHYLLIS NTANTALA

Prof. Jack Simons, struggle veteran, trusted adviser to Oliver Tambo and appointed chairperson of the Constitution Committee, conferring with the ANC president at the landmark Kabwe Conference in June 1985

Dr Zola Skweyiya is pictured here with Tambo and Sindiso Mfenyana at the 21st OAU summit in Addis Ababa in July 1985. Skweyiya was recalled as chief rep in Ethiopia to head the new Department of Legal and Constitutional Affairs and to serve as deputy chairperson of the Constitution Committee

Brigitte Mabandla, the only woman on the Constitution Committee and later the first woman to become justice minister in South Africa

Zingisile Ntozintle 'Jobs' Jobodwana was at the core of the Committee's work as its secretary

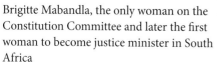

iv) During our presence in Swaziland we were informed that there is quite a number of our cars and property being held by the police and being sold very cheaply to the public. This includes two cars one of which is the one in which Cde Viva was killed in and according to reports it is relatively new, having been used for only 3 months. We are instructing Mr Matsebula to retrieve these cars and if possible arrange for their transportation to Lusaka.

Report compiled:

Ted Pekane

Zola Skweyiya

Date: July 20, 1987.

c.c. Cdes O.R. Tambo - President
     "   A. Nzo   - Secretary General
     "   T. T. Nkobi- Treasurer General
     PMC
     MHQ

Shadrack Lehlohonolo 'Teddy' Pekane, an MK veteran, undertook dangerous missions on behalf of the Committee and became ANC chief rep in Brussels in 1989

Kader Asmal, based at Trinity College in Dublin, specialised in international law. Pictured here with Enuga Reddy, head of the UN Special Committee on Apartheid, and Diana Collins from the International Defence and Aid Fund which provided vast amounts of funding for legal support to victims of apartheid

Amandla!   Albie Sachs

Constitution Committee rapporteur Albie Sachs (*left*) pictured with the Committee's youngest member, Penuell Maduna (*dark jacket, centre*), during their days in Mozambique when they shared a flat

The Freedom Charter and the Constitution

Constitutional Prototypes

MCH91-31-1-6a

Almost all modern Constitutions have certain ~~common~~ elements in common. They set out the main institutions of public ~~power~~ (government), define their competence and indicate how the leadership of the country is to be determined (election, heredity, succession, religious unction). The constitutions contain s... the general principles while ~~an even great~~ it is even more common ... sections setting out ... of citizens, sometimes in ...

The Freedom Char... constitution, ~~(it is it)~~ ... not define the stru...

The Preliminary Nature of the Constitutional Document.

MCH91-31-1-7a

Any constitutional document drawn up at this stage must of necessity be incomplete and provisional. It will be incomplete because we still await clear guidelines on questions such as economic policy and education, and because we lack the ~~(important)~~ ~~(politico)~~ demographic information. ~~(interesting)~~ Thus, the ~~(it is it)~~ political strategy to be adopted in relation to the mechanisms for the re-distribution of wealth will have a considerable bearing on what will probably be the most scrutinised part of the Constitution, namely, the rights and duties attached to property. Similarly, though less fundamental, the phrase in the Freedom Charter: "The law shall guarantee the right to all to educate their children" raises important questions

As rapporteur, Albie Sachs, speaking here at Kabwe, drafted the first reports of the Constitution Committee for submission to Oliver Tambo and the NEC in January 1986

Secretary-general Alfred Nzo, treasurer-general Thomas Nkobi and Ruth Mompati were among the ANC NEC leaders involved in operational oversight of the Constitution Committee, along with Tambo, Jordan and others such as James Stuart and Anthony Mangalo

Together with Nzo and Nkobi, alliance leaders John Nkadimeng (SACTU) and Joe Slovo and Dan Tloome (SACP) formed part of the President's Council that helped Tambo guide the ANC through the strategic changes and restructuring plans it adopted from 1985 onwards

Insert: Simon Makana, a member of the NWC's constitutional sub-committee, alongside Jordan and Slovo

The **1909 SA Native Convention** sent a delegation to London to protest the colour-bar constitution of the new Union of South Africa

Historical Papers, Cullen Library, Wits

In **1943** twenty-six South African leaders were appointed by Dr A.B. Xuma to draw up the **Africans' Claims** document in response to Churchill and Roosevelt's Atlantic Charter

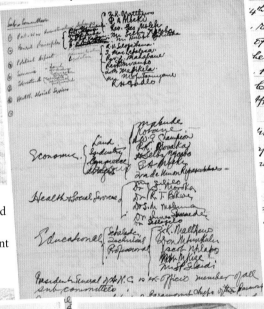

IF GOVERNMENT REFUSES NATIONAL CONVENTION...

ALL-IN CONFERENCE CALLS FOR ACTION

Mass Demonstrations On Eve of Republic

NEW AGE

AFRICA DAY SPECIAL

TREASON TRIAL MAY END THIS WEEK

Alf Khumalo, Bailey's African History Archives

Left: Various convention initiatives were launched in 1961 to demand a National Convention before South Africa became a republic

Above. Oliver Tambo at work with Chief Albert Luthuli. The latter grew up in the home of his uncle, Martin Lutuli, a founder of the Natal Native Congress as far back as 1900

14

'The Foundations of Government'

O N 16 SEPTEMBER 1986, eight months to the day after submitting its first report to the secretary-general's office, the Constitution Committee finally got the response it had been waiting for. However, what they received was no more than the two-page set of guidelines the NWC had agreed to back at its meeting on 20 February.[1] The document gave no explanation for HQ's long delay and the NWC had diplomatically held back Jordan's six-page report dealing with its internal discussions.

On seeing the NWC feedback, Simons and his colleagues would have wondered what the hold-up was all about. Jordan, Slovo and Makana had agreed with the Committee that it was not a good idea to draft a constitution at that stage, but rather a 'constitutional document' containing 'general principles' that could be 'quickly transformed into a constitution' when the correct political conditions materialised. The NWC also agreed that the Committee had phrased 'in very sound terms the objectives of such a constitutional document.'[2] There had been eleven of these objectives. To this the NWC added a new seventeen-point road map consisting of fifteen specific constitutional guidelines and two general points. The constitutional guidelines were listed under three headings – 'Basic principles', 'Political power and its exercise', and 'Economics'. The two general points noted that 1) a decision on a future system of government would await a fuller study and that 2) 'A legal system and judiciary consistent with these [guidelines] and dedicated to their pursuance must be created.'[3]

The guidelines showed the mix of influences on the debate in Lusaka. Some of them drew from the Skeleton the Committee had devised in January; for example, it referred to pluralism and a 'multiplicity of political parties', as well as the support for a Bill of Rights and the rejection of group vetoes. Both this last point and the one outlawing the advocacy or practice of racism, fascism, Nazism, tribalism or regionalism came straight from arguments in Jordan's 1985 paper. Other guidelines show the strong People's Power perspective articulated by Joe Slovo inside and outside the subcommittee discussions, such as the explanation that special constitutional provision would be made for mass organisations and the 'organs of popular power which are emerging during the course of the struggle', as well as the entrenchment of workers' participation in 'economic management'.

DRAFT TWO: NWC Guidelines, 18–23 February 1986[4]

The full NWC document read as follows:

1. Basic principles:
   a. Sovereignty in the democratic state will be vested in one central legislature, administration and executive within the context of a unitary state;
   b. The thrust of all state policy shall be toward the cultivation of a single national identity and loyalty binding on all South Africans irrespective of racial or ethnic origins;
   c. Consistent with the above considerations the state must recognise and encourage the linguistic and cultural diversity of the South African people;
   d. Consistent with (a) and (b) there will be provision made for the regional and local delegation of the powers of the central authority to smaller administrative units for purposes of more efficient and effective administration.

2. Political power and its exercise:
   a. There can be no entrenchment of minority group veto rights;
   b. A Bill of Rights guaranteeing the rights of individuals is acceptable but not group rights, mechanisms for their enforcement;
   c. The principle of one person, one vote will be fundamental;
   d. Complete outlawing of the advocacy or practice of racism, fascism, Nazism, tribalism, chauvinism or regionalism;
   e. Political pluralism permitting the existence of a multiplicity of political parties subject to the provisions (d);
   f. Entrenchment of the power of the electorate to exercise control over and its right of recall of all its elected representatives;
   g. Special provision shall be made for the representation and participation of organs of popular power which are emerging during the course of the struggle;
   h. Provision must be made for the participation of mass organisation, such as trade unions, in the governing and administration of the country.

3. Economics:
   a. The state shall have power to define and limit the rights and obligations relating to the ownership of land and all other forms of productive property;
   b. Entrenchment of the rights and protection of personal and non-exploitative property;

c. Entrenchment of the workers' participation in the way economic management and planning of all enterprises in which they are employed.
4. Choice between Presidential over Prime Ministerial system; proportional or direct representation; etc shall be adjourned until fuller study.
5. A legal system and judiciary consistent with these objectives and dedicated to their pursuance must be created.[5]

The Committee said that the NWC had 'presented us with a crisp set of guidelines, which we now take as our starting point'. They moved forward speedily and soon merged the Skeleton with the NWC response to form one new document called 'The Foundations of Government in a Democratic South Africa'. The Foundations had two subsections: the 'Objectives' of a new constitution and the 'Principles' on which it should be based.

The nine objectives were drawn from the eleven points listed under the 'Preamble' of the Skeleton on 14 January, minus the first two, which had consisted of the first and fourth sentences of the Freedom Charter. These nine points had, in turn, been culled from the minutes of the Constitution Committee meeting on 14 January and elaborated on in the 'Statement of the problem' in Sachs's short paper on 'The Preliminary Nature of the Constitutional Document' finalised that day.

The principles were based on the NWC's guidelines, which the Committee had reworked and reordered. The Constitution Committee also cut some formulations and inserted new points, to the extent that while it acknowledged that the NEC was the political driver of the process, it introduced new meanings to the guidelines. Some paragraphs were reworded and moved around, and some NWC formulations were left out. The new wording stated that 'the economy shall be a mixed one'; emphasised that religious freedom would be constitutionally protected; and, controversially, stated that 'Hereditary forms of political authority shall be abolished and the chiefs encouraged to participate in normal democratic life'. There was also a new paragraph saying that all state institutions would be obliged to 'eradicate apartheid in all its forms' and 'take measures to overcome its consequences'.

Out of the seventeen themes listed by the NWC, there were only two that the Committee had either not absorbed into the Foundations or on which it did not feel it necessary or advisable to publish anything at that stage. The first related to questions concerning a future political system, namely the kind of electoral system and the governmental system. These needed further research. The second concerned the right of voters to recall their representatives, 'since we feel this is a "paper right" difficult to define in practice and never, as far as we are aware, actually used in countries where theoretically it exists".[6] (However, as NEC member Reg September would contend, this kind of recall did happen in practice in the Soviet Union and, in his view, the section should be retained, as suggested by the NWC.)

After waiting eight months for the NWC to respond, the Constitution Committee took only four days to finalise its Foundations document. The final product had nine objectives and eighteen guidelines, expressed in tighter language with a smoother flow. It was forwarded to the NEC, together with an introductory memo and notes, on 20 September 1986.[7]

DRAFT THREE: Foundations of Government in a Democratic South Africa, drawn up by the Constitution Committee, 20 September 1986

OBJECTIVES of a new constitution
- The granting to the oppressed majority of their just national rights;
- The outlawing of racial discrimination in all its forms;
- The ensuring of the complete dismantlement of apartheid structures and their replacement by democratic ones;
- The prevention of the resurgence of racist policies, programmes and practices, whether in old form or new;
- The overcoming of the effects of centuries of racial domination and inequality by ensuring substantial redistribution of wealth and the complete opening up of facilities for all;
- The encouragement of the active involvement of all sectors of the population in government and economic and cultural life;
- The promotion of the habits of non-racial thinking, the practice of anti-racist behaviour and the acquisition of a genuine shared patriotic consciousness;
- The creating of the conditions for the speediest achievement of these goals with the least possible disruption to the tranquillity of the country and to the production of the goods and services necessary to enable all members of the community to lead a decent life; [and]
- The guaranteeing of the security necessary for the achievement of these goals.

The new constitution shall be based on the following PRINCIPLES
- South Africa shall be an independent unitary, democratic and non-racial state;
- Sovereignty shall belong to the people as a whole and shall be exercised through one central legislature, administration and executive;

- In the exercise of their sovereignty, the people shall have the right to vote under a system of universal suffrage based on the principle of one person, one vote;
- Every voter shall have the right to stand for election and be elected to all legislative bodies;
- The system of universal and equal franchise will apply also to the election of all regional and local bodies;
- It shall be state policy to promote the growth of a single national identity and loyalty binding on all South Africans; at the same time, the state will recognise the linguistic and cultural diversity of South African people, and provide facilities for free linguistic and cultural development;
- Hereditary forms of political power shall be abolished and the chiefs encouraged to participate in normal democratic life;
- The constitution will include a Bill of Rights based on the Freedom Charter guaranteeing the fundamental human rights of all citizens and providing appropriate mechanisms for their enforcement;
- The state and all social institutions shall be under a duty to eradicate apartheid in all its forms, as well as to take measures to overcome its consequences;
- The advocacy or practice of racism, fascism, Nazism, tribalism or regionalism shall be outlawed;
- Subject to the above, freedom of association and expression shall be guaranteed by the adoption of a multi-party system and an open press;
- Religious freedom shall receive special constitutional guarantee;
- Participatory democracy shall be encouraged by means of involving the community, and community and workers organisations, directly in public and economic administration;
- The state and all social institutions shall take active steps to redress as speedily as possible the economic and social inequalities produced by apartheid. In particular the unjust division of the land shall be corrected;
- The economy shall be a mixed one with a public sector, a cooperative sector, a private sector and a family sector;
  - The public sector shall be subjected to democratic control;
  - Cooperative forms of economic enterprise and the family sector shall be supported by the state;
  - Property for personal use and consumption shall be constitutionally protected;
  - The state shall have the right to determine the general context in which economic life takes place and to define and limit the rights and

obligations attaching to the ownership and use of private productive capacity;

- The state shall promote the acquisition of managerial and entrepreneurial skills, and provide facilities to encourage commercial and industrial activities amongst all sections of the population;
- Workers and trade union rights shall receive special constitutional protection;
- All organs of government, justice and security shall be transformed so as to make them representative of the people as a whole, democratic in their structure and functioning, and dedicated to defending the principles of the Constitution.

For the first time, nearly nine months after the Committee was established, there were proposed guidelines in place for a future South African constitutional dispensation arising from the combined efforts of the Constitution Committee and the NWC. What would the full NEC have to say about these?

15

The Leadership Has Its Say

THE NEC WAS quick to respond to the Foundations document: within a fortnight it had called for a meeting with the Committee to take the discussion further. The meeting, held on 2 October 1986 in Lusaka, was attended by twenty-five of the thirty NEC members who'd been elected at Kabwe. The Constitution Committee was represented by its five Lusaka-based members: Jack Simons, Zola Skweyiya, Penuell Maduna, Teddy Pekane and Jobs Jobodwana.

Most of the twenty-five NEC participants had already been involved, one way or another, in the secret backroom work of the Constitution Committee. Tambo and Nzo had overseen the establishment of the think tank; Ruth Mompati (SG's office and PMC), James Stuart (ECC secretariat) and Tony Mongalo (Tambo's administrative secretary and a member of the NAT directorate) had liaised with the Committee; Pallo Jordan, Simon Makana and Joe Slovo had been appointed to process the Constitution Committee reports for the leadership; and the Lusaka-based NEC members had attended at least two NWC meetings in January and February to consider the report and provide further guidelines to the Committee.

The other members of the leadership core, occupying key positions in the wide range of ANC operations, would be equally important in the spread of the new constitutional planning perspectives. To start with, there were the military leaders Joe Modise, Chris Hani and Steve Tshwete; the intelligence and security chiefs Joe Nhlanhla, Jacob Zuma and Sizakele Sigxashe; the underground commanders, such as Cassius Make (head of logistics, soon to be assassinated in Swaziland), Mac Maharaj, and Josiah Jele from the political HQ (falling under the PMC); the head of international affairs and former ANC spokesperson at the United Nations in New York, Mfanafuthi 'Johnny' Makatini; those based in other continents such as Aziz Pahad and Francis Meli working out of London; and finally, influential individuals such as Dan Tloome (SACP chairperson and head of the Tribunal Review Board), the SACTU general secretary John Nkadimeng, John Motshabi, Henry Makgothi, Robert Manci, Gertrude Shope, Jackie Selebi and Reg September.

Thabo Mbeki was absent, and from the documents it seems that he did not participate in any constitutional discussions that year. At that time, he was also a member of the Central Committee of the SACP, and no less than ten of their Central Committee members participated in this important meeting in their capacity as ANC NEC leaders. They were Tloome (SACP chairperson), Slovo (SACP general secretary), Nkadimeng (wearing three hats, since he was also general secretary of SACTU), Hani, Jele, Meli, Makgothi, Pahad, September and Sigxashe. This cross-cutting involvement of the leaders of the three exiled alliance partners in the debates about the constitutional guidelines meant that everyone was in the loop from the start.

In the chair was 'Cde TG': treasurer-general Thomas Nkobi. He started proceedings by welcoming the five members of the Constitution Committee present, congratulating them on their work and inviting them to speak to the memorandum they had sent to the NEC on 20 September.[1]

Simons and the Committee outlined the procedure they had followed. Since January they'd produced a considerable number of papers on topics related to constitutional developments. Some of these represented a consensus within the Committee, while others were presented for circulation and discussion. The full set of papers was tabled for consultation by the NEC. The Committee proposed, however, that discussion of these papers wait for another occasion. Given that they'd only received the NWC subcommittee's response on 16 September, it was much more important to deal with issues raised in the response first.

The Constitution Committee repeated the point that it had used the NWC's 'crisp set of guidelines' as 'our starting point' and had included all but two of the NWC's seventeen points in the new Foundations document. Skweyiya emphasised that the Committee now wanted the NEC to consider adopting and publishing the guidelines in the form of a document titled 'Proposed Foundations of Government in a Democratic South Africa'. This could then be presented to the people of South Africa as a whole, inviting their active participation and contribution towards preparing a final document.

Skweyiya explained that, while the Committee concurred with the NWC subcommittee that it would be unwise to draw up a constitution at present, they wanted the Foundations to be aired and debated. They felt that, apart from the proposed basic guidelines, a selection could be made of other documents that the Committee had already prepared or were planning to prepare for publication in *Sechaba* or distribution as autonomous pamphlets for discussion by ANC units. Jobodwana had already written to Tambo on 14 August asking for a regular column in *Sechaba* called the 'Constitutional Forum'.[2] In particular, the Committee wished to have a workshop of the broad membership to discuss the future constitution. These were issues already raised in early Committee meetings and correspondence to HQ. Finally, once the basic guidelines had been agreed upon, the Committee wanted the debate opened up to involve lawyers and others at home, and friendly lawyers in the international community.

As had been agreed at the prior Constitution Committee meeting, each of the other members addressed the NEC individually. Maduna answered the question of why the ANC should be involved in a constitutional debate, stating that 'People at home are looking at us for guidance', and 'this would enable the ANC to counter the propaganda against us'. He warned of the 'think tanks working for the *Boers*', referring to the KwaZulu-Natal Indaba and other such initiatives. His position was later supported by Pallo Jordan, who added that since constitutional discussions were already going on in the country, it would be 'dangerous to shelve or to keep quiet on some of the issues'.

Pekane explained the meaning of the terms used in paragraph 2(a) of Foundations, which referred to a future South Africa being an 'independent, unitary, democratic and non-racial state' – there seemed to be a call for clarity on the use of the words 'independent' and 'unitary' in it. The author found no further information on this, but independence would have been considered a complex issue, as South Africa was suffering under what the ANC typified as 'colonialism of a special type' in which the colonisers would not be leaving.

Skweyiya spoke again to explain the use of the term 'mixed economy', as this was a much more specific wording than that received from the NWC. In their accompanying notes, the Committee stated that in the absence of guidelines from the Economics Committee, and on the basis of preliminary ideas from the NWC subcommittee, 'we have on our own outlined a tentative series of propositions on the question of economic activity and property rights, which we are sure will be looked at with special attention by the NEC'.

Maduna then took on the point that referred to the 'place and role of chiefs' and advocated for 'the abolition of hereditary forms of political power'. Here, too, they had 'not received guidelines on the future constitutional position of the chiefs'; therefore, the fairly radical proposal was 'a tentative one'.

Finally, Jobodwana, the scribe and secretary, outlined the practical actions needed in matters requiring further research. The priority here was to conduct a full demographic/political survey of South Africa as soon as possible so that the Committee could respond to NWC queries about what kind of electoral and governmental systems should be put in place. Only then would the Committee and the NEC be able to answer questions relating to the electoral system and the presidential/prime ministerial debate. In addition, there were three other questions that still needed addressing: the constitutional evolution in Eastern Europe after World War II; the land questions; and the problem of positive discrimination or affirmative action to close South Africa's gap between rich and poor, white and black. Jobodwana said the ANC's Education Committee also needed to look urgently at the future status of private and church schools 'in case attempts are made to secure them special constitutional protection'. Finally, regarding the last guideline on transforming the organs of government, justice and security, the Committee felt that more attention should be given to the character and composition of the army, police force and prison service, as well as to the civil service and the judiciary.

'Meeting now open for the participation of NEC members,' Jobodwana noted in his minutes. Altogether seventeen members of the ANC leadership spoke.

First up was Steve Tshwete, a gravelly voiced ex–Robben Islander and underground activist from Peelton near King William's Town. In 1985, when Lennox Sebe's security police came knocking on the front door, he jumped over the back wall of his property and fled into exile. Promoted to the military High Command, he was soon to take over from Chris Hani as national commissar of MK. To the meeting, Tshwete declared: 'This is a very important discussion. I wish to commend the comrades of the Constitution Committee for the excellent work they have done. South Africa is a colony of a special type. The form of our struggle is national but the content [is] class. We have to get rid of the bourgeoisie.'

MK chief of staff and SACP general secretary and theoretician Joe Slovo covered several points, warning about the media and monopoly control of the economy. He expressed reservations about including the reference to an 'open press' in the paragraph dealing with freedom of speech. His concern was that an open press could be used to sow counter-revolutionary ideas. The press was controlled by those who could afford it. He did not have an alternative formulation but argued that television and radio had to be owned and controlled by the government. On the subject of a mixed economy, Slovo felt strongly that there was a need to break the stranglehold of monopolies over the economy. He referred to a distinction that an expert had drawn between the concepts of nationalisation and socialisation. 'In any event, we do not have to be nervous about the inclusion of a paragraph on that. [Fifty per cent of] investment is now controlled by the government in racist South Africa.' At the same time, Slovo cautioned against 'the use of the phrase "democratic control" when it comes to the control of the public sector ... [You] cannot control industry by voting'.

Next in line was Pallo Jordan. He cautioned against explicitly talking about nationalisation. 'We should guard against including in this document or constitution a clause or undertaking that will tie us; we can general[ise] on this issue.' Similarly with the media: 'We can keep quiet on this issue, some of these are already in the hands of the state. They can be inherited by the democratic state.'

Several other speakers weighed in on the topic of the economy and nationalisation. Chris Hani's views got the most space in the minutes. He said the questions that needed to be asked were:

Who is fighting in South Africa today? Who is sacrificing and making major contributions in our struggle?

Our calls to destroy state apparatus are directed to the ordinary people, workers, peasants etc. It is therefore important that the aspirations of the major contributors in our struggle are given special attention. Therefore, the Constitution document, as a mobilising instrument, should say something about Monopolies, Trust etc. There are people who are now jumping onto the bandwagon because they see the situation is favouring us.[3]

London-based Francis Meli (Alan Madolwana), editor of *Sechaba* and author of *South Africa Belongs to Us*, an unofficial ANC history, argued on similar socialist lines but acknowledged the multiclass nature of the ANC's nationalist phase of the revolution. He noted that 'Constitutions are there to protect the ruling class. Ours perhaps might be a coalition of classes, where we shall have the Motsuenyanes, who are pretending to be with [us] now. But after independence they will aspire to big bourgeoisie positions... Added to this we should include the anti-imperialist character in this constitution.'

This specific point was supported by NAT director Joe Nhlanhla: 'The document has to reckon with imperialism, especially in the USA. We are pandering to their interests but we are doing everything in consideration of using tactical reasons to enable us to take power.'

James Stuart and the ANC's chief diplomat Johnny Makatini cautioned against taking too strong a position when nuance was needed. Stuart said the 'principle of temporary alliance' applied to the petty bourgeoisie in the same way as it did to other sectors of society. For his part, Makatini reminded his colleagues 'that this document is a mobilising instrument. Therefore the intention is to unite all the people irrespective of class etc.'

Gertrude Shope expressed both an understanding of the need to be tactical and a revolutionary scepticism about supporting liberal democracy when she asked, 'Why should we announce a multiparty system? Why should we talk about it at the present moment? It is premature. PAC and other reactionary elements will exploit the loophole.'

The next hotly debated topic was the role of the chiefs or traditional leaders. In the absence of guidance from the NWC, the Constitution Committee memo recommended that hereditary chieftainship be done away with when democracy arrived: 'Hereditary forms of political power shall be abolished and the chiefs encouraged to participate in normal democratic life.' Meli came out in support of the proposal: 'We are against tribalism but not ethnicity. Ethnic interests do exist – they can be promoted. However we are against institutionalisation of the... tribal structures.'

Slovo spoke against the Committee's suggestion. He objected to the use of the word 'abolish' and 'preferred' the term 'phasing out' on the basis that the paragraph would 'shock the chiefs too much'. Simon Makana agreed: 'I think we should leave out the section on Chiefs otherwise it shall be misunderstood.'

Nhlanhla backed them up: 'Chieftainship is not an abolishable institution. We only need to think as to how we can harness it in the interest of our struggle. We want to give out this document as a mobilising factor, so if we now talk of abolishing the institution, we shall be mobilising against us a section of the population. It is necessary to learn from the experience of Zambia as to how the matter was treated ... Mobilisation is central. Land question is central. It is a fact that people participate in the revolution for their own interest. We accept these forces on that understanding for the time being.'

Jordan didn't quite support the Committee's recommendations but took issue with Nhlanhla's point: 'These people have been harnessed by the regime and are now being used for extremely counter-revolutionary purposes. Of course, we have the Sabatas and the Ndamases, but these are exceptions not the rule. Let us not romanticise Chieftainship. There are some dangers in retaining Chieftainship ... The experience of Zambia cannot be compared with the situation in South Africa.'

The speakers who followed agreed with Slovo, Makana and Nhlanhla. Reg September commented that whether they used the term 'abolish' or 'phase out', 'the effect is the same – as long as the section appears in print, it will cause us problems'. James Stuart added, 'We can neither speak of abolishing nor phasing out of chiefs, but we can put the paragraph in such a way as to mobilise the chiefs so that they do not think we shall throw them away.' Aziz Pahad suggested simply leaving out the paragraph on chiefs, and Makatini agreed that it 'should disappear from the document ... We should not put obstacles in front of us, the image of the African National Congress should be very clear.'

Jacob Zuma, deputy director of NAT and head of intelligence, empathised with tradition:

> We should not abolish Chieftainship, the problem should be solved politically. The Chief had been with us in the forefront, history can bear me out. Ours is to trace stages and ask how through racist machinations Chiefs became enemies of the people. We would like to see the system of chieftainship being in unison with the democratic system.[4]

Oliver Tambo came down on the side of caution in his concluding summary on this issue, taking sides with neither the defenders nor the antagonists. 'We have to say something about the Chiefs,' he said. 'A kind of formulation has to be found.

I had thought roughly of the following: "The institution of Chiefs will be converted to the service of the people."'

This suggestion was taken up in the revised list of constitutional principles that emerged from the meeting. The wording became: 'The institution of hereditary rulers and Chiefs shall be transformed to serve the interests of the people as a whole in conformity with the democratic principles embodied in the constitution.'

On foreign policy, Joe Slovo asked 'whether we should not include in the document a provision of inter-state relations, how we shall relate ourselves with other states, whether we shall be non-aligned or not. In short, our international relations.'

On the paragraph stating that 'Workers and trade union rights shall receive special constitutional protection', he argued that the word 'workers' should be removed from the draft, 'otherwise we should open ourselves to attack, as other classes, e.g. "peasants", would demand also special protection in the constitution'.

Finally, on organs of government (i.e. state apparatus), he felt that 'we need to state that Army, Police etc. shall be put under control of the people'.

On voting rights, Reg September objected to extending this right to people found guilty of the crime of apartheid and suggested that they 'now prepare a dossier of the names and particulars of all those people found guilty of the crimes of apartheid'.

On regionalism, Slovo and September supported the creation of regional administrations. Slovo said there was a need for these regional bodies, which 'will take care of the cultural and linguistic uniformities inside the country'. September concurred, saying these would 'help in the development of languages and cultures'. He said that 'in the USSR they do not have a single nation but a variety of national groupings'. Pahad, on the other hand, said that the term 'regionalism' was superfluous and should be removed. Ruth Mompati felt this matter would have to be tackled fully and clarification would be needed on what type of regional bodies were being considered.

Alfred Nzo raised concern about the paragraph stating that 'religious freedom shall receive special constitutional guarantee'. He said that churches like the Dutch Reformed Church 'are perpetuating racism and are agents of apartheid' and that, although he was not against freedom of worship in principle, those who preached racism should not be given guarantees. Pahad asked: 'Why must there be special guarantees of Churches and Trade Unions? This opens demands from other organisations which will seek special treatment in the constitution.'

After the NEC members had completed their contributions, Tambo summed up. He commended the Constitution Committee for its work, saying, 'We can now talk concretely about the future.' He added that there was a great need to consult widely, internally and internationally. It was necessary, therefore, to take seriously

Skweyiya's request for visits to the USSR and GDR, plus Joe Nhlanhla's mention that the invitations from these countries had long been open without any response from the ANC, and similar recommendations by Nzo. Tambo said the GDR could provide more practical information based on the post–World War II transitional stage, namely the interim period after the defeat of Nazism and before the GDR was established formally as a socialist state with the Communist Party at the helm.

Tambo went on to recommend that the demographic or political survey suggested by the Committee be followed up proactively. The Swedes had made an open offer of projects, and money should not be a problem: 'We do not have to be conservative.' Tambo knew what he was talking about. He and Thabo Mbeki had met Swedish prime minister Olof Palme in February 1986, ten days before his assassination, and the latter had agreed to back the ANC proposal to start planning strategically and systematically for a post-apartheid South Africa.[5] This resulted in the Planning for an Alternative South Africa (PASA) programme (also referred to as the Post-Apartheid South Africa project), which Zola Skweyiya and the DLCA/Constitution Committee became closely involved with, co-organising events and sending in their first application for support within four months of this NEC meeting. 'Structure of government and constitutional affairs' became one of PASA's six priority focuses. This involvement was clearly Tambo's intention from the start, given the work the Committee was undertaking.[6]

Tambo accepted the proposal of an ANC internal seminar on a future constitution. When this seminar happened, the NEC should be in a position to lead the discussion. He agreed with the Constitution Committee that it was essential to publish the ANC's ideas on the constitution but cautioned that the ANC needed to proceed carefully: 'We have to say how long this debate should go on. It is necessary before then to have consulted the Movement at large. It is necessary to bring in the democratic movement at home to participate, because they will have to defend our ideas inside the country.'

Tambo sympathised with Chris Hani's analysis, which argued that workers and peasants had been at the forefront of the struggle and that their interests should therefore be primary in the constitution. It was also necessary to deal with the monopoly control of the economy. But, he added:

We are at a stage when we have to lead. The way we lead must have a mobilising effect not a demobilising one. In my view, if there is a constitution being debated, we have to shift imperialism without abandoning our objective. What is important is to come up with something acceptable to the majority of our people, our working people, without necessarily frightening the others. That does not mean prematurely throwing tactical advantages to the enemy. The general proposition in this document is to scrutinise it so that it is not negative to the aspirations of our people.[7]

On Shope's concern about announcing multiparty democracy, Tambo said it was difficult to keep quiet on this point because the enemy was harping on this and forever saying the ANC was in favour of a one-party state. To resolve Secretary-General Nzo's objection to freedom of religion being used to accommodate or promote hate speech, he suggested combining the paragraph promoting freedom of religion with the paragraph that forbade hate speech.

A subcommittee would be set up to finalise the document, taking into account the views expressed in the deliberations. Tambo closed the meeting 'promptly at one o'clock'. Having completed what they knew to be a historic meeting, the leaders of the ANC and their five colleagues on the Constitution Committee retired for lunch.

Pallo Jordan, Zola Skweyiya and Penuell Maduna sat down straight afterwards to redraft the Foundations of Government. This revised version left twelve paragraphs of the Constitution Committee's memorandum of 20 September intact and made alterations to six, one of which was purely a rearrangement of the subsections. The changes in the other five are recorded below.

DRAFT FOUR: Foundations of Government in a Democratic South Africa, revised by a subcommittee of the NEC and the Constitution Committee after their joint meeting on 2 October 1986[8]

Original clauses	New and revised clauses (changes in italics)
Sovereignty shall belong to the people as a whole and shall be exercised through one central legislature, administrature and executive;	Sovereignty shall belong to the people as a whole and shall be exercised through one central legislature, administrature and executive;
	Provision will be made for the regional and local delegation of the powers of the central authority to smaller administrative units for purposes of more efficient and effective administration;

Hereditary forms of political power shall be abolished and the chiefs encouraged to participate in normal democratic life;

The institution of hereditary rulers and chiefs shall be transformed to serve the interests of the people as a whole in conformity with the democratic principles embodied in the constitution;

The state and all social institutions shall be under a duty to eradicate apartheid in all its forms, as well as to take measures to overcome its consequences;

The state and all institutions shall be under a duty to eradicate apartheid in all its forms, as well as to take measures to overcome its consequences;

The advocacy or practice of racism, fascism, Nazism, tribalism or regionalism shall be outlawed; Subject to the above, freedom of association and expression shall be guaranteed by the adoption of a multi-party system and an open press;

The advocacy or practice of racism, fascism, Nazism, tribalism or regionalism shall be outlawed; Subject to the *[previous two clauses] (i) and (j)* above, freedom of association and expression shall be guaranteed by the adoption of a multi-party system and an open press;

Religious freedom shall receive special constitutional guarantee;

Also subject to clauses *(i) and (j)* above, *freedom of religion, worship and conscience shall be given* special constitutional guarantee *by the state;*

The state and all social institutions shall take active steps to redress as speedily as possible the economic and social inequalities produced by apartheid. In particular the unjust division of the land shall be corrected;

The state and all social institutions shall take active steps to redress as speedily as possible the economic and social inequalities produced by apartheid. In particular the unjust *dispossession of the African people of their land shall be corrected through the abolition of all legislation restricting land ownership and use on a racial basis and all other apartheid measures designed to deprive the people of their land and live-stock. The victims of forced removals carried out by the apartheid regime shall be given proper redress by the state. In particular they shall be given the right to return to their land or ancestral homes wherever possible.*

By the end of 1986, Zola Skweyiya was effectively driving the administrative and advocacy functions of the Constitution Committee. Now that the NEC had endorsed the objectives and principles of the Foundations document, the Committee's aim was to have it made official and published as soon as possible. Skweyiya and the other members hoped that Oliver Tambo's 8 January statement for 1987 would launch the constitutional debate. It would be an ideal occasion: the seventy-fifth anniversary of the oldest liberation movement on the African continent.[9]

In preparation, the Constitution Committee drew up a document titled 'Statement of Intent by the African National Congress (SA): A Proposed Constitution for a Liberated South Africa'. Its objective was to expand on the propositions in the Foundations. The idea was that these two documents, together with extracts from the 8 January speech, would be signed off by the NEC, published and presented for discussion. This would launch and publicise the ANC's plans regarding a future constitution for a free South Africa. The Committee proposed 'to present this document to our cadres for discussion, to our people at home and also [to] all our friends for deliberation and further suggestions'.[10]

Skweyiya and Jobodwana had already suggested to the leadership that *Sechaba* start publishing a regular column called 'Constitutional Forum' that would make public the discussion pieces drawn up by the various members of the Constitution Committee. Editor Francis Meli was amenable, so all that was needed was the approval of HQ.[11]

Finally, the Committee asked the president and the NEC to give the go-ahead for the major internal seminar for members of the ANC in exile that had been agreed to at the October 1986 meeting. They wanted this seminar to take place as early as March 1987, in preparation for a bigger constitutional seminar for a wider constituency outside the ANC, which would be held later that year.[12]

16

Oliver Tambo Meets Mikhail Gorbachev

WITHIN A MONTH of the NEC's meeting with the Constitution Committee, Oliver Tambo flew to Moscow to meet with Soviet leader Mikhail Gorbachev. Accompanying him were SACP leaders Joe Slovo and Chris Hani, as well as his head of office and close aide, Thabo Mbeki, who was also a member of the SACP Central Committee. When Tambo met Gorbachev in the Kremlin on 4 November 1986, however, only Mbeki was with him.[1] Gorbachev welcomed them warmly, saying that he had received approaches from the Pretoria regime to engage in talks, but he had recommitted the Soviet Union to supporting the ANC. It was agreed that an ANC mission with full diplomatic status would be set up in Moscow. Simon Makana, who was part of the trio on the NWC constitutional subcommittee, was made chief representative and given full ambassadorial status. This gave him diplomatic immunity, the right to a radio channel for secure communications, an official car, and permission to fly the ANC flag at the Moscow mission.[2]

At the October 1986 NEC meeting, a message had come through to the Constitution Committee that the Soviets were eager to have South African academic scholars weigh in on the unfolding situation in the country. Jack Simons had already gone to Moscow in June to meet with prominent Soviet academics involved in southern African studies, taking formal leave from the Committee to do so. He was disappointed by the discussions that followed. The Soviet scholars saw the struggle in South Africa as one that was either for civil rights or a campaign for socialism and the ending of capitalism. They did not think the conditions were ripe to encourage a struggle for socialism, which meant that, in their view, the campaign was one for civil rights. What they didn't understand was the nature of what, in ANC circles, was called the National Democratic Revolution. This was for far more than civil rights, or things such as the right to eat at lunch counters or attend cinemas. The prime goal was to destroy the monopoly that whites had on the franchise and the instruments of power, together with legally reserved ownership of nearly 90 per cent of the land. It was to restore land to the dispossessed. It was to restore dignity, language rights and cultural rights. It was to reconstruct the whole nature of the country, to decolonise it in a profound sense. And it was not only Soviet academics who couldn't understand this point. Some in the OAU also took the simple position that, since South Africa was already an independent country, the struggle was one for civil rights. Simons agreed with one suggestion from the Soviet Union comrades, though: in addition to including the Freedom Charter in a future constitution, there should be clauses taken from various UN conventions on human rights.[3]

Simons' trip was followed up by a similar visit by Albie Sachs, together with Alpheus Manghezi and Rob Davies of the Centre for African Studies at Eduardo Mondlane University in Maputo. They were warmly received by Apollon Davidson and Irina Filatova at the Lomonosov Moscow State University. Davidson was the doyen of Africanist scholars in the Soviet Union and a long-time friend of the ANC. Davies records that they were also invited to visit Kazakhstan, one of the Asian republics of the Soviet Union, where the first explicitly ethnic protests against Soviet rule had recently occurred. This would enable them to experience for themselves how 'the national question' was being dealt with in a community, Asian in appearance, with a distinctive language, culture and historical background.[4] They also asked to meet with South African students studying at the Patrice Lumumba University in Moscow. Named after the murdered fighter for Congolese independence and the country's first prime minister, the university catered to students from 'Third World' countries.

The team flew to Alma-Ata, the capital of the Socialist Republic of Kazakhstan. Davies notes that they were 'told frankly that ethnic Kazakhs were underrepresented in all areas of economic and social life', and that 'racial and ethnic identity mattered, and that we needed to find a model that would accommodate the demands of ethnic minorities'.[5] Sachs recalls:

Alma Ata was something of a surprise and a disappointment. There was very little in the architecture or physical layout that looked distinctively Asian. What was wonderful was seeing a performance of Swan Lake given by people of the most diverse appearance. Coming from apartheid South Africa, it was uplifting for us to see an Asian-looking woman dancing the role of the white swan. And the ensemble on the stage and diversity of extremely enthusiastic audience was captivating. But outside of the concert hall, nothing seemed to be working. Shops were closed on week days. It was like a city asleep.[6]

The ANC students at Lumumba University, on the other hand, were very lively. After saying how much they appreciated the opportunity to study, they asked tentatively if it was permissible for them to speak about things that did not seem correct. The visiting comrades said they certainly should. 'They then told us that, very sadly, they encountered racism from some of the lecturers. In addition, some of the lecturers demanded bribes to enable them to pass. We thanked them for telling us the truth and encouraged them to use ANC channels to pass on this information.' Was this the kind of thing, Sachs and his colleagues wondered, that Gorbachev and perestroika were designed to deal with? And, more generally, what implications would perestroika have for their struggle and a future constitutional order in South Africa?[7]

The new legal and constitutional department under Skweyiya soon became an active part of the ANC's impressive international operational front, its members going in and out of the Frontline States – Botswana, Zimbabwe, Mozambique, Swaziland and Lesotho – and travelling further abroad on a regular basis. For example, in August 1996 Skweyiya, Maduna and Asmal were in Europe working on international solidarity, arranging meetings and a major conference with internal lawyer networks, and seeking funds for legal defence cases at home, working in tandem with the IDAF in London, the Swiss-based World University Service and the Swedish International Development Agency (SIDA).[8] In November, Sachs visited Columbia University in New York en route to Nicaragua to study the constitutional lessons from the overthrow of the vicious forty-six-year Somoza dictatorship by the Sandinistas in 1979, which had become a poster child for the anti-imperialist struggles of the seventies and eighties. Returning via Portugal, which also had a recent experience of setting up a post-fascist democracy, he brought back some important lessons from Nicaragua for the Constitution Committee's fourth plenary meeting in early January 1987. The struggles of the Sandinistas and various other groups involved in the armed resistance were driven by different political perspectives, but they agreed on 'about five basic principles that they could all make into a common platform', thus paving the way for victory. These tactics corresponded significantly with ANC broad-front strategies and bolstered the idea of the guidelines laid down in the Foundations of Government document recently approved by the NEC.[9]

While in New York, Sachs organised for representatives of the DLCA to be invited to Columbia as well and received the promise of a photocopier, which – the department reported proudly – it would be happy to share with the secretary-general and others at the Alpha offices.[10]

At the same meeting that took Sachs's report, the committee approved a visit to the unitary GDR and federal Czechoslovakia for Pekane, Jobodwana and Maduna so that they could familiarise themselves with Eastern European one-party state constitutional models and the transitional arrangements that brought them into being after World War II. Beforehand, the 'amount of information to be released' was carefully discussed and discussion topics were sent to the respective embassies and the chief reps in Berlin and Prague.[11] Maduna's twenty-two-page report on the trip was comprehensive but somewhat bland and descriptive, lacking in new insights the three comrades had gained. The main issues dealt with were land and agrarian reform, the party and state relationship, nationalisation, and 'socialist management', with visits to 'party schools' and projects included. One of the main contacts for the ANC trio was with 'Cde Prof' Pezolt, head of the Department of State Law and Government in the Central Committee of the GDR's Socialist Unity Party of Germany (SED), who had been in Angola from 1977 to 1980 as a 'consultant on State Power and the Party'. Pezolt, who still visited Angola annually for four to six weeks, 'undertook to do some assignments for the DLCA and the [Constitution Committee]'. Maduna explained that communication to him and others in the GDR should be 'sent to and through the Central Committee of the SED'.[12]

Meanwhile the Constitution Committee members were kept busy checking constitutions from other countries and arranging further study visits. With Tambo's permission, Maduna was delegated to take up an invitation from Professor Jack Greenberg for the ANC to participate in a six-week seminar on South Africa and its constitutional development at Columbia University.[13] It involved solid spells in the university library and him challenging a pro-SA government speaker from the Heritage Foundation. He noted that the 'US society' was subjected to a 'barrage of anti-ANC and anti-communist propaganda'. Maduna also met Harvard professor Robert Seidman, who helped SWAPO with the drafting of a Namibian constitution.[14] Kader Asmal, too, found himself on sabbatical in New York in the first half of the year.[15]

In addition, the Constitution Committee members participated in several other roadshows and conferences. In 1987 there were two trips to Geneva for gatherings of UN commissions on human rights and for the 'prevention of discrimination and the protection of minorities', one to Washington for a symposium on 'children in detention', and related meetings on 'uprooted people' and refugees in Lusaka and Harare in June.[16] There was also a steady stream of approaches from international civil society and university-based groups from 1986 onwards. Some came from suspected right-wing initiatives linked to the South African establishment, such as the Institute for Social Inventions in London and the Foundation for International Conciliation in Geneva. These were rebuffed.[17]

The volume of this Constitution Committee and DLCA work necessitated it meeting with Johnny Makatini, the ANC's shadow minister of foreign affairs from the international department, to clarify mutual protocols. It was agreed that 'the two departments are not meant to be parallel machineries in the international work of the movement', and the DLCA gave the assurance that 'it was not competition but co-operation which would enhance the work of the movement'.[18]

17

The Chief Checks In and
Skweyiya Presses Ahead

FINALLY, AFTER A full year had passed, the Constitution Committee was able to have a meeting with their founder, Oliver Tambo. It took place in Lusaka on 6 January 1987, at the tail end of the Committee's fourth plenary gathering.

The Chief attended the meeting alone. At the outset, he told them that the ANC was under pressure to produce clear constitutional proposals for the future. He was due to deliver his 8 January speech two days hence, and later in the month he was scheduled to meet US secretary of state George Shultz in the ANC's first high-level contacts with the US government.[1] 'We should be prepared for any eventuality,' he said. 'In all discussions and debates, the ANC should occupy a high ground. The NEC shall naturally rely on the Constitution Committee to achieve [t]his position.'[2]

When the Committee expressed the hope that his 8 January speech would include launching the constitutional debate, the president merely stated that his speech was ready but embargoed.

The Committee's primary purpose in this meeting was to explain to the president their new document – the 'Statement of Intent by the African National Congress (SA): A Proposed Constitution for a Liberated South Africa' – which it had drawn up following the fruitful discussions about the Foundations of Government at the joint meeting with the NEC three months earlier.[3] The Committee wanted the Statement of Intent to serve as an introduction to the Foundations document and proposed that the two documents be circulated simultaneously to start public discussion. For this they needed the president and NEC's buy-in.

Skweyiya took the meeting through the eleven sections of the six-page Statement. The first declared that 'The time has come' – the strength of the struggle and crisis of apartheid had reached a stage where it was now time to initiate discussions about the foundations of a future government in liberated and democratic South Africa following the 'transfer of power from the minority racist regime to the democratic forces of the people'. While a democratically elected constituent assembly would determine the final provisions of the Constitution, 'the embryo of the new constitution is already being shaped in the struggle against the old', and it was the 'Right and Duty' of the ANC to involve the 'people at large' in a 'nationwide consultation' where they could articulate the basic objectives, principles and rules they wished to live under. This second point was that the constitution had to come from the people themselves. Thirdly, the 'Freedom Charter' had been the product of the kind of participation now required and would be central in plotting the way forward, but it needed to be enriched and complemented.

Then followed specific goals in sections four to eight. The headings reiterated the message:

- 'Abolish apartheid' and its different manifestations and structures;
- Implement the principles of 'No discrimination' irrespective of 'race, colour, sex or ethnic origin';
- Institute 'Affirmative action', including the restoration of land rights to victims of land removals;
- Legalise 'Votes for all; and
- Provide 'Fundamental rights' for all South Africans, including the freedom to live, move and work where they wanted, together with freedom of conscience and the principle of the separation of church and state – so that they could be 'secure in their houses, choose their friends and marriage partners, establish families, [and] enjoy leisure, sport, cultural activities without interference'.

In terms of 'The economic order' (section 9), the ANC believed in a mixed economy for the purpose of doing away with racial discrimination and to bring about the rapid elimination of the gap between rich and poor, black and white. Section 10 on 'International relations' stated that South Africa should be a country whose foreign policy fulfilled the aims of the charters of the UN, the OAU and the Non-Aligned Movement, and which – given the background of apartheid destabilisation – promotes the harmonious development of southern Africa and the entire African continent. Finally, the Committee suggested that the ANC end the Statement of Intent in section 11 by explaining that while the Foundations of Government expressed in point form the organisation's fundamental principles and objectives, it was not final and therefore needed to be 'enriched' by suggestions, criticisms, comments and proposals by ANC members and 'anti-apartheid forces within and beyond South Africa'. The Constitution Committee was pressing the NEC to let the debate begin.[4]

A second part of the 6 January meeting related to proposals for a Bill of Rights made by the KwaZulu-Natal Indaba in its scenario planning. The Indaba had been organised on the initiative of the Buthelezi Commission, named after its initiator, Chief Mangosuthu Buthelezi, with whom Tambo had been in contact from time to time. Buthelezi had once been an ANC member and the organisation had hoped he would grow his organisation, Inkatha, into a body supporting the liberation struggle. This would have been in the manner of the Comrade King, Sabata Dalindyebo in the Transkei, and more recently of Bantustan leaders such as Enos Mabuza of KaNgwane, who had started to speak to the ANC. But the Committee members were convinced that Buthelezi was a Bantustan leader who was trying to set himself up as a centre-right political alternative to the ANC and doing so with the help of big business in South Africa and conservative leaders such as Thatcher, Reagan and Kohl internationally. The Indaba's thirty-five participating organisations, which included commercial bodies and the official white opposition, the Progressive Federal Party (PFP), had met regularly in 1986. The UDF and COSATU, both ANC-aligned, were among nine bodies that rejected an invitation to participate.[5]

Tambo and the Committee were at one that the Indaba's proposed Bill of Rights was fundamentally flawed. It did not repudiate the apartheid system but entrenched fundamental aspects of it, including ethnic local structures, and left racist property relations undisturbed. Kader Asmal pointed out that what the Indaba's proposed Bill of Rights did was 'privatise apartheid'.[6] The state would no longer enforce apartheid through racist statutes, but the constitution would entrench spatial apartheid by granting forms of self-government to local communities living in racial group areas. In addition, an entrenched principle of freedom of association would allow whites to continue to reserve for themselves owner-ship of the well-appointed white suburbs and control of the whites-only schools. Furthermore, there would be strong entrenchment of existing property rights, in terms of which more than 80 per cent of the land was by law reserved for whites only.

Tambo and the Committee felt strongly that the Indaba proposals should 'not be made a centre of debate in international fora', as the United States and 'other imperialist agents' wanted, thereby giving Buthelezi 'third force' status. In any case, the democratic forces at home had rejected and laid the Indaba's Bill of Rights to rest.[7]

Two days after meeting with the Constitution Committee, Tambo gave his 8 January statement and designated 1987 as the 'Year of Advance to People's Power'. Seated by his side at the event in Lusaka were President Kenneth Kaunda, Prime Minister Kebby Musokotwane of Zambia, SWAPO leader Hage Geingob, and representatives of the OAU and the Palestine Liberation Organization. Tambo said that, on this seventy-fifth anniversary of the ANC, the main issue facing South Africans and the international community was 'how soon and at what cost we

shall succeed to end the apartheid system and rebuild South Africa as a democratic country'. The issue was now the transfer of power. The future lay with the
mass democratic movement and the people. Referring to constitutional matters,
Tambo declared:

> As we mark the seventy-fifth anniversary of our movement, we reiterate our
> commitment to seize any opportunity that may arise, to participate in a nego-
> tiated resolution of the conflict in our country. This we would do in the interests
> of the masses of our people and those of Southern Africa as a whole, with the
> specific aim of creating a democratic, non-racial and united South Africa.
>
> Let those in our country who, in the face of our mounting offensive, have
> started talking about negotiations, commit themselves publicly to this perspec-
> tive. In addition, and of decisive importance, they must demonstrate by practical
> deeds their commitment to this objective as well as their acceptance of the rapid
> and irreversible process leading to the emergence of such a South African society.[8]

Tambo further stressed the need for internal and international unity against
apartheid and all its structures, including the Bantustans. He said that, going back
to 1912, the ANC saw itself as a parliament of the people rather than a party representing one political or ideological school of thought. While underlining that
the masses of black workers, peasants, youth and students, women, professionals
– the entire oppressed people – constituted the motive force that had to engage
the enemy in a united and uninterrupted offensive, Tambo also called on white
South Africans to join the move towards democracy.

Mac Maharaj and Pallo Jordan state in their book *Breakthrough* that, alongside the constitutional principles being developed in the Foundations document,
Tambo's 8 January address was a key milestone on the road to negotiations.[9]
Tambo said the ANC would 'seize any opportunity that may arise, to participate
in a negotiated resolution of the conflict in our country'. But those saying they
were in favour of this needed to match words with action and ensure an irreversible process to full democracy was set in motion. Though not mentioning the
Foundations document, Tambo put unity, individual freedoms and multiparty
democracy – as envisaged in the drafts discussed by the NEC and Constitution
Committee in October – at the centre of the future vision for South Africa.

> We must unite all these forces, both black and white, around the democratic
> perspectives for which so many people have already laid down their lives. Once
> more we reaffirm that in the new South Africa, the people – all the people –
> shall govern.

He stressed that 'the revolution will guarantee the individual and equal rights of all' regarding a wide range of freedoms – including 'speech, assembly, association, language, religion, the press, the inviolability of family life and freedom from arbitrary arrest and detention without trial' – and concluded that 'the victorious revolution demands and must ensure thorough-going democratic practice'.[10]

Sachs recalls the excitement of the Committee members present at the delivery of the 8 January statement and at the press conference afterwards. They weren't used to the idea of a revolutionary movement having a press conference. Though disappointed that Tambo didn't say anything about circulating the Committee's documents, it was the first time he had attended a press briefing and it was refreshing to see the deft way in which he dealt with questions from the media. According to Maharaj and Jordan, 'The ANC was taking occupation of specific strategic sites in the terrain: the battle for positions had begun on a battlefield named "negotiations".'[11]

The Constitution Committee's goal now was to move forward with the constitutional seminars. At the end of January, Skweyiya sent Tambo a project proposal for two seminars. The first would be an In-House Seminar in Lusaka for ANC members. The second would be a bigger Constitutional Seminar in Zambia or Zimbabwe and involve delegations from home and international friends of the ANC. He stated that the balance of forces had never been better for the ANC. The liberation struggle had assumed dimensions unheard of before, and because of the sustained national revolt and the growth of People's Power, 'the long-cherished goal of replacing the obnoxious apartheid system with a democratic and humane system of government is no more a faraway dream … Far-sighted people and influential groups are beginning to look to the future'. Specialists, apartheid think tanks, Western governments, NGOs and universities had all been hard at work on different constitutional proposals and models; it was time for the ANC to act.[12] Skweyiya contended that it behoved the ANC

> as the leading force, and organiser of the struggle against apartheid and as the legitimate representative and champion of the oppressed to seize the initiative in this constitutional debate and [move ahead] with the following aims:
> (i)   Focusing the thinking of our people on a future constitutional model for a post-apartheid South Africa.
> (ii) Involving them in the constitutional debate with an aim of increasing and sharpening their political consciousness for the final thrust against apartheid and increasing their resolve to free themselves from apartheid colonialism.

(iii) Galvanising the present offensive against apartheid inside South Africa.

(iv) Further isolate the racist regime both internally and internationally.

(v) Deepen and strengthen international solidarity with the struggle against apartheid at the crucial phase of South African history.[13]

The goals of the two seminars would be to achieve a consensus on constitutional proposals and the eventual draft of a constitution for a future democratic South Africa. The intention was to bring South Africans of all walks of life (lawyers, social workers, factory workers, etc.) together for the purpose of discussing constitutional options acceptable to all.[14]

Included in his letter was a request for a budget of US$117 469 for the In-House Seminar. Among other things, this sum was needed to ensure the participation of 115 ANC representatives in thirty countries, together with a core of sixty-five people from the Lusaka HQ. Besides a small budget for general expenses, the costs were to go towards return flights from Accra, Addis Ababa, Algiers, Antananarivo, Cairo, Dakar, Dar es Salaam, Gaborone, Lagos, Luanda, Manzini, Maseru, Maputo, Washington, Stockholm, London, Bonn, Moscow, Berlin, Havana, Montreal, Copenhagen, Oslo, Rome, Budapest, Sofia, Bucharest, Amsterdam, Brussels and Helsinki.[15]

Skweyiya was aware that during a decade when the ANC's foreign missions grew from twenty to more than forty,[16] these participants would do more than just offer ideas on constitutionalism from around the world. They would also see to it that the ANC's constitutional proposals were communicated both within the organisation and across the globe.

In sum, by late January 1987, Tambo and the NEC had received an updated Foundations of Government document accompanied by the new Statement of Intent and the concrete proposals for two seminars. In the meantime, since 1985, the ANC had become increasingly busy on another front – receiving 'safaris' from South Africa.

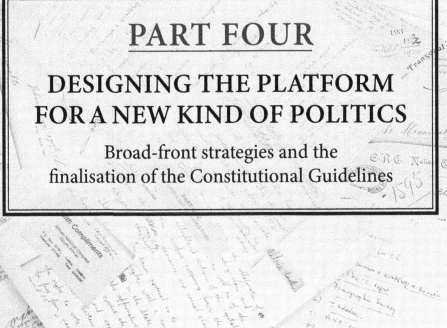

PART FOUR

DESIGNING THE PLATFORM
FOR A NEW KIND OF POLITICS

Broad-front strategies and the
finalisation of the Constitutional Guidelines

PART FOUR

DESIGNING THE PLATFORM
FOR A NEW KIND OF POLITICS

18

'How Do You Speak to an Archbishop?'

THE WORD SAFARI typically refers to a trip to a natural wildlife reserve in Africa. In the mid-1980s it adopted an additional meaning: a visit, open or clandestine, to meet with the ANC in Lusaka.

The ANC's constitution-making process was one of two interlinked strategic initiatives launched post-Kabwe. The other was a diplomatic offensive to build a platform for a political settlement and a triumphant return home. The ANC gave special attention to building a broad political front consisting of its existing base and the UDF-aligned democratic movement and other sympathetic organisations of the oppressed inside the country. It started reaching out, too, to traditionally hostile constituencies at home and in Western countries that had propped up the regime.

The leading liberation organisation had been typified by the Botha government and its apartheid-supporting allies as a violent, communist-inspired 'terrorist' proxy of the Soviet Union intent on upending Western values – even Western 'civilisation' – in South Africa. This was typical of the 'total onslaught' language of the time, grounded in colonial mentalities and decades of Cold War competition.

Reflecting well the misjudgements made by the regime and its allies, Britain's hard-line Margaret Thatcher asserted that anyone who thought the 'communist terrorist' ANC would get into power was living in 'cloud cuckoo land'.

However, as resistance against apartheid peaked from 1983 to 1985, and after P.W. Botha failed dismally to cross the Rubicon as promised, the prospects for change became tangible. Democratically minded South Africans started travelling beyond the borders to meet with the ANC, facing the severe penalties for communicating with the illegal organisation in their own country, or being caught reading or quoting its banned literature. From late 1985 to 1989 some two hundred such taboo-breaking encounters took place in Harare, Lusaka and other cities in the world, and the word 'safari' enjoyed new currency as the term for these risky trips. They weakened both the regime-imposed isolation of the ANC and the legitimacy of the repressive apartheid order, and rapidly dissolved boundaries between 'inside' and 'outside'. The first group of political safari-goers could not have been more 'respectable'. On 14 September 1985, Gavin Relly and an entourage of businessmen and newspaper editors took a private jet to Zambia to test the waters of an ANC-led future in South Africa. The trip came in the aftermath of

P.W. Botha's Rubicon speech, which had led to a flight of capital and confidence from South Africa. Relly was head of the mighty Anglo American Corporation, by far the biggest company listed on the Johannesburg Stock Exchange. He had approached President Kaunda to facilitate a meeting with Tambo.[1] Tambo's team included Thabo Mbeki, Chris Hani, Mac Maharaj, Pallo Jordan and James Stuart. The encounter took place at a safari lodge. Tony Bloom, one of the visiting business leaders, was amused to note that the businessmen were all dressed in safari outfits to meet the ANC guerrillas, while the jacketed ANC delegates were dressed more for business.[2]

While the engagement with Relly's team had importance in itself, it also set a precedent for many meetings with struggle-based ANC sympathisers and allied organisations. Though not illegal, these organisations faced the prospect of being banned. Many of their activities were restricted by state-of-emergency proclamations. Their members endured constant harassment, intimidation, arrest, detention without trial, jail and assassination. They were in the front trenches of the struggle. Because of the nature of the media under apartheid, however, the visiting groups that attracted the most publicity in the South African press were the white businesspeople, students, journalists and academics. The ANC welcomed these white South Africans as pioneers – the 'New Voortrekkers'.[3]

COSATU and the UDF were key participants at safari meetings. Within weeks of COSATU's formation in Durban on 1 December 1985, its secretary-general, Jay Naidoo, had conferred with the ANC leadership in Harare and issued a joint statement that created widespread publicity. This was followed by a meeting between delegations from COSATU and heavyweight ANC and SACTU leaders a few months later. Tambo, MK leaders Joe Slovo and Chris Hani, trade unionists John Nkadimeng and Stephen Dlamini, and key PMC underground strategist Mac Maharaj were among the latter. The COSATU team included Cyril Ramaphosa, Sydney Mufamadi, Jay Naidoo, Chris Dlamini, Alec Erwin and John Gomomo. They represented a potent new force and a new generation of leadership inside the country. The parties issued a statement saying 'only the national liberation movement, headed by the ANC, and the entire democratic forces in the country, of which COSATU is an important and integral part' could provide 'lasting solutions' to the crisis in South Africa. The internal trade union movement's relationship with the ANC and UDF had deepened to the extent that COSATU adopted the Freedom Charter as a guiding document in 1987, openly aligning it with the other internal pro-ANC forces.[4]

In January 1986, UDF leaders had met with an ANC delegation led by Tambo in Stockholm. Tambo had been accompanied by secretary-general Alfred Nzo, treasurer-general Thomas Nkobi, Mac Maharaj and the diplomats Thabo Mbeki and Aziz Pahad. The UDF contingent had included Arnold Stofile, Valli Moosa, Cheryl Carolus, Sydney Mufamadi, Ismail Mohamed, Raymond Suttner and Hoffman Galeng from the Huhudi Civic Association. According to the UDF's history, the January trip to Stockholm marked a significant departure from previous engagements and involved for the first time substantial discussion on strategy and tactics between the two informal allies.[5]

From late 1985 into 1986, the gates opened. Delegations travelled to Harare and Lusaka from all over, and included members from the Soweto Parents' Crisis Committee (SPCC); the leader of the official opposition in Parliament; the top hierarchies of various churches; an entire Bantustan government; the National African Federated Chamber of Commerce (NAFCOC); various university leaders, including the vice-chancellors of UCT, the University of the Western Cape, the University of the North; and the white National Union of South African Students (NUSAS),[6] among other groupings.

Chief Minister Enos Mabuza from KaNgwane arrived with a large twenty-person delegation from the Inyandza National Movement. This included his whole cabinet. The visit sent out the signal that the ANC message for those working within the Bantustans and other arms of the system to join the broader struggle was being heard.[7]

Frederik Van Zyl Slabbert, leader of the Progressive Federal Party, the official white opposition, resigned from Parliament after his first visit to Lusaka, and then visited twice more in 1986, along with colleagues including Alex Boraine, Peter Gastrow and Dick Enthoven. After he and Boraine left Parliament, they formed the Institute for a Democratic Alternative in South Africa (IDASA) to promote dialogue between establishment and extra-parliamentary groupings.[8] Before year end, the ANC in Lusaka also hosted Jules Browde, convenor of the National Convention Movement, which aimed to unite 'moderate' anti-apartheid opinion, including Inkatha, later leading to the formation of the Democratic Party.

Also very important were the delegations of leaders from the Southern African Catholic Bishops' Conference (SACBC), the South African Council of Churches and the Lutheran Church led by Dean Tshenuwani Simon Farisani. The SACBC team was headed by Archbishop Denis Hurley, accompanied by Bishop Wilfrid Napier of Kokstad, Bishop Mansuet Biyase of Eshowe and Father Smangaliso Mkhatshwa, who had just emerged from a gruelling detention in the Ciskei Bantustan.[9] The SACBC agreed with the ANC on their 'common commitment to bring a speedy end to the evil system of apartheid and to transform South Africa into a united, democratic and non-racial country'. The leaders said that while the Catholic Church could not identify with the armed struggle, it 'understood the reasons why the ANC resorted to force'.[10] Dr Manas Buthelezi headed the SACC team, which included several heads of member churches, as well as prominent anti-apartheid clerics like Beyers Naudé, Wolfram Kistner and Charles Villa-Vicencio.[11] Again, the organisations expressed strong solidarity with each other.

NAFCOC came in May 1986 to talk business with the ANC. Its delegation was led by its president, Gabriel Mokgoko, and included the pioneering business leader Sam Motsuenyane. A second meeting took place in Europe shortly afterwards, followed by several other such engagements between the two organisations. Thabo Mbeki later explained how the need to win over the black middle class had been brought home at these safari meetings with NAFCOC. Initially they were hostile to the way the ANC had translated the nationalisation clauses in the Freedom Charter, but they left convinced that liberation would help them, via struggle-based affirmative action, to find a place alongside the all-embracing power of monopoly capital in the country.[12] Pallo Jordan's path-breaking 1985 paper had made the same point: that the interests of the black middle class lay with the liberation movement rather than with the 'New Face of Counter-Revolution'. He wrote a detailed paper specifically on the evolution of NAFCOC in 1987, showing that its growing voice and clout in 1980s debates could be attributed to the gains made through the popular working-class and student struggles from Soweto onwards.[13]

In 1987 the contacts between Lusaka and home escalated, with Desmond Tutu, newly appointed Archbishop of Cape Town, and many others joining the safaris.

The interaction was two-way. Although the delegations making the pilgrimage to Lusaka were coming out to get direction, they increasingly ended up providing both knowledge and counselling to the struggle luminaries in exile, who had often been cut off from home for many years.

Many of the groups had significant influence and constituencies at home. The SACC, a key moral and on-the-ground support arm of the struggle, would in 1988 declare that it was legitimate for Christians to take up arms against oppressive systems such as apartheid. The Soweto Parents' Crisis Committee sought the ANC's help in getting children back in school after a long school boycott inspired by the slogan 'No education without liberation'. The ANC office in Lusaka soon issued a statement pointing out that education was a crucial part of liberation. The issue of schooling was then taken further with the UDF, and the outcome was the formation in South Africa of the National Education Crisis Committee (NECC), which paid a visit to Lusaka in March 1986.

In addition, the ANC learnt from COSATU, the UDF and others about the realities of myriad mini negotiations that were constantly being undertaken on the ground. In factory-floor and strike negotiations, a new style of engagement was unfolding, as activists worked with lawyers to circumvent restrictions or win space, while marching and petitioning authorities.

When a nationwide state of emergency was declared in June 1986, resulting in extreme state repression, the UDF, COSATU, NECC, SACC and SACBC united under the Campaign for National United Action. The goal was to oppose the emergency publicly, to revive the momentum of national resistance, and to broaden the scope of resistance by forging a close working alliance with COSATU.[14] All five of these organisations had consulted formally with the ANC outside the country in 1986. Using the organising capacity of COSATU, they undertook the biggest general strike in South African history when 2.5 million workers refused to go to work at the time of the whites-only general election in 1987. Here was the making of the broad front the ANC desired.

The author of the UDF's commissioned history has noted that COSATU and the UDF, the churches and other internal mass democratic formations were 'actually the mechanism through which the ANC, in exile for thirty years, effected its successful return, adaptation and reintegration as South Africa's post-apartheid government'. Without them, the ANC and its politics in the 1990s would have been 'entirely different'.[15]

As old boundaries between inside and outside dissolved, another highly significant dimension of the cross-border contacts between the ANC in Lusaka and people back home was the development of the secret underground ANC network inside South Africa. By 1989, the number of full-time ANC organisers in the underground had reportedly grown to 1225.[16] These underground activists were in constant contact with the legal and semi-legal internal activists and organisations. They functioned under the direction of the ANC's PMC, which was responsible for coordinating internal activities. Key members of this council included Josiah Jele, Jacob Zuma and Mac Maharaj, who also participated in many of the meetings with the safari-goers.

Underground activists and the special-interest groups now making direct contact with the ANC also influenced the formation of new sectoral bodies intended to broaden the base of the struggle into every sphere of South African life. A host of new ANC-aligned organisations emerged from 1986 onwards to extend the struggle base. They included the United Women's Congress (UWCO), the Congress of Traditional Leaders of South Africa (CONTRALESA), the South African Youth Congress (SAYCO), the National Association of Democratic Lawyers (NADEL), the National Sports Congress (NSC) and the South African Musicians' Alliance (SAMA).[17] Underground operatives also encouraged the adoption of new policy positions and the launch of local campaigns, which were often backed up, where possible, with 'armed propaganda' or strategic MK attacks timed to coincide with local demands.[18] ANC underground activities were not only about armed struggle; they also acted as conduits for political work, including the growing debate about negotiations, constitutional principles and options for the future.

The safaris had a considerable impact on the work of the Constitution Committee. Its members and the DLCA were involved in many of the meetings. Underground follow-up contacts were a logical next step. Skweyiya discussed with the SACC its extensive programme for 'legal defence and social welfare of the victims of apartheid persecution', and he reported to Tambo that the churches were involved in resettling victims of forced removals on their properties and 'this seems to be quite an interesting experiment from which the movement might gain some experience'.[19] The forced-removals issue discussed here also cropped up in the interactions between the Constitution Committee and Jordan's NEC subcommittee over finalising the constitutional principles in the Foundations document. And before the In-House Seminar that the Committee had requested, Skweyiya was able to report that 'It has involved the PMC, SACTU, UDF and COSATU in constitutional discussions'.[20]

The meetings with the groupings from home were all emotive events, holding immense meaning for both the ANC and the people coming from inside the country. Zola Skweyiya recalled the newness of the experience for many:

> we were going to meet Archbishop Hurley and we didn't know, you know; how do you speak to an Archbishop? What should our line be? If you want to make a good speech about the revolution, we know exactly what to say. 'Comrades we must rise up and overthrow the tyranny of oppression, we must seize power.' But we can[not] speak like that to the Archbishop ... And OR said, first of all, you put on a suit ... any kind of a suit and a tie. And then he said, right at the beginning of the meeting, Oliver Tambo said, 'Archbishop it would be very wonderful if you could open this meeting with a prayer' ... That simple but honestly, deeply felt subtle thing ... just establish[ed] the tone.[21]

While these political safaris took place, Tambo and the ANC proceeded on a parallel track with new and long-standing international engagements. The objective was to build on and develop existing alliances with the Frontline States in southern Africa, the OAU, UN, Non-Aligned Movement, the Soviet bloc, Scandinavian social democracies, and Western civil society and NGOs. By 1986, Tambo was reaching out beyond the ANC's traditional solidarity support base to more conservative forces. These would eventually provide the direct link to the apartheid regime. In that year he thrice made contact in Britain with powerful captains of industry from there and South Africa. In April, he also sent an ANC delegation to New York at the invitation of Franklin Thomas of the Ford Foundation. The meeting was attended by Mbeki, Maharaj ('secretary of the political underground') and Jordan.[22] In addition, Mbeki had a confidential meeting on the sidelines with Professor Pieter de Lange, chairperson of the Afrikaner Broederbond and rector of the Rand Afrikaans University. De Lange was motivated to push for discussions within the Broederbond about a negotiated settlement.

Numbers drawn up by Professor Mike Savage indicate that these meetings in Zambia and elsewhere with groups from South Africa grew from nineteen known meetings in 1985, to twenty-seven in 1986, down to twenty-three in 1987, then up again to thirty-two in 1988 and thirty-nine in 1989, although he himself noted that these numbers were far from complete. The number of unreported and informal contacts, particularly with mass-movement sympathisers, was much higher than that. Well over a thousand South Africans participated in this process of engagement.[23] All returned to South Africa with direct information about the character of the ANC and its general political positions. They also increasingly took with them information about the ANC's vision for a future democratic South Africa. Crucially, as Maharaj had noted, the ANC was also receiving and being influenced by fresh intelligence from within the country. A solid platform for a new form of engagement politics was being built.

19

Encounters in Dakar

THE GROWING LINKAGES, meetings and increasingly subtle coordination of the strategic direction of the struggle across international boundaries, merging legal and illegal opposition to apartheid, went to a higher level in July 1987. A seventeen-person ANC delegation under Thabo Mbeki met with a group of sixty-one Afrikaner 'dissidents' in Dakar, Senegal, in a conference that generated massive publicity and blew out of the water the apartheid regime's attempts to cocoon internal constituencies from having any contact with the ANC 'terrorists'. Kader Asmal and Penuell Maduna of the Constitution Committee and Pallo Jordan of the NWC subcommittee were part of the action.

Barely two months before, the National Party had won its biggest ever election victory, with 74 per cent support from a white population that had bought into the 'total onslaught' fears of communist revolution. As a result, the Dakar safari – four days of talks held between 9 and 12 July 1987 – created a sensation in South Africa and attracted global media coverage.[1] International television stations carried the story and it made front-page news in the *New York Times* and *Washington Post*. The South African media devoted thousands of columns of text to it. The government-supporting *Beeld* dedicated ten front-page headline stories to Dakar in twenty-one days. Newspapers like *The Star*, *Die Burger* and *The Citizen* were not far behind. A media review of these four titles showed that over a three-week period they gave an average of 134 column-centimetres of copy to it per day, not including headlines and cartoons. The national discourse was dramatically shifted.[2] A massive MK bomb that wrecked the headquarters of the SADF in the centre of Johannesburg on 30 July 1987 raised the temperature of the debate.

Inaccurately quoting the classic Marxist texts, P.W. Botha called the sixty-one Afrikaner 'Dakarites' the 'useful idiots' about whom Lenin had spoken when referring to members of the ruling class who could be persuaded to do things that supported the revolution. The extreme right-wing Afrikaner Weerstandsbeweging (AWB) declared the visit to be treason and said it would be waiting for the participants when they arrived home. Botha wanted to have them all arrested on their return but was persuaded by his advisors not to do so.[3] The group included former parliamentary opposition leaders Frederik Van Zyl Slabbert and Alex Boraine, who were then heading the newly created IDASA; the poet Breyten Breytenbach, who had spent years in jail for his anti-apartheid activities; his colleague from the Afrikaans 'Sestigers' group of writers, André Brink; their literary scholar friend Ampie Coetzee; SACC secretary-general Beyers Naudé; former Springbok rugby captain Tommy Bedford; Braam Viljoen, the identical twin brother of SADF chief Constand Viljoen; and an array of opposition MPs, actors, writers, journalists, lawyers, businesspeople, student leaders and academics.

Several academic lawyers specialising in constitutional law also attended. They were Professors Lourens du Plessis (Potchefstroom University), Gerhard Erasmus (Stellenbosch University) and future Constitutional Court judge Johann van der Westhuizen (Pretoria University), who had planned to meet with the ANC in Lusaka earlier that year but was stopped from doing so by his university after the security police intervened.[4]

Significant attention was focused on the academic quartet of Professors André du Toit and Hermann Giliomee; the German–Canadian sociologist Heribert Adam; and Lawrence Schlemmer, one-time director of the Inkatha Institute. Du Toit and Giliomee – effectively pushed out of Stellenbosch University for their *oorbeligte* ('over-exposed') views and now at the University of Cape Town – made major presentations from the side of the IDASA delegates. Giliomee had co-authored various books with Schlemmer and Adam, and all three had been members of the KwaZulu-Natal Indaba since the early 1980s, promoting Buthelezi as the moderate, pro-free-market, 'group rights', 'third way' alternative for South Africa.[5] Besides the Indaba, these scholars were well connected to a circle of influential liberal scholars, institutions and discussion groups, including the monthly Synthesis discussion group organised by mining executive Clive Menell; Professor David Welsh, who was head of UCT's Political Science Department, close to parliamentary liberals; the English press; the circle-driving *Die Suid-Afrikaan* journal; and the well-resourced, Yale-based South African Research Program (SARP) in the USA, which attracted many South African academics.[6] Pallo Jordan now found himself face to face with some of the purportedly liberal and *verligte* think-tank members whom he had, in his 1985 paper, identified as the new face of the counter-revolution. Though liberal-minded and some perhaps even supporting the long-taboo one-person, one-vote scenario, they were uniformly anti-ANC and sought group solutions based on ethnicity, consociationalism, federalism, the KZN Indaba, etc., all of which would preserve historic patterns of privilege and inequality in South Africa. As late as May 1988, Colin Eglin, the 'liberal' leader of the official opposition, expressed his opposition to one person one vote in a unitary South Africa in conversation with Margaret Thatcher. These establishment reformists professed liberal ideological perspectives founded on the fundamental value of individual freedom but, ironically, it was the revolutionary 'communist'

ANC, through its guidelines in the Foundations document, rather than they, that had decided unambiguously to promote the individual freedom approach and argued strongly against entrenching group rights.[7]

Among the South Africa–based intellectuals were political scientists Willem van Vuuren, Jannie Gagiano, André du Pisani and Ian Liebenberg; journalists Max du Preez, Chris Louw and Riaan de Villiers; photojournalists Rashid Lombard and Jimi Matthews; and delegations from UWC and the Cape Peninsula Technical College (Pentech) headed by their respective rectors Professors Jakes Gerwel and Franklin Sonn. As Afrikaans-speakers from the community classified as 'coloured', both Gerwel and Sonn loved the language and supported IDASA and other bodies promoting progressive Afrikaans-language initiatives. Teachers' Union leader Randall van der Heever, theologian Prof Jaap du Rand and dozens of others completed the line-up.

The ANC delegation included five NEC members: Mac Maharaj, Aziz Pahad and *Sechaba* editor Francis Meli, in addition to Mbeki and Jordan. Women were under-represented on both sides, but culture chief Barbara Masekela and Lindiwe Mabuza, a poet who had headed the Scandinavian mission, made powerful interventions during the four days. Barbara Masekela was unmistakably feminist. She came from a family whose first languages were Afrikaans and isiNdebele, and held a master's degree in English from Rutgers University. She had lived in Ghana, Britain, Zambia and the US.[8] Determined to escape Bantu Education, she left home on an exit permit in 1963, memorably meeting Maya Angelou as a 'confused' twenty-two-year-old in Accra that year. Masekela became an influential voice in the ANC in the late 1980s, and was involved in the planning for the easing of sanctions in the soft areas of culture and sport (see Chapter 21) in order to strengthen the hand of progressive, internal, ANC-aligned groupings.[9]

Mabuza was cut from the same cloth. Raised in Newcastle in today's KwaZulu-Natal, she did her undergraduate studies at Roma College in Lesotho before receiving two master's degrees from Stanford and Minnesota universities in the US. She became editor of the ANC's *Voice of Women* and in 1978 co-edited an anthology of poetry by ANC women. Mentored by Tambo, she was given the task of setting up the ANC's important Scandinavian mission in Stockholm the following year. In 1986 she took up the responsibility of opening an ANC office in Washington, and at Dakar, she was a charismatic presence.[10]

Adding intellectual muscle to the senior figures and Constitution Committee members already mentioned were struggle theoretician Professor Harold Wolpe from the University of Essex and sociologist Professor Bernard Makhosezwe Magubane from the University of Connecticut, who had taught at the University of Zambia in the 1960s. Magubane set aside a room for Oliver Tambo in his family home in Lusaka, before taking up teaching appointments in the USA. Completing the line-up were the likes of Manala Manzini (head of the youth section), Essop Pahad (information), Steve Tshwete (MK, attached to the president's office) and the invaluable backroom team of Selwyn Goss and Tony Trew, who apparently wrote up the delegation's report.

Just as Jordan had identified the internal *verligte* and business think tanks as new faces of the counter-revolution, so Magubane (best known for his book *The Political Economy of Race and Class in South Africa*) had long been a critic of the influential liberal South Africanist scholars at the South African Research Program at Yale University, to which Du Toit, Giliomee, and Adam were closely linked. In his autobiography, he devotes a long chapter to critiquing SARP and in particular Leonard Thompson, Jeffrey Butler and Heribert Adam as prime examples of scholars who 'largely through their control of institutional and foundation resources, passed as filters of African views and attitudes', while promoting what amounted to neo-apartheid solutions.[11]

Though unseen in the overall political drama of Dakar, this intellectual line-up of writers, artists and academics, and of the ANC constitutional planning team members versus the KZN Indaba and *verligte* and liberal think-tank academics, was an important subtext to the gathering in Senegal, giving a sense of how well-grounded the ideas articulated there were.

The conference was opened by Senegalese president Abdou Diouf and jointly chaired by the suave pair of Mbeki and Van Zyl Slabbert. Du Toit kicked off the debate on the first day with a paper on 'Strategies for Change', in which he expressed his personal opposition to the armed struggle and asked if it was not now time for the ANC to prioritise political approaches over militant ones. Giliomee was next from the IDASA side with an input on the mirror nature of competing African and Afrikaner nationalisms and the need, therefore, for power-sharing and a group-based accommodation between them. The implications of this approach were that the new constitutional arrangement in South Africa should be based on notions of power-sharing between leaders of the ethnically segmented groups, who would have certain veto powers. In reply, Mbeki, Maharaj and Jordan outlined the ANC's perspective on its struggle and a future constitutional vision in ways that mesmerised the South Africans from home.[12] Mbeki introduced himself by declaring, 'I am an Afrikaner.' He unambiguously underlined that the armed struggle was a non-negotiable part of the ANC's four-pronged political struggle, but also made a surprising statement, to an anxious group of Afrikaners after a tense first day, that 'the political process would be unlocked by the mere fact of the release of Mandela'.[13]

Jordan followed with an elaboration of the ANC's political guidelines for the future, including the importance it attached to non-racialism, multiparty democracy and an entrenched Bill of Rights. It was not against whites, and the organisation had underlined this point throughout its long history. When he referenced his 1985 paper and echoed one of the guidelines in the still-unreleased Foundations document of May 1987 – that the ANC would show a 'liberatory intolerance' to expressions of 'racism and fascism' in a democratic South Africa – there was a buzz. He made it clear that parties based on race would not be allowed. Jordan's comrades later rebuked him for being 'unnecessarily provocative'. In the ANC's 'Notes on the Dakar Conference', the rapporteurs noted that the same point could have been made differently.[14] Was it healthy self-criticism on the part of the delegation or perhaps also partly a clash between the 'think tank' lawyers and intellectuals on one side, and Mbeki and the diplomats running the 'talks' arm of the Tambo initiatives on the other?

At Dakar the ANC made probably its clearest statement yet on negotiations. In the joint conference communiqué on 12 July 1987, the ANC's seventeen-person delegation put its signature to a declaration that both parties had 'unanimously expressed a preference for a negotiated resolution of the South African question'. Thus, negotiations were no longer framed as an unlikely but possible option but were now 'the preference' for the ANC, according to the so-called Dakar Declaration.[15]

The ANC report of the conference observed that the Afrikaners were impressed by 'the freedom with which our delegates participated, with evident lack of regimentation but in total consistency'.[16] The ANC's position, well-honed in the two years since Kabwe, was that under no circumstances would it be co-opted into a regime-driven process of negotiation and change. Instead, it drew a clear line: negotiations could happen only if they accelerated the journey to liberation. In other words, there should be national self-determination through a universal franchise for the dispossessed and disenfranchised majority. The end point would be a united, non-racial democratic South Africa. The armed struggle remained an essential part of the broader political struggle, but that did not exclude negotiations. The organisation rejected anything to do with group rights. The basis of citizenship would be broad-ranging individual freedoms for every citizen, regardless of colour, creed or other differences, protected by law through a Bill of Rights and nurtured through multi-party democracy. The ANC did not expect the Afrikaner delegates to pick up AK-47s or take instructions from the organisation, but they needed to be clear about where they situated themselves.[17] The Dakar Declaration ended on the affirmative note that further contacts were necessary and these should 'involve more and more sections of the South African people in order to dispel misunderstanding and fear, and to reinforce the broad democratic movement'.[18]

The Dakar conference was a public relations coup for the ANC. It was legiti-mised as the most important actor in the political process next to the government. More than that, delegates went home singing the praises of its sophisticated leadership. Professor Jakes Gerwel of UWC commented on their 'honesty' and 'anguishing questions'. He left with the impression that the delegation from home did not have sufficient historical understanding or basic knowledge of the history of a 'broader South Africa'.[19] Decorated author André Brink summed it up as fol-lows: 'The thorough knowledge of history (both world history and South African history) among members of the ANC stood in alarming contrast with the lack of true historical insight among most of the "internal" group members.'[20] This was to be a recurring observation from ANC ranks in the next few years of interactions with people from the white establishment. In contrast, Hermann Giliomee, one of the few centre-right participants who remained unmoved, later summed up Dakar as an out-and-out propaganda victory for the ANC.[21]

Reflecting on Van Zyl Slabbert's motivations, close colleague Peter Gastrow said he had two main goals in organising Dakar with Mbeki: to 'white ant' P.W. Botha by selecting Afrikaners from 'apex institutions' to undermine apartheid and govern-ment policy, and to help create a climate for negotiations.[22] The two sides would have been equally pleased with the outcome. Steve Tshwete said the ANC had taken Dakar very seriously: 'We believe it is going to set new initiatives in motion in resolving the [national political] issue.'[23] A *Business Day* editorial observed that 'The people of this country stand at the beginning of a long, inevitably tedious process known loosely in diplomatic usage as "talks about talks". Afterwards come talks about the shape of the table and, finally ... the talks.' Dakar was 'a significant move in the process', the newspaper concluded.[24]

The ANC archives and the meeting notes, drawn up by Selwyn Goss and Tony Trew, provide insights into the ANC's careful preparation for the encounter. Its pre-conference planning was done via Pallo Jordan in Lusaka and Aziz Pahad in London. Jordan insisted that the initial agenda be changed so that both sides com-pleted their presentations before discussion followed. He said, 'We do not see it as fruitful that we are responding to their intervention.'[25] Upon arrival in Dakar, the delegation sat for a two-day pre-conference strategy session. Another change to the agenda followed: the ANC brought their key discussion topics (strategies for change) forward. Rapporteurs were appointed for each session. Every evening, after hours of discussion, the ANC delegates would retreat discreetly for an evalu-ation of the day, then reconnect and mingle with their guests from home. The socialising and convivial side talks would continue into the early hours of the morning.

Criticism and self-criticism were the order of the day, as when Pallo Jordan, citing Constitution Committee positions, was taken to task for speaking about the 'liberatory intolerance'. Maduna was also rapped over the knuckles for not letting Johann van der Westhuizen 'get a word in sideways' in a discussion on the Bill of Rights. Maduna agreed that he should have listened more rather than going on the offensive, and the situation was rectified by both him and Asmal engaging with the professor from Pretoria.[26]

After Dakar, the safari continued with most of the ANC and Afrikaner delegations jointly visiting two other West African countries: Burkina Faso and Ghana. Thousands of cheering Burkinabé lined the streets in Ouagadougou, chanting 'apartheid abas!' or 'down with apartheid', to welcome the delegations. President Thomas Sankara and vice-president Blaise Compaoré (who was involved in Sankara's assassination just a few months later) personally entertained the visitors. In Ghana, the delegation from home was told (probably not wholly accurately) that they were the first white South Africans to be officially allowed into the country since 1961. One of the highlights of that part of the visit was a robust public discussion held in Accra where Thabo Mbeki eloquently defended the concept of non-racialism and explained why the ANC was speaking to white South Africans.[27]

The contacts made at Dakar produced results that went well beyond the communiqué. On the post-conference tour to Burkina Faso, in the hotel pool in the blazing heat of Ouagadougou, IDASA delegates (among them Beyers Naudé and Max du Preez) discussed the need to launch an alternative Afrikaans-language newspaper. This resulted in *Vrye Weekblad*, vigorously edited by Du Preez, which provided a platform for progressive young Afrikaners and made its mark as an outstanding example of late-twentieth-century South African journalism. Among its accolades were the exposés of government death squads by a relatively unknown investigative journalist named Jacques Pauw, which shook the country.[28]

New, more universalist ideas were beginning to penetrate sections of the white population. The notion of Afrikanerdom was undergoing seismic changes. A younger generation of Afrikaners sought to break free from history and redefine themselves culturally as individuals with a broader South African identity and vision. To fans and followers of the Voëlvry ('free as a bird') music movement and Bernoldus Niemand's song 'Snor City' (about the apartheid capital, Pretoria), Afrikaners were far from homogenous, ideologically or temperamentally. They would have identified – with wholehearted laughter – with the definition of Afrikaners concocted much later by Dakarites Breytenbach, Brink, Van Zyl Slabbert and Ampie Coetzee:

Daar [is] bruin en bleek, kommuniste en Boere en boere en bittereinders en
liberale, Dakar-pelgrims en agnostici en Boedhiste en afvalliges en wederstrewi-
ges en skrumskakels en alkoholiste en kerkmuise en kultuurkokkerotte en moffies
en mekênieks en vissermense sonder kwotas en vorige grensvegters en boepbe-
woners en nihiliste en diakens en geselinne en filosowe en koffiedrinkers, kortom,
daardie ruie en ongetemde maar lewenskragtige verskeidenheid onafhanklikes
en bywoners en sinmakers en 'useful idiots' wat met reg daarop aanspraak kan
maak dat hulle die 'meerderheid' Afrikaners is (maar nooit so aanmatigend sal
wees om te dink hulle is 'verteenwoordigend' nie).[29]

There are brown and pale, communists and Boers and boer farmers and bitter-
enders and liberals, Dakar-pilgrims and agnostics and Buddhists and back-
sliders and contrarians and scrum-halves and alcoholics and church mice and
culture-cockroaches and queers and mechanics and fisherpeople without quo-
tas and former border-war fighters and beer-bellies and nihilists and deacons
and escorts and philosophers and coffee-drinkers, in short, that rough and
untamed but vibrant variety of independents and hangers-on and pundits and
'useful idiots' that can justly claim that they are the 'majority' Afrikaners (but
would never be so presumptuous as to think that they are 'representative').[30]

Tommy Bedford – former Springbok rugby captain and nephew of the writer
Laurens van der Post, advisor to Prince Charles and Margaret Thatcher – told
Van Zyl Slabbert he would join the Dakar safari on the condition that he get a
private meeting with the ANC leadership. On the first evening in Senegal, there
was a knock on his door. Bedford was called to Thabo Mbeki's hotel room, where
he offered to set up meetings between the ANC and the South African Rugby
Board. Mbeki, working in tandem with Sam Ramsamy of SANROC and internal
allies in the nascent National Sports Congress, subsequently initiated talks in
Harare between the different South African rugby bodies. It was this liaison with
Bedford that helped trigger the rugby unity process in the country.[31]

Similarly, Albert Koopman and Christo Nel, consultants for big business in
South Africa, went back after the conference and set up the Consultative Business
Movement (CBM). This played an important part in the early nineties as a forum
for change-friendly business to meet with struggle-related interest groups. It helped
in the setting up of the National Peace Accord and acted as the secretariat for the
negotiations at CODESA.[32]

After Dakar, Mbeki and Van Zyl Slabbert met with Zimbabwean government
officials to set up ongoing dialogue opportunities between people inside South
Africa, the ANC and Zimbabwean interest groups. The Zimbabwe Institute for

Southern Africa (ZISA) became IDASA's Zimbabwean partner, and the first exchanges were organised on Cold Comfort Farm. The farm was started in the 1960s as a transformative land experiment by independent-minded Englishman Guy Clutton-Brock, who was later deported by the Smith regime. Located on a mission station 150 kilometres from Harare, Cold Comfort Farm became a kind of Mecca for the Zimbabwean liberation movements. Through the ZISA partnership, IDASA facilitated more than fifty meetings with groups from South Africa in the six years after Dakar. They mainly involved university students and staff, particularly from Stellenbosch, as well as church, business and community groups.[33]

Inside South Africa, delegates held well over a hundred report-back meetings, generating further miles of newspaper columns. At the international level, President Reagan and the US State Department congratulated President Senghor for taking the initiative of hosting 'an unprecedented conference'.[34]

In February 1988, Professor Jakes Gerwel received a secretly hand-delivered letter from Lusaka-based NEC member John Nkadimeng, saying that the ANC had identified him as a key internal leader. The NEC had resolved to adopt 'a new strategy whereby your acclaimed accountability will play a very important and decisive role'. This was a moment when 'we need people of your calibre and capabilities', Nkadimeng added. Therefore, he asked, would Gerwel come to Swaziland the following month (under the pretext of going on holiday) to discuss 'sensitive issues which need urgent attention'? The 'strictest security measures would apply' and 'appropriate contact' would be made with him once he arrived at the Mbabane Holiday Inn so that 'Comrades Keith and Solly' could brief him on the NEC decisions.[35]

Thus, it came to be that within a year of Dakar, Gerwel helped Mbeki set up an internal, undercover academic think tank for the ANC inside South Africa, again using Zimbabwean contacts. In June 1988, the author accompanied him to a meeting at the home of Essop and Meg Pahad in London. Here they talked deep into the night with Mbeki, Aziz Pahad, Brian Bunting, poet Mongane Wally Serote and ex-Robben Islander Saki Macozoma, then working for the SACC. One of the issues discussed was the urgent need for Gerwel to send a trusted academic to Harare the next day for a meeting about setting up this think tank.

Historian Randi Erentzen was given the task, and later that same year the new Centre for Development Studies (CDS) was set up at UWC, with Erentzen as national coordinator. Its formation was part of the Swedish-supported Planning for a Post-Apartheid South Africa (PASA) project initiated by Oliver Tambo's meeting with prime minister Olof Palme in February 1986, shortly before the latter's assassination. The purpose was to set up 'an organisational structure that will initiate and co-ordinate research work on behalf of the National Liberation

Movement'.[36] Pallo Jordan and Thabo Mbeki were prominent members of the steering committee. After follow-up conferences in Harare and Bommersvik in Sweden in 1986/7, the ANC and its Swedish partners finalised key participant research and planning areas that could provide back-up to the ANC and its partners in the mass democratic movement. Key areas included health, education, the economy, local government and constitutional development. This related directly to the work of the DLCA and the Constitution Committee. Zola Skweyiya was one of the main participants in the discussions and planning. Stimulated by these developments, the ANC Economists Unit was upgraded to the new ANC Department of Economics and Planning (DEP) in September 1987, with Max Sisulu as head, to look seriously at post-apartheid economic policy.[37]

Two independent research units were set up to conduct the PASA work. The first was the South African Studies Project (SASPRO), based in Lusaka and headed by ANC projects coordinator Barney McKay (real name Goitsimolimo Leonard Pitso). The other was the UWC-based CDS. Both units aimed to network with international and domestic research groups to help develop ANC policy options for the future.[38] The CDS started working in tandem with progressive academics, grassroots organisations, and the leaderships of the UDF, COSATU and other formations of the MDM. By 1989, this internal structure was in place with six regional coordinators, and it was busy establishing eight study commissions. The one on the economy, for example, had Professors Vishnu Padayachee and Andrew Black as rapporteurs. South Africans working with the CDS were well represented and presented papers at conferences on land and local government in Harare and Amsterdam. The Harare minutes noted that 'ANC and related research units EROSA [Economic Research on South Africa], SASPRO and SAERT [South Africa Economic Research and Training] were present'.[39] CDS delegates returned from these conferences armed with a 'summary of research topics' to be pursued, including legal and constitutional aspects of local government, alternative housing policy and 'strategies of the state, capital and MDM'.[40]

Erentzen explained that the 'CDS can be compared to the British Labour Party who had to prepare for government by doing shadow reports on various aspects of policy'.[41] The Constitution Committee had, since January 1986, repeatedly called for the NEC to arrange for demographic and other surveys to help it make informed decisions on future constitutional options. Now, despite state repression and the illegal status of the ANC, there were organisations in place inside and outside South Africa meant to conduct this research.

From the above we can see that the preparatory, strategic, broad-front interventions by the ANC and its internal discussion partners were politically effective, delivering concrete outcomes. Dakar participants from both sides deliberately downplayed its significance, but these meetings were becoming key to advancing the ANC's position. While P.W. Botha and the Afrikaner establishment typified Dakar and other safaris in total-onslaught terms as dangerous and foolhardy adventures by opportunists who had no political relevance, these 'adventures' wounded a politically flat-footed regime and its supporters. Riaan de Villiers has opined that Dakar's real impact was on a socio-psychological level, helping Afrikaners to break through the cordon of censorship and security legislation and their ingrained 'obedience complex', derived partly from Afrikaner nationalism's Calvinist underpinnings. Some commentators have even claimed that 'our democracy would not have arrived' had the safaris not helped to crack the monolith of white politics.[42] The fact that the state changed its approach towards exploring the possibility of talks from late 1987 to early 1988 onwards (described in succeeding chapters) would seem to underline the point. From then on, Botha, his NIS head Niël Barnard, influential NP-supporting Broederbond intellectuals and the apartheid state as a whole had to retreat step by step, politically and ideologically, from a hard-line base policy of engineering change on their terms via repression and socio-economic upliftment without losing political control. This political retreat continued until the National Party was forced out of office only seven years later, in a scenario it had never thought possible.

20

Assassination in Swaziland

THE CONSTITUTION COMMITTEE members were living in complex and tragic times. On the morning of 12 July 1987, Kader Asmal, Penuell Maduna and other members of the ANC's delegation made their way to the harbour in Dakar, together with the Afrikaner 'dissidents' from home. They were bound for 'the place of no return' on Gorée Island, from which enslaved people had been transported to the Americas.[1] Everyone on the trip was aware that Govan Mbeki, father of one of the ANC team members, was serving his twenty-third year of incarceration with a thousand comrades on another island with a similar stained legacy at the tip of the continent.

Shortly before the delegates boarded a boat for the short journey across, tragic news came through: Cassius Make, the youngest member of the NEC, had been assassinated by a regime hit squad in Swaziland.[2] His comrades in Dakar were devastated. Make (the 'travelling name' of Job Tlhabane) had been chief of ordinance and logistics at military HQ and a member of the PMC. He and two comrades, Paul Dikeledi (Sello Motau) and 'Comrade Tsinini', had been picked up by a 'taxi' at Matsapha Airport and taken to a spot where all three met their end. By pure coincidence, underground operative Vusi Mavimbela was driving by on the same side road to avoid detection when he saw a car slowly sliding into a gully. The onlookers at the scene were most likely the killers.[3]

Back at Constitution Committee HQ in Lusaka, Zola Skweyiya and Teddy Pekane were tasked with going to Swaziland to identify the bodies. They, too, entered at Matsapha Airport, where police protection had been arranged for them via diplomatic channels. But, as Skweyiya later reported, when they arrived at Manzini police station, a criminal investigations officer 'point-blankly told us that the boers do what they like in Swaziland and that we should see to our own security as they were not in a position to provide us with such.'[4] They immediately switched hotels, as it was clear that 'we are on our own'. Despite the danger, they visited the mortuary and learnt when the post-mortems would be completed. With the help of Winnie Mandela, Paul Dikeledi's family had come to fetch his body for burial at home, but the undertaker's car was refused entry when it reached the South African border and had returned to Mbabane with the body. Skweyiya and

Pekane arranged for a chartered plane from Lusaka to fetch them and the three caskets. The plane took off on 17 July.

Despite the dangers of exposure, Skweyiya and Pekane also risked going to the Mbabane magistrate's court, where three ANC operatives were on trial for possessing arms of war. The Swazi capital was crawling with informers, askaris and regime hit squads. The police were selling ANC cars and property items cheaply to the public, including the new car in which 'Cde Viva' had been killed. 'According to our observation,' Skweyiya reported, 'the situation in Swaziland has deteriorated and it has become more dangerous than it has ever been.'[5]

Plans for war and plans for peace were marching forward step by step that July, as both the Dakar conference and the daring venture to the killing fields of Swaziland showed. The Constitution Committee and Skweyiya's DLCA bore witness to both as 1987 unfolded.

21

Harare, Arusha, Amsterdam

THERE'S A CLIP in *Breaking the Fetters*, a documentary on Dakar by Anli Serfontein, that shows the delegation landing in Senegal. Three people receive the Afrikaner delegation on the tarmac: ANC chief rep Aggie Qunu, a Senegalese official, and Penuell Maduna, the youngest member of the Constitution Committee. At first glance, Maduna's presence might seem incongruous, but the moment is a cue for understanding what was happening in the backroom revolution.

While the Committee worked on the ANC's constitutional proposals in the shadows, both it and the closely related DLCA were very much involved in the ANC's strategic planning around contacts, talks, negotiations and legal support for 'illegal' operations at home.

Looking at Dakar and the different safaris, some distinctive patterns become discernible, starting with the fact that each contact almost inevitably resulted in follow-up actions that advanced the struggle. One went on these safaris with a serious purpose, not for a holiday. Each meeting was preceded by meticulous preparations and consultation with senior structures of the organisation. As noted earlier, when Zola Skweyiya organised the meeting with lawyers from inside in Harare in 1986, he followed protocol by liaising with the offices of the president, secretary-general and treasurer-general, as well as with James Stuart of the ECC, Ruth Mompati of the NEC Secretariat and Joe Nhlanhla, the head of NAT intelligence and security, as well as secretary of the PMC responsible for internal operations. This kind of reporting and strategising for the meetings was routine.

Secondly, the message at each meeting was remarkably consistent with ANC goals and non-negotiable demands since 1985. The ANC's template for negotiations and the constitution-making processes was in place at an early stage. The bottom lines were always clear: Under no circumstances would the ANC agree to be co-opted into a regime-driven process of negotiation and change. Negotiations could happen only if they sped up the journey to 'liberation' or, in other words, national self-determination through a universal franchise for the dispossessed and disenfranchised majority. The end point was unambiguous: a multiparty, united, non-racial, democratic South Africa with a constitution that would allow for the thorough transformation of society.

To this end the ANC played two winning cards. Firstly, the need for national unity and a united front to replace apartheid and its divisions. This was in line with its historic mission of having been an all-embracing 'native parliament' accommodating different constituencies and perspectives from the start in 1912. Secondly, the basis of citizenship was non-negotiable. The organisation rejected anything to do with group rights. Citizenship would be based on broad-ranging individual freedoms for every citizen, regardless of colour, creed or other differences, protected in law through a Bill of Rights and nurtured through multiparty democracy. This was a master stroke that in the South African context clearly drew the line between those who sought to uphold the status quo and those who sought what would amount to revolutionary change.

At every encounter with groups from home, the ANC dealt in one way or another with the possibility of negotiations and constitution-making – always within the context of intensifying its interlinked four-pronged strategy of underground work, armed struggle, mass mobilisation and building international solidarity.

In the months following the July 1987 conference in Dakar, this approach was powerfully marketed by three other landmark conferences held in Harare, Arusha and Amsterdam. Each was aimed at a particular audience and each was a step forward in building a platform for a new kind of politics in South Africa. And on each occasion, Constitution Committee members were involved as organisers or participants.

The first was the conference on Children, Repression and the Law in Apartheid South Africa, held between 24 and 27 September 1987 in Harare. Emanating from its contacts with its international solidarity network, including the World University Service (WUS), the event was 'de facto' planned and organised by the DLCA and IDAF during consultations between Skweyiya, Asmal and Maduna in London in August 1986, approved by the NEC.[1] Maduna and Teddy Pekane – the latter seconded to temporarily relocate to Harare – were made ANC coordinators, and when Dakar happened they were already hard at work organising what would turn out to be another eye-catching international event, one that had special symbolism for the mass democratic movement inside the country.

The Children's Conference, Harare

'This must stop!' Oliver Tambo declared to a full-throated roar of approval in Harare.

He was speaking about the detention of more than ten thousand children in state-of-emergency South Africa in 1986 and 1987.[2] Traumatised young people had given first-hand testimony of the violence inflicted upon them by apartheid state security forces, and the audience applauded when Tambo condemned these acts. But Kader Asmal recalled that when Tambo turned to the subject of necklacing, there was a hush. Angry township residents had been using this method to kill people perceived to be betraying the struggle by spying for the regime. Tambo was unequivocal in his denunciation of it: 'This must stop!'[3]

Don Foster – co-author of a study on *Detention and Torture in South Africa*, and who presented at the conference – described it as 'the most moving political gathering I've ever been to'. And it culminated in Tambo's speech. 'One could hear a pin drop,' said Foster. 'He spoke magnificently.'[4]

Tambo quoted 'The Child Is Not Dead', a moving poem by Ingrid Jonker, to highlight the poignancy of the conference theme – and to make the point that despite apartheid atrocities South Africans would not be denied their freedom:

The child is not dead
The child lifts his fists against his mother
Who shouts Afrika! shouts the breath
Of freedom and the veld
In the locations of the cordoned heart.

The child lifts his fists against his father
in the march of the generations
who shouts Afrika! shout the breath
of righteousness and blood
in the streets of his embattled pride

The child is not dead
not at Langa nor at Nyanga
nor at Orlando nor at Sharpeville
nor at the police post at Philippi
where he lies with a bullet through his brain

The child is the dark shadow of the soldiers
on guard with rifles Saracens and batons
the child is present at all assemblies and law-givings
the child peers through the windows of houses and into the hearts of mothers
this child who wanted only to play in the sun at Nyanga is everywhere
the child grown to the man treks through all Africa
the child grown into a giant journeys through the whole world

Without a pass.[5]

According to *Children of Resistance*, 'Almost 300 South Africans, the majority of whom had come from inside the country, met with over 200 representatives from

more than 150 organisations from all over the world.'[6] Among the internal groupings were the UDF, the Detainees' Parents Support Committee, the new National
Medical and Dental Association (NAMDA) and the Organisation for Appropriate
Social Services in South Africa (OASSSA). Top figures in the freedom struggle
attended, including Beyers Naudé and Reverend Frank Chikane of the SACC,
who had recently been acquitted of treason charges brought against him by the
apartheid regime. They spoke forcefully on the role of the churches in the intensifying struggle.

The DLCA had made a concerted effort to build relationships with progres-
sive South African lawyers. A full list of Harare attendees is not available, but the
lawyers present included Pius Langa (who presented a paper on 'South African
Security Laws Versus the Child'), Marumo Moerane, Dullah Omar, Essa Moosa,
Nicholas Haysom, Enver Daniels, Ramesh Vassen, Johnny de Lange, Ismail Ayob,
Peter Harris and Professor David McQuoid-Mason, who presented a paper on
'Children and the Law in South Africa: The Child in the Dock.'[7] Other speakers
included doctors, psychologists, social workers, teachers, and community and
religious field workers.

The final conference declaration specifically criticised 'the lawyers and judges
who lend legitimacy to an illegitimate system and the medical practitioners who
conspire to keeping secret the brutality against children.'[8] The world, it said,
'should sever all relations with professional bodies which fail to condemn these
practices'. Various international organisations promptly followed, and critical resolutions were adopted by the European Union, the British House of Commons,
the United States Senate and the United Nations.

For many attendees, the highlight of the conference was when Tambo introduced the NEC members, about two-thirds of whom were present, to their fellow
countrymen and women in a closed session for the South African delegates only.
'It was an electric moment,' Foster recalls. They spoke openly – 'This is who we
are' – explaining their positions and saying how moved they had been to meet
with people from inside.[9] Victoria Brittain reported that the ANC 'showed an
openness the banned organisation had never chosen to display before.'[10]

Between and after sessions there was intense socialising between the ANC
exiles and the large number of South Africans from home. Foster went on to say
that the formal proceedings were, in a sense, a front, with the real talking often
happening afterwards in informal gatherings. 'People were together in rooms
until well after midnight. Certain NEC members were delegated to liaise with
particular regions. Joe Slovo, Ruth Mompati and James Stuart were delegated to
us ... Joe Slovo got a guitar out and I played a bit. James Stuart was in the forefront
singing *moppies*' (Cape carnival songs).[11]

Beyers Naudé noted: 'The heart is so full of so many emotions of joy ... of being together here in a way in which we never dreamed would have been possible ... Such a spirit is unconquerable. No action of the state, however repressive, however brutal it may be, can ever in any way conquer that spirit.'[12] These dizzying flashes of connection were features of the safaris: through struggle, solidarity, danger and the throwing off of taboos, people got a heightened sense of what unity and freedom could bring.

After the conference, apartheid minister of law and order Adriaan Vlok held several press conferences and produced a propaganda film to refute the revelations about the number of children in detention and their treatment. To avoid further embarrassment to the state, many children were quietly released.

International Unity Against Apartheid Conference, Arusha
In 1967, President Julius Nyerere of Tanzania launched his Ujamaa plans for socialism with an African face at Arusha. The Arusha Declaration was discussed throughout the continent and thoroughly studied in ANC circles. In 1987 Nyerere was in Arusha once again, telling 500 delegates from sixty countries, north, west, east and south, that there was no such thing as apartheid with a human face. The occasion was an ANC conference organised on the theme 'People of the World United against Apartheid for a Democratic South Africa'. The objective was to connect and recalibrate strategy with the international solidarity network built up over the quarter century since Tambo had been sent out of the country to start an external mission. The delegates came from the UN, the OAU and their agencies, as well as from numerous national governmental and anti-apartheid movements.[13]

Tanzania, a relativity poor country with scant resources, had been particularly generous in its support of the liberation struggle. In 1960, more than a year before independence, Nyerere insisted that the British allow Tambo to establish headquarters in Dar es Salaam. Three years later, Tanganyika united with Zanzibar to create Tanzania. As the new flag was raised, the anthem rang out: 'Mungu ibariki Afrika' – 'God Bless Africa', the Swahili version of South African composer Enoch Sontonga's hymn 'Nkosi Sikelel' iAfrika'. For many years, Dar es Salaam served as the ANC's external base. Later, the leadership moved to Morogoro, 156 kilometres to the west. In 1965 there were 600 MK guerrilla trainees at the Kongwa camp, deeper in the interior. The Luthuli Detachment proceeded from there to Zambia, after which they crossed the Zambezi to enter Rhodesia for what became the Wankie Campaign. At a later stage, the Solomon Mahlangu Freedom College (SOMAFCO) was set up in Mazimbu, near Morogoro. Over the years, thousands of children of ANC parents studied there. Some hard lessons were learnt at

SOMAFCO on matters such as whether to use corporal punishment, how to deal with abusive conduct by staff, whether girl children who fell pregnant should be excluded, and how to teach South African history. In 1976, Albie Sachs taught at the notably progressive law school at the University of Dar es Salaam, along with Dani Nabudere from Uganda, Pheroze Nowrojee from Kenya, and Joe Kanywanyi and Issa Shivji from Tanzania. The university had become a centre for anti-racist, anti-colonialist scholar activists from around the world, such as Walter Rodney from Guyana.[14]

Now in Arusha, 'this historic city of the African revolution', in the presence of the retired Mwalimu (Nyerere), his successor President Ali Hassan Mwinyi and conference chairperson 'our brother' Salim Ahmed Salim, who had been blocked from becoming UN secretary-general by Ronald Reagan because of his support for international liberation struggles, Tambo spoke to the assembled members of the support network that had sustained the exiled ANC for decades. He described it as a world parliament against apartheid, the first opportunity the ANC had to invite 'the rest of the world to come and consider, together with us, the issues on our agenda'. Thanks to the depth of international support, the illegitimate regime was in the process of being completely isolated, Tambo said. It was talking about negotiations, but only because it was trying, at all costs, to avert a terminal crisis and stay in power. Apartheid had failed. 'That is why even its architects proclaim its death while they try desperately to defend it with brute force.' Therefore, sanctions needed to be tightened. He explained that the ANC was not averse to negotiations but, as explained in the NEC's recent statement in October (Chapter 24), certain bottom-line demands needed to be met. The purpose would have to be the transfer of power to the people through a one-person, one-vote system in a unitary, non-racial, democratic state. It could not be about making amendments to the apartheid system. Tambo also pointed out that some Western countries – i.e. the US, Britain, France and West Germany – wanted to 'appropriate as their own' the issue of negotiation and this had to be guarded against.[15]

One of those present was the Constitution Committee's Kader Asmal, vastly experienced in liaising with international organisations on sanctions and other actions to end apartheid. A special feature of the event was the participation of a delegation of insiders from South Africa, who gave speeches in both the plenary sessions and the sessions devoted to the work of four commissions. Among them were representatives from COSATU, the newly formed National Association of Democratic Lawyers (NADEL), and the religious and women's sectors. Johnny de Lange announced that the Freedom Charter was gaining popularity in South Africa and that NADEL saw itself as part of the nascent organs of people's power. It was busy canvassing lawyers to join and initiating plans to redraft legislation.[16]

Tambo explained that the mass democratic movement now needed to be seen as part of the international coalition of forces against apartheid.

Arusha underlined once again that the ANC, with its many missions all over the world, had solid international support. As Roelf Meyer was later to observe, the ANC had set up more diplomatic missions than the regime since going into exile, the numbers growing from nine in the 1960s, to twenty by 1980 and forty-one in 1989.[17] Arusha gave Tambo and the ANC the opportunity to connect and plan with its international base. It prepared international allies for a diplomatic offensive to come and underlined the message from the host, Nyerere, that Botha's sham attempts at reform could not give apartheid a human face.

Endorsing the ANC's strategy, Nyerere said the armed struggle and the political struggle were intertwined and needed to stay that way until negotiations, which had to be about 'fundamentals', resulted in a government of the people sitting in Pretoria. Furthermore, negotiations had to take place at a two-sided table, with the genuine leaders – 'as free men and women' – on one side and the apartheid authorities on the other.[18] Until these goals had been met, the world had to keep isolating the apartheid government. The conference issued its own Arusha Declaration, and one of its sixteen points stated that 'Any negotiations would have to address the central question of political power and not how to give apartheid a more acceptable face'.[19] Tambo and his team – representing the 'people's camp', at home in an African continental base – had made another decisive move in the high-stakes diplomatic chess game unfolding between it and the regime and its local and foreign backers.

Taking Over the Royal Theatre in Amsterdam

Mayor of Amsterdam Ed van Thijn was a strong supporter of the Anti-Apartheids Beweging Nederland (AABN) and declared Amsterdam an 'apartheid-free zone'. It was his way of celebrating the fact that Amsterdam had been named the cultural capital of Europe for 1987. Working together with the AABN and the ANC, he organised the Culture in Another South Africa (CASA) conference in December that year, just after Arusha. It was yet another sectoral intervention, connecting a large group of South African writers, musicians, artists, actors, filmmakers, photographers and cultural workers from home with their exiled and international counterparts. Over 300 participated, highlighting the growth of resistance in South Africa and the unity between the ANC, the internal mass struggles and the international anti-apartheid movement.

One of the organisers noted that for ten days the South Africans took over 'the royal theatre and opera, the discos and the restaurants and the city hall and parliament'. Dozens of talks, exhibitions and performances were organised. The rhythm and the beat took in a wide range of South Africa's top talent: the African Jazz Pioneers, Letta Mbulu and Caiphus Semenya, Basil Coetzee and Sabenza, Jonas Gwangwa and Arekopaneng, Mr Mac and the Genuines, Ntsikana, Abdullah Ibrahim, Chris McGregor, Dudu Pukwana, Dolly Rathebe, various theatre and dance groups, the COSATU choir and the Amandla Cultural Ensemble of the ANC. Also featured were *The Hidden Hand* photographic exhibition; a full programme of documentaries by photographers and filmmakers operating on the frontlines of struggle under the state of emergency; a colloquium on South African journalism; plays such as *Woza Albert!* by Percy Mtwa, Mbongeni Ngema and Barney Simon, *Blood Knot* by Athol Fugard, *Bopha!* by Percy Mtwa and *Asinamali* by Mbongeni Ngema; and writers' and poetry events involving Nadine Gordimer, Lewis Nkosi, Don Mattera, Mandla Langa, Breyten Breytenbach, Njabulo Ndebele, Vernon February, Cosmo Pieterse, Willy Keorapetse Kgositsile, Lindiwe Mabuza and others. It was truly 'a mix of exiles from all over the world and "insiders" working and living in South Africa'.[20]

Still grieving from the pain of losing both his wife and daughter to a parcel bomb sent to their exile home in Angola, Marius Schoon wrote that that December in Amsterdam, 'though foreign to my bones', felt like 'home, surrounded by my own'.[21]

Writer Mandla Langa explained that 'There was electricity in the air, energy generated by South Africans meeting freely for the first time in years.' Langa noted also how the need to work for gender equality was 'discussed at length' as being necessary for a democratic culture to emerge.[22]

ANC participants included NEC members Thomas Nkobi, Alfred Nzo, Thabo Mbeki, Aziz Pahad, Pallo Jordan and Barbara Masekela, as well as Langa, Kgositsile and Mabuza. There were members of the Botswana underground who had been involved with the Medu Art Ensemble and the 1982 Culture and Resistance Festival in Gaborone – Kgositsile, Barry Gilder, Patrick Fitzgerald, Angela Brown (pseudonym of Louise Colvin), Gordon Metz and many of the others listed here.[23]

Barbara Masekela, head of the ANC's cultural department, opened the conference and stressed the social responsibilities of artists and cultural practitioners. In a message to the conference, the poet Serote, just back from a course of military training in the Soviet Union but unable to attend because of problems getting his travel documents cleared in Britain, wrote: 'Now we enter history ... and as we seek to define freedom, we become part of humanity'. In the popular imagination, the regime was bankrupt. Every piece played or enunciated by Ntemi Piliso, Basil 'Manenberg' Coetzee, Dudu Pukwana and the resistance artists became part of the heartbeat of the revolution. And in the CASA resolutions, the call went out for cultural workers to organise themselves and find ways in which culture could enhance the struggle.

Pallo Jordan, himself a former member of the Mayibuye Cultural Ensemble, explained in the keynote address that the ANC was not trying to impose a 'line' or insisting that artists become political pamphleteers or sloganeers. Rather, this was part of a 'continuing dialogue' and they should 'pursue excellence in their respective disciplines – to be excellent artists and to serve the struggle for liberation with excellent art'. Quoting Oliver Tambo, he added that artists should use their craft 'to give voice not only to the grievances, but also to the profoundest aspirations of the oppressed and exploited'.[24]

Much like the writer and soon-to-be president Václav Havel was doing in Czechoslovakia, where an old Soviet Union satellite system was dying as popular resistance welled up in parallel struggles, these artists sought to define freedom and envisioned a new birth in ways that had instant political resonance. They had key roles to play in popularising and legitimising systemic change.

Many participants pointed out that the gatherings in Amsterdam underlined how culture had come to mirror the organic nature of the struggle for liberation in South Africa. Not one struggle event or mass funeral for victims of state brutality went by without popular expression through music, dance, song, spoken-word poetry and visual imagery.

At CASA, decisions were taken about the international cultural boycott of apartheid South Africa. A total boycott had been instituted to isolate the regime. Now, it was decided that the growth of democratic forces within the country required that 'the cultural boycott as a tactic needs to be applied with a degree of flexibility which takes into consideration the developing situation within the country'. This would 'recognise and strengthen the emerging democratic culture in South Africa'. The CASA resolutions committee consisted of ANC people closely linked to the new terrain of constitutional planning – Pallo Jordan (the conference keynote speaker), Thabo Mbeki and Aziz Pahad, together with Krish Naidoo from the UDF. The outcome of this action was to further integrate unfolding ANC and domestic strategies, including setting up the UDF cultural desk under Sefako Nyaka and Jabu Ngwenya, forming the South African Musicians' Alliance under the presidency of Victor Ntoni, and refining and employing more effectively the long-standing, crucially important international sanctions weapon.[25]

Seven months after CASA, Jonas Gwangwa, Hugh Masekela, Miriam Makeba, Jonathan Butler, the Amandla Cultural Ensemble and Amampondo joined scores of the world's most celebrated artists in the massive Nelson Mandela 70th Birthday Tribute concert at Wembley Stadium in London. Seventy-two thousand people attended, most of them youths. They belted out the international hit song 'Free Nelson Mandela', and the event was broadcast to sixty countries and one of the biggest television audiences in history. Prisoner number 466/64 and his cause went global. Winnie Mandela wrote, 'We now know with absolute certainty that the whole world is with us in our struggle.'[26]

Despite government repression, the inside–outside linkages became highly effective in promoting sectoral mobilisation intended to cover every aspect of South African life. In line with the call to arms at Kabwe, Tambo's annual 8 January statements, and the late-1985 consolidation of trade union struggles into one new super federation – COSATU – a host of new legal organisations emerged from 1986 onwards to broaden the base of struggle in South Africa. Several of these were formed directly as a result of the meetings between internal people and the ANC.

In line with the theme for 1987 – the 'Year of Advance to People's Power' – the new formations joined existing sympathetic sectoral groups such as the important faith-based SACC, the SACBC and the Call of Islam (and later Jews for Justice) in making sure that the MDM was able to operate on a deeper level within South African culture and society. The SACC would in 1988 declare that it was legitimate for Christians to take up arms against oppressive systems such as apartheid.

The conferences in Dakar, Harare, Arusha and Amsterdam set a precedent not only in bringing together large numbers of internal South Africans and the ANC in large-scale conferences that were often well publicised, but also in allowing individuals and groups with cross-cutting interests and views to discuss sector-specific issues with the ANC. Tens of sectoral conferences followed in the next two years – for lawyers, writers, artists, women, religious bodies, sports people, social workers and medics, university and student groups, defence-force specialists, white democrats, and so on. An understanding of the various networks involved in these ANC–insider talks helps clarify the role of specific actors and positions coming to the fore in the unfolding process of constitution-making from the mid-1980s onwards as Oliver Tambo and the ANC took the initiative in opening up new terrains of struggle.

Some narratives by those associated with the apartheid regime portray Dakar and the other safaris as well-infiltrated jamborees that were more about heady adventurism than serious politics and strategy. These claims are disproven by the concrete actions that followed the conferences. This book attempts to expose the shallowness of such claims and challenges what are argued to be self-justifying narratives constructed by authors from the apartheid establishment such as Niël Barnard and Willie Esterhuyse about enlightened sectors of a reforming, almost omnipotent state that were all the while forward-looking and in control of the process.[27] No: African agency and democratic impulses were shaping the change agenda by the end of 1987, and a repressive, politically incapacitated state was being reactive rather than driving or co-authoring the process. Like its authoritarian counterpart in the GDR, with its supposedly all-seeing Stasi apparatus, the South African state depended on its repressive National Security Management System to maintain control. By 1989 it would reveal itself to be far from omnipotent, and politically in a deep-seated crisis.

Organisers of these various gatherings worked on the assumption that the NIS or Military Intelligence in South Africa would have informers at these events. It later emerged that the lawyer Vanessa Brereton was the apartheid spy at the Harare conference. No one doubts that there was an informer from the inside at Dakar as well – in addition, probably, to Francis Meli from the ANC side, who was later unmasked as a spy.[28] The same applied, for example, when student delegations visited the ANC (Mark Behr) and when the ANC had talks with scholars in divinity and philosophy from home.[29]

Each of these many conferences lifted old veils, opened up contacts for the ANC and ramped up its popularity as the leading force in the South African liberation movement. Each of these events delegitimised apartheid and further collapsed the mechanistic 'reform' plans of a repressive Botha government. The substantive process initiated by Oliver Tambo and the ANC in 1985 was creating a platform for a new kind of politics to which the state would be forced to react, rather than be able to pre-empt and stop it.

Particularly important for the constitutional planning process was the large presence of progressive lawyers who attended the 1987 Harare conference, a clear signal that the ANC was establishing dynamic contacts with progressive internal legal networks behind the scenes. Its links to NADEL, formed a few months earlier in May 1987, and to Pius Langa and Dullah Omar who would establish themselves as NADEL's main leaders, were especially significant, strengthening the ANC's constitutional planning capacities considerably in the years to come.

22

NADEL Broadens the Anti-Racist Legal Front

S IXTEEN-YEAR-OLD PIUS LANGA, South Africa's future chief justice, stood naked in a line of black men waiting to be hosed down and have their testicles examined. That morning he had taken a 'Native' bus from his home in a 'Native' location, as townships were called then, to the Native Affairs Department in downtown Durban to get his first 'Native' pass. It was a deeply unpleasant experience, but he was young and resilient, and without the pass he could not get a job. Furthermore, if he didn't have a pass he could be arrested at any time of day or night, in his home or on the street. What he could not bear was seeing men old enough to be his father or grandfather being subjected to this treatment.[1]

Langa's first job was at a shirt factory. Son of an itinerant preacher, he was gifted with words and languages and so was able to move on to a position as a messenger and interpreter in the Department of Justice. Here, he slowly worked his way up the ranks to become a prosecutor and then a junior magistrate. Studying by distance learning at the University of South Africa, he obtained BJuris and LLB degrees and left the department to become an advocate of the Supreme Court of South Africa. He became one of the small group of black advocates at the Durban Bar, working on the seventh floor of Salmon Grove Chambers, 407 Smith Street. His peers there included Sandile Ngcobo, Justice Poswa, Marumo Moerane, Achmat Jappie, Vuka Tshabalala, Shyam Gyanda, Chiman Patel, 'KK' Mthiyane, Leonard Gering and Zak Yacoob.[2] Langa's clients included various civic bodies, trade unions and people charged with political offences under the oppressive apartheid security laws.[3]

One of his brothers, Mandla Langa, served time in prison for ANC activities, then left the country to receive military training in an MK camp in Angola and went on to become a distinguished novelist.[4] Another activist brother, Ben Langa, was a poet and a member of the ANC underground inside the country. He met a tragic end when security police agents infiltrated the underground structure in which he was working and planted false information to make it appear that he had been working for the apartheid regime. On the basis of this material, he was declared an enemy agent and executed in May 1984 by two of his comrades. These comrades, in turn, were captured by South African security, put on trial and hanged. The whole episode was a terrible blow for the struggle and a catastrophe for the Langa family.[5]

Fighting down despair following the loss of his brother, Pius continued with his legal work. He also intensified his political activities within the structures of the UDF. In 1987 he became a founding member of NADEL. The following year he was elected its president.

Pius was well known in Lusaka thanks to his family connections and his defence of cadres arrested for their involvement in the resistance. Indeed, he travelled there to question the ANC leadership about the circumstances surrounding Ben's death, and when he was in Lusaka soon after NADEL's founding, Penuell Maduna asked Oliver Tambo to grant him an 'audience'.[6]

Dullah Omar worked closely with Langa as NADEL's vice-president at a key moment in its existence. He grew up in District Six, before this diverse Cape Town neighbourhood in central Cape Town was declared a white area, its inhabitants expelled and its buildings demolished, leaving a scar that remains to this day. He matriculated at Trafalgar High School, where he was strongly influenced by his English teacher, Ben Kies, a leading member of the Non-European Unity Movement. While studying for a BA and LLB at UCT, he became a prominent and respected Unity Movement activist on the unsettled campus. When he finally qualified as a lawyer, he found that the Group Areas Act prevented him from opening an office in the city, close to the courts. He defiantly joined a practice set up by Cadoc Kobus in Langa township, but here, too, he was thwarted: in terms of the Native Administration Act, he was obliged to get a permit to enter the location. Eventually Omar opened an office in Woodstock, a working-class area adjacent to the city centre where traces of a more cosmopolitan, pre–Group Areas Act past still existed.[7]

Though he remained an active member of the Unity Movement throughout the 1970s and early 1980s, he was widely admired in the anti-apartheid community for his willingness to represent people from all the different currents of the struggle. One of the few attorneys prepared to take on political trials, he defended people from the Poqo (loosely translated as 'pure' or 'alone' in isiXhosa) wing of the Pan Africanist Congress (PAC), which planned armed attacks on police stations and white civilians. He also made regular trips to Robben Island to represent ANC leaders incarcerated there. Then, when the authorities began to crack down on the Black Consciousness Movement (BCM), he acted for the Black People's Convention (BPC) and SASO.

When he married Farida Ally, an activist from a strongly pro-ANC family, people wondered which political current would become dominant in their home. The answer emerged from their relationship with Winnie and Nelson Mandela. When Mandela was transferred from Robben Island to Pollsmoor Prison in 1982,

Farida was sent to pick Winnie up at the airport and take her to Pollsmoor. It was their first meeting, and Farida describes how she and Winnie embraced and laughed. Afterwards, Winnie frequently stayed at the Omars' home in Rylands, and Dullah eventually became Nelson's unofficial spokesperson. When the UDF was established in 1983, Dullah joined the organisation, later becoming its western Cape chairperson and one of its most prominent public faces.

During this period his movements were restricted by government banning orders and he was detained without trial. In the eyes of the apartheid government's secret hit squad, known as the Civil Cooperation Bureau (CCB), he had clearly aligned himself with the ANC, and they therefore made two attempts to assassinate him. In the first instance he was to be killed by rifle shot, but the assassin – who went by the unlikely name of 'Peaches' Gordon – could not get a clear shot because Farida walked in front of Dullah as the couple emerged from their home. Generally, wherever Omar went there were apartheid agents hovering around him. On another occasion, Farida became suspicious of the drugs given to him during a hospital stay and refused to let him take them. Subsequent evidence proved her right: a commission of inquiry heard that his heart medication was to be substituted with poison pills.[8]

One of the DLCA's primary tasks was to unify progressive anti-apartheid lawyers at home. In addition, Skweyiya and his colleagues were eager to explore the possibility of initiating a countrywide debate on the constitutional future of South Africa. They had been concerned, too, about organising speedy defences for arrested ANC activists in order to boost the morale of cadres in detention, dealing with challenges like welfare assistance to the dependants of prisoners and detainees, and making sure 'recalcitrant lawyers' did not charge 'exorbitant fees'.[9]

The ANC had proposed forming a national body for democratic lawyers in South Africa at the initial Harare engagement with Lewis Skweyiya and Kwenza Mlaba in May 1986 (see Chapter 12). It then continued lobbying and meeting with Congress-oriented lawyers in places as diverse as Geneva, London and Lusaka with the aim of building a 'progressive alliance'. Skweyiya noted that 'There were subsequent meetings thereafter with other lawyers from different regions of South Africa'.[10] In January 1987, he wrote to the ANC top three – Tambo, Nzo and Nkobi – as well as Joe Nhlanhla of the PMC and James Stuart of the ECC. In this letter, he stated that he had 'requested friends of our movement' at the UN Commission on Human Rights (UNCHR), the World Health Organization and the World Council of Churches to invite 'a group of lawyers and ministers of religion' to Geneva for the sessions of the last-mentioned UNCHR.[11] Pius Langa's name was among those mentioned.

This was all part of the ANC's strategy for creating sectoral bodies in as many areas of life as possible – from religion, sport, trade unions and the economy, to education and the law. This way the organised challenge to apartheid could become more deeply rooted in society, going beyond the formal political level.

By early 1987, Skweyiya was confident that the DLCA had identified a core of progressive lawyers inside the country who could make unity a reality. Mathole Motshekga, a constitutional law lecturer at UNISA who used his university connections to meet secretly with the ANC at the University of Zambia, had been introduced to Skweyiya during a visit to Lusaka in 1986 to meet with Jacob Zuma and Joe Nhlanhla. He returned in February 1987 to consult with, among others, the Constitution Committee's Teddy Pekane and Penuell Maduna.[12] After their meeting, Pekane and Maduna confirmed that a new national non-statutory body of progressive lawyers was due to be formed in mid-March. It would be called the South African Association of Democratic Lawyers (SAADEL). Some had wanted this body to use 'Congress' in its title, but others argued that this would be divisive, and the idea was dropped.

Thus, the idea of forming one progressive body for South African lawyers had gained traction. Consultative meetings were held in Bisho, near eQonce (King William's Town), as well as in Johannesburg and Durban. A SAADEL steering committee was set up by 'a loose federal body of the existing lawyers' bodies', consisting of two delegates from each of them.[13] There were several small regional bodies that were pro-ANC and popularising the Freedom Charter. Among them were the Democratic Lawyers Association (DLA) in Natal, which had affiliated to the UDF, the Democratic Lawyers Organisation (DLO) in the western Cape, the Democratic Lawyers Congress (DLC) in the Transvaal and Orange Free State, and the Eastern Cape Democratic Lawyers Association (ECDLA).[14] A number of progressive white lawyers were active in the MDM-aligned bodies, including Nicholas Haysom, Halton Cheadle, Greg Nott and Peter Harris (Johannesburg), Ilan Lax (Durban), Clive Plaskett (eastern Cape), and Derrick Fine and Johnny de Lange (Cape Town).

The plan was for this 'progressive alliance' to oversee the formation of SAADEL and draw up a constitution for it. The steering committee met at the Riverside Hotel in Durban, with several prominent figures present: Dullah Omar, the western Cape regional leader of the UDF; Silas Nkanunu, a leading sports administrator from Port Elizabeth; Pius Langa and Krish Govender from Durban; Mahmood Cajee and Kader Hassim from Pietermaritzburg; and Mathole Motshekga, Krish Naidoo and Ismail Ayob (Mandela's personal lawyer) from Johannesburg.[15]

The goal of achieving broad unity on the legal front faced a particular challenge. The Black Consciousness–oriented Black Lawyers Association based in

Johannesburg was the biggest alternative grouping at the time. Could SAADEL help facilitate the formation of a single body uniting all the streams of anti-apartheid lawyers for Zola Skweyiya and the DLCA? Would it be possible for them all to work with the BLA within a broad front?

Those who'd been involved in the February briefing in Lusaka were confident that this broad-front planning would be successful. In their report 'Black Consciousness and the Perspective of Non-Racialism', Pekane and Maduna disclosed that 'Whereas it was initially thought that the BLA would be a problem in this regard, this hurdle was easy to jump and the organisation espouses non-racialism'. Moreover, chairperson Dumisa Ntsebeza, a lawyer and activist who had been subjected to severe repression in the Transkei Bantustan, was 'very good at articulating the cause of non-racialism'.[16] The main problem foreseen was that the BLA had, in the previous four years, managed to accumulate 'property and money and a legal aid clinic in Johannesburg, which they want to control and possess separately'. Others felt that these assets should be put in the SAADEL pool (and that the same should be done with money channelled from abroad for the defence of political trialists and their families). The ANC middlemen foresaw a compromise being reached on this score.[17]

Nelson Mandela, then into the third decade of his imprisonment, was strongly in support of the new unity plans between the lawyers of different ideological persuasions. As early as 1985 he was in correspondence with Victoria Mxenge (soon to be brutally assassinated by an apartheid hit squad, like her husband before her), enquiring about the emerging legal bodies.[18] Later he sent a letter from prison to Krish Naidoo, conveying his support for unity.[19]

Mandela had a personal relationship with two key figures in the BLA: Dikgang Moseneke, a future deputy chief justice of South Africa, and Godfrey Pitje, the BLA's founding president.

Dikgang Moseneke had been arrested and imprisoned on Robben Island at the age of fifteen for furthering the aims of the PAC. He found that the only way he could escape the extremely harsh prison life was through his mind and study. While standing around during the day, as there were no seats, and reading secretly under his blanket at night, he completed his junior certificate and matric exams. In his late teens, when he was pushing wheelbarrows filled with limestone in the Robben Island prison quarry, he would call out Latin verb conjugations to Mmutlanyane 'Uncle Stan' Mogoba, an older prisoner with a flair for classical languages who had become Moseneke's Latin tutor on the island. 'I would say *amo, amas, amat* [I love, you love, he/she/it loves, and then] *amamus, amatis, amant* [We love, you love (plural), they love],' wrote Moseneke, 'and he would call out the correct Latin word when I stuttered and nod approvingly when I got it right.[20] The Latin was necessary when Moseneke later completed a law degree with UNISA via distance learning. By that stage he'd served half of his ten-year sentence.

His interest in law had been sparked at the age of nine when he accompanied his father on a visit to Mandela and Tambo's offices in downtown Johannesburg. His father had come to consult Mandela regarding a compensation claim for his family's forced removal from their home in Lady Selborne in Pretoria, which had been declared a white area. Moseneke writes: 'Inside the entrance of Chancellor House there was a brass plaque that read "Mandela and Tambo Attorneys". [I]t left an indelible impression on me ... I remained in the rather congested but quiet waiting room as my father was called into an office.'[21]

After being released from prison and successfully completing his law degree, he set about becoming registered as a legal practitioner. The Transvaal Law Society opposed his application, saying that he was not a South African citizen but, as a Setswana-speaker, a citizen of the so-called homeland state of Bophuthatswana. Moseneke had never even been to Bophuthatswana. The judge who heard his application rejected the Law Society's position and invited Moseneke to step forward to take the prescribed oath. Moseneke describes the moment:

> The inside of my mouth dried up. I could feel my heart pounding as if it would pierce through my ribcage and I would have to pick it up from the floor ... My nostrils took in huge gulps of air as I strained to master this incredible moment in my life ... Even before the two judges rose and disappeared, loud applause broke out in the courthouse.[22]

Moseneke writes that all the professional challenges facing black lawyers occurred within a context of ever-increasing state repression and racial injustice. They were oppressed because of race, class and gender, and bore the responsibility of closing ranks with other progressive forces and liberating themselves. Moseneke stresses the importance of self-liberation:

> It was not open to oppressed lawyers to outsource their push for dignity, equality and freedom. They had to step up to the plate and become their own liberators. They had to agonise and wrestle with their miserable lot in a way only they could understand. They knew that activist lawyers could rightly earn the respect and support of white fellow-travellers only when they themselves took up cudgels against their wretched condition.[23]

BC and Africanist-inclined people like him had turned to Godfrey Pitje, who was regarded as the 'near natural leader' of this self-liberation project.[24]

While at Fort Hare, Pitje had been elected for a short time as president of the ANC Youth League and had gone on to become a lecturer in anthropology. He later became a schoolteacher and, in 1953, emerged as a leader in the resistance to Bantu Education. When facing the threat of expulsion from his teaching job, he sought advice at the only black legal firm in the country: Mandela and Tambo's. They urged him to consider becoming an articled clerk at their firm, adding that they were constantly being restricted, locked up and harassed, and that they would like him to stay out of politics to keep the firm alive. Pitje followed their wishes and kept a low political profile. When Tambo found himself threatened with a charge of contempt of court for refusing to obey a command from a magistrate to move away from the place where white lawyers addressed the court, to another section reserved for black practitioners, he sent Pitje as his clerk to explain why he would not appear in court under those conditions. Later, when most members of the firm, Tambo, Mandela, Mompati and Mendi Msimang, had ended up in exile or in prison, the clerk ended up leading it, earning huge respect for his work.[25]

Even when entering court buildings, black lawyers had to use a separate entrance. Once inside, they had to stand in separate queues to file and collect documents. The magistrates, prosecutors and senior orderlies were all white. More than 90 per cent of legal practitioners were white, while accused people were overwhelmingly black. A young white witness would be addressed as Mr or Mrs, while an elderly black person would be referred to by their first name. Many magistrates were openly hostile. In some cases, the blatant enmity they showed to Pitje as a black practitioner turned out to be advantageous to his clients: their decisions were so clumsily worded that it was easy to overturn them on appeal.

In June 1977, Pitje phoned around and sent a few faxes to black practitioners inviting them to a discussion in his office in Johannesburg. His modest premises overflowed with young and old lawyers, and the discussion led to the decision to form the BLA. Moseneke and Seun Moshidi were asked to draft a constitution for a more formal inaugural meeting.[26] Based mainly in Johannesburg and Pretoria, they started work in Black October 1977, the month in which Steve Biko was murdered in detention and many Black Consciousness organisations were banned.

The BLA was formally constituted at a meeting at the Seshego Hotel in Pietersburg on 1 September 1980, where the constitution drawn up by Moshidi and Moseneke was accepted. By that time, the BLA had already developed into a vibrant organisation providing for the steady stream of black lawyers who had emerged from the 1970s onwards.[27] 'Nearly every admitted black attorney or advocate joined', writes Moseneke, claiming 'the right to practise law for both personal gain and public service', and opting for viable formats of practice that went beyond the subsistence patterns of black practices in the 1950s and 1960s.[28] Moseneke goes on to say that the core group reached out to all practitioners who had been discriminated against and that the BLA espoused a non-racial stance while making its primary concern quite plain – 'the vital interests of black practitioners and the people they were intent on serving'. Legal figures such as Phineas Mojapelo, Justice Moloto, Mojanku Gumbi, Dolly Mokgatle, Ishmael Semenya and Vincent Maluleka became prominent in BLA educational and publishing programmes.

The BLA focused on training and capacity-building. Their objective was to enable black lawyers to break through the barriers to professional advancement. To raise the funds necessary for their work, Moseneke flew to New York with a proposal for Franklin Thomas, the new president of the Ford Foundation. Thomas was an African American who had played a significant role in the US movement against racial segregation and for social change. Moseneke gatecrashed his office, boldly bypassing a junior programme officer with whom his appointment had been made. Fortunately, Thomas listened to Moseneke's impassioned presentation explaining why the BLA was so vital to the fight against apartheid. Within weeks, the Ford Foundation's cheque had reached the BLA, and for many years afterwards the foundation assisted the BLA in its work.[29]

Meanwhile, the attempt to create a broad front among progressive anti-apartheid lawyers in 1987 got off to a good start when Lawyers for Human Rights (LHR) agreed to join the new umbrella organisation after some 'relatively easy' meetings with the steering committee. However, discussions with Godfrey Pitje, Dikgang Moseneke and others from the BLA proved to be more complicated. Firstly, there were clearly ideological differences, as the BLA was inclined more towards the thinking of the BCM, PAC and Unity Movement than the ANC and UDF. Secondly, the BLA was not keen to give the LHR equal status from the outset. According to Krish Naidoo's account, the BLA argued that it and SAADEL should 'join forces and then absorb the LHR on our terms'. Thirdly, the BLA felt that since SAADEL was a 'pressure group' rather than an organisation, its supporters should join the BLA as individual members.[30] Finally, the issue of the BLA holding on to its property and resources remained a sticking point.

After a few months of interaction, which set back the planned formation date, the BLA nevertheless agreed to come onto a joint steering committee to form a single organisation of progressive anti-racist lawyers. A constitution was drawn up for the new body, which was to be given a different name: NADEL instead of SAADEL. However, the consensus between the groups had not been sustained.

Despite pleas for representation for each of the different bodies on the new executive committee, the BLA was strong enough to dominate the elections for the leadership at NADEL's founding meeting in Durban on 1 May 1987. Only Dullah Omar (vice-president) and Ismail Ayob (secretary) from the 'progressive alliance' steering committee made it onto the executive committee. Advocate Dumisa Ntsebeza became NADEL's first president.[31]

Johnny de Lange, who represented the DLO on the joint steering committee and who attended the NADEL launch in Durban, clarified that two main points of contestation arose:

> Firstly, how to create an NEC that comprised all the constituent bodies that were integrated into NADEL. This battle we lost. The BLA position that the national executive should be decided by a vote of all participants present at the launch, won the day. This meant that the [Freedom] Charterist forces only had two members appointed to the NEC. Secondly, out of the blue, the BLA proposed that all white males should be excluded from membership of NADEL. This took us by surprise as during the work of the steering committee this issue was never raised and all the constituent bodies being integrated into NADEL, except the BLA, had white lawyers as members. The BLA proposal stated that no person who was legally obliged to serve in the SADF would be entitled to membership of NADEL. At the time the law stated that each white male South African was obliged to serve in the SADF or face a recurring prison term of five years imprisonment. So, if the BLA proposal was agreed to, all white males would automatically be excluded from membership of NADEL. After heated and long discussions, the other constituent bodies placed an ultimatum before the BLA. NADEL membership will remain non-racial or they would not become part of NADEL. On that day, the BLA backed down and the principle of non-racialism won the day. NADEL was launched with a non-racial membership.[32]

The first NADEL election, however, was a blow to the ANC. Zola Skweyiya wrote to Oliver Tambo on 4 May conveying the 'shocking news' that the 'DLCA received a report that none of its people or members of the progressive alliance was voted on to the National Executive body'. Moreover, it also had a new name and was no longer SAADEL, as had previously been decided on in the planning with the ANC. Skweyiya told Tambo: 'We believe the situation warrants a discussion of the organisation and its leaders ... at your earliest convenience'.[33] Copies of the letter were sent to the PMC and ECC heads, Nhlanhla and Stuart.

Skweyiya then called Langa, Mlaba, Linda Zama of the DLC and Motshekga of the DLA to Harare for a post-mortem within a fortnight. The DLCA had not been able to call further consultative meetings after the February meeting with Motshekga as it had been fully occupied with trying to arrange the Harare conference (originally planned for April 1987[34]), and it had only heard of the NADEL launch at the last minute.[35] The DLCA reported back in its dissection that 'the elections were vigorously fought on political alliance' and that the 'progressives' had been caught off guard and unprepared.[36] A plan was hatched in Harare to seize back control from what was termed the 'conservative alliance'. Meanwhile a middle course would be taken with NADEL. The ANC would explain to its international allies and funders that it would be adopting a wait-and-see attitude to the new organisation while attempting to quietly block international travel opportunities, contacts and funding for its executive, while promoting figures from the progressive alliance instead.[37] So although the ANC had deepened its organisational links with UDF-aligned comrades, a political struggle for control in NADEL had commenced.

The role of white lawyers in NADEL was specifically discussed at the May 1987 post-mortem in Harare. Those present agreed unambiguously that they should be welcomed into the organisation:

> African lawyers, coming as they do from the most oppressed section of our people, but at the same time proceeding from the perspective of non-racialism, have an even greater role to play in the mobilisation of all lawyers into the struggle for national liberation. They should therefore never shirk their responsibility in this regard. On this basis, white lawyers who are prepared to make common cause with blacks are not to be excluded from the ranks of NADEL.[38]

This was a key moment for NADEL. The organisation quickly pulled in white anti-apartheid legal activists, significantly broadening the anti-apartheid and constitutional planning front and bolstering it with some outstanding jurists.

Prominent among the white-led bodies were the Centre for Applied Legal Studies (CALS), the LHR, the LRC and the Centre for Human Rights (CHR) at the University of Pretoria. Each had its own history, function and personality. Taken together, they broadened the front on which apartheid was being attacked, even if they were not necessarily NADEL or ANC members.

The LHR was part of a network of interlinked legal organisations led by liberal and radical white lawyers, which redefined legal strategies and activities to counter apartheid laws more effectively. It had emerged in 1979, after the establishment of CALS at Wits University in 1978 and the first International Conference on Human Rights in South Africa in 1979. The latter was a groundbreaking meeting that attracted over 300 participants. Anti-racist lawyers had spoken about the nation's need for an organisation of legal professionals committed to human rights. When the LHR was started, it was under the motto 'justice for all'. John Dugard, a legal academic from Wits specialising in international law, had not only helped to set up both CALS and the LHR but saw to it that their work was oriented towards the broad struggles being waged by the MDM and, more specifically, the workers' movement. Dugard had grown up steeped in the ambience of Healdtown, the school where both his parents had taught. Mandela, who studied there too, recalls:

> Located at the end of a winding road overlooking a verdant valley, Healdtown was ... beautiful and impressive ... It was, at the time, the largest African school south of the Equator, with more than a thousand learners, both male and female. Its graceful ivory colonial buildings and tree-shaded courtyards gave it a feeling of a privileged academic oasis, which is exactly what it was.[39]

Journalism pioneer John Tengo Jabavu matriculated there in the 1870s. He was one of hundreds of early African leaders produced by this institution, followed generations later by PAC president Robert Sobukwe and three of the eleven Rivonia Trialists – Mandela, Govan Mbeki and Raymond Mhlaba.

Growing up at Healdtown had instilled in Dugard a deep respect for African culture and intellectual aspirations. Armed with a Cambridge PhD in international law, he bravely pronounced that the Bantustans and South Africa's occupation of South West Africa (Namibia) were illegal. He also guided CALS in developing processes in court to sabotage the cruel and grinding ways that pass laws and other racist statutes were producing rule *by* law rather than rule *of* law.

Dugard had provided leadership on the LHR's national council, together with some of the most sought-after advocates at the Johannesburg Bar – Arthur Chaskalson, George Bizos and Jules Browde. Initially, the organisation was purely a voluntary association of lawyers who performed pro bono work in their spare time, but by 1985 the LHR had grown to include nearly 800 members from across the country. Up-and-coming lawyers like Brian Currin, Peter Mothle, Nicholas 'Fink' Haysom, Halton Cheadle, Clive Thompson, Paul Benjamin, Dolly Mokgatle (who later became prominent in the BLA), Modise Khoza, Martin Brassy, Edwin Cameron, Jody Kollapen and Dennis Davis all cut their teeth in this legal milieu. Chaskalson, Bizos, Haysom and others were later to become involved with the ANC's Constitution Committee. The LHR did pioneering legal and educational work in relation to censorship and capital punishment.[40]

The founding of the Legal Resources Centre followed hard on the heels of CALS and the LHR. John Dugard, together with Felicia and Sydney Kentridge, approached

Arthur Chaskalson in 1979 to give up a lucrative legal practice to become the founding director of this new organisation. It would be a public-interest body modelled largely on the Legal Defense Fund of the National Association for the Advancement of Colored People (NAACP) in the US. Chaskalson had been junior counsel at the Rivonia Trial. He also helped with the defence of Bram Fischer, who had the unusual distinction of having been chair of the Johannesburg Bar Council while also being acting chair of the underground Communist Party. Described by a colleague as 'the most cerebral of advocates, Chaskalson's manner was formal, even cold – a devastating cross examiner, clear but soft-spoken in argument. His manner may have dissuaded an easy camaraderie, but he was a natural leader at the Bar.'[41] Yet those who worked closely with him were soon enamoured of his warmth, courtesy, openness of mind, intellectual brilliance and sense of honour. Above all, he hated the way in which the law was being used in South Africa to sustain racial oppression and hound opponents of apartheid.

Supported by Geoffrey Budlender, who had been a prominent activist in NUSAS, Chaskalson set about creating a completely new legal institution in South Africa. Its objective was to pursue strategic litigation in the courts to help undermine the pass laws, the Group Areas Act and other apartheid statutes through the adroit use of administrative law. In the process, this would undermine the doctrine of parliamentary sovereignty, which the judiciary had long used to avoid responsibility for the harshness and cruelty of the laws they enforced. Parliamentary sovereignty had left no space for bringing applications to strike down apartheid laws that were overtly racist and discriminatory or that granted unrestricted powers of search, seizure and detention to security officials, but the LHR, CALS and the LRC showed that a carefully prepared court action could put a spoke in the wheels of arbitrary, racist and oppressive statutes by challenging the manner in which they were being applied.[42]

The Harare conference in September 1987 showed that the ANC's broad-front efforts were beginning to produce results. As mentioned, a phalanx of progressive South African lawyers had attended, headed by figures like Pius Langa, Dullah Omar, Essa Moosa and Nicholas Haysom. Each of these men would later become members of the Constitution Committee. Their presence underlined a growing identification of progressive South African lawyers with evolving ANC initiatives. In the final conference declaration, they openly aligned themselves with ANC goals and called on international professional legal bodies to impose sanctions against those upholding the apartheid legal system.[43]

The BLA felt left out; it had not been invited to the Harare conference, so the next month it requested a meeting with the ANC. This meeting took place on

20 November 1987 in Lusaka. A big, twelve-person BLA delegation full of distinguished names made the trip north. The president, Dumisa Ntsebeza, had had his passport confiscated by the South African government, but Godfrey Pitje and Dikgang Moseneke were in the party, together with George Maluleka, Willie Seriti, Abram Motimele, Mojanku Gumbi, Keith Kunene, Justice Moloto, J. Moloi, Phineas Mojapelo and Moses Mavundla.[44] However, the fault lines were in place and the meeting failed to traverse the impasse. The BLA stayed separate from NADEL and its ally the ANC.

The different ideological positions manifested themselves again at the next elective conference of NADEL in 1988. Efforts before and during the conference to include both BLA and UDF-aligned people on the executive had been unsuccessful, a development about which Mandela, writing from prison, expressed his unhappiness.[45] This time, all the executive positions were taken by UDF-aligned members, with Pius Langa becoming president and Dullah Omar his deputy. Though there was some overlap of membership between the BLA and NADEL and large areas of common concern existed, the two organisations differed in terms of ideology, activities and alliances.

Zola Skweyiya and the DLCA in Lusaka were delighted with Langa and Omar's election. Both were high-profile figures linked to the UDF, meaning that the ANC could rely on them. This was what they had organised for. The election thus set NADEL back on the course that the ANC had planned for it. A new alliance with some of the best legal minds inside South Africa was taking shape.

The many contacts and the developments at home in 1987 had helped create heightened interest in the constitutional planning process of the DLCA and the ANC and a strong network of support for it. But Jack Simons and the Committee were feeling frustration over one important matter – lack of movement on its key document: the Foundations of Government.

23

Constitution Committee Plans in Cold Storage

THE YEAR 1987 was an extremely busy one for the Constitution Committee. According to the dates on Jack Simons' handwritten notes, no less than eight Constitution Committee meetings were held in the first half of the year. The secretariat functioning in the DLCA office also met every week, took decisions in between plenary sessions and met delegations from democratic lawyers' organisations to discuss the idea of initiating a countrywide debate on the constitutional future of South Africa.[1]

The DLCA members also saw to internal matters and organised and participated in several roadshows and conferences. Yet for all this non-stop activity, no progress was made on getting the Foundations of Government document into circulation. The Constitution Committee was struggling to make any progress at all in the very area it had worked hardest and been set up to deal with: preparing an outline of the constitutional principles that would underpin a future democratic dispensation in South Africa.

The Committee had started the year with an understanding that the Foundations document had been accepted after the joint meeting with the NEC in October 1986, and that it could now be distributed and discussed publicly. The Committee members had also taken the president through their documents and plans on 6 January 1987. Immediately afterwards, they forwarded their revised Statement of Intent – meant to complement the updated Foundations of Government – to the NEC for approval. The NEC endorsed it on 14 January 1987.[2] A fortnight later, Skweyiya sent the detailed project proposals and budget for the agreed-to In-House Seminar to the president for the NEC's approval to discuss the document.[3] The NEC was also asked formally to approve the plan for a bigger conference of international allies and internal groups to follow later in the year.

Weeks went by with no answer received. Finally, on 9 March, a letter came from Tambo saying that the request 'is receiving our attention'.[4] A few days later, on 13 March 1987, the NWC met in a special session to discuss the Foundations and the Statement of Intent. Their critique (which reached the Committee's secretary, Jobodwana, only on 15 April) declared that the Statement was unclear in its purpose and intended audience, and could be harmful if it reached the wrong audience. It was also much too long, repeating parts of the Foundations, and at least five sections could be happily excised. The NWC's critique added that the document was a bit self-congratulatory and the most that could be done with it was to use it as an introduction for the Foundations.[5] This was valid criticism, and the Statement of Intent (though clarifying what the Constitution Committee wanted the ANC to communicate to a broader audience) did not survive to become an official ANC constitutional document.

The NWC also had criticisms of the latest version of the Foundations document, despite it having been drafted after the joint Constitution Committee and NEC meeting in October 1986, and the fact that it included clauses that the NEC itself had insisted be added to the initial September 1986 draft. The NWC admitted that, in some cases, members had changed their minds about the issues they felt so strongly about at the October meeting. The NWC now wanted additional changes to seven paragraphs. Their criticisms are listed below in italics.

DRAFT FIVE: Amendments to certain paragraphs in The Foundations of Government in a Democratic South Africa, proposed by the NWC, 13 March 1987

OBJECTIVES of a new constitution
- The creating of the conditions for the speediest achievement of these goals with the least possible disruption to the tranquillity of the country and to the production of the goods and services necessary to enable all members of the community to lead a decent life; [and]
- The guaranteeing of the security necessary for the achievement of these goals.

These should be combined so that the issue of maintaining tranquillity and avoiding disruption in the period of transition, is dropped. The item could then read: 'the creation of the conditions and guaranteeing of the security necessary for the achievement of these goals'.

The New Constitution shall be based on the following PRINCIPLES
- The state and all institutions shall be under a duty to eradicate apartheid in all its forms, as well as to take measures to overcome its consequences;
- The advocacy or practice of racism, fascism, Nazism, tribalism or regionalism shall be outlawed;
- Subject to the previous two clauses, freedom of association and expression shall be guaranteed by the adoption of a multi-party system and an open press;

Objections were raised with regard to the term 'open press'. Various suggestions were made about its reformulation to accommodate such concepts as 'a people's press'. Fears were expressed as to the power of the monopolist press being left intact so that it may be used in opposition to the people's government. It was proposed that some formulation be found which while not placing a ban on a free press can not leave this tool in the hands of the monopolies.

- Also subject to those clauses, freedom of religion, worship and conscience shall be given special constitutional guarantee by the state;

It was felt that the use of 'special constitutional guarantee' implies that the other 'ordinary' guarantees are not as weighty. If the quality of the guarantee is considered good, why the need to qualify some as 'special'?

- The state and all social institutions shall take active steps to redress as speedily as possible the economic and social inequalities produced by apartheid. In particular the unjust dispossession of the African people of their land shall be corrected through the abolition of all legislation restricting land ownership and use on a racial basis and all other apartheid measures designed to deprive the people of their land and livestock. The victims of forced removals carried out by the apartheid regime shall be given proper redress by the state. In particular they shall be given the right to return to their land or ancestral homes wherever possible.

Reference to the victims of forced removals it was felt should be dropped since all blacks are in one sense or another victims of forced removals.

- [Formatting only rearranged] The state shall have the right to determine the general context in which economic life takes place and to define and limit the rights and obligations attaching to the ownership and use of private productive capacity. The economy shall be a mixed one with a public sector, a cooperative sector, a private sector and a family sector. The public sector shall be subjected to democratic control. Cooperative forms of economic enterprise and the family sector shall be supported by the state. Property for personal use and consumption shall be constitutionally protected;

Questions were raised as to why only the public sector should be under democratic control. Should not the private sector also be subject to control? Why should the family sector be given state support?

- The state shall promote the acquisition of managerial and entrepreneurial skills, and provide facilities to encourage commercial and industrial activities amongst all sections of the population;

Add to the item after 'population', 'especially the African people'.

199

> Finally, the NWC made a new point: *'no mention is made of special programmes regarding the rights of women and children. The DLCA should examine the possibility of inserting such a clause.*[6]

The NWC feedback came as a jolt to the Constitution Committee. Some of the required amendments had Joe Slovo's signature written all over them. The NWC's disquiet with the Committee's support for an 'open press' resurrected the same criticism Slovo had levelled at Simons over the phone in January 1986, in the first NWC response in February 1986 and at the joint meeting with the NEC in October 1986.

Committee secretary Jobs Jobodwana wrote to Simons, saying, 'I think it is high time we change our strategies now in the way we approach our work.' It was his personal opinion only, he said, but 'from the comments made it would seem as if our suggestions or proposals are too mild to merit acceptance by the NEC'.[7] Skweyiya and Maduna were at that time in Harare, planning the Children's Conference, and it was suggested the local members meet as soon as possible after their return.

Just over a month later, the Committee was ready with its response. It sought to hold the line on its basic thinking while acting on the suggestions from its political and line-function superiors. The result of this further round of engagement was a tidier, clearer version of the Foundations document with some key additional provisions. Revisions were made to five paragraphs, two were effectively binned, and a completely new one was added. Writing to Secretary-General Nzo, Skweyiya attached the revised and amended version of the Foundations and explained that they'd tried 'by all means to meet the criticism by the NWC and reflect their views'. He stated that most of the amendments were based on the NWC's formulations, but in response to the NWC's proposal that the reference to victims of forced removals 'be dropped since all blacks are in one sense or another victims of forced removals', Skweyiya (whose own family had been affected) wrote back:

> On the question of forced removals, rather than remove the passage from the original document, we should explain why we advise very strongly [that] it should be retained. While admittedly all blacks are in one way or another victims of forced removals, the concept has a particular meaning in the current situation in the country. If omitted, the document will be devoid of an attempt to address itself to the centuries' grievance of our people regarding the land. The Constitution Committee feels very strongly that if any changes are made, it will lose its mobilising effect on the masses of our people.[8]

The Committee also explained to the NWC why they felt that the family sector should be supported by the state: this would alleviate unemployment, provide services not catered for by the centrally administered economy and give support to a sector that did not hire labour, as opposed to the private sector, which did. Like all other parts of the economy, the family sector was exposed to financial risks, straits and economic disasters.

The most important addition to the new draft of the Foundations was a new final clause (r) regarding the rights of women and children, following the reminder by the NWC in March that it should consider inserting such a clause. None of the three initial documents drawn up by the Committee since January 1986 – the Freedom Charter analysis, the Skeleton or the Foundations – nor the NEC or NWC inputs until then, had made mention of this issue. The Constitution Committee had inserted a 'No Discrimination' section that specifically forbade discrimination regardless of 'race, colour, sex or ethnic origin' in the Statement of Intent in January, but the Statement itself would never become an official ANC document. Now, however, clause (r) of the Foundations stated that 'Steps will be taken to introduce a uniform system of family law relations, including marriage, divorce and succession, with equal rights for women and the provision for the protection of children'. This new guideline would itself be criticised and expanded in due course.

The updated version of the Foundations document was sent by Zola Skweyiya to Alfred Nzo on 8 May 1987. Copies were also circulated for the president and all the members of the NEC present in Lusaka at that time.

DRAFT SIX: 'The Foundations of Government in a Democratic South Africa', updated by the Constitution Committee, following the fifth round of inputs from the NWC in March 1987, and forwarded to the ANC secretary-general, 8 May 1987. (Changes indicated in italics.)

OBJECTIVES of a new constitution
(a)   The granting to the oppressed majority of their just national rights;
(b)   The outlawing of racial discrimination in all its forms;
(c)   The ensuring of the complete dismantlement of apartheid structures and their replacement by democratic ones;
(d)   The prevention of the resurgence of racist policies, programmes and practices, whether in old form or new;
(e)   The overcoming of the effects of centuries of racial domination and inequality by ensuring substantial redistribution of wealth and the complete opening up of facilities for all;
(f)   The encouragement of the active involvement of all sectors of the population in government and economic and cultural life;
(g)   The promotion of the habits of non-racial thinking, the practice of

anti-racist behaviour and the acquisition of a genuine shared patriotic consciousness;

(h) *The creation of the conditions and guaranteeing of the security necessary for the achievement of these goals.*

The New Constitution shall be based on the following PRINCIPLES

(a) South Africa shall be an independent unitary, democratic and non-racial state;

(b) *[Two paragraphs joined into one without change to the wording]*
   (i) Sovereignty shall belong to the people as a whole and shall be exercised through one central legislature, administrature and executive;
   (ii) Provision will be made for the regional and local delegation of the powers of the central authority to smaller administrative units for purposes of more efficient and effective administration;

(c) In the exercise of their sovereignty, the people shall have the right to vote under the system of universal suffrage based on the principle of one person, one vote;

(d) Every voter shall have the right to stand for election and be elected to all legislative bodies;

(e) The system of universal and equal franchise will apply also to the election of all regional and local bodies;

(f) It shall be state policy to promote the growth of a single national identity and loyalty binding on all South Africans; at the same time, the state will recognise the linguistic and cultural diversity of South African people, and provide facilities for free linguistic and cultural development;

(g) The institution of hereditary rulers and chiefs shall be transformed to serve the interests of the people as a whole in conformity with the democratic principles embodied in the constitution;

(h) The constitution will include a Bill of Rights based on the Freedom Charter guaranteeing the fundamental human rights of all citizens and providing appropriate mechanisms for their enforcement;

(i) The state and all institutions shall be under a duty to eradicate apartheid in all its forms, as well as to take measures to overcome its consequences;

(j) The advocacy or practice of racism, fascism, Nazism, tribalism or regionalism shall be outlawed;

(k) *Subject to clauses (i) and (j), the democratic state shall guarantee the basic rights and freedoms such as freedom of association, expression, worship, press and a multi-party system;*

(l)   Participatory democracy shall be encouraged by means of involving the community, and community and workers organisations, directly in public and economic administration;

(m) The state and all social institutions shall take active steps to redress as speedily as possible the economic and social inequalities produced by apartheid. In particular the unjust dispossession of the African people of their land shall be corrected through the abolition of all legislation restricting land ownership and use on a racial basis and all other apartheid measures designed to deprive the people of their land and . live-stock;

The victims of forced removals carried out by the apartheid regime shall be given proper redress by the state. In particular they shall be given the right to return to their land or ancestral homes wherever possible;

(n) *[Rearranged]* The state shall have the right to determine the general context in which economic life takes place and to define and limit the rights and obligations attaching to the ownership and use of private productive capacity;

The entire economy shall be placed under democratic control and direction to ensure that it serves the interests and well-being of all sections of the population.

Cooperative forms of economic enterprise and the family sector shall be supported by the state.

Property for personal use and consumption shall be constitutionally protected;

(o) The state shall promote the acquisition of managerial and entrepreneurial skills, and provide facilities to encourage commercial and industrial activities amongst all sections of the population, *especially the Africans*;

(p) Workers and trade union rights shall receive special constitutional protection;

(q) All organs of government, justice and security shall be transformed so as to make them representative of the people as a whole, democratic in their structure and functioning, and dedicated to defending the principles of the Constitution;

(r) *Steps will be taken to introduce a uniform system of family law relations, including marriage, divorce and succession, with equal rights for women and the provision for the protection of children.*

Skweyiya wrote that most of the NEC members had indicated that they agreed to the amended formulations in principle. This included Pallo Jordan, who reacted positively on behalf of the NWC, as well as Jordan's NWC subcommittee colleague Simon Makana and Treasurer-General Nkobi, who would provide the funding for the In-House Seminar. Makana, Nkobi and other members of the NEC had advised the Committee to go ahead and make arrangements for the seminar, adding that once the Foundations document was typed up, it should be given to the general membership through the eleven regional PMCs for discussion and amendment where possible. The Committee wanted the In-House Seminar to happen in Lusaka by the beginning of July 1987.[9]

Having received no response by the time the Committee met again in mid-June, three weeks before the Dakar conference, Skweyiya sent the secretary-general a follow-up letter informing him that the Committee had decided to proceed with its preparations. The proposed date for the seminar would now be October 1987. He added that 'it is taken for granted that the document ... would be circulated in the present form and is accepted by the NEC'. The treasury had long since given them the green light, and the Committee would now depend on the SG's assistance and cooperation as it implemented its proposals.[10]

Skweyiya asked that the president or SG open the seminar and for the NEC to commission one of its members to present a paper on the 'constitutional proposals for a democratic South Africa', based on the Constitution Committee's document'. The Committee also wanted Thabo Mbeki to deliver a piece on a post-apartheid economy, because 'Cde Thabo has been involved and more exposed to the broader discussion both internationally and internally with the mass democratic movement at home regarding ... this aspect'. For the rest, the Committee members would present papers on key questions, while eight different ANC departments in Lusaka would be asked to give inputs on their areas and to join the preparatory committee.[11]

This letter to Nzo, written a full eighteen months into the constitution-planning process, is the first archival evidence the author has found about Mbeki's involvement with the Committee and its work, even though he would become a key player in the drive for a negotiated settlement in South Africa.[12]

There was still no response from the NEC, though. In early October, ahead of an important NEC meeting to discuss the issue of negotiations, the full Committee met again with the item 'Memo to NEC' on the agenda.[13] On the same day, 7 October, Simons and Skweyiya again complained to Tambo that the NEC had failed to greenlight the publication of the document and the holding of seminars.[14] The Committee's plans appeared to be in cold storage.

24

NEC Debate: To Negotiate or Not to Negotiate?

I N HIS 8 January statement of 1987, Tambo had raised the prospect of negotiations. In the Dakar Declaration that July, the ANC had indicated a preference for negotiations. In addition, Thabo Mbeki had rounded off a day of heated discussions with the suggestion that releasing Nelson Mandela would unlock the political process. The ANC had firmly placed the release of Mandela and other political prisoners on its agenda in international campaigns. This was directly connected with the issue of whether to negotiate with the apartheid regime. In the wake of Dakar, P.W. Botha touched on the issue of negotiations in a major speech in Parliament on 13 August 1987. Despite blustering about the treachery of the ANC and the stupidity of those who had attended, he nevertheless dropped the precondition of renouncing violence for the release of political prisoners.

This was with a view to releasing the aged Govan Mbeki from Robben Island, ahead of discussions about the future of Mandela and other political prisoners. The apartheid government was aware that it would be a public relations disaster should any liberation leaders die in prison. Botha now also hinted that 'every generation will have to examine South Africa's problems anew, deal with them and, on that basis, negotiate and make amendments if we are seeking freedom and peace'. Sifiso Ndlovu has seen this moment as the first 'de facto recognition of the ANC' by the regime, though its preconditions were still unacceptable and aimed at destroying and disabling the movement rather than reaching accord with it.[1]

Tambo's 8 January address for 1987 had made the ANC's first major statement on the topic (see Chapter 17). With negotiation discussions speeding up at home and internationally, the NEC met on 9 October 1987 to discuss the question in depth. This came shortly after two-thirds of the NEC members had crossed from Zambia to attend the successful Harare conference.

Mac Maharaj and Pallo Jordan describe Tambo's 8 January statement and the one to emerge from this October 1987 NEC meeting as constituting two of 'the critical beacons guiding the democratic forces as they navigated their way through unchartered waters'. The third would be the constitutional guidelines being developed between the Constitution Committee and the NWC, encompassed at this stage in the draft Foundations of Government document.[2]

According to Maharaj, Tambo introduced the subject of negotiations in a way that encouraged NEC members to give their views. It was the best NEC discussion, in his opinion, since the careful preparations for the first business delegation in 1985, with Tambo characteristically listening carefully before giving his summary.[3]

The NEC reaffirmed its position since Kabwe. It had never been opposed to a negotiated settlement, but the regime had raised the prospect only to defuse the struggle inside South Africa and to avoid biting international sanctions. It had neither the desire nor the intention to enter genuine negotiations. In other words, the regime was sending out bogus signals. It was determined to control any process of change, including through the deepening repression against those fighting apartheid. However, genuine negotiations had to lead to a transfer of power. 'This, and only this, should be the objective of any negotiation process', the NEC emphasised in its statement following the October 1987 meeting:

> Once more, we would like to reaffirm that the ANC and the masses of our people as a whole are ready and willing to enter into genuine negotiations provided they are aimed at the transformation of our country into a united and non-racial democracy. *This, and only this, should be the objective of any negotiation process.* Accordingly, no meaningful negotiations can take place until all those concerned, and specifically the Pretoria regime, accept the perspective which we share with the whole of humanity ...[4]

The ANC was also determined not to be dragged into an interminable process that led nowhere:

> Being fully conscious of the way the Pretoria regime has, in the past, deliberately dragged out negotiations to buy time for itself, we maintain that any negotiations would have to take place within a definite time-frame to meet the urgent necessity to end the apartheid system and lift the yoke of tyranny from the masses of our people who have already suffered for too long.

The ANC saw no prospect yet for genuine negotiations because

> the Botha regime continues to believe that it can maintain the apartheid system through force and terror. We therefore have no choice but to intensify the mass political and armed struggle for the overthrow of the illegal apartheid regime and the transfer of power to the people.

As the ANC saw it, the regime and its policies lay at the heart of the problem and it was holding out false hopes of a just political settlement, which it had every intention to block. The reality was that the Botha government was conducting a determined campaign of repression that included the assassination of leaders, mass detentions, military occupation of townships and a programme of pacification carried out by the so-called Joint Management Centres (JMCs) under the National Security Management System (NSMS). The regime was out to terrorise people into submission, crush their democratic organisations and force them to surrender. These efforts would fail and only serve to sharpen the confrontation inside the country, bringing to the fore the prospect of the bloodiest conflict the continent had ever seen.

The NEC rejected outright Botha's most recent proposal for resuscitating a reform process that was already in tatters, namely the creation of a national statutory council that would advise government on future constitutional proposals. To make it worse, these proposals could then be legislated into being by the white-dominated Tricameral Parliament. This would entrench and legitimise the unrepresentative organs of the apartheid structures of repression. These structures could not be used to liquidate the very same system they had been established to maintain.

The NEC said the ANC's struggle would not end until South Africa was transformed into an equal society and a united, democratic and non-racial country. It went on to lay down six conditions that had to be met for such negotiations to take place. Paraphrased, the ANC declared that:

- The question of whether to negotiate, and on what conditions, should be put to the entire leadership, including those who are imprisoned (and who should be released unconditionally). While considering this question, the ANC leadership must be free to consult and discuss with the people 'without let or hindrance'.

- The ANC rejects unequivocally the cynical demand of the Pretoria regime that it unilaterally abandon or suspend the armed struggle. The source of violence in the country is the apartheid system. It is that violence which must end. Any cessation of hostilities must be negotiated and would entail agreed action by both sides as part of the process of the creation of a democratic South Africa.

- The ANC rejects all efforts to dictate to it who its allies should or should not be, and how its membership should be composed. Specifically, it will not bow down to pressures intended to drive a wedge between it and the South African Communist Party, a tried and tested ally in the struggle for a democratic South Africa. Neither will it submit to attempts to divide and weaken the movement by carrying out a witch hunt against various members on the basis of their ideological beliefs.

- The conflict is, in essence, between the forces of national liberation and democracy on the one hand, and those of racism and reaction on the other. Any negotiations will have to be conducted by these two forces as represented by their various organisational formations.
- An essential part of the apartheid system is the definition and division of the people according to racial and ethnic groups, dominated by the white minority. To end apartheid means, among other things, defining and treating all the people as equal citizens of the country, regardless of race, colour or ethnicity. To guarantee this, the ANC accepts that a new constitution for South Africa would include an entrenched Bill of Rights to safeguard the rights of the individual. They are, however, opposed to any attempt to perpetuate the apartheid system by advancing the concept of so-called group and minority rights.
- The region is fully conversant with the treacherous and deceitful nature of the apartheid regime. There are more than enough examples of agreements the regime has shamelessly dishonoured. Taking this experience into account, the ANC insists that before any negotiations take place, the apartheid regime must demonstrate its seriousness by implementing various measures to create a climate conducive to such negotiations. These would include the unconditional release of all political prisoners, detainees, captured freedom fighters and prisoners of war, as well as the cessation of all political trials. The state of emergency must be lifted, the army and the police withdrawn from townships and confined to their barracks. Similarly, all repressive legislation and all laws empowering the regime to limit freedom of assembly, speech, the press and so on must be repealed. Among these would be the Riotous Assemblies Act, the Native Administration Act, the General Laws Amendment Act, the Unlawful Organisations Act, the Internal Security Act and similar Acts and regulations.[5]

The reference to the Bill of Rights and the rejection of 'so-called group or minority rights' in a future constitution was clearly aligned to core provisions of the Foundations document, which the Committee was still attempting to get the NEC to sign off on and publicise.

Finally, the NEC called on the international community to implement comprehensive and mandatory sanctions that would bring the system down and reduce the amount of blood that would otherwise have to be shed to achieve this goal. The way to go, it said, was to follow the example of the OAU, which had recently adopted the Declaration of Southern Africa in support of the strategies the ANC was proposing.

———

According to one biography of Chris Hani, he complained after Dakar that some NEC members had only learnt of the event when the blaze of media publicity erupted. They were 'embarrassed', he said, 'to say to our members that we don't know these things'.[6] Caught up in fluid, quick-moving internal regional and international geopolitical developments, differences emerged in the NEC discussions. But this was a normal 'war of position' going on in internal debates, claim Maharaj and Jordan: 'Chris took part in the meeting with the Relly delegation of businesspeople in 1985 and some of the others that followed, and he never once opposed formal NEC decisions on the issue. Anyone who claims differently must show proof.' They point to the fact that his biographers, Houston and Ngculu, do not provide a valid source for his supposed Dakar complaint.[7]

Nevertheless, there were clearly tensions within the leadership and membership over differing perspectives towards negotiations. These could be seen in the debates within *Sechaba* and the *African Communist*, the journals of the ANC and SACP, which Sylvia Neame deals with at length in her study *Drama of the Peace Process in South Africa*. Jobs Jobodwana remembers that 'even comrades were very much suspicious of the work of the Constitution Committee'. 'Writing a constitution and whose mandate?'. Even words like 'sell-out', 'we are fighting and you are negotiating', or 'putting the cart before the horse' were used. But, Jobodwana says, they were 'not unduly worried or easily shaken by such accusations'. The reason? Zola and Ted were founder members of MK and 'I received my military engineering training ... in East Berlin', learning about 'blasting techniques', military intelligence and counter-intelligence.[8]

The paragraph in the NEC statement opposing any secret negotiations must be seen in this context of contending perspectives. There was still a significant degree of scepticism about taking this route. Individuals in the organisation could not be running around doing their own thing. 'We firmly believe that the people themselves must participate in shaping their destiny and would therefore have to be involved in any process of negotiations', the NEC concluded.

Given the author's inability to source the minutes of the NEC meeting, Maharaj volunteered that on the specific question of Mandela's release, three broad positions came out:

1. Accept the release offers and do everything possible to get them out.
2. We want them out, but let us probe the offers further.
3. This is nonsense; let's not engage with the regime now.[9]

An educated guess of NEC perspectives at this stage would put Thabo Mbeki in the first camp, Maharaj and Jordan in the second, and Hani and Slovo in the third.

In any case, if meaningful negotiations became an option, they would require the maximum amount of back-up from the various other complementary pillars of struggle, coupled with concerted efforts to intensify internal mass mobilisation, armed attacks, underground activities and international solidarity. Mbeki himself had already pointed out that the simultaneous deepening of the armed struggle 'might create the conditions for a bargained settlement'.

As historian Tom Lodge puts it, 'commitments to flexible pragmatism' at this stage were beginning to make sense, especially with the outreach through the safaris to white and 'moderate' South Africans and increasing diplomatic success in isolating the regime in the USA and Europe. The goal Mbeki pointed out was to create fundamental realignments that would lead to a loss of support for the regime and force it – even if it was not overthrown – 'to do what Ian Smith did': cede power in a negotiated settlement.[10]

In summary, it was too early for the movement to show its hand. The key strategic issue for the ANC would be to decide when the time was ripe and right to come out openly in favour of negotiations. This would depend on the changing balance of forces – the relative strengths and weaknesses of the main adversaries in the period ahead – and what favourable preconditions the ANC would be able to secure. Until then, there would be a necessary ambiguity in the debates as the internal war of position in the ANC played itself out. The NEC's statement on the question of negotiations underlined the point. But intriguingly, besides issuing this statement, the NWC meeting held the following week also passed a resolution on negotiations. It was minuted as secret, so whatever it was, the issue was becoming increasingly pressing.

25

Tambo's Special Christmas Gift

A FEW DAYS AFTER Christmas 1987, Oliver Tambo offered a very special gift to the Constitution Committee: his personal comments on the Foundations of Government document. For the first time since he had set up the Committee almost two years before, he was putting in writing his own views on the issues raised in the text. The background to his intervening at last was as follows.

Jack Simons, Zola Skweyiya and the DLCA secretariat in Lusaka had organised a Constitution Committee meeting two days before the NEC 'negotiations' meeting in October that year. They fired off a letter of reminder to the leadership – yet another of their numerous pleas for action on the proposed seminars since late 1986.[1]

The letter was from Simons but signed by Skweyiya and directed to the president. They informed him that the Committee had considered using the NEC session to put forward their proposal for a post-apartheid constitutional framework. The Committee had now prepared a final version of the Foundations, a document on which they'd been working since early 1986. To their regret, the strategy to discuss and release it more broadly had not materialised because the NEC had thus far failed to give them the green light.

They pointed out that, when meeting with the Committee in both January 1986 and January 1987, the president had warned that if the ANC did not take the initiative and provide a framework for the future, Western powers friendly to the regime would intervene and start dictating the terms. That moment had arrived, said Skweyiya. A week before, on 29 September, US secretary of state George Shultz had, in a statement on 'The democratic future of South Africa', made 'a direct appeal to South Africans to build a new future' through 'negotiations between the racist government and "interested parties"'. The result, Simons and Skweyiya said, was that 'the wind has been taken out of our sails'. They attached a draft memorandum for the In-House Seminar on a future constitution. This would be for the long-awaited discussions with ANC members, hopefully to be held in February 1988. They added that 'the NEC response will be quite instructive' given 'the source and pressure that is brought to bear on us'.[2]

Skweyiya also discussed the matter with ANC leaders, including Thabo Mbeki. On 12 October he sent a follow-up letter, appealing to Mbeki at the Department of Information and Publicity (DIP) to put the Foundations into 'a more accept-able journalistic style' as the Committee intended to circulate the document to the general membership as soon as possible.[3]

When the local members of the Committee met on the morning of 10 December 1987 (sans Teddy Pekane, who was discussing with the Swedes how the constitu-tional seminar would be fitted in under the umbrella of the PASA project), there were signs of progress. Simons recorded in his notes: 'Jobs reads letters written to OR and Thabo' and, though no reply had yet been received, 'Zola says we'll have the document before the end of the month.'[4]

More important was the fact that Tambo was back in Lusaka after a long period on the road.

The president had had another gruelling year. Apart from constant shuttles in Africa and returning from the Arusha conference only a few days earlier, he had visited at least eleven countries outside the continent: the United States, Australia, Sweden, Britain, Jamaica, Nicaragua, Venezuela, Canada, Zimbabwe, the Soviet Union and the German Democratic Republic. His biographer Luli Callinicos notes that, when arriving back in Lusaka that December, 'Tambo was left with three weeks in which to organise and prepare for the next 8 January speech, which was now being delivered to larger numbers of avid listeners, both in South Africa and abroad.'[5] He made time to attend to Constitution Committee issues as part of these preparations. On 11 December, starting at 8.45 a.m. Tambo had a two-hour meeting with the Committee at HQ. Both parties emerged fully updated and in agreement on how to proceed.[6]

Turning to the Committee's burning issue at hand, Simons outlined plans for a full 'plenary' meeting of the Committee in January (around the time of the 8 January statement), followed by the In-House Seminar in March and then the publication of 'our constitutional proposals'. At this stage, Simons noted, 'OR phones Ruth [Mompati] about publication of the const[itutional] proposals'. Zola Skweyiya then spoke about the speakers, asking 'OR' to open the seminar. 'Press Freedom; Women's Section [and] Women's Rights' were added to the plans. The purpose of the seminar would be to 1) inform the ANC, and 2) open research at home and plan for a follow-up meeting in the Frontline States with people from home. Skweyiya said this was part of PASA's 'Post-Apartheid activity and will be funded from this source'. Teddy Pekane, who'd discussed PASA and the seminar with the Swedes the day before, suggested the University of Zambia as the venue for the In-House Seminar, but this would need to be discussed with the chancellor first.[7]

Tambo supported the publication of the proposals, saying, 'We must have a document to confront [constitutional affairs minister Chris] Heunis & co.' and this would be 'of great interest to the world'.

Although Simons noted that there were certain things on which Mbeki had not briefed Tambo, this meeting on 11 December was constructive and was quickly followed by two major steps forward. Eleven days later, Alfred Nzo sent out a circular to chief reps and heads of department giving notice of an In-House Seminar to be held on 1–4 March. Nzo's circular conveyed also that Teddy Pekane and Penuell Maduna would be heading the preparatory committee.[8] The seminar had been greenlit and given dates at last.

Then, Tambo found time in the period between Christmas and New Year to devote special attention to the Committee's Foundations of Government document, and he sent his comments directly to Simons. The three tightly typed pages reflected the attention to detail for which Tambo was known.[9] This can be regarded as the seventh draft of the ANC's working constitutional document. He pointed out a degree of overlap (and therefore confusion) between the objectives and principles. He suggested tightening up certain formulations, indicating that 'overcoming centuries of racial domination and inequality' would be stronger than just 'the inequalities produced by apartheid'. Instead of 'anti-racist behaviour', he suggested 'habits of non-racial thinking and behaviour'. He asked why there were inconsistencies in phrasing, with the document referring to both 'constitutionally protected' rights and rights that were given 'special constitutional guarantees'. He also made suggestions for grammatical and stylistic improvements.[10]

Summing up, he asked questions and expressed the view that there remained substantive political issues that needed more attention. For example, to what extent was the Freedom Charter incorporated into the objectives and principles of the document? Did the principles fall short by not 'incorporating what would amount to a Bill of Rights [expressly] based on the Freedom Charter'? Finally, Tambo said, 'It is ... necessary that our document does three things':

a) demolish the positions of the enemy;
b) point the way forward for all to follow who seek a genuine solution; and
c) seek to rally international opinion to our point of view.[11]

On demolishing the enemy's positions, he said there were various ideas the regime and its allies were toying with, which the ANC should explore in its document. The most serious was group rights.

In the statement of the principles on which a new constitution will be based we should launch a frontal attack on and not evade the group concept so central to 'Afrikaner Thinking'. Whether we have group or individual rights is absolutely fundamental to our concept of a new constitution. We should permit of no vagueness on the matter.[12]

The president's concluding assessment was forthright: 'I am not satisfied that the document as it stands meets these requirements.' He suggested to Simons and his team that they also do a comparative analysis, looking at the constitutional plans of the Broederbond, the business establishment through its business charter, and the Buthelezi Indaba to see how they compared with the Freedom Charter.[13]

Simons replied the next day, 30 December, saying he found the president's comments 'very much to the point, positive and salutary'. He said the Committee would take note of his criticisms and incorporate them in a revised draft 'if the Committee agrees'.[14]

The Constitution Committee did agree and had the eighth updated version of its Guidelines document ready by 10 January 1988. This version had a new title and a new format that made it easier for readers to follow the progression of thought. 'The Foundations of Government for a Democratic South Africa' became the 'Constitutional Guideline[s] for a Democratic South Africa'.[15]

The newest Guidelines replaced the eight bullet points of the objectives with a preamble of some 565 words, incorporating all Tambo's key points. It included the warning that while the multicultural and multifaith nature of South Africa would be 'handled with special constitutional sensitivity', there would be no constitutional protection for group rights, which could be used in the South African context as 'an excuse for the entrenchment of racial privilege' and for keeping the majority of the people 'constitutionally trapped in poverty' and as perpetual 'outsiders in the land of their birth'. The preamble also envisaged 'corrective action which guarantees a rapid and irreversible redistribution of wealth and opening up of facilities to all'.[16]

The principles had by now grown to twenty-two in number, but there was clear continuity with previous Constitution Committee documents.[17] These twenty-two clauses were now, for the first time, neatly highlighted under nine clear categories to help popularise the Guidelines as a political programme. These sections were the state, franchise, national identity, a Bill of Rights and affirmative action (including Tambo's suggestion that the Bill of Rights be based on the Freedom Charter), economy, workers, women, the family and international affairs.[18]

26

The SG Calls the Cadres to Lusaka

A FTER THE INTERACTION with Tambo, the Constitution Committee forwarded the 'newly-named Constitutional Guideline[s] for a Democratic South Africa' to the NEC. The document was discussed at the NEC's meeting on 14 January 1988, and ten further amendments were suggested: three small changes to the preamble and seven adaptations to four of the principles. These amendments, which were draft nine of the Guidelines, were sent to the Constitution Committee, which met a week later to discuss the new issues raised by the NEC. All the Lusaka-based members of the Committee were present.[1]

The Committee conceded to two of the changes, one of which added 'the right to strike and bargain collectively' under clause (t) in Section F on workers' rights. On the other seven points they tried to hold the line, objecting forcefully in three cases. The Committee was against the deletion of 'the principle of non-discrimination in relation to national groups' in the preamble, because the approach on group rights had been at the insistence of the president and this formulation had been suggested by him. Dealing with clause (k) in the Bill of Rights and affirmative action (Section D), the Committee also queried why the NEC had – 'not for the first time' – removed reference to land and forced removals, and said it 'would like an explanation'. It was similarly unhappy about the removal of the phrase 'democratic control' in clause (n) in Section E on the economy: 'We feel this term should be used because it indicates one of the ways of coping with private enterprise.' Its parting query in its memorandum to the NEC was why, in the commitments to 'achieving world peace and nuclear disarmament' in clause (v) of the international section, the NEC now wanted to drop the second of these.[2] The result of this engagement was a synthesis of the two positions and a further reworking of the draft Guidelines into a tenth draft.

Meanwhile, the NEC had endorsed the plans for the much-delayed In-House Seminar to be held in Lusaka starting on 1 March 1988. Preparations began. In late January, Jobs Jobodwana sent out an invite to ANC department heads to attend a briefing at Alpha, the SG's office, a week later, with a programme attached.[3] Shortly afterwards, Teddy Pekane confirmed with them the detailed allocation per department of delegates to the forthcoming seminar. The ANC's constitutional planning process was finally going to move beyond the narrow circle in which it had been discussed so far, namely the dozen or so insiders involved since the first Constitution Committee meeting in early January 1986, and the roughly forty NEC and alliance leaders and their office staff who had been drawn into the debate since then.[4] Now, after ten drafts since January 1986, the updated eleventh version of the Guidelines document, finalised and printed, was going out to the broad membership of the organisation, with care taken to involve all its sections.[5]

The turnout was significant. The attendance registers show that more than 100 representatives of different parts of the movement converged on the University of Zambia, some seven kilometres from the city centre on the Great East Road, less than a kilometre from Jack and Ray Simons' home in the Roma suburb. They had come from all parts of the world, intrigued by the invitation to spend five days at what was called an In-House Seminar on Constitutional Guidelines. (See the full list of attendees in the appendix after the last chapter.)

In his December letter of notice, Alfred Nzo had said that attendance was expected of the NEC, chief reps, heads of departments and sections, and delegates from the 'training centres' (that is, the MK camps).[6] Teddy Pekane elaborated afterwards that there was an allocation per department, ranging from the Department of Information and Publicity, the PMC, Military HQ and National Intelligence, located under the president's office, to the numerous sections falling under the line-function responsibility of the secretary-general. The latter included the Women and Youth sections, the Education and Health departments, Economic Planning, Arts and Culture, Religious Affairs, Radio Freedom, the ECC, and the Departments of Political Education, Manpower Development and International Affairs. Care had been taken to invite a delegate from each of the eleven Regional Political Committees scattered across the globe.[7] In addition, participants from the SACP and SACTU had been invited.[8]

The whole process was overseen by a steering committee headed by Dan Tloome (leader of the SACP) and John Nkadimeng (leader of SACTU); Tambo was taking his alliance partners with him. Assisting them were NEC members Joe Slovo, James Stuart and Pallo Jordan, and Constitution Committee deputy head Zola Skweyiya, with further back-up coming from Kader Asmal, Lindiwe Mabuza and Mendi Msimang.

In December, the Central Committee of the SACP had set up their own constitution committee under Joe Slovo to formulate an update of its political positions, and in February 1988, shortly before the In-House Seminar, it published a position paper called the 'ANC Platform for Negotiations'. The paper supported ANC positions, foreseeing the possibility that the revolutionary struggle would end at the negotiating table, followed by the implementation of the National Democratic Revolution (NDR) as an interim step towards the ultimate goal of a socialist South

Africa.[9] Twenty-one SACP members had been elected to the new ANC NEC at Kabwe and at least ten from the Central Committee had participated in the October 1986 NEC discussion on the Foundations document. Now, in addition to Slovo and Tloome, Nkadimeng, Ray Simons and Thabo Mbeki were among the top leadership of the SACP present at the In-House Seminar.

Oliver Tambo was scheduled to give the opening address on 1 March 1988 but it was Nzo who delivered it. The two drafts of the speech in the archives are virtually identical but with different headings.

The speech was being given only a few days after the regime had banned the UDF and sixteen other organisations. Nzo declared that the open violence of the state against the democratic forces was an immediate challenge facing the ANC. He warned that, as the enemy continued with its attempt to destroy the ANC, there was the greatest need for organisational, material and intellectual consolidation in its ranks so that the foundations of the people's advance to the ultimate breakthrough would be strengthened. The enemy's latest onslaught, however, was not a sign of strength: the regime was on the defensive and every step Botha took showed it was moving into an ever-deepening all-round crisis from which it would never extricate itself.

The secretary-general went on to recognise the significance of 'this historic meeting to lay the foundations for the future democratic non-racial South Africa'. He said the gathering would be the basis for future broad consultations within the ANC and the MDM at home on the drawing up of 'the fundamental law of our future democratic state, by a democratically constituted assembly of all the free peoples of our country'.[10]

Reconnecting to the constitutional traditions of the ANC in the decades before it was banned, Nzo pointed out that the question of a constitution and constitution-making had been on the organisation's agenda ever since it came into being. He paid tribute to 'the founders' who had taken up the cudgels on behalf of 'a sorely oppressed people' with a 'firmness, adherence to principle, and avoidance of rhetorical claims [which] has characterised our movement throughout its history'.

We honour our predecessors for their persistent attempts to advance the rights of our people through negotiation combined with effective goals on the road to final emancipation. Nation-building had the first place in the 20 objectives set out in the [first official 1919 ANC] Constitution. Congress undertook to defend the freedom, rights and privileges of all Africans, strive to remove colour bars and achieve equitable representation in parliament and legislative bodies. There was no wavering after 1919 on the need for direct representation in parliament.[11]

The first-generation drafters of the first ANC constitution also issued the first African Bill of Rights in 1923, Nzo explained. This document proclaimed the need for 'democratic principles of equality of treatment and equality of citizenship in the land irrespective of race, class, creed or origin', as well as 'unrestricted ownership of land' for Africans in 'the land of the fathers'. Moreover, they had 'the constitutional right of an equal share in the management and direction of the affairs of this land of their permanent abode, and to direct representation by members of their own race in all the legislative bodies ... there can be no taxation without representation'.[12]

Nzo then turned to the 1940s era of Dr A.B. Xuma, when the ANC was revitalised and the struggle compass reset. In difficult times during World War II and its aftermath, the Congress adopted the Africans' Claims document, a clause-by-clause response to Churchill and Roosevelt's Atlantic Charter, which laid out the basis for a post–World War II era of human rights and freedoms, giving rise to the formation of the UN and the adoption of the Universal Declaration of Human Rights in 1948.

The Africans' Claims document included a comprehensive Bill of Rights, which set the benchmark for the future by unequivocally demanding full citizenship rights for all; rights to equal justice, freedom of residence, freedom of movement and freedom of the press; recognition of the sanctity of the home; the right to own land and 'engage in all forms of lawful occupations' and work in public employment on equal terms with whites; and, finally, the right of every child to free and compulsory education, as well as equality of treatment in social services and social security schemes.[13] As Nzo put it, this was 'a new Charter from the standpoint of Africans ... setting forth a list of claims similar to those in the Guidelines before us'.[14]

The third stage of internal constitutional development of the ANC, Nzo continued, was its 1959 constitution issued under the names of Chief Albert Luthuli and the drafter, Oliver Tambo himself, who was at that time its secretary-general. The 1959 constitution also had a four-point programme of objectives.

> They represented an important advance in style and content over the Constitution of 1943. Congress undertook to unite the African people in a powerful instrument to secure their complete liberation from all forms of discrimination and national oppression; promote African interests, strive for a universal adult suffrage and the creation of a democratic South Africa on the principles of the Freedom Charter; support the cause of national liberation and the right to independence of nations in Africa and the rest of the world.[15]

A fourth stage followed at Kabwe in 1985. That consultative conference had adopted internal constitutional guidelines that took account of the tremendous growth of the organisation in the intervening years, and in particular its emergence as the leader and unifier of all revolutionary democratic, anti-racist and patriotic forces in the country.

Nzo then went on to frame the launch of the Constitutional Guidelines as the fifth stage of the ANC's internal constitutional evolution over nearly eight decades. And, he observed, the Freedom Charter of 1955 stood out through all these phases of the ANC's constitutional development, including the one that was being launched at the seminar. From a constitutional perspective, the Charter had dual value. It was part of the ANC's constitutional DNA and had been adopted as a constitutional programme by the most extensive array of democratic forces representing the backbone of the struggle at home. Secondly, it projected a vision arising out of the struggles and demands of the people, which would underlie a future constitution for South Africa. Nzo said:

> We honour our predecessors for their persistent attempts to advance the rights of our people through negotiation combined with effective goals on the road to final emancipation ... [It is] precisely the task of our generation to convert that programmatic vision into a constitutional reality, and this is the context in which this historic seminar takes place.
>
> We are not here to draft a constitution or even to discuss a draft constitution. That task belongs finally and exclusively to the people of South Africa, properly represented and at a democratically chosen National Convention.
>
> But we are here to carry the Freedom Charter a step forward, to distil its essence in a set of formulations specifically declaring what we in the ANC believe the foundations of government in a liberated South Africa should be.
>
> Accordingly, the NEC of the ANC, presents to you for consideration and discussion the document entitled 'Constitutional Guidelines for a Democratic South Africa'.[16]

The Guidelines, he emphasised, had one basic theme: democracy.

Underlining the fact that all sections of the movement were represented, Nzo explained that this was not to be a conference that adopted new policy directions, but would serve as a sounding board where the NEC could get the members' feelings about the concrete application of an important aspect of long-standing policy. The title 'In-House Seminar' was being used so that the discussion within the organisation could be as representative as possible. This would be the first of many extensive consultations. He added that while the Constitutional Guidelines before them were the product of much debate and analysis by the NEC, ably assisted by the Constitution Committee since 1986, it was 'not a sacrosanct text'.

> To succeed in these tasks, we must have democracy in our own ranks. Hence we place this document before you for your unconstrained appraisal.
>
> We urge you to analyse its terms, to tell us how it can be enriched, to indicate if you think it should be replaced or supplemented by another document. Tell us if it corresponds to what you believe in, what you are fighting for, tell us if you think the overall thrust and balance it represents is as it should be.[17]

Every ANC member would be expected to study the Guidelines and analyse the meaning of the document. The goal was to show it to friends so that they could understand precisely what the ANC positions were. It would be used especially to mobilise supporters in the ANC and MDM, and to isolate the regime. The Guidelines were also there to encourage those who were taking their first steps towards genuine anti-racist positions to move further and faster along that road. Finally, the Guidelines would be used to counteract the enemy's propaganda and help the ANC take the initiative in presenting its own positions directly to the world.

> We want the document to be studied boldly and also realistically, since in South African conditions, every revolutionary has to be a realist, just as every realist has to be a revolutionary.[18]

The secretary-general ended by saying that 'through our constitutional proposals, we project the vision of a totally different South Africa built on different principles'. Therefore, the challenge for the democratic forces 'as we enter the decisive period ahead' was to 'aim for and achieve the greatest possible mobilisation, organisation and united action of the ... mass of black workers, peasants, youth and students, women, professionals, the entire oppressed people'.

27

'For Your Unconstrained Appraisal': The In-House Seminar

A FTER HIS OPENING address, Alfred Nzo tabled the Constitutional Guidelines as an NEC document for the 'unrestrained appraisal' of the membership, and so began the five-day programme. The discussions were led by the ANC's top leadership, members of the Constitution Committee and influential mid-level leaders in various operational spheres of the organisation. Twenty-six papers were read, and two major oral presentations were made from notes.[1] The presentations covered all nine sections of the principles in the Constitutional Guidelines.

First on the schedule was Constitution Committee rapporteur Albie Sachs, who explained the structure, character and status of the Guidelines.[2]

Second was Thabo Mbeki, dressed in the short-sleeved Cuban guayabera shirt favoured by many South African revolutionaries, and speaking with his characteristic cadences and qualifications. Skweyiya had asked months before that he give the input on the economy, a key issue.[3] 'All manner of forces are engaged in an ideological struggle to determine what the outcome of our revolution shall be,' Mbeki said. 'Everybody is participating in this thing except ourselves. I find that rather strange.' After mentioning that Max Sisulu would be speaking on economic policy later in the programme, he offered some general thoughts of his own.

Mbeki's biographer says this off-the-cuff speech was one of the bravest, most provocative and most important interventions Mbeki was to make during his exile years. For someone who tended to operate diplomatically behind the scenes rather than get involved in polemical debates within the ANC, he pushed beyond orthodox ANC positions, challenging easy notions of nationalisation and a control economy. The demand in the Freedom Charter to restore the wealth to the people was quite correct, he observed, but how prepared was the ANC to govern?[4] How would it harness the intellectual and scientific resources needed to manage large sectors of the economy?

> On day one of the revolution ... who manages the enormous public sector, central ... to the South African economy, the banks, the mines, monopoly industry? ... Gorbachev says there's a need for new methods of management and control in all branches of the Soviet economy. Perestroika as restructuring.

[He says] we should start from the upper echelons... [They should be] connected with the scientific and technological revolution ... What prospects do we have on day one of the revolution to set up [a central planning body] made up of prominent scientists and intellectuals? ... South Africa [has] a cadre which is politically well prepared, committed to the revolution, but scientifically under-prepared. And the other side has ... a cadre which is scientifically well-prepared but hostile to the revolution ... We'll have a [central planning body] made up of politicians, like the chairman and myself, who know nothing about running an economy. The result is counter-revolution, when the people can't get food, can't get clothes, when they can't get the material results of the revolutionary transformation.[5]

Having gone through the Freedom Charter clause by clause, Mbeki then dealt with what he called 'some of the implications of these rather heretical things I think I'm saying'. He noted that the Freedom Charter called for the mines to be nationalised (although this is not the specific wording contained in the Charter). The objective was quite correct, he declared, but what policies would be developed to achieve this objective? What about the equipment that had to be used, the drills and shafts: who would supply them? The great bulk of this equipment was manufactured abroad. In 1968, the government of Zambia correctly decided that the wealth of Zambia had to belong to the people of Zambia. They took 51 per cent ownership of the copper mines, but they didn't have personnel to run the mines and asked Anglo American to continue to manage them. Mbeki added that the result was a disaster for the Zambian economy, and though the Zambian government was a majority shareholder it had no way of holding to account a company registered in the Bahamas.

Mbeki passed on to comrades, too, stories about his and Tambo's meetings with Mikhail Gorbachev and Fidel Castro. Castro had told them in 1986 about the Cubans' experience with Bacardi rum, 'the prince of rums for people who drink rum'. After the Cuban Revolution in 1959, the Bacardi family emigrated to Bermuda, where they registered the trade name 'Bacardi'. Instead of the people of Cuba benefiting from the sale of internationally renowned Bacardi rum, which had been matured according to age-old tradition in vats in Havana, it was the Bacardi family in Bermuda who benefited. The Cubans had to sell the original blend, under the lesser-known name 'Havana Club'. The new revolutionary government in Cuba also realised that they had not registered their legendary cigars as Cuban, so they rushed off, sweating, to Madrid, where international tobacco brands were registered, and secured their products under a Cuban trademark. Mbeki also mentioned that Gorbachev had asked Tambo what the ANC's relationship was with the intelligentsia in South Africa, saying that if it had the working class and intelligentsia on its side, 'nothing would stop the ANC'.[6]

Mbeki's talk started a lively debate. The next morning, the following had been chalked up on the seminar-room blackboard: 'When asked by certain workers, "How can we manage the economy when we have no experience?", Comrade Lenin replied, "We have never run the state before, and we are managing that."' No one felt bold enough to erase these words, and they stayed there till the end of the seminar.[7] But the message from Mbeki got across. Max Sisulu, head of the Department of Economics and Planning, followed along the same lines on the second day, with Mbeki joining him in getting the discussions 'oriented'. The rapporteurs wrote that their inputs

> graphically highlighted the huge lacuna in the movement's knowledge of our country – particularly details of the mechanism of the SA economy. Also showed that all manner of forces, institutions and governments are busy toying about with models for a future South Africa, and yet we pay no attention to what sort of country we would like to bring about.[8]

The ANC's Economists Unit was set up in 1984 as part of the movement's decision in the late 1970s to establish what it called 'professional bodies' or units in the areas of education, economics, arts and culture, health and law. The unit was meant to cost the implementation of the Freedom Charter that Pallo Jordan had referred to in his important 'Submission on Negotiations' in 1985. It was revived and relaunched as the Department of Economics and Planning in 1987, with Sisulu as its head and cadres like Patrick Magapatona, Rob Davies, Vella Pillay and Tito Mboweni involved.[9] Jack Simons reported that by 1987 the ANC had completed six papers on the South African economy – besides the Constitutional Guidelines – dealing with international trade and trade policy, electricity, coal, the chemical industry and the internal financial system.[10]

The In-House Seminar called for much more such work to take place. It recommended the systematic training of future specialists; the need to 'win over onto our side forces from non-monopoly capital in the country'; and the importance of undertaking urgent research in various areas, 'including how to revamp the declining economy'. These actions would facilitate the clear formulation of the economy section in the Constitutional Guidelines.[11]

Pallo Jordan's paper on day three of the seminar, described by the rapporteurs as a 'New Look at the African Petty Bourgeoisie', would have linked directly with the inputs by Mbeki and Sisulu on the need for the ANC to move towards a multi-class, mixed-economy scenario in future.[12]

Kader Asmal followed the Mbeki presentation with a paper titled 'Electoral Forms: A Critical Survey'. He started by saying that electoral systems could evolve through incremental extension of the franchise or be established following a constitutional disruption such as a war. In all cases, the system chosen was not based on abstract principles of fairness but on what was consistent with the objectives of those in charge of society at the time. He then outlined several electoral modalities.

In Britain and countries that were once part of the British Empire, the plurality or first-past-the-post system had been adopted. There would be territorial divisions in the country and people would be chosen to represent particular districts or constituencies. Usually, it was the person who got the greatest number of votes, even if this was not a 50 per cent majority of the total votes cast. In a single-transferable-vote system, multiple representatives stood and local voters could list their preferences in sequence from, say, one to ten. Thirdly, in the list system and proportional representation, parties would be represented in terms of the percentage of the total votes they received. Asmal did not argue in favour of any particular model or combination of models. He simply alerted the delegates to the kinds of decisions that would have to be made in future.[13]

Zola Skweyiya followed with a fully footnoted paper titled 'Parliamentary and Presidential Systems of Government'. Should a liberated South Africa follow a prime ministerial system of government, such as that adopted in India, Australia and Canada, where the top political leader in the country would be the prime minister, chosen by Parliament? Or should South Africa have a president chosen directly by the people, such as in the United States? He argued, on balance, for a presidential regime on the basis that this was well known in Africa. People were used to personalised leadership. It would bring to the fore national leadership within the framework of a constitutional system. The fixed term of office provided for stability and continuity, and a stable government would be important during a period of change.[14]

Next from the Constitution Committee was Jack Simons, who gave a presentation on the National Question. He dealt with Afrikaner nationalism and African nationalism, relating both to the issue of class exploitation. He emphasised that nation-building was a historical process. In South African conditions, it required the ending of racist forms of regionalism, in particular the Bantustans. But it needed more than that. It required not creating federal arrangements that consolidated white hegemony in some areas and black leadership in others. The nation could not be built on the basis of keeping South Africa racially and spatially divided, keeping African people ethnically divided, and subjecting the working class to continued exploitation. At the heart of the freedom struggle was the national liberation of the black majority. It was not simply a struggle for civil rights, such as the right to exercise the vote and enjoy access to facilities. It was a struggle to bring down the multiple forms of law and practice that kept the African majority oppressed.[15]

The next speaker, London-based Tony O'Dowd, could not be present, so his paper on the legal system and the judiciary was delivered by Nat Masemola. His paper set out the different areas of law, establishing the place of constitutional and administrative law in the total picture. It stated that the most difficult question in constitutional law was whether the highest law-making authority in the land could itself be made subject to law. In the US, the Supreme Court could declare Acts of Congress to be unconstitutional and strike them down. In the UK, on the other hand, Parliament reigned sovereign and supreme. It made the law and the courts simply had to carry it out. They had some supervisory power to review the validity of regulations made under an Act of Parliament, but they could not say that Parliament itself had overstepped the mark.

O'Dowd's piece argued that South Africa would need to consider creating a separate Constitutional Court to serve as an impartial authority to decide if the constitution's Bill of Rights was being observed. In his view, this court did not need to sit every day and could be staffed by part-time judges. One possibility would be to have one or two judges from the higher reach of the judiciary, together with some senior political figures and eminent persons from different walks of life who would not have to be lawyers.

The paper pointed out that of the 130 superior court judges in South Africa, all were white and all except one were male. In future, special attention would have to be given to how judges were chosen.[16]

Penuell Maduna presented an extensively footnoted paper with the oblique title 'Non-Central Government Structures in South Africa Today'. The delegates understood that this terminology had been chosen to avoid engaging directly with the F-word – federalism. They were aware that there was a widespread campaign by conservative forces inside and outside South Africa to retain white privilege under the guise of developing federal structures. Their objective was to keep the country territorially divided, maintain Bantustans and prevent any nationwide efforts towards the redistribution of land and wealth. Despite these distortions, provision would have to be made for a territorial political division into clearly defined local and regional/provincial levels of government. But these structures would have to be developed in a way that would reflect 'the will of the majority of the people'. They should be anti-colonialist and anti-racist. They should promote a relatively smooth way of proceeding to a non-exploitative society and could play a crucial role in the resolution of the National Question, uniting all our people into a single family and abolishing national inequalities flowing from centuries-old colonial domination and capitalist exploitation.

After referring to the importance of defining the different levels or tiers of government, Maduna went on to deal with the role of traditional leaders. Account had to be taken of the recent emergence of the Congress of Traditional Leaders of South Africa. In some countries in Africa, such as Guinea, Benin, the Congo and Tanzania, where colonialists had used traditional institutions to preserve control, these institutions were fully liquidated in order to develop and sustain national unity after independence. (This was the position the Constitution Committee had proposed in its October 1986 meeting with the NEC.) On the other hand, there were countries, such as Zambia and Zimbabwe, where the institution of traditional rulers had a place in their new constitutions. Though Maduna did not think it necessary to mention that Britain was still a monarchy with a largely ceremonial queen, he did say that the British themselves had preserved an archaic institution based on hereditary power, namely the House of Lords.[17]

Women's voices had been absent from the constitutional planning process since the January 1986 launch of the Committee. Now they were here speaking for themselves for the first time. In the last session on the second day, Ruth Mompati made a 'Statement by the Women's Section on the Gender Question' by way of introducing a paper by Ivy Matsepe-Casaburri on 'Constitution, Law and the Gender Question'. Matsepe-Casaburri was assisted in her presentation by Brigitte Mabandla, who had been a legal advisor for the DLCA since 1986, undertaking a trip to Botswana that June to assist cadres needing support.[18]

Ruth Mompati and the long-serving Gertrude Shope were the only two women on the NEC, alongside twenty-nine men. Women were still struggling to get recognition in an organisation that had for decades been solidly patriarchal, and Mabandla was one of those who complained about this fact. She had given up her studies at the University of the North in the 1970s after becoming involved in the Black Consciousness struggles of the time. After going into exile, she qualified with a law degree from the University of Zambia in 1979. From there she moved to Botswana, where she lectured in law and English at the Polytechnic and Institute of Administration and Commerce in Gaborone between 1981 and 1986. When back in Lusaka, she complained to Tambo about being left out of meaningful involvement by her comrades in the DLCA. Tambo proposed that she take special responsibility for the area of women and children, and she subsequently became integrated into the work of the Constitution Committee.[19] She was also appointed as an ANC judge – that is, a member of the ANC's National Tribunal – but she asked the president's office to reconsider the appointment in late 1987, as she felt there would be a conflict of interest in working for the DLCA while acting as a judge.[20]

The first and second ANC Women's Conferences were organised by the ANC Women's Section in Luanda, Angola, in 1981 and in September 1987. These set a firm agenda for the recognition of women's rights in the organisation and in the country for which they were fighting.[21] This was premised on the ANC recognising that most women in South Africa suffered from triple oppression, facing systemic exclusion and discrimination on the basis of race, class and gender.[22]

The pressing need to attend to women's rights in the organisation was also driven home by various international conferences on gender that ANC activists regularly attended (such as the 1985 World Conference on Women in Nairobi) as well as a growing focus on women's issues in the trade union movement and the mass democratic movement at home.[23] Women comrades had been making calls for a revolution within a revolution in the ANC for a long time. In 1971, Zanele Dhlamini wrote a powerful paper titled 'Women's Liberation', declaring that

> [the] way to deal with the feminist problems amongst the oppressed is to launch a revolution within the revolution so that women in the South African struggle can participate as a massive, conscious and equal partner in solving all the problems that affect the re-education and 'consciousness raising' of both men and women towards a transformation of social roles affecting both public and private lives. It will be the women's responsibility to make sure that the successes achieved carry on to the resulting government and are not reversed by the new masters as has been experienced elsewhere.[24]

Now, at the In-House Seminar, Mompati declared that the emancipation of women 'must be and is' an integral part of the struggle for national liberation. Therefore,

> the Constitution of post-apartheid South Africa must address, in the same way, the racist, class and gender oppressive character existing today with a view to eliminating this oppression.
> Just as every aspect of the law and legal institutions will have to be examined in order to eliminate specific and effective racism, so too they must be examined to eliminate sexism.[25]

The experiences of independent African countries showed that it was not good enough just to say there will be formal equality and then replicate a system that is exclusionary in practice. Colonial subjugation had severely stifled women's participation in the running of the state and in social and economic life, so institutions had to be made effectively accessible to women. Their understanding of their own oppression was deepening their understanding of and visions for the future.

Mompati was a thoughtful, well-organised, quiet and composed person at the centre of the ANC's administration. Known for her diplomacy and great people skills, she surprised and stirred the audience with the fierceness of her words, challenging the comrades who had drafted the Guidelines for their failure to grasp the nettle of sexism.

As Sachs recorded:

> Those of us who regarded ourselves as liberated men expected a pat on the back for the clause that said women should have equal rights in the sphere of public and private life, and the state shall take affirmative action to eliminate sexual inequalities. Instead, waving the Guidelines in the air, Ruth demanded to know why centuries of racial domination and inequality were mentioned but nothing was said about gender inequality. Nothing about the effect that patriarchy had had going back even longer than colonial domination. The Guidelines said nothing about sexism. They spoke about not allowing any advocacy of racism, fascism and Nazism, but nothing about prohibiting sexism. Her use of the word 'sexist' was surprising and electric, sending a shock wave through all of us present.[26]

Ivy Matsepe-Casaburri then spoke on 'Constitution, Law and the Gender Question'. Born in Kroonstad in the Free State, she would one day be president of South Africa for fourteen hours. Her father was a school principal, musician and sportsman and her mother was a teacher and a social and community worker. Matsepe-Casaburri obtained a BA from Fort Hare University. After going into exile, she worked in Swaziland, first as a teacher then for a firm of lawyers, which gave her a special interest in studying the oppression of women in society. She obtained a PhD in sociology from Rutgers University in the United States. In her 1986 article 'On the Question of Women in the South African Struggle' (which she referred to in the seminar presentation), she looked at the ways in which women from different races and ethnic groups are oppressed. She went on to work for the United Nations Institute for Namibia (UNIN) in Lusaka as a lecturer and registrar. It was while working at UNIN that she became active in the ANC Women's Section.[27]

The paper she presented (and which the Women's Section had circulated to the delegates) contained a large amount of factual information about the extent to which women in South Africa were being held back, both in the public and private spheres. For example, the number of women in domestic service had grown from 55.02 per cent of the total in 1911 to 90 per cent in 1980, with 83 per cent of this number being African women. (White 'servants' went from 4.79 per cent to virtually zero in this time.) Matsepe-Casaburri said the 'gender question cannot be wished away' at this conjuncture when the Freedom Charter was moving from a 'vision for the future [to] a constitutional reality ... Neither can it perfunctorily be dealt with ... The present nature of the struggle', she emphasised, 'its forms and its content, our strategies and tactics, demand that the question be dealt with in great depth, and with better understanding of the issues involved.'

Having laid out the bottom line, Matsepe-Casaburri then explained the historical legacy of women's oppression in South Africa, how to ensure the future status of women – given the inevitable limitations of a constitution – and fourteen specific issues that needed to be addressed to make this happen.

Four paragraphs of the Constitutional Guidelines were specifically identified as needing to be changed: (i), (j), (k) and (r). While the Guidelines spoke of the need for the constitution to provide for corrective action to 'guarantee rapid and irreversible restructuring', there should be 'a special dispensation in favour of women as well'. These paragraphs related to the constitution promoting 'the habits of non-racist behaviour', but they 'certainly should also promote anti-sexist thinking and behaviour'. She said the Bill of Rights and affirmative action must not pay 'lip service' to equality and special provisions for women: 'anti-sexism (like anti-racism) must be entrenched in the constitution so that the law or practice (administrative or otherwise) that discriminates on the grounds of gender can be declared unconstitutional'.[28]

The ANC women stressed that while they understood the constitution could not be too detailed or too specific, it nevertheless 'cannot be ambivalent about what rights it specifically has to protect', about 'what it entrenches'. Comparative examples in the GDR, South Africa, the USSR and USA showed that '[h]istorical moments at which constitutions are drawn, determine what the constitution will be like'. In the USA, discrimination against women remained so general it took centuries before 'successful challenges were made in the courts'.

This paper, Matsepe-Casaburri said, did not pretend to be exhaustive, but 'raises issues that sensitise us to the enormity and the complexity of the task ahead of us'. It listed very specific and meaningful aspects of women's lives and rights. All laws and legal institutions had to be examined 'to eliminate specific and effective racism and sexism. The constitution had to make sure that retrogressive aspects of culture and religion relating to women did not overrule 'the constitutional human rights of all individuals'. It also had to entrench full participation of women in electoral life or else post-apartheid South Africa would have little meaning for them. Because of high levels of illiteracy among women (and because white women 'have been socialised into non-democratic political participation'), permanent voter-education programmes would be needed to educate and prepare more than 50 per cent of the population to play their role in society. The paper pointed out that 'Other forms of discrimination against women abound in the experiences of the states around us', and these would need to be studied carefully and eliminated.

The workplace was another key area. While the paper welcomed the provision in the Guidelines for a workers' charter, 'protection of both genders against all work harmful to their reproductive capability and capacity and health must be entrenched'. Specific threats to women workers, such as sexual harassment, also needed attention. Women's free choice in choosing occupations and their equality in training, access and pay had to be addressed constitutionally. The overt commercialisation and sexual harassment of women had to be opposed, too.

Crucially, the paper emphasised, care should be taken to ensure that 'the much vaunted "privacy" of the family, does not retain the clandestine quality of subverting the serious and critical efforts at founding a truly non-racial and united democratic South Africa'. In this respect, the GDR was a good model of the 'egalitarian protection of the family'. The ANC women were emphatic on this point:

> The protection of the family is absolutely necessary. However, the nature of that family is usually much more problematic than it has been assumed. Family and kin relations are not as harmonious and conflict-free as may have been earlier. The rapid increase in the divorce rate and family violence is indicative of this.
>
> Protection of the family must therefore not be to the exclusion of constitutionally guaranteed human rights of [its] members. The right of the privacy of the family should not be allowed to be the 'theatre for the secret oppression of women and girls'.[29]

Finally, Matsepe-Casaburri concluded, women's rights to 'shelter, land, property and residence have historically been tied to men – their fathers, husbands and male kin' and fundamental human rights were undermined in this matter, as some exiles living in Zimbabwe had experienced (with inheritance laws and the like).

This was a powerful statement on the position of women in society and in relation to the Constitutional Guidelines. Mompati, Matsepe-Casaburri and Mabandla had put women's rights firmly on the agenda, saying it was time for the ANC to move from rhetoric to reality on this issue. The results were one or two small but important changes to the Guidelines, as well as another seminar twenty-one months hence, where women's issues were much more strongly spotlighted and acted on, leading to additional changes to the Guidelines and greater roles for women in the ANC (see Chapter 36).

Vusi Pikoli remembers the impact of the women's inputs on the more traditionally minded men in the very patriarchal ANC. 'When delegates sought out the bathrooms afterwards, there was a buzz and Baba [Jacob] Zuma was one of those who said they perhaps went too far in critiquing African traditions like polygamy,' Pikoli recalls.[30]

On the third day, Albie Sachs gave an impromptu presentation on the topic 'Group Rights, Federalism and a Bill of Rights'. He opened by saying that it was necessary to attack apartheid on all fronts. In the case of the struggle on the political, legal, ideological and constitutional front, you had to know the terrain, as the military comrades were always saying. This terrain was not established by individuals but by history. And you had to know your weapons. Just like people had to learn to use limpet mines, they had to study constitutions, systems of electoral practice and forms of government.

Because the seminar had been so preoccupied with the question of nationalisation, he continued, the comrades had not even reached the core political/ideological issue: the question of so-called guarantees for so-called minorities. This was a battle that the ANC had to win inside the country and internationally, in the Frontline States, in Africa – with their friends in the world and not only with the West. It was now being widely accepted that apartheid had to be dismantled, but the question was always posed as to what guarantees could be offered to the whites and, sometimes, to coloured people, Indians, Zulus and so on.[31] The argument from the racists was that, if you had black-majority rule, the new black government would take everything away from the whites, kill them and destroy everything that was functioning. A more sophisticated argument was that the whites were in power, they had the guns, and if you wanted them to give up their power, you had to offer them guarantees of a secure future. Examples of the guarantees being requested included the federalist option of dividing the country into small groups, which would retain the Bantustans and keep the black population divided. Another guarantee would be to ensure that in any new parliament, different ethnic groups would have vetoes over any legislation dealing with what were called their 'Own Affairs', that is, matters of deep and special interest to themselves.

Sachs's heart was racing when he came to address the delegates on the centrality of a Bill of Rights for the ANC.[32] There were three reasons for its importance. The first was diplomatic – it made the ANC look good. Instead of presenting themselves as a group hungry for power, they would be projecting themselves as democrats aiming for a law-governed society. The second reason was strategic and dealt with the core issue of giving guarantees to minorities. A Bill of Rights would answer the claims being advanced in favour of group rights and power-sharing. There was no problem, in principle, with group rights for workers, women, children, or members of language groups and faith communities. But to introduce group rights as the foundation of formal structures of government would bring apartheid right into the heart of the new constitutional order. Instead, a Bill of Rights would secure people's fundamental rights, not because they belonged to a majority or a minority but because they were human beings.

In his book *We, the People: Insights of an Activist Judge*, Sachs explains the third reason as the one that really made his heart beat: 'It was advancing this, perhaps the most profound and deeply principled reason of all ... We needed a Bill of Rights, I said, against ourselves.' But, he wondered,

> What would the delegates think? It was easy for me, a lawyer who had grown up with the privileges that went with a white skin, to come up with these ideas ... I looked into the eyes of the audience. To my joy, instead of hostility or repudiation, I saw looks of delight. It was as though they all felt a sense of reassurance [from] the creation of institutional mechanisms against any abuses of power from any quarter whatsoever ... We were living in societies where many people who had fought very bravely for their freedom had gone on to become authoritarian heads of state themselves ... We had seen [that] our own organisation ... had from time to time been obliged to take firm and principled initiatives against unacceptable forms of conduct and abuses of power.[33]

Sachs has also recorded in his book *Oliver Tambo's Dream* that he (and the likes of Asmal) sometimes got the praise (or blame) for having introduced the Bill of Rights into the ANC.[34] He points out that it was the other way round: he had been a rights-sceptic, inclined to the view that it was wrong for essentially political issues to be decided by the courts. It was the ANC, and Tambo in particular, who persuaded him that, in South African conditions, a Bill of Rights could enunciate the quintessence of all they had been struggling for. It could convert the Freedom Charter into an operational document and become the cornerstone of the country's new constitutional order. The judiciary would then become a crucial instrument for ensuring that core elements of political morality would be maintained in the new society. Independent judges would also have a role to play in seeing to it that the rights of workers, women, children, the disabled and the poor were respected.[35]

In his seminar presentation, Sachs then went on to explain why a group of students from the ranks of the oppressed had set up an anti–Bill of Rights committee:

it was a response to the fact that certain quarters had called for a Bill of Rights to protect existing property rights.

> And by property they don't just mean your furniture, your clothing, your car, your own personal effects. They mean the huge shareholdings. They mean the enormous tracts of land, the agribusinesses. All this will be constitutionally protected in terms of a race-free constitution, which will freeze the results of centuries of apartheid and block any movement towards change.[36]

Sachs concluded that, on the contrary, the Bill of Rights should be fashioned in such a way as to become an emancipatory instrument to advance the interests of all in society, and should include the use of affirmative action to bring about economic and social equality, as envisaged by the Freedom Charter.

After all the seminar papers had been presented and discussed, a report was delivered by a Resolutions Committee that had been set up to review the work of the seminar and make recommendations. Chaired by Simons, this committee included Sachs and Jobodwana, as well as Brigitte Mabandla and Nat Masemola, who had both been accepted into the work of the Constitution Committee in 1987/88. One of the first ANC arrivals in Lusaka, Masemola became town clerk of the city before moving on to London, where he headed the Albert Luthuli Foundation, which provided scholarships to black students from South Africa.[37] Joining them on the Resolutions Committee were Jackie Selebi (head of the ANC Youth League) and Tambo's loyal aide and ECC secretary James Stuart.

A committee of rapporteurs appointed for the seminar helped Simons and the Resolutions Committee to record and collate opinions. This group was from a younger generation and included several women comrades. The coordinator was Sipho M. Dlamini, who worked at the Centre for African Studies at Eduardo Mondlane University in Maputo and had co-authored a struggle history dedicated to an analysis of the problems of socialist transition in Mozambique in the context of South Africa.[38] Dlamini, who had also served in intelligence structures in Angola, was supported by Nelson Miya (vice-coordinator). The other rapporteurs were Khosi Msimang, a doctor from one of the socialist countries; Sowetan Lucy Thandeni, from the Women's Section; Miranda Qwanyashe, who had been active in the women's and community formations in the UDF struggles in Cape Town before going into exile and becoming a member of a specialised structure of the Botswana Regional PMC concentrating on the western Cape; Sipho Majombozi; Thami Bolani; Martha Motaung; Sikose Mji; Don Ngubeni; Solly Mpoli; and Lusaka-based Dr Prem Naicker, who was the ANC's deputy secretary of health.[39]

The Resolutions Committee delivered initial feedback in the report-back session on the last day of the In-House Seminar. It was then given two weeks to report formally. As per instructions, it typed up and submitted a formal report for the Constitution Committee and the NEC to consider.[40] This was followed by a longer but similarly worded Constitution Committee memorandum on the Guidelines and the seminar, which was sent to the president on 12 April 1988, effectively the twelfth input.[41] In the memorandum, Simons and Skweyiya 'welcomed the idea and opportunity to discuss the outcome of the In-House Seminar' further.[42] Presumably the Constitution Committee then had further discussion on the Guidelines with sections of the leadership before Pallo Jordan, head of the NEC secretariat, sent out this thirteenth draft 'as amended by the DLCA seminar' to NWC and NEC members for consideration at their meetings on 22–23 and 27 June 1988 respectively.[43] It included only a few small but significant modifications.

After the NEC lightly tweaked this June draft, the Constitutional Guidelines were formally adopted as ANC policy after going through fourteen iterations since the Skeleton was first drafted in January 1986. They appeared as an official ANC public document for the first time in the August 1988 edition of the organisation's monthly journal, *Sechaba*.[44]

The two post-seminar reports stressed the successes of the meeting, noting that 'the discussion was generally of a high level and the interest of the participants was extremely strong'.

> The participants showed an excellent grasp of the objectives of the Movement and the problems we encounter in bringing our struggle to a point where control of our country would be transferred to a people's democracy as it is contemplated in the Guidelines.[45]

The 'general consensus' among them was also that the Guidelines were skilfully prepared and would inspire further discussion and action. The seminar had 'succeeded completely in opening up important themes for debate and satisfying in a small way the immense thirst of the membership for organised discussion on fundamental issues facing the movement'.[46] Most of the Guidelines were approved without opposition. The preamble and the sections on the state, franchise and national identity – paragraphs (a) to (g) – were accepted. This included the 'soft' formulation on the position of traditional leaders proposed by Tambo at the October 1986 NEC meeting in response to the discussion about the possible abolition of the chieftaincy. On the section on the Bill of Rights and affirmative action – (h) to (l) – it was generally accepted that the provisions had a sufficiently progressive character.[47]

The four issues that generated particular excitement and needed extra attention in the post-seminar amendments related to the economy, the land issue, and workers' and women's rights. An unnamed rapporteur noted that 'great and animated debates were occasioned by the presentations on the economy, the Bill of Rights, culture and language and the land'.[48]

Despite the strong inputs by Thabo Mbeki and Max Sisulu, the greatest reservations and critiques in the discussions were still about the economy. Many of the delegates felt that, by not openly propagating nationalisation, the Guidelines were a retreat from the Freedom Charter, which 'was made worse by a complete absence of reference to the theme of land and land-distribution'.[49] The Constitution Committee itself shared this criticism. At its 21 January meeting, members had, for a second time, challenged the NEC's insistence on removing references to land and forced removals from the Guidelines.[50] There was 'almost universal feeling', the final report of the Resolutions Committee said, 'that the land question needs to be directly addressed, so as not to give the impression the ANC is running away from it and its historic commitment to restore the land to those who work it'.[51]

This theme echoed a comment in an unsigned, handwritten report by one of the rapporteurs on the session led by presenters Barney Mackay and Tessa Marcus: 'It was strongly argued that the land question formed the backbone of the being of the ANC and of the struggle, and that it must, therefore, of necessity, be reflected in any and all Constitutional Guidelines for any such exercise to be meaningful to the overwhelming majority of our people.'[52] The result was that the NEC and Constitution Committee added a new heading and a new clause on 'Land' in the eleventh draft of the Guidelines in June 1987:

(u)   The state shall devise and implement a Land Reform Programme that
       will include and address the following issues:
       i.   Abolition of all racial restrictions on ownership and use of land.
       ii. Implementation of land reform in conformity with the principle of
            Affirmative Action, taking into account the status of victims of forced
            removals.[53]

Some delegates expressed fears that, by propagating the mixed-economy scenario, the ANC 'appeared to be accepting the existence of capitalism in post-apartheid South Africa'. However, the Resolutions Committee added that 'many of the participants were prepared to accept a mixed economy' on the understanding that the shape of the economy would eventually be determined by the prevailing balance of forces inside and outside the organisation. If there was a strongly organised workers' movement and strong government control, then the economy could be moved in a progressive direction.

Following this discussion, the NEC built in a new, seventh paragraph, (p), under 'Economy' in its post-conference finalisation of the Guidelines:

> (p)   The private sector of the economy shall be obliged to co-operate with the state in realizing the objectives of the Freedom Charter in promoting social well-being.[54]

Democratic control over the private sector was a point that the Constitution Committee had made in its January 1988 draft of the Guidelines. The NEC removed it in the next version – a decision the Committee had challenged – but was now putting it back in the form quoted above.

A further promise of protection by the future state came after the discussion on workers. There was general satisfaction with the text, although some felt that further rights spelt out in the Freedom Charter, but not in the Guidelines, should be included. The 'right to work' was one example. This led to the NEC adding a second sentence in the fifth clause, (l), of the 'Bill of Rights and affirmative action' section. It now read:

> Subject to clauses (i) and (k) above, the democratic state shall guarantee the basic rights and freedoms, such as freedom of association, thought, worship and the press.
>
> Furthermore, the state shall have the duty to protect the right to work, and guarantee education and social security.[55]

The paragraph on workers' rights emphasised 'the rights of workers to strike and bargain collectively' by adding the word 'especially' before the quoted words.

The conference report mentioned that, as the internal debate got going, many ANC, SACP and SACTU members were conflicted about the contradictions between the multiparty-state idea that Tambo, the Committee and now the NEC were pushing, versus the one-party People's Power constitution concept that prevailed in Mozambique, Angola, Cuba and the Soviet Union. Some delegates asked whether 'in a liberated South Africa there should be a multi-party parliamentary system with freedom for parties that did not violate the [Bill of Rights clauses] *i* to *k*, but which were reactionary and anti-people'. Another question concerning state structures was 'how the organs of local people's power would fit into the scheme'. The fundamental conceptual contradictions between people's democracies and a multiparty system based on individual rights therefore remained unresolved. The

Committee's report even seemed to lean towards the former, as the earlier quote above indicates.[56]

Finally, the hard push by Ivy Matsepe-Casaburri and others for greater attention to women's rights led initially to only one addition to the Guidelines: 'non-sexism' was added to 'non-racialism' in the preamble as a value that the constitution should promote. The Resolutions Committee reported that the conference accepted without change the section on women in the Guidelines – paragraph (w) – 'save that the speakers dealing directly with this theme urged strongly that the struggle against sexism be expressly referred to in the preamble and the section on a Bill of Rights and affirmative action'.[57] Simons and Skweyiya's report to Tambo was more specific: this section was 'wholly accepted save that the author of the paper on the gender question [Matsepe-Casaburri] felt that the struggle against sexism should receive equal treatment, attention and emphasis in the Guidelines with all other forms of discrimination'.[58] An extra phrase forbidding discrimination between the sexes was added only in the final August 1988 draft: 'eliminate sexual inequalities' was replaced by 'eliminate inequalities and discrimination between the sexes'. It thus read:

> Women shall have equal rights in all spheres of public and private life and the
> state shall take affirmative action to eliminate inequalities and discrimination
> between the sexes.[59]

When Matsepe-Casaburri's call for stronger wording in the Bill of Rights and affirmative action section was ignored, the concerned women continued to protest. They called a further meeting where those in attendance 'went through the guide-lines, clause by clause' and wrote up their views in a memorandum on 'Matters of Particular Concern'.[60] While the initial lobbying bore only minimal results in 1988, the persistence of these women members would in the following year lead to substantive additions to the Constitutional Guidelines (see Chapter 36).

Simons and Skweyiya declared that the seminar was 'highly successful' and the report stated that it should become the 'starting point for wide-ranging discussions' on key themes of the Constitutional Guidelines. Ways needed to be found of placing the Guidelines before the 'entire membership of the Movement and the democratic Movement inside the country', together with the papers presented and other explanatory documents. The Resolutions Committee were confident that the new Constitutional Guidelines

> will provide the basis for profound debates which will promote unity and enable
> the membership and the people as a whole to feel that they 'know what is going

on' and are contributing to the evolution of the solutions ... The whole question of the inter-relationship between realism and tactical considerations, on the one hand, and clear revolutionary goals to fight for and die for, if necessary, is a difficult one to resolve and requires more rather than less debate.[61]

The two Constitution Committee leaders made two practical proposals to the president to ensure this process was bedded down. 'More elaborate seminars' on the issue of the land question, the economy and the role of culture in building national unity should be organised as soon as possible, they suggested. Secondly, making known the Swedish-supported PASA project and working in cooperation with the University of Zambia would 'go a long way in facilitating the smooth exchange of views and information between the ANC external mission and the democratic movement at home'.[62]

Thus it was that after two years and two months of work by the Constitution Committee, and fourteen drafts and revisions necessitated by vigorous engagements with the NWC, the NEC, the president and, ultimately, the delegates at the In-House Seminar, the 'Constitutional Guidelines for a Democratic South Africa' were ready for final approval by the NEC.

The timing was perfect because big challenges lay ahead – war in Angola, continuing states of emergency, assassinations, bombings, and engagements about possible talks about talks between the ANC leaders and the Botha government. The Guidelines would become an important tool in helping the movement advance decisively in the twenty-one months before the end of the tumultuous eighties.

DRAFTS SEVEN TO FOURTEEN: Constitutional Guidelines for a Democratic South Africa, published in *Sechaba*, August 1988

Final consolidated document incorporating the input from Oliver Tambo, 29 December 1986; Constitution Committee updated Guidelines document, 10 January 1987; NEC amendments, 14 January 1987; further Constitution Committee response and update 21 January 1987; the printed Constitutional Guidelines document circulated for discussion at the ANC In-House Seminar, 1–5 March 1988; recommendations from the seminar and report of the Constitution Committee, 12 April 1987; draft of the Guidelines, June 1988; and subsequent small changes by the Constitution Committee and the NEC before publication of the fourteenth and final draft in August 1988. (See endnotes for individual sources mentioned.)

PREAMBLE

The Freedom Charter, adopted in 1955 by the Congress of the People at Kliptown near Johannesburg was the first systematic statement in the history of our country of the political and constitutional vision of a free, democratic and non-racial South Africa.

The Freedom Charter remains today unique as the only South African document of its kind that adheres firmly to democratic principles as accepted throughout the world. Amongst South Africans it has become by far the most widely accepted programme for a post-apartheid country. The stage is now approaching where the Freedom Charter must be converted from a vision for the future into a constitutional reality.

We in the African National Congress submit to the people of South Africa, and to all those throughout the world who wish to see an end to apartheid, our basic guidelines for the foundations of government in a post-apartheid South Africa. Extensive and democratic debate on these guidelines will mobilise the widest sections of the population to achieve agreement on how to put an end to the tyranny and oppression under which our people live, thus enabling them to lead normal and decent lives as free citizens in a free country.

The immediate aim is to create a just and democratic society that will sweep away the centuries-old legacy of colonial conquest and white domination, and abolish all laws imposing racial oppression and discrimination. The removal of discriminating laws and eradication of all vestiges of the illegitimate regime are, however, not enough: the structures and the institutions of apartheid must be dismantled and be replaced by democratic ones. Steps must be taken to ensure that apartheid ideas and practices are not permitted to appear in old forms or new.

In addition, the effects of centuries of racial domination and inequality must be overcome by constitutional provisions for corrective action which guarantees a rapid and irreversible redistribution of wealth and opening up of facilities to all. The Constitution must also be such as to promote the habits of non-racial and non-sexist thinking, the practice of anti-racist behaviour and the acquisition of genuinely shared patriotic consciousness.

The Constitution must give firm protection to the fundamental human rights of all citizens. There shall be equal rights for all individuals, irrespective of race, colour, sex or creed. In addition, it requires the entrenching of equal cultural, linguistic and religious rights for all.

Under the conditions of contemporary South Arica 87% of land and 95% of the instruments of production of the country are in the hands of the ruling class, which is solely drawn from the white community. It follows, therefore, that constitutional protection for group rights would perpetuate the status quo and would mean that the mass of the people would continue to be constitutionally trapped in poverty and remain as outsiders in the land of their birth.

Finally, success of the constitution will be, to a large extent, determined by the degree to which it promotes conditions for the active involvement of all sectors of the population at all levels in government and in the economic and cultural life. Bearing these fundamental objectives in mind, we declare that the elimination of apartheid and the creation of a truly just and democratic South Africa requires a constitution based on the following principles.

PRINCIPLES

The State
a. South Africa shall be an independent, unitary, democratic and non-racial state.
b. Sovereignty shall belong to the people as a whole and shall be exercised through one central legislature, executive, judiciary and administration. Provision shall be made for the delegation of the powers of the central authority to subordinate administrative units for purposes of more efficient administration and democratic participation.
c. The institution of hereditary rulers and chiefs shall be transformed to serve the interests of the people as a whole in conformity with the democratic principles embodied in the constitution.
d. All organs of government, including justice, security and armed forces, shall be representative of the people as a whole, democratic in their structure and functioning, and dedicated to defending the principles of the constitution.

Franchise
e. In the exercise of their sovereignty, the people shall have the right to vote under a system of universal suffrage based on the principle of one person/ one vote.
f. Every voter shall have the right to stand for election and be elected to all legislative bodies.

National Identity
g. It shall be state policy to promote the growth of a single national identity and loyalty binding on all South Africans. At the same time, the state shall

recognise the linguistic and cultural diversity of the people and provide facilities for free linguistic and cultural development.

Bill of Rights and Affirmative Action

h. The constitution shall include a Bill of Rights based on the Freedom Charter. Such a Bill of Rights shall guarantee the fundamental human rights of all citizens, irrespective of race, colour, sex or creed, and shall provide appropriate mechanisms for their protection and enforcement.

i. The state and all social institutions shall be under a constitutional duty to eradicate race discrimination in all its forms.

j. The state and all social institutions shall be under constitutional duty to take active steps to eradicate, speedily, the economic and social inequalities produced by racial discrimination.

k. The advocacy or practice of racism, fascism, Nazism, the incitement of ethnic or regional exclusiveness shall be outlawed.

l. Subject to clauses (i) and (k) above, the democratic state shall guarantee the basic rights and freedoms, such as freedom of association, thought, worship and the press. Furthermore, the state shall have the duty to protect the right to work and guarantee the right to education and social security.

m. All parties which conform to the provision of (i) and (k) above shall have the legal right to exist and to take part in the political life of the country.

Economy

n. The state shall ensure that the entire economy serves the interests and well-being of the entire population.

o. The state shall have the right to determine the general context in which economic life takes place and define the limit to the rights and obligations attaching to the ownership and use of productive capacity.

p. The private sector of the economy shall be obliged to cooperate with the state in realising the objectives of the Freedom Charter in promoting social well-being.

q. The economy shall be a mixed one, with a public sector, a private sector, a co-operative sector and a small-scale family sector.

r. Co-operative forms of economic enterprise, village industries and small-scale family activities shall be supported by the state.

s. The state shall promote the acquisition of management, technical and scientific skills among all sections of the population, especially the Blacks.

t. Property for personal use and consumption shall be constitutionally protected.

Land

u. The state shall devise and implement a land reform programme that will include and address the following issues:
  - Abolition of all racial restrictions on ownership and use of land;
  - Implementation of land reform in conformity with the principle of affirmative action, taking into account the status of victims of forced removals.

Workers

v. A charter protecting workers' trade union rights, especially the right to strike and collective bargaining, shall be incorporated into the constitution.

Women

w. Women shall have equal rights in all spheres of public and private life and the state shall take affirmative action to eliminate inequalities and discrimination between the sexes.

The family

x. The family, parenthood and children's rights shall be protected.

International

y. South Africa shall be a non-aligned state committed to the principles of the Charter of the OAU and the Charter of the UN and to the achievement of national liberation, world peace and disarmament.

Creating the platform for a broad front and a new kind of politics. *Above*: A struggle meeting in Johannesburg in 1987. The urban revolt and internal mass struggles of the mid-to-late 1980s, headed by the UDF and COSATU working closely with the ANC, changed the face of South Africa. *Below*: The Constitution Committee's Kader Asmal and Barbara Masekela, Thabo Mbeki and Lindiwe Mabuza leading the 17-strong ANC delegation in song at the highly publicised Dakar conference in Senegal in June 1987. Penuell Maduna is just behind them

September 1987
NOMMER 11
R1.99 PLUS AVB

DIE SUID-AFRIKAAN

Dakar: die volle ver...

More than 200 safari meetings, given momentum by the conferences at Dakar, Harare, Amsterdam and Arusha in 1987, helped dissolve boundaries between internal and external anti-apartheid groupings and blew away the regime's attempts to demonise and isolate the ANC through its 'total onslaught' strategy

Top: The platform party at the Harare Conference on children and repression in South Africa, including Kader Asmal, Abdul Minty, Oliver Tambo and Beyers Naude, applaud conference patron Archbishop Trevor Huddleston. *Middle*: Children were present in Harare to testify about their detention and life experiences. *Bottom*: Barbara Masekela, Barry Gilder and Pallo Jordan speaking at the big CASA culture gathering in Amsterdam where important strategic decisions were taken to exempt allied democrats from the boycott

Oliver Tambo and Salim Salim at the Arusha Conference in December 1987, where a wide range of governments and international agencies and solidarity groups pledged their support for the ANC's political initiatives and efforts to further isolate the regime

Tambo with a close ally, the Swedish prime minister Olof Palme. Sweden was a major funder of the liberation movement and the first Western European country to impose economic sanctions on apartheid South Africa. Just days before Palme's assassination in 1986, they agreed to initiate the Planning for an Alternative South Africa (PASA) programme, which involved the Constitution Committee

Above: The president shares a light moment with Cuban leader Fidel Castro, a staunch ally of the liberation movements. Castro cautioned Oliver Tambo in early 1986 about the pitfalls of nationalisation in a future South Africa. *Below*: When Tambo, accompanied by Thabo Mbeki, met Soviet leader Mikhail Gorbachev for the first time in November 1986, three years before the fall of the Berlin Wall, the ANC had already decided on a future constitution ensuring multiparty democracy with a Bill of Rights that gave equal protection to all South Africans

Rare footage from the historic In-House Seminar on the Constitutional Guidelines in Lusaka in March 1988. Above: Thabo Mbeki speaking, with Mendi Msimang and Alfred Nzo sharing the podium. Below: Max Sisulu makes a point from the floor, while in front of him new member of the Constitution Committee Nathaniel Masemola, Sipho 'FAPLA' Dlamini, Ruth Mompati and Yusuf Salojee listen intently.

9	Susan Mnumzana	
0	Ncithe	
1	Rufus mbilini	
2	Vusmzi Pikoli	
3	Tami Bolani	
4	Lobster Ntabeni	
35	CHISELENGA C CHARLES (OOP) ZAMBIA	
36	Captain LEROLE	
37	Page Boikanyo	
38	Sipho Dlamini	
39	Jack Simons	
40	Mathlepule Moloto	
41	addie Funde	
42	Mpho Sebeko	
43	Lindiwe Mabuza	
44	MPHO SEFATE	
45	Joh Davies	
46	A. MASONDO	
47	M. MABILETSA	
48	T. Marcus	
49	SOLLY Mpoli	
50	Ray Simons	
51	Benny Leviread	
52	MAX MLONYENI	
53	THEMBA THABETHE	
54	Brigitte Sylvia Mabandla	
55	Albie Sachs	
56		

© Albie Sachs Collection

© Kader Asmal Papers, UWC

CONSTITUTIONAL GUIDELINES
FOR A DEMOCRATIC SOUTH AFRICA

ANC

The People Shall Govern

All National Groups Shall Have Equal Rights

There Shall be Work and Security

The People Shall Share in the Country's Wealth

All Shall be Equal Before the Law

The Land Shall be Shared Among Those who Work It

The Doors of Learning and Culture Shall be Opened

All Shall Enjoy Equal Human Rights

© Albie Sachs Collection

© UWC/RIM Mayibuye Archives

A constitution written in blood

Constitution Committee rapporteur Albie Sachs
moments after the car bomb attempt on his life in
Maputo, April 1988. He survived but lost his right
arm and sight in his left eye. This was only weeks
after speaking at the ANC's historic In-House
Seminar in Lusaka to finalise the Constitutional
Guidelines. *Opposite page*: Sachs holding up
the Guidelines with the arm he would soon lose

Sachs's colleagues wrote to Tambo five days after
the attack, in words of revolutionary outrage and
resignation written as an obituary:
We make no apology for putting into words our sense
of shock and outrage at the murderous assault
on Albie by the same hand that murdered Dulcie
[September]. He was close to us – a dear friend and
esteemed colleague whose contribution to the work
of our committee and indeed the entire movement
is beyond praise. We wish to condole with you and
through you all the devoted members of our great
enterprise for the liberation of our country from a
tyrant who is evil personified but whose end is certain

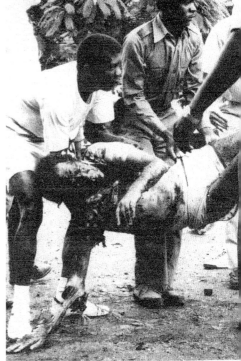

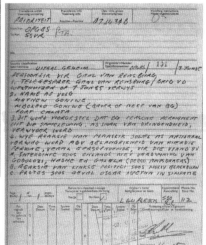

DETENTIONS!!!!
UDF LEADERS DETAINED
BANNINGS!!!!!!
MEETINGS IN 22 AREAS BANNED
REPRESSION!!!
PEOPLE SHOT DEAD IN TOWNSHIPS
[ ]MENT!!!
UDF
WE WILL NOT BE SILENCED

Above: Dulcie September, ANC chief rep in France, was assassinated only nine days before the attempt on Albie Sachs's life in Maputo

Above: 'PRIORITY. HIGHLY SECRET'. The signal sent out on 7 June 1985 by the State Security Council for the 'permanent removal from society, as a matter of urgency' of Cradock activists Matthew Goniwe, Mbulelo Goniwe and Fort Calata. Their murders were confirmation that the regime was using extra-legal terror to get rid of its opponents

Lawyers Griffiths and Victoria Mxenge were brutally murdered within a few years of each other, as state-sponsored hit squads became a feature of the political landscape in the 1980s

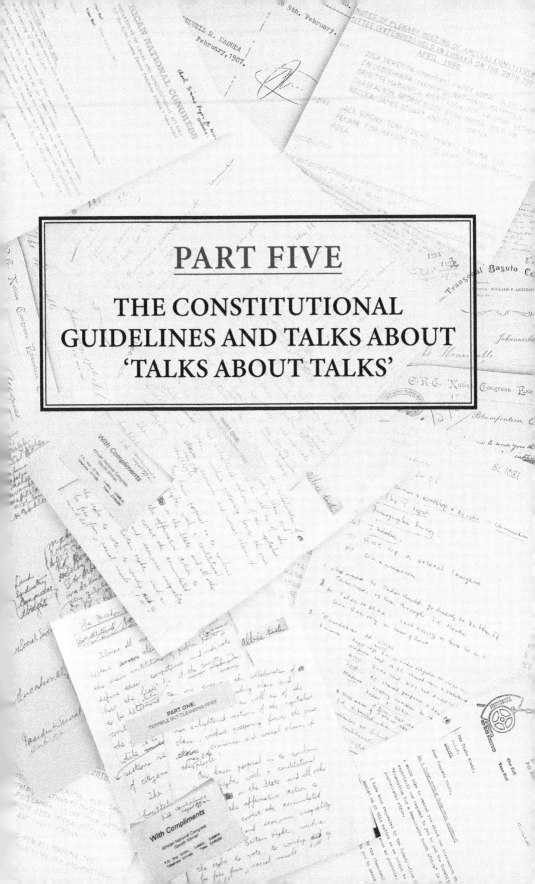

PART FIVE

THE CONSTITUTIONAL GUIDELINES AND TALKS ABOUT 'TALKS ABOUT TALKS'

28

Cuito Cuanavale

B EFORE THE HISTORIC Kabwe conference, it had been the inaptly named
'Guns of Gaborone'. This time, in March 1988 – days after the landmark
In-House Seminar on the Constitutional Guidelines in Lusaka – it was the Battle
of Cuito Cuanavale. This battle in a minor town in a rural expanse in south-east
Angola, so far off the beaten track that the Portuguese referred to it as 'the land at
the end of the Earth', became the military event marching in step with the advance
of the liberation movement's political struggles. Nelson Mandela, then imprisoned,
later referred to it as 'a turning point for the liberation of our continent and my
people'.[1]

In the previous year, Angolan government troops, guided by Soviet military
personnel, had driven south to capture Jonas Savimbi at his headquarters in Jamba
close to the Caprivi Strip, which runs from Namibia to Zambia. Savimbi was the
leader of UNITA (União Nacional para a Independência Total de Angola), which
was being strongly supported by the CIA and the SADF, intent on destabilising
the newly independent state hosting ANC military training camps. At first the
Angolan government troops advanced rapidly and inflicted defeats on the UNITA
combatants. But then the SADF intervened with massive firepower and annihilated
the advancing forces. Bedraggled stragglers retreated to Cuito. However, instead
of advancing, capturing the town and seizing the initiative to split Angola in two,
the SADF stayed in place. A small contingent of Cuban troops rushed to Cuito
to help organise the defences. A ferocious siege developed. Pounding Cuito with
155mm G5 howitzers, the SADF staged attack after attack led by 61 Mechanised
Battalion, the crack 32 Battalion and, later, the 4th South African Infantry Battalion.
The defenders held out, reinforced by 1 500 elite troops who arrived from Cuba in
December 1987. By 23 March 1988, the last major attack on Cuito was 'brought to
a grinding and definite halt'. In the words of 32 Battalion commander Colonel Jan
Breytenbach, 'The Unita soldiers did a lot of dying that day ... The full weight of
[the enemy's firepower] was brought down on the heads of the Regiment President
Steyn.'[2]

Ronnie Kasrils, who was then a senior officer in MK intelligence, heard views
on this battle from both Fidel Castro, on the one hand, and General Kat Liebenberg,
a South African army chief, on the other. According to General Liebenberg, the

SADF could have taken the town, but its objective was not to seize it but rather to keep it under constant bombardment to prevent its airstrip from being used. Implicit in his approach was the SADF narrative that it had won the battle.

Castro's analysis – fitting in with the liberation struggle narrative – was rather different. At a briefing in Havana's Defence Ministry at the end of 1988, he outlined the drama on a huge tabletop sand model of southern Angola. Kasrils recalls:

> Our delegation, headed by South African Communist Party leader Joe Slovo, hung on his every word. Castro observed that the SADF was far too cautious ... After their early success, they could have quickly taken the town. [But] the defenders not only saved the day, but bought the time to enable the Cuban-Angolan side to turn the tables, and by April 1988, launched a breathtaking offensive in the south-west that changed the course of history.
>
> On his table-top model, Castro pointed out the amazing feat of a 40 000-strong Cuban [-Angolan government] and Swapo troop deployment [on] a front which stretched from Namibe on the coast, along a railway line ... to Cuito Cuanavale in the east. The SADF forces at Cuito were sidelined ... as powerful forces (armed with the latest Soviet weaponry and under superior air cover) moved west towards the Namibian border. Angola's southern ... provinces were liberated after years of SADF control.[3]

Kasrils adds that a masterstroke was the rapid construction of airstrips by Cuban engineers within 300 kilometres of the Namibian border. Soviet MiG-23s flown by Cuban pilots had demonstrated their superiority over South Africa's aged Mirage fighters, whose obsolescence was the result of UN sanctions. Once the Cuban pilots commanded the skies, the network of SADF bases in northern Namibia was at their mercy. Showing quiet pride in this achievement, Castro used what became his famous boxing analogy to explain the carefully formulated strategy: Cuito in the east represented the boxer's defensive left fist that blocked the blow, while in the west the powerful right fist had struck, placing the SADF in a perilous position. The SADF's end was signalled when a squadron of MiGs bombed the hydroelectric dam systems on the Cunene River, cutting the water and power supply to Ovamboland and its military bases. Before returning to base, a MiG-23 executed a neat victory roll. Kasrils continues in romantic vein:

> It is fitting that at Freedom Park outside Pretoria, the names of the 2 070 Cuban soldiers who fell in Angola between 1975 and 1988 are inscribed alongside those of the South African revolutionaries who died during the decades-long liberation struggle ... After 13 years, defending Angolan sovereignty, the Cubans

took nothing home except the bones of their fallen and Africa's gratitude ... For most of those years, uMkhonto we Sizwe combatants engaged their adversary in many parts of Angola ... [They] aided in the interception and translation of Afrikaans radio traffic and provided invaluable intelligence on the SADF following an historic agreement signed between Angolan President Eduardo dos Santos and the ANC's Oliver Tambo ... One hundred and thirty MK combatants lost their lives in action during that time, as did possibly as many white SADF troops as well as several thousand Unita and other surrogates under SADF command.[4]

Inside South Africa, minister of finance Barend du Plessis was reporting to cabinet that the country could not continue to support the costs of the war in Angola. At the same time, newspaper stories were coming out about South Africa's secret war. Young white men who refused to be conscripted started the End Conscription Campaign, whose imaginative activism against 'total onslaught' ideas touched a nerve. They were willing to go to jail rather than fight in what were being called 'border wars' or take part in military manoeuvres in the townships. Playing on the senselessness of apartheid militarism as well as the increasing psychological damage it was doing to young conscripts, one End Conscription poster depicted a young man with a primed hand grenade for a head and the words 'Apartheid maak malletjies', meaning that compulsory military conscription and apartheid propaganda were creating a disturbed and dangerous generation of young people.[5]

At the international level, negotiations between the Soviet Union and the United States aimed at reducing Cold War tensions in different parts of the world, including Africa. With the USA acting as an intermediary and the USSR as observer, formal multilateral negotiations commenced in London in May 1988 between Cuba, Angola and South Africa, to find a solution to the Namibian conflict and its attendant geopolitical impacts on southern Africa. These talks led to the signing of the Brazzaville Protocol on 22 December 1988, which paved the way for the independence of Namibia. In return, the agreement provided for the withdrawal of Cuban forces from Angola, as well as the obligatory removal of MK combatants, who were moved to rear bases in Uganda.[6]

Meanwhile, in Lusaka, Tambo set up a special committee to ensure that the ANC would remain responsive and proactive in relation to geo-political developments. This included Peter Mayibuye (aka Joel Netshitenzhe), Ngoako Ramatlhodi and Neo Mnumzana. Their task was to provide advice and draft a programme and plan of action around which the ANC and its allies could mobilise international support.[7] At the heart of this document would be two major ANC instruments: the Constitutional Guidelines and the NEC policy document on negotiations.

29

Murder in Paris and a Car Bomb in Maputo

O N 29 MARCH 1988, just six days after the end of the Battle of Cuito Cuanavale and scarcely three weeks after the In-House Seminar in Lusaka, Dulcie September, the ANC's chief representative for France, Luxembourg and Switzerland, was shot from behind with a silenced .22 calibre rifle as she unlocked the door of the ANC's fourth-floor office at 28 Rue des Petites-Écuries in Paris. She was discovered lifeless with five bullet wounds in her body.[1]

September grew up in Athlone on the Cape Flats. Despite her father's decision to end her formal schooling halfway through Standard 8 (Grade 10), she persevered and went on to become a teacher. In the 1950s, education was one of the principal terrains of struggle, due to the imposition of Bantu education and coloured education, and in September's first year of teaching, a close friend recruited her into the newly established Cape Peninsula Students' Union (CPSU). It was an affiliate of the Non-European Unity Movement, a strong proponent of revolutionary class struggle and non-racialism, which had strong support among educators in Cape Town.

September eventually parted ways with her Unity Movement mentors. The Sharpeville massacre and the consequent political crisis that gripped the country had awakened a militant attitude among many. In 1962, September aligned herself with Dr Neville Alexander and several other young radicals who formed a study group known as the Yu Chi Chan Club (YCCC). 'Yu Chi Chan' was the Chinese name for guerrilla warfare used by Mao Tse-Tung. The YCCC, however, disbanded at the end of that same year and was replaced by the National Liberation Front (NLF) in January 1963. In October that year, September was arrested for her NLF activities and detained without trial at Roeland Street Prison. After being convicted for her underground activities, she spent five years in jail.[2]

Three years after her release, she left South Africa for London. She joined the ANC and slowly advanced in the organisation to become its chief representative in Paris, becoming known inside and outside the organisation as a strong opponent of gender discrimination.[3] During apartheid, France and major French corporations were some of the most loyal supporters of the South African government. French companies became the second-largest suppliers of arms to South Africa. There was some pushback from within both France and South Africa.

In 1985, representatives from the French and South African communist parties met to discuss solidarity. However, the French government continued to supply arms to apartheid South Africa, violating the arms embargo for which Tambo had tirelessly worked and on which Kader Asmal had published extensively.

In June 1986, September was instrumental in organising an international conference against apartheid. Tambo's opening address for the event spoke of France's moral obligation to impose comprehensive sanctions against South Africa. His words were not heeded. Less than five months later, France, the United States, Germany, Israel and Britain voted against an oil embargo against South Africa at the United Nations.

By 1987 it became evident that September had formed an effective anti-apartheid lobby. By mounting a strong pro-sanctions and disinvestment campaign, not only in France but also in Switzerland and Luxembourg, she forged strong links with pressure groups and left-wing politicians in all three countries. At the time she was assassinated, September was gathering evidence to show how powerful networks involving European banks, international arms dealers, shipping companies and middlemen were enriching themselves by arming apartheid in violation of the mandatory UN embargo. Much of the trade was coordinated through the South African embassy in Paris. The mid-1980s saw increased aggression in South African military actions against ANC external missions. She was certain that her office was under surveillance and her telephone bugged, and that unknown agents had gained access to her office. She reported that she was being watched and feared an attempt on her life.[4]

Her assassination was flagrant. It was a sign of the deepening violence of the political system of apartheid in its dying days. For such a high-ranking official of the organisation to be shot down in a major European city was deeply shocking to her comrades. She was fifty-two years old. Her murder has never been solved.

Just nine days after Dulcie September was shot, South African security agents attempted to assassinate Albie Sachs. After the In-House Seminar in Lusaka in early March, Sachs flew back to Maputo. From Mavalane airport, where you had to report hours early though the plane often left late, it was a few miles back to his apartment. He was living alone on the third floor of a building in Julius Nyerere Avenue, which had been his home since shortly after he arrived in Maputo in 1977. Maputo's recently renamed streets were lessons in unfolding history, replacing the names of Portuguese soldiers, bishops and traders with Nyerere, Engels, Lumumba, and so on.

He loved Mozambique. 'This is where I became African,' he says plainly. It was where he had got in touch with his laughter and passion again after a marriage that broke down and ten years in the cold of another hemisphere. He felt rehumanised.

On 7 April 1988, a public holiday in Maputo – O Dia da Mulher Moçambicana, the Day of the Mozambican Woman – Sachs decided to go to the beach. He skipped down the three flights of stairs and walked to his red, left-hand drive Honda. As he opened the car door:

> Oh shit. Everything has abruptly gone dark, I am feeling strange and cannot see anything. The darkness is not clearing, this is something serious ... a terrible thing is happening to me, I am swirling, I cannot steady myself as I wait for consciousness and light to return. I feel a shuddering punch against the back of my neck, and then what seems like another one ... This is the moment we have all been waiting for, the few ANC members still working in Mozambique, with dread and yet with a weird kind of eagerness ...
>
> The darkness is total, but still I hear tense staccato speech.
>
> 'Lift him up, put him there.'
>
> I am not a him, I am me, you cannot just cart me around like a suitcase. But I am unable to struggle any more, I just have to go along and accept what happens, my will has gone ...
>
> All is very still and calm and without movement or voices or muscular activity. I am wrapped in complete darkness and tranquillity. If I am dead I am not aware of it ...
>
> 'Albie ...' through the darkness a voice, speaking not about me but to me, and using my name and without that terrible urgency of all those other voices.
>
> '... Albie, this is Ivo Garrido speaking to you ...' the voice is sympathetic and affectionate, I know Ivo, he is an outstanding young surgeon and a friend '... you are in the Maputo Central Hospital ... your arm is in a lamentable condition ...' he uses a delicate Portuguese word to describe my arm, how tactful the Mozambican culture is compared to the English one, I must ask him later what that word is '... we are going to operate and you must face the future with courage.'
>
> A glow of joy of complete satisfaction and peace envelops me, I am in the hands of Frelimo, of the Mozambican Government, I am safe.
>
> 'What happened?' I am asking the question into the darkness, my will has been activated in response to hearing Ivo's voice ...
>
> A voice answers, close to my ears, I think it is a woman's, '... a car bomb ...' and I drift back, smiling inside, into nothingness.[5]

His would-be assassins had placed a bomb under the front right-hand-side seat of the car, where drivers in southern Africa generally sit. His left-hand-drive Honda had turned out to be his saving grace. A television crew in the vicinity had filmed his body on the ground, placed him in their van and driven him to the Maputo Central Hospital.

When Sachs's comrades on the Constitution Committee submitted their report on the In-House Seminar to Oliver Tambo on 12 April 1988, it was only five days after the bomb blast, and less than a fortnight after Dulcie September's assassination. They wrote passionately about their colleague in a statement of revolutionary outrage. They did not yet know whether he would survive. In fact, reading these words one senses resignation; they take the past-tense form of an obituary:

> We make no apology for putting into words our sense of shock and outrage at the murderous assault on Albie by the same hand that murdered Dulcie. He was close to us – a dear friend and esteemed colleague whose contribution to the work of our committee and indeed the entire movement is beyond praise. We wish to condole with you and through you all the devoted members of our great enterprise for the liberation of our country from a tyrant who is evil personified but whose end is certain.[6]

Sachs survived and was flown to London for further treatment, and in case a second attempt was made on his life:

> I look towards the airport buildings and can dimly make out the visitors' balcony against the glare of the lights. We are half-way up the steps ... A soldier stands close by with his AK gun, the first thing I saw when I landed in Maputo ten years ago; it was a real person, not a poster – I wanted to dance and cry, and the word that came to my lips ... was: Victory. How rarely could we say that, how many times had African people been trampled underfoot because of inferior firepower. Now I have seen so many guns, the war has dragged on for so long, so many problems have beset the army, that I no longer enthuse over the uniform or the arms in the same way, but something of that initial respect will always remain ...
> I raise my head a little, lift my arm in a final farewell and wave towards the balcony. The air is warm and the lights are confusing. Suddenly, amazingly and beautifully, there are hundreds and hundreds of arms waving back to me, and I feel the cantata of love and affection swelling out towards me again. The people of this city and I are in joyous, spontaneous communion, my friends, my colleagues are there, but also hundreds of strangers, it is a beautiful hallucination, as I raise my arm in a last farewell from my mummy-like body, all those arms swaying and rolling against the glare of the lights.

The nurses pause at the top of the staircase ... Khanimambo, Maputo, thank you, until we meet again ... and then carry me into the plane.[7]

Not long after his arrival at the London hospital, Sachs received a handwritten note from Tambo expressing outrage at this 'dastardly deed'.[8] Another note came from a comrade telling him not to worry; he would be avenged. But the idea of an eye for an eye, a tooth for a tooth, an arm for an arm, filled him with anguish. The only kind of vengeance that could assuage the loss of his arm was a historical one, victory for the things they had been fighting for, the triumph of their ideals.[9]

Some weeks later, after he had been discharged from hospital, Albie met with Jacob Zuma and John Nkadimeng, who had been mandated to bring him greetings on behalf of the NEC. 'Zuma was laughing as he received me into his arms at the front door, while comrade John had grave, sad eyes despite my exclamation of pleasure on greeting them.' Touching on the many-sided aspects of life and struggle and the poignancy of the meeting, Sachs recalled:

> There are times for solemnity, times for earnestness, times for passionate calls
> to battle, and times for laughter. This is a time for laughter, the listener partici-
> pating in the story by means of almost continuous and celebratory laughter ...
> As I launch into my story, Zuma sits close by and watches me intently, ready
> to respond with warm chuckles and vigorous swings and shakes of his body
> to each statement I make. When I describe how, lying on the ground in Julius
> Nyerere Avenue, I shouted ('but politely') in English and Portuguese he almost
> falls off the chair. He knows that area well, for ten years he was one of our
> leaders in Maputo ... I start describing the part when I thought I was fighting
> for my life against kidnappers from Pretoria when really I was making a few
> feeble flaps with my shoulders against my Mozambican rescuers, and he lets
> out roars of supportive laughter, not waiting to the end of the sentence but, as
> if to underline and share with me the poignant hilarity of the situation, accom-
> panying the climax of my words with happy explosive gurgles. I look across at
> comrade John, trying to force him with my vivacity to join in the mirth, but he
> stares back at me with sad, moist eyes.[10]

John Nkadimeng had been a trade unionist since his father's day and Albie had known him 'since I was a child'. Sachs wanted the older man 'to celebrate my survival with me, the arm is a detail, not the main thing', but he had to remember that Nkadimeng himself 'lost one of his sons to a similar bomb blast [in Gaborone in 1985], and perhaps I remind him of his slain child'.

In the archival papers of the In-House Seminar, an unsigned handwritten note states that, in disseminating the Guidelines, 'Discussion [would necessarily be] subject to security'. Those involved in shaping the historic text understood that, given the dangers of exile and revolutionary underground work at the time, this was not just another academic debate taking place. Just below this comment was another observation: the 'State of Emergency has been a school for underground organisation'.[11]

Historian Linda Colley has written in *The Gun, the Ship and the Pen* that constitutions often emerge in the midst of profound conflict. Far from the staid picture of them being birthed through the rational discourse of elevated literary society and conference halls, they are constituted in creative cultural ways, emerging from poems, plays, journalism and plain survival during times of violence and instability.[12]

Colley's observations have a resonance with 1988 when the finishing touches were being put to the Constitutional Guidelines and a slowly recovering Albie Sachs sought to make sense of what it would mean to be fully 'human' in the new South Africa. He reflected, amid the dangers of that time, on the profound personal journeys and thinking involved in the process of imagining a new country:

> It is as if the camera is healing me by recording my image, counteracting the terrible hatred contained in the bomb ... This is my vengeance, my way of fighting back, not by killing others but by transmuting bad into good, using my heart and brains to project as much as possible a vision of survival, struggle, triumph and humanity.[13]

Sachs went on to ask 'if the apertures in our eyes are wide enough', if South Africans had the 'cultural imagination', to grasp 'the full dimensions of the country struggling to give birth to itself'. Or were they 'still trapped in the multiple ghettoes of the apartheid imagination', not yet ready for freedom, preferring to be angry victims? His subsequent book, *The Soft Vengeance of a Freedom Fighter*, is a testament to the depth of thinking and the freshness and often counter-intuitive nature of the ideas produced by those at the heart of the ANC's constitutional-planning project in the 1980s. Like Pallo Jordan in his 1985 paper, he punctured stereotypes and dogma, imagining newness beyond the constraints and boundaries of the present. Nobel literature laureate Nadine Gordimer described the book as 'the rarest of reading ..., a revelation of an aspect of political activism ignored or denied', but which should be obvious: 'that to risk oneself to change the world for the better is to have a capacity for the splendid tender joys of the body as well as spirit and mind'.[14] In a similar vein, Sachs went on to suggest in a paper on culture and the Constitutional Guidelines presented in Lusaka that in order to fully promote free speech and counteract self-limiting censorship 'we should ban ourselves [for five years] from saying culture is a weapon of struggle'.[15]

It generated much debate and publicity, with colleague Kader Asmal among those who took issue with him. These are readings and intimate insights that sceptics about the transformational thinking and goals of the 1980s process, who wish to better understand it, would do well to engage with.

Later in 1988 the Constitution Committee gave Sachs a task that fitted in perfectly with his desire for soft vengeance. On a rainy day he found himself seated at a kitchen table in the home of Kader and Louise Asmal at 20 Beech Park Road, Dublin, with a ballpoint pen raised over a blank sheet of paper. They had been asked to draft an outline of a Bill of Rights for a democratic South Africa. Asmal remembered:

> Albie flew to Dublin to work with me on the draft ANC bill of rights. As always it was raining in Dublin, and I remember having my repeated smoke breaks outside in the rain because the smoke hurt Albie's damaged eyes. Seated at my kitchen table, with Albie struggling to learn to write with his left hand, we resumed work together on drafting our country's bill of rights. We decided that Albie would start first on the substantive rights and I on their mechanisms for enforcement. Then we would read each other's drafts and integrate them into one document. Albie and I worked without any sources – on purpose. We didn't want our thinking to be predetermined in any way. We wanted to put down what it meant to be a human, a South African, who has fundamental rights. We were strongly aware of being part of a process of writing history; this was going to be the text of a document that would become a lodestar for the ANC during the negotiation process. It was also the precursor for the Bill of Rights that now proudly adorns South Africa's democratic Constitution. I will forever remember those interactions and arguments with Albie, which often went on deep into the night.[16]

Sachs recalls:

> I sat down at that table with a clean piece of paper – no books, no documents, no charters, no constitutions, no preambles – the idea being that a Bill of Rights should speak from inside of you ... I was writing with my left hand – I had to learn to write with my left – and I jotted down a number of fundamental rights the people of South Africa would have. Afterwards, Kader and I checked against the great instruments of the world, and all the fundamental rights were there.

It wasn't because we were particularly clever or astute. It was because we'd been so deeply immersed and involved in a struggle, with millions of people taking part and expressing their demands, that we were able to find the language.[17]

After decades of denouncing apartheid and trying to bring it down, and despite the intense turmoil and violence all around, Sachs was beginning to experience a new set of emotions of hope, healing, building and reconstruction. The Asmals' photograph of the family protectively surrounding a smiling and clearly recovering Albie in the family home at the time of this assignment in Dublin is emblematic of the moment.

This drafting session in Dublin between the one-armed bomb victim, learning anew to write, and the chain-smoking Trinity College law dean has entered the realm of romantic myth. This was the moment when two gifted exiled intellectuals wrote the first words of a Bill of Rights for a country that had been plagued by colonialism and apartheid for longer than three centuries, sitting at Louise and Kader's kitchen table with only a blank piece of paper in front of them and without any references so they could do justice to the uniqueness of the task and the lived experiences of South Africans.[18] And, fittingly, from anti-colonial perspectives, this happened in a small island nation that had long borne the brunt of colonial brutality from neighbouring Britain.

In writing about this historic moment, some questions immediately arise. Surely those first words did not emanate from a tabula rasa or blank sheet? What were the words? And which of the 1988 formulations found their way into the Constitution of democratic South Africa in 1996? Finally, if only from inquisitiveness, what happened to the table?

The first question is easy to put to bed. That rainy August in Dublin was certainly not the first time that these two legally skilled freedom fighters applied their minds to the question of what a Bill of Rights for South Africa should contain. For years they had been immersed in this very debate. Their papers show it. Furthermore, the Constitution Committee had already discussed the need for a Bill of Rights and a preamble for a future constitution at its first meeting in January 1986. Asmal had articulated the Committee's criticisms about the undemocratic nature of the KwaZulu-Natal Indaba's draft Bill of Rights at length in its meeting with Oliver Tambo in January 1987. Some months later, in June 1987, Sachs wrote to the ANC president from Maputo, enclosing for his attention 'a copy of a manuscript I have prepared on a Bill of Rights for a Democratic South Africa'. Some of the chapters had previously been published while others were 'completely new'. Sachs added that, 'I am sending copies to the Legal and Constitutional Department and asking if there is any objection to the book's publication (it would be strictly in my name and not that of the ANC)'.[19] The Constitution Committee minutes for that month show also that the Committee had tasked Sachs with preparing 'a paper on a Bill of Rights' in the run-up to the In-House Seminar.[20] So in Dublin, in a way, Sachs was picking up the writing he'd been busy with before the bomb blast. This work eventually came to be published by Oxford University Press in 1991 as *Protecting Human Rights in a New South Africa.*

The second and third questions above cannot currently be answered. Sachs and Asmal had deliberately not developed the draft Bill of Rights from notes prepared in advance, so the only document to emerge was their final handwritten text. In that time before personal computers, Louise Asmal typed up the document for them, together with some carbon copies.[21] Strangely, none of the handwritten first drafts, nor the typed-up version – hammered out on what was then the latest-model golf ball typewriter – nor any printed versions generated from the originals have been preserved. Nor are there any marked-up drafts that show the evolution in thinking and formulation from 1988 to the publication in November 1990 of 'A Bill of Rights for a New South Africa', the Constitution Committee's first pub-lished suggestions for a draft Bill of Rights.[22] Revised versions of the booklet were later published in 1992 and 1993.[23] Despite both authors having kept voluminous paper records that are well preserved in collections named after them at the University of the Western Cape, there is no sign of these documents.

The charismatic Asmal is no longer with us to help fill in the gaps concern-ing the original text written and typed up at his home in Dublin, or the way it morphed into the ANC draft Bill of Rights for a democratic South Africa. He offered only cryptic answers in his autobiography. The first was that 'although we had drawn up the draft bill of rights, we kept it close to our chests through most of the negotiations period'. The big silence about work on the document before the unbannings in February 1990 remains. Asmal also offered that 'Only its bare outline was included in the 1993 Interim Constitution because we didn't want it to be anticipated at a subsequent stage'. Even then, he said, it was not presented as a template for the negotiated Interim Constitution of 1993, in keeping with the ANC's long-held position that only a democratically elected body could produce the country's constitution. It 'became one of many documents drawn on at the time of writing the final Bill of Rights and we wanted it to be incorporated in a way that would best serve South Africa'.[24]

It is easy to understand why Sachs did not keep a record at that stage. He had boarded a plane in Maputo on a stretcher with only a small bag of clothing to accompany him. When he emerged from hospital in London, he had no home or office and stayed with friends. When the Dublin weekend was over, he flew back to London, leaving it to the Asmals to send the document to the ANC.[25] Presumably the typed original would have been posted to the ANC office in London for delivery to the Constitution Committee in Lusaka. There are many points at which it could have been mislaid.

And what about the kitchen table on which the first draft was written? The Asmal family are not sure what happened to it. Louise believes it ended up in Greece, where her sister stayed. But a blue plaque, unveiled by the Irish Taoiseach, was placed on the front wall of the house at 20 Beech Park Road in Foxrock, Dublin, to mark its place in the evolution of South Africa's constitutional democracy.

30

'Only Free Men Can Negotiate'

WAR IN ANGOLA, murder in Paris, murderous state-of-emergency hit squads, disappearances and mass detentions at home in South Africa, and a car bomb attack in Mozambique on one of the key crafters of the ANC's Constitutional Guidelines ... By early 1988 the political crisis in South Africa was deepening and the pressure was growing for the ANC and the apartheid government to start talking to each other.

On Sunday 3 July 1988, Mac Maharaj, the NEC member in charge of underground operations, together with senior MK commander Siphiwe Nyanda, operating under the *nom de guerre* 'Gebuza', secretly entered South Africa to launch the long-planned-for Operation Vula.

Maharaj had built an elaborate cover since being appointed commander in 1986. He was photographed with a walking stick at the highly publicised Dakar conference in 1987 and the legend was that he was seriously ill and receiving treatment in the Soviet Union. At the start of Operation Vula, he travelled to Moscow, where he was fitted out with false passports, including an Indian passport in the name of Robin Das, and some sophisticated disguise equipment. He then flew to Amsterdam to meet with Nyanda. Their main objectives were to coordinate underground ANC political activity in South Africa and create conditions for an insurrection to overthrow the apartheid regime. One of their specific goals was to make contact with Mandela in prison. After arriving in South Africa, Maharaj established his main base in Durban, where there was an expanding underground network, and set up a remarkable system of communication with Lusaka.[1]

Three years earlier, on 31 January 1985, President Botha had offered Mandela his freedom on condition that he 'unconditionally reject violence as a political weapon'. This was the sixth reported offer of release made to Mandela. Previous offers had been conditional on his going to live in the Transkei Bantustan. Mandela rejected them all on the grounds of ANC policy, which refused to acknowledge the status of the Bantustans and those who collaborated with them. His daughter Zindzi read his response to this latest offer at a UDF mass meeting at Jabulani Stadium, Soweto, on 10 February 1985. After a stirring introduction, she proclaimed the following words on his behalf:

I am a member of the African National Congress. I have always been a member of the African National Congress and I will remain a member of the African National Congress until the day I die. Oliver Tambo is much more than a brother to me. He is my greatest friend and comrade for nearly fifty years. If there is any one amongst you who cherishes my freedom, Oliver Tambo cherishes it more, and I know that he would give his life to see me free. There is no difference between his views and mine.

I am surprised at the conditions that the government wants to impose on me. I am not a violent man. My colleagues and I wrote in 1952 to Malan asking for a round table conference to find a solution to the problems of our country, but that was ignored. When Strijdom was in power, we made the same offer. Again it was ignored. When Verwoerd was in power we asked for a national convention for all the people in South Africa to decide on their future. This, too, was in vain.

It was only then, when all other forms of resistance were no longer open to us, that we turned to armed struggle. Let Botha show that he is different to Malan, Strijdom and Verwoerd. Let *him* renounce violence. Let him say that he will dismantle apartheid. Let him unban the people's organisation, the African National Congress. Let him free all who have been imprisoned, banished or exiled for their opposition to apartheid. Let him guarantee free political activity so that people may decide who will govern them.

I cherish my own freedom dearly, but I care even more for your freedom. Too many have died since I went to prison. Too many have suffered for the love of freedom. I owe it to their widows, to their orphans, to their mothers and to their fathers who have grieved and wept for them. Not only I have suffered during these long, lonely, wasted years. I am not less life-loving than you are. But I cannot sell my birthright, nor am I prepared to sell the birthright of the people to be free. I am in prison as the representative of the people and of your organisation, the African National Congress, which was banned.

What freedom am I being offered while the organisation of the people remains banned? What freedom am I being offered when I may be arrested on a pass offence? What freedom am I being offered to live my life as a family with my dear wife who remains in banishment in Brandfort? What freedom am I being offered when I must ask for permission to live in an urban area? What freedom am I being offered when I need a stamp in my pass to seek work? What freedom am I being offered when my very South African citizenship is not respected?

Only free men can negotiate. Prisoners cannot enter into contracts ... I cannot and will not give any undertaking at a time when I and you, the people, are not free.

Your freedom and mine cannot be separated.[2]

These were Mandela's first public utterances in twenty years and his words were met with uproarious applause. The text of his statement was published by the ANC in London. His message to the Kabwe conference similarly raised 'indescribable emotions'.[3]

Mandela's goal was to ensure that neither sceptics within the movement nor adversaries outside of it would be able to drive a wedge between him and Tambo. In his statement he insisted that formal negotiations could only happen with the ANC leadership in exile; the government had to talk to them directly because only Tambo and the leadership in Lusaka had a mandate to talk. Thus, Mandela had sought, from the start, to open a direct channel of communication between himself, Lusaka and the internal mass democratic movement – first through messages via his trusted lawyers, secondly through regular meetings with UDF and other internal leaders, and finally by using Operation Vula and the secret underground channels that Maharaj had opened.

Early in 1986, Mandela's direct emissary and lawyer, George Bizos, travelled to Lusaka to brief Tambo that Mandela had spoken informally to minister of justice Kobie Coetsee while in hospital for surgery the previous year. This followed a chance meeting between Coetsee and Winnie Mandela during a flight, where she encouraged him to speak to the imprisoned icon. Mandela had been sending constant reminders to Coetsee and General Willemse that he wished to engage with President Botha about the need for negotiations between the ANC and the regime. Some forward movement could be seen in his being allowed to meet in prison with Nigerian president Olusegun Obasanjo from the Commonwealth's EPG mission in February 1986. Then Coetsee allowed him a few visitors. Bizos, speaking of his visit to Lusaka to speak to Tambo as an envoy for Mandela, later wrote:

Oliver Tambo came to my room at 10 p.m. and remained until past three ... [H]is security men had been pacing up and down the passage worried that the meeting was becoming a security risk. It was February 1986. We had not seen, spoken, or written to one another for 26 years ... We embraced and remained silent for a while, looking intently into one another's eyes, fighting back tears of both joy and sorrow. Oliver was anxious to know about the state of Nelson's health ... He asked what lay behind the rumours of his possible release. Would his illness and isolation lead to any embarrassing arrangement? I assured him that Nelson was in touch with political developments ... He had access to the leaders of the UDF, and legal opinion. He could listen to the radio and watch television. There would be no early release. He stood by the speech Zindzi had read out in Soweto ... Oliver knew the speech well. He mentioned the references Nelson had made to him. He even wondered if it mightn't have been better if Nelson had gone into exile rather than him.[4]

The next morning, Bizos and his colleague Ismail Ayob were taken to the guest cottage in State House where Tambo lived as the guest of President Kenneth Kaunda. When Kaunda arrived, he embraced Tambo and shook hands with Bizos and Ayob. When Bizos conveyed Mandela's greetings and gratitude for what the Zambian president had been doing for the people of South Africa, Kaunda wiped away tears with his white handkerchief and said, 'Tell my friend Nelson that none of us in Africa feel free while he is in jail.' During the lunch that followed, an aide came in and whispered something in Tambo's ear. Shaken, Tambo informed the group that Olof Palme, the prime minister of Sweden and a great friend of his, had been assassinated. Tambo had just returned from meeting and sharing a plat-form with Palme in Sweden. At one stage, it had been the only Western European country to support economic sanctions against South Africa.

At the airport lounge before Bizos' flight home, Tambo asked the visitors not to divulge where he was living. South Africa's hit squads had already assassinated ANC leaders in Botswana, Lesotho, Swaziland, Mozambique and Zimbabwe, and unsuccessful attempts had been made in Zambia.[5]

The following month, March 1986, Mandela met with Coetsee twice. Then, in 1987, after several further promptings from Mandela and a long wait without any concrete follow-up from the apartheid government, Mandela had 'several private meetings' with Coetsee at the justice minister's private residence in Cape Town. Altogether, the two met at least fifteen times while Mandela was in prison.[6] Coetsee was his most senior and regular government contact and had finally proposed to President Botha that the government 'appoint a committee of senior officials to conduct private discussions with me.'[7]

Botha accepted Coetsee's advice and set up the special committee, which met with Mandela in May 1988. The four members were NIS head Dr Niël Barnard, his director-general Mike Louw, director-general of justice (under whose jurisdiction prisons fell) Fanie van der Merwe, and commissioner of prisons General Willie Willemse.

From then on, the level of contact escalated. 'I met them almost every week for a few months,' Mandela noted, 'and then the meetings occurred at irregular intervals, sometimes not for a month, and then suddenly every week.'[8] Initially, these discussions were primarily information-sharing sessions at which Mandela tried to educate the apartheid officials about the nature of the ANC and the desirability of negotiations. By this time, he'd become a global figure and even the regime's closest friends were pressing for him to be released. State sources mention that forty-eight meetings between Mandela and this state-appointed committee took place between May 1988 and February 1990.

For a decade on Robben Island, Mandela and his colleagues performed hard labour on a sparse diet that included one loaf of bread once a year at Christmas. They washed in cold *brak water,* slept on the concrete floor with a thin mat and two blankets, and wore short pants and sandals – no shoes, socks, underpants or long trousers, even in the wet Cape winters. Only gradually did conditions improve. Then, to facilitate these talks about talks, the government moved Mandela from Robben Island, first to his own section in Pollsmoor Prison in 1982, and then to Victor Verster Prison near Paarl in December 1988. There, he was accommodated in a house meant for prison warders.

For Mandela there were three issues that needed immediate addressing when the more formal talks process started in mid-1988. One was to consult with his closest comrades who had been moved from Robben Island to Pollsmoor: Walter Sisulu, Raymond Mhlaba, Andrew Mlangeni and Ahmed Kathrada. Another was to communicate the news to Tambo in Lusaka. The third was to draft a memorandum to P.W. Botha, 'laying out my views and those of the ANC on the vital issues before the country'.[9]

At the meetings with his fellow Rivonia trialists, he sketched his plans in broad terms. Mhlaba and Mlangeni were enthusiastic; his closest confidants, Sisulu and Kathrada, less so. Sisulu said he would have preferred the initiative to come from the regime. Kathrada was unhappy with Madiba's plans of talking to government, feeling that it could be seen as a sign of weakness.[10]

In an exchange of smuggled letters with a concerned Tambo, Mandela assured his comrade in exile that he 'was talking to the government about one thing and one thing only: a meeting between the National Executive of the ANC and the South African government'.[11]

Operation Vula commander Mac Maharaj sent a message to Tambo that, in the light of the developing situation, it was important that there be a direct and safe line between him and Madiba. The first contact was around September/October 1988. 'I recall informing OR that the possibility of setting up a mechanism of contact with Madiba had arisen before I took action,' says Maharaj. 'By the time OR responded, saying I should not take risks and jeopardise Vula, I had already reached Madiba and was able to reply, informing him that I had set up the line of communication.' Tambo then sent a succinct appraisal of the current situation for Maharaj to transmit to Mandela.[12]

Using a small laptop equipped with a modem, Maharaj transmitted coded messages from public telephone booths to contacts in London and Amsterdam, who then retransmitted them to Lusaka. The coding system was sophisticated but easy to use – a computerised version of a self-erasing 'one-time pad', which meant that the code for each message changed automatically once the message was sent, so that the next message was encoded differently. The receiver had a set of decoding systems set up in the same order. This meant that if messages were intercepted, the interceptor could not break the code by tracing consistencies from message to message – they were all different.[13]

'We would put our message on a tape recorder, go out at night to find a phone booth, put an acoustic coupler on the mouthpiece, and play the tape,' Maharaj explains. 'We would collect our messages in the same way, then run them from the tape into the computer through the decoding process and get the message in a printout. It could handle four to six pages in three minutes.'[14] So, for the first time, ANC exile headquarters in Lusaka were in direct and regular contact with a senior underground agent inside South Africa. The two old law-firm partners were thus communicating in real time using new technology emerging from the nascent digital revolution.[15]

Later, Maharaj established a way of communicating with Mandela in prison, and it became a unique three-way contact that proved invaluable in the events to come. 'When I sent Tambo his first report from Mandela he got so excited that he immediately bombarded me with a ten-page reply,' Maharaj recalls. Tambo said to Mandela, 'Look, there is only one problem: don't manoeuvre yourself into a situation where we have to abandon sanctions. That's the key problem. We are very concerned that we should not get stripped of our weapons of struggle, and the most important of these is sanctions. That is the trump card with which we can mobilise international opinion and pull governments over to our side.'

'Communicating with Mandela was in fact a lot simpler than the computer talk with Tambo,' says Maharaj. 'I would print out a message in a small typeface on a thin strip of paper that could be folded in such a way that you could pass it to him while you were shaking hands,' he explains. 'It was a trick we had learned on Robben Island. The courier would carry a small tape recorder in his pocket with a concealed microphone, so that Mandela could dictate his reply as though conversing with the courier. By nightfall, the reply would be in Tambo's hands in Lusaka.'[16]

31

The Consgold Talks and the
Constitutional Guidelines: Round One

T HE THREE AFRIKAANS-SPEAKING Stellenbosch professors from the NP's
intellectual establishment were in an apprehensive mood when they arrived
at the Compleat Angler hotel in Marlow, Oxfordshire. One of them must have been
particularly nervous: he had just completed a training course with the NIS so that
he could report back to them on the proceedings. It was late October 1987 – just
months after Dakar and scarcely a fortnight since the NEC had issued its statement
on negotiations – and they were there for the first meeting of what would become
known as the 'Consgold discussions' with the ANC. Their ANC counterparts were
equally wary: as a group of activist-intellectuals connected with the ANC office in
London, they had been ordered to engage with the professors and report back on
whether they were reasonably trustworthy and truly had the ear of the South African
regime. Could they serve as a conduit opening the way to future negotiations?

The story of the Consgold discussions had started in earnest in June 1986, when
Tambo attended a second meeting with a group of British business tycoons. This
gathering was arranged by Anthony Sampson, his Johannesburg contemporary and
a former *Drum* magazine editor. Sampson had written several books on Britain,
beginning with *The Anatomy of Britain* (1963), and was highly connected in
London. Among the British participants was Michael Young of Consolidated
Gold Fields (Consgold), a former advisor to conservative prime ministers Sir Alec
Douglas-Home and Edward Heath. According to Sampson, Young had 'surpris-
ingly invited himself' to the first such meeting the year before and, at the 1986
follow-up meeting, was 'so impressed by the small, elegant precise man' (Tambo)
that he approached him asking how he could help.[1] Young recalls that

> Tambo thought for a while, holding my hand for what seemed like an eternity,
> and then asked if I could help him build a bridge between the ANC and those
> Afrikaners close to government. He told me that no means of communication
> existed and, without this, progress was impossible.[2]

Young claims he then persuaded his hard-nosed boss at Consgold, Rudolph Agnew,
to support this process. Described by some as a business 'buccaneer' and an 'appall-

ing old reactionary', Agnew had headed Consgold since 1933 and was an 'ardent admirer' and friend of Margaret Thatcher.[3] The business itself had been co-founded by Cecil John Rhodes and was the 'most die-hard company of all', as Sampson put it, with a long history at the core of South Africa's exploitative mining industrial complex.[4] With an obvious stake in the country's future, it agreed to set aside a kitty of up to one million pounds for Young to follow up on the request.[5]

In Young's telling, these events of feel-good happenstance unfolded innocently, involving actors who were enlightened, farsighted and wanted to help. Yet the evidence suggests that something more purposeful had been on the go, with conservative Anglo–South African business and political interests setting out to protect their investments against the consequences of the achievement of universal franchise in South Africa. They wanted a foot in the door so that they could, if needs be, derail any radical ANC plans to undermine their economic hegemony.

Fleur de Villiers, one of Young's colleagues at Consgold and a former deputy editor at the virulently anti-ANC *Sunday Times* in Johannesburg, pointed him in the direction of Stellenbosch professors Willie Esterhuyse (philosophy) and Sampie Terreblanche (economics). Esterhuyse was also friends with the newspaper's editor Tertius Myburgh, who was later unmasked as a government spy.[6]

Esterhuyse had been a Jeugaksie youth leader of the South African Bureau for Racial Affairs (SABRA), an Afrikaner Broederbond initiative that sought to give academic and theoretical justification to apartheid policy. According to a confidential source, he admitted to being part of a planning meeting held at Betty's Bay for the Tricameral Parliament, the thoroughly discredited three-tiered assembly that presided over the last decade of apartheid. He was also an open defender of South Africa's military aggression in Namibia and visited troops on the border.

Sampie Terreblanche grew up in an ultra-Afrikaner nationalist family. His father participated in the 1914 rebellion and became a general in the fascist-inclined Ossewabrandwag (OB). A young Sampie proudly carried his 'junior-OB' card and later graduated to being a member of the Broederbond. He was vice-chairperson of the South African Broadcasting Corporation (SABC) under the Verwoerdian ideologue Piet Meyer.[7] He served in that role for fifteen years, from 1972 to 1987, during a time when the corporation played an inglorious role as a 'total onslaught' apartheid propaganda mouthpiece.

Esterhuyse and Terreblanche regarded themselves as *verligtes*, so-called enlightened Afrikaners, but their departure point had nevertheless been that the NP had to be the vehicle for change.[8] They were both long-standing P.W. Botha supporters and members of the secret Afrikaner Broederbond. Having nominated Botha to be chancellor of Stellenbosch University in 1985, they turned down an invitation to visit Lusaka after Botha forbade them from meeting with the 'ANC murderers'.[9]

In a well-publicised debate in the Afrikaans press, they attacked their *oorbeligte* (overexposed) colleagues on campus, accusing figures like Hermann Giliomee and André du Toit (who had argued that forces outside of the party might be avenues for reform) of using revolutionary language and propaganda that should not 'be spread unpunished under the guise of intellectualism'. Both Giliomee and Du Toit subsequently moved to UCT, having been effectively chased out of Stellenbosch.[10]

In Terreblanche's disarmingly honest words, he and Esterhuyse were part of the 'patronage [net]work' of the NP establishment.[11] Although ostensibly reform-ists, it was only in 1987 that they openly challenged Botha and the parameters he'd set. They did this via their Stellenbosch discussion circle, Besprekingsgroep 85, and by becoming supporters of an anaemic regional variant of white NP parlia-mentary breakaway politics allied to Dr Denis Worrall's Independent grouping.[12] These *verligte* Broederbonders and the English-speaking right-wing liberals, well connected to the conservative British establishment, had been perfectly described by Pallo Jordan in 'The New Face of Counter-Revolution' as middle-of-the-road and big-business insiders supportive of 'reform', but only in a limited way, on narrow ruling-class terms. They were light years away from where progressive opinion was in seeking to create a new political paradigm – until Michael Young and Consgold, acting on Tambo's request, presented them with a serendipitous opportunity.

Within weeks of Young's approach, the NIS asked Esterhuyse to work with them and report back about the process. He agreed. They codenamed him 'Gert' and gave him several months of intensive training under a group of NIS handlers using safe houses in the Stellenbosch and Somerset West area, 'some of which belonged to private owners', including a 'prominent cleric'. The university rector and one of Esterhuyse's departmental colleagues were made privy to his NIS work. One of his postgraduate students was enlisted to help with the project and 'saw to it that minutes and appointments were kept'.[13]

During apartheid, Stellenbosch University was embedded, Stasi-like, in the Afrikaner *volksbeweging* (people's movement) as well as party and state structures. These included the Broederbond; its junior branch, the Ruiterwag or mounted guard; the Rapportryers or mounted messengers, a front of prominent business and cultural figures; the Federasie van Afrikaanse Kultuurvereniginge (FAK); the NIS; and other intelligence agencies and parastatal groups like the Censorship Board (responsible for banning just under 40 000 books during the apartheid years).[14] D.F. Malan had said that Stellenbosch 'stood for an idea'. That idea was apartheid. The university's professors and student leaders heavily populated the above-mentioned bodies, and Esterhuyse was not the only academic at Stellenbosch working for the NIS at this time. In his writings, he makes light of his decision to work with the apartheid intelligence services as if this was somehow unique, linked to higher motives and removed from historical context. In fact, his actions were very much in keeping with what was expected of a pillar of the establishment at a *volksuniversiteit*. Esterhuyse's original secret reports for the NIS and the minutes and transcriptions of meetings made by his postgraduate aide would make interesting reading next to his later published writings about how the process unfolded. The latter would have to be read against the former before any assessment can be made about his self-proclaimed enlightened liberal ideas and *voorpunt* (cutting-edge) diplomacy.[15]

After being contacted by Young, Esterhuyse persuaded Terreblanche and political science professor Willie Breytenbach, also an academic with 'civil service experience, even within the State Security Council', to join him.[16]

Young chaired the first Consgold encounter. He encouraged an open-ended approach, with informal discussions and plenty of time for social interaction. All the ANC knew about the professors was that they considered themselves to be bridge-builders and go-betweens, and had hinted that they were able to convey messages to the highest levels.[17] The ANC members at these discussions were Aziz Pahad, Wally Serote, Tony Trew and Harold Wolpe. Poet and writer Serote had just completed a military training course in the Soviet Union. Trew, grandson of a police commissioner, had studied philosophy at Stellenbosch University, where the writings of Jean-Paul Sartre inspired him to join the African Resistance Movement (ARM). He'd been imprisoned in South Africa for blowing up electricity pylons and was now working for the IDAF in London. Both Trew and Wolpe had been part of the ANC delegation at Dakar. Wolpe was a lawyer who, at the time of the Rivonia arrests, had escaped from John Vorster Square and skipped the country dressed as a priest before reinventing himself as an Essex University sociologist and leading Marxist theoretician.

The first meeting was a trial run. No NEC leaders had come from Lusaka, and Pahad and his ANC team had been tasked with assessing whether it would be worthwhile for the ANC to engage with the academics. The atmosphere was uncomfortable and tense at first, but the talk about home and a relaxed atmosphere over dinner created a more conducive climate for discussions the next day. Pahad recalled that the domestic situation, the economy and the release of political prisoners were the three main issues discussed. Trew took the role of ANC rapporteur and his notes state that, in their view, it was worth continuing with the discussions.[18]

The second Consgold meeting was held from 21 to 24 February 1988 at the

Eastwell Manor Hotel in Kent. Thabo Mbeki, who had not attended the icebreaker in Oxfordshire, took charge of the ANC team at this meeting.

After the excitement from the Dakar, Harare, Arusha, Amsterdam and other gatherings the year before, the idea of negotiations became less outlandish to the ANC, but what would these discussions deliver? As Pahad explains in *Insurgent Diplomat* and Mandela observes in *Long Walk to Freedom*, the prison and Consgold processes essentially covered the same thematic and substantive ground that many of the ANC's previous meetings with internal and international groups from the time of Kabwe had done. The same topics had cropped up in all of them – the armed struggle, the role of the SACP, majority rule, group rights, nationalisation and so forth. The ANC felt that their interlocutors always sought 'to find strategic and political differences among us that could be exploited in order to sow divisions in the ANC'. However, Pahad notes:

> It remains a remarkable matter of principle that, while there might have been differences in emphasis and tactical approaches, fundamental policies on negotiations could not be changed outside the leadership collective, something Mandela understood all too well.[19]

Pahad also comments on how surprised he was that the professors were ignorant of the work of the Constitution Committee and the ANC's perspectives on issues such as a Bill of Rights. Why had they not been informed about the many meetings the ANC had been having with diverse sections of South African society, where ANC policies on all these issues had been thoroughly canvassed and explained? Mandela made similar observations in his prison discussions with Niël Barnard and the state-appointed interlocutors. He said that his 'new colleagues' were largely ignorant of South African politics outside of their narrow minority-white world and that they 'knew little about the ANC [although] they were all sophisticated Afrikaners, and far more open-minded than nearly all of their brethren'. He concluded that 'they were victims of so much propaganda that it was necessary to straighten them out about certain facts'. This included Barnard, who was highly qualified academically and whose job was to be on top of the subject but who 'could not help but be infected by the same biases'. Clearly 'he received most of his information from police and intelligence files, which were in the main inaccurate and sullied by the prejudices of the men who had gathered them'.[20]

Nevertheless, Pahad left the second Consgold meeting in February 1988 feeling that the academics had a better sense of what the ANC's positions were.[21] According to Esterhuyse, much time was devoted to constitutional issues at this meeting, including the ANC's insistence on 'one person one vote in a unitary state'. Marinus Wiechers, a constitutional law professor from UNISA, had joined Esterhuyse and Terreblanche, and the topic would have been one of special interest to him. Constitutional issues cropped up, even if indirectly, as the discussions went back and forth about the positions of the NP and the ANC regarding the future of the country. 'Mbeki went out of his way to explain the ANC's position', wrote Esterhuyse. The message was unambiguous: 'It quickly became clear that the idea of a multiparty democracy in a unitary state was non-negotiable to the ANC.'[22]

Mbeki recalls a discussion about the Freedom Charter with Esterhuyse's group, when they asked:

When the Freedom Charter says 'the people shall govern', what does that mean? We debated [this] with them for a long time. He was saying what it actually means is the ANC shall govern? We were saying, 'No, it literally means what it says – that *the people* shall govern.'[23]

The third Consgold meeting took place after a break of six months, from 21 to 24 August 1988 at the gold mining company's Mells Park estate near Bath in the Gloucester countryside. It put firmly on the table the subject of the Constitutional Guidelines, which the ANC had in the meanwhile adopted after the In-House Seminar that March. This time, Esterhuyse and Terreblanche were joined by Dr Willem de Klerk, who had coined the ubiquitous *verligte/verkrampte* terms used to describe the political divisions among Afrikaners. De Klerk had edited several newspapers and was the brother of senior NP cabinet minister and member of the State Security Council F.W. de Klerk.

Both Esterhuyse and Pahad confirm in their books that a long discussion of the Guidelines took place.[24] Pahad explained the background to their publication and the document was circulated for discussion. The author has been able to examine the original meeting reports by Young and Trew, which Mbeki and his team of Consgold participants still hold close to their chests. These allow for a more in-depth analysis of the discussions and their meaning than the published books to date, revealing for a start that the 'secret' discussions were being relayed back to both P.W. Botha and Margaret Thatcher and the British and South African governments – details generally played down in accounts of the process by the ANC participants. Tambo had given the ANC members the go-ahead to talk, but they did not have an NEC mandate to speak to either the NIS or South African and British government proxies. Young and author Robert Harvey were aware of sensitivities around British involvement in the process and would have wanted to avoid negative portrayals about the discussions.

Trew remembers taking a call in the public 'tickey box' outside his workplace at the IDAF in Islington, in which Young said P.W. Botha conveyed that 'the talks should resume'.[25] And Young started his August 1988 report by noting that Esterhuyse and new arrival Dr Wimpie de Klerk 'were charged by both the State President and Dr Niël Barnard ... to make certain proposals to the ANC'.[26] Wimpie de Klerk confirmed later that he reported back to his younger brother after every meeting: 'I would write him a little memo, and he acknowledged it' (but claimed he would not read it because he was opposed to talking to the ANC).[27] On the British side, Young's covering letter to his record of the next set of 'Bilateral Talks' in December 1988, marked 'Secret', was copied to both Rudolph Agnew and the private secretary to the British minister for overseas development, Chris Patten, with the comment that he 'much look[ed] forward to discussing how we progress the matter with No. 10 Downing Street'.[28]

Secondly, it is clear that 'the people from home' (as Trew described them for security reasons) had read the Constitutional Guidelines in the months since the In-House Seminar in March 1988 – and Esterhuyse and Wimpie de Klerk appeared to be on a fishing expedition on behalf of the apartheid government to see if the Guidelines could be the starting point for formal negotiations. During the afternoon session on 22 August 1987, Pahad and Mbeki outlined how the ANC wanted the Guidelines discussed and expanded more broadly. Dr de Klerk, whose probing was particularly direct, immediately jumped in and said:

But then one must move towards a negotiating conference and a concept of power-sharing. Would you like to put this on the negotiating table – do you want to negotiate on this?[29]

In the final session two days later, Wimpie de Klerk came back to the issue: they 'were ready to take back messages, and that it is important that there should be no misunderstanding on the messages or incorrect perceptions'.[30]

Was he conveying a possible government strategy and tactic as middleman, as Young's notes seem to imply? Was he trying to tie the ANC into early negotiations around a set of guidelines and then to push back on certain issues such as group rights, the economy and power-sharing in order to extract concessions from it? Mbeki, who would prove highly astute in holding ANC strategic positions, was quick to dismiss any such notion:

No. We are speaking here of a broad conference constituted by a wide range of forces ... which would agree to a more final form of guidelines (and which might present other documents?).[31]

The ANC was not going to be drawn into premature commitments that strengthened the state's hand. Pahad explained that 'As an organisation the ANC wanted
to be fully prepared for eventual constitutional negotiations'. Therefore, 'The
Guidelines would be discussed as widely as possible, also within South Africa, so
that an inclusive process of basic principles and values could crystallise'.[32] The
ANC held the political initiative.

Esterhuyse's criticism of the Constitutional Guidelines was that the white
community, which had negative views of the ANC and 'extra-parliamentary movement', would find them vague and insincere. Terreblanche concurred: 'What is
missing is anything on implementation – it is an end product, but there is no
indication of how we get there'.[33] Revealing itself here was the same impatience
for a quick-fix solution that Wimpie de Klerk had shown, but Mbeki answered:

> The objective was to start a process [on the guidelines] – or rather to join it – of
> achieving the broadest consensus possible on basic issues. How to implement
> it will be discovered in struggle. The question is how do we test it? How is
> discussion to be organised?[34]

Pahad backed him up, saying that the ANC foresaw that it and the mass democratic movement would discuss the Guidelines. That 'others' would have to
discuss them 'within their own formations', beyond the extra-parliamentary groupings. Then there could be a 'move towards a broad conference to put final form to
the document'.[35]

After the Guidelines were adopted at the In-House Seminar in March 1988,
reports about them had filtered back into the country despite the ban on the ANC
being quoted inside South Africa. David Niddrie, writing in the left journal *Work
in Progress*, and Tom Lodge, in *Leadership SA*, were among the first insiders to
review them, both describing the Guidelines as a major development.[36] Esterhuyse
reported that they had also been published in *Business Day* and *South* newspapers
and had even been discussed by the Afrikaner Broederbond front Rapportryers,
who, he said, had no 'objection to a broad acceptance of the guidelines'. The
problem for the 'white minority', added Wimpie de Klerk, was how they would
be accommodated. Knowledge of the Guidelines would strengthen 'the middle
ground and the [Afrikaner] left'.[37]

The ANC team addressed a succession of questions on the contents of the
Guidelines:
- Did the section on the devolution of administration 'contain a hint of
  federalism'? No. Devolution was different from federalism, which in the
  South African context was being used to limit the sovereignty of the state and

therefore of 'the people as a whole', said Trew. And, Mbeki added, devolution had in mind also 'the importance of grassroots participation'.

- Was there any element of compromise in the document? Here Terreblanche chipped in to answer his colleagues without the ANC needing to say anything. The purpose of the Guidelines was to set out goals. If compromises happened, this would be 'at the stage of implementation'.

- Regarding white fears of a 'unitary majoritarian state', 'Is there anything in the document that will help us in the event of a takeover of power?' Trew countered the question with several of his own: 'Concretely, what are the fears? What is it that is to be protected by such arrangements that is not set out in the ANC's guidelines? If more is being asked for, is it not a demand to protect privileges under the existing set up?'

  Firing rapidly, Wimpie de Klerk asked what the ANC felt about:
  - the protection of mineral rights;
  - proportional representation in a transitional set-up (backed up by Esterhuyse, who said there had to be a 'transitional phase' to allay white fears);
  - checks and balances; and
  - veto rights.

- Terreblanche the economist, who seemed in certain respects to be ploughing a course independent from De Klerk and Esterhuyse, focused in on the economic sections of the Guidelines, making statements rather than asking questions. The section on the economy needed fleshing out. The affirmative action clause (j) should drop the racial qualification. The land issue was not important in a 'modern economy' and needed to be taken out of the special section and subsumed under job opportunities. Clause (d) seemed to hint at nationalisation and was unnecessary. The Guidelines conflated the welfare and developmental functions of the state, and these needed to be separated, as South Africa with 40 per cent unemployment would not be able to guarantee the right to work like developed economies. Economic growth was crucial – redistribution and transformation in a declining economy could not be achieved 'without engendering social conflict'. The only chance for putting South Africa on a growth curve was for 'a credible government to give commitment to a set of goals like those in the constitutional guidelines', he concluded – this would open up the way to the normalisation of international relations and the possibility of aid for South Africa through a variation of the Marshall Plan.[38]

Trew commented on the contradictions that appeared during the discussion on the Guidelines. While the ANC could not accept elements of the status quo staying in place, all three Broeders argued that whites needed some guarantees and a 'phasing out' of white rule. Trew's conclusion was that 'Striking a balance between these conflicting interests is vital to selling the package'.[39]

During the final session on 24 August, the two groups reviewed the discussions so far and asked, 'What next?' Wimpie de Klerk offered a six-point summary of what he understood the key issues to be: the 'controlled release of Mandela into political life' – possibly scheduled for as early as the spring of 1989; a moratorium on violence; a transitional phase for the introduction of a new order; and the rejection of violence by the ANC and its acceptance that compromises and secret negotiations would be necessary. Also, 'The ANC wishes to have some informal discussions with government officials to discuss the Constitutional Guidelines'. He proposed that both sides refer back to their principals in order to move matters forward.[40]

Mbeki once again clarified that the ANC was not ready to have formal meetings with government officials. Unofficial discussions, yes, to clear obstacles to the release of Mandela and problems that 'the government may have', but not formal talks:

> the release should not be made conditional on the meeting, nor should it be subordinated to the objective of arranging a meeting. Nor should such a meeting be assumed to be the first of a sequence of meetings with a list of issues on the agenda.[41]

Dealing specifically with the Constitutional Guidelines, the ANC team underlined that 'We are not talking of anything that requires talks with government officials, which would be a constitution-making exercise'. They reiterated the point that the Constitution Committee had articulated from the beginning: the Guidelines needed to be discussed as widely as possible – 'we want everyone to discuss it'. As for the future, 'The further stages of the process are still to be worked out', the ANC team explained. 'This is not negotiation, but trying to widen the debate and break down divisions so that South Africans can begin to act together.' The ANC had the idea of 'some conference of South Africans, as broad as possible' sometime in the future, but the 'forms and mechanisms' still had to be worked out.[42] This was the follow-up to the In-House Seminar that Skweyiya and the Constitution Committee had been crying for since 1986 in letters to the NEC; and this debate also perhaps signalled that the ANC already had in mind the idea of a broad-front meeting that would eventually take the shape of the Conference for a Democratic Future in December 1989.

The ANC had no intention of going straight into talks with government officials on a fixed set of constitutional principles. The first priority was to get Mandela released, which would in turn lead to the freeing of other prisoners and the unbanning of the ANC and other organisations. At this stage the Constitutional Guidelines were for discussion, not negotiation. Furthermore, the release of Mandela should be seen not as *part* of a negotiations process but as a preliminary step to *starting* negotiations. In ANC parlance, these confidential Consgold discussions were not the beginning of talks with the regime; they were preliminary discussions with go-betweens who had the ear of the regime about how to get to talks about talks. As Tony Trew explained, the 'Mells talks were not even pre-negotiations'.[43]

Still, it can be argued that the meeting at Mells Park in August 1988 was the moment the ANC began to operationalise phase two of its negotiations strategy: of making contact with the state itself after having done a great deal of groundwork from mid-1985 to mid-1988. The Mells Park meeting also gave an early indication of the importance that the Constitutional Guidelines would come to assume. The twenty-five principles were now the formal framework for the ANC vision and arguments for a future South Africa. Any negotiation with the state or its allied thinkers would have to proceed from the basis of the Guidelines.

32

The Consgold Talks and the Constitutional Guidelines: Round Two

THE *HOLLYWOOD REPORTER* describes the film *Endgame* (2009) as 'a hypnotically gripping account' about how three brave men – Willie Esterhuyse (William Hurt), Thabo Mbeki (Chiwetel Ejiofor) and Michael Young (Jonny Lee Miller) – 'brought racial warfare to an end' in South Africa.[1] *DVD Talk* marketed the film as 'a piece of work that's somehow both accurate and stimulating ... replicating the events that occurred with a precision that emphasizes every line of dialogue, every movement towards freedom'.[2]

The film is based on British conservative MP Robert Harvey's narration of Michael Young's role at the Consgold talks.[3] Tony Trew, trusted scribe of the discussions, was asked to read and check the film script. Mbeki advised him to make sure the basic facts were correct but not to interfere with the drama of the story. Nevertheless, one inaccuracy concerns Mbeki himself, who repeatedly states in the film that the ANC was prepared to start negotiations without any preconditions, which was the direct opposite of ANC policy.[4]

The 'three brave men' claims of the *Hollywood Reporter* and some of the participants in the film's making need to be challenged. Though conservative forces in South Africa and the UK failed to colonise the negotiations process, they seem to have got away with colonising the narrative retrospectively through books and film. What is particularly unfortunate in the view of the author is that, to maximise the importance of their own role, Professor Esterhuyse and NIS director Niël Barnard trivialised the contributions made by other individuals and groups, including those who showed enough courage and foresight to go on the safaris to engage with the ANC. From a reading of their work, they seem to have done this particularly with the Afrikaners who went to Dakar. In the process they deny, too, the importance of the ANC's strategy of creating a broad anti-apartheid front through its many meetings with people from home.

The notes of the proceedings from the ANC side give a far more sardonic account of the role played by the professors. And it was only towards the end of 1988, at the fourth Consgold meeting, held at Flitwick Manor Hotel in Bedfordshire from 16 to 18 December 1988 – that the talks began to shift from an exploratory talkshop to more serious discussions of mutual positions held by the ANC and the regime. By then, the Guidelines occupied a central place on the agenda.

Just four days before this fourth round of Consgold talks, the Constitution Committee met in London – the only time between 1986 and 1990 that they met at a venue outside of Lusaka. They had chosen London to accommodate a recovering Albie Sachs. Besides showing solidarity with their comrade, being in the British capital would have given Skweyiya et al. the opportunity to consult and strategise with Mbeki and Pahad, as well as to coordinate fundraising and legal support plans with the IDAF and other backers.[5]

Besides the Constitutional Guidelines, the items for the December 1988 meeting included:

- 'Where are we now?' (following the signing of the Geneva Protocol by the governments of Angola, South Africa and Cuba in August, bringing closer Namibian independence, and the apartheid municipal elections in October 1988);
- Discussions on a planned new party of scattered parliamentary groups to the left of the NP, with which, to different degrees, De Klerk, Terreblanche and Esterhuyse had all been involved;
- Nelson Mandela's release;
- The 'Regional Situation'; and
- Assessing the 'International Perspective'.[6]

Esterhuyse, Terreblanche and Wimpie de Klerk largely stuck to the same topics and positions they had raised in August with regard to the Guidelines. This indicated (with perhaps Terreblanche excepted) that they had probably come to the table with ideas caucused beforehand with the NIS and government-linked groups where, they reported, 'there is also a debate going on'.[7] Esterhuyse again criticised the 'lack of procedure for implementation' in the document and the conception of the state, which, he said, conflicted 'with a democratic account'. Terreblanche backed off from his previous statement on the land issue, having visited Zimbabwe in the meantime. He stuck to the reformist position that 'Ideally we should have a sequence of re-education, reconstruction in a booming economy and gradual democratisation'.

Wimpie de Klerk's input on the Guidelines once again covered a detailed list of points:

- Arrangements for 'minority groups' should allow for participation based on language and cultural group rights instead of 'race'.
- The multiparty state was only implied and 'the guarantee of civil rights is tied to too many conditions'.

- There was no entrenchment of the judiciary, while the wording on the mixed economy undermined the idea because it gave the state the 'right to determine the general context in which economic life takes place'.
- There were concerns that workers' rights would be 'accorded only to ANC-oriented workers organisations'.
- Non-alignment in international affairs 'in concrete reality means anti-western'.
- One response was that the Guidelines were 'a paradox – a camouflaged one-party Marxist state containing important tentacles of western democracy'.
- In what areas could there be compromise? Did they include Marxism/capitalism, language rights and individual/group rights?[8]

The people from home pressed further. Esterhuyse said, 'There is a need for ancillary guidelines, or discussion documents on the various sections [of the Guidelines] to flesh things out.' Moreover, management of the discussion of the Guidelines needed to be broader. It had to go beyond IDASA and MDM focus points, such as had been exemplified by a recent conference on the Freedom Charter organised by UCT-based James Polley, a close ally of Breyten Breytenbach. Esterhuyse's reaction here was consistent with the anti-Dakar sentiments he maintained throughout. Finally, the three professors asked:

> What about a discussion or seminar between us? There is a need for a conference of several days, involving not only South Africans but also people like Heribert Adams [sic], the Jubilee Centre and so on, maybe in Zimbabwe.[9]

They added that there was a 'need to promote cross-fertilisation' involving the likes of the Broederbond, Rapportryers and a nascent 'new party' being set up, which Wimpie de Klerk, Terreblanche and, to a lesser extent, Esterhuyse supported. This planned party aimed to bring together the Progressive Federal Party (which had been weakened after Frederik Van Zyl Slabbert and Alex Boraine's departure) and the Afrikaner Independents led by Denis Worrall and Wynand Malan, under the leadership of business tycoon Zach de Beer from Anglo American. It 'intended to represent a leap in white politics' and was seeking to become a base both for uniting white opinion to the left of the NP, as well as creating a 'forum for negotiation involving all the [black political] actors from COSATU to Inkatha'. It therefore had 'a white system agenda and a black struggle agenda which must link up', the three explained, adding that 'The forum of the new party will have to take note of the Guidelines and to formulate its own'. And 'the debate is going to increase over the next twelve months and ANC position papers will be useful'.[10]

These positions indicated that the three professors were going well beyond their initial role of serving as objective and disinterested intermediaries between the ANC and the regime. They were now participating in processes to create new political formations. Instead of the ANC being seen as the principal leader of the liberation struggle seeking to get its message through to those who held power in the white system, they would be invited to submit the Guidelines to a large conference of multiple organisations to be organised by the envisaged new party.

Mbeki, Pahad and Trew's response was clear: the ANC would not help recalibrate white politics. They poured cold water on the idea of the broad front for the new party – seemingly conceived of as a version of the middle-ground interim governments put in place during the transitions under Bishop Abel Muzorewa in Zimbabwe and the Democratic Turnhalle Alliance in Namibia respectively. Mbeki stated that, from the ANC perspective, a 'national forum' already existed in the form of the MDM with COSATU at its core, and was 'the outcome of two years of unity talks'. The new party should therefore 'position itself not so much as *the* agent of change, but as a participant in change'. From that perspective it would be acceptable to the ANC and, Mbeki mentioned, 'the ANC would wish to be more involved in the process of the new party than merely as detached observers'.[11]

In response to the inputs and questions on the Constitutional Guidelines, the ANC representatives said the professors from home 'tend to be mistaken in two directions'. Firstly, certain questions, such as the need for the Guidelines to conceptualise more clearly what was meant by 'the state', mystified more pressing issues by dwelling on the abstract. Secondly, there was a demand for more details in some cases where only general guidelines could be provided at this stage. This was because 'detailed implementation can only be determined at the specific moment when a new order can be established, and the details will depend on the balance of political forces at that time'. In addition, the ANC retorted, certain objections could not be directly responded to because they flowed from cynicism and mistrust of the movement: 'It is clear that some of the objections are expressions of a desire to preserve existing privileges.' Whichever way they further developed the Guidelines, the same response was likely.[12]

In his notes on the December 1988 discussions at Flitwick Manor, Trew summed up his belief that the South African government was in deep trouble:

All the signs are that the government is experiencing crisis – an economic crisis, a negotiating crisis, a desertion crisis to both left and right; a succession crisis; an acceptance crisis with respect to its constitutional model based on race-group as a building block; and a management crisis as its policies become clearly unfeasible and unaffordable.[13]

This crisis of apartheid was reflected in the report-back from the three insiders; it confirmed that Botha had run out of ideas. In order to counter the 'total onslaught', the security system had been restructured to give the military more power and the country was being run via the State Security Council (SSC), which became a kind of 'second cabinet' or 'shadow government' undermining the normal constitutional process, with tentacles going down to local level. It was chaired by the president and included his senior cabinet minister, as well as the leadership of the police, the military, the NIS and the departments of foreign affairs and justice, meeting every second Monday at the Union Buildings or at Tuynhuys to assess the situation in the country. From here, instructions for immediate follow-ups were sent to localised Joint Management Committees in whichever areas action was needed.[14] The hawks who wanted to divide and destroy the ANC were in charge and believed their own propaganda, including that 40 to 50 per cent of the black population would support its idea of a 'race federation' in an election.[15] All the Botha government could offer as a constitutional option to the African people at this stage were derisory variants of its tricameral model, such as its proposed national council, which had no support.

The final 'what's next?' session of the December 1988 Consgold meeting at the Flitwick Manor Hotel ended with three actions being decided on: the group's next meetings; the ways in which discussions on the Constitutional Guidelines would be taken forward; and the matter of the non-ANC participants reporting back on the discussions to the British government and the NIS, which had even asked if one of its members could attend future meetings. It was agreed that Michael Young 'would convey to the Foreign Office [FO] the points made about the conditions for a constructive role by Britain'.[16] This decision would have raised eyebrows at ANC leadership level, to say the least, if Mac Maharaj's comments in the margins of Trew's notes are anything to go by. He scribbled in pencil: 'Talks hidden from NEC/NWC but not from FO in UK! What about OR's insistence on excluding MT [Margaret Thatcher]?' Young noted that Thatcher needed 'to improve her standing with the ANC and others' if she wished to 'have the capacity to act as an honest broker'. He was clearly pushing hard for her to act as a 'catalyst' and was due to meet with her soon afterwards. The ANC trio did not hide its scepticism. Trew recorded that, given her long-standing support for Botha and Buthelezi, she would have to change 'not merely her image, but her actual stance in relation to South Africa'.[17]

In light of what the notes of this meeting reveal, it has to be asked whether Young's uninvited appearance at Tambo's first meeting with the British business-people in October 1985, and his offer to Tambo at the second one in 1986, as well as Rudolph Agnew's approval and huge budget of up to a million pounds for the Consgold process, were as innocent as the narratives painted by the Consgold participants, including some from the ANC side, have implied.

The NIS's Niël Barnard, with clearance from P.W. Botha, also asked the Consgold participants if his deputy could sit in on the next meeting, or part of it. 'After discussion all believed this to be acceptable, provided the deputy could speak freely and articulate for the agency.'[18] In the end, the meeting decided in the final session that because Wimpie de Klerk and Terreblanche supported the plans for a new party to the left of the NP, an NIS presence could compromise the discussions. Therefore, both sides would bring more delegates to the next meeting and 'any participation of anyone from NIS should take place separately and be discussed separately'.[19] Neither the new party nor the *verligte* professors would take part in these further discussions. Mbeki, Pahad and Trew were skilfully guiding discussion towards the framework that the ANC wished to see implemented. However, as we will see below, their ANC colleagues in the NEC and NWC expressed frustration that Mbeki was not keeping them in the loop. Tambo and Mbeki, it seems, were keeping the engagements in England as secret within the ANC as a Chris Hani MK op or the Vula plans led by Mac Maharaj.

Maharaj's reading of Young and Trew's Consgold notes is that they tell a 'great story of how the regime reacted' to the Constitutional Guidelines and how it sought (and failed) to water down the contents in the hope of blunting the impact of the Guidelines at home and internationally, especially among Western countries.[20] The ANC delegation itself noted that 'At present one sees only a strategy for buying time by making limited concessions to international forces in the hope of being able to control and limit the internal consequences.' The government's plan was 'so foolish and so dead, one asks what can PWB hope to achieve?'[21]

Nevertheless, after years of ANC conversations with a wide range of interest groups, Consgold was now regarded by Tambo and those in the know in the ANC as its main conduit for seeking the release of Mandela with a view to loosening up a broader process of negotiations and change. But it would only be six months later (in July 1989, when Botha met Mandela) and nine months later (in September 1989, when Mbeki and Zuma met an NIS delegation in Switzerland via the Consgold link) that the table was laid for concrete 'talks about talks'. These developments themselves were the outcome of multiple forms of politics and pressure on the regime.

In the safari meetings, in the negotiations with Mandela in prison and in the Consgold talks, two vastly different world views based on vastly different lived experiences met. Esterhuyse acknowledged very late – in the second half of the 1980s – that the future would be based on a one-person-one-vote system in South Africa.[22] It was a big step for him but could hardly be described as an exceptional revelation for a university professor in the last years of that decade. Yet, in the current literature and in *Endgame*, he is portrayed in great-man style as a far-seeing, enlightened thinker (constantly on the alert to the supposed security police surveillance he was under) who, with a handful of others, was somehow the co-architect of South Africa's democracy. He has sought to reinforce this position in his own writings while conspicuously leaving out his embeddedness all along in the ideas and system of apartheid, and airbrushing others out of the narrative.

Esterhuyse goes so far as to claim in his book (with the same name as the film), and in his later *Die Tronkgesprekke*, that through his Besprekingsgroep 85 of Stellenbosch academics and by supporting Dennis Worrall, who was standing as an independent in the whites-only 1987 Somerset West by-election, he and Terreblanche were chisels that 'struck a blow to the heart of the Botha regime'. He claims that they played roles far more important than the Dakar conference and the work of Van Zyl Slabbert and IDASA. Oliver Tambo, the ANC and the mass struggle in South Africa are reduced to bit pieces in this apartheid trope. In March 1987, the Besprekingsgroep clashed verbally with Botha, and we are told that 'In Lusaka, more notice was taken of this than anything else. Hope of a negotiated settlement was kindled – also in Pollsmoor, where Mandela was in conversation with Kobie Coetsee by that time.'[23]

Ironically, this was when the NIS, intent on promoting the government agenda and destabilising the ANC, was recruiting Esterhuyse to join them. The NIS, it has been reported, paid Esterhuyse for his transport and hotel costs and for his time.[24]

Some of the fiercest denunciations of Esterhuyse's self-proclaimed role as an influential figure who acted decisively to bring about an end to apartheid came from his Stellenbosch colleagues. Already in the early 1980s, they critiqued his book *Apartheid Must Die* for endorsing the iniquitous 'homelands' system and concluded that, by praising NP reform in his writings, he in fact became 'an obstacle to fundamental reform'.[25]

Much later, journalist and editor Chris Louw denounced the shallowness of Esterhuyse's claims in his hard-hitting newspaper missive and book, saying '*Boetman is die bliksem in*'. He angrily pointed the finger at the *verligte* '*Ooms*' (uncles) of the 1980s, explicitly naming the Consgold participants, for having served the system their whole lives and been complicit in its tricameral farce and border-war violence only to jump ship in 1988 and once more claim authority.

These very late awakenings and moves were opportunistic and 'smelled of dis-honesty', Louw said, 'the dishonesty of self-justification'.[26] Louw concluded that when tested against their pronouncements over decades – which kept in line and harmed the lives and prospects of an entire generation of compliant young Afrikaners – as well as against Esterhuyse's preparations with the NIS to neutral-ise and divide the ANC at Consgold and stop it from winning power, the political mission of the *Ooms* had indeed been a failure.

In particular, the writings of Esterhuyse and Barnard show a visceral, almost Freudian determination to trivialise and write out of the grand narrative the sig-nificance of the Dakar encounters and the efforts of Dr Frederik Van Zyl Slabbert and like-minded Afrikaners. Van Zyl Slabbert broke the rules of the establishment in 1986 when he resigned as leader of the opposition, declaring white parliamen-tary politics to be 'irrelevant', and went on to found IDASA and organise the 1987 Dakar conference. Esterhuyse has dismissed events like Dakar for being ad hoc and marked by adventurism, referring to them as much-hyped publicity stunts with little concrete effect.

In a 1990 book titled *The ANC and Its Leaders* (compiled with Philip Nel), Esterhuyse referred to the Dakar conference in a subsentence only. According to *Boetman*: 'It was important that the *ontmoetings* [meeting of people] at Dakar should not get acknowledgement, for the sake of the illusion later that it was indeed the establishment that took the initiative for the reforms that lay ahead.'[27]

Similarly, Barnard and his NIS colleagues echoed P.W. Botha's description of the Dakarites as *vlentergatte* (ragged arseholes), 'injudicious' idealists, and 'do gooders' who were 'very dangerous'. 'Some perhaps' had good intentions, others had 'no more than an eye on their own interests'.[28]

For all his bravado, Barnard gave away in an interview with Mark Gevisser, Mbeki's biographer, his nonchalantly expressed but real fear that the safaris to the ANC 'were threatening to take over from the government, so we had to act quickly'.[29]

Maharaj and Jordan have also commented on how Esterhuyse has been 'obsessed' with pitting the discussions he was involved in against the many more prison talks – both the Mandela–Coetsee meetings and the encounters between Mandela and the committee of bureaucrats – 'with a bent to write into history [contrary to the evidence], that the Mbeki talks were the real talks and that these preceded talks with Mandela'.[30] Tony Trew has reiterated that the 'Mells talks were not even pre-negotiations',[31] but Esterhuyse (and Barnard, in a broader sense) has somehow claimed a central role in the 1980s struggles, brushing off Mandela's prison discussions with Coetsee and the in-depth ANC initiatives and struggles that pushed them into talking in the first place, despite their late (reactive) entry in the constitutional debates initiated by Tambo and the ANC in Lusaka years earlier.

In their book *Prisoner 913*, based on the extensive Kobie Coetsee archive, Riaan de Villiers and Jan-Ad Stemmet are highly sceptical of Barnard's 'rival claim to ownership of the secret discussions' and therefore his determining role in history. Both they and Maharaj and Jordan also point out that Barnard somehow managed (many years later) to quote extensively from secret tapes of meetings while at the same time claiming that these records either did not exist or had been destroyed. He was either lying or 'Perhaps Barnard has a truly exceptional memory', the authors of *Prisoner 913* suggest. Barnard also maintains that the routine bugging of Mandela's conversations by the secret services, which was used to spread disinformation and division within his family and the struggle, was done with an ethical purpose – to 'protect' Mandela.[32] He further gives himself the credit for one of the 'great successes' of the secret talks in March 1989: getting Mandela's 'buy-in that the peace process would be led and implemented by South Africans'. He comes to the astounding conclusion that 'Through this, we ensured his commitment to South Africa's sovereignty in the negotiation process'. Moreover, 'Perhaps it was the deep emotional connection we both had with South Africa that brought home both Mandela's and my realization that negotiations, like a healthy marriage, had no room for outsiders'. All the time, meanwhile, wary of the Lancaster House experience and the delayed Namibian independence process, this had been the ANC's clear position all along, at least since 1985. In addition, the ANC had also already at that time insisted that any talks about talks should be at a two-sided table so that the regime could not try to manipulate the process by involving supposed 'third-way' proxies as happened in Zimbabwe and Namibia.[33]

It is time that these apartheid intelligence-rooted versions of the transition are overturned and put into perspective. Ditto the conservative British and American tellings of the story by Robert Harvey and others.[34] As Trew warned at the first private screening of *Endgame*, this essentially South African story was 'a dramatization by English artists of an interpretation by a British historian [and Tory MP] of the record of the talks by the English facilitator'.[35] Riaan de Villiers recently noted that in South Africa 'there is still a disconnect between a "colonial" and a largely submerged "indigenous" political discourse, morphing into "outsider" and "insider" reporting ... not confined to the media alone, but symptomatic of the gulf between the colonial and indigenous worlds that continues to bifurcate South African society'.[36]

In the telling of the history of the negotiated transition, the 'submerged' discourse is still woefully under-represented. It is time for its green shoots to break the surface and grow so that those who made this history can wrench back a story that has been stolen from them.

33

The Guidelines Move to Centre Stage, 1989

THE CONSGOLD DISCUSSIONS in August and December 1988 marked the ANC's filtering of the Constitutional Guidelines into the contacts between it and the apartheid government's middlemen in preparation for more formal engagements between the two parties. The ANC also now began, in earnest, to engage in public debates over the Guidelines, in the way the Constitution Committee had been asking for since mid-1986.

The Guidelines were listed as number one in the action plan drafted during that final session at Flitwick Manor Hotel. The group agreed that an 'open discussion/ seminar' was desirable. But the ANC team intimated that this would be in the medium term only – six months or so hence.[1] For the moment, they brushed off the idea of negotiations around the Guidelines with government officials. And, even when it involved less formal contacts, the ANC remained lukewarm to the idea of being drawn in to organise discussions about the Guidelines with government-linked people. Mbeki's team said the idea of writing explanatory 'ANC Green Papers' relating to certain sections of the Guidelines (which the Constitution Committee had, in effect, already drawn up in 1986) was possible, but the issue was not straightforward:

> To whom would they go? Resources for this are not available on the scale suggested. We need to focus on how to organise and co-ordinate discussion and the formulation of the final document, to establish a 'clearing house' for commentary and discussion.[2]

It was agreed that both the venue – Maputo or Harare – and the latter point about establishing a 'clearing house' would be left to the ANC. As the pages below show, however, Mbeki was purposefully leaving Esterhuyse and his team in the dark. Having blocked the idea of negotiations with a government delegation over the Guidelines and now placing the planned seminar for the Consgold parties into an unspecified medium-term schedule, Mbeki said nothing about the fact that the Constitution Committee was already finalising plans for a January meeting with South African lawyers to be hosted by the Zimbabwean government. In line with the DLCA's efforts to broaden its engagement with lawyers from inside South Africa, Brigitte Mabandla and Vusi Pikoli had met, as far back as September, with Gerhard Erasmus from Stellenbosch University (who had been at Dakar) and his former colleague Hugh Corder, now at UCT, to plan for the forthcoming January 1989 event. It would take place in Harare, but it was not the Maputo or Harare event mooted at the Consgold talks.

The ANC had a concrete reason for driving the Constitutional Guidelines separately from the Consgold conversations. Firstly, it was aiming to unite influential sections of the legal fraternity in the country behind its constitutional proposals, building the capacity of the movement for the contestations that lay ahead in this terrain. Secondly and more importantly, it was planning to work closely with the leadership of the MDM and international anti-apartheid allies to ensure that the Guidelines were woven into strategies and plans that would push the regime politically into a corner it could not get out of. In this respect, developments would soon be unfolding at breakneck speed.

Emmerson Mnangagwa, who was then Zimbabwe's minister of justice, opened the ANC's Harare lawyers conference.[3] Its theme was 'The role of law in a society in transition' and the Constitutional Guidelines were the focus of the discussions. Mnangagwa declared to the thirty South African lawyers who had travelled to Harare to confer with ANC legal thinkers that this was 'an opportunity for lawyers who are frequently involved in fundamental decision-making to confront, in advance, major problems facing South Africa, such as its transition from apartheid.'[4]

The five-day meeting started on 31 January 1989 and was hosted by the dean of law at the University of Zimbabwe, Professor Reg Austin (who had been one of Penuell Maduna's lecturers when he studied there). Austin was a UCT graduate and had long fought against the racist minority regime of Ian Smith in what had then been Southern Rhodesia. The Constitution Committee had kept in close contact with the Zimbabwean legal fraternity ever since the Ghanaian and Zimbabwean governments helped Constitution Committee vice-chairperson Zola Skweyiya organise the first formal meeting with lawyers from home in Harare in mid-1986.[5]

The ANC delegation in Harare underlined the seriousness with which the ANC was approaching constitutional issues. It was headed by NEC members Mbeki, Zuma, Jordan, Tshwete and Kasrils; an expanded eight-person Constitution Committee now also drawing in Brigitte Mabandla, Tony O'Dowd, Nathaniel Masemola and Harare-based Vusi Pikoli; as well as chief rep Stanley Mabizela and Ngoako Ramatlhodi from Tambo's office, who would later help draft the Harare Declaration.[6] Albie Sachs, on his first trip back to Africa after the traumatic loss of an arm and the sight of an eye in the horrific car bombing nine months before, was given a special welcome back by Steve Tshwete, which got the gathering off to an emotional start.[7]

The meeting was packed with legal academics from at least six South African universities. Among them were Professors Johann van der Westhuizen and Christof Heyns from the CHR at the University of Pretoria; the Oxford-educated Rhodes Scholar Edwin Cameron, who worked at the Centre for Applied Legal Studies at Wits University; Kobus Pienaar from the Legal Resources Centre; Professor David McQuoid-Mason from Natal University, who had presented a paper at the 1987 Harare conference; UCT law professors Hugh Corder, Christina Murray, Dennis Davis, Danie Visser and Dirk van Zijl Smit; and from UWC, Professor Nico Steytler, the son of Elsa Joubert, one of the foremost novelists writing in Afrikaans. The delegates also included three Stellenbosch academics who had been at Dakar: Jannie Gagiano, Lourens du Plessis and Gerhard Erasmus.[8]

Van der Westhuizen and Heyns, who set up the CHR in 1986, were among the first legal scholars in South Africa to have sought a meeting with the ANC. Jack Simons had written to Van der Westhuizen in August 1986 enquiring about papers at a symposium on a Bill of Rights in Pretoria he had written about in *De Rebus* law journal.[9] Van der Westhuizen and some of his colleagues were then invited to meet with the Constitution Committee over the New Year in 1987.[10] But the day before their departure he was informed by the rector that, at the behest of senior members of the security police, the university had withdrawn permission for him to go to Lusaka. Nevertheless, Van der Westhuizen went to Dakar soon afterwards and had met with the ANC several times by the end of 1989.[11]

Women, as usual, formed only a tiny part of the gathering. Representing the ANC with Brigitte Mabandla were struggle veteran Phyllis Naidoo and sociologist Tessa Marcus, one of four members of a well-known ANC activist family in exile. Marcus had presented at the In-House Seminar and her research focused on farm workers in commercial agriculture, the land question and, later, HIV/AIDS.[12] The only woman from inside was Christina Murray from UCT.

In a statement that underlined his awareness of fast-moving South African political developments going into 1989, Zola Skweyiya explained in his paper to the conference that the Constitutional Guidelines were 'a clarification of our objectives in our present struggle' and were 'meant to strengthen the confidence of the liberation forces'. The regime 'has been shaken to its foundations' and the Guidelines were meant to increase the pressure on it and 'make our force irresistible'. 'They are a response to the demands the struggle has reached.'[13]

The academic lawyers were energised by the connections they were making with the ANC Constitution Committee and leadership. At stake was the prospect of revolutionising the South African legal system from top to bottom. The implications for their work and for their country were enormous. Within the framework of constitutional legal discourse, they were exploring profoundly political issues. Some had given activist support to trade unions, community organisations, women's groups and victims of forced removals. Others had written and taught about the manner in which the legal system in South Africa was being used to further apartheid and exploitation, rather than protect the rights of the most vulnerable. Now they were being invited to envisage a role for themselves as lawyers helping to shape the basic concepts and institutions of a new non-racial democratic South Africa. Although they came from different law schools with different legal and academic traditions, they got an intensely heady sense of scholarly solidarity after spending five days together in the same hotel in Harare and sharing ideas among themselves and with ANC lawyers.[14]

In broad terms, the academic lawyers expressed strong enthusiasm for the content and spirit of the Constitutional Guidelines and for the fact that they were being invited to contribute their own views and positions.

A joint communiqué was issued, stating that the participants agreed that the legal community had a responsibility to participate in ending the system of apartheid. Consensus was reached on the need for a new constitutional order, a justiciable Bill of Rights and an independent judiciary. The conference stressed the urgency for a negotiated end to apartheid and recognised as an undeniable fact the stature and vital role of the ANC in this process.[15]

Following the Constitution Committee meeting in London in December, Zola Skweyiya wrote to their Dear Comrade President asking that he include the by now 'widely discussed' Constitutional Guidelines in his 8 January statement for 1989. Although they were already a 'public issue', they had 'hitherto not been launched formally by the NEC'. Therefore, the 'draft guidelines lack that essential NEC stamp that would give them their proper status'. Tambo obliged. Tony Mongalo, secretary for presidential affairs, let Skweyiya know on 3 January that the statement 'has a section dealing with the matter'.[16] The president's 8 January statement for 1989 clarified that

> In keeping with the intensified efforts to address the question of power, the ANC has tabled for consideration by all the people of the country a set of Constitutional Guidelines. We urge everybody to discuss these and make proposals so that finally a position emerges which reflects the broadest national consensus. In building that consensus, the possibility will be created for all of us to advance more purposefully together for the birth of the new South Africa which, we together, will have to define.[17]

Two days after the annual statement, Maduna, taking the role of 'acting administrative secretary', wrote to Tambo on behalf of the Committee asking that he and the SG 'get all the regions of the ANC to start discussing the document'. They wanted this process to start by the end of January and for the membership to be given 'at most' five months to do this and report back. This would allow the ANC to call the big conference it planned in one of the Frontline States, which would 'involve the mass democratic movement as well as labour organisations from home'. Tambo instructed Mongalo to act, scribbling on the letter, 'Tony, please attend to this.'[18] On 25 January, Maduna followed up with Alfred Nzo's office, asking that the SG rope in the PMC, the Internal Political Committee (IPC) and SACTU to make 'an earnest drive ... to get the debate started by and within the various popular and labour formations within our country'.[19] The ANC clearly had plans to mobilise internal support for the Guidelines as well.

Two months later, Tambo wrote to Skweyiya noting that the Constitutional Guidelines had been circulated for discussion and comment at home, and that newspapers such as the *Weekly Mail* had taken the initiative to open debate about them. But 'as far as we know, we have had no comprehensive response from our people on the ground'. President Tambo then asked, 'At what stage should we insist on feedback so that we can begin to prepare the final document?'[20]

In fact, the Constitutional Guidelines were being widely discussed in South Africa. Views were increasingly vented across various media platforms, including newspapers, political journals, and academic and legal publications such as the *South African Journal on Human Rights*.[21] Following on the Constitution Committee's Harare conference of lawyers in January, IDASA published the Guidelines in February 1989, alongside the Freedom Charter,[22] and in the next few months hosted at least eight follow-up workshops around the country, starting with Durban and Pietermaritzburg in March, followed by East London, Port Elizabeth, Johannesburg, Bloemfontein and Cape Town. Responding to the ANC's invitation for feedback on the Guidelines and its stated position that they were not fixed but needed to be 'extended, revised and given a content that reflects the wishes of the people of South Africa', IDASA actively sought to contribute as a facilitator in the debate. It commissioned various papers on the Guidelines document and published these as well as inputs and analyses in relation to some of the specific guidelines in it.[23] Meanwhile the ANC itself was meeting with dozens of delegations from South Africa, and the Constitution Committee held a workshop on the Guidelines with a joint UDF/Cosatu delegation in Harare in May (see below).

At the IDASA workshop in Natal in March, participants from the KZN Indaba initiated by Chief Mangosuthu Buthelezi argued strongly for free-market approaches and federalism.

In a specially arranged follow-up to these two early seminars, IDASA, together with the Departments of Economics and Sociology at the University of Natal, hosted a seminar on 'The Economic Implications of the African National Congress's Constitutional Guidelines for a Democratic South Africa' on 28 June 1989, where leading economists and left scholars, including Ari Sitas and Daryl Glaser, put the Guidelines under the microscope.[24]

At the Johannesburg seminar on 23 May, Advocate Mathole Motshekga from the Institute for Foreign and Comparative Law at UNISA, who had been working behind the scenes with the DLCA since 1986, responded to IDASA's Alex Boraine. Quoting extensively from Zola Skweyiya's input at the recent ANC lawyers conference in Harare, he started off by rebutting Boraine's understanding that the future negotiating parties would have the government on one side and *all* opposition groupings on the other. Rather, the negotiations would have to be between the government on one side and the 'national liberation movement led by the ANC' on the other. This was because the 'democratic forces' had forced the government 'to make Negotiation Politics their buzzword'. And their struggles were the cause of growing consensus on the need in future for a united South Africa and 'a deeper appreciation of the importance of a bill of rights'.[25]

At IDASA's Cape Town seminar, there were strong critiques from a gender perspective. Dr Dorothy Driver of UCT commented positively that the assertion concerning franchise – where universal suffrage is referred to by means of the principle one person, one vote, and the general plural 'people' is used rather than the singular term 'man' – seemed to be a particularly striking instance of a progressive or anti-sexist stance. But she went on to critique the explicit inclusion of the category women in clause (w), asking why the rights of women should be located in a single section of the Bill of Rights:

> suppose that in the ANC Guidelines the terms 'person', 'people' and so on recognise the presence of women in all their multiplicity in this country: Women agriculturalists, women journalists, women teachers, policewomen, traffic officers, domestic workers, hawkers, typists, doctors, academics, housewives, squatters, the unemployed. Yet we wonder, when we come to clause (w) of the Constitutional Guidelines, if this is really the case ... We may wonder why there is a special clause for women, if there has not been one for men. We wonder if perhaps *woman* has been *absent* all the time, that they – we – need a special mention.[26]

A better approach, she argued, would be for every section of the Bill of Rights to be looked at in a gender-sensitive manner. 'Rewriting the language is crucial if the legal system and administrative practices are to run along non-sexist lines,' she declared.[27]

Left critiques were starting to appear as well. Smaller groupings like the PAC, AZAPO, the New Unity Movement and the BC-aligned National Council of Trade Unions (NACTU) were ideologically opposed to the ANC and the prospect of negotiations. Left academics in the universities inclined against the nationalism of the ANC also raised their voices. The PAC had issued a position paper on 'Some Considerations in Respect of the So-called Dialogue with White-Ruled South Africa through its Government' in 1988, ridiculing the idea of negotiations and intensifying its commitment to all-out armed struggle. It also criticised the Frontline States for standing in fear of white South Africa and the USA and 'dreaded the prospect of the PAC's passing of men and weapons through their countries to reach the hot spot'. Kwandiwe Kondlo, author of a PAC history, said the organisation failed to read and understand the changing geopolitical context and 'rendered themselves [politically] irrelevant as a result'.[28] Ian Liebenberg of IDASA observed that Trotskyites and committed scientific socialists on one hand, and unbridled free marketeers and apartheid- and fascist-inclined whites on the other, would not easily identify with the Guidelines – nor would the proponents of a 'new-style minority multiracial government'.[29]

Meanwhile, the ANC itself had at least thirty-nine recorded meetings with inside groups from home in 1989. The number was probably much higher given the many secretive MDM and underground-linked meetings now being held. For example, the MDM's Murphy Morobe and Valli Moosa had participated in the ANC NWC meeting on 8 January 1989 – the ANC's 77th birthday[30] – and one activist recalls clearly going three times to Lusaka and Harare in 1989 for meetings that have not been recorded. Jack Simons also noted in May 1989 that the ANC was working on arranging the planned follow-up discussions recommended at the 1988 In-House Seminar in the four key areas – culture, the economy, women's rights and the land issue – identified as needing further attention in the Constitution Guidelines and ANC planning processes.[31] Some of these planning assignments involved people from inside.

Barbara Masekela and the culture section of the ANC first held an internal seminar on culture in Lusaka, and then it was off to the Victoria Falls between 8 and 12 July to meet a large delegation of South African writers and academics, mainly Afrikaans-speakers, at this creatively chosen venue. The twenty-person ANC delegation was backed by heavyweights like Mongane Wally Serote, Willie Kgositsile, Mandla Langa, Baleka Mbete-Kgositsile, Breyten Breytenbach (as a special invitee) and the constitutional planners Jordan and Sachs.[32]

At the same time, a colloquium on the South African economy was held in

Lausanne, Switzerland, between 8 and 13 July 1989. Fifty-seven prominent econo-
mists and academics participated (twenty from the ANC and twenty-six from
'inside'). Tito Mboweni, a future Reserve Bank governor and finance minister, was
in the ANC delegation. Seen in action here, taking up issues flagged at the 1988
In-House Seminar, was Tambo and Palme's PASA initiative and the SASPRO–
CDS connection initiated by Thabo Mbeki and UWC rector Jakes Gerwel.[33] In
November, a second big meeting on the economy took place in Paris. Mbeki and
Jordan once again led a delegation that included Mabandla, Maduna and Sachs.[34]

Dealing with another unresolved issue from the In-House Seminar, and
announcing that funds were available, the secretary-general also 'assigned' the
Women's Section the leading role in convening a seminar on 'Women and Children
in a Future Constitutional Order'. They had to report by the end of November 'in
time for consultations with the internal structures' of what he called the Democratic Movement and the Labour Movement.[35]

A 'small ANC group' had also been working on the related land issue. It consisted of Barney Mackay and Tessa Marcus (the presenters in March 1988), as well
as Tanya Abrahamse, Albert Dlomo, Helena Dolny, Masiphula Mbongwa, Bongiwe
Njobe, Sachs and Skweyiya. By early 1990 the group were 'of the opinion that it
had reached the stage where it should be transferred into a Commission as foreseen in the SASPRO–CDS plans'.[36]

A noticeable feature of the attendance lists at these large gatherings in 1989 was
the presence of many of the ANC names and lower-level leaders who had attended
the In-House Seminar in March 1988. For example, in June 1989, a phalanx of sixty
ANC members headed by Tambo and Nzo conferred in Lusaka with 115 white
democrats from the Johannesburg-based Five Freedoms Forum, to which the assassinated David Webster and other prominent anti-apartheid activists belonged. The
Constitutional Guidelines were prominent in the discussions and the meeting
ended with a joint communiqué endorsing them.[37] Those closely involved in the
development of the Guidelines were present in numbers, including Pallo Jordan,
Ruth Mompati, James Stuart and the Constitution Committee's Skweyiya, Sachs,
Pekane, Jobodwana, Mabandla and Masemola.[38]

The Guidelines and the diplomatic offensive that they were part of was being
bedded down. MDM and COSATU leaders were in and out of Lusaka throughout the year, underlining the close contact being maintained between HQ and
the internal forces at home. Murphy Morobe, Mohammed Valli Moosa, Albertina
Sisulu, Cheryl Carolus, Sister Bernard Ncube, Raymond Suttner and Jessie Duarte
all came and went.[39] In May 1989, a UDF/COSATU delegation met with the ANC
in Harare and Zola Skweyiya reported that the internal allies participated in a
workshop on the 'programme around the Constitutional Guidelines'.[40] Borders had

stopped being borders. South Africans previously cut off from each other feasted on opportunities to engage. What did the NIS's Niël Barnard think about all this, one wonders. The sluice gates had been opened.

The meetings with lawyers at home and further afield were also continuing, including the first meeting between the ANC and judges serving in the apartheid courts.

In the late eighties, Professor Ronald Dworkin was one of the most eminent political philosophers of the age, holding dual positions at New York University and Oxford. It was he who organised the latest unusual meeting with the judges, and he'd been working on the idea with Oliver Tambo's permission for some time.[41] The Constitution Committee showed some concern that Nat Masemola in London had 'left the matter in Dworkin's hands', and that he had personally sent out the invitations himself,[42] but they had come around. There were good responses from a number of judges too. But when the news of the upcoming meeting between the judges and the ANC hit the headlines, minister of justice Kobie Coetsee sent a statement to chief justice Michael Corbett, requiring him to instruct judges not to meet with people planning the violent overthrow of the government. The chief justice responded that he would not attend such a meeting but that he had no authority to prohibit other judges from doing so and would leave the matter to the individual conscience of each one. Most decided to go ahead.

Dworkin was also a friend of Albie Sachs, who spent many hours planning the meeting with him. A keen theatregoer, Dworkin was delighted by the idea that Sachs had been able to acquire the apartment in Ashworth Mansions, Maida Vale, London, with funding from a special benefit performance of the *Jail Diary of Albie Sachs* at the Young Vic Theatre, with the participation of four British actors who had played the part of Sachs in other productions of the play. But the normally debonair, quick-tongued and buoyant Dworkin was uncharacteristically subdued one day when he stepped through the door of Sachs's flat in early 1989. Visibly embarrassed, he told Sachs that there was bad news. The judges had, at the last minute, introduced a new condition for their attendance – they would not go if Sachs was part of the ANC delegation, and gave no reason for this. To them, he surmises, he was part of the *rooi gevaar* – a white, Jewish communist, like Slovo. Of course, Dworkin added, this was unacceptable, and the meeting would have to be called off. Sachs responded that of course the meeting should go on without him, but it would be good if he could later meet some of the visitors socially. The result was that two encounters were arranged: a formal legal engagement, followed by an informal social gathering.[43]

The formal first meeting, held in July 1989 at Nuneham Park in Oxfordshire, focused on the new constitutional ideas and brought together judges and an array of public-interest lawyers, legal academics and practitioners from within South Africa.[44] The judges included Laurie Ackermann, John Didcott, Hannes Fagan, John Milne, Les Rose-Innes and Andrew Wilson. Milne was the judge who had acquitted Maduna in 1976 following the Soweto uprising. Wilson had appeared as defence counsel in a number of trials of ANC and other political activists. Didcott was known for never having passed a death sentence, as well as for his willingness to give a full hearing to allegations of police torture. The public-interest and other lawyers included George Bizos, Edwin Cameron, Arthur Chaskalson, John Dugard, Pius Langa, Ismail Mahomed, Hugh Corder, Dennis Davis and Etienne Mureinik. They were joined by Constitution Committee members Zola Skweyiya, Kader Asmal and Penuell Maduna, as well as the intellectually polished Frene Ginwala, who had been admitted to the Bar at the Inner Temple and had a doctorate from Oxford.

The exchanges at the meeting were positive. The visiting judges were impressed by the seriousness with which the ANC team discussed constitutional matters and the importance given to the Bill of Rights and the role that an independent judiciary would play in the new dispensation.

The later social gathering took place at the home of David Astor, who had been editor of the *Observer* newspaper for twenty-seven years. It was attended by the advocates and academics but not the judges (because it was not a formal working engagement). Added to the Constitution Committee delegation were Tambo, Mbeki and Sachs.[45]

The social encounter proved to be extremely emotional. Sachs recalls that Tambo was radiant in an elegant dark blazer. He was linking up with legal colleagues he had last seen three decades earlier when in practice with Nelson Mandela in Johannesburg. Encouraged by the warmth of the encounter, he was convinced that in the not-too-distant future a new constitutional order would be in place in South Africa. Instead of the law being used to divide and oppress, it would serve to protect the dignity and fundamental rights of all. Contributing to the emotional charge of the occasion was the fact that colleagues who had worked with Sachs when he had been practising as an advocate at home were seeing him with his shortened right arm for the first time. The visiting lawyers indicated that they were deeply energised by the meetings and would do everything within their power to ensure that the Guidelines were taken seriously back in South Africa.[46]

Two months later, an ANC delegation consisting of Tambo, Mbeki, Slovo, Jordan and the Constitution Committee's Simons, Skweyiya, Maduna and Brigitte Mabandla met a delegation from Lawyers for Human Rights, including Jules Browde (president) and Brian Currin (director) in Lusaka. Delegate John Dugard, director of the Centre for Applied Legal Studies at Wits, was 'impressed with the commitment of the ANC to a constitutional democracy that included a Bill of Rights'.[47]

A further big conference on a future constitution for South Africa was held at Columbia University Law School in New York in September that year. This conference, organised by Professors Jack Greenberg, Stephen Ellmann and Paul Martin of Columbia University, with support from Ronald Dworkin, was yet another opportunity for top lawyers from South Africa, many of them present at earlier meetings, to meet with the ANC.[48] The heavyweight lawyers were met by an equally authoritative ANC delegation comprising Thabo Mbeki, Kader Asmal, Frene Ginwala, Lindiwe Mabuza, Penuell Maduna, Tebogo Mafole, Seretse Choabi, Nathaniel Masemola, Albie Sachs, Zola Skweyiya and Raymond Suttner, a recently released internal underground cadre who had suffered torture and isolation while in lengthy detention without trial. There were about a hundred attendees, including American academics. Using Sachs's Columbia University connections, several of the Constitution Committee members had spent periods of time at Columbia since 1986.[49] This was the university where Pixley Seme had studied, and it was the first in the USA to divest from South Africa.

Since the completion of their Foundations of Government document in October 1986, the Constitution Committee had sought to stimulate broader discussions about the Constitutional Guidelines beyond the ANC. This process was now well and truly under way. And, by keeping the Constitutional Guidelines open to critique and inviting contributions to their development, the DLCA and ANC leadership was able to mobilise around the document both within South Africa and internationally. In this way, they succeeded in switching the discourse away from the convoluted power-sharing, group-rights and federalist notions coming from conservative quarters and towards one centred on the vision in the Guidelines for a united, non-racial South Africa.

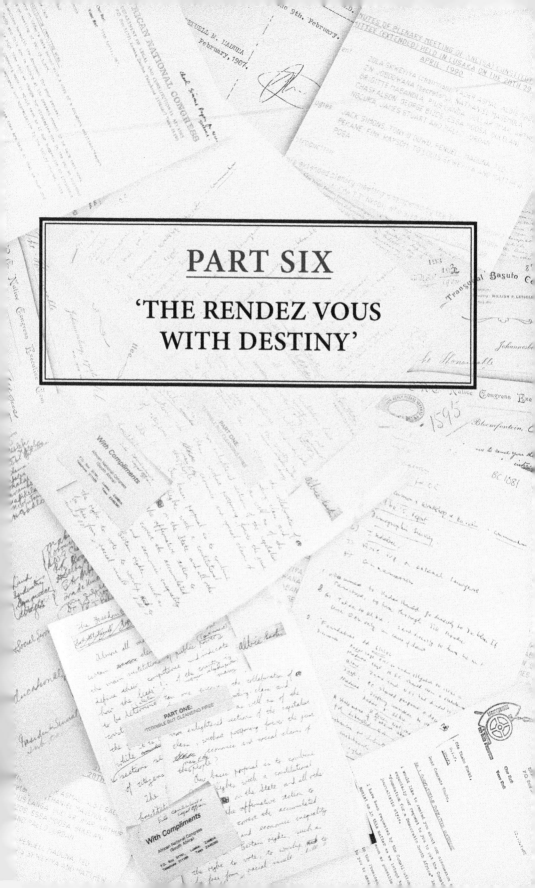

PART SIX

'THE RENDEZ VOUS
WITH DESTINY'

34

Taking Charge of
'What Needs to Be Done in Our Country'

IN MAY 1989, Oliver Tambo contacted his underground commander, Mac Maharaj, via the secret, encrypted Vula communications network and informed him that 'The race for who will control developments in our country has started in earnest, & we should be in the lead'.[1] Namibia was moving towards independence under international supervision. South Africa, Britain, Angola, Cuba, the UN and the superpower observers – the United States and Soviet Union – were all involved in the discussions.

In addition, Mikhail Gorbachev and Ronald Reagan had met in Reykjavik and agreed that, to reduce Cold War tensions, neither of their countries would continue supporting any attempt at the military overthrow of any government anywhere in the world. This had implications for the armed struggle in South Africa.[2] One consequence would be the Soviet Union limiting its support for MK. In his message to Maharaj, Tambo noted: 'We're under intense pressure from friends and allies.'

Pallo Jordan had warned way back in his 'Submission on Negotiations' to the NEC in November 1985 that the ANC would have to be ready when this moment arrived. The trigger point for the ANC's 'rendez vous with destiny' was at hand. His words still had resonance: 'Everything depends on our tactical acumen ... We cannot fail.'

After a UDF/COSATU delegation had visited Lusaka as part of its regular coordination meetings, COSATU noted in a memorandum to its members:

Zambia has been strongly pushing that ANC must find a negotiated settlement as Frontline States can no longer provide bases to ANC on their soil. They have said that if the ANC does not find a negotiated solution, then it will have to fight the war against apartheid from within the country. The Frontline States have said that, after there is a settlement in Namibia, they will call a conference and lead in the settlement of SA. Kaunda has already indicated that he is willing to talk to FW De Klerk.[3]

President José Eduardo dos Santos of Angola warned the ANC that 'negotiations are coming soon'. He had been approached by the French government to help in this direction.[4]

The pressure was coming from numerous quarters. In his communication to Maharaj, Tambo stressed: '[We do not want] to leave the running to MT & other allies of the regime'. 'MT' was Margaret Thatcher, who had sent the opportunistic Sir Robin Renwick to be her ambassador in South Africa. Tambo continued:

> The question being pressed on us from every corner is 'what is to be done?' What is the new strategy, or new approach? We need to evolve a kind of [United Nations Resolution] 435 for South Africa, formulated by us (ANC & MDM), sold to the FLS [Frontline States] & used to control & channel pressures, including MT and co, that [demonstrates] we can take charge of what needs to be done in our country.[5]

Resolution 435 of the UN Security Council formed the basis for the deployment of a UN peacekeeping force to Namibia in April 1989 to monitor the peace process and elections there. The title of this peacekeeping force, which took over control of Namibia, was the United Nations Transition Assistance Group (UNTAG). Resolution 435 had been adopted in 1978 with the objective of ensuring 'the withdrawal of South Africa's illegal administration from Namibia and the transfer of power to the people of Namibia with the assistance of the United Nations'. The purpose was to secure 'the early independence of Namibia through free elections under the supervision and control of the United Nations'.[6] Ten years of delay and bitter warfare had followed before the Battle of Cuito Cuanavale precipitated extensive meetings to bring about a ceasefire and the deployment of UNTAG.

A body called the Western Contact Group (WCG), representing Canada, France, West Germany, the United Kingdom and the United States, had been set up way back in 1977 to ease the fears of both South Africa and the internal parties that were collaborating with it in its occupation and control of Namibia – then called South West Africa.

The UN and WCG had established minimum guarantees for Namibia's constitutional process and for the eventual constitution. These principles would provide for a Bill of Rights, an independent judiciary and a multiparty democracy.[7] The principles were accepted by South Africa, the internal parties and, eventually, by SWAPO.

The ANC's NEC and Constitution Committee would have been acutely aware of the dangers of an externally imposed plan such as this; Jack Simons had been an advisor for SWAPO in Lusaka, where the UN Institute for Namibia was based. One of the biggest worries of the ANC leadership was that if the Western countries intervened in the process of negotiations in South Africa, they would do so to protect white-minority rights. This is what had happened at Lancaster House where talks sponsored by the Commonwealth had taken place to establish what was called 'black majority rule' in Zimbabwe. 'When we talk about a non-racial South Africa,' Thabo Mbeki recalls, their instincts would be to protect white-minority rights, so 'they would be talking about group rights, essentially in support of positions that have been taken by the National Party. This was a central issue. It would impose a post-apartheid South Africa which would be unacceptable.'[8] It was for these reasons that one of Jack Simons' first handwritten notes at the first Constitution Committee meeting in January 1986 had been 'Keep ahead (avoid Lancaster House)',[9] and why the ANC was against the idea of an external peace-keeping force being introduced to supervise and manage the transition. At the same time, the ANC could count on the fact that the apartheid regime did not want any external force to step in and undermine its NSMS-driven military control of the country.

In his missive to Maharaj, Tambo explained that the NWC and others at head-quarters were working intensively on the ANC's own '435' idea and that the drafting team was doing a redraft of its embryonic document or declaration (the name it would be remembered by) tailored for the international community. Among the support team were Neo Mnumzana (ANC chief rep at the UN), Joel Netshitenzhe, up-and-coming SACP intellectual Jeremy Cronin, Penuell Maduna, and the president's deputy PA, Ngoako Ramatlhodi. Key NEC members would be involved as well. Tambo and his team packaged the ANC's Constitutional Guidelines, the NEC's preconditions and strategies for negotiations, and its goals for the transfer of power into the new document. It was developed over a period of several months after intense consultations within the ANC, and with both its internal MDM and international allies. And, according to Maduna, the Constitution Committee was involved in the process as well.[10]

The ANC was now in a position to take the initiative because it had clear positions. Mac Maharaj says, 'The question was always, if the signal comes will we read it right?'

By 31 May 1989, the new thinking had been sent into the country to the under-cover Mac Maharaj. Following the ANC/MDM workshop on the Constitutional Guidelines with Skweyiya and others in Harare in May, the NEC met with MDM and COSATU leaders, including Frank Chikane and Sydney Mufamadi, in Lusaka on 6 June 1989 to formally consider the ANC's declaration and the joint strategies required in the rapidly changing situation. They agreed that they should jointly attempt 'to take control of the process and ensure that negotiations, should they come about, are genuine and serious'. The plan was to:

• adopt 'the same agreed positions' inside and outside South Africa;

- make sure those who sought to intervene 'have to deal with our position', not the other way around;
- build an 'all Africa position', which was 'crucial to our ability to influence the rest of the world'; and
- find ways to use the issue of negotiations 'to further divide/disrupt the ruling class rather than have the issue divide us'.[11]

The ANC had the democratic movement – the foot soldiers on the ground – on its side, and it was agreed that the MDM would launch a 'defiance campaign with a mass character' to challenge the state of emergency, demand the release of Mandela, call for negotiations that would lead to a transfer of power and, generally, 'fire up the imagination' and take the struggle to new levels. The internal leaders were worried about how the idea of negotiations would be received inside the MDM and unions, and stressed the need to explain that the struggle had 'pushed the enemy into a corner and we therefore have to consolidate this gain'.[12]

Following this key strategy session, the NEC met on 8 June and amendments were made to the draft international declaration. An updated document called 'ANC Discussion Paper on the Issue of Negotiations' was ready by 16 June. It noted that the time had arrived to address such issues as

> the aim of negotiations, the pre-conditions for genuine negotiations, the nature of the mechanism for negotiations and therefore the question of who would sit at the negotiating table, the cessation of hostilities by both sides, the possibility of the formation of a transitional government, the duration of the negotiations and the role of the international community in any negotiated resolution of the South African Question.[13]

It was passed on to a dozen or so selected internal leaders on a confidential basis to seek their input. Drafts were also sent to Cuba and the Soviet Union. Tambo sent his commander Maharaj the updated document on the same day and tasked Vula with getting comments from Mandela and some of the individuals across South Africa within ten days.[14] The MDM also circulated the document as a position paper and study document for its activists inside the country, and a copy appeared in the press soon afterwards. By this time the ANC was having regular contact with the UDF and others from home, so it was no problem getting the draft document to people inside the country.

Those in the know included UDF heavyweights Chikane, Mufamadi, Murphy Morobe, Mohammed Valli Moosa, Albertina Sisulu, Archie Gumede, Cassim Saloojee and Dullah Omar, as well as COSATU leaders Elijah Barayi and Jay

Naidoo; NUM's James Motlatsi and Cyril Ramaphosa; and the recently released Robben Islanders Govan Mbeki and Harry Gwala.[15] Linda Zama, who was a young lawyer acting as a courier at the time, described the excitement she felt taking messages from Tambo to Mbeki in Port Elizabeth and Harry Gwala in Pietermaritzburg, and how she accompanied the latter to visit Mandela in prison.[16]

The NECs of the UDF and COSATU met on 26 June, the anniversary of the Freedom Charter, to work out a programme of action in support of the ANC's plans.[17] Preparations were made to launch the defiance campaign in August to intensify the pressure on the state.

Mandela was also making progress with his talks in prison.[18] On 5 July 1989, he met with P.W. Botha for the first time. For more than three years he'd insisted that he wanted to 'talk to the man with the power, and that is P.W. Botha',[19] and after submitting a memorandum in March, his request was finally granted. Mandela thought 'South Africa reached a point of no return that day'. According to *New York Times* journalist Patti Waldmeir, 'He was dressed in a tailored suit and was met by an unfailingly courteous, deferential and friendly Botha, who personally poured his tea.'[20]

Meanwhile, in Lusaka, the ANC forged ahead with the declaration. The plan was for it to secure the broadest possible international support. The first parties that needed to be persuaded were the leaders of the Frontline States. These leaders would be attending a summit meeting of the OAU ad hoc committee on the question of South Africa, due to be held in Harare on 10 August 1989. The meeting was being convened specially to adopt an African position on negotiations in South Africa.

Mbeki describes how Tambo and his team finalised the Declaration: 'We discussed it with [Tambo]. And then I think I made a draft ... and other people were there – Penuell Maduna, Pallo Jordan, Steve Tshwete. So we would draft, and then get together with him, look at the draft. If this thing looks okay, right, now this is what we are going to take to the Frontline States.'[21]

Mbeki recalls:

OR was an intellectual in the best meaning of that word. He was a person of reason, a person of rational thought and rational action. It's a great ability, a great gift, that gift of reason. And I think it was central to OR's make-up and central to his behaviour. With Oliver Tambo, you had a person who could deal with both the concrete and the abstract, the specific, the particular and the general; between tactics and strategy – that dialectical interaction, OR understood very well.[22]

Tambo engaged severely with his own reflections before any meeting or discussions, according to Mbeki:

> OR is a very thoughtful person. He ... would stand up there and make a speech for 20 minutes ... off the cuff. [But] he would have sat for two or three days writing copious notes – writing down and then scratching ... [G]enerally, that's how he worked. Even in terms of meetings, almost always he would speak last. Particularly if there's a major issue on the agenda of the National Executive Committee. He would always speak last having listened to everybody, comment on everybody to say it's a very good point that was made but he doesn't agree with it, then go on. And always he would ... reflect on the discussion ... But on each of the major points he would have made preparations for days and days. You wouldn't think so, sitting at the meeting [where he'd be] sitting and discussing as a member of the Executive Committee. ... In fact, he would prepare a lot, not through discussion with anybody, [but] sit with himself and pen and paper.[23]

Others close to him have testified that Tambo strove for perfection in his formulations and would redo statements over and over:

> OR was very careful with his language. He did not like jargon. And would not hesitate to return a draft four or five times. He would fill a waste paper basket with discarded formulations. In the age before 'delete' and 'insert' technology, the to-and-fro of draft rewrites required a dedicated team of drivers, typists and proof readers.[24]

Now, in the early days of August 1989, the drafting of the document was in its final stages. Tambo had worked ceaselessly with great strategic and tactical acumen during the four years since the ANC had decided to explore constitutional options for the future in the wake of Kabwe, despite his failing health. He and his team were putting the finishing touches to the plan they had embarked upon to take power and transform South Africa into a united non-racial democracy. It would entail one last dash through the Frontline States to check that their leaderships were on board – and this precipitated the final collapse of Tambo's health.

The Declaration had to be one that 'becomes the proper expression of the South African people' he had said, 'and then, secondly, the region'. There was little time left, as the draft document had to be submitted to the OAU committee scheduled for 10 August.

First stop on the four-country, three-day, sleep-deprived shuttle was Dar es

Salaam, to meet with Julius Nyerere. Accompanying the president were his head of office, Mbeki; NEC administrative secretary Jordan; former MK commissar Tshwete, now an NEC member based in the president's office; Maduna of the Constitution Committee; and Ramatlhodi, Tambo's deputy PA and part of the drafting team.

Tambo was approaching his seventy-second birthday. He not only participated fully in the drafting process until the end but also jumped in to help make arrangements for the meetings ahead. He was preoccupied with the diplomatic and logistical details, seeking and confirming flights and landing permission for the small plane arranged by Kenneth Kaunda (commercial flights would have taken too long). He personally reconfirmed appointments with regional heads of state.[25]

The high regard that they had for Tambo was what made it possible to arrange these meetings at very short notice. Over nearly thirty years he'd developed brotherly relations with the leaders of the Frontline States. They were first-generation heads of state and former liberation-movement leaders.

The year before, Nyerere had hosted and spoken with Tambo at the Arusha conference for the ANC's international supporters. Five years before this, in 1984, it had been the Nkomati Accord demanding their attention. The Frontline States had asked Samora Machel to account for the Nkomati Accord signed with P.W. Botha, which committed the Mozambican government 'to chase our [ANC] people out of Mozambique except for a diplomatic presence of ten'. That 1984 meeting was held in Tanzania and chaired by Nyerere too. Machel had asserted that the Accord, by which the apartheid regime had agreed to stop backing RENAMO (the counter-revolutionary Mozambican national resistance movement), was a victory for the Mozambican revolution. But Kenneth Kaunda had responded by giving an example of how he and Nyerere had agreed that, after independence, neither of them would allow their countries to fall into the clutches of the International Monetary Fund (IMF) and the World Bank. 'Yet, even as we are sitting here, there's an official of the IMF who is sitting at the Department of Finance in Lusaka,' Kaunda had said. 'We can't take any major decision without his approval.' It had been a defeat for Zambia, he'd said, and Nkomati, too, was a defeat that should not be treated as a victory.[26] Nyerere called for a tea break and afterwards said: 'Now Oliver, we haven't heard you on this thing.'

Thabo Mbeki relays Tambo's response: 'This is a product of the aggression of the apartheid system. Samora here and our colleagues there in Mozambique have really had to stand up to [it]. Sure, this thing is a reversal. But our challenge is not to be criticising Samora Machel and the others for a reversal. Our challenge is to be supporting them in this hour of need.'[27]

In a moment of irony, humour and admiration, Nyerere replied, 'Oliver, I don't understand you. Because we are busy getting angry in terms of what Samora has done and you are saying, "I support him". I never understand you and your ANC.'[28]

Nevertheless, Tambo's large vision won over the leaders and became the official position at the summit that day. Mbeki observes: 'That was OR and he could interact like that. So I am saying that in terms of the region, he would have *that* access and *that* influence.'

Tambo and his team flew from Lusaka to Dar es Salaam, having worked on the draft up to the night before in the Mbekis' flat in the suburb of Kabulonga, with Maduna on the computer.[29] Maduna recalls:

> As luck would have it, we start with Tanzania, Julius Kambarage Nyerere, Mwalimu, the teacher. So we land there and we are with the likes of Salim Ahmed Salim and Joseph Warioba. ... Nyerere listens to us ... We thought we knew it all ... Nyerere listens carefully, an adjournment is asked for and after the adjournment he tells Tambo that we need a new document. So he outlines the defects ...[30]

Thabo Mbeki picks up the story, recalling how Nyerere told them:

> What you people are talking about ... I believe and think you are correct. At some point these negotiations are going to come. But they come in a situation in which you have not defeated the apartheid regime and neither has it defeated you. And so you are going to have to negotiate a compromise. What you are proposing, this business of yours of saying, let's have an agreement for a constituent assembly which would draft the constitution. You will win the elections. You will be the dominant party in that constituent assembly. Why must the other side agree? Because you are saying you will draft the constitution because you're the majority.[31]

He thus suggested a two-staged process to winning power. Nyerere agreed that the bottom line was that the constitution must be negotiated and drafted by elected representatives after a democratic election. But the first stage must be to negotiate and win over the other side to the idea of participating in an election with a universal vote that would lead to their loss of power, and key in this was to agree on binding constitutional principles beforehand. These the ANC already had – the Constitutional Guidelines, the NEC conditions for negotiations, et cetera. Maduna recalls that after the session with Nyerere they returned to the drawing board, working into the night to adjust the draft to incorporate his input, which became part of clause 21 of the declaration.

In the morning the team presented the new draft to Nyerere for his approval and then flew on to Gaborone in Botswana. Here, they met with Quett Masire, followed by Eduardo dos Santos in Angola. Tambo made a full presentation and the team accepted what turned out to be small changes at each stop. They then returned to Lusaka, where they had extensive consultations with Kaunda.

When the team met with Robert Mugabe in Zimbabwe, he told them that he was very happy to receive the document and that, instead of it going out in the name of the ANC, it should rather be adopted by the OAU at the upcoming summit meeting in Harare. Zanele Mbeki, who went on this part of the trip, recalls how during this leg, 'At 4 a.m. when all were fast asleep, [Tambo] called me to reconfirm various logistical arrangements for the next stop. I don't think that he slept that night.'[32]

The delegation finally returned to Lusaka from its intensive round of presentations at 6 a.m. on 7 August. By 10 a.m. they were back in Mbeki's flat, drafting the final version. Tshwete said that Tambo '[l]ooked after every comma, every word, every spacing and what it looked like on paper'. He was tired and the team persuaded him to go home and rest.

The next day, 8 August, Tambo was not well and arrived late at the NWC meeting due to start at 10 a.m. It was postponed to the afternoon. Two drafts of the document were prepared, one slightly different, in case the OAU didn't like the final ANC suggestions. Afterwards, Tambo went to John Nkadimeng's house to meet a comrade from home, and then back to his office until late.

The NWC, consisting of the NEC members in Lusaka, met again on the morning of 9 August. A final session of drafting followed, and the document was finalised and adopted. Tambo closed the meeting at 12.30 p.m. The ANC had made the OAU deadline. Then it was back to the office at HQ for the president. He had a meeting with Thenjiwe Mtintso, the MK camp commander in Uganda. She explained the dire conditions existing in the new facilities there after the withdrawal of cadres from Angola, and told of how she had to sleep in a truck while trying to scrounge for food for the troops in Kampala.

It was dark by the time she left HQ. When Zola Skweyiya joined him for a meeting, Tambo collapsed, falling to the floor. Skweyiya called for help as he tried to make the Chief comfortable on a couch.[33] Maduna recalls:

> The chief steward [of the Harare Declaration] ... Oliver Tambo, the old man with thick glasses, with the black and red pens marking our work as though he were a school principal, had had a stroke.[34]

But not before he'd dotted all the i's and crossed all the t's.

Kaunda arranged for a plane to rush Tambo from Lusaka to London. Pallo Jordan and Tony Mongalo accompanied him on the flight, alongside his trusted bodyguards.[35]

35

The Harare Declaration

A GROUNDBREAKING, HUGELY COMPLEX exercise, filled with drama, pitfalls and personal tragedy, ended with beautiful simplicity. In the absence of the stricken president, Alfred Nzo, secretary-general of the ANC, flanked by members of the drafting team, presented the Declaration to the summit meeting of the Ad-Hoc Committee on Southern Africa of the Organisation of African Unity in Harare on 10 August, the day after Oliver Tambo's stroke. The OAU adopted the Harare Declaration as its own document on 21 August 1989. Demonstrating the now solid bonds between the internal and exiled movements, Murphy Morobe and other MDM leaders were present to celebrate the occasion.

In early September, the Declaration was adopted in Belgrade, Serbia, by the Non-Aligned Movement, a forum of 120 states, mostly from what is now referred to as the Global South, which were not formally aligned with or against any major power bloc. Next, at a meeting in Kuala Lumpur in October, despite any qualms Margaret Thatcher might have had, it was adopted without opposition by the Commonwealth heads of state in the presence of Thabo Mbeki and Reverend Allan Boesak, representing the united exiled and internal democratic forces.

Inside South Africa, from 9 to 11 December 1989, the UDF, COSATU and the broad MDM convened a Conference for a Democratic Future (CDF) in Johannesburg to garner internal support for the Declaration. At this 1980s equivalent of the Congress of the People, the updated plan for national liberation and a constitutional democracy based on the Freedom Charter, the Constitutional Guidelines and the Harare Declaration were endorsed.

Finally, with the backing of four major multilateral global groupings and coupled internally with the enthusiastic endorsement of the MDM, the Harare Declaration took wings to the UN in New York. Mbeki remembers the occasion. The General Assembly established a negotiating team drawn from the different regions of the world, the African group choosing its delegates, the Americas choosing theirs, the European Union choosing theirs, and so on.

There were two of us from the ANC. You couldn't say, 'This is an OAU document, please endorse.' We had to sit with them for two days. It was very difficult. We have the EU and [then] we have the Americas. [Each] would sit for three hours and knock off and go to sleep. And then a new team would take over. But we couldn't do that. We had to sit with them right through. And the last day it was actually right through the night.[1]

Finally, on 14 December 1989, the document, without many changes of substance, was adopted by the General Assembly by acclamation. This meant that even the representatives appointed by Ronald Reagan and Margaret Thatcher, who for years had been resisting attempts to impose significant sanctions on the apartheid regime, went along with the strong formulations that had originally been outlined by Tambo's drafting team. If you compare the document as finally adopted by the UN to the original Harare Declaration, you'll find that no significant changes were made on its journey from Harare to New York. The text is almost the same, with identical words and phrasings being used throughout both versions. The only big difference is in the title, which was changed from the bland descriptor 'Harare Declaration' to the more forceful 'Declaration on Apartheid and Its Destructive Consequences in Southern Africa'.

Jack Simons had worked closely with Tambo to draft the extensive preamble,[2] in what could be seen as their joint swansong from the hurly-burly of struggle politics. After developing pneumonia and being hospitalised for nearly two months during a lecture tour of the GDR in the previous year, the long-standing, eighty-one-year-old confidant of Tambo asked the Constitution Committee to consult with the president about his 'withdrawal' from the position of chairperson in mid-1989.[3] It was appropriate that the Declaration would be their final major assignment together. Several of its clauses came from the Skeleton, which the Constitution Committee had sent to Tambo after its very first meeting in January 1986. The preamble established the historical and political setting for the Declaration, locating it in the context of African struggles for self-determination, emphasising the right of the people of South Africa to determine their own destiny and the system of government under which they wished to live. Africa could not be free until colonialism and apartheid were liquidated. Until such time, the objectives of justice, human dignity and peace on the continent would remain elusive. At President Kaunda's request, perhaps, it underlined that the Declaration was a genealogical successor to the Lusaka Manifesto of 1969, which outlined the conditions necessary for peace and stability in South and southern Africa, updated to meet current needs and circumstances. The preamble included a strong denunciation of the destructive consequences of apartheid and made extensive references to the way South Africa had destabilised countries of the region 'whether through direct aggression, sponsorship of surrogates, economic subversion or other means'. It also called for the eradication of apartheid and for negotiations that would lead to the transformation of South Africa into 'a united, democratic and non-racial country'. The preamble did, however, slightly soften the original text's reference to apartheid as 'a crime against humanity' to read as 'a crime against the conscience and dignity of mankind'.

The Harare Declaration followed with a section titled 'Statement of principles', as had been suggested by Julius Nyerere. It then set out that the outcome of the process should be a new constitutional order based on the following principles:

- South Africa shall become a united, democratic and non-racial state.
- All its people shall enjoy common and equal citizenship and nationality regardless of race, colour, sex or creed.
- All its people shall have the right to participate in the government and administration of the country on the basis of a universal suffrage, exercised through one person, one vote, under a common voters' roll.
- All shall have the right to form and join any political party of their choice, provided that this is not in furtherance of racism.
- All shall enjoy universally recognised human rights, freedoms and civil liberties, protected under an entrenched Bill of Rights.
- South Africa shall have a new legal system which shall guarantee equality of all before the law.
- South Africa shall have an independent and non-racial judiciary.
- There shall be an economic order which shall promote and advance the well-being of all South Africans.
- A democratic South Africa shall respect the rights, sovereignty and territorial integrity of all countries and pursue the policy of peace, friendship and mutually beneficial cooperation with all peoples.

All of these were taken directly from the Constitutional Guidelines. They appeared in identical terms in the UN Declaration (as paragraphs 16.1 to 16.9 and 17), save for three changes to the third point. The first alteration was the replacement of the phrase 'common voters' roll' with the phrase 'non-racial voters' roll'. The liberation movement's fight for a 'common voters' roll' came from South African history. In the Union of South Africa created in 1910, a significant number of men of colour in the former Cape Colony continued to have the right to vote even if they were prohibited from becoming members of Parliament. (When women were granted the franchise in 1930, only white women were allowed to vote.) In 1936, African men were removed from the common voters' roll and put on a separate roll to choose three whites as so-called Native Representatives. Finally, in the 1950s, the placing of coloured men onto a separate voters' roll gave rise to extensive constitutional litigation and the creation of the Torch Commando led by men and women who had fought against Hitler – hence the liberation movement's demand for 'a common voters' roll with one person one vote'. The later creation of Bantustans, with pseudo-independence being granted to what had formerly been called 'tribal homelands', intensified the demand for a single electoral system based on equal rights in the whole of South Africa. The UN chose to replace the specific contextualised phrasing of 'common voters' roll' with the term 'non-racial voters' roll'; 'non-racial' was a word that had become vogue in the 1980s as a result of the liberation struggle.

The second change was the deletion of the reference to universal suffrage being exercised through 'one person one vote'. In the South African context, colonial domination was achieved largely by reserving the right to vote for white people only. From time to time, proposals were advanced that some suitably qualified black persons should be allowed to vote. Political decolonisation of South Africa would accordingly be achieved not through secession and the creation of a separate state but by destroying the system of white supremacy and enabling all black people to vote as equals in a united South Africa. The demand for 'one person one vote' represented an insistence on having a universal franchise. The UN again felt the term 'non-racial' conveyed what was necessary. The third change was the addition of the words 'in a united and non-fragmented South Africa'. This made it clear that granting the franchise separately to people living in the Bantustans would not be acceptable, and the term 'by secret ballot' was added for good measure. The UN version thus referred to a long-standing preference among the majority of South Africans: that a political settlement would not be the amendment or reform of the apartheid system but its ending.

The UN also declared that acceptance of these fundamental principles could constitute the basis for an internationally acceptable solution that would enable South Africa to take its rightful place as an equal partner among the world community of nations. South Africa had been a founder member of the UN, but in 1974, because of the policy of apartheid, the South African government had been precluded from sending representatives to the body, where its chair remained empty.

The next section of the Declaration was called 'Climate for negotiations' and summed up the ANC's preconditions for speaking to the regime, which had been well-established by the NEC:

- Together with the rest of the world, we believe that it is essential, before any negotiations can take place, that the necessary climate for negotiations be created. The apartheid regime has the urgent responsibility to respond positively to this universally acclaimed demand and thus create this climate.

- Accordingly, the present regime should, at the very least:
  - Release all political prisoners and detainees unconditionally and refrain from imposing any restrictions on them;
  - Lift all bans and restrictions on all proscribed and restricted organisations and persons;
  - Remove all troops from the townships;
  - End the state of emergency and repeal all legislation, such as, and including, the Internal Security Act, designed to circumscribe political activity; and
  - Cease all political trials and political executions.
- These measures are necessary to produce the conditions in which free political discussion can take place – an essential condition to ensure that the people themselves participate in the process of remaking their country. The measures listed above should therefore precede negotiations.

The UN version is identical save for two relatively small points. The phrase 'apartheid regime' was changed to 'South African regime' and the statement that 'the measures listed above should therefore precede negotiations' was removed.

The practical implications of the demands made in this section were enormous. They required not only the release of Nelson Mandela and all other political prisoners but also the unbanning of the ANC, the PAC and the Communist Party, the return of exiles and the dismantling of the entire apparatus of political repression. The global community was imposing severe and specific obligations on the South African government that called for immediately visible practical action.

The section that followed addressed key questions on the 'Process of negotiations'. They set out the need to create a mechanism to draw up a constitution and an interim government to supervise elections and the transition to democracy. Without making any substantive changes to their content, the UN version condensed and summarised the Guidelines as follows:

The process of negotiations should commence along the following guidelines:
- Agreement on the mechanism for the drawing up of a new constitution, based on, among others, the principles enunciated above.
- Agreement on the role to be played by the international community in ensuring a successful transition to a democratic order.
- Agreed transitional arrangements and modalities for the process of the drawing up and adoption of a new constitution and for the transition to a democratic order, including the holding of elections.

The last section of the Harare Declaration was titled 'Programme of action' and was intended to guide the international community and multilateral organisations, including the UN, to keep up pressure to isolate the regime and ensure the end of apartheid. It called for a stepping up of support for the South African liberation movement and campaigns in the rest of the world. The UN document combined these two into the term 'opponents of apartheid'. Next, it called for the intensification of mandatory and comprehensive sanctions against apartheid South Africa, mobilising against the rescheduling of Pretoria's debts, working towards the imposition of a mandatory oil embargo and full observance by all countries of the arms embargo. This was the one paragraph where, to get universal agreement, the text was notably softened to read as follows: 'To use concerted and effective measures, including the full observance by all countries of the mandatory arms embargo, aimed at applying pressure to ensure a speedy end to apartheid.'

The next four clauses called upon the African continent not to relax existing measures for the total isolation of apartheid South Africa, to continue to support SWAPO in Namibia, extend support to the governments of Angola and Mozambique, and offer general support to the Frontline States to enable them to withstand Pretoria's aggression and destabilisation efforts. These clauses were adopted and to some extent augmented in the UN Declaration. The support southern African countries had given the liberation movements in the 1980s came at a tremendous cost to them. As part of its efforts to 'safeguard and perpetuate apartheid through its "total strategy", South Africa had systematically destabilised the subcontinent since 1980 in military, economic, diplomatic and political terms.' A report by the UN Economic Commission on Africa in 1989 estimated that the cost of their 'full-scale defensive war' against South African aggression and proxy wars, and the consequent disruption of food production, especially in Angola and Mozambique, amounted to US$60 billion from 1980 to 1988, as well as the deaths of over one million people, and the displacement of twelve million from their homes at some stage. On an annual basis, this amounted to 'perhaps a quarter' of the 'non-war regional output' of these countries and up to 200 000 lives per year.[4] Finally, the Harare Declaration appealed to all people of goodwill throughout the world to support the programme of action as a necessary measure to secure the earliest liquidation of the apartheid system and the transformation of South Africa into a united, democratic and non-racial country. This statement was extended in the UN's December Declaration to include the following significant resolution and action point:

> The new South Africa shall, upon adoption of the new constitution, participate
> fully in relevant organs and specialised agencies of the United Nations...

We request the Secretary-General [Javier Pérez de Cuéllar] to transmit copies of the present Declaration to the South African government and the representatives of the oppressed people of South Africa and also request the Secretary-General to prepare a report and submit it to the General Assembly by 1 July 1990 on the progress made in the implementation of the present declaration.

For the ANC and Tambo, who was in hospital receiving speech and physical therapy, this was an unqualified triumph in relation to what they had set out to achieve. When asked what the impact of an earlier stroke might have been, Mbeki stressed the importance not only of Tambo's knowledge, skills and hard work but of the trust that people had in him. Everyone in the movement depended on his judgement. Putting it mildly, Mbeki said, without him, 'I think we would have had more problems within the ANC of people accepting the need to change in the light of the changed circumstances.'[5]

The UN had thrown its full weight behind the campaign to bring a rapid end to the system of apartheid. At the same time, the UN would not be sending its own troops and administration into the country as it had done in Namibia. Instead, it would be left to South Africans themselves to determine how the transition took place. It would be South Africans who told the international community how they could help.

The most important immediate consequences were to the pressure put on the South African regime to create conditions for negotiations to take place. This required it to take immediate, far-reaching and irreversible steps. The time frame was clear. The minority government was given six months to make real progress in implementing the Declaration's main demands. Political prisoners had to be released; exiles allowed to return; the ANC, PAC and the Communist Party had to be unbanned; troops had to be withdrawn from the townships; and free political activity permitted through the length and breadth of the country. The message of organised humanity to F.W. de Klerk and his government was unmistakable.

THE HARARE DECLARATION: Declaration of the OAU Ad-hoc Committee on Southern Africa on the question of South Africa, Harare, Zimbabwe, 21 August 1989. First version of the document agreed to by the ANC and the Frontline States that morphed into the United Nations Declaration on Apartheid and Its Destructive Consequences in Southern Africa adopted by the General Assembly on 14 December 1989 (Resolution A/RES/S-16/1, after being endorsed in turn by the OAU, the

Non-Aligned Movement, the Commonwealth countries and the MDM-initiated Conference for a Democratic Future within South Africa. Note that paragraphs 16 and 17 were taken from the Constitutional Guidelines.)

PREAMBLE

1. The people of Africa, singly, collectively and acting through the OAU, are engaged in serious efforts to establish peace throughout the continent by ending all conflicts through negotiation based on the principle of justice and peace for all.

2. We reaffirm our conviction, which history confirms, that where colonial, racial and apartheid domination exist, there can neither be peace nor justice.

3. Accordingly, we reiterate that while the apartheid system in South Africa persists, the peoples of our continent as a whole cannot achieve the fundamental objectives of justice, human dignity and peace, which are both crucial in themselves and fundamental to the stability and development of Africa.

4. With regard to the region of Southern Africa, the entire continent is vitally interested that the processes, in which it is involved, leading to the complete and genuine interdependence of Namibia, as well as peace in Angola and Mozambique, should succeed in the shortest possible time. Equally Africa is deeply concerned that the destabilisation by South Africa of all countries in the region, whether through direct aggression, sponsorship of surrogates, economic subversion and other means, should end immediately.

5. We recognise the reality that permanent peace and stability in Southern Africa can only be achieved when the system of apartheid in South Africa has been liquidated and South Africa transformed into a united, democratic and non-racial country. We therefore reiterate that all the necessary measures should be adopted now, to bring a speedy end to the apartheid system in the interest of all of the people of Southern Africa, our continent and the world at large.

6. We believe that, as a result of the liberation struggle and international pressure against apartheid, as well as global efforts to liquidate regional conflicts, possibilities exist for further movement towards the resolution of the problems facing the people of South Africa. For these possibilities to lead to fundamental change in South Africa, the Pretoria regime must abandon its abhorrent concepts and practices of racial domination and its

record of failure to honour agreements, all of which have already resulted in the loss of so many lives and the destruction of much property in the countries of Southern Africa.

7. We reaffirm our recognition of the rights of all peoples, including those of South Africa, to determine their own destiny, and to work out for themselves the institutions and the system of government under which they will, by general consent, live and work together to build a harmonious society. The Organisation of African Unity remains committed to do everything possible and necessary, to assist the people of South Africa, in such ways as the representatives of the oppressed may determine, to achieve this objective. We are certain that arising from its duty to help end the criminal apartheid system, the rest of the world community is ready to extend similar assistance to the people of South Africa.

8. We make these commitments because we believe that all people are equal and have equal rights to human dignity and respect, regardless of colour, race, sex or creed. We believe that all men and women have the right and duty to participate in their own government, as equal members of society. No individual or group of individuals has any right to govern others without their consent. The apartheid system violates all of these fundamental and universal principles. Correctly characterised as a crime against humanity, it is responsible for the death of countless numbers of people in South Africa. It has sought to dehumanise entire peoples. It has imposed a brutal war on the whole region of Southern Africa, resulting in untold loss of life, destruction of property and massive displacement of innocent men, women and children. This scourge and affront to humanity must be fought and eradicated in its totality.

9. We have therefore supported and continue to support all those in South Africa who pursue this noble objective through political, armed and other forms of struggle. We believe this to be our duty, carried out in the interest of all humanity.

10. While extending this support to those who strive for a non-racial and democratic society in South Africa, a point on which no compromise is possible, we have repeatedly expressed our preference for a solution arrived at by peaceful means. We know that the majority of people of South Africa and their liberation movement, who have been compelled to take up arms, have also upheld this position for many decades and continue to do so.

11. The positions contained in this Declaration are consistent with and are a continuation of those elaborated in the Lusaka Manifesto two decades

ago. They take into account the changes that have taken place in Southern Africa since that Manifesto was adopted by the OAU and the rest of the international community. They constitute a new challenge to the Pretoria regime to join in the noble effort to end the apartheid system, an objective to which the OAU has been committed from its very birth.

12. Consequently, we shall continue to do everything in our power to help intensify the liberation struggle and international pressure against the system of apartheid until this system is ended and South Africa is transformed into a united, democratic and non-racial country, with justice and democracy for all its citizens.

13. In keeping with this solemn resolve and responding directly to the wishes of the representatives of the majority of the people of South Africa, we publicly pledge ourselves to the positions contained hereunder. We are convinced that their implementation will lead to a speedy end of the apartheid system and therefore the opening of a new dawn of peace for all the peoples of Africa, in which racism, colonial domination and white minority rule on our continent would be abolished for ever.

STATEMENT OF PRINCIPLES

14. We believe that a conjuncture of circumstances exists which, if there is a demonstrable readiness on the part of the Pretoria regime to engage in negotiations genuinely and seriously, could create the possibility to end apartheid through negotiations. Such an eventuality would be an expression of the long-standing preference of the people of South Africa to arrive at a political settlement.

15. We would therefore encourage the people of South Africa, as part of their overall struggle, to get together to negotiate an end to the apartheid system and agree on all the measures that are necessary to transform their country into a non-racial democracy. We support the position held by the majority of the people of South Africa that these objectives, and not the amendment or reform of the apartheid system, should be the aims of the negotiations.

16. We are at one with them that the outcome of such a process should be a new constitutional order based on the following principles, among others:

16.1. South Africa shall become a united, democratic and non-racial state.

16.2. All its people shall enjoy common and equal citizenship and nationality regardless of race, colour, sex or creed.

16.3. All its people shall have the right to participate in the government and administration of the country on the basis of a universal suffrage, exercised through one person, one vote, under a common voters' roll.

16.4. All shall have the right to form and join any political party of their choice, provided that this is not in furtherance of racism.

16.5. All shall enjoy universally recognised human rights, freedoms and civil liberties, protected under an entrenched Bill of Rights.

16.6. South Africa shall have a new legal system which shall guarantee equity of all before the law.

16.7. South Africa shall have an independent and non-racial judiciary.

16.8. There shall be an economic order which shall promote and advance the well-being of all South Africans.

16.9. A democratic South Africa shall respect the rights, sovereignty and territorial integrity of all countries and pursue the policy of peace, friendship and mutually beneficial co-operation with all people.

17. We believe that agreement on the above principles shall constitute the foundation for an internationally acceptable solution which shall enable South Africa to take its rightful place as an equal partner among the African and world community of Nations.

CLIMATE FOR NEGOTIATIONS

18. Together with the rest of the world, we believe that it is essential, before any negotiations can take place, that the necessary climate for negotiations be created. The apartheid regime has the urgent responsibility to respond positively to this universally acclaimed demand and thus create this climate.

19. Accordingly, the present regime should, at the very least:

19.1. Release all political prisoners and detainees unconditionally and refrain from imposing any restrictions on them;

19.2. Lift all bans and restrictions on all proscribed and restricted organisations and persons;

19.3. Remove all troops from the townships;

19.4. End the state of emergency and repeal all legislation, such as, and including, the Internal Security Act, designed to circumscribe political activity; and

19.5. Cease all political trials and political executions.

20. These measures are necessary to produce the conditions in which free political discussion can take place – an essential condition to ensure that the people themselves participate in the process of remaking their country. The measures listed above should therefore precede negotiations.

GUIDELINES FOR THE PROCESS OF NEGOTIATION

21. We support the view of the South African liberation movement that upon the creation of this climate, the process of negotiations should commence along the following lines:

    21.1. Discussions should take place between the liberation movement and the South African regime to achieve the suspension of hostilities on both sides by agreeing to a mutually binding ceasefire.

    21.2. Negotiations should then proceed to establish the basis for the adoption of a new Constitution by agreeing on, among others, the Principles enunciated above.

    21.3. Having agreed on these principles, the parties should then negotiate the necessary mechanism for drawing up the new Constitution.

    21.4. The parties shall define and agree on the role to be played by the international community in ensuring a successful transition to a democratic order.

    21.5. The parties shall agree on the formation of an interim government to supervise the process of the drawing up and adoption of a new constitution; govern and administer the country, as well as effect the transition to a democratic order, including the holding of elections.

    21.6. After the adoption of the new Constitution, all armed hostilities will be deemed to have formally terminated.

    21.7. For its part, the international community would lift the sanctions that have been imposed against apartheid South Africa.

22. The new South Africa shall qualify for membership of the Organisation of African Unity.

PROGRAMME OF ACTION

23. In pursuance of the objectives stated in this document, the Organisation of African Unity hereby commits itself to:

    23.1. Inform governments and inter-governmental organisations throughout the world, including the Non-Aligned Movement, the

United Nations General Assembly, the Security Council, the Commonwealth and others of these perspectives, and solicit their support;

23.2. Mandate the OAU ad-hoc structure on Southern Africa acting as the representatives of the OAU and assisted by the Frontline States to remain seized of the issue of a political resolution of the South African question;

23.3. Step up all-round support for the South African liberation movement and campaign in the rest of the world in pursuance of this objective;

23.4. Intensify the campaign for mandatory and comprehensive sanctions against apartheid South Africa; in this regard, immediately mobilise against the rescheduling of Pretoria's foreign debts; work for the imposition of a mandatory oil embargo and the full observance by all countries of the arms embargo;

23.5. Ensure that the African continent does not relax existing measures for the total isolation of apartheid South Africa;

23.6. Continue to monitor the situation in Namibia and extend all necessary support to Swapo in its struggle for a genuinely independent Namibia;

23.7. Extend such assistance as the governments of Angola and Mozambique may request in order to secure peace for their people;

23.8. Render all possible assistance to the Frontline States to enable them to withstand Pretoria's campaign of aggression and destabilisation and enable them to continue to give their all-round support to the people of Namibia and South Africa;

24. We appeal to all people of goodwill throughout the world to support this Programme of Action as a necessary measure to secure the earliest liquidation of the apartheid system and the transformation of South Africa into a united, democratic and non-racial country.

36

A Revolution Within the Revolution

'[T]he ANC would not be true to its principles and values if it did not now seri-ously address the question of the emancipation of women within the ANC, the liberation movement, and in post-apartheid South Africa.'
– ANC Women's Section paper, Lusaka, December 1989[1]

A T THE VERY moment that the Harare Declaration was being signed, sealed and cemented as the bottom-line template document for change in South Africa, another key step in the thinking about the future of the country was being taken. Amid intensifying international geopolitical developments and internal struggles, women in the ANC called for gender equality to be recognised in an unequivocal way in the organisation and within society. After more than two decades of work by ANC feminist activists and a year of careful planning,[2] includ-ing an ANC women's meeting on 'Feminism and national liberation' in London in August, around 100 delegates assembled from 8 to 12 December 1989 at the Mulungushi International Conference Centre in Lusaka for a seminar on Women, Children and the Family in a Future Constitutional Order.[3]

The objectives were stated as follows:

- To formulate cogent policy guidelines on the gender question in the South African struggle.
- To review a proposal for structural modification aimed at strengthening the integration of women/gender issues in all aspects of ANC organisational work.
- To entrench issues specific to women in the Constitutional Guidelines for a post-apartheid South Africa.
- To review the United Nations Convention on the Elimination of All Forms of Discrimination Against Women (CEDAW) with the aim of binding the ANC to its provisions.
- To ensure protection of the rights of the child and of the family in a future constitutional order.
- To identify future areas of research.[4]

Revising the text of the current 'Constitutional Guidelines for a Democratic South Africa' was specified as one of the 'immediate and practical' goals to be achieved by the end of the seminar.

The event was structured along the lines of the March 1988 In-House Seminar where the Constitutional Guidelines had been finalised for publication, and where Ivy Matsepe-Casaburri, Ruth Mompati and Brigitte Mabandla had seized the opportunity to call for women's rights to be fully inscribed into any future constitution. At the second ANC National Women's Conference in Luanda in September 1987, and in planning this 1989 Women's Seminar, the women's lobby within the ANC had successfully pushed for introducing strong elements of gender awareness into the Constitutional Guidelines.[5] In these discussions, certain tensions had surfaced in the organisation between women and men – for example in MK, with its hierarchical male structure and traditional gender attitudes; between older and younger generations of women members; and between the Women's Section – seen by some to be playing a motherly support role that reinforced the subordination of women – and younger feminists who wished to link up with women's debates and struggles inside the country and internationally. 'The "unity of women" in the ANC was visibly fractured', according to Hassim. Some women comrades had also challenged the Constitution Committee and leadership about the final wording of the Constitutional Guidelines decided on after the March 1988 In-House Seminar in Lusaka. Now the time had come to turn the rhetoric of gender equality in the ANC into something substantive.[6]

A particular feature of the seminar was the fact that it was given the status of a decision-making policy conference. This meant that any policy positions adopted would not simply be recommendations; they would be binding on the ANC. While day one would be dedicated to introductory papers, the format for days two and three was changed to panel discussions and round tables focusing specifically on policy proposals and a programme of action.

The seminar was organised by the DLCA, the Women's Section and the ANC's earlier-mentioned Swedish-supported and PASA-linked South African Studies Project.[7] A thick conference pack was prepared for the delegates. One of the most important documents in it was a two-page summary of precedent-setting constitutional clauses on women's rights. These came from the Freedom Charter, the 1988 Constitutional Guidelines, the SA Law Commission (1989), the US Equal Rights Amendment, the Canadian Charter of Rights and Freedoms, the Instrument of Government in Sweden, the progressive article 36 of the Ethiopian Constitution and article 10 from the newly drafted constitution for independent Namibia, as well as the 1979 UN Convention on the elimination of discrimination against women. This was backed up by the comprehensive set of resolutions and recommendations on women's emancipation from the second ANC Women's Conference in Luanda in September 1987 and the first National Women's Conference of COSATU in April 1988, running to nine and seventeen pages respectively. The delegates were being prepared for concrete action. The COSATU documents were yet another example of the growing synergy in thinking and action taking place between the movement in exile and the MDM. This synergy introduced new directions that were being pointed to by the younger generation's internal mass struggle, and this momentum carried even further, as the internal struggle often gave direction to the ANC as the undisputed leader of the revolution.

Zola Skweyiya was in the chair when the seminar proceedings started. Jack Simons, Kader Asmal, Penuell Maduna, Albie Sachs and Brigitte Mabandla were all actively involved.[8] Of the around 100 people present, two-thirds were women.[9]

After a welcome from Gertrude Shope (head of the ANC Women's Section) and a keynote address by secretary-general Alfred Nzo, acting as leader in Tambo's place, several speakers made presentations. First up was Frene Ginwala on the situation of women in South Africa. Ginwala had grown up in a Parsi family in Johannesburg that had a business interest in Mozambique. She had completed a law degree at London University and then completed her PhD in philosophy at Oxford. Instead of pursuing a career in the United Kingdom, however, she moved to East Africa to assist ANC people escaping the crackdowns that followed the Sharpeville massacre. One of the first people she assisted had been Oliver Tambo, with whom she was to work closely for many years. She worked as a journalist and broadcaster in Zambia, Mozambique and Tanzania, and was the managing editor of *The Standard* and the *Sunday News* in Tanzania. In Tanzania, she was founder and editor of *Spearhead*, a monthly journal highlighting the liberation struggle. The title was a reference to Umkhonto we Sizwe – 'the spear of the nation'. During her time in exile, Ginwala wrote extensively on the subject of sanctions, defending her argument with references to international law and the responsibility of the democratic world. Highly respected as a forceful and independent-minded comrade, Ginwala never ceased to drive home to the overwhelmingly male ANC leadership the extent to which the creativity and wisdom of women members was being suppressed by traditional sexist expectations and behaviour.

The next presentation was by Penuell Maduna, who spoke on the patriarchal nature of South African society. He was followed by Ivy Matsepe-Casaburri, whose presentation addressed the question, 'What do women want?'

Next to present was poet and writer Baleka Mbete-Kgositsile. Born in 1949 in Clermont, Durban, she studied at Lovedale Teacher Training College in Alice before returning to teach in Durban, where she became active in Black Consciousness organisations and established contact with the ANC's underground structures. She went into exile in Swaziland in 1976 and then went on to Tanzania, where she became the first secretary of the regional Women's Section of the ANC. She married fellow writer Keorapetse Kgositsile in 1978, and in 1981 joined him in Nairobi, where writer Ngũgĩ wa Thiong'o was among those they befriended. Following Ngũgĩ's arrest in 1976, along with other progressive intellectuals in Kenya, Mbete-Kgositsile moved to Botswana, where she became the lead singer in Jonas Gwangwa's band Shakawe, and head of the writing and music units of the Medu Art Ensemble in Gaborone, until the murderous SADF raid in 1985 put an end to their activities. She recalled this time as a golden space during her period of exile, allowing her to develop her creative skills.[10]

After attending the 1985 World Conference on Women in Nairobi and spending time in Zimbabwe, where she became a member of the Regional Political Committee, Mbete-Kgositsile was called to Lusaka to head the preparations for the 1987 Women's Section national conference. Now, two years later, this strong African feminist took a cue from Matsepe-Casaburri's 1988 presentation at the In-House Seminar and made a presentation on the post-independence experience of women and the need to be on guard to avoid maintaining old discriminatory practices after freedom arrived.

Finally, the Constitution Committee's Kader Asmal gave his views on the United Nations CEDAW Convention, after which the seminar broke up for two and a half days of round-table discussions, policy-making and action-oriented discussions. One motif that ran through all the discussions was the triple oppression of black women. Mbete-Kgositsile presented again – on the structure of the ANC Women's Section. She was followed by Tessa Marcus, who delivered a 'Baseline Survey Report' on women in South Africa. Marcus was born in Johannesburg and went into exile in London with her activist family in 1969 at the age of fourteen. She became personally active in the anti-apartheid movement as an undergraduate student of sociology in the UK, and went on to obtain a PhD in Poland. She later moved to Lusaka, where she undertook research into agriculture, agrarian problems, the conditions of farm workers, the land question, and the terrible effects of the Bantustan system on the lives of women and children in particular.[11]

The round tables were meant to allow for concentrated collective discussions. Each had a chairperson and rapporteur. They discussed a range of issues, including the legal, political, socio-economic and sociocultural issues affecting women. For example, the commission on women's emancipation, with Matsepe-Casaburri, Ginwala, Mbete-Kgositsile, Monica Mosia, Ann Davis and Saeeda Naidoo taking the lead, discussed a 'Background Paper No. 10' titled 'Programme of Action of the ANC: Towards the Emancipation of Women in South Africa', and came up with twelve concrete recommendations for the NEC, which were formally adopted by the seminar.[12]

THE RENDEZ VOUS WITH DESTINY'

The list of those chairing the sessions and round-table discussions included many who would later rise to prominence in South Africa, among them Barbara Masekela, head of the ANC's Arts and Culture Department; MK camp commander Thenjiwe Mtintso; Tito Mboweni, then a PhD student in economics, who had done his undergraduate studies at the University of Lesotho; and Mavivi Manzini, a core member of the ANC's feminist group, who had graduated with a degree from the University of Zambia after going into exile.[13] Senior and mid-level leaders such as John Nkadimeng; Stanley Mabizela, the ANC's deputy head of International Affairs;[14] ANCYL head Jackie Selebi; and Dr Ralph Mgijima, head of the health secretariat, were also prominent. Many of those who spoke and attended had also participated in the historic In-House Seminar that adopted the Guidelines twenty-one months before.

Like Mbete-Kgositsile, the well-travelled and USA-educated Barbara Masekela has written a beautifully textured memoir, *Poli Poli*, which testifies to the networks, wealth of experience and intellectual depth to be found among the delegates in Lusaka in December 1989. Explaining the rich milieu in which she as a young woman grew up in the late fifties and early sixties, it weaves together her life and schooling in Witbank, Alexandra and the Inanda Seminary with her growth in consciousness and her journey to feminism. As a child in Alex, she listened in passing to the 'TG' – treasurer-general Thomas Titus Nkobi – and other ANC leaders speaking 'at the square ... near 12th Avenue in Alex'. At Inanda, one of her teachers was Edith Sibisi, wife of ANC provincial secretary M.B. Yengwa, who was arrested during the Treason Trial. She and her fellow pupils had a brief unforgettable encounter with the banned Albert Luthuli. And among her strong role models at Inanda were Joyce Sikhakhane and one of her prefects, Manto Mali (later Tshabalala), who would end up in exile with her.[15]

Another influential presence at the seminar was Zanele Dhlamini-Mbeki, who had helped raise funds for the event. She, too, was born in Alexandra, in 1938. Her mother was a dressmaker and her father a Methodist priest. She studied social work at the University of the Witwatersrand and the London School of Economics before being awarded a scholarship to study at Brandeis University in Massachusetts in the United States. Dhlamini gave up her PhD studies to link up with the ANC in London, where she met and married Thabo Mbeki in 1974. After returning to Lusaka, she worked for the International University Education Fund. She resigned in 1980, shortly before her boss, Craig Williamson, was exposed as a South African spy and the fund was closed down. After this, Dhlamini-Mbeki lectured at the University of Zambia for two years and then worked for the UN High Commissioner for Refugees in Nairobi. Meanwhile, she was also elected to the ANC Women's League and wrote for the Women's League publication *Voice of Women*.

The final two days, 11 and 12 December, were devoted to the issue of children and the family. The discussion on children's rights followed on the International Conference on Children that the ANC had organised in Harare two years earlier. It strongly affirmed the need for children in the new South Africa to be freed from the afflictions that apartheid society was imposing on them. Following Kader Asmal's input, special attention was given to the UN Convention on the Rights of the Child.

It was well known that many Western feminists at the time took strong issue with women being identified simplistically in terms of their roles as mothers and wives. These feminists saw the family as the archetypal institution of women's oppression. They repudiated any idea of a special link between women and children, emphasising that childcare should be as much a male as a female responsibility. Two days at the Women's Seminar were devoted to the themes of children and the family, so the delegates were clearly interested in hearing how these controversial issues would be approached. New faces presenting in this section were Patricia McFadden, Lyndall Shope-Mafole and Lulu Gwagwa.

A radical African feminist, sociologist, writer, educator, and publisher from eSwatini, McFadden studied at the University of Botswana, Lesotho and Swaziland before completing her master's in sociology at the University of Dar es Salaam and her doctorate at the University of Warwick in the United Kingdom. Her main areas of inquiry were sexuality, reproductive and sexual health, and identity, violation and citizenship for African women.

Born in Johannesburg, Shope-Mafole lived with her aunt in Zimbabwe because her parents, Gertrude and Mark Shope, had already fled into exile when she was three years old. Although she needed the fingers on both hands to count the number of countries she lived in during her early years, she spent most of her youth in Cuba and obtained a master's in telecommunications engineering at the José Antonio Echeverría Higher Polytechnic Institute in Havana in 1983. It was no surprise that she was asked to speak on 'Children in Exile (ANC)'.

Nolulamo 'Lulu' Gwagwa was born in a rural village near Umzimkulu in KwaZulu-Natal. From time to time she would visit her widowed grandmother in her domestic-servant's quarters in Durban. Although barely literate, her grandmother held the family together with very firm values. Gwagwa was a bright student and graduated from Fort Hare in 1976. She was awarded a scholarship to study town planning at the University of Natal, where she became involved with Black Consciousness activists. When her fiancé, who was an underground ANC operative, went into exile, Gwagwa was detained under security laws. Eventually she left the country. In 1989 she completed her master's dissertation at the London

School of Economics on the same topic as her presentation.[16] Her paper showed familiarity with the most recent readings on the topic, quoting both ANC material and that of well-known feminist scholars inside South Africa such as Jacklyn Cock, Josette Cole, Sandra Burman, Pamela Reynolds, Debbie Gaitskell and Shireen Hassim.[17]

Gwagwa opened her presentation at the Women's Seminar by saying that the ANC was not against the family. On the contrary, the people were fighting for the right to live in families. It was apartheid that, through the migrant labour system and the pass laws, was destroying black families in South Africa. The burning issue for African women, therefore, was not whether or not to have families. Rather, they posed two critical questions: what forms the family could take, and what the relationships within the family should be. Regarding the first question, Gwagwa argued, the nuclear family should not be seen as the model structure for family life. Families existed in a multiplicity of forms with a great variety of relationships. There were extended families, single-parent families, and families in which grand-parents played a particularly important role. It was crucial to acknowledge and protect the diversity of family formations.

The main thrust of her presentation dealt with relationships *within* the family, in particular the need to achieve equality between women and men. This, she said, was a big battle that African feminists had to wage.

The delegates expressed enthusiastic approval of her analysis. It reconciled the strong emphasis that African people placed on the importance of family rela-tionships based on mutual interdependence, and solidarity with the indignation that many African women felt living under what they experienced as the yoke of patriarchy. Confidently articulated by a young black woman, her affirmative African-feminist conception of the family helped to fuse the women's struggle with the national liberation struggle, so that each dimension enriched the other.

Gwagwa was following a tradition going back twenty-five years in the ANC. In a paper written in 1971, Zanele Dhlamini had responded to the demands of the women's liberation struggle in North America and Europe from her vantage point as a young black woman from South Africa. She expressed her broad support for the goals of the women's movement while asserting that the position of women in South Africa was markedly different in several key respects. She pointed out that the number of white women in government service, the military, industry and management was negligible. Divorce laws, laws governing succession, illegitimacy and administrative promotions were biased in favour of men.

Their experience, however, can never be comparable to that of a black woman. [They] have been put on a pedestal ... based on false and mythical bourgeois standards: that they are fragile, decorative, weak (feminine) and incapable of the simplest work that black women perform daily for both their masters and for themselves. The white men feed the illusion with minor 'gentlemanly' tasks of door opening and cigarette lighting.[18]

On the other hand, black women in South Africa – and here she, in Black Consciousness terms, included women from the coloured community and women of Indian descent – bore a 'triple yoke of oppression'. They suffered all the degradations of white racism. They were exploited as workers and peasants. And they were females in a clearly patriarchal family structure where precedence was given to males in both public and private life. She writes:

Problems of survival have taught the black man that the black woman, who traditionally took the back seat, is no frivolous nit wit incapable of caring for herself and family in his absence, that is when he is unemployed, in prison, detained or has fled the country for political reasons. She has had to work for wages, feed and clothe the family and educate the children to the limits that the South African situation will permit.[19]

Drawing on work by Jack Simons, Mbeki concluded that

Black women live under three legal systems (customary law, Native law and European law), none of which accord her a position equal to that which she in fact holds by virtue of her influence, her economic independence and her social and political dynamism ... The sexism black women suffer most is from the white establishment. Black male prejudices have not dehumanised, degraded and brutalised black women to remotely the same extent that white racism and capitalist exploitation are doing. Black men are no index of equity for black women. They do equally dreary jobs for a pittance ... South African black women would not better their condition much by acquiring the status of black men ... It is obvious that feminist issues exist in South Africa, but black women will have to work out their own priorities according to their experience and the future society they wish to see.[20]

Lulu Gwagwa remembers that, fresh from completing her master's/doctorate, she was invited to speak at the Lusaka seminar by Frene Ginwala, who had attended a presentation of hers at the Institute of Commonwealth Studies headed by Professor Shula Marks. Ginwala was so impressed she invited Gwagwa home. She recalls, 'It was the first time I had been in a flat with all white carpets'. Ginwala mentored the young scholar, taking her to the Lusaka event and then to the USA and Venezuela. During the Lusaka seminar, Gwagwa shared a session with Albie Sachs and remembers being 'terrified and overawed'. But it went very well and there was plenty of discussion.[21] Sachs's detailed thirteen-page paper, 'Judges and Gender', dealt with the constitutional rights of women in a future South Africa in his usual eloquent way, starting with the comment that 'It is a sad fact that one of the few profoundly non-racial institutions in South Africa is patriarchy'.[22]

Indeed, one of the papers strongly criticised the ANC's NEC for appointing an all-male Constitution Committee to draft the Constitutional Guidelines. Using unflattering comparisons with the apartheid establishment, the unnamed writer(s) of 'Formulating National Policy on the Emancipation of Women and the Promotion of Women's Development in Our Country' said that the current constitution of South Africa had been drafted by 'seven white men, six of them Afrikaners'. Similarly, the changes then being suggested by the SA Law Commission included a Bill of Rights 'couched in male language and reflecting male perceptions'. It was bad enough that the NEC appointed only men but 'far worse' was that 'this decision met with no protest (except a very few individual voices) from the members of the constitution committee itself or from any of the structures of the organisation including the Women's Secretariat and the National Women's Executive Committee'. The paper concluded that 'This is a measure of the problem within the organisation itself which confronts us'.[23] The fact that Brigitte Mabandla had joined the Constitution Committee in 1987 did little to diminish the sting of the critique.

The above-mentioned paper on national policy and women's emancipation reflects the systematic preparation and purposeful approach of the delegates in Lusaka. The drafters went through the key questions one by one. They declared unambiguously that 'the argument frequently put forward that raising the [women's] question before liberation is divisive and deflects energy/attention away from the main issue, i.e. the struggle for liberation[,] has no validity'.[24] The message was that the ANC now had to act on an issue that was akin to racism and should never be separated from it in constitutional planning.

Albie Sachs documented the major impact the women's seminar had on revising the text of the Constitutional Guidelines from a gender perspective, listing no fewer than twelve changes.

> In the 'Preamble', the following sentence was added: 'Special attention has to be paid to combatting sexism, which is even more ancient and as pervasive as racism.'

A DOCUMENT TO CREATE A CLIMATE OF UNDERSTANDING

MR PRESIDENT, I HOPE THAT MINISTERS KOBIE COETSEE AND GERRIT
VILJOEN HAVE INFORMED YOU THAT I DEEPLY APPRECIATE YOUR
DECISION IN TERMS OF WHICH EIGHT FELLOW PRISONERS WERE FREED
ON 15 OCTOBER 1989 AND FOR ADVISING ME OF THE FACT IN
ADVANCE.   THE RELEASE WAS CLEARLY A MAJOR DEV
RIGHTLY EVOKED PRAISE HERE AND ABROAD.

IN MY VIEW, IT HAS NOW BECOME URGENT TO TAKE O!
TO END THE PRESENT DEADLOCK, AND THIS WILL CER1
ACHIEVED IF THE GOVERNMENT FIRST CREATES A PROP
FOR NEGOTIATION FOLLOWED BY A MEETING WITH THE

THE CONFLICT WHICH IS PRESENTLY DRAINING SOUTH /
LIFEBLOOD, EITHER IN THE FORM OF PEACEFUL DEMONS
ACTS OF VIOLENCE OR EXTERNAL PRESSURE WILL NEVER
UNTIL THERE IS AN AGREEMENT WITH THE ANC. TO TH__ END 1
HAVE SPENT MORE THAN THREE V___
NEGOTIATE
WITH EMPTY

THE GOVERNM
COMMITMENT '
THIS IS THE
GOVERNMENT W

THE OUTSET THAT THE ANC WILL NEVER MAKE SUCH A COMMITMENT AT
THE INSTANCE OF THE GOVERNMENT, OR OF ANY OTHER SOURCE FOR
THAT MATTER. WE WOULD HAVE THOUGHT THAT THE HISTORY OF THIS
COUNTRY'S LIBERATION MOVEMENT, ESPECIALLY DURING THE LAST 41
YEARS, WOULD HAVE MADE THAT POINT PERFECTLY CLEAR.

THE WHOLE APPROACH OF THE GOVERNMENT TO THE QUESTION OF
NEGOTIATION WITH THE ANC IS TOTALLY UNACCEPTABLE, AND
BE DRASTICALLY CHANGED. NO SERIOUS POLITICAL
WILL EVER TALK PEACE WHEN AN AGGRESSIVE WAR IS
AGAINST IT. NO PROUD PEOPLE WILL EVER OBEY
THOSE WHO HAVE HUMILIATED AND DISHONOURED THEM

The above identikit image of the imprisoned Nelson Mandela,
who had not been seen by the world for more than a quarter of
a century, was drawn up around the time he initiated contact
with the government and was based on descriptions from his
lawyer. In some 40 meetings between 1988 and 1989, Mandela
held to the line that for South Africa to have lasting peace the
Botha government would have to negotiate with the banned
ANC leaders in Lusaka

Release Nelson Mandela
and all political prisoners of South Africa and Namibia!

Anti-Apartheid Movement 13 Mandela St London NW1 0DW 01-387 7966

IN-HOUSE SEMINAR OFFICIALS

A. __PREPARATORY COMMITTEE__ : Comrades 1) PEKANE

2) P.M. MADUNA

B. __STEERING COMMITTEE:__

Chairman: Cde Dan Tloome

Vice-Chairman: Cde John Nkadime

Members

Cdes: Joe Slovo
James Stuart
Pallo Jordan
Zola Skweyiya
Kader Asmal
Lindiwe Mabuza
Mendi Msimang

C. __RESOLUTIONS COMMITTEE__

Chairman: Cde Jack Simons

1. Nathaniel Masemol
2. Albie Sachs
3. Z.N. Jobodwana
4. Jackie Selebi
5. James Stuart

6. Brigette Maband

© Facebook

Input from Ruth Mompati (*above*), Ivy Matsepe (*middle*) and Brigitte Mabandla (*bottom*) at the In-House Seminar on the Constitutional Guidelines in Lusaka in March 1988 strongly brought to the fore still-unattended issues relating to the position of women in the ANC and society in general

Sipho M Dlamini

Vice   Nelson Miya

Members
1. Khosi Msimang
2. Lucy Thandeni
3. Miranda Qwanyasi
4. Sipho Majombozi
5. Thami Bolani
6. Martha Motaung
7. Sikose Mji
8. Don Ngubeni
9. Solly Mpoli
10. Pren Naicker

E. __TRANSPORT:__ Cdes Boza, June, Maqabane

ENQUIRIES COMMITTEE: Cdes Zola, Jobs, Maduna, Teddy.

The follow-up In-House Women's Seminar in Lusaka in November 1989 led to significant changes in the Constitutional Guidelines. It was an important step towards securing protection for women's and gender rights in South Africa's democratic constitution. *Top, right*: Gertrude Shope and, on her right, Frene Ginwala made important contributions at the 1989 seminar. *Middle*: In the first 78 years of the ANC, only four women served on its NEC. L-r: Lilian Ngoyi, Florence Moposho, Shope and Mompati. *Below*: Women joining MK in greater numbers from 1976 onwards strengthened the calls inside the ANC for policies that would ensure gender equality

Above: In August 1988, Kader Asmal and Albie Sachs – who was still recovering from the bomb blast and learning to write left-handed – were tasked with drafting a Bill of Rights for a future South Africa. They are pictured with Louise, Rafique and Adam Asmal at the Asmal's home in Dublin

Left: The Constitution Committee's Teddy Pekane was promoted to the position of ANC chief rep in Brussels in 1989. Pictured here with Lord Plumb, president of the European parliament

1989 was the year in which the Constitutional Guidelines were widely discussed with activists, scholars, lawyers and judges from South Africa. Here, Zola Skweyiya and Penuell Maduna are pictured with legal academics Gerhard Lubbe, David Maquoid-Mason, Edwin Cameron and an unidentified colleague in Harare in January 1989

Talks about the possibility of official 'talks about talks'

As part of the ANC's broad-front strategies, engagements with internal groups and constitutional planning, Mandela (separately in prison) and Tambo in Lusaka sought to initiate formal contacts between the ANC and the apartheid government. Two main channels had developed by 1988. Firstly, Mandela's prison meetings with the justice minister and a committee of state officials that led to his meeting with P.W. Botha in May 1985. And secondly, the Consgold discussions in Britain between an ANC team led by Thabo Mbeki and Afrikaner intellectuals with links to government, chaired by a British businessman, which resulted in the first meeting between the ANC and the NIS in Switzerland in September 1989. See Chapters 30–32 for new light on these discussions

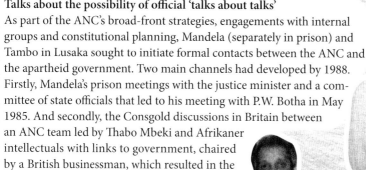

Thabo Mbeki, Aziz Pahad and Tony Trew (*standing*) formed the tight-knit core of the small ANC team at the Consgold meetings

© A.Pahad, *Insurgent Diplomat* (Penguin, 2014)

© N. Barnard, *Secret Revolution* (Tafelberg, 2015)

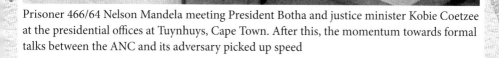

Prisoner 466/64 Nelson Mandela meeting President Botha and justice minister Kobie Coetzee at the presidential offices at Tuynhuys, Cape Town. After this, the momentum towards formal talks between the ANC and its adversary picked up speed

The template for South Africa's future constitution was shaped in African exile. The support of the Frontline States for the liberation movements came at a high cost to those countries. Tambo is photographed here with 'brother-presidents' Sam Nujoma (Namibia), Kenneth Kaunda (Zambia) and Julius Nyerere (Tanzania)

Freedom in sight: February 1990
Key ANC figures in the constitutional planning debates, Pallo Jordan, Chris Hani, Albie Sachs and James Stuart, waiting at Lusaka Airport for the arrival of Nelson Mandela. The latter was taking his first trip out of South Africa two weeks after his release, to report to ANC HQ and thank the Zambian people for their support on a day that was declared a national holiday

Opposite page: The Defiance Campaign of 1989 was part of a joint strategy by the ANC and the internal MDM to force the apartheid regime to the negotiating table behind the values and preconditions outlined in the Constitutional Guidelines and the Harare Declaration, giving rise to fears in government circles of popular uprisings similar to those taking place in Eastern Europe at the time (*insert*)

Jack and Ray Simons were the first exiles to return home, on 2 March 1990. Pictured at Lusaka Airport (*above*) and arriving in Cape Town hours later to a joyful welcome from struggle veteran Francis Baard under a blaze of television lights (*right*)

The start of the second phase of constitution-making in 1990, with the ANC operating as a legal organisation inside South Africa for the first time in thirty years. The Constitution Committee's Penuell Maduna and Jacob Zuma (*circled*) were the first ANC officials sent back to the country to open up negotiation channels with the regime, and they were present when high-ranking delegations from the ANC and the regime, under Nelson Mandela and F.W. de Klerk respectively, met for the first time at Groote Schuur on 2–4 May 1990

The provision dealing with 'The state' was amended in three respects.

Firstly: 'South Africa shall be an independent, unitary, democratic, non-racial and non-sexist state *based on the principle of equal rights for all.*'

Secondly: 'The institution of hereditary rulers, chiefs *and chieftainesses* shall be transformed to serve the interests of the people as a whole in conforming with the democratic principles embodied in the Constitution.'

Thirdly: 'All organs of government including justice, security and armed forces shall be representative of the people as a whole, *men and women*, democratic in their structure and functioning and dedicated to defending the principles of the Constitution.'

The section dedicated to 'Franchise' was changed to read: 'In their exercise of their sovereignty *all men and women* shall have the right to vote under a system of universal suffrage based on the principle of one person one vote.'

Under 'National identity', a sentence was added to read as follows: 'It shall be state policy to promote the growth of a single national identity and loyalty binding on all South Africans. At the same time, the state shall recognise the linguistic and cultural diversity of the people and provide facilities for free linguistic and cultural development. *Such cultural diversity shall not be the basis for discrimination.*'

Two new sentences were added to the section headed 'A Bill of Rights and affirmative action' to read as follows: 'The constitution shall include a Bill of Rights based on the Freedom Charter. Such a Bill of Rights shall guarantee the fundamental human rights of all citizens irrespective of race, colour, sex or creed, and shall provide appropriate mechanisms for their enforcement. The state and all social institutions shall be under a constitutional duty to eradicate race discrimination in all its forms [and ...] *to work towards the rapid elimination of inequality based on gender and to combat sexism in all its forms.*'

Finally, in the sixth and last clause in this section, it was decided that '*The basic rights and freedoms set out above shall be enforceable through the courts and the principle of ensuring equal access to the legal system shall be followed.*'

A provision in the section on 'Economy' was altered to read: 'The state shall promote the acquisition of managerial, technical and scientific skills among all sections of the population, especially the blacks *and shall take special steps to remove the barriers to women participating fully in economic life.*'

The heading of a section formerly called 'Women's rights' was changed to 'Women and men' and the text was changed to read as follows: '*A charter of gender rights shall be incorporated into the constitution guaranteeing* equal rights *between men and women* in all spheres of public and private life and requiring the state *and social institutions* to take affirmative action to eliminate inequalities, discrimination and *abusive behaviours based on gender.'*

The provision on 'The family' was amended to read: 'The family, parenthood and *equal rights within the family* shall be protected.'

A new section was added titled 'Children's rights', which reads: 'The principles of the International Convention on the Rights of the Child shall receive constitutional respect.'[25]

Although not specifically emphasised, the ANC's policy on sexual orientation and gay rights was also fundamentally revised and clarified in the process. Joseph Jackson has shown in his research that some delegates at the In-House Seminar manifested homophobic biases typical of the times, suggesting, for example, the 're-education' of minors who had engaged in homosexual sex in all-male mining compounds. But the conference came to 'an unequivocal decision against discrimination on grounds of sexual orientation'.[26] Thanks to the Women's Conference, this now became official ANC policy.

The organisers of the seminar had appointed a strong writing team with a view to preparing an extensive report on the proceedings. Edwin Mabitse, one of Tambo's speech writers and secretaries, who was part of a special committee in the president's office with Ngoako Ramatlhodi and Simons, was delegated to coordinate the rapporteurs and prepare the draft final report. They were to be supported by seventeen other comrades. It was expected that it would take several months to finalise the report. However, the writing process was interrupted and overtaken by events unfolding in South Africa and the final report was never completed. Nevertheless, the December 1989 Women's Seminar in Lusaka opened the door for significant changes in gender relations within the ANC and in society more widely. The suggested changes to the Constitutional Guidelines became core values in the 1996 Constitution of democratic South Africa.

The momentum was taken further the following month when ANC women met with activists from home at the Malibongwe Conference in Amsterdam in January 1990.[27] When the ANC held its first national conference back in South Africa in 1991, the number of women on the NEC jumped from only four (Lilian Ngoyi, Florence Mophosho, Gertrude Shope and Ruth Mompati) in the first seventy-eight years of the ANC to eight members comprising 16 per cent of the leadership in 1991 (including Shope and Barbara Masekela, who were participants at this seminar). The extended 1991 NEC also included representatives of a newly constituted ANC Women's League from each of the fourteen ANC regions in South Africa, taking the total to 24 per cent women. This unambiguously signalled a new trend in South African public life and society.[28]

37

'Eight Is Not Enough!': The Final Push and an Unexpected Announcement

'Whatever the expectations of the National Party might have been, from that moment on they were following the Harare Declaration text book.'
– Pieter Mulder[1]

T HE EPIC RUSH of drafting and diplomacy to put the Harare Declaration in place and the assertive voices of the ANC women at the Lusaka seminar would have a long-term impact on South Africa. But, just as significant was the mobilisation of the ground troops of the mass movement inside South Africa in late 1989. They were key to the liberation movement's final push as a country in flux careered through the last months of a turbulent decade. This was going to be a summer of change and things were moving fast.

On 14 August 1989, just over a month after meeting Nelson Mandela and six days after Oliver Tambo's workload finally drained away his health, P.W. Botha was forced to resign as president by the National Party caucus. The Harare Declaration would be adopted a week later. That same month, the MDM and UDF announced that they were unbanning themselves and launched a defiance campaign to complement the ANC's international diplomatic initiatives. Fifteen days into September, F.W. de Klerk was elected to succeed Botha as state president.

The defiance campaign had been decided on in Lusaka during the June meeting between the ANC and its internal allies, and its purpose was to challenge the ongoing state of emergency, demand the release of Mandela and push for substantive negotiations that could lead to the transfer of power. Though hobbled by the emergency restrictions, the MDM was riding the wave of popular support. On 2 August it duly proceeded as planned with its hunger strikes, deliberately 'illegal' mass marches, invasions of segregated beaches, demands for treatment at whites-only hospitals, campaigns against whites-only schools, stayaways to protest against the white elections and generally making known that the people's organisations were 'unrestricting' themselves from the apartheid police-state's shackles.

God's beaches were not made for one community, Archbishop Desmond Tutu declared as he led activists past the whites-only signs onto the white sands of the 'fairest' Cape in Table Bay. Known fondly as 'The Arch', this diminutive, fun-loving man with the stature of a giant was arrested during the protest marches in Cape Town, along with his wife Leah Tutu and other leaders, thereby raising international attention and putting the government on the back foot. Mass marches also occurred in Johannesburg (20 000), Uitenhage (80 000), East London (40 000), Durban (20 000), Port Elizabeth (50 000) and even small towns like Oudtshoorn (8 000), according to figures provided by the unsympathetic South African Institute of Race Relations. Before De Klerk even stepped into his official residence at Groote Schuur, the ANC and its allies had given him notice that there would be no backtracking on the demands for real change.[2]

The day after the NP elected him to succeed Botha and four days before his inauguration on 20 September, the new president discovered that the NIS had met directly with Thabo Mbeki and Jacob Zuma in Switzerland the week before. The two sides met at the Palace Hotel in Lucerne with the aim of clarifying issues relating to Mandela's release and a possible talks process. Mbeki and Zuma, travelling under the assumed names of John and Jack Simelane, represented the ANC. Fanie van der Merwe, Botha's director-general for constitutional affairs, and NIS deputy director Mike Louw headed the regime's intelligence service contingent. The meeting confirmed for the NIS the willingness of the ANC to negotiate and opened concrete channels of communication for acting on future negotiation-related issues.[3] This is when formal talks about talks between the ANC and the regime can be said to have started.

The prison discussions and the talkshop with the 'Broeders' via Consgold had finally delivered what Mandela, Tambo and Mbeki had been working towards for at least eighteen months – namely, direct contact between the ANC and the regime. From now on it would be direct two-sided talks between these two main role players because 'one of the first "agreements"' reached between the NIS and ANC 'was about the exclusion of persons and bodies that were "outside" the informal and formal settlement process'.[4] Thus, from September 1989 onwards, the platform created by the ANC through its Constitutional Guidelines, the Harare Declaration and the multifaceted discussions with many different actors since 1985 finally converged into formalised, direct interactions between the ANC on the one hand and the apartheid government on the other.

There would be two or three more meetings of the Consgold circle, slightly expanded to include a few South African businesspeople, but the meetings had served their purpose. According to Aziz Pahad, Esterhuyse's group complained that the Harare Declaration had fixed the situation rather than leaving it open-ended for negotiation.[5] The group of academics and businesspeople – indeed the white political establishment – were effectively sidelined politically by the ANC having established, through their relationships with African countries, a set of processes and conditions that they felt should have been discussed with them first.

From now on the ANC and the NIS would talk directly to each other. Penuell Maduna of the Constitution Committee would be one of the earliest participants (see Chapter 38).

When the NIS agents reported to De Klerk days after the meeting, he was suspicious about having been left out of the loop, but from then on he became fully involved in the process of possible negotiations with the ANC.[6] The new president was regarded as a dyed-in-the-wool conservative who was part of NP royalty. His father, Jan de Klerk, had left his position as a school principal to organise Afrikaans-speaking workers, inter alia opposing the leadership of the Garment Workers' Union led by Solly Sachs (father of Albie Sachs).[7] He went on to hold top positions under J.G. Strijdom and Hendrik Verwoerd in the heyday of apartheid, notably as a particularly conservative minister of labour. However, F.W. de Klerk turned out to be a different kind of politician to P.W. Botha. He consolidated his power by bringing together those who were discontented with Botha's notoriously cantankerous nature and his reliance on a shadow state controlled by the military.

Pieter de Lange, head of the Broederbond, had met with Mbeki in New York in 1986. After De Klerk became leader of the NP, De Lange helped set up meetings for him with businesspeople and moderate reformers. They warned De Klerk that the party and country would be staring a scorched-earth future in the face if they did not embark on serious reforms. He also set out to meet with foreign leaders, starting with Kenneth Kaunda and Joaquim Chissano of the Frontline States, Mobutu Sese Seko of Zaire and Hastings Banda of Malawi. He then travelled to Europe to have discussions with Germany's Helmut Kohl and Britain's Margaret Thatcher, arch-enemy of the ANC. Thatcher was amenable to De Klerk's idea of controlled reform from above, along a Swiss system of group representation at cabinet level. The plan was to reluctantly include the ANC, but make sure it was marginalised as far as possible.[8]

De Klerk started putting together his structure and strategies for negotiations. The focus shifted from the State Security Council to the cabinet and its subcommittees. He announced a new cabinet, with the reform-minded former Broederbond chief and university rector Professor Gerrit Viljoen as his chief negotiator with the extra-parliamentary political forces. Viljoen's deputy was Roelf Meyer, who, as deputy minister of police, had been in charge of managing the day-to-day responses of the State Security Council to developments on the ground. Together with Dr Oscar Dhlomo of the Inkatha Freedom Party, Meyer headed an eight-person committee set up by the government and Inkatha to pursue the idea of creating a new interracial alliance. They agreed that Mandela would have to be released and the ANC unbanned. At the same time, as it later came to light, the state was busy training Inkatha vigilantes in the border areas of Namibia to be unleashed on the ANC and MDM in the brutal fight for political control that was then happening in Natal.[9]

Meanwhile, the MDM's defiance campaign was on the go with its mass marches and other strategies. On 15 October, five of the Rivonia Trialists – Walter Sisulu, Ahmed Kathrada, Raymond Mhlaba, Andrew Mlangeni and Elias Motsoaledi – were released to rapturous receptions after twenty-five years in prison – as were Wilton Mkwayi and Oscar Mpetha of the ANC and Jafta Masemola of the PAC. After having spent more than a quarter of a century in apartheid prisons, they discovered for the first time what faxes were and found a world where people went up and down tall buildings in glass elevators. And they discovered adulation! Tens of thousands of people welcomed them back, and with the by now white-haired senior statesman of the ANC, Walter Sisulu, in front, they immediately tuned in to the ANC and MDM campaigns. At their first major rally in Johannes-burg, a message was read out from their president, Oliver Tambo, who sent the unambiguous message that the Harare Declaration provided the road map to a genuine political settlement.

Bulelani Ngcuka remembers that there was a sitcom on TV at the time called *Eight Is Enough*, and Allan Boesak, speaking on behalf of the MDM at a meeting in Cape Town, together with Archbishop Tutu, played on these words in a call that was taken up by the foot soldiers:

Eight is NOT enough. For as long as Mandela is in prison, eight is not enough. For as long as there are shacks in Khayelitsha, eight is not enough. For as long as there is apartheid, eight is not enough. Eight is not enough! Eight is not enough! Eight is not enough![10]

The political flux and speed of events were causing consternation in the ranks as well. The ANC's NWC met on 26 and 27 October 1989 in Lusaka following leaks in South African newspapers about the secret Consgold talks in England. The indisposed Tambo and Mbeki were absent. An intense debate ensued. Pahad recorded that strong reservations were expressed about how the ANC was pro-ceeding. Old complaints surfaced: Why was Mbeki not reporting to the NEC about the meetings? There were fears that its powers were being usurped. NEC members said that leadership was chaotic and lacking in cohesion, and there had to be greater accountability at all levels. One immediate result of the debate was that Jacob Zuma soon afterwards briefed the NWC about the meeting with the NIS in Switzerland, but the absence of the indisposed president and unifier was already being sorely felt.[11] Alfred Nzo (acting in Tambo's place) and Thomas Nkobi were accused of inertia and a lack of direction, and divisions over strategy in the NEC sharpened. They were not the leaders the organisation needed just then.

Three key anomalies in the ANC intersected at the very moment that the organisation was facing one of its biggest historic challenges. Firstly, while the ANC and allies on the ground in South Africa maintained an attachment to insurrection and the revolutionary language of seizure of power, the logic and implications of its multitracked planning and diplomatic outreach since the Kabwe conference were torpedoing it into a new dimension of struggle. For four years, Tambo and the NEC had prepared systematically to activate the constitutional option when the changing balance of forces required this and struggle journals had been publishing articles about 'Fighting with new weapons' since the Constitutional Guidelines had been published,[12] but given long-standing struggle cultures and the fluid uncertainty of the times, implementation was always going to be a complex challenge. Secondly, speculation about secret talks was rife in the organisation and this was leading to a loss of morale and exacerbating the uncertainty. There was justified frustration at chief diplomat Thabo Mbeki's failures to attend and report back to NWC and NEC meetings – and suspicions about his 'individualism and private agendas'.[13] However, the evidence points to Mbeki, who became ANC head of international affairs after Johnny Makatini's death in late 1988, indeed having a mandate for his diplomatic forays from Tambo and the senior alliance leaders in the previously mentioned President's Committee, and that he did report back to them. Members of the President's Committee like Tloome, Nzo, Nkobi and Nkadimeng were prominent as patrons in all the key constitutional planning meetings discussed in this book and the Constitution Committee personally copied them in on correspondence at times. In 1985, and again in 1988, the NEC had given this Committee a brief to propose how the organisation could be restructured with a view to increasing the efficiency of ANC operations. Minutes and other evidence back up the existence and important backroom role of this committee.[14] I believe it is fair to say that in the same way that Hani was running sensitive military operations or that Maharaj was secretly leading Operation Vula inside the country without the knowledge of the NEC, Mbeki was proceeding with diplomatic initiatives on a familiar, underground, need-to-know basis. As even his sometime critics have pointed out, internal ANC processes were inevitably constrained by the illegal and dangerous conditions under which the struggle was waged, and perspectives regarding strategy and tactics in ANC ranks were seldom simply about 'revolution' or 'negotiation'; rather there were numerous criss-crossing ideas being shaped by constantly changing dynamics in which emphases on the best options differed.[15] Finally, various historians have made the point that the ANC was, in certain respects, in organisational and bureaucratic disarray at the time. This reality, acknowledged by the NEC itself, as we have seen above, did not, however, trump the fact that by the end of 1989 this resilient movement and its internal allies had firmly grabbed the political initiative from the apartheid government – and that the balance of forces was tilting decisively in its favour and would remain so for the next four years until democracy arrived and the NP was removed from power.

The ANC may have been a non-state actor with limited resources operating in a difficult environment, but neither was the repressive power of the apartheid state a guarantee of its ability to maintain control, as the citizens in the GDR were at that very moment demonstrating as they marched in Leipzig and Berlin, soon to take over the House of Ministries in Wilhelmstrasse and other once impregnable spaces.

On 9 November 1989, the Berlin Wall came crashing down. This contributed dramatically to the end of the Cold War, which had dominated international politics since the end of World War II. As far as the ANC was concerned, this event had relatively little impact on its immediate thinking and strategy in relation to negotiations. The Harare Declaration setting out the organisation's vision, the principles to be embodied, the conditions to be complied with and the processes to be followed was already on its way via the Commonwealth and the Non-Aligned Movement to the UN. For De Klerk, the fall of the Berlin Wall had a double impact. On the one hand, the apartheid government could no longer rely on support from Western countries as a bastion against the supposed spread of communism. On the other, it was extremely propitious in enabling the new leader to overcome his own party's bitter resistance to allowing communists to walk free in South Africa. The return of communist exiles, such as Chris Hani and Joe Slovo, and the unbanning of the Communist Party would therefore be less problematic for him. Of more concern was a cabinet-level government report warning that

> radical groups have the capacity to exploit situations in order to radicalise the masses. Recent events have also shown that peaceful protests could degenerate into violence. Should the capacity to mobilise the masses be fully exploited, events such as those in Eastern Europe and [the Tiananmen Square protests in] China would not be far-fetched.[16]

Ministers were informed that there was a 'well-organised, collective leadership structure in place' to guide the struggle:

> MDM leaders and members of the ANC's NEC were in constant contact, and the ANC has begun to relocate its 'Political Military Committees', which co-ordinate military activities from the Frontline States, to the Republic ... The central theme during talks in Lusaka between MDM representatives and the ANC NEC on 21 to 23 November 1989 was that the 'struggle' in the Republic had to be intensified.[17]

From 3 to 5 December 1989, De Klerk took his ministers and the provincial administrators on a retreat to the D'Nyala game reserve near the Botswanan border to formalise a strategy for the future. His finance minister warned that the economy was on a precipitous slope. De Klerk said that they could still hold out for ten or fifteen years, but that there would be sanctions, sabotage and terror. Is that what they wanted? He argued that they should rather seize the golden moment and start negotiating now than be forced to concede under pressure in ten to fifteen years. It was agreed that the strategy would be to try to create 'a normal process of open politics' where people and organisations with different opinions would be able to canvass political support and negotiate solutions where problems existed – all the while making sure that the government maintained control of the process.[18]

Four days later, between 9 and 11 December, in line with the strategy of the liberation movement forces to keep the regime under pressure, some 4 600 delegates from 2 000 organisations – including representatives from the Black Consciousness Movement – met at the Conference for a Democratic Future in Johannesburg, which was seen as a modern-day Congress of the People, where the Freedom Charter had been adopted. The purpose was to demonstrate the internal support for the Constitutional Guidelines and the Harare Declaration. The conference also agreed on a programme of action to back up the demands in these documents, including mass protests against a forthcoming sanctions-defying 'rebel' cricket tour from England.[19] COSATU and the UDF, which had morphed into the MDM, once again showed their central role in legitimising the ANC and coordinating the ground troops of the revolution. The MDM's Murphy Morobe said the basic goal was to keep overall pressure on the government and to 'begin working on the creation of a constituent assembly'.

On 13 December 1989, as the ANC team met with the UN General Assembly to promote the Harare Declaration, De Klerk agreed to meet the imprisoned Nelson Mandela for the first time. Mandela was brought to De Klerk's office in Tuynhuys, the presidential office next to Parliament. The meeting lasted for two hours and fifty-five minutes.[20] 'I think Niël Barnard was there, General Willemse was there, Kobie Coetsee was there ... but after brief handshakes, they all withdrew and ... Mandela and I had a one-on-one discussion', De Klerk later recalled.[21] The men had never met before, and like everyone else, De Klerk had no real idea of what Mandela looked like; for more than twenty years, only a few secretly snatched photos of him had been seen. De Klerk wrote later that Mandela was taller than he expected, dignified, courteous and self-confident. Mandela for his part wrote to his ANC colleagues in Lusaka that he had 'taken the measure of Mr De Klerk, just as I had with new prison commanders when I was on Robben Island'. Mandela said: 'You can release me, but I will do exactly what you arrested me for if you don't unban my organisation.'[22] He gave no undertakings on the issues that had always been raised from the government's side, namely violence, relations with the Communist Party and the fear of majority rule.

The next day, 14 December 1989, the UN General Assembly approved the Harare Declaration in the form of the UN Declaration on Apartheid and gave the apartheid government six months to fulfil the demands in the document. The secretary-general was instructed to report back after that time to ensure it was complying.[23] The ANC had backed the regime into a political corner, as planned.

The new president thus made a bold move. South Africa was in a dead-end street. He would rescind the prohibition of the ANC, the PAC, the Communist Party and allied organisations, as well as the emergency restrictions on the UDF, COSATU and thirty-three other internal organisations; suspend the death sentence; lift certain restrictions on the media, educational institutions and detainees; release certain categories of political prisoners – including Nelson Mandela; and try the way of negotiations to hold in check his opponents and their demands for one-person, one-vote democracy.

He made the unexpected announcement of these decisions at the opening of Parliament on 2 February 1990.[24] Many were caught off guard. The ANC leadership in Lusaka had been in touch with Mandela and the underground and MDM leadership right up to the announcement,[25] but the extent of the reform initiative came as a surprise, causing Jack Simons to later remark that the ANC had not been prepared for its banning in 1960 and was not ready for its unbanning in 1990.[26]

Pieter Mulder of the right-wing Vryheidsfront recalls the drama of the moment:

Everything changed at that very moment. We were in the chamber when the announcements were made by Mr De Klerk. We realised it's a new ball game from that very moment on. I think most parties then moved directly to their caucus room to discuss the implication of what was announced. Later on we heard from National Party people that they were also not informed before the announcements were made in the chamber.[27]

Seasoned correspondent Allister Sparks commented:

> In those thirty-five minutes De Klerk unleashed forces that within four years would sweep away the old South Africa and establish an altogether new and different country in its place. Another country with another constitution and another flag and another national anthem. And above all another ethos.[28]

Sparks would have been more accurate in his observations if he had added the rider that De Klerk was responding to the forces and specific strategies for creating another country with another constitution and another flag and another national anthem, and above all another ethos, that had emanated from Lusaka in the wake of Kabwe nearly five years earlier and culminated in the events in Johannesburg and New York only weeks before.

De Klerk's announcement was directly in keeping with the demands made in the Harare Declaration. These were the basic measures necessary to producing the conditions in which free political discussion could take place and ensure that the people themselves could participate in the process of remaking their country.

By making the concessions, the last apartheid president hoped to control the change process and forestall a democratic dispensation that would lead inevitably to majority rule, or what he termed a 'winner take all' outcome. However, as Sparks noted, the genie was out of the bottle. He had unleashed a force far beyond his imagination and control.

In their book on Mandela's release, subtitled 'Revelations from the Kobie Coetsee Archive', Riaan de Villiers and Jan-Ad Stemmet made a close study of Mandela's last few weeks in prison and the drafts of De Klerk's 2 February speech. They conclude that it underlined that the Harare Declaration 'played a far more important role in shaping the government's actions at that stage than has generally been acknowledged':

> It was perhaps understandable De Klerk did not refer to the declaration; he could hardly be seen as acknowledging that the government was responding to terms dictated to it by the ANC and the United Nations. However, a close reading, against the background of the secret memorandums, reveals the extent to which the declaration had come to dominate government strategy at that time and, eventually, De Klerk's renowned address.[29]

They conclude:

> The proceedings in parliament on 2 February, then, were dominated by two
> absent figures: Prisoner 913, who was watching them on a TV set in his cottage
> at Victor Verster prison; and Oliver Tambo, who was recovering from his stroke
> in a clinic in Sweden.[30]

The second of February 1990 has to be put in its proper context. As Pieter Mulder
was later to sardonically observe, whatever the NP's expectations might have
been before the speech, from that moment on they were following the Harare
Declaration textbook.[31] And although it was De Klerk's moment, the political
victory belonged to the ANC, as the event nine days later brought home.

De Klerk did not announce a date when Mandela would be released. The speculation and haggling continued behind closed doors – until Sunday 11 February.
Then people poured into the streets. The news was spreading that 'Mandela is
going to be released today'. It was one of those events where everyone remembers
where they were and what they were doing.

I was due to play a cricket match that Sunday, but both teams agreed this was a
day like no other. We abandoned the match when it was confirmed that the legend
had left his final place of imprisonment in the Cape Winelands and was on his
way to Cape Town's gathering place on the Grand Parade in front of the City Hall.

As it happened, we could have played on a while longer. The crowd – which
looked and felt a hundred thousand strong – were kept waiting for five, six hours
in the hot sun ... and still no Mandela.

In his entourage there were fears for his security. He was being driven by
'Comrade Rose' – UDF leader Mzunani Roseberry Sonto – in a second-hand
Toyota borrowed from the Western Cape Traders Association, without whom
the UDF would not have been able to afford all the creative T-shirts and posters
they produced over the years. As the motorcade neared Cape Town's Parade, the
extent of the crowd dawned on them. Mandela's minders, including COSATU's
Cyril Ramaphosa, spoke to event coordinator Willie Hofmeyr, not long out of
a hunger strike of several weeks during the defiance campaign, and decided to
retreat to nearby Rondebosch for a tête-à-tête. Someone asked one of the other
drivers, 'Saleem, don't you live near here?' And thus the procession made its way
to the Mowzer family house undetected. His sister, Nishaad, responded to the
knock on the door to see with surprise that it was Madiba. And that is how it
happened that the world's most famous person on that day had his first cup of tea
as a free man at 44 Haywood Road in modest Rondebosch East.

Now what to do? In those days before mobile phones, the comrades got onto the landline. One of the options was to call off Mandela's appearance altogether. Madiba borrowed spectacles to do some reading, probably his speech. In the rush, he had apparently left his behind somewhere.

Meanwhile, back at the Parade the people remained happy, good-natured. Friends in their struggle T-shirts greeted each other and waited with delicious expectation for history to happen. Squashed together, balancing precariously on statues, scaffolding, dustbins, lampposts and whatever other vantage points could be gained, even on the roof of American senator Jesse Jackson's abandoned limousine, they waited. Only as dusk approached did they become restless. Dr Allan Boesak, the orator, tried to keep the party spirit alive, saying, don't worry, comrades, he is coming. But they were tired, wanting only Madiba now.

The entourage asked, was it safe for him to come to the Grand Parade? The whole world is here, was the answer they got from the likes of Archbishop Tutu and Dullah Omar.

Then, suddenly, there he was on the balcony. Fists rose with the ANC's emblematic chant: *Amaaandla!* Total bedlam. The trusted Walter Sisulu at his side. Those attending knew they were present for something that only happened once in a lifetime.

Finally, Mandela spoke, the world waiting for his words: 'I greet you not as a prophet but as a humble servant of you, the people.' This time he was borrowing Winnie's specs to read his speech. Recommitting himself to serve the people after twenty-seven years of incarceration, even if it meant dying for the cause of freedom, he said, 'I therefore place the remaining years of my life in your hands.'[32] South Africa would never be the same again. It was entering a whole new phase of its history. Mandela proceeded on his journey from prisoner to global icon and to president in a few short years, carrying impossible expectations on his shoulders. His first trip outside the country, taken within a fortnight of his release, was to Lusaka to report to the comrades at HQ and to thank President Kaunda for the support Zambia had given the liberation movement. Zambia declared the day a national holiday. *Sechaba* reported that 'Every well-wisher and supporter among the more than 50,000 who were there to meet him, was overwhelmed by the enormousness of the event.'[33]

At a two-day NEC meeting held in Lusaka, Mandela was elected deputy president of the ANC. He was the effective, unchallenged new leader. He would bestride the globe like a colossus in the 1990s. The vacuum left by Tambo's stroke six months earlier was being filled. A new era lay ahead.

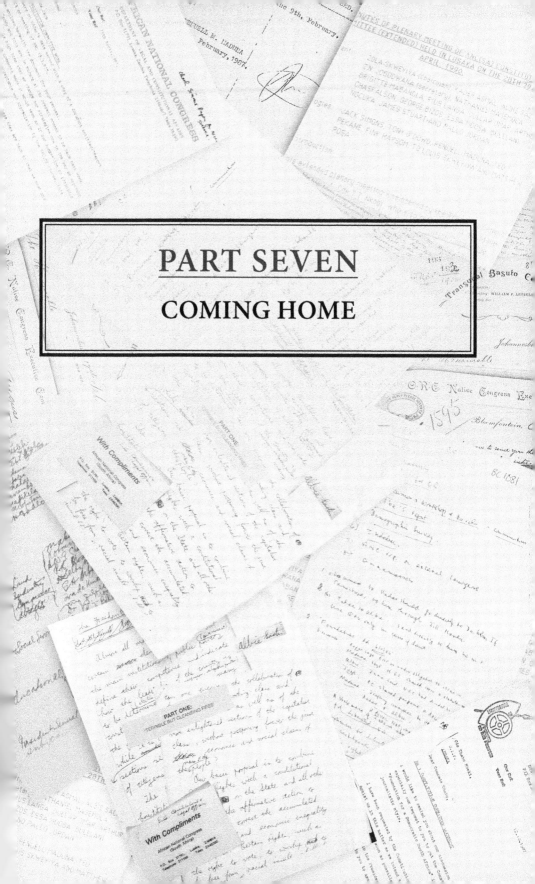

PART SEVEN

COMING HOME

38

Return of the First Exiles

J ACK SIMONS AND Ray Alexander got permission to go home without delay
and were the very first exiles to return to South Africa. Jack had believed as late
as 1989 that he would never return home in his lifetime. They arrived back in Cape
Town on 2 March 1990, exactly a month after F.W. de Klerk's announcement.
By then, Jack had ceded the leadership of the Constitution Committee to Zola
Skweyiya. This made sense in light of his advanced age, the two months he spent
in hospital in East Berlin in 1988, and the quickening pace of work and diplomatic
engagements in 1989, in which Zola was prominent. Skweyiya was very much at
the centre of things now, as his appointment by the NEC as head of the Task Force
on Negotiations early in 1990 was to show.[1]

When Simons and Alexander bought the property at 250 Zambezi Road in
Lusaka more than two decades earlier, they'd called it Entabeni after their home
under the great mountain in Cape Town, and fixed to the entrance was the name-
plate they had taken with them into exile. They had earned the right to settle back
in Vredehoek in the city centre of Cape Town, where they'd left behind their
two daughters and son, now all middle-aged. They were accompanied on the emotional flight back by a team of notable bodyguards, including Albertina Sisulu
and Sister Bernard Ncube, a fearless struggle nun. After landing, they were warmly
welcomed by joyous crowds in struggle T-shirts, under the glare of television
lights.

They settled into a happy routine in Cape Town. Their interlinked studies
overflowed with cuttings, papers and books, spilling over into the spaces where
they received never-ending adulatory visits from a steady trail of younger struggle pilgrims eager to engage in discussion. Less than three weeks after returning,
they were present as special guests at the Namibian independence celebrations in
Windhoek on 21 March 1990, in recognition of the support they had given in
their home to the founders of SWAPO forty years earlier.

Penuell Maduna was also among the advanced guard of returnees. He and Jacob
Zuma arrived home on 21 March 1990, the thirtieth anniversary of Sharpeville
and the day Namibia became independent. MK underground commander and
lawyer Mathews Phosa (aka Freddie Dlamini) followed a week later, and the trio

were chosen to be the first of the returned ANC cadres to establish communications and 'handle negotiations' with the regime.

Maduna recalls: 'We were met by the National Intelligence Service people as well as General Basie Smit at the Jan Smuts Airport and they took us to a safe place where we stayed and started the Talks about Talks.'[2] They were under the protection of the NIS because of the very real threat of them being eliminated by right-wingers. The volatility of the situation in South Africa became evident five days later when the police opened fire on a crowd of about 50 000 protestors from the Sebokeng township, killing eleven people and injuring more than 300. The protest march was to the local offices of the ruling NP, and focused on high rents and racially segregated local facilities, calling for the resignation of township councillors.[3] After calls for a judicial inquiry, F.W. de Klerk appointed Justice Richard Goldstone to head the investigation into the massacre.

After the Sebokeng massacre, Maduna and Zuma were spirited back to Lusaka: 'we went back to Lusaka to report and a decision was taken that we must continue'. Their subsequent preparations back home led to the Groote Schuur meeting on 2 May 1990, the symbolic beginning of formal talks between delegations from the government and the liberation movement.

39

Last Meeting in Lusaka

L ESS THAN A week before the Groote Schuur talks, when implacable enemies shook hands on manicured lawns before the world's press to effectively start the negotiations process, the ANC's Constitution Committee reconstituted itself. A heavyweight grouping of the best legal thinkers available to the ANC from exile and 'inside' got together at the Pamodzi Hotel in Lusaka on 28–29 April to strategise on how best to take the Committee's work forward in the wholly changed context of the party's legalisation in South Africa.[1]

Albie Sachs recalls how he and Dullah Omar gave each other a long hug. His passport restored, Omar had flown up to Lusaka for the first time with an excited team of five other lawyers from home who would be taking their seats as newly appointed members of the Committee. They had been urgently summoned to HQ in Zambia while some of them were preparing to organise the huge welcoming rally the UDF was arranging for the returning leaders in Mitchells Plain the same day – fittingly this was the place where the UDF had been formed a short seven years before.[2]

With Omar were Pius Langa, 'the soft-spoken, self-contained president of the National Association of Democratic Lawyers, with a wry and gentle sense of humour'; Omar's two close comrade lawyers from Cape Town, Bulelani Ngcuka and Essa Moosa; and the formidable Johannesburg duo of Arthur Chaskalson and George Bizos. Sachs noted that it was especially emotional meeting his two former counterparts at the Bar from the 1960s and that 'there was a wonderful bond between the tall, laconic Arthur and the shorter, rounder and more gregarious George.'[3]

While people were finding their places, Bizos, a well-known raconteur, told everyone present that when he was appointed to the Committee he asked if he would have to apply for a membership card and was told that this would not be necessary. Cyril Ramaphosa said he would arrange an exemption from toyi-toying. 'I was never sure if this was granted,' says Bizos. 'As a precaution, I've refrained from the toyi-toyi in the presence of the media.'[4]

In the absence of Oliver Tambo, ANC treasurer-general Thomas 'TG' Nkobi arrived to open the meeting. He was supported by James Stuart and Pallo Jordan, two of the NEC members who had been most involved since 1985 in overseeing the constitutional planning process. Four of the founder members of the Constitution Committee attended: Zola Skweyiya, Kader Asmal, Jobs Jobodwana and Albie Sachs. Jack Simons and Penuell Maduna had returned to South Africa and Ted Pekane was now ANC chief rep in Brussels. The four were joined by more recent recruits from the exile community: Brigitte Mabandla, Nathaniel Masemola and Mathews Phosa. The meeting was informed that three more lawyers from home who had been appointed to the Committee were unable to attend: Lewis Thembile Skweyiya, Fink Haysom and Edwin Cameron.

After Nkobi had reviewed the work of the Committee since 1986, Skweyiya stated that its entire role would have to be reviewed and redefined in the light of unfolding developments, starting with its role in negotiations and constitution-making. Secondly, they would have to define a future relationship with the ANC's Task Force on Negotiations. This body had been set up by the NEC, with Skweyiya as its chairperson, to prepare for the ANC's preliminary talks with the regime at the presidential residence, Groote Schuur, in a few days' time.[5]

The first item on the agenda was to find out which of the members, old or new, sitting around the table, would be available to serve on the Constitution Committee, full-time or otherwise, when it located itself back home in South Africa.

Zola Skweyiya, Jobodwana and Mabandla, all of whom were working full-time for the DLCA in Lusaka, said they would be available to work full-time with the Committee back home. London-based Masemola said that he was not at that time able to leave his position as head of the Luthuli Trust Fund, which provided scholarships to enable black South African students to study in Britain. Phosa indicated that he would soon be joining Maduna in Johannesburg to help create conditions for exiles to return and prisoners to be released. This meant he would be working for the ANC in a legal capacity, but in a different context.

Sachs reported that he was in the hands of the Committee and in cases of emergency would be one hundred per cent available, but hoped to spend half his time with his newly created Centre for South African Constitutional Studies in London, and the other half in South Africa. Asmal said he was making himself available to the ANC on a full-time basis. After a quarter of a century in Dublin with his British wife, he was prepared to give up his deanship at Trinity College and 'commence with his duties' as soon as the European summer exams were over.

Next to speak was Ngcuka. He had completed his BProc degree at the University of Fort Hare in 1977. In 1980 he was admitted to the legal profession as an attorney after doing his articles in Durban with Griffiths Mxenge, a senior ANC underground figure who was brutally stabbed and hacked to death the following year. Soon after burying his mentor, Ngcuka was arrested and sentenced to three years' imprisonment for refusing to testify against Patrick Maqubela, later a judge, who had been charged with high treason. While in Helderstroom Prison near Caledon, Ngcuka had furthered his studies with the University of South Africa and completed an LLB degree. On his release, he spent two years working for the International Labour Organization in Switzerland and completed an MA in International Relations with the University of Webster. When he returned to South Africa, he joined a law firm in Cape Town, became active in UDF activities, including the 1989 defiance campaign, and was detained several times under the emergency regulations. He had served as chairperson of the UDF in the Western Cape and became a leading figure in NADEL.[6] Ngcuka told those present that it would be extremely difficult for him to leave private practice, but that he was prepared to participate in plenary sessions of the Committee.

Essa Moosa followed. Born in District Six in 1936, he had been admitted to practice as an attorney in Cape Town in 1962. Specialising in human rights issues, he was a rooted UDF 'struggle lawyer' who brought challenges to detentions without trial and repressive restrictions of freedoms of association, expression and movement. Community groups and activists all over the country sought him out to defend their cases under apartheid and emergency laws.[7] Archbishop Desmond Tutu often told the story of being in a jail cell packed with clergy and activists who had been detained by apartheid security forces for marching through the streets of Cape Town without permission. It was 1989. Tutu turned to the officer in charge and said: 'I want our lawyer.' Normally, this would have necessitated a phone call. Instead, a soft voice from the back of the cell floated over the hubbub: 'I am also here.'[8]

Moosa had played an instrumental role in starting NADEL and had chaired its Human Rights Committee. Advocate Dumisa Ntsebeza, the BLA-supported first president of the association, said he didn't notice Moosa at first 'because Dullah [Omar] was larger than life ... [Essa] had a quiet demeanour. You could almost miss him. He wasn't a fire-eater like the rest of us.'[9] Moosa was also a founding member and trustee of community-based media initiatives including Bush Radio, Grassroots Publications, *Saamstaan* newspaper (Southern Cape) and *South* newspaper. He told the Committee that he was running a large practice, which he had to keep together, but that he was prepared to do work on the plenary committee and avail himself for specific tasks.

When it came to his turn, Bizos stated that, although not formally a member of the ANC, he had been asked by Mandela to make himself available for the work of the Committee. He had handled a large number of political cases involving ANC members and had served as one of Mandela's personal lawyers. He was frequently called upon to act as a reliable messenger between the ANC and government, and felt that he could lose that role if he became a full-time ANC functionary. He said that he would, however, like to be involved in plenary meetings and other important Committee tasks.[10]

Chaskalson explained that he was anxious to do what he could, essentially as a technician, analyst and draftsman. He could make time for specific jobs, such as spending short periods looking into proposals coming back and forth. Langa reported that he spent a great deal of his time doing unpaid MDM work, so he had to make a living and could not easily leave his practice. However, he wished to know everything being done by the Constitution Committee and wanted ready access to its core people.

Omar, who had been elected vice-president of NADEL at its founding, was prepared to do the work he was called upon to do. At the invitation of UWC rector Jakes Gerwel, he was busy setting up the Community Law Centre at the university. Part of its work was related to the work of the Constitution Committee, and his services would be at the disposal of the Committee. He added that he 'enjoy[ed] working with Arthur, George, Pius, Bulelani and Essa', and looked forward to doing so in future.

After everyone had explained their degrees of availability, it was agreed that there should be a core of full-time functionaries based inside South Africa. As long as uncertainty remained about the timing of the ANC members' return from exile, it would be appropriate for Omar and Langa, 'the leader of the group of participants from South Africa', to head the internal core. This core would be complemented by part-time members to form a broad plenary group.[11]

The 'committee restructuring' included the establishment of eight commissions, which would be 'entrusted with areas of research and be called upon from time to time to do specific jobs for the Constitution Committee or ANC'. The main purpose of the commissions was 'to broaden the spectrum of participation and to introduce some form of specialisation'. It was decided that 'the identified personnel need not necessarily be members of the ANC'. The Committee identified a convenor for each commission, who would be 'at liberty to engage the services of other people after consultation' with the Committee.

The eight commissions and the accompanying 'assignment of duties' (convenors mentioned first) were:
- Electoral process – Asmal and Bizos
- Future economy, land and affirmative action – Masemola with Omar, Skweyiya, Mabandla and Jobodwana
- Structural constitution set-up – Skweyiya with Chaskalson, Sachs and Langa
- Bill of Rights–enforcing mechanism – Moosa with Sachs, Ngcuka and Jobodwana

- Court structures or systems – Ngcuka with Maduna and Jobodwana
- Labour – Maduna with Haysom and Cameron
- Gender – Mabandla with Maduna and Sachs
- Overall constitutional framework – Skweyiya with Chaskalson, Langa and Sachs[12]

On the electoral process, it was pointed out that the majority of South Africans had never voted or even seen what a ballot box looked like. It was therefore an urgent priority to educate the people, as well as to carry out the demographic survey and research the Constitution Committee had been calling for since its formation in January 1986, and for which the ANC's Swedish-backed PASA project had been initiated a month later. From 1988, aspects of the PASA plans began to be implemented via SASPRO under Barney McKay from the ANC's projects office in Lusaka and with the CDS under Randi Erentzen at UWC.[13]

It was recorded that land, the future economic system, the redistribution of wealth and affirmative action were going to be key in the negotiation process. It would be vital to include research on maritime resources, mining and mineral resources, and ecology law. On the land issue, it was noted that 'all [our] papers are inadequate', implying that the ANC needed to put in place a clear policy on this key, complex topic.

On the question of group rights, it would be necessary to ensure that the regime did not find models – like its proposed 'second chamber' of parliament – that would serve as a means of 'protecting minority rights and privileges'.

The minutes record that 'the question of the oppression of women, more especially the triple oppression of African women, can no longer be avoided ... [M]ore educative work amongst members of our community has to be done in this regard'. The Women's Seminar in Lusaka four months earlier had clearly brought that point home.[14]

Several immediate tasks were allocated. Omar and Asmal were asked to draft an interim Bill of Rights that could be used to test the extent to which restrictive laws and regulations were being employed to limit free political activity. Chaskalson undertook to look into the emotive South African Indemnity Bill that had been drafted by De Klerk's legal advisors to skew the granting of indemnity in favour of government operatives and to limit the class of freedom fighters who would be classified as 'affected persons' entitled to indemnity. The text of this Bill would have to be reformulated to ensure that the definition included activists from the ANC and other organisations who had taken up arms.

Langa was mandated to prepare a dossier on the activities of Inkatha and of 'reports of all Inkatha's atrocities against the people'. The bitter internecine fighting in Natal had led to the loss of around 2 400 lives by the end of 1989. It was a huge issue for the ANC at this time. They understood that there was a key battle ahead. On one side would be the allied NP and Inkatha, with their inclination towards a federal, group-rights solution. On the other was the ANC with its emphasis on equal individual rights protected by a Bill of Rights in an undivided democracy. Inkatha 'third force' vigilantes were trained secretly in the Caprivi Strip by the SADF and acted as its proxies in the state's attempts to crush the ANC. IFP leader Mangosuthu Gatsha Buthelezi, a former ANC member, was seen as having betrayed the struggle. The members felt that a 'wide and effective publicity campaign' was needed so that 'Gatsha's nefarious role in the Natal killings should be explained and publicised in a sustained way to the people and the international community'.[15]

In discussing how to remove the obstacles to negotiations, the Committee drew on a dossier prepared for them by Fink Haysom,[16] as well as the experiences of Namibia and Zimbabwe. They identified eight areas that needed to be dealt with:

- the definition of political prisoners;[17]
- amnesty for political prisoners;
- the suspension of political trials and indemnity for political offences;
- safe conduct and immunity for returned exiles;
- the repeal of security and emergency legislation;
- the removal of troops from the townships;
- the cessation of hostilities; and
- the Natal conflict with Inkatha.

The Constitution Committee set itself three immediate tasks:

- to assist the negotiating team in the first stage by dealing with the removal of obstacles and creating a healthy climate for negotiation;
- to service the negotiating team involved in, first, talks about talks and, second, in the actual negotiations themselves; and
- to assist in the actual constitution drafting.[18]

There was 'a strong suspicion' in the ANC and the Constitution Committee 'that the regime is already having a draft constitution'. Therefore, the Committee felt, these tasks had to be 'tackled simultaneously' in an integrated, urgent way. It would have to establish a solid database of various sources relevant to its work, and this 'should be made available to the members for analysis and sharing'. To ensure efficiency, members were asked to always reply and acknowledge the receipt of such material. 'As part of our preparation for hard negotiations', the Committee would also have to draw up 'a glossary of constitution related concepts, principles and other opinions' for the ANC negotiating team. The Committee recognised also that it would have 'to do some field work, going to people and various structures and formations and ask[ing] them to draft something on various topics'. Thus, 'on religion, the SACC [South African Council of Churches] can be asked to mobilise its structures and affiliates'. The same would apply to the different educational constituencies, women's organisations, trade unions and youth structures, et cetera. Members would be expected to do 'given assignments', including convening meetings, research and 'specific jobs'. The view was that 'it is not enough' for members to participate 'generally' – focused work in key areas was required.[19] They were now entering an uncertain new era of legality. The Constitution Committee and the ANC would have to be absolutely goal-focused to ensure that the organisation achieved its objectives.

After the meeting, Omar, Ngcuka and Moosa took Sachs aside and Omar said, 'Comrade Albie, you chaps are taking much too long to get home. Give us a week and we'll fly you in to Cape Town to give some lectures at UWC. Farida and I have a spare room. We'll make sure you get back to London.'[20] Omar explained that he was busy setting up the new Community Law Centre on the UWC campus, thereby activating plans – several years in the making – for the Committee to have an institutionalised base within the country. They also made similar approaches to Asmal, Skweyiya (also originally from Cape Town) and the other exiled members of the Committee.

The reconstituted Constitution Committee was now set to move to South Africa. It provisionally scheduled its next meeting for the end of May 1990. On home soil!

40

A Soft Landing in Cape Town

ALBIE SACHS FELT elated as he reached the back summit of Table Mountain. He'd been imagining this moment for more than twenty-four years. It was the fulfilment of a vow he'd made to himself every day of his exile. He'd arrived on a Saturday morning in early May at what was then called D.F. Malan Airport, had tea with his mother, whom he had seen only twice in the past twenty-four years, and put on his *takkies* to climb the mountain. He was driven to Constantia Nek and, accompanied by a number of ANC athletes, he walked up a broad path to the summit. Overjoyed, he traversed the undulating mountaintop plateau, descended to the Pipe Track above Camps Bay, and ended up exhausted and happy at Kloof Nek. Afterwards, he attended a crowded tea hosted in his honour at the home of NADEL lawyer Dines Gihwala in Rylands on the Cape Flats, a group area designated for Indians. Eventually, overwhelmed with emotion, he collapsed onto his bed in the special room for visiting comrades in the nearby house of Dullah and Farida Omar. He was back home.[1]

The next day Omar took him to the Great Hall at UWC to address a crowd of nearly a thousand Muslims from all over South Africa who had gathered to consider what their future would be when democracy came to the country. 'What we in the ANC envisage,' he told the Muslim Judicial Council leaders and others present, 'is that when you come into the new non-racial democracy, you don't leave Islam behind; you bring your beliefs in with you.' This was his first public engagement, reconnecting him with South Africans on home soil. The mood was jubilant.[2]

Omar was also there for Asmal when he landed at D.F. Malan Airport. The pilot had made a special point of circling over Robben Island for the passengers. Then followed the busy round of introductions and engagements: a visit to District Six; a meal of salted snoek, the local delicacy; and a poetry reading by wildfire student poet Sandile Dikeni at a welcoming dinner – 'a very emotional event'.[3] Asmal wanted to visit the naval base in Simon's Town as well, 'to see for myself the effects of the arms embargo' he had fought so hard for as a leader for a quarter of a century in the British and Irish anti-apartheid movements.[4] Cape Town was completely strange to Kader and to his English-born partner, Louise, but by 1991 he was settled at UWC as professor in human rights. Their first task was to find a place where they and their two sons, Adam and Rafiq, could live. The law was not clear on whether they could legally live together. Although the Immorality Act and the Mixed Marriages Act had been repealed in 1985, the Group Areas Act, which imposed strict residential segregation, remained intact.[5] F.W. de Klerk had announced in April that the government would repeal the Group Areas Act, but although people were actively flouting it at that moment in time, the legal situation remained unclear. Kader and Louise managed to find a house in Mowbray with relatively easy access to the UWC campus via the N2. Soon enough, they were calling Cape Town home and the Asmal house became something of a centre of sociability in the city, exuding South African warmth and openness, Indian conviviality and Irish expressivity.

Sachs and Asmal's links with UWC in the northern suburbs of Cape Town were part of plans to give the Constitution Committee an institutional home in a supportive environment back in South Africa. In anticipation of needs to come, Professor Jakes Gerwel, the rector of UWC, who had already helped Thabo Mbeki and the ANC establish the Centre for Development Studies on campus in 1988, invited Dullah Omar to set up a new Community Law Centre at the university to act as a South African base for the Constitution Committee. With funds from the Ford Foundation, Omar had been able to move from his practice to the campus in 1990 to become the new centre's first director. Bulelani Ngcuka also left his practice to become its deputy director. Before and after the Constitution Committee's first meeting back in South Africa on 11 June 1990, other members started returning as well.

In his unfussy way, Zola Skweyiya, the senior organiser in Lusaka, slipped back into what had been the punishing city of his youth. The Group Areas Act had led to the destruction of his home at what had been known as Luyolo near Simon's Town. He was added to the staff of the Community Law Centre and continued to provide laconic but focused leadership to the growing band of Constitution Committee members in Cape Town. Similarly, Brigitte Mabandla joined the centre and was one of the key organisers of a well-attended follow-up conference to the 1989 women's seminar in November 1990, opened by Mandela. This led to the publication of the influential *Women's Rights: A Discussion Document* by the centre, taking the protection of women's rights in the Bill of Rights of the future constitution a stage further.

Within months, no less than six members of the restructured Constitution Committee – Omar, Sachs, Asmal, Skweyiya, Ngcuka and Mabandla – found themselves ensconced at their new base at UWC. Later, they were joined by internal newcomer Yvonne Mokgoro, who, although not a formal member of the Constitution Committee, became actively involved in its work. Born in Galeshewe township in Kimberley, she was encouraged by Robert Sobukwe, during the time of his banishment there, to think of a career in law. She moved from being a nursing assistant to becoming a clerk in the Department of Justice, studying by correspondence and eventually becoming a lecturer and associate professor at the University of Bophuthatswana (now North-West University). Later she received an LLM at the University of Pennsylvania in the United States.[6]

Thanks to forward planning, and the deep networks of underground struggle, the Committee was thus able to make a soft landing in South Africa. The bulk of the Committee now had an academic institutional home in South Africa in keeping with the think-tank role originally envisaged by Tambo. As Omar put it, 'They wanted the former exiles to feel *at home* at home.' Not far away on the campus, the Centre for Development Studies, directed by Randi Erentzen, was on hand to partner with the Committee, fund constitutional workshops, and establish direct connections with progressive South African academics and MDM formations throughout the country. The Constitution Committee had noted at its last meeting in Lusaka that 'with the assistance of other structures', it now had to 'look for financial resources as its work will now demand enormous funding' and 'the initial funding would be coming from CDS after due consultations'.[7] This was the goal of the PASA project agreed to by Oliver Tambo and Swedish premier Olof Palme in February 1986 to help the ANC's planning for a future South Africa come to fruition.

The Committee's strategy was to develop a joint programme of national workshops in different parts of the country and with an international outreach. Themes to be explored were:

- electoral systems;
- the question of land;
- affirmative action;
- whether to have a constitutional court; and
- the issue of regions and the inclusion of social and economic rights in the Bill of Rights.[8]

The idea was for input from these workshops to be fed into the formal negotiations process by members of the Committee. Significant funding support was made available by the Friedrich Ebert Foundation, set up by the Social Democratic Party in Germany.

Meanwhile, Pius Langa was offered a position at the University of Natal where Linda Zama, another protégé of slain lawyer Victoria Mxenge, provided considerable assistance for his Constitution Committee work.[9]

The Constitution Committee was now in a position to serve as a feeder for the

ANC leadership in developing the principles and structures of South Africa's new constitutional order. After fifty-two months of unheralded backroom preparation by the Constitution Committee and the NEC in Lusaka, the Committee had no fewer than seven people working full-time with organisational and academic structures to help develop constitutional concepts as talks proceeded on South African soil on how to carry the negotiations process forward.

Meetings of the full Committee took place at Shell House, the ANC headquarters across the way from Joubert Park in downtown Johannesburg. It was arranged that members from Cape Town and Durban would fly up to meet with Johannesburg-based Arthur Chaskalson, George Bizos and Fink Haysom. In addition to supervising the programme for workshops, the Committee started work on a preamble for a new constitution and on determining possible structures of government in a new democratic South Africa.

On the face of it, the resources available to the ANC team were miniscule compared to those of the existing South African government. The government's Department of Constitutional Development had about eighty staff members and 'the benefit of unlimited state resources for the appointment of consultants and experts from various universities' – both local and international. Yet, the Constitution Committee members had an immense sense of certainty. The manifest justice of their cause, the huge international and internal support for the ANC, and its consistency with international standards and values counted a great deal. In the five years of its existence, the NEC and the Committee, working in collaboration, had been able to develop a clear, coherent and convincing vision for a new democratic South Africa.[10]

So, when an official from the US State Department offered the Committee support 'to level the playing field', the Committee politely replied that if they wished to level the playing field, they should rather support the South African government.

The official in fact arranged for renowned American law and political science professor Donald L. Horowitz to offer advice by telephone to a workshop organised by the Constitution Committee. The professor opened his remarks by saying that the problem with lawyers was that they never gave a straight answer; they always said, on the one hand a certain remedy was required and on the other hand something else had to be taken account of. 'What you need in South Africa to get a good constitution,' he said, 'is a one-armed lawyer.' Everyone at the workshop burst out laughing because the Constitution Committee had just that.[11]

41

Tambo Arrives Home

THIRTY YEARS AND eight months since he had crossed the border into then Bechuanaland, Oliver Tambo was preparing to fly back home. On 22 March 1960, the day after the Sharpeville massacre, he had followed ANC instructions to leave the country and mobilise international support to bring down the apartheid regime. Bechuanaland (today Botswana) was still under unsympathetic British control and his goal had been to get to Tanganyika (today Tanzania). To do so, he had to traverse Southern Rhodesia (Zimbabwe), Northern Rhodesia (Zambia) and Nyasaland (Malawi). All these territories were still British colonies, with a white-minority government effectively in charge of Southern Rhodesia. On arrival in Bechuanaland, Tambo, accompanied by writer Ronald Segal, had met up with Yusuf Dadoo, chair of the Communist Party of South Africa, who had also clandestinely crossed the border. The problem facing Tambo, Dadoo and Segal was that even if they could avoid being kidnapped by apartheid agents or deported by British officials in Bechuanaland, they still had to cross more than 2000 kilometres of colonial territory to Dar es Salaam, and they had no travel documents or any means of transport. Frene Ginwala had been sent to East Africa sometime before to make preparations for such an eventuality. She secured legal opinions from progressive lawyers in London to prevent the three from being deported back to South Africa:

> That night, I received Dr Dadoo's call at a telephone kiosk on the university [of Dar es Salaam] campus and immediately started speaking in Gujerati. I explained that they should go to Palapye [in Bechuanaland] where someone would meet them with transport and papers. My knowledge of the language was rudimentary and as we were speaking... I realised I did not know the word 'airplane' or 'pilot'. I improvised. And for years thereafter I was teased by both Dr Dadoo and Oliver Tambo as the word I used 'chakh' is a tiny Indian bird.[1]

At daybreak on the allotted day, Ginwala travelled from Dar es Salaam to Salisbury (now Harare) to meet the pilot who would be picking them up in Bechuanaland. She gave him a package of legal opinions as well as blank Indian *laissez-passer* passports to which the three were to attach their pictures on the flight from

Bechuanaland. The plane would not have enough fuel to get to Dar es Salaam, so she instructed the pilot not to land anywhere in Southern Rhodesia but to proceed to Blantyre in Nyasaland. Later, she discovered that Rhodesian warrants of arrest had been sent from Salisbury to Blantyre. However, they were not valid for Nyasaland, and with assistance from Nyasaland African Congress members, they had avoided arrest. The flight took off from Blantyre early the next morning, before new, valid warrants could be issued. The plane arrived safely in Dar es Salaam. The next day, Tambo was embraced by Julius Nyerere, then leader of the Tanganyika African National Union.

From then on Tambo's life was a whirl of international travel and activity. His first trip was to Tunis via Nairobi and Rome. His biographer recalls the impact:

> For the first time in his life, Tambo was exposed to the sheer cosmopolitanism of Africa. Here in the north, ebony blue-black men spoke fluent French and Italian, yet wore their dress of vibrant textiles, design, colour and stitchwork. Colonised as most unmistakably were, they were also located in a nexus where Africa met the Mediterranean and the Levant, the cultural product of centuries of vigorous trade, war and religious transaction.[2]

It was a culture shock that made him realise the challenges ahead, and 'He had now to reconstruct his identity in a world of new diversity'. As did his organisation. Exile added immeasurably to the rich texture of the ANC's culture and thinking. Before returning home, Albie Sachs described this organisational 'personality' as follows:

> African tradition, church tradition, Gandhian tradition, revolutionary socialist tradition, all the languages and ways and styles of the many communities in our country: we have black consciousness; and elements of red consciousness (some would say pink consciousness these days), even green consciousness... Now with the dispersal of our members throughout the world, we also bring in aspects of cultures of all humanity. Our comrades speak Swahili and Arabic and Portuguese and Russian and Swedish and French and German and Chinese, even Japanese, not because of Bantu Education but through ANC education. Our culture, ANC culture, is not a picturesque collection of separate ethnic and political cultures lined up side by side, or mixed in certain proportions, it has a real character and dynamic of its own ... This must be one of the greatest achievements of the ANC, [its universal perspectives and] that it has made South Africans of the most diverse origins feel comfortable in its ranks.[3]

This book has deliberately focused on the central role played by the ANC in the late 1980s. This is not due to an assumption that the ANC alone made the decisive push for freedom; multiple forces and personalities outside of the ANC contributed meaningfully to the constitutional transition of South Africa from being a despised apartheid state to becoming an admired constitutional democracy. This point needs to be emphasised. A special space must be given to the amorphous MDM, led by the UDF and the muscular COSATU, who were the ground troops who connected the ANC with home in ways that had not been possible before. Closely connected to the urban revolts that transformed South Africa in the 1980s, the MDM's grassroots struggles and its new-generation voices and methods energised, educated and strengthened the democratic forces, giving direction to the ANC and South Africa in fundamental ways at a key moment in history. Then there were many others who helped make a different South Africa possible – like the multiple formations inspired by Robert Mangaliso Sobukwe acting under the banner of Africanism, as well as members of the Black Consciousness Movement who followed the ideas of Stephen Bantu Biko. There were also a great number of non-aligned trade unions, community and civil society groupings, and faith and human rights organisations. The churches, with the likes of Beyers Naudé, Archbishop Desmond Tutu, Allan Boesak, Malusi Mpumlwana, Brigalia Bam and many others in the forefront, were a massive social support army for the struggle, delegitimising apartheid and providing leadership, resources and comfort to communities under siege.

There is a narrative claiming that it was famous enlightened individuals, or the regime, or anti-communists in the West, or communists in the Soviet Union, who were the key catalysts and main drivers of change in creating a new country. *Dear Comrade President* decolonises that narrative. It was Africans who were the main force for change. Furthermore, as Heinz Klug asserts in the introduction to Juta's *Constitution of the Republic of South Africa, 1996*,

> The origins of South Africa's negotiated revolution are to be found in the countless acts of confrontation, negotiation and compromise between the proponents and the opponents of the status quo that began as early as the 1970s. These interactions – between workers and employers in the union movement; between communities and local peace committees; between activists organising consumer boycotts and local business leaders; and finally, between the imprisoned and exiled leaders of the liberation movements and the apartheid government itself – produced a wealth of negotiating experience that made success possible.[4]

Another important ingredient to this long walk to freedom was the huge international support that was mobilised to secure the release of Nelson Mandela and all other political prisoners, bring down apartheid, and replace it with a non-racial democracy.

The skill of Tambo's team lay precisely in its capacity to coordinate and direct all these pro-change energies into support for a focused and direct programme to end over three centuries of colonialism, apartheid and minority rule.

In his three decades of wanderings in exile, Tambo took a multitude of different forms of transport in different parts of the world. In the 1970s, on the first leg of his flight from Vietnam back to his exile base in Zambia, he flew on a Soviet Aeroflot plane, dependable rather than comfortable, with boxes full of his handwritten notes and comments on how to mobilise all possible resources in advancing the People's Revolutionary War.[5]

Conny Braam, leader of the Dutch anti-apartheid movement, speaks of how terrified she felt when cycling through Amsterdam to a Boycott South Africa meeting, carrying on her handlebars President Oliver Tambo of the ANC.[6]

How different it was in New York in early 1986. Tambo brought a thousand people to their feet in the Riverside Church with a passionate and lyrical eulogy to his great friend Olof Palme, the social democratic prime minister of Sweden assassinated a mere week after the two had last met. Then, much to the chagrin of the meeting's organisers, boxing promoter Don King placed an arm around him and whisked him off in a white stretch limousine parked near the entrance.[7]

Now, Tambo was about to return on an ordinary commercial flight to South Africa with his wife Adelaide and their children: Thembi, Dali and Tselani. He was worried that when he touched down in Johannesburg, his post-stroke speech would be too indistinct for the expectant crowd at the airport to understand. To help him recover his speech, he had asked for the support of someone close to him. The ANC had sent his trusted private secretary Ngoako Ramatlhodi to London to help with his vocal exercises. Ramatlhodi had been head of the Regional Political and Military Council of the ANC's Zimbabwe Mission when Tambo recruited him as his speechwriter in the late 1980s. 'The good thing about him – he was a fighter,' says Ramatlhodi, who with long practice was able to get Tambo to read out loud the text of speeches they had prepared.[8]

Tambo returned at the end of 1990, landing to a great welcome – reputedly the largest welcoming crowd ever to gather at Johannesburg's Jan Smuts Airport, which was later to be named after him. The MDM had jumped into action like only it could. Among those present was Nelson Mandela, who recorded that

The day was a Thursday, 13 December 1990, a summer's day in South Africa. I was, of course, among those there to meet OR, along with our comrades. We sat and spoke in the back of a motor car for a while before Oliver, who was very frail by then, got out to acknowledge the thunderous welcome of the crowds that had gathered. I had the honour to tell those crowds: 'Our President wishes to say he is happy to be home.' I remember the widest grin on Oliver's face as the crowd erupted.[9]

Tambo lifted his right arm with his left to wave. Thousands of right arms rose into the air with clenched fists in response.

Mouthing his words carefully, Tambo said, 'I have devotedly watched over the organisation all these years. I now hand it back to you, bigger, stronger – intact. Guard our precious movement.'[10] After thirty years of wanderings far and wide, Dear Comrade President was back home.

Afterword: 'Freedom and Bread'

T HE RELEASE OF Mandela and the return of Tambo brought to an end the first phase of focused constitutional planning for a free South Africa by the ANC and its allies between late 1985 and early 1990, as described in this book. Working from its Lusaka exile, the movement had succeeded in putting in place an internationally endorsed template for the future. Through the Constitutional Guidelines and the Harare Declaration – and multiple interrelated strategies and struggles – it established the ground rules for political freedom and a constitutional democracy strongly supported by the global community. The template that Tambo's team finalised in 1989, and which the ANC then successively got the Frontline States, the OAU, internal forces, the Non-Aligned Movement, the Commonwealth countries and the UN to adopt, was followed almost step by step from 1990 onwards.

Phase two of the constitution-making process played itself out in a wholly different context of a legal ANC operating inside South Africa. Talks about talks were held to decide who should be represented when actual talks began, where they should take place and how decisions should be made. These resulted in the onset of formal negotiations, involving 228 delegates representing seventeen political organisations, when the Convention for a Democratic South Africa (CODESA) met for the first time at Johannesburg's Kempton Park in December 1991.

The negotiations process took place in a highly charged and unstable environment. Over 14 000 people died because of political violence between 1990 and 1994 – a higher toll than for the whole of the eighties. At the same time as they were talking, the governing NP and its proxies were destabilising the democratic opposition in the most intense ways yet. The continuous violence outside reached the negotiation chamber itself when the AWB used an armoured car to crash through its glass windows and take over the proceedings. In April 1993, Chris Hani was assassinated. People in townships were slaughtered in their beds by masked armed impis, and there was a terrible massacre at Bisho and a mutiny in Bophuthatswana. But a feature of the negotiating process was the way in which the ANC, with its more than four years of focused pre-planning, outmanoeuvred opponents determined to block true democracy.[1] The idea of majority rule coupled with a Bill of Rights in a non-racial democracy, on the side of the ANC, led to a breakdown. Rolling mass action in the streets secured a resumption of negoti-ations. There was a moment where Mandela and De Klerk slung insults at each other. A provision for amnesty had to be arranged, and last-minute changes made to get the IFP to participate in the elections. A threat by 40 000 armed white right-wing men to launch a civil war was averted by a deftly drafted constitutional provision. A short-term Government of National Unity and sunset clauses played a role. The outcome was an interim constitution and the country's first democratic elections, held on 27 April 1994. In four short years, three centuries of colonial and apartheid rule were formally annulled. Mass mobilisation kept the pressure on the regime to the end. The ANC's Harare Declaration and Constitutional Guidelines for a Democratic South Africa continued to act as the guide. The dis-enfranchised mass of South Africans at last reclaimed their national sovereignty and ushered in full-scale political democracy. 'Freedom', at least at the political level, arrived amid unprecedented scenes of national joy and celebration.

The third phase in the making of the Constitution followed the historic elec-tions in which the ANC won an overwhelming mandate from the people to form South Africa's first-ever democratic government. The world's most famous political prisoner became president in May 1994. The 490 democratically chosen represent-atives in the new Parliament formed themselves into a Constitutional Assembly to draft a new democratic constitution.[2] This constitution was not written secretly by negotiators in secluded hotel rooms in other parts of the world. It was drafted openly on South African soil, as had been envisaged by the Constitution Commit-tee at its first meeting in Lusaka in January 1986. Most of the assembly had been involved in the struggle, suffered the pains of oppression and shared the dreams of liberation. Well-organised women's movements were strongly represented, and there was a big bloc of passionate trade unionists. They drafted what was hailed as one of the most progressive constitutions in the world. Building on ideas ten years in the making, it was signed into law by Mandela in Sharpeville on 10 December 1996.[3] Not only did it guarantee the rights of every citizen via its Bill of Rights, but it also had a transformative character at its very core, emphasising the import-ance of second- and third-generation social and economic rights and the need for historical redress in a fractured and unequal society.

The Constitution Committee's Penuell Maduna summed up the goals at the time when he said:

> The ANC adopts a holistic approach to human rights and seeks a bill of rights
> that will guarantee to the individual both 'freedom and bread'. It is aware that
> the failure to meet the basic social and economic needs of the majority of
> South Africans will undoubtedly spell doom for any future government. It is

conscious of the fact that the mere removal of every vestige of apartheid from the statute book, though absolutely necessary, and the guarantee of civil and political rights alone, would not suffice.[4]

Two hundred years after the French Revolution, South Africa was undergoing its own revolution from colonialism and apartheid to twentieth-century democracy. In a paper presented at the International Conference on the Bicentenary of the Rights of Man and the Citizen, organised by UNESCO in Paris in 1989, Kader Asmal similarly explained that colonialism and apartheid with its Bantustans mocked the notion of self-determination and said that the will of South Africans was to 'create a single African nation' which gave expression to the rich cultures and aspirations of South Africa's people. Therefore:

> The achievement of popular sovereignty in the context of national oppression ... presupposes more than the mere incorporation or integration into an existing political structure, as the civil rights thesis would imply. It presupposes restoration of usurped land and wealth, an end to national humiliation in all its forms, an affirmation of the culture and personality of the oppressed. A return to the structures of the past when society has moved on would be a negation of the right to control one's own destiny, which is set in the present.

Asmal ended by explaining that 'Precisely how the goals of national liberation should be attained is a matter which would have to be left to the new sovereignty'.[5] *Dear Comrade President* deals only with the first phase of this remarkable ten-year journey between 1986 and 1996. Phases two and three deserve their own books and historians so that more of the texture, nuances and simple details of these times are known. As historians such as Christopher Saunders have pointed out, there is an almost complete dearth of serious scholarship on how South Africa's new constitutional order was brought into being.[6] His words point to the need for a new generation of historians, political scientists and lawyers to start writing about and engaging with the stories of these different phases. Valuable material in the form of a complete set of documents and transcripts of tapes about the negotiation and Constitutional Assembly processes will soon become available through the ambitious Constitution Hill Trust project, which will enable multiple experiences and voices to be presented in a variety of different formats.

When the full stories of the constitution-making process come to be written, it will be seen that although the Constitution Committee continued to have a significant role after its return from exile, other structures became pre-eminent. It will also be noted that the respect enjoyed by the constitutional planners who'd endured the hard years in Lusaka from 1986 to 1990 was well demonstrated at the ANC's first national conference on South African soil in three decades, held in Durban in July 1991. Eighty-six per cent of the roughly two thousand voting delegates voted Pallo Jordan in at number five, and he was joined (in order) by new members Albie Sachs, Dullah Omar, Kader Asmal and Zola Skweyiya from the Constitution Committee. The younger generation of Penuell Maduna, Brigitte Mabandla and Mathews Phosa would move up later.

Soon after the Durban conference, the new NEC, headed by Nelson Mandela, set up a Negotiations Commission to serve as the engine room for the ANC's preparations and strategising in the new era of negotiations. Cyril Ramaphosa and his colleague from the pre-1990 MDM core leadership Mohammed Valli Moosa were made chairperson and secretary. This meant they were charged with leading the operational aspects of negotiations. All other nine members were leaders from exile. Represented here were MK's Joe Modise and Joe Slovo; underground Vula commander Mac Maharaj; Jacob Zuma and Joe Nhlanhla from intelligence; Barbara Masekela and Baleka Mbete-Kgositsile from the specifically identified women's constituency; Thabo Mbeki; and another younger leader and former Tambo aide, Joel Netshitenzhe. According to coordinator Mohammed Valli Moosa, the Negotiations Commission met 'more than 200 times between February 1992 and the first democratic elections on 27 April 1994', providing 'regular written reports' to the NWC and also bringing out a Negotiations Bulletin to 'publicly confirm the ANC's positions' and 'report on progress'.[7]

The new Negotiations Commission was, in effect, a beefed-up version of the NWC subcommittee set up in Lusaka in 1986, supplemented by people from the old coordinating structures. Joe Slovo was still there, providing continuity, but Jordan, who had played the link between the Constitution Committee and the leadership as administrative secretary to the NEC, was not on it.

The Constitution Committee, which had in exile reported to Tambo and the NWC subcommittee, now reported to this Negotiations Commission. This new commission also took reports and representations from the political structures of the ANC and its alliance partners, as the pool of inputs on home soil expanded massively to include ANC regions and community and special-interest groups. The Negotiations Commission, as the NWC working committee had done in Lusaka, then reported up to the ANC NWC and NEC, where the strategic decisions were taken.

Nelson Mandela, Walter Sisulu, Cyril Ramaphosa, Thabo Mbeki and other top officials became *ex officio* members of the new Negotiations Commission, which indicates that the reporting lines in the constitution-making and negotiations process were clearly established for the key strategic battles to come in the next two and a half years. It was this period of work inside South Africa that would constitute phase two in the making of the Constitution after the Lusaka years described in this book.

Constitution Committee members Zola Skweyiya, Penuell Maduna and Mathews Phosa were brought on to the Negotiations Commission to cement the traditional link in what would be a vastly expanded brief. Kader Asmal and Albie Sachs were regularly invited to contribute and attend. The five now found themselves involved at all three levels – NEC, Negotiations Commission and Constitution Committee. Thus, while the Constitution Committee carried on as an out-of-sight think tank, its members played key roles in different capacities in the bigger negotiations and constitution-making structures. The subsequent careers of Zola and Lewis Thembile Skweyiya, Mabandla, Maduna, Omar, Asmal, Phosa, Pekane, Haysom, Chaskalson, Langa, Sachs and Mokgoro – constituting five cabinet ministers, a provincial premier, a senior figure at the UN, three ambassadors and five justices of the Constitutional Court – underlined the point.

Parliament and the president set up the new Constitutional Court in 1994 to both certify the Constitution and to ensure that from then on South Africa would be governed by the democratic rule *of* law rather than by the undemocratic rule *by* law of the colonial and apartheid periods. At their first meeting, sitting on borrowed chairs in temporary accommodation, the justices unanimously decided to advise counsel to dispense with addressing them as 'My Lord' or 'My Lady'. They made several other egalitarian decisions: that seating of the judges should not be based on hierarchy and seniority, and in court should rotate, save that the chief justices and deputy chief justices should remain at the centre to preside over the hearings; that the eye level of counsel standing should be the same as that of the judges seated; that the logo of the court should not be based on imported heraldry or the figure of a blindfolded woman holding the scales of justice, but should rather depict justice under a tree, the traditional African way of settling disputes; and that the Constitutional Court building should not be austere and forbidding but warm and friendly. They went on to choose the site of the Old Fort Prison, redolent of African pain and struggle for justice, as the permanent home of the court.[8] They did not loudly use the language of decolonisation. They went ahead and created a decolonised home for the court. Among their decisions that went on to achieve world renown were those dealing with capital punishment, the rights to housing and to health, same-sex marriages, prisoners' right to vote, and living customary law. Its decisions in holding the president to account placed it firmly in the spotlight.

As the above indicated, democracy and the new Constitution became institutionalised and brought many benefits to South Africans, starting with six free and fair general elections, presidents stepping down when they knew Parliament would reject them, and government stepping aside to let the opposition govern when it lost independently verified local and provincial elections. The new state implemented policies and measures to affect historical redress on multiple levels. One of these was a new system of social grant protection, which was extended to some fifteen million people under minister Zola Skweyiya, former member of the Constitution Committee. South Africans openly speak their minds through song, comedy, theatre, art and social media, as well as through political parties and civil society movements. There is a robust critical media and strong investigative journalists and a bold judiciary. Books are not banned. South Africans are not detained without trial. The country does not have states of emergency, even when there is an emergency. There is no death sentence. Same-sex couples can openly express their love. These are not trivial things. They are all connected with the Constitution – and by now most of these new protections are simply taken for granted by the citizenry.

When Teddy Pekane died in 2016, the Johannesburg church where his funeral took place was packed with his old-time comrades. In a poignant gesture, former members of MK's Luthuli Detachment formed a guard of honour around his coffin as his biological and ANC family paid tribute.[9] Zola Skweyiya tried to get the SABC to cover Pekane's funeral. The broadcaster, however, was under the control of the state capture faction of a by now divided ANC, deeply saturated with corruption. It decided that the passing of one of the shapers of the Constitution 'is not news' and did not send a reporter. In response to this lack of interest, Skweyiya said in his eulogy that 'Our history must not be written in sand. It must be inscribed in stone.'[10]

South Africa and the public mood in the 2020s are very different than in the 1990s. Those upbeat moments seem far away. The country is troubled, facing multiple crises. People across the board are angered by revelations of state capture, coupled with daily experiences of governmental failure. The idea of constitutional democracy has received a bashing – an unsettling turbulence has come about through a confluence of two completely different streams. The one has its deep origins in the fact that democracy has not distributed its benefits widely enough to meet the needs of the marginalised majority. Poverty and inequality remain endemic. As Professor William Gumede of the School of Governance at Wits University has noted, '[w]ithout fixing broken governance, an equitable and peaceful society is not possible'.[11] The source of the other is that those involved in the very process of state capture and corruption that contributed to the breakdown seek to achieve impunity through undermining the efficacy of the rule of law and law enforcement, in particular by denigrating the courts and Constitution. The result is that South Africans now live in a time of great public anger and loudly divisive national debate triggered by widespread corruption and manifest failures of the ANC in government to fulfil its undertakings to ensure a better life for all. Past and present members of the organisation are among those from many sectors of society involved in the denunciations of corruption and incompetence.

At the centre of the debate is the Constitution. Has it been a doorway to the full achievement of human freedom and happiness in South Africa, or has it been an obstacle to change? The young and the excluded are asking questions. As part of the 'epistemic disobedience' that accompanied the Rhodes Must Fall and Black Lives Matter student protests from 2015 onwards, decolonial inter-pretations gained strength. Does the Constitution have an African philosophical grounding, or is it stuck in fossilised Western modernist and authoritarian Eastern European frameworks and complacency? Is the Constitution, fitted to capitalism's purpose – rather than the poorly performing government and political classes – the reason why systemic inequality and exclusion persist? Young social scientists are posing the question of how 'the *human*' was conceptualised in the Constitution and interrogating humanist notions that underpin it, such as 'dignity, ownership, freedom, self-expression and equality'. Does its human rights emphasis help main-tain rather than disrupt old colonial and apartheid power relations? Does it allow for the voices and aspirations of the poor and colonised 'other' to find expression?[12] Would it not be better to have a popular-will parliamentary democracy rather than the legal restraints of constitutional democracy? Which invites an immediate counter question: but then how do you protect the security and rights of citizens against the kind of impoverishing populism and misgovernance associated with state capture?

A Constitution cannot build houses, create wealth, and ensure ethics, account-ability and delivery on its own. But knowing how it was fought for and shaped, how the words in it came to be written, enables people themselves to take respon-sibility for the future. It is right that these questions are posed. There is no other way than to continue generations-old struggles to create dignity and safety from harassment, fear and deprivation for people in a country burdened by history. Healthy critique can benefit a political system and constitution rooted in struggles for change. This book is intended to help provide some historical context to cur-rent debates. Without an understanding of the formative 1980s thinking described here, and the deep century-old intellectual and struggle networks and traditions that underpinned it, it is not possible for such debates to reach the critical depth they need to.

This book, then, provides an explanatory framework for understanding how African agency shaped the transition from apartheid to self-determination and democracy, how the first steps in the making of the Constitution were taken, and what views underlay the template put in place. It argues that the decade-long process that started in the backrooms off Cha Cha Cha and Cairo Roads in Lusaka was rich, complex, multidimensional and ultimately inspiring. That the way in which South Africans constructed and formalised, politically and legally, a counter-hegemonic vision and a new constitutional order for South Africa is a remarkable story of African imagination, intellect, sacrifice and struggle, and of success – even political genius – against huge odds, including having to prise loose the suffocating (systemic) tentacles of three centuries of dispossession and having to overcome superpower hostility.

In facing the often-frightening challenges of the present, this past needs to be engaged with and understood. Let us not forget or dismiss the remarkable journey that brought South Africa its modern political order. Likewise, in recognising the achievements of the past, it is necessary to look straight-eyed at the challenges of the present, not gloss over them, or ignore the poverty – in economic terms, and of leadership, governance, attitudes and behaviour – that litters the landscape of South Africa today.

The sometimes almost anti-intuitive reflections of Pallo Jordan's in his *Letters to My Comrades*, the writings of actors like Oliver Tambo and Ivy Matsepe-Casaburri – examining the women's question at the 1988 and 1989 seminars – and the imaginings of a recuperating Albie Sachs in *The Soft Vengeance of a Freedom Fighter* on what it would take to be fully human in a future South Africa remind us of the wealth of this legacy.[13] Critical thinking, literature, culture, internationalism, African inventiveness and courageous action were all part of the indigenous constitutional tradition since its inception in the 1880s.

As the historian and prominent legal figure Tembeka Ngcukaitobi has noted: 'Let us never forget: The South African constitution is written in blood'. And, he adds, 'By recalling the true origins of constitutionalism in our country, we can make sense of the Constitution's promise and it can – perhaps once again – play its redemptive role.'[14]

Appendix

Provisional list of ANC members involved in drawing up the Constitutional Guidelines, 1986–1989, comprising the Constitution Committee, the NEC and known delegates to the March 1988 and December 1989 In-House Seminars. (Some 100 names still missing and others from handwritten attendance registers still subject to correction.)

Jaya Appalraju, Kader Asmal, Page Boikanyo, Thami Bolani, F. Boza, George Chaane, Chiselenga C Charles, Louise Colvin (nom de guerre Angela Brown), Gemma Cronin, Benny Nato de Bruyn, Rob Davies, Ann Davis, Frans Dibakwana, Sipho M. Dlamini, Steve Dlamini, Zanele Dhlamini-Mbeki, Patrick Fitzgerald, Sonwabo Eddie Funde, Frene Ginwala, Reverend Fumanekile 'Ncutshe' Gqiba, Nolulamo 'Lulu' Gwagwa, Mzimkulu Gwentshe, Chris Hani, Ntozintle 'Jobs' Jobodwana, David Johannes, D. Johnson, Z. Pallo Jordan, Ronnie Kasrils, Captain Lerole, Barry Levinrad, Hermanus Loots (James Stuart), Brigitte Mabandla, Edwin Mabitsela (Mabitse), Martin Mabiletsa, Stan Mabizela, Tiksie Mabizela, Lindiwe Mabuza, Penuell M. Maduna, Tebogo Mafolo (Dan Cindi), Ben Magunya, Mac Maharaj, Sipho Majombozi, Simon Makana, Johnny Makatini, Cassius Make, Henry Makgothi, Jimmy Makgoti, Herbert Malinga, Z. Mamba, Jan Mampane (Reddy Mazimba), P. Manana, Robert Manci, Mavivi Manzini, Tessa Marcus, Barbara Masekela, Nathaniel Masemola, Andrew Masondo, Ivy Matsepe (later Matsepe-Cassaburi), Thabo Mbeki, Rufus Mbekini or Mbileni, Baleka Mbete-Kgositsile, Tito Mboweni, Patricia McFadden, Francis Meli, Peter Mfene, Ralph Mgijima, Nelson Miya, Sikose Mji, Max Mlonyeni, M. Mnvamana, Billy Modise, Joe Modise, Yolise Modise (nee Bokwe), Ben Mokoena, Jackie Molefe, Ruth Mompati, Anthony Mongalo, Victor Moshe, Susan Mnumzana, Max Moabe, U. Mokebi, Moatsi Mokhali, Ben Mokoena, Pappie Moloto, Motlalepale Moloto, A. Moray, Ivy More, D. Mosupeti, Mojo Motaung, Monica Mosia, Walter Motaung, Mpho Motsamai, Zakes Motse, Solly Mpoli, Antonio Mqhawe, Dr Makhosazana 'Khosi' Msimang, Mendi Msimang, Thenjiwe Mtintso, Prem Naicker, Saeeda Naidoo, S. Ndaba, Thomas Ndhlela (Tom Moyane), Don Ngubeni, Thami Ngwevela, Joe Nhlanhla, Mavis Nhlapo, M.Winchi Njobe, Mandise Njobe, John Nkadimeng, Thomas Nkobi, R. Nkuku, Thembi Nobadula, Ben Nqunye, Lobster

Ntabeni, Alfred Nzo, Tony O'Dowd, Aziz Pahad, Shadrack Lehloehonholo 'Teddy' Pekane, Girlie Pikoli, Vusumzi Pikoli, Mzwai Piliso, Goitsimolimo Leonard Pitso (Barney McKay or Mackay), Matthews Phosa (Freddie Dlamini), A. Qono, Miranda Qwanyashe, Albie Sachs, Yusuf Saloojee, Mpho Seboko, Patrick Seboko, Mpho Sefate, Mpho Sejako, Jackie Selebi, Reg September, Sizakele Sigxashe, Gertrude Shope, Lyndall Shope-Mafole, Solly Simelane, Jack Simons, Ray Simons, Max Sisulu, Zola Skweyiya (Zola Bona), Joe Slovo, Solly Smith, Themba Thabethe, Oliver Tambo, Lucy Thandeni, Dan Tloome, Manto Tshabalala-Msimang, Steve Tshwete, Miranda Vilakazi, T. Williams, Jacob Zuma.

Notes

ACKNOWLEDGEMENTS

1. See S. Forman and A. Odendaal (eds.), *A Trumpet from the Housetops: The selected writings of Lionel Forman* (London: Zed Press, Athens: Ohio University Press and Cape Town: David Philip, 1992).

2. For the books written by Sachs, see *The Jail Diary of Albie Sachs* (London: Harvill Press, 1966); *Stephanie on Trial* (London: Harvill Press, 1968); *Justice in South Africa* (Berkeley: University of California Press, 1973); *Sexism and the Law*, with Joan Hoff Wilson (Oxford: Martin Robertson, 1978); *Island in Chains*, with Indres Naidoo (Harmondsworth: Penguin, 1982); *Liberating the Law, Liberating the People*, with Gita Honwana Welch (London: Zed Press, 1990); *The Soft Vengeance of a Freedom Fighter* (London: Grafton Books, 1990 and Oakland: University of California Press, 2014, with new preface and epilogue); *Protecting Human Rights in a New South Africa* (Cape Town: Oxford University Press, 1991); *Advancing Human Rights in South Africa* (Oxford: Oxford University Press, 1992); *The Free Diary of Albie Sachs*, with Vanessa September (Johannesburg: Random House, 2004); *The Strange Alchemy of Life and Law* (New York: Oxford University Press, 2009); *We, the People: Insights of an Activist Judge* (Johannesburg: Wits University Press, 2016); *Oliver Tambo's Dream* (Cape Town: African Lives, 2018).

INTRODUCTION

1. UWC/RIM Mayibuye Archives, Albie Sachs Collection, MCH91-31-1-4a: Minutes, Constitution Commission [Committee], Lusaka, 8 January 1986, p. 2.

2. Albie Sachs interview with Penuell Maduna, Johannesburg, 29 April 2019, 00:44:11:08 – 00:46:28:01.

3. M. Sparg, J. Schreiner and G. Ansell (eds.), *Comrade Jack: The Political Lectures and Diary of Jack Simons, Novo Catengue* (Johannesburg, STE Publishers, 2001), p. 113.

4. UFH, NAHECS, ANC Archives, LM/021/0154/11, 'Letter to participants', 'Seminar objectives' and 'Programme', [no date].

5. C. Saunders, 'The Making of Democratic South Africa's Constitution: A Critical Literature Review', Commissioned by ASCAROL, Cape Town, 2016, p. 1.

6. See L. Callinicos, *Oliver Tambo: Beyond the Ngele Mountains* (David Philip, Cape Town, 2015), Chapters 16–18; M. Gevisser, *Thabo Mbeki: The Dream Deferred* (Johannesburg: Jonathan Ball, 2007), Chapters 32–33; SADET (eds.), *The Road to Democracy in South Africa*, Vol. 4 [1980–1990], Parts 1 and 2 (Pretoria: UNISA Press, 2010), pp. 63–132; David Welsh, *The Rise and Fall of Apartheid* (Johannesburg: Jonathan Ball, 2009), Chapters 9–11; T. Simpson, *History of South Africa: From 1902 to the Present* (Cape Town: Penguin, 2021), Chapters 18–22.

7. Interview with Brigitte Mabandla, Johannesburg, 6 October 2019.

8. J. Dugard, *Confronting Apartheid: A Personal History of South Africa, Namibia and Palestine* (Auckland Park: Jacana, 2018), p. 133.

9. N. Mandela, *Long Walk to Freedom: The Autobiography of Nelson Mandela* (Abacus: London, 1994), p. 640; A. Pahad, *Insurgent Diplomat: Civil Talks or Civil War?* (Johannesburg: Penguin, 2014), p. 215.

10. See, for example, the following writings by the author: 'The Development of African Organisational Politics in South Africa, with Particular Emphasis on the Responses of Africans to the Process of Unification' (MA dissertation, University of Stellenbosch, 1980); 'African Political Mobilisation in the Eastern Cape, 1880–1910' (PhD dissertation, University of Cambridge, 1983); *Vukani Bantu! The Beginnings of Black Protest Politics in South Africa to 1912* (Cape Town: David Philip, 1984 and Totowa: Barnes and Noble, 1984); '*Mayibuye iAfrika Nakwimbali Yelizwe*: Towards Decolonising the History of Early African Politics in South Africa' (departmental seminar, Department of History, University of South Africa, June 1984); 'Power in Print', *City Press* (Sunday edition), 11 November 1984; '"History is on our side": Historical Perspectives on Constitutional Change and African Responses in South Africa' in *The Political Economy of Race* (Institute for Social Development, UWC, 1985); 'Liberalism and the African National Congress' (paper presented at the Conference on Liberalism in South Africa, Houw Hoek Inn, 30 June – 3 July 1986); 'South Africa's Black Victorians: Sport and Society in South Africa in the Nineteenth Century', in J.A. Mangan (ed.), *Pleasure, Profit, Proselytism: British Culture and Sport at Home and Abroad, 1700–1914* (London: Cass, 1988); also published in *Africa Perspective*, new series 1(7/8) 1989 and in *The Societies of Southern Africa in the 19th and 20th Centuries*, Vol. 15, collected seminar papers no. 38 (University of London, Institute of Commonwealth Studies, 1990); *The Story of an African Game: Black Cricketers and the Unmasking of One of Cricket's Greatest Myths, South Africa, 1850–2003* (Cape Town: New Africa Books and Human Sciences Research Council, 2003); *The Founders: The Origins of the ANC and the Struggle for Democracy in South Africa* (Auckland Park: Jacana, 2012; and Lexington: University Press of Kentucky, 2013); A. Odendaal, K. Reddy, C. Merrett and J. Winch, *Cricket and Conquest: The History of South African Cricket Retold*, Vol. 1, 1795–1914 (Cape Town: Best Red/Human Sciences Research Council, 2016); '"Native Lives" Behind *Native Life*: Intellectual and Political Influences on the ANC and Democratic South Africa' in S.J. Remington, B. Willan and B. Peterson (eds.), *Sol Plaatje's Native Life in South Africa: Past and Present* (Johannesburg: Wits University Press, 2016); and 'Lived Experience, Active Citizenry and South African Intellectual History: Reflections on a Colloquium on "The intellectual heritage and inherited values of the Eastern Cape"', in *Transformation: Critical Perspectives on Southern Africa*, No. 97, 2018.

11. See 'Part of a Global Dialogue' in Odendaal, *The Founders*, Chapter 25.

12. Odendaal, *The Founders*, Chapter 42.

13. D.D.T. Jabavu and C.W. Manona (trans.), *In India and East Africa/E-Indiya nase East Africa: A Travelogue in isiXhosa and English*, edited by T. Steiner, M.W. Jadezweni, C. Higgs and E.M. Mwangi (Johannesburg: Wits University Press, 2020), pp. 35–6.

14. T. Karis and G. Carter (eds.), *From Protest to Challenge: A Documentary History of African Politics in South Africa, 1882–1964*, Vol. 2, Hope and Challenge, 1935–1952 (Stanford: Hoover Institution Press, 1973), pp. 217–18.

15. See *Fighting Talk*, Vol. 15, No. 3, April 1961, pp. 2–3.

16. See Odendaal, '"Native Lives" behind *Native Life*', pp. 131–2.

17. Z. Jolobe, 'Getting to CODESA: An Analysis of Why Multi-Party Negotiations in South Africa Began, 1984–1991' (PhD dissertation, University of Cape Town, 2014), p. 168.

18. Callinicos, *Oliver Tambo*, p. 619.

CHAPTER 1: THE 'COUNCIL OF WAR' AT KABWE

1. 'Opening statement of Comrade President Oliver Tambo' in *Documents of the Second National Consultative Conference of the African National Congress, Zambia, 16–23 June, 1985* (London, ANC, no date), p. 4.

2. For details, see J. Smith and B. Tromp, *Hani: A Life Too Short* (Johannesburg: Jonathan Ball, 2009), Chapter 7; H. Macmillan, *Chris Hani: A Jacana Pocket Biography* (Auckland Park: Jacana, 2014), Chapter 4; G. Houston and J. Ngculu, *Voices of Liberation: Chris Hani* (Cape Town: HSRC Press, 2014), pp. 17–19, 75–83.

3. See A. Odendaal, 'Resistance, Reform and Repression in South Africa in the 1980s' in O. Badsha, G. Mendel and P. Weinberg (eds.), *Beyond the Barricades: Popular Resistance in South Africa in the 1980s: Photographs by Twenty South African Photographers* (London: Kliptown Books, 1989); A. Odendaal, 'The Liberation Struggle in South Africa, 1948–1994' in Y.N. Seleti (ed.), *Africa Since 1990* (Cape Town: New Africa Education, 2004), pp. 180–90.

4. For details, see 'Gross Violations of Human Rights Committed in ANC Ranks and in Exile' in *Truth and Reconciliation Commission of South Africa Report* (Cape Town: TRC, 1998), Vol. 2, pp. 347–66.

5. A.L. Sachs and A. Dodd edit, Cape Town, 10 September 2020.

6. J. Ancer, *Spy: Uncovering Craig Williamson* (Auckland Park: Jacana, 2017), pp. 190–92.

7. Evidence of H. Phahle to the HRV hearing in Alexandra, 30 October 1996, TRC original report, Vol. 6, p. 122. sabctrc.saha.org.za/reports/volume6/section2/chapter4/subsection2.htm?t=%2BGaborone+%2Braid&tab=report. Accessed February 2019.

8. J. Mattison, *God, Spies and Lies: Finding South Africa's Future Through its Past* (Vlaeberg: Missing Ink, 2015), pp. 213–18.

9. Ancer, *Spy*, pp. 191–2.

10. *Medu* is a Sepedi word meaning 'roots'.

11. S. Manong, *If We Must Die: An Autobiography of a Former Commander of uMkhonto we Sizwe* (Nkululeko Publishers, 2015), p. 233.

12. C. Nqakula, *The People's War: Reflections of an ANC Cadre* (Johannesburg: Mutloatse Arts Heritage Trust, 2017), p. 14.

13. Ibid., p. 23.

14. For lists of attendees, registration forms and NEC nomination lists, see UWC/RIM Mayibuye Archives, ANC Papers, MCH01-45-1, 2 and 3.

15. H. Macmillan, *The Lusaka Years: The ANC in Exile in Zambia, 1963 to 1994* (Auckland Park: Jacana, 2013), pp. 166, 188–90.

16. Manong, *If We Must Die*, p. 233.

17. 'Political report of the National Executive Committee' in *Documents of the Second National Consultative Conference*, pp. 11–13, 17–18.

18. B. Magubane with M. Mzamane, *Bernard Magubane: My Life and Times* (Scottsville: University of KwaZulu-Natal Press, 2010), p. 304.

19. 'Communiqué of the second ANC National Consultative Conference' in *Documents of the Second National Consultative Conference*, p. 39.

20. 'The ANC is with you. Call to the People of South Africa', in *Documents of the Second National Consultative Conference*, p. 47.

21. 'Press conference, Lusaka, 25 June 1985', in *Documents of the Second National Consultative Conference*, p. 42.

22. Nqakula, *The People's War*, p. 32.

23. 'The ANC is with you. Call to the People of South Africa', in *Documents of the Second National Consultative Conference*, p. 47.

24. UFH NAHECS, ANC Archives, LSM/014/0053/03: 'Typed report from the Commission on Strategy and Tactics [1985]', p. 5.

25. H. Klug, 'ANC Constitutional Committee, 1985–1995' (Chapter 3 of unpublished manuscript, 2018), p. 1.

26. See K. Asmal and A. Hadland, with M. Levy, *Politics in My Blood: A Memoir* (Auckland Park: Jacana, 2011), Chapter 4, especially pp. 91–8.

27. Nqakula, *The People's War*, p. 20.

28. Ibid.

29. UFH, NAHECS, ANC Archives, LSM/014/0053/02: ANC National Consultative Conference June 1985: Reports of the Commission on National Structures, Constitutional Guidelines and Codes of Conduct, p. 7. Also quoted in Nqakula, *The People's War*, p. 20.

30. UFH, NAHECS, ANC Archives, LSM/014/0053/02: ANC National Consultative Conference June 1985: Reports of the Commission on National Structures, Constitutional Guidelines and Codes of Conduct, p. 15.

31. UFH, NAHECS, ANC Archives, LSM/014/0053/04: Report of the Commission on Cadre Policy and Ideological Work, pp. 13–14.

32. SADET, *The Road to Democracy*, Vol. 4 [1980–1990], Part 2, p. 1007.

33. Macmillan, *The Lusaka Years*, p. 137.

34. UFH, NAHECS, ANC Archives, LSM/014/0053/04, Report of the Commission on Cadre Policy and Ideological Work, pp. 12–13.

35. 'Political report of the National Executive Committee' in *Documents of the Second National Consultative Conference*, pp. 35–6.

36. Ibid., p. 36.

37. Ibid., p. 36.

38. 'Conference communiqué' in *Documents of the Second National Consultative Conference*, p. 39.

39. Albie Sachs Papers (home): Sachs interview with Maduna, April 2019, 0035:37:00 – 00:39:32:05.

40. See also *Selected Writings on the Freedom Charter: A Sechaba Commemorative Publication* (London: ANC, 1985).

41. 'Conference, communiqué' in *Documents of the Second National Consultative Conference*, p. 41.

42. Ibid., p. 42.

43. 'Press conference, Lusaka, 25 June 1985' in *Documents of the Second National Consultative Conference*, p. 43.

CHAPTER 2: 'WILL COMRADE KING SABATA PLEASE COME TO THE MICROPHONE'

1. See Nqakula, *The People's War*, pp. 63–4.

2. For a full account of this remarkable early period of regional and national mobilisation, see Odendaal, *The Founders*. Chapters 20–21 and 32 show the direct role that the early SANC played in helping to shape a new national movement from the 1890s onwards.

3. J. Opland and A. Nyamende (eds.), *Isaac Williams Wauchope: Selected Writings, 1874–1916* (Cape Town: Van Riebeeck Society, Second Series no. 39, 2008), pp. 164–9.

4. Odendaal, *The Founders*, pp. 135–6.

5. Ibid., pp. 83–5, 135–6, 200–203.

6. Ibid., pp. 16, 83–6, 136, 152–3, 201–3, 382, 461.

7. X. Mangcu, *Mandela: The Aristocrat and the Revolution* (unpublished manuscript, 2017), Chapters 1, 4.

8. B. Ngcaweni and S.J. Ndlovu Gatsheni, *Nelson R. Mandela: Decolonial Ethics of Liberation and Servant Leadership* (Trenton USA: Africa World Press, 2018), pp. 1–12.

9. X. Mangcu, 'Mandela: The Untold Heritage', in C. Bundy and W. Beinart (eds.), *Reassessing Mandela* (Auckland Park: Jacana, 2020), Chapter 2, especially p. 74.

10. 'Transkei Opposition Continues' and 'This is Sabata's Constitution', *New Age*, 10 May 1962, pp. 1, 6.

11. 'The Transkei: Battleground Against Apartheid', *Fighting Talk*, Vol. 17, No. 1, January 1963, pp. 2–3.

12. See ibid., p. 3.

13. For Matanzima's persecution of Sabata, as well as his bizarre night-time snatching and burial of Sabata's body when it was returned from Lusaka, see T. Gibbs, *Mandela's Kinsmen: Nationalist Elites and Transkei's First Bantustan* (Auckland Park: Jacana, 2014), pp. 107–10, 137–40.

14. Ibid., p. 109.

15. 'The Transkei: Battleground Against Apartheid', *Fighting Talk*, Vol. 17, No. 1, January 1963, pp. 2–3.

16. Nqakula, *The People's War*, p. 64.

17. Sachs and Dodd edit, September 2020.

18. See L. Calata and A. Calata, *My Father Died for This* (Cape Town: Tafelberg, 2018); and C. Nicholson, *Permanent Removal: Who Killed the Cradock Four?* (Johannesburg: Wits University Press, 2004).

19. Nqakula, *The People's War*, pp. 36–7.

20. Conversation with Dr Peter Mtuze at the Colloquium on Re-thinking South African Canonical Writing and Centring the isiXhosa Writings of the 19th and Early 20th Centuries, Rhodes University, 21–22 June 2018.

21. Nqakula, *The People's War*, p. 70.

22. J.A. Chalmers, *Tiyo Soga: A Page of South African Mission Work* (Edinburgh, 1878).

23. D. Williams, *Umfundisi: A Biography of Tiyo Soga, 1829–1871* (Alice: Lovedale Press, 1978), pp. 33–4.

24. Nqakula, *The People's War*, pp. 104–7.

CHAPTER 3: A NEW DIMENSION OF STRATEGY AND ANALYSIS

1. https://www.washingtonpost.com/archive/politics/1985/09/14/s-african-businessmen-meet-with-exiled-guerrilla-leaders/33; M. Maharaj and Z.P. Jordan, *Breakthrough: The Struggles and Talks that Brought Apartheid South Africa to the Negotiating Table* (Cape Town: Penguin, 2021), pp. 103–5. Feelers for this meeting had already been put out in April of that year.

2. T. Bell, 'South African women's rights activist Phyllis Ntantala-Jordan dies at 96 in the US', *Mail & Guardian*, 20 July 2016, http://mg.co.za/article/2016-07-20-south-african-womens-rights-activist-phyllis-ntantala-jordan-dies-at-96-in-the-us. Accessed 12 January 2017.

3. P. Ntantala, *A Life's Mosaic: The Autobiography of Phyllis Ntantala*, UWC Mayibuye History Series No. 6 (Cape Town: David Philip and Mayibuye Books, 1992), pp. 135–44, 182–3.

4. 'Archibald Campbell Jordan', https;//en.wikipedia.org/wiki/Archibald_Campbell_Jordan. Accessed 12 February 2017.

5. E. van den Bergh and T. Kraan (compilers), *Koekemakranke: Die Pad van Vernie February (1938–2002)* (Leiden: African Studies Centre, 2002).

6. Z. Mda, *Sometimes There Is a Void: Memoirs of an Outsider* (Johannesburg: Penguin, 2011), pp. 8–13.

7. Conversation with Brigalia Bam and Barney Pityana, Hogsback, 8 August 2016.

8. UFH, NAHECS, ANC Archives, O.R. Tambo Papers: Z.P. Jordan, 'Marxism and National Liberation in South Africa: A Review of *Class and Colour in South Africa* by Jack and Ray Simons (unpublished paper, London, March 1970), pp. 1–2. My thanks to Dave Alexander for the copy of this unnumbered document.

9. J. Mosavel, Speech to Suid-Oosterfees, Artscape, Cape Town, 27 April 2017.

10. See W. Pick, *The Slave Has Overcome* (Cape Town: self-published, 2007).

11. See Z.P. Jordan, *Letters to My Comrades: Interventions and Excursions*, compiled by K. Kgositsile and M. Mutloatse, African Lives No. 8 (Auckland Park: Jacana, in association with African Lives, 2017), pp. xi–xv.

12. H. Dolny, *Banking on Change* (Sandton: Viking, 2001), p. 36.

13. As conveyed to the author by Wolfie Kodesh after his return to South Africa.

14. UFH, NAHECS, ANC Archives, LSM/020/0147/01, ANC and SACP brochure in tribute to Ruth First, [1983], pp. 1–25. For more on the South African connection with CEA, see N. Manghezi, *The Maputo Connection: ANC Life in the World of Frelimo* (Auckland Park: Jacana, 2009), pp. 86–94; SADET, *The Road to Democracy in South Africa*, Vol. 5, African Solidarity, Part 2 (Pretoria: UNISA Press, 2014), pp. 758–9.

15. R. Davies, *Towards a New Deal: A Political Economy of the Times of My Life* (Johannesburg: Jonathan Ball, 2021), p. 35.

16. News24, '"Dr" Pallo Jordan: Why I Did It', 24 August 2014. http://www.News24.com/South Africa/Politics/Pallo-Jordan-Why-I-did-it-20140824. Accessed 7 June 2022.

17. UFH, NAHECS, ANC Collection, O.R. Tambo Papers, Box 34, Folder B4.5.3, Z.P. Jordan to O.R. Tambo, 26 July 1985, attaching 'The New Face of Counter-Revolution: A Briefing Paper', p. 12. See also Jordan, *Letters to My Comrades*, pp. 50–74.

18. Jordan, 'The New Face of Counter-Revolution', p. 3.

19. Ibid., p. 7. For aligned views on the relationship between the ANC and the liberal establishment at the time, see also A. Odendaal, 'Liberalism and the African National Congress' (paper presented at the Conference on Liberalism in South Africa, Houw Hoek Inn, 30 June – 3 July 1986), pp. 11–13, 20–23.

20. On Huntington, see also G. Mbeki, *Sunset at Midday, Lathon' ilanga emini* (Bloemfontein: Nolwazi, 1986), Chapter 6; H. Giliomee, *Die Laaste Afrikanerleiers: 'n Opperste Toets van Mag* (Cape Town: Tafelberg, 2012), pp. 186–8, 211–13.

21. Jordan, 'The New Face of Counter-Revolution', p. 10.

22. Ibid., p. 25.

23. Ibid., pp. 25–6.

24. Ibid., p. 26.

25. Ibid., p. 26.

26. Ibid., p. 8.

27. Ibid., p. 11.

28. See section on Jordan in A. Odendaal, 'Lived Experience, Active Citizenry and South African Intellectual History' in *Transformation*, pp. 100–106.

29. For example, despite the title of the book *Democratic Liberalism in SA: Its History and Prospect* edited by J. Butler, R. Elphick and D. Welsh (Middletown, Connecticut: Wesleyan

University Press, 1987), and the contributors taking on the role of intellectual leaders of the liberal project, the book (as Christopher Saunders points out) has not one chapter in it dealing with constitutional options for the future.

30. UFH, NAHECS ANC Collection (on file): O.R. Tambo to NEC members, no date [1985].
31. Macmillan, *The Lusaka Years*, p. 168.
32. UWC/RIM Mayibuye Archives, ANC Papers, MCH01-9-2: Typed report of the second National Consultative Conference of the African National Conference, held in Zambia, 16–23 June 1985, pp. 7, 9.
33. Telephonic interview with Pallo Jordan, Cape Town, 13 August 2021. See also Maharaj and Jordan, *Breakthrough*, pp. 97–9.
34. See Z. Pallo Jordan Collection (on file with author): Pallo Jordan, 'Submission on Negotiations [1985]'; 'A Submission on the Question of Negotiations', Lusaka, 27 November 1985 – Document 129 in G.M. Gerhart and C.L. Glaser, *From Protest to Challenge: A Documentary History of African Politics in South Africa, 1882–1990*, Vol. 6: Challenge and Victory, 1980–1990 (Auckland Park: Jacana, 2013), pp. 589–92.
35. Jordan, 'Submission on Negotiations', p. 2.
36. 'A Submission on the Question of Negotiations', in Gerhart and Glaser, *From Protest to Challenge*, Vol. 6, p. 589.
37. Jordan, 'Submission on Negotiations', pp. 2–4.
38. Ibid., p. 6. See pp. 3–4, 8 and 'A Submission on the Question of Negotiations' in Gerhart and Glaser, *From Protest to Challenge*, Vol. 6, p. 592, for the comparative international assessments.
39. Jordan, 'Submission on Negotiations', p. 8.
40. 'A Submission on the Question of Negotiations', in Gerhart and Glaser, *From Protest to Challenge*, Vol. 6, pp. 591–2.
41. For one paper already produced on a key subject by the ANC research team working with Jordan, see Pallo Jordan Collection: Z.P. Jordan to A. Odendaal, 24 October 2021, attaching ANC Department of Research, 'Operationalising the Economic Clauses of the Freedom Charter'. This provides insight into the thinking in the NEC at the time on the future economy and the land issue.
42. Jordan, 'Submission on Negotiations', p. 10.
43. UFH, NAHECS, ANC Collection, O.R. Tambo Papers, Box 34, Folder B4.5.3: Z.P. Jordan to O.R. Tambo, 26 July 1985.
44. Gerhart and Glaser, *From Protest to Challenge*, Vol. 6, p. 592. For possible reasons for Mbeki's absence, see the partial picture painted in Gevisser, *Thabo Mbeki*, pp. 533, 535.
45. In their book, *Breakthrough*, Maharaj and Jordan refer to this committee headed by Jack Simons as the Constitutional Commission, and though the minutes of its first meeting use the same designation, Tambo there gave it the name Constitution Committee, which it used without exception for the next few years. In my opinion, the Constitutional Commission more accurately applies to the NEC's own sub-committee headed by Jordan, which supervised the work of the Constitution Committee.
46. Jordan, 'Submission on Negotiations', p. 11.

CHAPTER 4: A HISTORIC GATHERING IN A
BUILDER'S YARD OFF A SANITARY LANE IN LUSAKA

1. UWC/RIM Mayibuye Archives, ANC Papers, MCH01-26-3: Message of the NEC of the ANC on the occasion of 8th January 1986, delivered by comrade president O.R. Tambo.

2. Personal communication with Luyanda Mpahlwa, Robben Island Museum Memorial Lecture, 18 July 2018.
3. UWC/RIM Mayibuye Archives, Albie Sachs Collection, MCH91-31-1-4a: Minutes, Constitution Commission [Committee], 8 January 1986, p. 1; UCT, Jack Simons Papers, BC1081, P25.1: ANC Constitution Committee report to the NEC, 16 January 1986.
4. UCT, Jack Simons Papers, BC1081, P25.1: ANC Constitution Committee report to the NEC, 16 January 1986; UWC/RIM Mayibuye Archives, Albie Sachs Collection, MCH91-103-6: A. Sachs, Third annual Ruth First lecture – Part II: Towards the reconstruction of South Africa – The constitutional dimension, 27 September 1985.
5. UCT, Jack Simons Papers, BC1081, P25.1: ANC Constitution Committee report to the NEC, 16 January 1986.
6. UWC/RIM Mayibuye Archives, Albie Sachs Collection, MCH91-31-1-4a: Minutes, Constitution Commission [Committee], 8 January 1986, p. 1. In addition to the formal minutes, see also Jack Simons' handwritten notes in UCT, Jack Simons Papers, BC1081, P25.1: 'Constitution Committee, resume of opening meeting', 9 to 13 January 1986.
7. UWC/RIM Mayibuye Archives, Albie Sachs Collection, MCH91-31-1-4a: Minutes, Constitution Commission [Committee], 8 January 1986, pp. 1–2.
8. Ibid., p. 2.
9. Ibid., p. 7.
10. H. Klug, 'ANC Constitution Committee, 1985–1995' (unpublished draft manuscript, Chapter 3), p. 3. My thanks to Heinz, a partner in ASCAROL's project to research the making of the Constitution, for sharing ideas and material with me – in this case, a page missing from my archival material.
11. UCT, Jack Simons Papers, BC1081, P25.1: 'Constitution Committee, Resume of opening meeting', 9 January 1986.
12. 'Short note for André Odendaal from Ntozintle Jobs Jobodwana', Glenwood Estate, Pretoria', 4 September 2021.
13. See K. Keable, *London Recruits: The Secret War Against Apartheid* (Pontypool, Wales: Merlin Press, 2012), pp. 301–10. Thanks to Pallo Jordan for explaining this link to the garage.

CHAPTER 5: 'KK', 'OR' AND COMRADE JACK

1. Emphasising this deep constitutional tradition, Luthuli grew up in the house of his uncle Martin Lutuli, secretary to Dinuzulu in the 1880s and a founder of the Natal Native Congress in 1900. Matthews was the son-in-law of John Knox Bokwe, the famous composer and leader of the Native Education Association based at Lovedale from the 1860s through to the 1890s, and he was a signatory to the Africans' Claims document in 1942. Matthews proposed the idea of drawing up the Freedom Charter at a Congress of the People in 1955.
2. A. Sachs, *Justice in South Africa* (Berkeley, University of California Press, 1973), p. 213.
3. Sachs and Dodd edit, September 2020.
4. A. Sachs, 'The Quiet South African', in Z.P. Jordan (ed.), *Oliver Tambo Remembered: His Life in Exile* (Johannesburg: Macmillan, 2007), p. 252.
5. R.S. Levine, *A Living Man from Africa: Jan Tzatzoe, Xhosa Chief and Missionary, and the Making of Nineteenth Century South Africa* (New Haven: Yale University Press, 2010), p. 154.
6. Odendaal, *The Founders*, Chapter 25.
7. Z. Jaffer, *The Beauty of the Heart: The Life and Times of Charlotte Maxeke* (Bloemfontein:

Sun Press, 2016); M. McCord, *The Calling of Katie Makanya* (Cape Town: David Philip, 2000), Chapters 1–5.

8. R. Rive and T. Couzens, *Seme: The Founder of the ANC* (Johannesburg: Skotaville Publishers, 1991), p. 71; B. Ngqulunga, *The Man Who Founded the ANC: A Biography of Pixley ka Isaka Seme* (Cape Town: Penguin, 2017), pp. 25, 27–30. See also T. Ngcukaitobi, *The Land is Ours: South Africa's First Black Lawyers and the Birth of Constitutionalism* (Cape Town: Penguin, 2018).

9. See N. Masilela, *An Outline of the New African Movement in South Africa* (Trenton: Africa World Press, 2013); N. Masilela, *The Historical Figures of the New African Movement*, Vol. 1 (Trenton: Africa World Press, 2014).

10. See, for example, P. Abrahams, *The Coyaba Chronicles: Reflections on the Black Experience in the Twentieth Century* (Cape Town: David Philip, 2000).

11. Sparg, Schreiner and Ansell (eds.), *Comrade Jack*, pp. 213–34.

12. Albie Sachs Papers (home): Sachs interview with Maduna, April 2019, 0054:42:00 – 00:56:08:10.

13. H. Macmillan, *Jack Simons: Teacher, Scholar, Comrade* (Auckland Park: Jacana, 2016, 2nd impression), pp. 106–7. See also Sparg, Schreiner and Ansell (eds.), *Comrade Jack*, pp. 111–15.

14. Macmillan, *Jack Simons*, pp. 115–16.

15. Ibid., pp. 73–4.

16. UWC/RIM Mayibuye Archives, Albie Sachs Collection, MCH91-31-1-4a: Minutes, Constitution Commission [Committee], 9 January 1986, p. 4.

17. UWC/RIM Mayibuye Archives: Transcriptions of Albie Sachs interviews with Stanley Sello re: his Albie Sachs Collection (transcribed by Pat Fahrenfort), 2007, Tape 1–1, pp. 10–11.

18. UCT, Jack Simons Papers, BC1081, P25.1: Jack Simons' handwritten notes, 'Constitution Committee, 9 January 1986'.

19. UWC/RIM Mayibuye Archives, Albie Sachs Collection, MCH91-31-1-4a: Minutes, Constitution Commission [Committee], 8 January 1986, p. 7.

CHAPTER 6: THE QUARTET IN SHEKI-SHEKI ROAD: THE CORE OF THE CONSTITUTION COMMITTEE

1. Editorial, 'Saluting Skweyiya', *Cape Times*, 12 April 2018.

2. S. Phaliso, 'Skweyiya's Work on Constitution Recalled', *Cape Times*, 20 April 2018.

3. S. Mfenyana, *Walking with Giants* (Cape Town: South African History Online, 2017), pp. 88–91.

4. Smith and Tromp, *Hani*, pp. 45–58; Macmillan, *Chris Hani*, pp. 25–7.

5. See Skweyiya's profile in http://www.mbeki.org/2018/04/13/statement-of-the-thabo-mbeki-foundation-on-the-passing-of-comrade-zola-themba-skweyiya/; C. Barron, 'Zola Skweyiya ... 1942–2018', *Sunday Times*, 15 April 2018, p. 19; and https://omalley.nelsonmandela.org/omalley/index.php/site/q/03lv00017/04lv00344/05lv00389/06lv00501.htm. Accessed February 2019.

6. Conversation with Ike Mamoe at NAHECS, University of Fort Hare, March 2017.

7. See T. Nthite, 'Another struggle stalwart dies' and editorial on 'Saluting Zola Skweyiya', *Cape Times*, 12 April 2018; Barron, 'Zola Skweyiya', *Sunday Times*, 15 April 2018; obituary by M. Motshekga, *Sunday Independent*, 15 April 2018; obituary by G. Manyya, *City Press*, 22 April 2018.

8. Two interviews form the basis of this profile: Albie Sachs Collection (home): Sachs interview with Maduna, April 2019, 00:01:15:05 – 00:13:55:08; Luli Callinicos Collection: L. Callinicos interview with P. Maduna, Pretoria, 6 June 1994 (transcribed by Mukoni Ratshitanga), pp. 1–3.
9. Callinicos interview with Maduna, 6 June 1994, pp. 1–3.
10. Sachs interview with Maduna, 29 April 2019, time code 01:46:44:00 – 01:50:41:00.
11. Ibid., 00:19:02:08 – 00:22:03:18.
12. Callinicos, *Oliver Tambo*, p. 584; H.W. van der Merwe, *Peacemaking in South Africa: A Life in Conflict Resolution* (Cape Town: Tafelberg, 2000), p. 140.
13. 'Personal Profile: Penuell Maduna, Minister of Justice', http://www.armsdeal-vpo.co.za/special_items/profiles/profile_maduna.html. Accessed 28 April 2018.
14. Odendaal, 'African political mobilisation in the Eastern Cape, 1880–1910', pp. 143, 209–10.
15. Telephonic interview with Z.N. Jobodwana, 29 July 2021, and 'Short note from Ntozintle Jobs Jobodwana', September 2021.
16. See 'Massacre at Maseru: South African Aggression Against Lesotho' (International Defence and Aid Fund, London, 1985, Fact paper on Southern Africa No. 12), pp. 1–36.
17. Telephonic interview with Jobodwana, 29 July 2021.
18. 'Short note from Ntozintle Jobs Jobodwana', September 2021.
19. Ibid.
20. Telephonic interview with Pallo Jordan, 13 August 2021.
21. Sachs and Dodd edit, September 2020.
22. See S. Hayes, 'Ted Pekane – South African freedom fighter, died Dec 2016' (on file). https://groups.google.com/forum/#!topic/soc.culture.south-africa/H_pyR1MEp_8. Accessed 28 July 2021. Quoting from the funeral programme, edited by Elinor Sisulu.
23. S. Hayes, 'Ted Pekane – South African freedom fighter, died Dec 2016'.
24. See UFH, NAHECS, ANC Archives, LSM/014/0053/02: ANC National Consultative Conference June 1985, Report of Commission on National Structures, Constitutional Guidelines and Codes of Conduct, pp. 10–13.
25. Sachs interview with Maduna, 29 April 2019, 00:41:53:00 – 00:41:48:20.
26. Sachs interview with Maduna, 29 April 2019, 00:39:43:05 – 00:42:11:15.
27. 'Short note from Ntozintle Jobs Jobodwana', September 2021.
28. UWC Archives, Kader Asmal Collection, Box 57: African National Congress (SA), DLCA report on the visits to the German Democratic Republic and the Czechoslovak Socialist Republic, prepared by P.M. Maduna, 16 February 1987.
29. 'Short note from Ntozintle Jobs Jobodwana', September 2021.
30. T. Pekane and F. Reyntjens, 'The Realization of the Constitutional Guidelines for a Democratic South Africa', *Afrika Focus*, Vol. 5, Nos. 1–2, 1 March 1989. https://doaj.org/article5of3Od7c18b etc.

CHAPTER 7: THE TWO INSIDERS FROM OUTSIDE LUSAKA
1. UFH, NAHECS, O.R. Tambo Papers, Folder B4.5.3, Box 34: Z.P. Jordan to O.R. Tambo, 26 July 1985.
2. Gordon Metz Collection, 16Y07M21-006: Gordon Metz and André Odendaal interview with Albie Sachs, Clifton, Cape Town, 21 July 2016, transcript, p. 7.
3. Kader and Louise Asmal Papers (home): Kader Asmal curriculum vitae, September 1998; the degree of Doctor of Laws (LLD) honoris causa, Kader Asmal, University of Pretoria

graduation brochure, Pretoria, 12 April 2010; M. Maher, 'One Couple's Crusade to End Apartheid', *The Irish Times*, 20 March 1990; and various other biographical notes.

4. See, for example, Kader and Louise Asmal Papers (home): K. Asmal, 'Representing the African National Congress of South Africa', 'The liquidation of racism and apartheid: An urgent task of our time', meeting of jurists at Baku, Azerbaijan, 11–15 September 1978 (organised by the Association of Soviet Lawyers and the International Association of Democratic Lawyers); draft programme for OAU conference on anti-apartheid and solidarity movements on sanctions against South Africa, Addis Ababa, Ethiopia, 17–20 June 1985.

5. Asmal, Hadland and Levy, *Politics in My Blood*, Chapter 4, especially pp. 91–8.

6. See Kader and Louise Asmal Papers: ANC (SA), 'The legality of the use of force by National Liberation Movements', Lusaka, 5 February 1982.

7. Asmal, Hadland and Levy, *Politics in My Blood*, p. 97; Kader and Louise Asmal Papers: Statement by Mr O.R. Tambo, President of the ANC of SA, on the occasion of the making of the declaration of adherence to the Geneva Conventions, 28 November 1980.

8. Kader and Louise Asmal Papers: J. Bruce to K. Asmal, 25 October 2005, with attachments, including secret report by P. Keating to H.J. McCann, secretary, Department of External Affairs, 23 September 1964; H.J. McCann to Ambassador J.G. Molloy, 7 October 1964; 'Spy tried to bribe me, says Irish author', *Evening Press*, 3 November 1971; D. Mulhall, staff office, University of Dublin to A.K. Asmal, 19 May 1988.

9. Academy of Achievement, Albie Sachs. https://achievement.org/achiever/albie-sachs/. Accessed 5 April 2016.

10. See D. Goldberg, *The Mission: A Life for Freedom in South Africa* (Johannesburg: STE Publishers, 2010), pp. 7–9, 48–51, 59–60.

11. Sachs and Dodd edit, September 2020.

12. A. Sachs and G. Honwana Welch, *Liberating the Law, Liberating the People: Creating Popular Justice in Mozambique* (London: Zed Books, 1990).

13. Sachs and Dodd edit, September 2020.

14. UWC/RIM Mayibuye Archives, Albie Sachs Collection, MCH91-31-1-4a: Minutes, Constitution Commission [Committee], 8 January 1986, pp. 1–3.

15. *Documents of the Second National Consultative Conference of the African National Conference, Zambia 16–23 June 1985*, pp. 28–9, 50. See also the two thirtieth anniversary commemorative publications: *Selected Writings on the Freedom Charter: A Sechaba Commemorative Publication*; and R. Suttner and J. Cronin, *30 Years of the Freedom Charter* (Johannesburg: Ravan Press, 1986).

CHAPTER 8: TRANSLATING THE VISION OF THE FREEDOM CHARTER INTO A CONSTITUTIONAL DOCUMENT

1. UWC/RIM Mayibuye Archives, Albie Sachs Collection, MCH91-31-1-4a: Minutes, Constitution Commission [Committee], [8 and 10 January 1986], composite quote from pp. 3, 11, 12.

2. UWC/RIM Mayibuye Archives, Albie Sachs Collection, MCH91-31-1-4a: Minutes, Constitution Commission [Committee], [10 January 1986], p. 10; MCH91- 31-1-5a: [A. Sachs on behalf of the Constitution Committee], 'The Freedom Charter and the constitution'. Three different drafts of this document exist.

3. UWC/RIM Mayibuye Archives, Albie Sachs Collection, MCH91- 31-1-5a: 'The Freedom Charter and the constitution'. For some light on the views of different members on this

debate about the Charter and a constitution, see Jack Simons' handwritten notes in UCT, Jack Simons Papers, BC1081, P25.1: 'Constitution Committee, resume of opening meeting', 9 January 1986.

4. See Jack Simons' handwritten notes in UCT, Jack Simons Papers, BC1081, P25.1: 'Constitution Committee, resume of opening meeting', 10 January 1986. These notes give more information than the formal minutes about the different speakers in the meeting.

5. UWC/RIM Mayibuye Archives, Albie Sachs Collection, MCH91-31-1-4a: Minutes, Constitution Commission [Committee], [10 January 1986], pp. 10–11.

6. UWC/RIM Mayibuye Archives, Albie Sachs Collection, MCH91- 31-1-5a: 'The Freedom Charter and the constitution'.

7. UCT, Jack Simons Papers, BC1081, P25.1: Handwritten notes, 'Constitution Committee, resume of opening meeting', 9 to 13 January 1986.

8. UWC/RIM Mayibuye Archives, Albie Sachs Collection, MCH91-31-1-4a: Minutes, Constitution Commission [Committee], 8 January 1986, p. 13.

CHAPTER 9: THE SKELETON

1. Sachs and Dodd edit, September 2020.
2. My thanks to Mac Maharaj for this information, gleaned from documents in his possession.
3. Conversation with Albie Sachs, Clifton, 14 May 2018.
4. UWC/RIM Mayibuye Archives, Albie Sachs Collection, MCH91-31-1-5a: 'The Freedom Charter and the constitution'.
5. UWC/RIM Mayibuye Archives, Albie Sachs Collection, MCH91-31-1-2a: [A. Sachs on behalf of the Constitution Committee], 'The preliminary nature of the constitutional document', p. 1.
6. UWC/RIM Mayibuye Archives, Albie Sachs Collection, MCH91-31-1-4a: 'Minutes, Constitution Commission [Committee], 8 January 1986, p. 14.
7. UWC/RIM Mayibuye Archives, Albie Sachs Collection, MCH91-31-1-2a: 'The preliminary nature of the constitutional document', p. 3.
8. UWC/RIM Mayibuye Archives, Albie Sachs Collection, MCH91-31-1-4a: 'Minutes, Constitution Commission [Committee], 14 January 1986, p. 14.
9. For the different headings, see ibid., pp. 14–16.
10. For the Committee's comments on each of these headings, see ibid., pp. 15–16 and MCH91-31-1-2a: 'The preliminary nature of the constitutional document'.
11. UCT, Jack Simons Papers, BC1081, P25.1: Jack Simons' handwritten notes, 'Constitution Committee, 9 January 1986'.
12. UWC/RIM Mayibuye Archives, Albie Sachs Collection, MCH91-31-1-2a: 'The preliminary nature of the constitutional document', pp. 10–14.
13. Ibid., pp. 14–16, Annexure 3 to the minutes.
14. The need for demographic and political surveys was to be a continuing theme. This concern for informed research was to lead to the PASA project and the formation of the Centre for Development Studies at UWC in 1988/1989, as we will see in Chapters 15, 19, 27, 36 and 39–40.
15. UWC/RIM Mayibuye Archives, Albie Sachs Collection, MCH91-31-1-2a: 'The preliminary nature of the constitutional document', pp. 17–18. The quote is from page 18.
16. Ibid., pp. 8–9.
17. Ibid., pp. 8–9.
18. Ibid., pp. 9–10.

CHAPTER 10: JOE SLOVO'S MISGIVINGS

1. UCT, Jack Simons Papers, BC1081, P25.1: Handwritten notes, 'Constitution Committee, resume of opening meeting', 9 January 1986; UWC/RIM Mayibuye Archives, Albie Sachs Collection, MCH91-31-1-4a: 'Minutes, Constitution Commission [Committee], 8 January 1986, p. 3.

2. UCT, Jack Simons Papers, BC1081, P25.1: ANC Constitution Committee Report to the NEC, 16 January 1986.

3. See MCH91-31-1-5a: The Freedom Charter and the constitution', pp. 1–2; MCH91- 31-1-5a: 'Our objectives in drafting a constitution', pp. 1–2; MCH91-31-1-2a: 'The preliminary nature of the constitutional document', pp. 1–18. Sachs wrote all three of these documents on behalf of the Constitution Committee. But, as Jobodwana's minutes and Simons' handwritten notes indicate, the documents reflect the general contributions by the team in its six days of intense deliberations. For handwritten drafts of these documents, see also MCH 91-31-1-5a, 6a and 7a.

4. UWC/RIM Mayibuye Archives, Albie Sachs Collection, MCH91-31-1-4a: Minutes, Constitution Commission [Committee], 14 January 1986, p. 6; UCT, Jack Simons Papers, BC1081, P25.1: Jack Simons' handwritten notes, 'Constitution Committee, resume of opening meeting', 14 January 1986.

5. H. Klug, 'ANC Constitution Committee, 1985–1995' (unpublished draft manuscript, 2017), Chapter 3, citing J. Simons to O.R. Tambo, 14 January 1986; UCT, Jack Simons Papers, BC1081, P25.1: Draft covering letter by Jack Simons for ANC Constitution Committee report to NEC, 16 January 1986.

6. UWC/RIM Mayibuye Archives, Albie Sachs Collection, MCH91-31-1-5a:, 'The Freedom Charter and the constitution'.

7. UWC/RIM Mayibuye Archives, Albie Sachs Collection, MCH91-31-1-2a: 'The preliminary nature of the constitutional document'.

8. UWC/RIM Mayibuye Archives, Albie Sachs Collection MCH91-31-1-5a: [A. Sachs on behalf of the Constitution Committee], 'Our objectives in drafting a constitution'.

9. See UFH, NAHECS, ANC Archives, LSM/014/0053/02: 'National Structures' in ANC National Consultative Conference June 1985: Reports of the Commission on National Structures, Constitutional Guidelines and Codes of Conduct, pp. 1–2.

10. UCT, Jack Simons Papers BC1081, P25.1: 'Report of the NWC sub-committee on the Report of the Constitutional Commission [sic]', no date.

11. https://www.anc.org.za/contentanc-structures-and-personnel-1960-1994.

12. V. Shubin, The Hot 'Cold War': The USSR in Southern Africa (London and Scottsville: Pluto Press and University of KwaZulu-Natal Press, 2008), pp. 256–7.

13. UCT, Jack Simons Papers, BC1081, P25.1: J. Simons' handwritten notes, 16h00, 21 January 1986, pp. 1–2.

14. Ibid., p. 2.

15. Ibid., p. 2.

16. UWC/RIM Mayibuye Archives, Albie Sachs Papers, MCH91, Box 57: First section of the 'Report of the NWC sub committee on the report of the Legal and Constitutional Commission' from Z.P. Jordan (convenor), 23 February 1986, pp. 2–4. See also the second section, 'Discussion in N.W.C.', on pp. 5–6.

17. UCT, Jack Simons Papers, BC1081, P25.2: J. Simons to O.R. Tambo, 27 January 1986.

18. UCT, Jack Simons Papers, BC1081, P25.1: J. Simons to R. Mompati, 30 January 1996.

19. UCT, Jack Simons Papers, BC1081, P25.2: R. Mompati to J. Simons, 30 January 1986.

20. Obituary: 'Mendi Msimang, December 8 1918 to December 3 2018', *City Press*, 9 December 2018, p. 5.
21. https://www.anc.org.za/contentanc-structures-and-personnel-1960-1994.
22. UCT, Jack Simons Papers, BC1081, P25.2: R. Mompati to J. Simons, 7 February 1986.
23. Ibid.
24. Ibid.
25. UCT, Jack Simons Papers, BC1081, P25.2: J. Simons to R. Mompati, 11 February 1986.
26. UCT, Jack Simons Papers, BC1081, P25.2: J. Simons to R. Mompati, 12 February 1986. See also BC1081, P25.4.3: J. Simons to members of the Constitution Committee, 12 February 1986.
27. UCT, Jack Simons Papers, BC1081, P25.2: J. Simons to Z.N. Jobodwana, 9 February 1986.
28. UCT, Jack Simons Papers, BC1081, P25.4.3: J. Simons to members of the Constitution Committee, 12 February 1986, p. 2.

CHAPTER 11: A CALL FOR CLEAR POLITICAL GUIDANCE

1. UCT, Jack Simons Papers, BC1081, P25.2: J. Simons to Z.N. Jobodwana, 9 February 1986; P25.1: J. Simons' handwritten diarised notes, no date.
2. UWC/RIM Mayibuye Archives, ANC Collection, MCH01, Box 57: Third and final section of the 'Report of the NWC sub committee on the report of the Legal and Constitutional Commission' from P. Jordan (convenor), 23 February 1986, pp. 7–8.
3. UCT, Jack Simons Papers, BC1081, P25.2: African National Congress (South Africa) Internal Memorandum, Jack Simons to Comrade President, 28 February 1986.
4. UCT, Jack Simons Papers, BC1081, P25.2: Z.N. Jobodwana to administrative secretary, NEC, ANC, 3 April 1986.
5. Sachs and Dodd edit, September 2020.
6. UCT, Jack Simons Papers, BC1081, P25.1: Minutes, second plenary session of the Constitution Committee, 7 April 1986, p. 1.
7. Ibid.
8. UCT, Jack Simons Papers, BC1081, P25.1: Minutes, joint NWC/Constitution Committee, 8 April 1986 and 9 April 1986.
9. Ibid., p. 1.
10. UCT, Jack Simons Papers, BC1081, P25.1: Proposed agenda for the joint NWC/ Constitution Committee meeting held on 8 April 1986, with annotations by Simons.
11. UCT, Jack Simons Papers, BC1081, P25.1: 'Constitutional Commission', continuation of [joint NWC/Constitution Committee] meeting, 9 April 1986, pp. 3–4.
12. ANC Archives (on file): Z.N. Jobodwana to secretary-general, 11 May 1986, counter-signed by Z. Skweyiya.
13. ANC Archives (on file): Z.N. Jobodwana to Comrade President, 3 April 1996, attaching 'Revised agenda of the Constitution Committee meeting to be held from the 7th to the 10th April, 1986, at Alpha Building, Lusaka'.
14. ANC Archives (on file): Z.N. Jobodwana to secretary-general, 11 May 1986, counter-signed by Z. Skweyiya.

CHAPTER 12: CONFIDENTIAL AND URGENT:
OPENING UP CHANNELS WITH LAWYERS FROM HOME

1. UFH, NAHECS, ANC Archives (on file): O.R. Tambo to Z. Skweyiya, 19 April 1986.
2. See Constitutional Court of South Africa, profile of Justice Thembile Skweyiya. Accessed 4 January 2022.

3. UFH, NAHECS, ANC Archives (on file): Draft agenda of meeting between DLCA, advocate Skweyiya and attorney Mlaba, signed by Z.N. Jobodwana, 9 May 1986.

4. UFH, NAHECS, ANC Archives (on file): Z.N. Jobodwana, to secretary-general, 11 May 1986, counter-signed by Z. Skweyiya.

5. UFH, NAHECS, ANC Archives (on file): Confidential and urgent. Report of the Department of Legal and Constitutional Affairs on their meeting with advocate Lewis Skweyiya and attorney Kwenza Mlaba held in Harare on 18 May 1986, pp. 1, 12.

6. UFH, NAHECS, ANC Archives (on file): Telegram from ANC – Harare to Cde Zola Bona, 25 May 1986.

7. UFH, NAHECS, ANC Archives (on file): Confidential and urgent. Report of DLCA meeting with Lewis Skweyiya and Kwenza Mlaba, Harare,18 May 1986, p. 6.

8. Ibid., pp. 10–12.

9. UFH, NAHECS, ANC Archives (on file): Telegram from ANC – Harare to Cde Zola Bona, 25 May 1986.

10. UFH, NAHECS; ANC Archives (on file): Z.S.T. Skweyiya to secretary-general ANC, 31 July 1986. The preparatory committee included representatives from the DLCA; the president, secretary-general and treasurer-general's offices; the Politico-Military Council; the External Coordinating Committee; and the trade union alliance partner SACTU.

11. UFH, NAHECS, ANC Archives (on file): Z.S.T. Skweyiya to R. Mompati, 30 July 1986, and Z.S.T. Skweyiya to president, ANC, 29 September 1986.

12. *Staffrider*, Vol. 10, No. 3, 1992, pp. 36–41.

13. UFH, NAHECS, ANC Archives (on file): Z.S.T. Skweyiya to president, ANC, 29 September 1986.

CHAPTER 13: YHE DILEMMA

1. UCT, Jack Simons Papers, BC1081, P25.2: R. Mompati to J. Simons, 7 February 1986.

2. Callinicos, *Oliver Tambo*, p. 623.

3. Gevisser, *Thabo Mbeki*, p. 537.

4. UCT, Jack Simons Papers, BC1081, P25.1: Z.N. Jobodwana to secretary-general, 11 May 1986, counter-signed by Z. Skweyiya.

5. UCT, Jack Simons Papers, BC1081, P25.2: J. Simons to Z.N. Jobodwana, 19 May 1986. See also J. Simons' note 'For CC', 23 September 1986, outlining the agenda for a discussion on 'Constitutional reforms and stalemate' following the EPG visit.

6. UFH, ANC Archives, numbering not clear (on file): 'Notes in preparation for the EPG', no date.

7. See R. de Villiers and J-A. Stemmet, *Prisoner 913: The Release of Nelson Mandela* (Cape Town: Tafelberg, 2020), Chapters 4–5.

8. Callinicos, *Oliver Tambo*, p. 597.

9. Luli Callinicos Collection: Luli Callinicos interview with Joe Slovo, Johannesburg, 5 and 7 January 1994. Transcribed by Thomas Mathole.

10. D. Glaser, 'National Democratic Revolution Meets Constitutional Democracy' in E. Webster and K. Pampallis (eds.), *The Unresolved National Question: Left Thought Under Apartheid* (Johannesburg: Wits University Press, 2017), Chapter 15; quotes from pp. 275, 294.

11. UCT, Jack Simons Papers, BC1081, P25.1: African National Congress Constitution Committee, Proposals for a National Front, Lusaka, 4 April 1986; ANC Archives (on file): Seminar paper on 'The Congress Alliance' delivered by J. Simons on the anniversary of the founding of SACTU, no date, p. 11.

12. UCT, Jack Simons Papers, BC1081, Part 25.4.2: [A. Sachs], 'People's Power constitutions', no date [1986].
13. UWC/RIM Mayibuye Archives, ANC Collection, MCH01, Box 57: First section of the 'Report of the NWC sub committee on the report of the Legal and Constitutional Commission' from Z.P. Jordan (convenor), 23 February, p. 1.
14. UCT, Jack Simons Papers BC1081, P25.4.3: Memorandum from J. Simons to members of the Constitution Committee, 12 February 1986, p. 3.
15. UCT, Jack Simons Papers, BC1081, P25.1: Jack Simons' handwritten notes, 'Constitution Committee', 9 January 1986.
16. UWC/RIM Mayibuye Archives, ANC Collection, MCH01, Box 57: First section of the 'Report of the NWC sub committee on the report of the Legal and Constitutional Commission' from Z.P. Jordan (convenor), 23 February, pp. 1–4.
17. 'UWC/RIM Mayibuye Archives, ANC Collection, MCH01, Box 57: Discussion in NWC, second section of the 'Report of the NWC sub committee on the report of the Legal and Constitutional Commission' from Z.P. Jordan (convenor), 23 February, pp. 5–6.
18. UWC Archives, Kader Asmal Papers, Box 177: Untitled paper sent by T. O'Dowd to K. Asmal, 4 June 1986.
19. Sachs and Dodd edit, September 2020. Sachs gives 1986/1987 as the date for this meeting, but unfortunately the author was not able to source NEC minutes to confirm either the date or substance of the NEC discussions.
20. Sachs and Dodd edit, September 2020.
21. Callinicos, *Oliver Tambo*, p. 601.

CHAPTER 14: 'THE FOUNDATIONS OF GOVERNMENT'
1. UWC/RIM Mayibuye Archives, ANC Collection, MCH01, Box 57: 'Report of the NWC sub committee on the report of the Legal and Constitutional Commission' from Z.P. Jordan (convenor), 23 February 1986, pp. 7–8.
2. Ibid., pp. 1–2.
3. Ibid., pp. 7–8.
4. Ibid., pp. 7–8.
5. Ibid., pp. 7–8.
6. UCT, Jack Simons Papers, BC1081, P25.5: 'Notes' in 'Foundations of Government in a Democratic South Africa', attached to memorandum to the NEC by the Constitution Committee, 20 September 1986.
7. UCT, Jack Simons Papers, BC1081, P25.5: 'Foundations of Government in a Democratic South Africa', attached to memorandum to the NEC by the Constitution Committee, 20 September 1986.

CHAPTER 15: THE LEADERSHIP HAS ITS SAY
1. ANC Archives (on file): Z.N. Jobodwana, minutes, joint NEC/CON-COMM meeting, 2 October 1986. The meeting details below all come from this document.
2. ANC Archives (on file): Z.N. Jobodwana to O.R. Tambo, 14 August 1986.
3. Ibid., p. 6.
4. ANC Archives (on file): Minutes, joint NEC/CON-COMM, 2 October 1986, p. 6.
5. P. Wastberg, 'An inner compass', in Jordan (ed.), *Oliver Tambo Remembered*, p. 319.
6. SADET, *The Road to Democracy in South Africa*, Vol. 3, International Solidarity, Part 1 (Pretoria: UNISA Press, 2008), pp. 515–17. See also related references below.

7. ANC Archives (on file): Minutes, joint NEC/CON-COMM, 2 October 1986, p. 8.

8. ANC Archives (on file): Final draft constitution document by Z.P. Jordan, S. Makana and Z. Skweyiya, [October 1986]; UFH, NAHECS, ANC Archives, LSM012/0016/09: 'Foundations of Government in a Democratic South Africa' [October 1986].

9. ANC Archives: (on file): Record of proceedings of a meeting held on 6 January 1987, DLCA-P[resident] ANC, p. 1.

10. Ibid.

11. ANC Archives (on file): Z.N. Jobodwana to O.R. Tambo, 14 August 1986.

12. ANC Archives (on file): Z. Skweyiya, 'chairman' [on DLCA letter head] to O.R. Tambo, 29 January 1987.

CHAPTER 16: OLIVER TAMBO MEETS MIKHAIL GORBACHEV

1. Shubin, *The Hot 'Cold War'*, pp. 256–9.

2. Ibid., pp. 256–7.

3. Sachs and Dodd edit, September 2020, drawn from Albie Sachs interviews on his ANC Constitution Committee documentation at the UWC/RIM Mayibuye Archives, 2007 (provisionally transcribed by Pat Fahrenfort, 2016), pp. 36–7. Unfortunately, the massive fire in 2020 at the UCT libraries where the Simons Papers are stored prevented me from following up on Jack Simons' own reports of the trip.

4. Davies, *Towards a New Deal*, pp. 49–50.

5. Ibid.

6. Sachs and Dodd edit, September 2020.

7. Ibid.

8. ANC Archives (on file): Z.S.T. Skweyiya to secretary-general, 31 July 1986; Z.S.T. Skweyiya to R. Mompati, 31 July 1986; Z.S.T. Skweyiya to O.R. Tambo, report on trip to London, 29 September 1986.

9. UWC/RIM Mayibuye Archives: Albie Sachs interviews on his ANC Constitution Committee documentation, 2007 (provisionally transcribed by Pat Fahrenfort, 2016), pp. 27–8, 31.

10. ANC Archives (on file): Z.S.T. Skweyiya to O.R. Tambo, 20 January 1987; Sachs and Dodd edit, September 2020.

11. UWC/RIM Mayibuye Centre, ANC Papers, MCH01, Box 57: DLCA report on the visit to the German Democratic Republic and the Czechoslovak Socialist Republic prepared by P.M. Maduna, 16 February 1987.

12. Ibid.

13. ANC Archives (on file): J. Greenberg to secretary, ANC Legal and Constitutional Committee, 9 December 1986.

14. UWC/RIM Mayibuye Archives, ANC Papers: P.M. Maduna report on Columbia Law School visit, 28 April 1987.

15. Adam Asmal, personal communication, 6 November 2020.

16. UFH, ANC Archives, LSM/012/0026/04, Annual report of the DLCA [1987], pp. 4–5.

17. ANC Archives (on file): Z.N. Jobodwana to A. Nzo, 13 May 1986.

18. UWC/RIM Mayibuye Archives, ANC Papers, MCH01-57-1-2: Meeting between DLCA and International Department, 20 June 1987.

CHAPTER 17: THE CHIEF CHECKS IN AND SKWEYIYA PRESSES AHEAD

1. ANC Archives (on file): J. Simons, 'The Congress Alliance', paper delivered on the anniversary of the founding of the South African Congress of Trade Unions, 17 March 1987, p. 2.

2. ANC Archives (on file): Record of proceedings of a meeting held on 6 January 1987 DLCA-P[resident] ANC, p. 1.

3. ANC Archives (on file): Constitution Committee draft 'Statement of Intent by the African National Congress (SA): A proposed constitution for a liberated South Africa', Lusaka, 5 January 1987, pp. 1–6.

4. ANC Archives (on file): Draft 'Statement of Intent by the African National Congress (SA)', 5 January 1987, pp. 1–6.

5. Kader and Louise Asmal Papers (home): T. Alberts to K. Asmal, 31 October 2005, with attached document on 'Our legacy of freedom'.

6. See ANC Archives (on file): 'Brief KwaZulu-Natal Indaba' in record of proceedings of a meeting held on 6 January 1987, DLCA-P[resident] ANC, p. 2.

7. ANC Archives (on file): Record of proceedings of a meeting held on 6 January 1987, DLCA-P[resident] ANC, p. 2.

8. ANC Archives (on file): Excerpts from the statement of the NEC of the ANC on the occasion of the 75th anniversary of the ANC, presented by President Oliver Tambo, 8 January 1987. See also 'Address by Oliver Tambo at the 75th anniversary meeting of the African National Congress, Lusaka, 8 January 1987', South African History Online, https://www.sahistory.org.za/archive/address-oliver-tambo-75th-anniversary-meeting -african-national-congress-08-january-1987. Accessed 7 June 2022.

9. Maharaj and Jordan, *Breakthrough*, pp. 99–100, 133.

10. 'Address by Oliver Tambo at the 75th anniversary meeting of the ANC, Lusaka, 8 January 1987, South African History Online.

11. A.L. Sachs and A. Dodd edit, Cape Town, 10 September 2020.

12. ANC Archives (on file): Project proposal document, ANC (SA) DLCA, for 'Seminar on a Future Constitution for a Democratic South Africa', attached to Z. Skweyiya 'chairman' to O.R. Tambo, 29 January 1987, p. 1.

13. Ibid., pp. 1–2.

14. Ibid., p. 2.

15. Ibid. The other estimated costs were for accommodation (120 Zambian kwacha per day, including lunch and supper), local transport (ZK3 600) and primitive conference materials by today's standards (Gestetner stencils and ink and stationery at ZK9 585).

16. SADET, *The Road to Democracy*, Vol. 4, Part 1, p. 126.

CHAPTER 18: 'HOW DO YOU SPEAK TO AN ARCHBISHOP?'

1. https://www.washingtonpost.com/archive/politics/1985/09/14/s-african-businessmen-meet -with-exiled-guerrilla-leaders/33.

2. Maharaj and Jordan, *Breakthrough*, pp. 104–5.

3. UFH, NAHECS, ANC Archives (on file): Excerpts from the statement of the NEC on the occasion of the 75th anniversary of the ANC, 8 January 1987, p. 1.

4. J. Naidoo, *Fighting for Justice: A Lifetime of Political and Social Activism* (Johannesburg: Picador Africa, 2010), pp. 104–7; J. Baskin, *Striking Back: A History of COSATU* (Johannesburg: Ravan Press, 1991), pp. 73–5, 94–5.

5. J. Seekings, *The UDF: A History of the United Democratic Front in South Africa, 1983–1991* (Cape Town: David Philip, 2000), pp. 166–7.

6. Andrew Boraine Collection: 'NUSAS Talks to the ANC' (booklet published and distributed by NUSAS, 1986).

7. M. Savage, 'Trekking outward: A chronology of meetings between South Africans and

the ANC in exile, 1983–1990' (unpublished article, second version September 2017, from the author).

8. F. Van Zyl Slabbert, *The Other Side of History: An Anecdotal Reflection on the Political Transition in South Africa* (Johannesburg: Jonathan Ball, 2006), pp. 46–51.

9. Transcript of the meeting, Document 80, in Gerhart and Glaser, *From Protest to Challenge*, pp. 437–47.

10. UFH, NAHECS, ANC Archives, LSM 016/0070/9: Minutes, ANC and RCC delegations, 15–16 April 1986; UWC/RIM Mayibuye Archives, ANC Papers, MCH01, Box 26.3: Joint communiqué of the meeting of the Southern African Catholic Bishops' Conference and the ANC, Lusaka, 16 April 1986.

11. Savage, 'Trekking outward'.

12. Gevisser, *Thabo Mbeki*, pp. 538–9.

13. Jordan, *Letters to My Comrades*, pp. 18–49.

14. Seekings, *The UDF*, pp. 202–3.

15. G. Gerhart, quoted in Seekings, *The UDF*, cover blurb.

16. G. Houston, 'The ANC's Internal Underground Political Work in the 1980s' in SADET, *The Road to Democracy*, Vol. 4, Part 1, p. 207.

17. Callinicos, *Oliver Tambo*, p. 571.

18. For details on the underground struggle, see R. Suttner, *The ANC Underground in South Africa to 1976: A Social and Historical Study* (Auckland Park: Jacana, 2008); S. Gunn and S. Haricharan (eds.), *Voices from the Underground: Eighteen Life Stories from Umkhonto we Sizwe's Ashley Kriel Detachment* (Cape Town: Penguin, 2019); H. Ebrahim, *From Marabastad to Mogadishu: The Journey of an ANC Soldier* (Auckland Park: Jacana, 2019); SADET, *The Road to Democracy*, Vol. 4, Part 1, pp. 133–438.

19. UWC/RIM Mayibuye Archives, ANC Papers, MCH01-57-1: Memorandum, Z.S.T. Skweyiya to O.R. Tambo, on the Uprooted People Conference, 8–12 June 1987, and other issues, no date, p. 2.

20. UFH, NAHECS, ANC Archives, LSM/012/0017/07: Constitution Committee report in minutes, ECC meeting, 11 February 1988, p. 5.

21. UWC/RIM Mayibuye Archives, A. Sachs interviews with Stanley Sello on his Constitution Committee documents. Provisionally transcribed by Pat Fahrenfort, 2016, p. 54.

22. A. Sampson, *The Anatomist: The Autobiography of Anthony Sampson* (Johannesburg: Jonathan Ball, 2008), p. 228; Callinicos, *Oliver Tambo*, pp. 594–5.

23. Savage, 'Trekking outward'.

CHAPTER 19: ENCOUNTERS IN DAKAR

1. See S.F. Ndlovu, 'The African National Congress and Negotiations' in SADET, *The Road to Democracy*, Vol. 4, Part 1, pp. 103–12.

2. See C. Louw, 'SA pers, ANC safari oopgevlek', *Die Suid-Afrikaan*, No. 11, September 1987, pp. 26–30.

3. W. Esterhuyse, *Endgame: Secret Talks and the End of Apartheid* (Cape Town: Tafelberg, 2012), p. 34.

4. Johann van der Westhuizen, personal communication, 5 November 2021; Kader and Louise Asmal Papers (home): Consultation in preparation for the meeting with the law professors from white South Africa, 31 December 1996, p. 1.

5. See R.W. Johnstone, obituary of 'Laurence Schlemmer, 1936–2011', *Natalia* 42 (2012), pp. 129–34.

6. H. Giliomee, *Historian: An Autobiography* (Cape Town: Tafelberg, 2016), pp. 66–7, 104–8, 118–25, 148–50.

7. *Rapport Weekliks*, 4 July 2021, p. 8.

8. For more details, see B. Masekela, *Poli Poli* (Johannesburg: Jonathan Ball, 2021); https://en.wikipedia.org/wiki/Barbara_Masekela. Accessed 29 September 2019.

9. P. Hain and A. Odendaal, *Pitch Battles: Sport, Racism and Resistance* (Rowman and Littlefield, Lanham, Boulder, New York, London, 2020), pp. 295–301.

10. Obituary by David Kenvyn, 6 December 2021; https://en.wikipedia.org/wiki/Lindiwe _Mabuza.

11. Magubane with Mzamane, *Bernard Magubane*, Chapter 9, especially pp. 249, 294–8.

12. See account of R. de Villiers, 'In die gesprek lê 'n nuwe vertrekpunt opgesluit', *Die Suid-Afrikaan*, No. 11, September 1987, pp. 14–19; H. Giliomee, *Historian*, p. 165.

13. Gevisser, *Thabo Mbeki*, pp. 512–13.

14. UWC/RIM Mayibuye Archives, ANC Collection, MCH01 (on file): 'Notes on the Dakar Conference', no date [1987].

15. André Odendaal Collection, Box C13: The Dakar Declaration, 12 July 1987.

16. UWC/RIM Mayibuye Archives; ANC Collection MCH01 (on file): [n.a.], 'Notes on the Dakar Conference'.

17. See, for example, 'Dakar Special: Forging a broad national unity – some questions', *UWC News*, September 1987, p. 5.

18. André Odendaal Collection, Box C13: The Dakar Declaration, 12 July 1987, paragraph 10.

19. Chris Louw, 'Van bekeering weet mens nou nie ...', *Die Suid-Afrikaan*, No. 11, September 1987, p. 11.

20. Pahad, *Insurgent Diplomat*, p. 134.

21. A. Mischke, 'Afrikaan en Afrikaner kyk mekaar in oe', *Rapport*, 24 December 2000.

22. Comments at the screening of the documentary *Breaking the Fetters*, produced and directed by Hennie and Anli Serfontein, STIAS, Stellenbosch University, 23 August 2018.

23. Riaan de Villiers interview with Steve Tshwete, Dakar, Senegal, July 1987 in *Die Suid-Afrikaan*, No. 11, September 1987, pp. 45–8.

24. 'Talks about talks', *Business Day*, 6 July 1987.

25. See UWC/RIM Mayibuye Archives, ANC London Papers, MCH01, Box 21: Z.P. Jordan letters to A. Pahad, 11 June 1987, and Z.P. Jordan to S. Smith, 2 July 1987.

26. UWC/RIM Mayibuye Archives, ANC Collection, MCH01 (on file): 'Notes on the Dakar Conference'.

27. André Odendaal Collection: Cutting from 'Talking about a new South Africa', *New Era*, [1987].

28. See M. du Preez, *Pale Native: Memories of a Renegade Reporter* (Cape Town: Zebra Press, 2004), Chapter 21.

29. See letter to *Die Burger*, 20 March 1999.

30. The last bit is a riff on P.W. Botha's aforementioned reference to Van Zyl Slabbert and others, whom he viewed as communist puppets.

31. Hain and Odendaal, *Pitch Battles*, pp. 298–9.

32. Van Zyl Slabbert, *The Other Side of History*, p. 81.

33. See http://www.sun.ac.za/.../seminars-and-workshops, TRU seminar, 21 November 2017; and T. Heard, 'Alex Boraine, a Prince of Peace', *Daily Maverick*, 10 December 2018. Christopher Makuvaza of the University of the Free State is writing a PhD on the IDASA/ ZISA dialogues.

34. Magubane with Mzamane, *Bernard Magubane*, p. 323.
35. Jakes Gerwel Papers (home): J. Nkadimeng to J. Gerwel, 15 February 1988.
36. UWC/RIM Mayibuye Archives, ANC Papers, MCH01-2-4: Reports on the Bommersvik, Sweden, workshop on research priorities for post-apartheid South Africa, including Annexure IV: Alpha meeting, 8 August 1987; Meeting to brief Comrades Zola and Max, 15 August 1987; Meeting to brief comrades from home, 15 August 1987; Meetings of the ANC delegation on 17 and 22 August 1987. For full details of PASA, see T. Sellström, *Sweden and National Liberation in Southern Africa: Solidarity and Assistance, 1970–1994* (Uppsala: Nordic Africa Institute, 1999), pp. 794–810.
37. UWC/RIM Mayibuye Archives, ANC Papers, MCH01-56: P. Magapatuna and M. Sisulu to administrative secretary, office of the treasurer-general, 20 February 1987; M. Sisulu to Bheki, 28 September 1987; Memo on the Department of Economics and Planning, no date or author.
38. UWC/RIM Mayibuye Archives, ANC Papers, MCH01-59: Memorandum by B. Mackay, PASA coordinator, on 'History and rationale of the CDS/SASPRO [PASA]', no date.
39. Zohra Ebrahim Papers: Minutes, CDS land and planning/local government commissions working group, 14 December 1989.
40. Zohra Ebrahim Papers: CDS, Local Government and Planning Study Commission, research proposal for 1990, December 1989.
41. Zohra Ebrahim Papers: L. Steyn, co-interim coordinator of land, CDS, to comrades, 2 August 1989, attaching Minutes, land sector CDS meeting, Community House, 2 July 1989. See also UFH, NAHECS, ANC Archives, LSM/021/0154/11: Conference package: 'II Seminar objectives'.
42. Heard, 'Alex Boraine', *Daily Maverick*; Magubane with Mzamane, *Bernard Magubane*, pp. 325–6, 328.

CHAPTER 20: ASSASSINATION IN SWAZILAND

1. G. Leach, 'The Biggest Journey of All', *The Listener*, 16 July 1987, p. 4.
2. T. Stirling, 'Top ANC Man Shot Dead', *The Citizen*, 11 July 1987.
3. V. Mavimbela, *Time is Not the Measure: A Memoir* (Johannesburg: Real African Publishers, 2018), pp. 187–9.
4. UFH, NAHECS, ANC Archives (on file): Report on mission to Swaziland by members of the DLCA, Z. Skweyiya and T. Pekane, 15–17 July 1987.
5. Ibid. For a similar, earlier visit, see also UWC/RIM Mayibuye Archives, ANC Papers, MCH01-57-1: Report of a trip undertaken by DLCA to Swaziland, 5–10 June 1987.

CHAPTER 21: HARARE, ARUSHA, AMSTERDAM

1. UWC/RIM Mayibuye Archives, ANC Papers, 01-57-1: Z. Skweyiya to ANC president, 'Report on trip to London', 29 September 1986, J. Jobodwana to ANC secretary-general, proposed conference: WUS-IDAF-ANC, Harare: Children under apartheid, 30 September 1986; and Z. Skweyiya to secretary, ANC-NEC secretariat, 2 February 1987; ANC Archives (on file): H. Rabkin to secretary DLCA, ANC, 30 September 1986.
2. A. Jeffrey, *People's War: New Light on the Struggle for South Africa* (Johannesburg: Jonathan Ball, 2009), p. 138.
3. K. Asmal, 'Our Lodestar', in Jordan (ed.), *Oliver Tambo Remembered*, p. 40.
4. Interview with Don Foster, Cape Town, 26 August 2016. See D. Foster, *Detention and*

Torture in South Africa: Psychological and Historical Studies (Cape Town: David Philip, 1987). My thanks to Don for allowing me access to his conference file.

5. Don Foster Papers: Statement by Oliver Tambo at the Conference on children, repression and the law in apartheid South Africa, Harare, 24–27 September 1987.

6. V. Brittain and A.S. Minty (eds.), *Children of Resistance: Statements from the Harare Conference on Children, Repression and the Law in Apartheid South Africa* (Kliptown Books, London, 1988), p. 138.

7. According to Mike Savage, there seems to be no available list of those who attended the conference, probably because of the danger such a list could have posed if discovered by the security police. However, among those who came from 'inside', besides those mentioned above, were Rashieda Abdulla, Ashraf Abrahams, Amiena Abrahams, Jean Benjamin, Vanessa Brereton, Barbara Creecy, Andy Dawes, Jo-Ann Collinge, Bruce Duncan, Farid Esack, Rev. Blessings Finca, Edith Fries, Joyce Gwabeni, Mongesi Gwabeni, Rev. Lionel Louw, Dr Zonke Majodine, Dr Greg McCarthy, Dorothy Mfako, William Modibedi, Glenn Moss, David Niddrie, Bishop Simon Nkoane, Farida Omar, Dr Wendy Orr, Hans Ramrak, Dr Freddy Reddy, Brian Robertson, Lisa Seftel, Tina Schouw, Illona Tip, Dr Ivan Toms, Cynthia Tinto, Monica Wittenberg, Chris Vick and Joanne Yawitch.

8. Brittain and Minty (eds.), *Children of Resistance*, pp. 122–3, 139.

9. Interview with Don Foster, Cape Town, 26 August 1986.

10. Brittain and Minty (eds.), *Children of Resistance*, p. 22.

11. Interview with Don Foster, Cape Town, 26 August 1986.

12. Brittain and Minty (eds.), *Children of Resistance*, p. 126.

13. South African History Online, https://www.sahistory.org.za/archive/african-national-con gress-%28sa%29-international-conference%2C-arusha%2C-tanzania%2C-1-4-december -1987. Accessed 26 January 2019; Ndlovu, 'The African National Congress and Negotiations' in SADET, *The Road to Democracy*, Vol. 4, Part 1, pp. 126–7.

14. Sachs and Dodd edit, September 2020.

15. South African History Online, 'Address by Oliver Tambo at the opening session of the ANC Conference, Arusha, 1 December 1987', https://www.sahistory.org.za/archive/ address-oliver-tambo-opening-session-anc-conference-arusha-1-december-1987. Accessed 7 July 2021. See also UWC Archives, Kader Asmal Collection, Box 177: B. Barrett, 'An analysis of recent constitutional developments within the African National Congress and its stance on negotiations', Inkatha Institute, September 1988, p. 13.

16. https://www.sahistory.org.za/archive/african-national-congress-%28sa%29-international -conference%2C-arusha%2C-tanzania%2C-1-4-december-1987. Accessed 26 January 2019.

17. ASCAROL Collection, 16Y10M14-001: Gordon Metz and André Odendaal interview with Roelf Meyer, Pretoria, 14 October 2018; Ndlovu, 'The African National Congress and Negotiations', in SADET, *The Road to Democracy*, Vol. 4, Part 1, p. 126.

18. Ndlovu, 'The African National Congress and Negotiations' in SADET, *The Road to Democracy*, Vol. 4, Part 1, pp. 126–7.

19. Ibid., p. 127.

20. For details, see W. Campschreur and J. Divendal, *Culture in Another South Africa* (London: Zed Books, 1989); UWC/RIM Mayibuye Archives, ANC Papers, MCH01-59-1: B. Masekela to secretary-general, 16 March 1988, with resolutions and correspondence. My thanks to Kier Schuringa for helping me to trace the original programme and a list of participants.

21. E. Groenink, *Incorruptible: The Story of the Murders of Dulcie September, Anton Lubowski and Chris Hani* (Cape Town: self-published, 2018), pp. 11–12.

22. M. Langa, 'The Quiet Thunder: Report on the Amsterdam Cultural Conference', *Sechaba*, March 1988.

23. Besides those mentioned above, other South African participants at CASA included Mmabatho Nhlanhla (singer), Zila (music group), Zakhene (dance group), Richard Carter (ballet), Peter Ngwenya and the Student Youth Drama Society, Mono Badela, Victor Moche, Howard Barrell, Pat Sidley, Sipho Khumalo and Joanne Collinge (all six were journalists), Nana Gutumela (UDF Cultural Desk), Robert Cavanaugh (theatre lecturer), Hessie Sibanyoni, Brian Abrahams (musician), Alfred Temba Qabula (poet and script writer), John Matshikiza and Barry Feinberg (filmmakers), Steve Gordon and Lloyd Ross (music producers), Thele Moema (ANC), Similo Makambi (singer/actor), Charlton George (actor), Libby Lloyd, Herbert Mabuza, Glenn Moss, David Niddrie, Jeeva Rajgopaul, Chris Vick, Paul Weinberg (photographer), Moss Gwenya (video maker), Farid Esack (Call of Islam), Anthony Akerman (theatre director), Thekwini Theatre group and Junction Avenue Theatre Company.

24. Campschreur and Divendal, *Culture in Another South Africa*, pp. 259–65.

25. See K. Naidoo, *Krish: Struggle Lawyer* (Crown Mines: self-published, 2019), pp. 196–200.

26. M. Benson and L. Nickson, *Free Nelson Mandela: Festival Concert book* (London: Penguin, 1988), p. 9.

27. See Chapters 30–32.

28. Meli's ANC comrades appear to have known by now that he was compromised by his heavy drinking. Jordan asked Solly Smith, with some disdain, why 'City' was included in the delegation when it was known the proceedings would be 'confidential'. He was probably referring to Meli and was to find out later that Smith himself had become an apartheid informer. See UWC/RIM Mayibuye Archives, ANC London Papers MCH01, Box 21: Z.P. Jordan to S. Smith, 2 July 1987.

29. C. Barron, 'Obituary: Charismatic Academic, Novelist, Spy', *Sunday Times*, 6 December 2015.

CHAPTER 22: NADEL BROADENS THE ANTI-RACIST LEGAL FRONT

1. Langa recounted this story to Albie Sachs as they drove past the building in central Durban after Sachs had returned from exile. Sachs and Dodd edit, September 2020.

2. Zak Yacoob, personal communication to Albie Sachs, July 2021.

3. 'Pius Nkonzo Langa', South African History Online, https://www.sahistory.org.za/people/pius-nkonzo-langa. Accessed 11 October 2021.

4. 'Mandla Langa', African Literary Profiles, https://aflitprof.blogspot.com/2015/09/mandla-langa.html. Accessed 11 October 2021.

5. R. Pather, 'Impimpi accusations are "reckless"', *Mail & Guardian*, 22 February 2021.

6. Ibid.; ANC Archives (on file): P.M. Maduna to O.R. Tambo, 22 October 1987.

7. 'Dullah Mohamed Omar', South African History Online, https://www.sahistory.org.za/people/dullah-mohamed-omar. Accessed 23 June 2020.

8. B. Pogrund, 'Dullah Omar: Politician of post-apartheid South Africa', *Independent*, 15 March 2004, https://www.independent.co.uk/news/obituaries/dullah-omar-38171.html. Accessed 21 July 2020.

9. UFH, NAHECS, ANC Archives, LSM/012/0026/009: Z. Skweyiya, annual report of the DLCA [1987].

10. UWC/RIM Mayibuye Archives, ANC Papers, MCH01-57-1: DLCA report on the formation of the Association of Democratic Lawyers (NADEL), 19 May 1987.

11. UWC/RIM Mayibuye Archives, ANC Papers, MCH01-57-1: Z. Skweyiya to A. Nzo, 28 January 1987.

12. UWC/RIM Mayibuye Archives, ANC Papers, MCH01-57-1: DLCA meeting with a leader of the DLC, 11 February 1987.

13. UWC/RIM Mayibuye Archives, ANC Papers, MCH01-57-1: DLCA report on the formation of NADEL, 19 May 1987.

14. See UFH, NAHECS, ANC Archives (on file): Confidential and urgent. DLCA report on their meeting with advocate Lewis Skweyiya and attorney Kwenza Mlaba, Harare, 18 May 1986, pp. 1, 12; UWC/RIM, ANC Papers, MCH01-57-1: DLCA meeting with a leader of the DLC, 11 February 1987, p. 1.

15. Naidoo, *Krish*, pp. 202–4. See his Chapter 11 for more details about the formation of NADEL.

16. UWC/RIM Mayibuye Archives, ANC Papers, MCH01-57-1: DLCA meeting with a leader of the DLC, 11 February 1987, p. 1. For more on Dumisa Ntsebeza's background, see M.M. Duka, *Matthew Goniwe on a South African Frontier: A Community History of an African Revolutionary* (Makhanda: ISER, Rhodes University, 2018), pp. 59–80.

17. UWC/RIM, ANC Papers, MCH01-57-1: DLCA meeting with a leader of the DLC, 11 February 1987, pp. 1–2, 6–7.

18. 'N. Mandela to V.N. Mxenge, 8 July 1985', in S. Venter (ed.), *The Prison Letters of Nelson Mandela* (New York: Liveright Publishing Corporation, 2018), pp. 471–5.

19. Naidoo, *Krish*, pp. 205–6.

20. D. Moseneke, *My Own Liberator* (Johannesburg: Picador Africa, 2016), p. 117.

21. Ibid., p. 207.

22. Ibid., p. 167.

23. Ibid., p. 215.

24. Ibid., p. 213.

25. Callinicos, *Oliver Tambo*, pp. 152, 163, 178–9, 271.

26. Moseneke, *My Own Liberator*, p. 213.

27. The Black Lawyers Association, https://www.blaonline.org.za/. Accessed 9 September 2019.

28. Moseneke, *My Own Liberator*, p. 215.

29. Ibid., p. 216.

30. Naidoo, *Krish*, p. 204.

31. Ibid., pp. 204–5.

32. Email from J. de Lange, 10 October 2021.

33. UWC/RIM Mayibuye Archives, ANC Papers, MCH01-57-1: Z.S.T. Skweyiya to O.R. Tambo, 4 May 1987. At this stage, the failure of the African lawyers from the DLC and DLA to be elected appeared to matter more than the fact that Omar and Ayob had made it onto the executive, which one DLCA report felt had fallen under the control of 'Trotskyites'.

34. UWC/RIM Mayibuye Archives, ANC Papers, MCH01-57-1: Z.S.T. Skweyiya to [Z.P. Jordan], the secretary, ANC-NEC secretariat, 2 February 1987.

35. UWC/RIM Mayibuye Archives, ANC Papers, MCH01-57-1: DLCA report on the formation of NADEL, 19 May 1987, pp. 1–3.

36. Ibid., pp. 4–5.

37. Ibid., pp. 2, 5–6.

38. Ibid., p. 8.

39. Mandela, *Long Walk to Freedom*, p. 43.
40. Dugard, *Confronting Apartheid*, p. 40.
41. For details, see S. Ellmann, *Arthur Chaskalson: A Life Dedicated to Justice for All* (Johannesburg: Picador Africa, 2019), Chapters 11–12; Sachs and Dodd edit, September 2020.
42. Ibid.
43. Brittain and Minty (eds.), *Children of Resistance*, pp. 122–3, 139.
44. UWC/RIM Mayibuye Archives, ANC Papers, MCH0157-1: P. Maduna, DLCA, to O.R. Tambo, 19 November 1987; ANC Archives (on file): P. Maduna to O.R. Tambo, 22 October 1987.
45. Naidoo, *Krish*, pp. 205–6.

CHAPTER 23: CONSTITUTION COMMITTEE PLANS IN COLD STORAGE

1. UFH, NAHECS, ANC Archives, LSM/012/0026/009: Z. Skweyiya, annual report of the DLCA [1987], p. 1.
2. Ibid.
3. ANC Archives (on file): Project proposal document, DLCA, for 'Seminar on a Future Constitution for a Democratic South Africa', attached to Z. Skweyiya to O.R. Tambo, 29 January 1987, p. 1; Reply, O.R. Tambo to Z. Skweyiya, 9 March 1987.
4. ANC Archives (on file): O.R. Tambo to Z. Skweyiya, 9 March 1987.
5. ANC Archives (on file): Z.N. Jobodwana to J. Simons, 15 April 1987, enclosing 'Report to DLCA on meeting of NWC, 13 March, 1987'. See also South African History Archive, Mark Gevisser Papers, AL 3284, G. 190: Minutes, NWC, 13 March 1987.
6. ANC Archives (on file): Report to DLCA on meeting of NWC, 13 March 1987.
7. ANC Archives (on file): Z.N. Jobodwana to J. Simons, 15 April 1987.
8. ANC Archives (on file): Z.S.T. Skweyiya to A. Nzo, 8 May 1987.
9. Ibid.
10. UWC/RIM Mayibuye Archives, ANC Papers, MCH01-57-2: Z.S.T. Skweyiya to A. Nzo, [no date, but mentioning Constitution Committee meeting of 17 June 1987].
11. Ibid.
12. See also UCT, BC1081, Jack Simons Papers, P25.4.3: Z.S.T. Skweyiya to T. Mbeki, 12 October 1987.
13. UCT, BC1081, Jack Simons Papers P25.1: Handwritten notes, Constitution Committee meeting, 7 October 1986.
14. UFH, NAHECS, ANC Archives, LSM/012/0016/03: J. Simons (signed by Z.S.T. Skweyiya) to O.R. Tambo, 7 October 1987.

CHAPTER 24: NEC DEBATE: TO NEGOTIATE OR NOT TO NEGOTIATE?

1. SADET, *The Road to Democracy in South Africa*, Vol. 4, Part 1, pp. 110–12.
2. Maharaj and Jordan, *Breakthrough*, p. 137.
3. Telephone conversation with Mac Maharaj, 4 December 2018.
4. 'Statement of the National Executive Committee of the African National Congress on the question of negotiations, October 9th, 1987', *Sechaba*, December 1987, p. 2. (Author's emphasis.)
5. Ibid., pp. 3–5.
6. Houston and Ngculu, *Chris Hani*, p. 34.
7. Jordan, coordinator of NEC planning from the Lusaka end, claims that Hani was, indeed, invited to join the delegation to Dakar (personal communication, December 2021).

8. 'Short note from Ntozintle Jobs Jobodwana', 4 September 2021, p. 4.
9. Telephone conversation with Mac Maharaj, 4 December 2018.
10. T. Lodge, *Red Road to Freedom: A History of the South African Communist Party* (Auckland Park: Jacana, 2021), pp. 415–16.

CHAPTER 25: TAMBO'S SPECIAL CHRISTMAS GIFT

1. UFH, NAHECS, ANC Archives, LSM/012/0016/03: J. Simons (signed by Z.S.T. Skweyiya) to O.R. Tambo, 7 October 1987, attaching 'Appendix: Draft memorandum on the In-House Seminar on a future constitution for a non-racial, independent, democratic and united South Africa'.
2. UFH, NAHECS, ANC Archives, LSM/012/0016/03: J. Simons (signed by Z.S.T. Skweyiya) to O.R. Tambo, 7 October 1987. The 'received' stamp in the president's office is dated 16 October 1987.
3. UCT, Jack Simons Papers, BC1081, P25.4.3, Z.S.T. Skweyiya to T. Mbeki, 12 October 1987.
4. UCT, Jack Simons Papers, BC1081, P25.1: Handwritten notes, Constitution Committee meeting, 10 December 1987.
5. Callinicos, *Oliver Tambo*, p. 624.
6. UCT, Jack Simons Papers, BC1081, P25.1: Handwritten notes, Constitution Committee meeting, 10 December 1987.
7. Ibid.
8. UWC Archives, Kader Asmal Papers, Box 177: A. Nzo to chief representatives and heads of department, 22 December 1987. Also in Albie Sachs Papers, MCH91-20.
9. UWC/RIM Mayibuye Archives, Albie Sachs Papers, MCH91-15: [O.R. Tambo] Comments on constitutional proposals, undated, unsigned [but clearly sent by Tambo on 29 December 1987 as per the content, Jack Simons' reply the next day, and the note 'From Chief' handwritten on the document]. Also in UFH, ANC Archives, LSM/012/0016/04.
10. UWC/RIM Mayibuye Archives, Albie Sachs Papers, MCH91-15: [O.R. Tambo] Comments on constitutional proposals, [29 December 1987], p. 1. For a point-by-point analysis of Tambo's changes, see J. Jackson, 'Roots of Revolution: The African National Congress and Gay Rights in South Africa', *Brooklyn Journal of International Law*, Vol. 44, Issue 2, 7 January 2019, pp. 639–45.
11. UWC/RIM Mayibuye Archives, Albie Sachs Papers, MCH91-15: [O.R. Tambo] Comments on constitutional proposals, [29 December 1987], pp. 2–3.
12. Ibid., p. 3.
13. Ibid.
14. UWC/RIM Mayibuye Archives, Albie Sachs Papers, MCH91-15: 'A constitution for liberated South Africa', J. Simons to O.R. Tambo, 30 December 1987.
15. UWC Archives, Kader Asmal Papers, Box 177: 'Con Comm draft' of 'Constitutional guideline for a democratic South Africa', signed by Z.N. Jobodwana, 10 January 1987.
16. The eight bullet points had originated from the January 1987 'Statement of Intent' and, before that, 'The Skeleton' of January 1986.
17. Sixteen of the twenty-two clauses were from the October 1986 Foundations draft, and another emanated from the Skeleton document of January 1986. There was also the one addition suggested by the NWC in May 1987.
18. UWC Archives, Kader Asmal Papers, Box 177: 'Con Comm draft' of 'Constitutional guideline for a democratic South Africa', signed by Z.N. Jobodwana, 10 January 1987.

CHAPTER 26: THE SG CALLS THE CADRES TO LUSAKA

1. UFH, NAHECS, ANC Archives, LSM 012/0016/02: Meeting of the Constitution Committee, 21 January 1988.
2. Ibid.
3. UFH, NAHECS, ANC Archives, LSM 012/0026/01: Z.N. Jobodwana for Z.S.T. Skweyiya, DLCA chairperson, to 'Head of Dept', 27 January 1988.
4. UFH, NAHECS, ANC Archives, LSM 012/0026/03: Circular to 'all heads of department' from T. Pekane, 18 February 1988.
5. UFH, NAHECS, ANC Archives, LSM 012/0016/10: 'Constitutional Guidelines for a Democratic South Africa', draft document. For a discussion of changes made to the Guidelines after the Constitution Committee's reply to the NEC on 21 January, see Jackson, 'Roots of Revolution', pp. 645–7.
6. UWC Archives, Kader Asmal Papers, Box 177: A. Nzo to chief representatives and heads of department, 22 December 1987.
7. UFH, NAHECS, ANC Archives, LSM 012/0026/03: Circular to 'all heads of department' from T. Pekane, 18 February 1988.
8. UWC Archives, Kader Asmal Papers, Box 177: Unsigned, handwritten draft 'Report on in-house seminar on "Constitutional guidelines for a Democratic South Africa", p. 1.
9. See UWC Archives, Kader Asmal Papers, Box 177: Barrett, 'An analysis of recent constitutional developments', pp. 23–4.
10. UWC Archives, Kader Asmal Papers, Box 177: Opening address by the secretary-general at the In-House Seminar on constitutional guidelines, p. 1.
11. Ibid., p. 2.
12. Email from Z.P. Jordan, 7 October 2021, attaching draft document on 'The ANC and the Bill of Rights: A seventy year survey' [published in the 1990s].
13. Karis and Carter (eds.), *From Protest to Challenge*, Vol. 2, Hope and Challenge, pp. 217–18.
14. UWC Archives, Kader Asmal Papers, Box 177: Opening address by the secretary-general at the In-House Seminar, p. 2.
15. Ibid., pp. 2–3.
16. Ibid., p. 3.
17. Ibid., p. 5.
18. Ibid., pp. 5–6.

CHAPTER 27: 'FOR YOUR UNCONSTRAINED APPRAISAL': THE IN-HOUSE SEMINAR

1. UWC Archives, Kader Asmal Papers, Box 177: Unsigned, handwritten draft 'Report on In-House Seminar', p. 6. Twenty-three of the papers presented can be found in the Asmal Papers and several others in the UWC/RIM Mayibuye Archives, ANC Papers, MCH01-57-2.
2. Sachs and Dodd edit, September 2020.
3. UWC/RIM Mayibuye Archives, ANC Papers, MCH01-57-2: Z.S.T. Skweyiya to A. Nzo, [no date, but mentioning Constitution Committee meeting of 17 June 1987], p. 2, number 7, as well as attached 'Draft memorandum on the In-House Seminar on a future constitution for a non-racial, independent, democratic and united South Africa'.
4. Gevisser, *Thabo Mbeki*, pp. 539–40.
5. Albie Sachs Collection: Film clips of the In-House Seminar, Lusaka, 1–4 March 1988. Provided to author by Steve Gordon.
6. Ibid.; Gevisser, *Thabo Mbeki*, p. 536.

7. Gevisser, *Thabo Mbeki*, p. 536; Sachs and Dodd edit, September 2020.

8. UWC Archives, Kader Asmal Papers, Box 177: Unsigned, handwritten contributions. Paper on 'Broad perspectives of future economy in South Africa' presented by Thabo Mbeki (1/3/88) and Max Sisulu (2/3/88).

9. Mfenyana, *Walking with Giants*, pp. 219–20, 226–8; Davies, *Towards a New Deal*, p. 51.

10. UCT, Jack Simons Papers, BC1081, P25.4.3: J. Simons to publications secretary, Institute for the Study of Public Policy, UCT, 26 January 1990.

11. UWC Archives, Kader Asmal Papers, Box 177: Unsigned, handwritten contributions. 'Broad perspectives of future economy in South Africa'.

12. UWC Archives, Kader Asmal Papers, Box 177: Unsigned, handwritten draft 'Report on In-House Seminar', p. 4. This report lists the speakers in the order they spoke. The title of Jordan's paper in the programme was 'Class and power structure'.

13. Sachs and Dodd edit, September 2020, drawing on Sachs's interviews with Stanley Sello on his Constitution Committee documents at the UWC/RIM Mayibuye Archives, Tape 6.1. Provisionally transcribed by Pat Fahrenfort, April 2016, pp. 59–60.

14. Ibid., p. 55.

15. Ibid., p. 59.

16. Ibid., p. 58.

17. Ibid., pp. 71–2.

18. ANC Archives (on file): Z. Skweyiya, DLCA, to B. Mabandla, 30 January 1987.

19. Brigitte Sylvia Mabandla profile in the Wayback Machine – http://web.archive.org/web/20081002000852/http://www.info.gov.za:80/gol/gcis_profile.jsp?id=1035. Accessed 30 January 2022; interview with Brigitte Mabandla, Johannesburg, 6 October 2019.

20. ANC Archives (on file): B. Mabandla to president's office, 10 November 1987.

21. See UFH, NAHECS, ANC Archives: LSM/021/0154/13: Programme of Action, Papers of National Women's Section (NWS) second national conference, Luanda, September 1987, pp. 36–43; UFH, NAHECS, ANC Archives, LSM/021/0154/02: Recommendations/resolutions of NWS second national conference, Luanda, September 1987.

22. For concise analyses of the history of the ANC Women's Section, gender dynamics in the ANC and the different perspectives among women members, see S. Hassim, *The ANC's Women's League: A Jacana Pocket History* (Auckland Park: Jacana, 2017, 3rd impression).

23. See, for example, various conference papers and material available in the Mayibuye Archives, Catalogues No. 7, ANC Papers (Lusaka and London, 1960–1991), pp. 3–16.

24. Z. Dhlamini, 'Women's liberation', 1971, South African History Online, https://www.sahistory.org.za/archive/womens-liberation-zanele-dhlamini-mbeki. Accessed 8 June 2020.

25. UWC/RIM Mayibuye Archives, ANC Papers MCH01-57-2: Statement by women's section on the gender question, undated, unsigned.

26. Sachs and Dodd edit, September 2020.

27. 'Ivy Matsepe-Casaburri: The SABC's new boss', *Speak*, 1993, pp. 5–8. Available at https://www.sahistory.org.za/sites/default/files/archive-files2/SpNov93.1684.5161.000.056.Nov1993.3.pdf. Accessed 9 June 2020.

28. UWC/RIM Mayibuye Archives, ANC Papers MCH01-57-2: [I. Matsepe-Casaburri and ANC Women's Section], paper on 'Constitution, Law and the Gender Question', In-House Seminar, Lusaka, 1–4 March 1988, pp. 3–4.

29. Ibid., p. 4.

30. Telephone conversation with Vusi Pikoli, 21 October 2021.

31. Albie Sachs Collection: Film clips of ANC In-House Seminar, Lusaka, 1–4 March 1988, provided to author by Steve Gordon.

32. A. Sachs, *We, the People: Insights of an Activist Judge* (Johannesburg: Wits University Press, 2016).

33. Ibid., p. 12.

34. A. Sachs, *Oliver Tambo's Dream* (Cape Town: African Lives, 2017), p. 16.

35. Sachs has explained that his initial scepticism was reinforced in the early 1960s, when Donald Molteno, a colleague at the Cape Bar, 'had in the name of liberalism produced a report associating a Bill of Rights with federalism and a qualified franchise which would permit all white adults to vote, while only a better-educated and property-owning black elite could do so'. In this context, a Bill of Rights would clearly be one of the constitutional mechanisms designed to protect the political and economic status quo. (Email from A. Sachs, 20 January 2022.)

36. A. Sachs, 'Towards a Bill of Rights for a Democratic South Africa', in *Hastings International and Comparative Law Review*, Vol. 2, No. 9, Winter 1989, pp. 289–324.

37. Macmillan, *The Lusaka Years*, p. 25.

38. See R. Davies, D. O'Meara and S. Dlamini, *The Struggle for South Africa: A Reference Guide to Movements, Organisations and Institutions* (London: Zed Books, 1984).

39. UWC Archives, Kader Asmal Papers, Box 177: List of In-House Seminar officials.

40. UWC Archives, Kader Asmal Papers, Box 177: Report of the Resolutions Committee, no date, pp. 1–2.

41. UWC/RIM Mayibuye Archives, ANC Papers, MCH01-57-3: Memorandum from J. Simons and Z.S.T. Skweyiya to O.R. Tambo, 12 April 1988, pp. 1–4.

42. Ibid., p. 1.

43. UFH, NAHECS, ANC Archives, LSM, 014/0056/02: Z.P. Jordan to comrade, 3 June 1988, attaching 'Draft constitutional guidelines for a democratic South Africa (N.B. all amendments are underlined)' and notice of NWC meeting for 7 June 1988; LSM 014/0056/03: Minutes, NWC meeting, 22–23 June 1988; LSM 014/0055/03: Draft agenda for NEC meeting 27 June 1988; LSM 014/0055/03: Z.P. Jordan to Cde Malume, notice of NEC secretariat meeting, 31 May 1988.

44. 'Constitutional Guidelines for a Democratic South Africa', *Sechaba*, September 1988.

45. UWC/RIM Mayibuye Archives, ANC Papers, MCH01-57-3: Memorandum from J. Simons and Z.S.T. Skweyiya to O.R. Tambo, 12 April 1988, p. 1.

46. UWC Archives, Kader Asmal Papers, Box 177: Report of the Resolutions Committee, no date, p. 1.

47. Ibid.; UWC Archives, Kader Asmal Papers, Box 177: Draft programme for In-House Seminar on 'Constitutional Guidelines in a Democratic South Africa', Lusaka, 1–4 March 1988.

48. UWC Archives, Kader Asmal Papers, Box 177: Unsigned, handwritten draft, 'Report on In-House Seminar', p. 6.

49. UWC Archives, Kader Asmal Papers, Box 177: Report of the Resolutions Committee, p. 1.

50. UFH, NAHECS, ANC Archives, LSM 012/0016/02: Minutes, Constitution Committee, 21 January 1988.

51. UWC/RIM Mayibuye Archives, ANC Papers, MCH01-57-3: Memorandum from J. Simons and Z.S.T. Skweyiya to O.R. Tambo, 12 April 1988, p. 2. See also Jackson, 'Roots of revolution', for his analyses of the various changes made to the Guidelines during this process.

52. UWC Archives, Kader Asmal Papers, Box 177: Unsigned, handwritten draft 'Report on In-House Seminar', p. 7.

53. UFH, NAHECS, ANC Archives, LSM 014/0056/02: 'Draft constitutional guidelines for a democratic South Africa (N.B. all amendments are underlined)', attached to Z.P. Jordan to comrade, 3 June 1998, clause (u).

54. Ibid., clause (p).

55. Ibid., clause (l).

56. UWC Archives, Kader Asmal Papers, Box 177: Report of the Resolutions Committee, no date, p. 1.

57. Ibid., p. 2.

58. UWC/RIM Mayibuye Archives, ANC Papers, MCH01-57-3: Memorandum from J. Simons and Z.S.T. Skweyiya to O.R. Tambo, 12 April 1988, p. 3.

59. See UFH, NAHECS, ANC Archives, LSM 014/0056/02: 'Draft constitutional guidelines for a democratic South Africa (N.B. all amendments are underlined)', attached to Z.P. Jordan to comrade, 3 June 1988, clause (w); 'Constitutional Guidelines for a Democratic South Africa', *Sechaba*, September 1988.

60. UWC/Rim Mayibuye Archives, ANC Papers MCH01-81: Memorandum on 'Matters of Particular Concern', no date, quoted in Jackson, 'Roots of revolution', p. 655.

61. UWC Archives, Kader Asmal Papers, Box 177: Report of the Resolutions Committee, no date, p. 2.

62. UWC/RIM Mayibuye Archives, ANC Papers MCH01-57-3: Memorandum from J. Simons and Z.S.T. Skweyiya to O.R. Tambo, 12 April 1988, p. 4.

CHAPTER 28: CUITO CUANAVALE

1. R. Kasrils, 'Cuito Cuanavale, Angola: 25th Anniversary of a Historic African Battle', *Monthly Review*, 1 April 2013. Available at https://monthlyreview.org/2013/04/01/cuito-cuanavale -angola/. On the battle, see also Shubin, *The Hot 'Cold War'*, Chapter 7; UWC/RIM Mayibuye Archives, Oral history section: Adrian Hadland Collection, Max du Preez interview with Jakkie Cilliers, Interview no. 22, Pretoria, 16 June 2006; 'Battle of Cuito Cuanavale 1988', South African History Online, https://www.sahistory.org.za/article/ battle-cuito-cuanavale-1988. Accessed 28 March 2022.

2. Kasrils, 'Cuito Cuanavale', p. 1.

3. Ibid., p. 4.

4. Ibid., p. 5.

5. See *Out of Step: War resistance in South Africa* (London: CIIR, 1989).

6. Jeffery, *People's War*, p. 201.

7. Callinicos, *Oliver Tambo*, p. 613.

CHAPTER 29: MURDER IN PARIS AND A CAR BOMB IN MAPUTO

1. E. Groenink, *Incorruptible: The story of the Murders of Dulcie September, Anton Lubowski and Chris Hani* (Cape Town: self-published, 2018).

2. 'Dulcie Evonne September', South African History Online, https://www.sahistory.org.za/ people/dulcie-evonne-september. Accessed 5 May 2020.

3. R. Bitsch and K-E. Koopman, 'The Erasure of Dulcie September', *Africa Is a Country*, 2019, https://africasacountry.com/2019/08/the-erasure-of-dulcie-september/?fbclid=IwAR 1kGIsNp_OJxXGp47JOw4s69LOVAkL2r4D78Pzmh7Z6vSMvqrX1SsDSYdo. Accessed 4 May 2020.

4. Ibid.
5. This and other extracts about the bomb blast and Albie's subsequent recovery are taken from A. Sachs, *The Soft Vengeance of a Freedom Fighter* (London: Souvenir Press, 2011). From Chapter 1 in this instance. This beautifully poignant book, also published in the USA by HarperCollins in 1990, won the Alan Paton Prize in 1991. We thank Souvenir Press for allowing us to republish the extracts (sometimes slightly modified).
6. ANC Archives (on file): Memorandum from the Constitution Committee to O. R. Tambo re: Constitution Guidelines and the In-House Seminar, 12 April 1988, p. 4.
7. Sachs, *Soft Vengeance*, Chapter 8.
8. Sachs and Dodd edit, September 2020.
9. Sachs, *Soft Vengeance*, p. 77.
10. Ibid., Chapter 22.
11. UWC Archives, Kader Asmal Papers, Box 177: Notes in file on seminar papers (unsigned, undated and untitled).
12. M. Taylor, 'Book of the day – *The Gun, the Ship and the Pen* by Linda Colley review – how the modern world was made', *Guardian*, 24 April 2021.
13. Sachs, *Soft Vengeance*, p. 136.
14. N. Gordimer, back-page blurb, in Sachs, *Running to Maputo*, the USA edition of *Soft Vengeance*.
15. See 'Preparing ourselves for freedom: Culture and the ANC Constitutional Guidelines', in A. Sachs, *Protecting Human Rights in South Africa*, p. 175.
16. Asmal, Hadland and Levy, *Politics in My Blood*, p. 114.
17. Sachs, *We, the People*, pp. 17–18.
18. Email from A. Sachs, 22 September 2021.
19. ANC Archives (on file): A. Sachs to Comrade President, 5 June 1987.
20. UCT, Jack Simons Papers, BC1081, P25.1: Handwritten minutes, Constitutional Committee, 3 June 1987; UWC/RIM Mayibuye Archives, ANC Papers, MCH01-57-2: Z.S.T. Skweyiya to A. Nzo, [no date, but mentioning Constitution Committee meeting of 17 June 1987], No. 7, p. 2, as well as attached 'Draft memorandum on the In-House Seminar on a future constitution for a non-racial, independent, democratic and united South Africa'.
21. Email from A. Sachs, 22 September 2021. Information on the kind of typewriter used was received from Louise Asmal, 2019.
22. 'A Bill of Rights for a new South Africa: A working document by the ANC Constitutional Committee' (Bellville: UWC, November 1990).
23. ANC draft Bill of Rights for a new South Africa, ANC Constitutional Committee (Bellville: Centre for Development Studies, UWC, 1993).
24. Asmal, Hadland and Levy, *Politics in My Blood*, pp. 114–15.
25. Email from A. Sachs, 22 September 2021.

CHAPTER 30: 'ONLY FREE MEN CAN NEGOTIATE'

1. P. O'Malley, *Shades of Difference: Mac Maharaj and the Struggle for South Africa* (Johannesburg: Penguin, 2008), Chapters 10–12.
2. The Nelson Mandela Centre for Memory: 'I am not prepared to sell the birthright of the people to be free', ZA COM MR-S-013, https://atom.nelsonmandela.org/index.php/za-com -mr-s-13. Accessed 5 May 2020.
3. Magubane with Mzamane, *Bernard Magubane*, p. 304.

4. G. Bizos, *Odyssey to Freedom* (Johannesburg: Random House, 2007), p. 420.

5. Ibid., p. 421.

6. Maharaj and Jordan, *Breakthrough*, p. 124.

7. Mandela, *Long Walk to Freedom*, p. 636.

8. Ibid., p. 641.

9. For the full text of Mandela's important memorandum to P.W. Botha in March 1988, see Maharaj and Jordan, *Breakthrough*, pp. 181–92.

10. Ibid., p. 638.

11. Ibid., pp. 637–9.

12. Email from Mac Maharaj, 9 July 2019; O'Malley, *Shades of Difference*, pp. 263, 304–5, 309–13.

13. O'Malley, *Shades of Difference*, pp. 254–5, 279.

14. Ibid., p. 255.

15. The brains behind this secret communications network was Tim Jenkin, a political prisoner who had successfully escaped from Pretoria Central prison and fled South Africa. His story forms the basis of *Escape from Pretoria*, a 2020 Hollywood film on these events.

16. O'Malley, *Shades of Difference*, pp. 311–13.

CHAPTER 31: THE CONSGOLD TALKS AND
THE CONSTITUTIONAL GUIDELINES: ROUND ONE

1. Sampson, *The Anatomist*, p. 226. Tambo's team at the meeting had comprised NEC members Thabo Mbeki, Mac Maharaj, Jacob Zuma and London Regional PMC head Aziz Pahad.

2. R. Harvey, *The Fall of Apartheid: The Inside Story from Smuts to Mbeki* (Basingstoke: Palgrave Macmillan, 2003), p. 23.

3. Ibid., pp. 16–19.

4. Sampson, *The Anatomist*, p. 226.

5. Harvey, *The Fall of Apartheid*, p. 20.

6. Mattison, *God, Spies, Lies*, pp. 213–18; Esterhuyse, *Endgame*, p. 53.

7. Sampie Terreblanche Papers: S. Terreblanche, 'My Stellenbosch Sprong na Vryheid (unpublished paper, 1990), pp. 2–3 and 'Prof. Sampie Terreblanche, 1933–2018: Sampie's life and work through the eyes of his family', no date. Terreblanche was a member of the Theron Commission, which was critical of certain aspects of government policy but had been approved by the Broederbond. From 1987 onwards, he started cutting his ties with the *volk* and Afrikaner establishment. Every strand cut, he recalled, was 'painful' and 'every time I had to leave a little blood'.

8. Esterhuyse's *verligte* credentials included two books with a limited reform agenda and spending time working with the Urban Foundation after 1985. For his profile, see Esterhuyse, *Endgame*, pp. 15–16, 351; South African History Online, https://www.sahistory .org.za/people/willie-esterhuyse; https://af.wikipedia.org/wiki/Willie_Esterhuyse; Giliomee, *Historian*, pp. 126–7.

9. Esterhuyse, *Endgame*, p. 52.

10. See Giliomee, *Historian*, pp. 126–33; Terreblanche, 'My Stellenbosch Sprong', p. 15.

11. Terreblanche, 'My Stellenbosch Sprong', p. 6.

12. See Esterhuyse, *Endgame*, pp. 53–4; Terreblanche, 'My Stellenbosch Sprong', pp. 6–8; D. Worrall, *The Independent Factor: My Personal Journey Through Politics and Diplomacy*

(Wandsbeck: self-published, 2018). Worrall declared he was neither for the government nor for the opposition, but for reconciliation.

13. Esterhuyse, *Endgame*, pp. 28–33.
14. See C. Merrett, *A Culture of Censorship: Secrecy and Intellectual Repression in South Africa* (Cape Town: David Philip, 1994); and J.H.P. Serfontein, *Brotherhood of Power: An Exposé of the Secret Afrikaner Broederbond* (London: Rex Collings, 1978).
15. Gordon Metz Collection, 16Y07M21-006: Gordon Metz and André Odendaal interview with Roelf Meyer, Pretoria, 14 October 2016; Giliomee, *Historian*, p. 107; Giliomee, *Ethnic Power Mobilised*, Chapter 3; J. Matisonn, 'How the Broederbond's tentacles penetrated deep into the heart of South Africa', *Daily Maverick*, 19 April 2022.
16. Esterhuyse, *Endgame*, p. 93.
17. Pahad, *Insurgent Diplomat*, pp. 142–3. UWC/RIM Mayibuye Archives, ANC Archives, MCH01-66A-2: [T. Trew], 'Notes on meeting of 31.10.87 to 1.11.87'.
18. Pahad, *Insurgent Diplomat*, pp. 142–5.
19. Pahad, *Insurgent Diplomat*, p. 215.
20. Mandela, *Long Walk to Freedom*, p. 640.
21. Pahad, *Insurgent Diplomat*, pp. 152–4.
22. Esterhuyse, *Endgame*, p. 131.
23. Gordon Metz and André Odendaal interview with Thabo Mbeki, Thabo Mbeki Foundation, Johannesburg, 19 October 2017, 26:00:03.
24. Esterhuyse, *Endgame*, p. 150; Pahad, *Insurgent Diplomat*, p. 163.
25. Conversation with Tony Trew, Tamboerskloof, Cape Town, 8 February 2019.
26. Michael Young Papers, YOU/1/1/5: Secret, bilateral discussion, 21–24 August 1988, p. 1.
27. Gevisser, *Thabo Mbeki*, pp. 544–5.
28. Michael Young Papers, YOU/1/1/6: Note for Mr R.I.J. Agnew, copied to Mr H. Wood and Mr A. Sykes, attaching 'Secret, Mells Park, Bilateral Talks', 6 January 1989.
29. Tony Trew report, 'Meeting with the people from home', 21–24 August 1988, p. 45.
30. Ibid., p. 54.
31. Ibid., p. 45.
32. Esterhuyse, *Endgame*, p. 150.
33. Tony Trew report, 21–24 August 1988, pp. 45–6.
34. Ibid., p. 45.
35. Ibid., p. 45.
36. D. Niddrie, 'Building on the Freedom Charter', *Work in Progress*, April/May 1988, pp. 3–6; T. Lodge, 'The Lusaka amendments', *Leadership South Africa*, Vol. 7, No. 4, 1987, pp. 17–20.
37. Tony Trew report, 21–24 August 1988, p. 44.
38. Ibid., pp. 44–8.
39. Ibid., p. 48.
40. Ibid., p. 54.
41. Ibid., p. 55.
42. Ibid., p. 55.
43. Conversation with Tony Trew, Tamboerskloof, 8 February 2019.

CHAPTER 32: THE CONSGOLD TALKS AND THE CONSTITUTIONAL GUIDELINES: ROUND TWO

1. See https://www.hollywoodreporter.com/review/film-review-endgame-92772. Accessed 23 November 2019.

2. *DVD Talk*, Reviews, T. Spurlin, *Endgame* (2009). Available at https://www.dvdtalk.com/reviews/40703/endgame/. Accessed 7 June 2022.

3. Harvey, *The Fall of Apartheid*.

4. Conversation with Tony Trew, Tamboerskloof, 8 February 2019. Thanks also to Tony for his 'Notes for introduction to the private viewing of *Endgame*', no date. In their review in *Politikon*, Vol. 41, Number 2, 2014, John Matisonn and Chris Saunders observe that the film typifies Esterhuyse as a 'conscience-stricken rogue outlier' while all along he was working for the NIS.

5. ANC Archives (on file): Z.S.T. Skweyiya to O.R. Tambo, 27 December 1988. See also Albie Sachs interview with Penuell Maduna, Johannesburg, 29 April 2019, transcript 01:02:50:03 – 01:03:02.00.

6. Michael Young Papers, YOU/1/1/6: 'Secret, Mells Park, Bilateral Talks', 6 January 1989, p. 1.

7. Tony Trew report, 'Meeting with people from home', December 1988, p. 74. Terreblanche had resigned from both the Broederbond and the National Party in February 1987.

8. Ibid., pp. 72–3.

9. Ibid., p. 74.

10. Ibid., pp. 66–7.

11. Ibid., pp. 67, 80. Emphasis in the quote by the author.

12. Ibid., pp. 73.

13. Tony Trew report, 'Meeting with people from home', [16–18] December 1988, p. 63.

14. N. Barnard, as told to Tobie Wiese, *Secret Revolution: Memoirs of a Spy Boss* (Cape Town, Tafelberg, 2015), p. 136.

15. Tony Trew report, December 1988, pp. 64–5.

16. Ibid., p. 80.

17. Ibid., pp. 77–9; Michael Young report, 6 January 1989, pp. 8–9.

18. Michael Young report, 6 January 1989, p. 9.

19. Tony Trew report, December 1988, p. 80.

20. Mac Maharaj, personal communication, 25 July 2021.

21. Tony Trew report, December 1988, p. 65.

22. Esterhuyse, *Endgame*, p. 27.

23. Esterhuyse, *Endgame*, pp. 52–4. See also pp. 34, 49.

24. Mattison, *God, Spies, Lies*, p. 215.

25. Giliomee, *Historian*, p. 127.

26. C. Louw, *Boetman en die Swanesang van die Verligtes* (Human and Rousseau, Cape Town, 2001), p. 7 and Chapters 10, 12, 13.

27. Louw, *Boetman*, p. 211.

28. Pahad, *Insurgent Diplomat*, p. 136. See also Esterhuyse, *Endgame*, pp. 34–5, 49, 91; Barnard, *Secret Revolution*, pp. 191–2.

29. Gevisser, *Thabo Mbeki*, p. 541.

30. Maharaj and Jordan, *Breakthrough*, p. 130.

31. Conversation with Tony Trew, Tamboerskloof, 8 February 2019.

32. De Villiers and Stemmet, *Prisoner 913*, pp. xiv, 28–32, 99–105; Maharaj and Jordan, *Breakthrough*, pp. 82–4. The quote is from page 105 of the first source here.

33. Barnard, *Secret Revolution*, pp. 192–4; Z. Pallo Jordan Collection (on file with author): Typed paper by Pallo Jordan titled 'Submission on negotiations', [1985], p. 11.

34. See also, for example, R. Renwick, *Mission to South Africa: Diary of a Revolution* (Johannesburg and Cape Town: Jonathan Ball, 2015).

35. Tony Trew Collection: T. Trew, 'Notes for introduction to the private viewing of *Endgame*', no date.
36. Riaan de Villiers, quoted in A. Odendaal, 'Lived experience, active citizenry and South African intellectual history' in *Transformation*, No. 97, 2018, p. 99.

CHAPTER 33: THE GUIDELINES MOVE TO CENTRE STAGE, 1989

1. Tony Trew report, 'Meeting with people from home', December 1988, p. 80.
2. Tony Trew report, December 1988, p. 80.
3. Mnangagwa succeeded Robert Mugabe as president of Zimbabwe in 2017.
4. ANC Archives (on file): 'Lawyers conference: The role of law in a society in transition, final communiqué', no date [4 February 1989].
5. See also Chapters 12, 19 and 20 for details about Zimbabwean support for the ANC's dialogue initiatives in the second half of the 1980s.
6. UWC/RIM Mayibuye Archives, ANC Papers, MCH01-57, secretary-general's office: Z.S.T. Skweyiya to A. Nzo, 4 January 1989.
7. Telephone conversation with former judge Johann van der Westhuizen, 22 January 2022.
8. Others attending included Charles Dlamini, Gerhard Lubbe, Johann Potgieter, Susan Scott, Louis van Huyssteen, Jannie van Rooyen, André van der Walt and Dawid van Wyk.
9. Jack Simons Papers, BC 1081, P25.2: J. Simons to J.V. van der Westhuizen, 20 August 1986.
10. Kader and Louise Asmal Papers (home): 'Consultation in preparation for the meeting with the law professors from white South Africa', 31 December 1996, p. 1; Johann van der Westhuizen, personal communication, 5 November 2021.
11. See K. Kriel, 'Retirement ceremony of Justice Johann van der Westhuizen', *De Rebus: Law Society of South Africa* (2016). Available at http://www.derebus.org.za/retirement -ceremony-of-justice-johann-van-der-westhuizen/. Accessed 27 July 2020.
12. https://www.up.ac.za/family-medicine/article/2330946/biography-prof-tessa-marcus#. Accessed 24 October 2021. Specialising in community-oriented primary healthcare, Marcus later became one of only a handful of social scientists ever awarded a professorship at a South African medical school.
13. Z. Skweyiya, 'The ANC Constitutional Guidelines: A vital contribution to the struggle against apartheid', paper presented at the Harare Conference of Lawyers, 31 January – 4 February 1989, p. 3, quoted in J.M. Rantete, *The African National Congress and the Negotiated Settlement in South Africa* (Pretoria: J.L. van Schaik, 1998), p. 148; UFH, NAHECS, ANC Archives, LSM/009/0020/01: M. Motshekga, 'The debate about guidelines for the future: Constitutional issues', paper at IDASA conference on 'Options for the future', Braamfontein Protea Hotel, Johannesburg, 13 May 1989.
14. Sachs and Dodd edit, September 2020.
15. ANC Archives (on file): 'Lawyers conference: The role of law in a society in transition, final communiqué', [4 February 1989].
16. ANC Archives (on file): Z.S.T. Skweyiya to O.R. Tambo, 27 December 1988; T. Mongalo, secretary for presidential affairs, to Z.S.T. Skweyiya, 3 January 1989.
17. Quoted in S. Neame, *Drama of the Peace Process in South Africa: I Look Back 30 Years* (Cape Town: Best Red, 2021), p. 163.
18. UWC/RIM Mayibuye Archives, ANC Papers, MCH01-57: P.M. Maduna, acting administrative secretary, to O.R. Tambo, 10 January 1989.
19. UWC/RIM Mayibuye Archives, ANC Papers MCH01-57: P.M. Maduna to secretary-general, 25 January 1989.

20. ANC Archives (on file): O.R. Tambo to Z.S.T. Skweyiya, 27 March 1989.
21. See, for example, *New Nation*, 21 July 1989; *New Era*, undated cutting (on file) 1989; *South African Journal on Human Rights* 129, 1989.
22. UWC/RIM Mayibuye Archives, Albie Sachs Papers, MCH91-70-2: *Constitutional Guidelines for a Democratic South Africa: African National Congress' Proposals – 1955 & 1988* (published by IDASA in the interests of working towards a negotiated democratic future, February 1989).
23. I. Liebenberg, 'Responses to the ANC Constitutional Guidelines', IDASA, occasional papers, No. 25, August 1989, p. 4.
24. André Odendaal Collection: Conference pack signed by Gary Cullen, convenor, no date.
25. UFH, NAHECS, ANC Archives, LSM/009/0020/01: M. Motshekga, 'The debate about guidelines for the future: Constitutional issues', paper at IDASA conference on 'Options for the future', Braamfontein Protea Hotel, Johannesburg, 13 May 1989.
26. D. Driver, 'Women and Language in the ANC Constitutional Guidelines for South Africa', *Die Suid-Afrikaan*, No. 23, 1 October 1989, pp. 15–18; S. Christie, D. Driver and E. van der Horst, 'Creating a Non-Sexist Constitution: Women's Perspectives', IDASA, occasional papers, No. 26, 1989.
27. Driver, 'Women and Language in the ANC Constitutional Guidelines', pp. 15–18.
28. See, for example, K. Kondlo, *In the Twilight of the Revolution: The Pan-Africanist Congress of Azania (South Africa)* (Basel: Basler Afrika Bibliographien, 2009), pp. 257–61. See also SADET, *The Road to Democracy*, Vol. 4, Part 2, Chapters 24–25 for the views of AZAPO and the BCM of Azania.
29. Liebenberg, 'Responses to the ANC Constitutional Guidelines', p. 19.
30. Nelson Mandela Centre for Memory, O'Malley Archives, Mac Maharaj Papers – Documents and reports: Minutes, NWC, 8 January 1989.
31. UCT, Jack Simons Papers, BC1081, P.25.1: Handwritten notes of 'Zola and Maduna' meeting, 10h30, 23 May 1989, p. 2.
32. M. Savage, 'A chronology of meetings between South Africans and the ANC in exile 1983–2000', South African History Online, https://www.sahistory.org.za/archive/chronology-meetings-between-south-africans-and-anc-exile-1983-2000-michael-savage. Accessed 13 May 2020.
33. Ibid.
34. Ibid.
35. UWC/RIM Mayibuye Centre, ANC Papers, MCH01-57: 'Seminar on women and children in a future constitutional order', unsigned and undated document, office of the secretary-general.
36. UWC/RIM Mayibuye Archives, ANC Papers, MCH01-57-1: Z. Skweyiya to A. Nzo, 11 April 1990.
37. SADET, *The Road to Democracy*, Vol. 4, Part 1, p. 113.
38. Savage, 'A chronology of meetings between South Africans and the ANC in exile 1983–2000'.
39. Ibid.
40. UWC/RIM Mayibuye Archives, ANC Papers, MCH01-57-1: Z. Skweyiya to A. Nzo, 11 April 1990.
41. ANC Archives (on file): R. Dworkin to O.R. Tambo, 26 October 1987 (document marked B2531).
42. UCT, Jack Simons Papers, BC1081, P.25.1: Handwritten notes of 'Zola and Maduna' meeting, 10h30, 23 May 1989, p. 1.

43. Sachs and Dodd edit, September 2020.
44. Dugard, *Confronting Apartheid*, p. 133. The judges were Milne, Didcott, Kriegler, Rose Innes, Fagan, King and Wilson.
45. Savage, 'A chronology of meetings between South Africans and the ANC in exile 1983–2000'.
46. Sachs and Dodd edit, September 2020.
47. Dugard, *Confronting Apartheid*, p. 133.
48. The lawyers from home included Laurie Ackermann, George Bizos, Pius Langa, Dikgang Moseneke, Lewis Skweyiya, Firoz Cachalia, Brian Currin, John de Gruchy, Gerhard Erasmus, Hugh Corder, Nicholas Haysom, Priscilla Jana, Felicia Kentridge, Anthony Mathews, Quraish Patel, John Samuel, Derek van der Merwe, Johann van der Vyver, Johann van der Westhuizen and Linda Zama.
49. ANC Archives (on file): Prof J. Greenberg to secretary, DLCA, 9 December 1986; A. Mangalo, secretary in the president's office to the chairperson, DLCA, 4 February 1987.

CHAPTER 34: TAKING CHARGE OF
'WHAT NEEDS TO BE DONE IN OUR COUNTRY'

1. P. O'Malley, *Shades of Difference*, p. 315. This work is a useful reference about interconnected developments within the ANC and MDM in mid to late 1989.
2. Albie Sachs interview with Penuell Maduna, Johannesburg, 29 April 2019, transcript, 00:54:40:03 – 00:54:42:00 (on file); Luli Callinicos Collection: Luli Callinicos interview with Penuell Maduna, Pretoria, 6 June 1994, transcribed by Mukoni Ratshitanga, p. 19.
3. Macmillan, *The Lusaka Years*, pp. 222–3.
4. G. Mbeki, *Sunset at Midday*, p. 103.
5. Nelson Mandela Centre of Memory, O'Malley Archives: Maharaj/Vula comms/1988/17 May 1989.
6. United Nations Resolution 435 (1978) of 29 September 1978. The Resolution was adopted at the 2 087th meeting by twelve votes to none with two abstentions (Czechoslovakia, USSR). China did not participate in the voting.
7. N. Horn, 'The Forerunners of the Namibian Constitution', p. 64. Available at https://www .kas.de/c/document_library/get_file?uuid=40888552-4a31-2602-6234-31a00e39866a&group Id=252038. Accessed 19 May 2020.
8. Gordon Metz and André Odendaal interview with Thabo Mbeki, Thabo Mbeki Foundation, Johannesburg, 19 October 2017.
9. UCT, Jack Simons Papers, BC1081, P25.1: 'Constitution Committee, resume of opening meeting', 9 January 1986.
10. Albie Sachs interview with Penuell Maduna, Johannesburg, 29 April 2019, transcript, 01:02:50:03 – 01:02:51.13 (on file); Callinicos, *Oliver Tambo*, p. 615; Gevisser, *Thabo Mbeki*, p. 549.
11. Seekings, *The UDF*, pp. 244–5.
12. P. O'Malley, *Shades of Difference*, p. 319.
13. UFH, NAHECS, ANC Archives, LSM/009/0033/01: ANC discussion paper on the issue of negotiations, 16 June 1989, p. 3.
14. O'Malley, *Shades of Difference*, pp. 317–18. For the intense interactions taking place between the ANC and internal groupings in June 1989, see Mac Maharaj – Vula Communications – 1989', https://omalley.nelsonmandela.org/omalley/index.php/site/q/03 lv03445/04lv03961/05lv03975/06lv03981.htm. Accessed 8 June 2022.
15. O'Malley, *Shades of Difference*, pp. 317–18.

16. C. Payet, 'I am privileged to have known Madiba', *Sunday Times*, 22 December 2013.
17. O'Malley, *Shades of Difference*, p. 38.
18. W. Esterhuyse and G. van Niekerk, *Die Tronkgesprekke: Nelson Mandela en Kobie Coetsee se Geheime Voorpunt-Diplomasie* (Cape Town: Tafelberg, 2018), Chapter 12.
19. P. Waldmeir, *Anatomy of a Miracle: The End of Apartheid and the Birth of the New South Africa* (New York, W.W. Norton and Company, 1997), p. 103.
20. Ibid., p. 106.
21. Gordon Metz and André Odendaal interview with Thabo Mbeki, Thabo Mbeki Foundation, Johannesburg, 19 October 2017, 18:09:00.
22. Quoted on back-cover blurb, Callinicos, *Oliver Tambo*.
23. Gordon Metz and André Odendaal interview with Thabo Mbeki, Thabo Mbeki Foundation, Johannesburg, 19 October 2017.
24. Zanele Mbeki in S.M. Ndlovu and M. Strydom (eds.), *The Thabo Mbeki I Know* (Johannesburg: Picador Africa, 2016), p. 122.
25. Jordan (ed.), *Oliver Tambo Remembered*, p. 125.
26. Gordon Metz and André Odendaal interview with Thabo Mbeki, Thabo Mbeki Foundation, Johannesburg, 19 October 2017.
27. Ibid.
28. Ibid.
29. Jordan (ed.), *Oliver Tambo Remembered*, p. 125.
30. Albie Sachs interview with Penuell Maduna, Johannesburg, 29 April 2019, transcript 01:04:35:13 – 01:14:33.03 (on file).
31. Gordon Metz and André Odendaal interview with Thabo Mbeki, Thabo Mbeki Foundation, Johannesburg, 19 October 2017; Gevisser, *Thabo Mbeki*, p. 550.
32. Jordan (ed.), *Oliver Tambo Remembered*, p. 125.
33. Callinicos, *Oliver Tambo*, pp. 615–19.
34. Albie Sachs interview with Penuell Maduna, Johannesburg, 29 April 2019, transcript 01:13:43:21 – 01:13:44.06.
35. Pallo Jordan, personal communication, October 2021.

CHAPTER 35: THE HARARE DECLARATION

1. Gordon Metz and André Odendaal interview with Thabo Mbeki, Thabo Mbeki Foundation, Johannesburg, 19 October 2017.
2. Callinicos, *Oliver Tambo*, p. 615.
3. Email from Hugh Macmillan, 22 March 2022; UCT, Jack Simons Papers, BC1081, P.25.1: Handwritten notes on 'Constitution Committee, 21 July 1989'.
4. Report on 'South African destabilisation: The economic cost of frontline resistance to apartheid', quoted in P. Sinclair, *Art from the Frontline: Contemporary Art from Southern Africa* (London: Karia Press, 1990).

CHAPTER 36: A REVOLUTION WITHIN THE REVOLUTION

1. UFH, ANC Archives, LSM/021/0154/01: [no author/s], paper on 'Formulating national policy regarding the emancipation of women and the promotion of women's development in our country'.
2. See UWC/RIM Mayibuye Archives, ANC Papers MCH01-57-2: Statement by women's section on the gender question, undated, unsigned; UWC/RIM Mayibuye Archives, ANC Papers, MCH01-57-2: [I. Matsepe-Casaburri and ANC Women's Section], paper on

'Constitution, Law and the Gender Question', In-House Seminar, Lusaka, 1–4 March 1988; UFH NAHECS, ANC Archives, LSM/021/0154/02: Recommendations/resolutions of NWS second national conference, Luanda, September 1987.

3. UWC/RIM Mayibuye Archives, Albie Sachs Papers, MCH91-82-5-1: Press statement on the seminar on 'Women, Children and the Family in a Future Post-Apartheid Constitutional Order'.

4. See UFH, NAHECS, ANC Archives, LSM/021/0154/11: DLCA/NWS/SASPRO National Preparatory Committee letter to participants, with 'seminar objectives', programme and 'chairpersons, rapporteurs and presenter[s]' attached.

5. See UWC/RIM Mayibuye Archives, ANC Papers, MCH01-57-2: Statement by women's section on the gender question, undated, unsigned; UWC/RIM Mayibuye Archives, ANC Papers, MCH01-57-2: [I. Matsepe-Casaburri and ANC Women's Section], paper on 'Constitution, Law and the Gender Question', In-House Seminar, Lusaka, 1–4 March 1988; UFH NAHECS, ANC Archives, LSM/021/0154/02: Recommendations/resolutions of NWS second national conference, Luanda, September 1987.

6. Hassim, *The ANC Women's League*, pp. 84–9.

7. UWC/RIM Mayibuye Archives, Albie Sachs Papers, MCH91-82-5-1: Printed programme; and MCH91-82-5-5: Proposed annotated agenda, as well as more detailed cyclostyled programme.

8. See, for example, UWC/RIM Mayibuye Archives, Albie Sachs Papers, MCH91-82-5-4: J. Simons, 'South Africa's family and marriage law reformed towards one system for all South Africans'.

9. UWC/RIM Mayibuye Archives, Albie Sachs Papers, MCH91-82-5-1: Press statement on the seminar on 'Women, Children and the Family in a Future Post-Apartheid Constitutional Order'.

10. B. Mbete, 'In for the long haul' in L. Ngcobo (ed.), *Prodigal Daughters: Stories of South African Women in Exile* (Scottsville: University of KwaZulu-Natal Press, 2012), p. 85; 'Baleka Mbete-Kgositsile', South African History Online, https://www.sahistory.org.za/ people/baleka-mbete-kgositsile. Accessed 10 June 2020.

11. Tessa Marcus, interview by Diana Russell, 1987, Alexander Street, https://search. alexanderstreet.com/preview/work/bibliographic_entity%7Cvideo_work%7C3424300. Accessed 11 June 2020.

12. UWC/RIM Mayibuye Archives, Albie Sachs Papers, MCH91-82-5-7: Commission Six – 'Women's emancipation', pp. 83e–83f.

13. 'Mavivi Myakayaka-Manzini', South African History Online, https://www.sahistory.org. za/people/mavivi-myakayaka-manzini. Accessed 29 September 2019.

14. 'Buzwe Stanley Mabizela', South African History Online, https://www.sahistory.org.za/ people/buzwe-stanley-mabizela. Accessed 29 September 2019.

15. B. Masekela, *Poli Poli* (Johannesburg: Jonathan Ball, 2021), pp. 216–17, 233, 240–41.

16. N.N. Gwagwa, 'The relationship between the State, the family and African women: Towards a post-apartheid South Africa' (unpublished MSc dissertation, London School of Economics and Political Science, 1989).

17. UWC/RIM Mayibuye Archives, Albie Sachs Papers, MCH91-82-5-7: N.N. Gwagwa, 'The family and women's emancipation in South Africa'.

18. Dhlamini, 'Women's liberation', South African History Online.

19. Ibid.

20. Ibid.

21. Telephone conversation with Lulu Gwagwa, October 2021.
22. UFH, ANC Archives, LSM/021/0154/10: [Albie Sachs], paper on 'Judges and gender: The constitutional rights of women in a post-apartheid South Africa', p. 1.
23. UFH, ANC Archives, LSM/021/0154/01: [no author/s], paper on 'Formulating national policy regarding the emancipation of women and the promotion of women's development in our country', p. 7.
24. Ibid., p. 1.
25. The twelve highlighted changes shown above are taken directly from A. Sachs, *Protecting Human Rights in a New South Africa* (Oxford University Press, 1991), Appendix B: 'The ANC's Constitutional Guidelines for a Democratic South Africa – Proposed changes after seminar on gender', pp. 197–201. Sachs wrote that 'these are the author's record of the proceedings and should not be regarded as the official [missing or undone] text'.
26. Jackson, 'Roots of Revolution', pp. 661, 664.
27. Hassim, *The ANC Women's League*, p. 93. For some reason, this book does not touch on the Lusaka seminar in December 1989.
28. UFH, NAHECS, ANC Archives, LSM/014/0055/04: NEC ballot count, no date [1991].

CHAPTER 37: 'EIGHT IS NOT ENOUGH!':
THE FINAL PUSH AND AN UNEXPECTED ANNOUNCEMENT

1. UWC/RIM Mayibuye Archives, Adrian Hadland Collection: Transcription of Max du Preez interview with Pieter Mulder, Interview number 3, Parliament, 14 November 2006.
2. Jeffery, *People's War*, pp. 217–19.
3. See Pahad, *Insurgent Diplomat*, pp. 218–22, for details of the meeting.
4. Esterhuyse, *Endgame*, p. 171.
5. Pahad, *Insurgent Diplomat*, p. 220.
6. Esterhuyse, *Endgame*, p. 255.
7. Sachs, *We, the People*, p. 2.
8. Giliomee, *Die Laaste Afrikanerleiers*, pp. 304–5, 315. See also H. Giliomee, 'Maggie se Marshall-plan vir SA', *Rapport Weekliks*, 4 July 2021, pp. 8–9.
9. Giliomee, *Die Laaste Afrikanerleiers*, pp. 314–15.
10. M. Sparg, *The Story of Bulelani Ngcuka: From Struggle Lawyer to Crime Fighter* (Johannesburg, Cape Town and London: Jonathan Ball, 2022), pp. 138–9.
11. Pahad, *Insurgent Diplomat*, p. 183.
12. For example, *New Era*, August 1988.
13. For the views of both Mbeki and his detractors, see ibid., pp. 184–6; Gevisser, *Thabo Mbeki*, pp. 552–3; and the endnote below.
14. For example 'Mac Maharaj – Documents and Reports', https://omalley.nelsonmandela. org/omalley/index.php/site/q/03lv03445/04lv04015.htm: Minutes, NWC, 9 March 1988, p. 1, that state that Mbeki was 'delegated by the President's Committee to meet with representatives and intermediaries acting on behalf of the regime'. See also Chapter 3 above and UWC/RIM Mayibuye Archives, ANC Papers, MCH01-56, LSM/011/0013/02: Extracts from the decisions of the NEC, July 1988; LSM/012/0017/12: Circular to all ECC Departments and sections by James Stuart, secretary, 10 March 1988; MCH01-57: DLCA report to the President's Committee, 11 March 1988; Gordon Metz and André Odendaal interview with Thabo Mbeki, Thabo Mbeki Foundation, Johannesburg, 19 October 2017, 14:00:04 – 16:00.06; Gevisser, *Thabo Mbeki*, p. 552; Callinicos, *Oliver Tambo*, p. 609.

15. See Maharaj and Jordan, *Breakthrough*, p. 135; SADET, *The Road to Democracy*, Vol. 4, Part 1, p. 114.
16. De Villiers and Stemmet, *Prisoner 913*, pp. 197–9.
17. Ibid., pp. 199, 206.
18. Giliomee, *Die Laaste Afrikanerleiers*, pp. 314–17.
19. Hain and Odendaal, *Pitch Battles*, p. 312; 'CDF calls for end of rebel tours' and 'Resolution on sports boycott and rebel tours to South Africa', *City Press*, 17 December 1989.
20. Nelson Mandela Memory Centre, Richard Stengel interview with Nelson Mandela. Footnote to transcript of recordings made in 1992/3 of interviews with Mandela as part of the research process for *Long Walk to Freedom*.
21. T. Cohen, 'From our vault: De Klerk and Mandela – what might have been', *Daily Maverick*, 11 February 2011. Available at https://www.dailymaverick.co.za/article/2011-02 -11-de-klerk-and-mandela-what-might-have-been/#gsc.tab=0. Accessed 15 June 2020.
22. De Villiers and Stemmet, *Prisoner 913*, p. 159. For this meeting and the detailed preparations for Mandela's release, including his discussions with the ANC in Lusaka, see Chapters 14–21.
23. Jeffery, *People's War*, pp. 230–31.
24. De Villiers and Stemmet, *Prisoner 913*, Chapter 24.
25. Ibid., pp. 190, 202.
26. Macmillan, *Jack Simons*, p. 143.
27. UWC/RIM Mayibuye Archives, Adrian Hadland Collection: Transcription of Max du Preez interview with Pieter Mulder, Interview number 3, Parliament, 14 November 2006.
28. A. Sparks, *Tomorrow Is Another Country: The Inside Story of South Africa's Negotiated Revolution* (Sandton: Struik Book Distributors, 1995), pp. 7, 13.
29. De Villiers and Stemmet, *Prisoner 913*, p. 237.
30. Ibid., p. 237. In a long interview, Roelf Meyer gave us four principal reasons for the regime's decision to change direction; three of these related directly to the ANC's multipronged strategy – the ANC's commanding international presence, its success in campaigning for sanctions (the most important), and the refusal of the internal MDM to lie down despite successive states of emergency. See Gordon Metz Collection: Gordon Metz and André Odendaal interview with Roelf Meyer, Pretoria, 14 October 2016.
31. UWC/RIM Mayibuye Archives, Adrian Hadland Collection: Transcription of Max du Preez interview with Pieter Mulder, Interview number 3, Parliament, 14 November 2006.
32. Narrative drawn from Hain and Odendaal, *Pitch Battles*, pp. 328–40.
33. Macmillan, *The Lusaka Years*, pp. 258–9.

CHAPTER 38: RETURN OF THE FIRST EXILES

1. UWC/RIM Mayibuye Archives, ANC Papers, MCH01-57: Z. Skweyiya to Treasurer General, [date unclear] April 1990.
2. Luli Callinicos Collection: Luli Callinicos interview with Penuell Maduna, Pretoria, 6 June 1994, transcribed by Mukoni Ratshitanga, p. 19.
3. 'Eleven protesters are killed in Sebokeng', South African History Online, https://www.sa history.org.za/dated-event/eleven-protesters-are-killed-sebokeng. Accessed 25 June 2020.

CHAPTER 39: LAST MEETING IN LUSAKA

1. UWC/RIM Mayibuye Archives, Albie Sachs Papers, MCH97-81: Minutes, Constitution Committee, Lusaka, 29–30 April 1990.

2. Sachs and Dodd edit, September 2020.

3. Ibid.

4. G. Bizos, *Odyssey to Freedom* (Johannesburg: Random House, 2007), p. 487.

5. UWC/RIM Mayibuye Archives, Albie Sachs Papers, MCH97-81: Minutes, Constitution Committee, Lusaka, 29–30 April 1990.

6. For Bulelani Ngcuka's biography, see M. Sparg, *The Story of Bulelani Ngcuka: From Struggle Lawyer to Crime Fighter* (Johanessburg: Jonathan Ball, 2022).

7. André Odendaal Collection: Brochure for memorial service of the late Judge Essa Moosa, 8 February 1936 – 26 February 2017; and Essa Moosa memorial lecture by Ebrahim Rasool, 'A legacy left behind, A guide to the future', Islamia Auditorium, Cape Town, 31 October 2018; S. Mzantsi, 'Hamba Kahle Judge Moosa' and editorial, *Cape Times*, 27 February 2017; 'Essa Moosa: Always ready to fight the good fight', *Bush Radio* blog, https://bushradio.wordpress.com/2017/02/26/5742/. Accessed 26 June 2020.

8. S. Kings, 'Obituary: The people's attorney – Judge Essa Moosa', *Mail & Guardian*, 2 March 2017. Available at https://mg.co.za/article/2017-03-02-obituary-the-peoples-attorney-judge -essa-moosa/. Accessed 26 June 2020.

9. Ibid.

10. UWC/RIM Mayibuye Archives, Albie Sachs Papers, MCH97-81: Minutes, Constitution Committee, Lusaka, 29–30 April 1990.

11. Ibid.

12. Ibid.

13. SADET, *The Road to Democracy*, Vol. 3, International solidarity, Part 1, pp. 514–17.

14. UWC/RIM Mayibuye Archives, Albie Sachs Papers, MCH97-81: Minutes, Constitution Committee, Lusaka, 29–30 April 1990.

15. Ibid.

16. Copies of 'Fink' Haysom's *Mabangalala: The Rise of Right-Wing Vigilantes in South Africa* were circulated and a discussion ensued about the situation in Natal where bitter internecine fighting was taking place.

17. The thinking on the definition of political prisoners was that it would include state 'hit squads'. 'On humanitarian grounds even the killer of the Pretoria nine, [Barend] Strydom, should be included.' The feeling was that Strydom was also a victim of apartheid.

18. UWC/RIM Mayibuye Archives, Albie Sachs Papers MCH97-81: Minutes, Constitution Committee, Lusaka, 29–30 April 1990.

19. Ibid.

20. Sachs and Dodd edit, September 2020.

CHAPTER 40: A SOFT LANDING IN CAPE TOWN

1. Sachs and Dodd edit, September 2020.

2. Ibid.

3. For his poems, see S. Dikeni, *Guava Juice*, Mayibuye History and Literature Series, No. 42 (Cape Town: Mayibuye Books, 1992).

4. Asmal, Hadland and Levy, *Politics in My Blood*, pp. 116–17.

5. The Immorality Act would have criminalised sexual intimacy between them, and the Mixed Marriages Act would have outlawed their marriage.

6. For Yvonne Mokgoro's profile, see https://www.concourt.org.za/index.php/judges/ former-judges/11-former-judges/63-justice-yvonne-mokgoro. Accessed 26 October 2021.

7. UWC/RIM Mayibuye Archives, Albie Sachs Papers, MCH97-81: Minutes, Constitution Committee, Lusaka, 29–30 April 1990.
8. Ibid.
9. H. Mzolo, 'The Inaugural Victoria Mxenge Annual Lecture', *Umlando: Durban Local History Museums*, Issue 4: December 2013, p. 17. Available at https://durbanhistorymuseums .org.za/wp-content/uploads/2015/05/Umlando4.pdf. Accessed 26 June 2020.
10. Sachs and Dodd edit, September 2020.
11. Ibid.

CHAPTER 41: TAMBO ARRIVES HOME

1. Jordan (ed.), *Oliver Tambo Remembered*, pp. 72–3.
2. Callinicos, *Oliver Tambo*, p. 252.
3. Quoted in Macmillan, *The Lusaka Years*, pp. 286–7.
4. *Constitution of the Republic of South Africa, 1996* (Juta Law, Cape Town, 14th edition, 2017), p. xiv.
5. Macmillan, *The Lusaka Years*, pp. 139–40.
6. Reminiscence of an anecdote told to Albie Sachs by Conny Braam, [10 September 2020].
7. Story relayed by Peter and Cora Weiss, organisers and hosts of Tambo's US visit, to Albie Sachs, 2019.
8. A. Chauke, 'The Oratory of Oliver Tambo: Ngoako Ramatlhodi on Oliver Tambo', *Brand South Africa*, 17 October 2017, https://www.brandsouthafrica.com/people-culture/history -heritage/oratory-oliver-tambo-ngoako-ramatlhodi-oliver-tambo. Accessed 9 July 2020.
9. Jordan (ed.), *Oliver Tambo Remembered*, p. 111.
10. Mandela, *Long Walk to Freedom*, p. 601.

AFTERWORD: 'FREEDOM AND BREAD'

1. For a brief timeline of the second phase of negotiated constitution-making between 1991 and April 1994, see M. Nicol, *The Making of the Constitution: The Story of South Africa's Constitutional Assembly, May 1994 to December 1996* (Cape Town: Constitutional Assembly/Churchill Murray Publications, 1997), pp. 16–19.
2. For the story of the Constitutional Assembly, the third phase in the making of the Constitution, see ibid. and M. Sparg (compiler), *The Constitutional Assembly Annual Report, 1996* (Cape Town: Typeface Media, 1996).
3. Nicol, *The Making of the Constitution*, pp. 60–65.
4. P.M. Maduna, 'Judicial Control of Executive and Legislative Powers of the Government' (University of the Witwatersrand: draft Master of Laws dissertation, 1992), p. 350.
5. Kader Asmal Papers (home): K. Asmal, 'Human rights and self-determination: The South African experience', paper presented at the International Conference on the Bicentenary of the Rights of Man and the Citizen, Its topicality and future, Unesco, Paris, 9–11 March 1989, p. 8.
6. C. Saunders, 'The making of democratic South Africa's constitution: A critical literature review' (Commissioned by the Albie Sachs Trust on Constitutionalism and the Rule of Law in South Africa, Cape Town, 2016, p. 1.
7. See draft manuscript on the Negotiations Commission 1992–1994 by its minute-taker, Hassen Ebrahim, later also executive director of the Constitutional Assembly. This and his more than twenty notebooks have been deposited at the Nelson Mandela Centre for Memory.

8. For the making of the Constitutional Court, see B. Law-Viljoen (ed.), *Light on a Hill: Building the Constitutional Court of South Africa* (Johannesburg: David Krut, no date); B. Law-Viljoen (ed.), *Art and Justice: The Art of the Constitutional Court of South Africa* (Johannesburg: David Krut, 2008); no author, *The Constitutional Court of South Africa: The First Ten Years* (Johannesburg: The Constitutional Court of South Africa, 2004); L. Segal, K. Martin and S. Kort, *Number Four: The Making of Constitution Hill* (Johannesburg: Penguin Books, 2006).

9. S. Hayes, 'Ted Pekane – South African freedom fighter, died Dec 2016'. https://groups.google.com/forum/#!topic/soc.culture.south-africa/H_pyR1MEp_8. Accessed 28 July 2021.

10. Ibid.

11. W. Gumede, 'The pillars of a new society after the pandemic', *Sunday Times*, 14 June 2020.

12. For some of these critical new voices, see UWC Centre for Humanities' call for workshop proposals on 'Transformative Constitutionalism: What human is imagined in the "Human Rights" contained in the South African constitution?', April 2022; T. Madlingozi, 'Roots of South Africa's Transformative contra Decolonising Constitutionalism', *Herri*, Number 2, 2020; J.M. Modiri, 'Conquest and constitutionalism: First thoughts on an alternative jurisprudence', *South African Journal on Human Rights*, Volume 34, Number 3, 2018, pp 300–325. My thanks to Lwando Scott and colleagues in the Centre for Humanities Research at UWC for this material.

13. See, for example, I. Matsepe-Casaburri and ANC Women's Section, Paper on 'Constitution, Law and the gender question', In-House Seminar, Lusaka, 1–4 March 1988; Z.P. Jordan, *Letters to My Comrades, Interventions and Excursions*, compiled by K. Kgositsile and M. Mutloatse (Auckland Park: Jacana, in association with African Lives – African Lives Series number 8 – 2017); A. Sachs, *The Soft Vengeance of a Freedom Fighter* (London: Souvenir Press, 2011).

14. *Mail & Guardian*, 10 November 2021, pp. 28–9.

Index